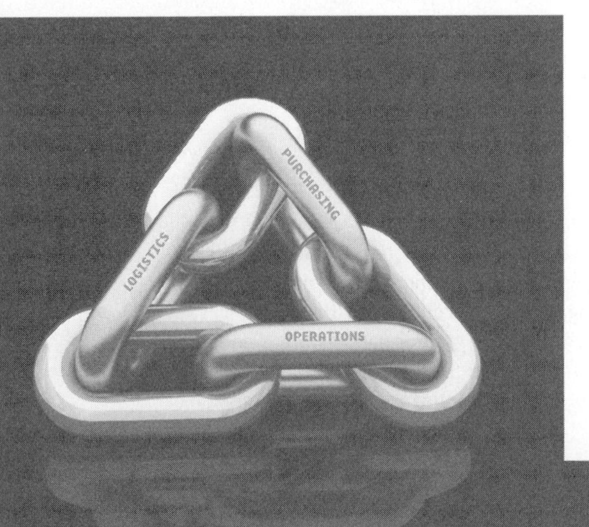

Principles of Supply Chain Management

A Balanced Approach | 4e

JOEL D. WISNER, PhD
University of Nevada, Las Vegas

KEAH-CHOON TAN, PhD
University of Nevada, Las Vegas

G. KEONG LEONG, PhD
California State University, Dominguez Hills

CENGAGE Learning

Australia • Brazil • Mexico • Singapore • United Kingdom • United States

Principles of Supply Chain Management: A Balanced Approach, Fourth Edition
Joel D. Wisner, Keah-Choon Tan, G. Keong Leong

Vice President, General Manager, Social Science & Qualitative Business: Erin Joyner

Product Director: Joe Sabatino

Associate Content Developer: Conor Allen

Senior Product Assisstant: Brad Sullender

Marketing Director: Natalie King

Marketing Manager: Heather Mooney

Marketing Coordinator: Eileen Corcoran

Art and Cover Direction, Production Management, and Composition: Lumina Datamatics, Inc.

Media Developer: Chris Valentine

Intellectual Property

Analyst: Christina Ciaramella

Project Manager: Betsy Hathaway

Manufacturing Planner: Ron Montgomery

Cover Image: © alxpin/E+/Getty Images

Library of Congress Control Number: 2014950273

Student Edition ISBN: 978-1-285-42831-4

Cengage Learning
20 Channel Center Street
Boston, MA 02210
USA

Cengage Learning is a leading provider of customized learning solutions with office locations around the globe, including Singapore, the United Kingdom, Australia, Mexico, Brazil, and Japan. Locate your local office at: **www.cengage.com/global**

Cengage Learning products are represented in Canada by Nelson Education, Ltd.

To learn more about Cengage Learning Solutions, visit **www.cengage.com**

Purchase any of our products at your local college store or at our preferred online store **www.cengagebrain.com**

Printed in the United States of America
Print Number: 01 Print Year: 2014

To CJ, Hayley, and Blake.

—*Joel D. Wisner*

To Shaw Yun, Wen Hui, and Wen Jay.

—*Keah-Choon Tan*

To Lin and Michelle.

—*G. Keong Leong*

Brief Contents

Contents

On the Companion Website

Preface

Welcome to the fourth edition of *Principles of Supply Chain Management: A Balanced Approach.* The practice of supply chain management has become widespread in all industries around the globe today, with both small and large firms realizing the benefits provided by effective supply chain management. We think this text is unique in that it uses a novel and logical approach to present discussions of this topic from four foundation perspectives: purchasing, operations, logistics, and process integration. We think this book is also somewhat different than the other supply chain management texts available, since we present a more balanced view of the topic—many of the texts available today concentrate primarily on just one of the three areas of purchasing, operations, or logistics.

The objective of the book is to make readers think about how supply chain management impacts all of the areas and processes of the firm and its supply chain trading partners, and to show how managers can improve their firm's competitive position by employing the practices we describe throughout the text. Junior- or senior-level business students, beginning MBA students, as well as practicing managers can benefit from reading and using this text.

There are several changes to this fourth edition that we hope you will find interesting and useful. There is a greater emphasis on environmental sustainability and technological advances throughout the text. Additionally, each chapter contains a number of SCM Profiles, beginning with a chapter opening profile, and then other smaller company profiles throughout the chapters. All chapter references throughout the text have been updated, with new and interesting storylines, to keep readers engaged and informed. Additionally, new end-of-chapter discussion, essay and project questions, and exercises have been added. Other ancillary materials are described below.

New with the fourth edition is a tie-in to a wonderfully engaging global supply chain simulation game called SCM Globe. A separate page dedicated to SCM Globe follows this preface. We are very excited about the simulation and hope instructors will take it for a test drive and then use it in their classes. Our textbook comes with a dedicated website containing teaching cases split among each major part of the book. Most of the case companies and situations are real, while some others are fictional, and the cases vary from easy to difficult and short to long. Cases are being added to the list as time progresses. Also on the website is a guide to supply chain management videos along with the YouTube website addresses for each video. Finally, Power Point lecture slides are available for downloading. Part of the website is protected and for instructors only, and this site contains sample syllabi, case teaching notes, answers to all of the end-of-chapter questions and problems, and a test bank. In the Chapter 1 Appendix, there is a discussion of the Beer Game, with inventory tracking sheets to allow instructors to actually play the game with their students. Finally, there are quantitative as well as qualitative problems and questions, essay/project exercises, and Excel problems spread throughout most of the chapters.

Part 1 is the overview and introduction to the topic of supply chain management. This chapter introduces the basic understanding and concepts of supply chain management, and should help students realize the importance of this topic. Core concepts such as the bullwhip effect, supplier relationship management, forecasting and demand management, enterprise resource planning, transportation management, and customer relationship management are briefly discussed. There is also a closing section on current trends in supply chain management.

Part 2 presents supply issues in supply chain management. This very important topic is covered in three chapters, building from an introduction to purchasing management, to managing supplier relationships, and then finally to ethical and sustainable sourcing. Within these chapters can be found sections on government purchasing, global sourcing, e-procurement, software applications, supplier development, ethical purchasing, and green purchasing.

Part 3 includes four chapters regarding operations issues in supply chain management. This section progresses from forecasting, resource planning, and inventory management to lean production and Six Sigma in a supply chain setting. Topics in this section include the basics of forecasting; collaborative planning, forecasting, and replenishment; material requirements planning; enterprise resource planning; inventory models; lean thinking; Six Sigma concepts and tools; and statistical process control techniques.

Part 4 presents distribution issues in supply chain management and consists of four chapters. This section begins with a review of domestic U.S. and international logistics with sections on green transportation, international logistics security, and reverse logistics. This is followed by chapters on customer relationship management, global location decisions, and service response logistics. Content in these chapters includes new software application discussions, social media and cloud computing in customer relationship management, sustainability in logistics, new location trends in the global economy, and cloud computing in services.

The final section is Part 5, which presents discussions of the integration issues in supply chain management and performance measurements along the supply chain. While cooperation and integration are frequently referred to in the text, this section brings the entire text into focus, tying all of the parts together, first by discussing internal and external process integration in detail, followed by a discussion of traditional and world-class performance measurement systems. The topics of supply chain risk management and expanded coverage of performance measurement models are also included.

We think we have compiled a very interesting set of supply chain management topics that will keep readers engaged and we hope you enjoy it. We welcome your comments and suggestions for improvement. Please direct all comments and questions to:

Joel D. Wisner: joel.wisner@unlv.edu (primary contact),

Keah-Choon Tan: kctan@unlv.edu, or

G. Keong Leong: gkleong@csudh.edu

ACKNOWLEDGEMENTS

We greatly appreciate the efforts of a number of fine and hard-working people at Cengage Learning. Without their feedback and guidance, this text would not have been completed. The team members are: Joe Sabatino, Product Director; Heather Mooney, Marketing Manager; Conor Allen, Associate Content Developer and day-to-day contact person; and Chris Valentine, media developer. We also would like to thank Joseph Malcolm and his team at Lumina Datamatics who put the manuscript into final copy form.

Additionally, we would like to thank all of the case writers who contributed their cases to this textbook. Their names, along with their contact information, are printed with each of the cases on the website. As with any project of this size and time span, there are certain to be a number of people who gave their time and effort to this textbook, and yet their names remain unknown and so were inadvertently left out of these acknowledgments. We apologize for this and wish to thank you here.

SCM Globe | A Supply Chain Simulation

SCM Globe is a serious supply chain game. Students can design supply chains from scratch or use the supply chains provided by the case studies to understand how different designs produce different operating results, and then how to manage those results. As SCM Globe progresses, students get an intuitive and analytical feel for how supply chains work.

SCM Globe is a real-time strategy game, and the goal is to create supply chains that meet customer demand for products, while attaining the lowest operating costs and inventory levels. This is accomplished by designing and combining four main entities that define the supply chain. Those entities are products, facilities, vehicles, and routes.

SCM Globe lets students create products, facilities, vehicles, and routes and combine them any way they want. Supply chains can be created that closely model actual company supply chains. SCM Globe leverages functions in Google Maps and adds further functionality and a user interface that enables the design of multiple supply chains, while simulating performance and analyzing results.

Users drag-and-drop facilities on a map of the world, specify the routes (road, rail, air, water) that connect the facilities, and then view and edit the routes on the map. Products are defined that relate to the facilities and vehicles that move products between facilities. Finally, SCM Globe lets students simulate the operation of their supply chains while showing them operating data and problem areas (where products accumulate or run out). Students can keep improving supply chain designs until they get the results they want.

SCM Globe is designed to be user friendly and works equally well for individuals and teams in the classroom. Teams can work together remotely utilizing a video conference link that offers screen sharing (e.g., GoToMeeting, Skype).

A concise user's manual and video tutorials are available to walk users through the basics of designing a supply chain and simulating its performance. A FAQ section and an internal WIKI provide additional help. There is also a library of case studies. Each case study is a bit more challenging than the last and illustrates supply chain operating principles. These principles and other issues are presented in a section for each case study.

SCM Globe is both engaging and useful. New features are continually being added based on feedback and comments from people using the application. Student versions of SCM Globe can be purchased for a modest price. To learn more about SCM Globe, to purchase your copy, or to test its features, go to www.scmglobe.com, or e-mail SCM Globe at info@SCMGlobe.com.

About the Authors

Joel D. Wisner is Professor of Supply Chain Management in the Lee Business School at the University of Nevada, Las Vegas. He earned his BS in Mechanical Engineering from New Mexico State University in 1976 and his MBA from West Texas State University in 1986. During that time, Dr. Wisner worked as an engineer for Union Carbide at its lush, forested Oak Ridge, Tennessee, facility and then worked in the oil industry in the wet, green Louisiana Gulf Coast and the dry, dusty West Texas areas. In 1991, he earned his PhD in Supply Chain Management from Arizona State University. He holds certifications in transportation and logistics (CTL) and in purchasing management (C.P.M.).

He is currently keeping busy teaching courses in supply chain management at UNLV. His research and case writing interests are in process assessment and improvement strategies along the supply chain. His articles have appeared in numerous journals including *Journal of Business Logistics, Journal of Operations Management, Journal of Supply Chain Management, Journal of Transportation, Production and Operations Management Journal,* and *Business Case Journal.*

Keah-Choon Tan is Associate Dean of Academic Affairs and Professor of Operations Management in the Lee Business School at the University of Nevada, Las Vegas. He received a BSc degree and an MBA from the University of South Alabama, and a PhD in Operations Management from Michigan State University. Prior to academia, Dr. Tan was a hospital administrator and an account comptroller of a manufacturing firm. He holds certifications in purchasing management (C.P.M.) and production and inventory management (CPIM).

Dr. Tan has published articles in the area of supply chain management, quality, and operations scheduling in academic journals and magazines including *Decision Sciences, Decision Support Systems, International Journal of Production Research, International Journal of Operations & Production Management, International Journal of Logistics Management, Journal of Supply Chain Management,* and *Omega*, among others. He has served as editor, co-guest editor, and on the editorial boards of academic journals. Dr. Tan has received several research grants and teaching awards, including the UNLV Foundation Distinguished Teaching Award.

G. Keong Leong is Associate Dean in the College of Business Administration and Public Policy at California State University, Dominguez Hills. He received an undergraduate degree in Mechanical Engineering from the University of Malaya and an MBA and PhD from the University of South Carolina. He was previously a member of the faculty at the University of Nevada, Las Vegas and the Ohio State University, and a clinical faculty member at the Thunderbird School of Global Management.

His publications appear in academic journals such as *Journal of Operations Management, Decision Sciences, Interfaces, Journal of Management, European Journal of Operational Research, and International Journal of Production Research*, among others. He has coauthored three books including *Operations Strategy: Focusing Competitive Excellence,* and *Cases in International Management: A Focus on Emerging Markets* and received research, teaching, and service awards including an Educator of the Year award from the Asian Chamber of Commerce in Las Vegas, Dennis E. Grawoig Distinguished Service award from Decision Sciences Institute, and OM Distinguished Scholar award from the

Operations Management Division, Academy of Management. He has been active in the Decision Sciences Institute, serving as President, Editor of *Decision Line*, At-Large Vice-President, Associate Program Chair, Chair of the Innovative Education Committee, Chair of the Doctoral Student Affairs Committee, and Manufacturing Management Track Chair. In addition, he served as President of the Western Decision Sciences Institute and Chair of the Operations Management Division, Academy of Management.

PART 1

Supply Chain Management: An Overview

Chapter 1

INTRODUCTION TO SUPPLY CHAIN MANAGEMENT

"Supply chain management traditionally has been a hard, analytical type of practice where you are involved in activities that are well-suited to operations research and hard analysis such as optimizing routes and minimizing inventory costs. Now, it requires a more coordinated effort working with numerous partners. What had historically been a support, cost-based focus has now become more of a people-management and leadership role."

— ***Chris Caplice, Executive Director of MIT's Center for Transportation & Logistics***[1]

"The faster you get products to market, the more full-price sales you get. If we can figure out a way to get a new product into the market prior to Target or Wal-mart, Kohl's, or J. C. Penney ... we get to enjoy full price sales for some period of time. This shows why speed to market is important, and the engine that drives speed to market is effective supply chain management."

— ***Greg Rake, Senior VP of Supply Chain, Pier 1 Imports***[2]

Learning Objectives

After completing this chapter, you should be able to

- Describe a supply chain and define supply chain management.
- Describe the objectives and elements of supply chain management.
- Describe local, regional, and global supply chain management activities.
- Describe a brief history and current trends in supply chain management.
- Understand the bullwhip effect and how it impacts the supply chain.

Chapter Outline

Introduction

Supply Chain Management Defined

The Importance of Supply Chain Management

The Origins of Supply Chain Management in the U.S.

The Foundations of Supply Chain Management

Current Trends in Supply Chain Management

Summary

Supply Chain Collaboration Means Success at Hologic

Successful supply chain management at medical technology firm Hologic requires collaborative relationships, both internally and externally. At 8 AM every day, Timothy Bye, director of supply chain, will be at a meeting discussing the firm's daily production plans with a team of buyers, materials managers, production planners, and operations professionals. Some of them are at the table with Bye, while others in various locations are on the phone.

It's just one of a series of cross-functional meetings Bye takes part in during the course of a day, week, or month. On a weekly basis, he'll be in meetings with teams in areas ranging from product development to purchasing to marketing. He'll personally meet with suppliers on a quarterly basis along with his commodity teams to review supplier performance, give them updates on Hologic's priorities, and outline its goals going forward.

Collaboration is central to any good supply chain strategy, and the best way to drive collaboration is by having everyone in on the same conversation at once. Because it has grown through acquisition and new product development, Hologic has a diverse product line and organization chart, so cross-functional collaboration in the supply chain doesn't happen naturally. It needs to be driven.

Hologic's physical plant sites are mostly in the Northeast U.S., with a new manufacturing site in Costa Rica. It has also acquired several companies, including Third Wave Technologies, BioLucent, and Cytc Corp. Product development, at its core, is a cross-functional process, with the supply chain team serving as the glue holding together all the other parts. Each new product has a "core team" assigned to its development that meets weekly. During the alpha and beta stages of product development, engineers make more of the supplier decisions, but Bye makes sure the purchasing team is in the loop from the ground floor, to better understand the engineers' selection of parts and suppliers.

Because of the nature of Hologic's product lineup, its supply base is relatively small and very specialized. Most are located in close proximity to Hologic's manufacturing sites and have to comply with strict guidelines, as much of Hologic's product lineup requires FDA approval before going on the market. Bye points out that relying on custom parts can create risk in the supply chain—if only one supplier can make a part and that supplier goes down, then it directly impacts Hologic's production. So, Hologic focuses on building strong relationships with those suppliers.

"Better relationships equate to better communication," Bye says. "We prefer to have suppliers involved in product development when possible. If you get suppliers' feedback early, it almost always makes a better product."[3]

INTRODUCTION

Operating successfully today requires organizations to become much more involved with their suppliers and customers. As global markets expand, labor, material, and fuel prices escalate and competition increases, making goods and services that customers want, at a price they are willing to pay, requires firms to be good at a number of things. Business managers must pay closer attention to where materials come from; how suppliers' products are designed, produced, and transported; how their own products and services are produced and distributed to customers; and what their direct customers and the end-product consumers really think of the goods and services they bought.

Thirty years ago, many large firms were vertically integrated, meaning they owned some of their suppliers and/or customers. Today, this practice is much less common due to the high cost and difficulty in managing such diverse business units. Firms are selling off business units to focus more on core capabilities while trying to create alliances or strategic partnerships with suppliers, transportation and warehousing companies, distributors, and other companies that are very good at what they do. This collaborative approach to buying, making, and distributing goods and services has become the best way for firms to stay successful—and it is central to the practice of supply chain management (SCM).

Several factors encourage and enable firms to work together more effectively than ever before. Communication and information exchange using enterprise resource planning (ERP) system applications (discussed further in Chapter 6) has made global collaboration not only possible but necessary for firms to compete. Communication technologies continue to change rapidly, making partnerships and teamwork much easier than ever before. Competition is also expanding rapidly in all industries and in all markets around the world, bringing new materials, products, people, and resources together, making it more difficult for many of the local, individually owned, "mom-and-pop" shops to keep customers. Additionally, the recent global recession made customers more cost-conscious while seeking higher levels of quality and service, which is requiring organizations to find even better ways to compete. Customers are also demanding more socially responsible and environmentally friendly goods and services from organizations. Considering all of these changes to the environment, it is indeed an exciting time for companies seeking to develop new products, find new customers and compete more successfully. Consequently, many job opportunities are opening up in the areas of purchasing, operations, logistics, and supply chain management.

As you read this textbook, you will be introduced to the many concepts of supply chain management and how to use these concepts to become better managers in today's global economy. Examples are used throughout the text to illustrate the topics discussed, and online cases for each section of the textbook are provided to enable you to test your problem-solving, decision-making, and writing skills in supply chain management. It is hoped that by the end of the text you will have gained an appreciation of the value of supply chain management and will be able to apply what you have learned, both in your profession and in future courses in supply chain management.

In this chapter, the term *supply chain management* is defined, including a discussion of its importance, history, and developments to date. The chapter ends with a look at a few of the current trends in supply chain management.

SUPPLY CHAIN MANAGEMENT DEFINED

To understand supply chain management, one must first begin with a discussion of a **supply chain**; a generic one is shown in Figure 1.1. The supply chain shown in the figure starts with firms extracting raw materials from the earth—such as iron ore, oil, wood, and food items—and then selling these to raw material suppliers such as lumber companies, steel mills, and raw food distributors. These firms, acting on purchase orders and specifications they have received from component manufacturers, turn the raw materials into materials that are usable by these customers (materials such as sheet steel, aluminum, copper, lumber, and inspected foodstuffs). The component manufacturers, responding to orders and specifications from their customers (the final product manufacturers), make and sell intermediate components (electrical wire, fabrics, plumbing items, nuts and bolts, molded plastic components, component parts and assemblies, and processed foods).

Figure 1.1 A Generic Supply Chain

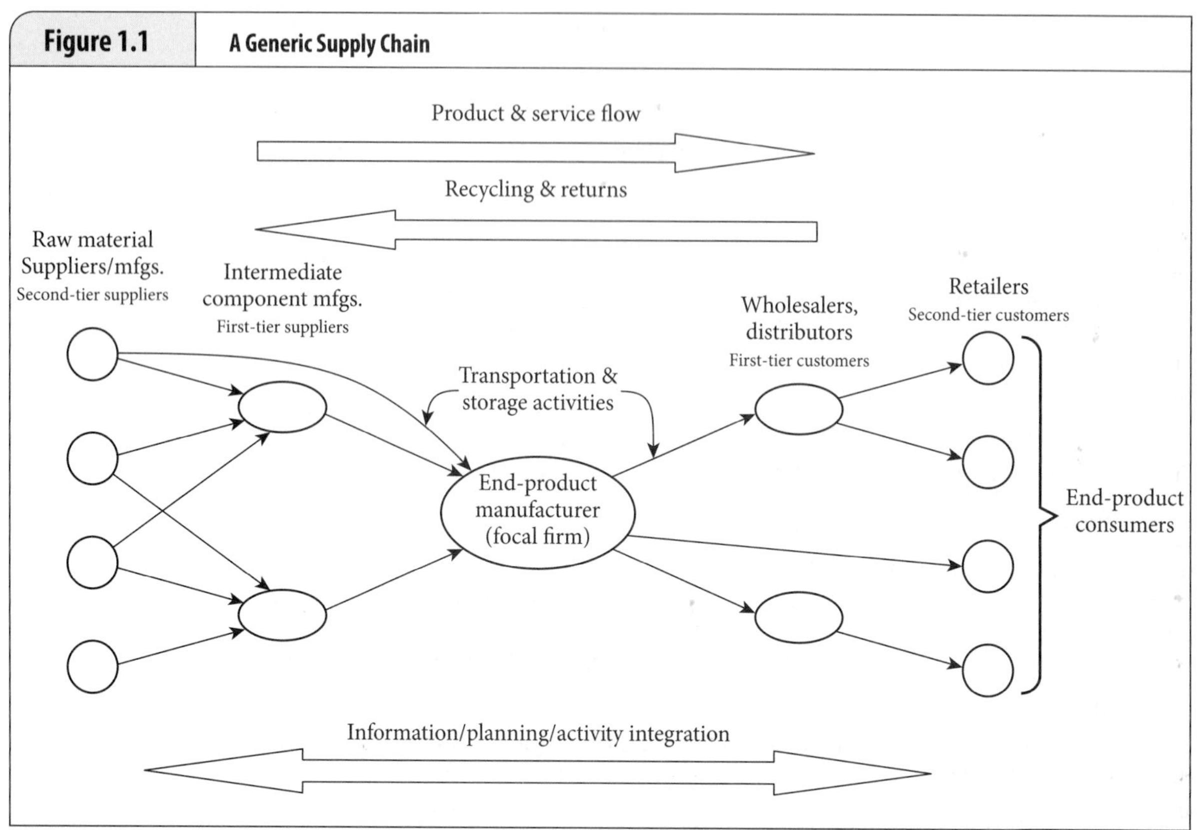

The final product manufacturers (companies such as Boeing, General Motors, and Coca-Cola) assemble the finished products and sell them to wholesalers or distributors, who then resell these products to retailers as their product orders are received. Retailers in turn sell these products to us, the end-product consumers.

Consumers buy products based on a combination of cost, quality, availability, maintainability, and reputation factors, and then hope the purchased products satisfy their requirements and expectations. The companies, along with their supply chains, that can provide all of these desired things will ultimately be successful. Along the supply chain, intermediate and end customers may need to return products or obtain warranty repairs, or they may just throw products away or recycle them. These reverse logistics activities are also included in the supply chain and are discussed further in Chapter 9.

Referring again to Figure 1.1, the firm in the middle of the figure is referred to as the *focal firm* simply because it is the firm being discussed here; the direct suppliers and customers of the focal firm are first-tier suppliers and first-tier customers. The first-tier suppliers' suppliers are thus the focal firm's second-tier suppliers, and the first-tier customers' customers are the focal firm's second-tier customers. Not all supply chains look exactly like the one shown in Figure 1.1. Some raw material and end-product manufacturers, for example, may sell directly to end consumers. Some supply chains, such as an automobile supply chain, might have many tiers, while others such as a law office's supply chain might have very few tiers.

Thus, the series of companies eventually making products and services available to consumers, including all of the functions enabling the production, delivery, and recycling of materials, components, end products, and services, is called a supply chain. Companies with multiple products likely have multiple supply chains. All products and services reach their customers via some type of supply chain—some much larger, longer, and more complex than others. Some may involve foreign suppliers or markets.

With this idea of a supply chain in mind, there really is only one true source of income for all supply chain organizations—the supply chain's end customers. Steve Darendinger, vice president of advanced sourcing and supply chain strategy for Cisco Systems of California, says the key to developing effective supply chain management programs is *keeping the customer in mind*. "The things that we do within our supply chain are driven around customer success," he says. "We provide opportunities and solutions for customers."[4] When companies make business decisions while ignoring the interests of the end customer and other chain members, these suboptimal decisions create additional risks, costs, and waiting time along the supply chain, ultimately leading to higher end-product prices, lower supply chain service levels, and eventually lower end-customer demand.

A number of other companies are also indirectly involved in most supply chains, and they play a very important role in the delivery of goods to customers. These are the many service providers, such as trucking and airfreight shipping companies, information system providers, public warehousing firms, freight forwarders, agents, and consultants. These service providers are extremely useful to the firms in most supply chains because they can help to get goods where they need to be in a timely fashion, allow buyers and sellers to communicate effectively, allow firms to serve outlying markets, enable firms to save money on domestic and global shipments, and in general allow firms to adequately serve their customers at the lowest possible cost.

So, now that a general description of a supply chain has been provided, what is **supply chain management (SCM)**? A number of definitions are available in the literature and among various professional associations. A few of these are provided here from various organizations connected to the practice of supply chain management:

- The Council of Supply Chain Management Professionals (CSCMP) defines supply chain management as:

    The planning and management of all activities involved in sourcing and procurement, conversion, and all logistics management activities. Importantly, it also includes coordination and collaboration with channel partners, which can be suppliers, intermediaries, third-party service providers, and customers.[5]

- The Institute for Supply Management (ISM) describes supply chain management as:

    The design and management of seamless, value-added processes across organizational boundaries to meet the real needs of the end customer.[6]

- The Association for Operations Management (APICS) defines supply chain management as:

    The design, planning, execution, control, and monitoring of supply chain activities with the objective of creating net value, building a competitive infrastructure, leveraging worldwide logistics, synchronizing supply with demand, and measuring performance globally.[7]

Consistent across these definitions is the idea of coordinating or integrating a number of goods- and services-related activities among supply chain participants to improve operating efficiencies, quality, and customer service. Thus, for supply chain management to be successful, firms must work together by sharing information on things like demand forecasts, production plans, capacity changes, new marketing strategies, new product and service developments, new technologies employed, purchasing plans, delivery dates, and anything else impacting the firm's purchasing, production, and distribution plans.

In theory, supply chains work as a cohesive, singularly competitive unit, accomplishing what many large, vertically integrated firms tried and failed to accomplish in years past. The difference is that independent firms in a supply chain are relatively free to enter and leave supply chain relationships if these relationships are no longer proving beneficial; it is this free market alliance-building that allows supply chains to operate more effectively than vertically integrated conglomerates.

For example, when a particular item is in short supply accompanied by rising prices, a firm might find it beneficial to align itself with one of these suppliers to ensure a continued supply of the scarce item. This alignment may become beneficial to both parties—new markets for the supplier leading to new, future product opportunities, and long-term continuity of supply and stable prices for the buyer. Later, when new competitors start producing the scarce product or when demand declines, the supplier may no longer be valued by the buying firm; instead, the firm may see more value in negotiating with other potential suppliers for its purchase requirements and may then decide to dissolve the original buyer–supplier alignment. As can be seen from this example, supply chains are often very dynamic or fluid, which can also cause problems in effectively managing them.

While supply chain management may allow organizations to realize the advantages of vertical integration, certain conditions must be present for successful supply chain management to occur. One important prerequisite is a melding of the corporate cultures of the supply chain participants so they are receptive to the requirements of supply chain management. More traditional organizational cultures that emphasize short-term, company-focused performance can conflict with the objectives of supply chain management. Supply chain management focuses on positioning organizations in such a way that all participants in the supply chain benefit. As described in the chapter opening SCM Profile of Hologic, effective supply chain management relies on high levels of trust, cooperation, collaboration, and honest, accurate communications.

Purchasing, manufacturing, and logistics managers not only must be equipped with the necessary expertise in these supply chain functions but also must appreciate and understand how these functions interact and affect the entire supply chain. Rebecca Morgan, president of Fulcrum Consulting Works, an Ohio-based supply chain management consulting firm, says too many companies go into agreements they call partnerships, then try to control the relationship from end to end. "A lot of the automotive companies did this in the beginning," she says. "They issued a unilateral ultimatum: you will do this for me if you want to do business with me, no matter what it means for you."[8] This type of supply chain management approach can lead to distrust, poor supplier performance, finding ways to "beat the system," and ultimately poor supply chain performance.

Boundaries of supply chains are also dynamic. It has often been said that supply chain boundaries for the focal firm extend from "the suppliers' suppliers to the customers' customers." Today, most supply chain collaboration efforts do not extend beyond these boundaries. In fact, in many cases, firms find it very difficult to extend coordination efforts beyond a few of their most important direct suppliers and customers (in one survey, a number of firm representatives stated that most of their supply chain efforts were with the firm's *internal* suppliers and customers only!).[9] However, with time and successful initial results, many firms are extending the boundaries of their supply chains to include their **second-tier suppliers**, **second-tier customers**, and logistics service providers. Some of the firms considered to be the best at managing their supply chains have very recognizable names. Each year, for example, the business advisory company Gartner, Inc. announces the twenty-five companies that exhibit the best supply chain management leadership. For 2013, the top ten companies on this list were Apple, McDonald's, Amazon.com, Unilever, Intel, Proctor & Gamble, Cisco Systems, Samsung Electronics, Coca-Cola, and Colgate-Palmolive.[10]

THE IMPORTANCE OF SUPPLY CHAIN MANAGEMENT

While all firms are part of a chain of organizations bringing products and services to customers (and most firms operate within a number of supply chains), certainly not all supply chains are managed in a truly coordinated fashion. Firms continue to operate independently in many industries (particularly small firms). It is often easy for managers to be focused solely on their immediate customers, their daily operations, their sales, and their costs. After all, with customers complaining, employees to train, late supplier deliveries, creditors to pay, and equipment to repair, who has time for relationship building and other supply chain management efforts? Particularly within the recent economic downturn, firms were struggling to just keep their doors open.

Many firms today, though, have worked through their economic problems and are encountering some value-enhancing benefits from their supply chain management efforts. Firms with large system inventories, many suppliers, complex product assemblies, and highly valued customers with large purchasing budgets have the most to gain from the practice of supply chain management. For these firms, even moderate supply chain management success can mean lower purchasing and inventory carrying costs, better product quality, and higher levels of customer service—all leading to more sales and better profits.

According to the U.S. Census Bureau's Annual Survey of Manufactures, the total cost of all materials purchased in 2011 exceeded $3.2 trillion among U.S. manufacturers, up from $2.8 trillion in 2010 and about the same as in 2008. The total 2011 end-of-year cost of

SCM Profile | IBM's Global Supply Chain Management Capabilities Evolve

IBM's global supply chains include hundreds of thousands of suppliers, from mainframe computers, servers, and other hardware to software, services, and spare parts. Managing such large and complex supply chains while achieving integration is no small task. In many respects, it came about as the company itself evolved. There was a point in time, for example, when IBM let every business unit in the company run itself. Later, as IBM became a global enterprise, their supply chains changed radically as well. Today, all supply chain processes are fully integrated on a global basis, from purchasing to manufacturing and logistics.

IBM realized that if their supply chains were going to be successful, they had to function in a circular and networked fashion and not in the older, linear model. "In the older, linear model, we began with goods coming into the process at the beginning of the supply chain and we finished with completed products coming out on the other end of the supply chain. Today, the supply chain is much more complex. It functions in more of a multi-point network configuration. The movements of goods, processes and communications are all network-centric and we use business analytics to manage the entirety of the process instead of trying to manage it through individual pipes of activity. This is a different vision," explains Mike Ray, VP of Business Integration and Strategy at IBM.[11]

inventories for all U.S. manufacturers was over $590 billion, up from $489 billion in 2009.[12] Thus, it can be seen that purchasing and inventory costs can be quite sizable for firms and represent areas where significant cost savings can be realized when using effective supply chain management strategies. In fact, in a 2010 survey of supply chain progress conducted by Michigan State University and *Supply Chain Management Review* magazine, 77 percent of the respondents reported an increase in their emphases on supply chain management as a way to counteract the global economic decline. Additionally, about 61 percent reported that their supply chain initiatives had a moderate to high impact on cost improvement.[13]

Supply chain management efforts can start small—for instance, with just one key supplier—and build through time to include more supply chain participants such as other important suppliers, key customers, and logistics services. Finally, supply chain management efforts can include second-tier suppliers and customers. So why are these integration activities so important? As alluded to earlier, when a firm, its customers, and its suppliers all know each others' future plans and are willing to work together, the planning process is easier and much more productive in terms of cost savings, quality improvements, and service enhancements. The nearby SCM Profile describes IBM's growth in supply chain management capabilities over the years.

On the other hand, lack of effective supply chain management can cause problems for organizations. Using a fictitious setting, Example 1.1 illustrates some of the costs associated with independent planning and lack of supply chain information sharing and coordination.

Grebson's safety stock, which they have built into their roller bearing purchase orders, has resulted in still additional safety stock production levels at the Pearson plant. In fact, some of the erratic purchasing patterns of Grebson are probably due to their leftover safety stocks causing lower purchase quantities during those periods. This, in turn, creates greater demand variability, leading to a decision at Pearson to produce an even higher level of safety stock. This same scenario plays out between Pearson and CJ Steels, with erratic buying patterns by Pearson and further safety stock production by CJ. This magnification of safety stock, based on erratic demand patterns and forecasts derived from demand already containing safety stock, continues to grow as orders pass to more distant suppliers up the supply chain.

The continuing cycle of erratic demand causing forecasts to include safety stock which in turn magnify supplier forecasts and cause production planning problems is known as the **bullwhip effect**. If Grebson Manufacturing *knew* its customers' purchase plans for the coming quarter along with how their purchase plans were derived, it would be much more confident about what the upcoming demand was going to be, resulting in little, if any, safety stock requirement, and consequently it would be able to communicate its own purchase plans for roller bearings to Pearson. If Grebson purchased its roller bearings from only Pearson and,

Example 1.1 Grebson Manufacturing's Supply Chain

The Pearson Bearings Co. makes roller bearings for Grebson Manufacturing on an as-needed basis. For the upcoming quarter, they have forecasted Grebson's roller bearing demand to be 25,000 units. Since Grebson's demand for bearings from Pearson has been somewhat erratic in the past due to the number of bearing companies competing with Pearson and also the fluctuation of demand from Grebson's customers, Pearson's roller bearing forecast includes 5,000 units of safety stock. The steel used in Pearson Bearings' manufacturing process is usually purchased from CJ Steels, Inc. CJ Steels has, in turn, forecasted Pearson's quarterly demand for the high-carbon steel it typically purchases for roller bearings. The forecast also includes safety stock of about 20 percent over what CJ Steels expects to sell to Pearson over the next three months.

Since Pearson Bearings does not know with full confidence what Grebson's roller bearing demand will be for the upcoming quarter (it could be zero, or it could exceed 25,000 units), Pearson will incur the extra costs of producing and holding 5,000 units of safety stock. Additionally, Pearson Bearings risks having to either scrap, sell, or hold onto any units not sold to Grebson, as well as losing current and future sales to Grebson if their demand exceeds 25,000 units over the next quarter. CJ Steels faces the same dilemma—extra materials, labor costs, and warehouse space for safety stock along with the potential stockout costs of lost present and future sales. Additionally, Grebson's historic demand pattern for roller bearings from its suppliers already includes some safety stock, since it uses roller bearings in one of the products it makes for a primary customer.

further, told Pearson what its quarterly purchase plans were, and if Pearson did likewise with CJ Steels, safety stocks throughout the supply chain would be reduced considerably, driving down the costs of purchasing, producing, and carrying roller bearings at each stage. Trade estimates suggest that the bullwhip effect results in excess costs on the order of 12 to 25 percent for each firm in a supply chain, which can be a tremendous competitive disadvantage. This discussion also sets the stage for a supply chain management concept called collaborative planning, forecasting, and replenishment, discussed further in Chapter 5.

As working relationships throughout the supply chain mature, key trading partners will feel more comfortable investing capital in better facilities, better products, and better services for their customers. With time, customers will share more information with suppliers, and suppliers will be more likely to participate in their key customers' new product design efforts, for instance. These, then, become some of the more important benefits of a well-integrated supply chain. In the following chapters of the text, other associated benefits will also become apparent.

THE ORIGINS OF SUPPLY CHAIN MANAGEMENT IN THE U.S.

During the 1950s and 1960s, U.S. manufacturers were employing mass production techniques to reduce costs and improve productivity, while little attention was typically paid to creating supplier partnerships, improving process design and flexibility, or improving product quality (see Figure 1.2). New product design and development was slow and relied exclusively on in-house resources, technologies, and capacity. Sharing technology and expertise through strategic buyer–supplier partnerships was essentially unheard of back then. Processes on the factory floor were cushioned with inventories to keep machinery running and maintain balanced material flows, resulting in large investments in work-in-process inventories.

Figure 1.2 Historic Supply Chain Management Events in the United States

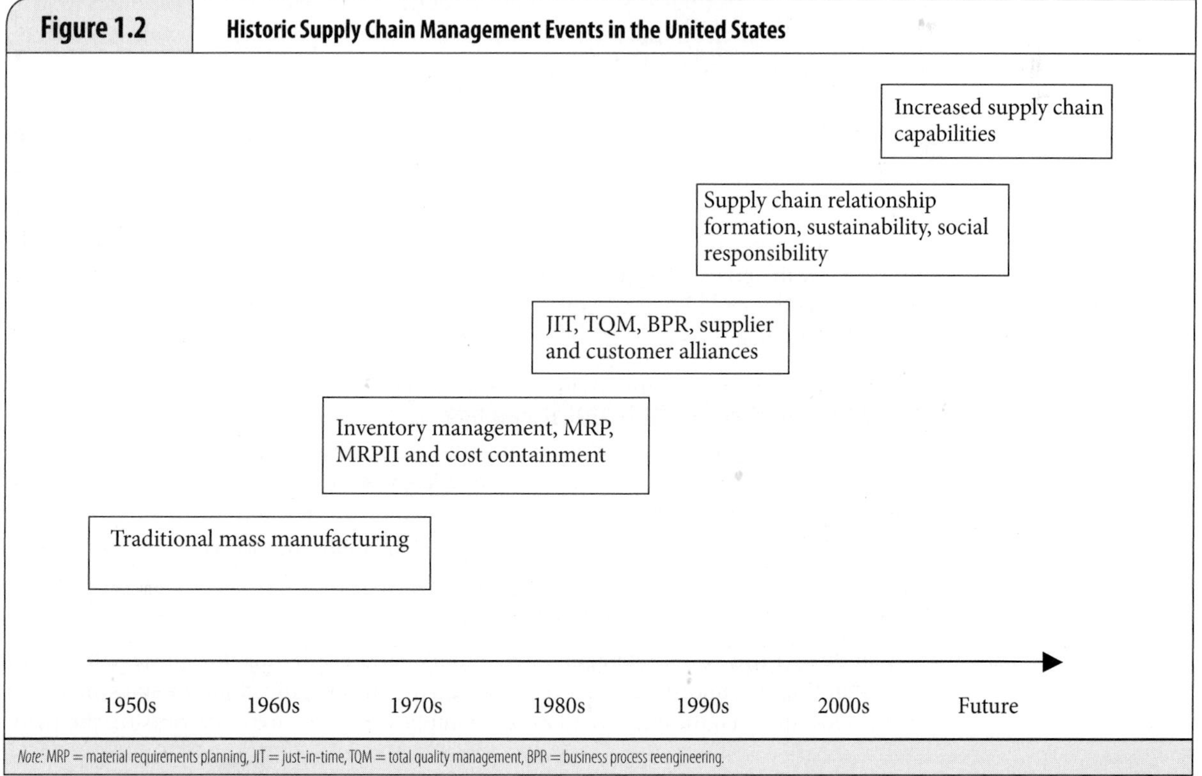

Note: MRP = material requirements planning, JIT = just-in-time, TQM = total quality management, BPR = business process reengineering.

In the 1960s and 1970s, computer technologies began to flourish and material requirements planning (MRP) software applications and manufacturing resource planning (MRPII) software applications were developed. These systems allowed companies to see the importance of effective materials management—they could now recognize and quantify the impact of high levels of inventories on manufacturing, storage, and transportation costs. As computer capabilities grew, the sophistication of inventory tracking software also grew, making it possible to further reduce inventory costs while improving internal communication of the need for purchased parts and supplies.

The 1980s were the breakout years for supply chain management. One of the first widely recorded uses of the term *supply chain management* came about in a paper published in 1982.[14] Intense global competition beginning in the 1980s (and continuing today) provided an incentive for U.S. manufacturers to make low-cost, high-quality products along with high levels of customer service. Manufacturers utilized just-in-time (JIT) and total quality management (TQM) strategies to improve quality, manufacturing efficiencies, and delivery times. In a JIT manufacturing environment with little inventory to cushion scheduling and/or production problems, firms began to realize the potential benefits and importance of strategic and cooperative supplier–buyer–customer relationships, which are the foundations of SCM. The concept of these partnerships or alliances emerged as manufacturers experimented with JIT and TQM.

As competition in the United States intensified further in the 1990s accompanied by increasing logistics costs and the trend toward market globalization, the challenges associated with improving quality, cost, customer service, and product design also increased. To deal with these challenges, manufacturers began purchasing from a select number of certified, high-quality suppliers with excellent service reputations and involved these suppliers in their new product design activities as well as in cost, quality, and service improvement initiatives. In other words, companies realized that if they started giving only their best suppliers most of their business, then they, in return, could expect these suppliers to provide continued benefits in the form of on-time deliveries; high-quality, low-cost products; and help with new product design efforts.

Interestingly, the general idea of supply chain management had been discussed for many years prior to the chain of events shown in Table 1.1. In 1915, Arch W. Shaw of the Harvard Business School wrote the textbook *Some Problems in Market Distribution,* considered by many to be the first on the topic of what we now refer to as supply chain management (Shaw never used this term). The text included discussions of how best to purchase raw materials, transport products, locate facilities, and analyze productivity and waste. He recommended a "laboratory point of view" or what could be termed a systematic study of supply chain issues.[15]

Business process reengineering (BPR), or the radical rethinking and redesigning of business processes to reduce waste and increase performance, was introduced in the early 1990s and was the result of a growing interest during this time in the need for cost reductions and a return to an emphasis on the key competencies of the firm to enhance long-term competitive advantage. As this fad died down in the mid- to late 1990s (the term became synonymous with downsizing and thus fell out of favor), the practice of supply chain management rapidly increased in popularity as a source of competitive advantage.

Also during this time, managers, consultants, and academics began developing an understanding of the differences between logistics and supply chain management. Up until then, supply chain management was simply viewed as logistics outside the firm.

As companies began implementing supply chain management initiatives, they began to understand the necessity of integrating key business processes among the supply chain participants, enabling the supply chain to act and react as one entity. Today, logistics is viewed as one important element of the much broader supply chain management concept.

At the same time, companies also saw benefits in the creation of alliances or partnerships with their customers. Developing these long-term, close relationships with customers meant holding less finished product safety stock (as discussed earlier in the bullwhip effect example) and allowed firms to focus their resources on providing better products and services to their best customers. In time, when market share improved for its customers' products, the result was more business for the firm.

Thus, supply chain management has evolved along two parallel paths: (1) the purchasing and supply management emphasis from industrial buyers and (2) the logistics and customer service emphasis from wholesalers and retailers. The increasing popularity of these alliances with suppliers and customers (and suppliers' suppliers and customers' customers) in the later part of the 1990s and continuing today has also meant a greater reliance on the shipping, warehousing, and logistics services that provide transportation, storage, documentation, and customs clearing services to many firms within a typical supply chain. Relationship building has also occurred increasingly with many of these **third-party logistics providers (3PLs)** to ensure a continuous, uninterrupted supply of goods. The need to periodically assess the performance of these relationships has also accompanied the growth of supply chain management. One of the challenges faced today by many firms involved in supply chain management is how to adequately assess overall performance in often extremely complex, global supply chains. This idea of evaluating supply chain performance from numerous perspectives including financial, sustainability, speed, and risk is explored in Chapter 14.

For the wholesaling and retailing industries, the supply chain management focus is on location, logistics, and customer service issues more often compared to manufacturing. Supply chain management in these industries has often been referred to as quick response, service response logistics, or integrated logistics. The advancement of electronic data interchange (EDI) systems, bar coding, Internet systems, logistics software applications, and radio frequency identification (RFID) technologies over the past two decades has greatly aided the evolution of the integrated supply chain concept. Retailers utilize supply chain management to help meet changing demands in the marketplace and to reduce inventories throughout their supply chains.

Most recently, the rapid development of client/server supply chain management software that typically includes integrated supply chain management and electronic commerce components has aided in the evolution and adoption of supply chain management. Sharing information with supply chain partners through the Internet has enabled firms to integrate stocking, logistics, materials acquisition, shipping, and other functions to create a more proactive and effective style of business management and customer responsiveness.

Today, an emphasis is being placed on the environmental and social impacts of supply chains. Customers are demanding that companies and their supply chains act in an ethically and socially responsible manner. This includes attention to how suppliers are hiring and training employees, how they are harvesting plants and other materials, how their activities impact the environment, and what sorts of sustainability policies are being utilized. With these practices in mind, supply chain managers today must also cope with maintaining the most flexible supply chain possible to take advantage of new markets, new sources of supply, and new customer demands.

THE FOUNDATIONS OF SUPPLY CHAIN MANAGEMENT

The foundation elements of supply chain management are introduced in this section. These elements essentially make up the table of contents for this textbook and are shown in Table 1.1 along with the chapters where they are discussed.

Supply Elements

Traditional purchasing strategies typically emphasized the use of many suppliers, competitive bidding, and short-term contracts. This often created adversarial buyer–supplier relationships with a focus primarily on the product's purchase price instead of the capabilities of the suppliers and how they could contribute to the long-term competitiveness of the buying organization. In many cases, purchasing was performed by a clerk. Over the past twenty or twenty-five years, there has been a shift toward a more strategic approach to purchasing, and this broader approach is more commonly referred to as **supply management**. Supply management professionals now most often perform the purchasing function. Effective supply management has resulted generally in smaller supply bases and the development of more long-term supplier relationships to achieve the competitive benefits described earlier.

Purchasing and the strategic concepts of supply management are one of the foundations of supply chain management, since incoming material quality, delivery timing, purchase price, product safety, and the impact of purchasing on the environment are all affected by the buyer–supplier relationship and the capabilities of suppliers. "The issues today are more challenging and global," observes Mohan Ponnudurai, industry solution director at software provider Sparta Systems. "The challenge is to manage suppliers, ensuring the right type of suppliers from a brand risk perspective while meeting your mission regarding safety, regulatory compliance, costs and a global presence."[16] Chapters 2 through 4 cover the topics associated with supply management.

The recent economic downturn added another problem to the supply side of businesses, namely how the focal firm will continue to produce when several key suppliers go out of business. "One of the lessons learned was that we often do a very good job of looking at the creditworthiness of our customers and their ability to pay us, but we don't do as good a job looking at the financial wherewithal of our suppliers," says Tom Murphy, executive vice president of manufacturing and wholesale distribution at Georgia-based RSM McGladrey, a professional services firm.[17] Thus, supply chain managers are busy building better visibility into their supply chains to spot these problems before they become unmanageable.

One of the more crucial issues within the topic of supply management is **supplier management**. Simply put, this means encouraging or helping the firm's suppliers to perform in some desired fashion, and there are a number of ways to do this. This involves assessing

Table 1.1 The Foundations of Supply Chain Management

FOUNDATION ELEMENTS	IMPORTANT ISSUES	CHAPTERS
Supply	supply base reduction, supplier alliances, SRM, global sourcing, ethical and sustainable sourcing	2, 3, 4
Operations	demand management, CPFR, inventory management, MRP, ERP, lean systems, Six Sigma quality	5, 6, 7, 8
Logistics	logistics management, CRM, network design, RFID, global supply chains, sustainability, service response logistics	9, 10, 11, 12
Integration	barriers to integration, risk and security management, performance measurement, green supply chains	13, 14

suppliers' current capabilities and then deciding if and how they need to improve them. Thus, one of the key activities in supplier management is **supplier evaluation**, or determining the current capabilities of suppliers. This occurs both when potential suppliers are being evaluated for a future purchase and when existing suppliers are periodically evaluated for ongoing performance purposes. A closely related activity is **supplier certification**. Supplier certification allows buyers to assume the supplier will meet certain product quality and service requirements covered by the certification, thus reducing duplicate testing and inspections and the need for extensive supplier evaluations. Farm implement manufacturer Deere & Company, for example, has its Achieving Excellence program wherein suppliers are evaluated annually across several performance categories. The idea is to reward high performers and provide feedback to promote continuous improvement. InnerWorkings, a print management solutions provider, recently was named a partner-level supplier for 2012 by Deere and was inducted into Deere's Supplier Hall of Fame for attaining partner-level status for five consecutive years.[18]

Over time, supplier management efforts allow firms to selectively screen out poor-performing suppliers and build successful, trusting relationships with the remaining top-performing suppliers. These suppliers can provide tremendous benefits to the buying firm and the entire supply chain. As discussed in greater detail in Chapter 2, greater purchase volumes per supplier typically mean lower per unit purchase costs (causing a much greater impact on profits than a corresponding increase in sales) and in many cases higher quality and better delivery service. These characteristics are viewed as strategically important to the firm because of their impact on the firm's competitiveness.

Suppliers see significant benefits from the creation of closer working relationships with customers in terms of long-term, higher-volume sales. These trading partner relationships have come to be termed **strategic partnerships** and are emphasized throughout this text as one of the more important aspects of supply chain management. Procter & Gamble, for example, has created strategic partnerships with several firms, including Accenture, Cisco, IBM, Microsoft, and Xerox. What distinguishes their strategic partners from other vendors is the ability to help strengthen P&G's capabilities in three strategic areas: visualization, digitization, and simulation. In simulation work, for example, physical product mock-ups can be replaced with virtual–reality applications, allowing marketers to virtually place products on the shelf next to those of competitors. This lets them evaluate packaging options more quickly and frequently, changing cycle time from weeks to hours.[19] Chapter 3 explores strategic partnerships and other topics associated with supplier relationship management.

Recently, the supply management discipline has come to include a closer emphasis on **ethical and sustainable sourcing**, or purchasing from suppliers that are governed by environmental sustainability and social and ethical practices. Companies are realizing that suppliers can have a significant impact on a firm's reputation and carbon footprint, as well as their costs and profits. Supply chain managers must therefore learn how to develop socially responsible and environmentally friendly sourcing strategies that also create a competitive advantage for the company. These topics along with other supplier management topics are discussed in detail in Chapter 4.

Operations Elements

Once materials, components, and other purchased products are delivered to the buying organization, a number of internal operations elements become important in assembling or processing the items into finished products, ensuring that the right amount of product is produced and that finished goods and services meet specific quality, cost, and customer service requirements. Along with supply management, operations management is also considered a foundation of supply chain management and is covered in Chapters 5 through 8.

During a calendar year, seasonal demand variations commonly occur. Firms can predict when these variations occur, based on historic demand patterns, and use forecasting techniques to guide weekly or monthly production plans. If demand does not occur as forecasted, then the focal firm is left with either too much inventory (or service capacity) or too little. Both situations are cost burdens to the firm and can result in permanent lost future business if a stockout has occurred. To minimize these costs, firms often rely on **demand management** strategies and systems, with the objective of matching demand to available capacity, either by improving production scheduling, curtailing demand, using a back-order system, or increasing capacity. In a recent survey of supply chain managers, stockouts were considered the most pressing issue in the use of demand management activities, followed closely by excess inventories and long lead times.[20]

Managing inventories is one of the most important aspects of operations and is certainly value enhancing for the firm. Firms typically have some sort of **material requirements planning (MRP)** software system for managing their inventories. These systems can be linked throughout the organization and its supply chain partners using **enterprise resource planning (ERP)** systems, providing real-time sales data, inventory, and production information to all business units and to key supply chain participants. These system configurations vary considerably, based on the number and complexity of products, size of the firm, and design of the supply chain. Retailers like Wal-Mart, for example, scan the bar codes of items when consumers make purchases, causing the local store's MRP system to deduct units from inventory until a preset reorder point is reached. When this occurs, the local computer system automatically contacts Wal-Mart's regional distribution center's MRP system and generates an order. At the distribution center, the order is filled and sent along with other orders to the particular Wal-Mart. Eventually, the inventory at the distribution center needs replenishing, and at that time, the distribution center's MRP system automatically generates an order with the manufacturer who sells the product to Wal-Mart. This order communication and **inventory visibility** may extend farther up the supply chain, reducing the likelihood of stockouts, excess inventories, and long lead times.

Another common form of inventory management is through use of a **lean production system** (lean production may also be referred to as just-in-time or the Toyota Production System). Implementing a lean system takes time but usually results in faster delivery times, lower inventory levels, and better quality. Missouri-based Barnes-Jewish Hospital applied the principles of lean production to reduce the time it took to treat stroke patients once they had arrived. When the changes were implemented in 2011, the so-called "door to needle" times decreased by 40 percent, and the percentage of stroke patients receiving care within the first hour of arrival increased from 52 to 78 percent.[21]

An important aspect of a lean production system is the quality of the incoming purchased items and the quality of the assemblies as they move through the various production processes. This is due to the characteristically low inventory levels of purchased goods and work in process in lean-oriented facilities. Thus, firms and supply chains employing concepts of lean production usually have a **Six Sigma quality management** strategy in place to ensure continued quality compliance among suppliers and with internal production facilities. The type of inventory control system used is especially important when considering the design of the supply chain (for instance, where to construct distribution centers, what transportation services to use, and how big to make production facilities and warehouses).

Logistics Elements

When goods are produced, they can be delivered to customers through a number of different modes of transportation. Delivering products to customers at the right time, quality, and volume requires a high level of planning and cooperation between the firm, its customers, and the various logistics elements or services employed (such as transportation, warehousing, and break-bulk or repackaging services). In contrast, services are produced and delivered to the customer simultaneously in most cases, so services are extremely dependent upon server capacity and successful service delivery to meet customer requirements. Logistics is the third foundation of supply chain management, and these topics are presented in Chapters 9 through 12.

Logistics decisions typically involve a trade-off between cost and delivery timing or customer service. Motor carriers (trucks), for example, are more expensive to use than rail carriers but offer more flexibility and speed, particularly for short routes. Air carriers are even more expensive but much faster than any other transportation mode. Water carriers are the slowest but are also the least expensive. Finally, pipeline transportation is used to transport oil, water, natural gas, and coal slurry. Many transportation services offer various modal combinations, as well as warehousing and customs-clearing services.

In a typical integrated supply chain environment where JIT deliveries are the norm, **third-party logistics services** or 3PLs are critical to the overall success of the supply chain. In many cases, these services are considered supply chain partners and are viewed as key value enhancers for the supply chain. From recent earthquakes, to tornadoes, to volcanoes, to floods, companies are teaming up with 3PLs to improve visibility and flexibility while reducing risk in their supply chains. "Globally, manufacturers and retailers are taking a renewed interest in redesigning and reengineering their supply chains in the wake of these events," says Jim McAdam, president of 3PL provider APL Logistics.[22]

The desired outcome of logistics is customer service at a reasonable price. In order to provide a desired level of customer service, firms must identify customer requirements and then provide the right combination of transportation, warehousing, packaging, and information services to successfully satisfy those requirements. Through frequent contact with customers, firms develop **customer relationship management** strategies regarding meeting delivery due dates, resolving customer complaints, communicating with customers, and determining other logistics services required. From a supply chain management perspective, these customer activities take on added importance because second-tier, third-tier, and end-product consumers are ultimately dependent on the logistics outcomes at each stage within the supply chain.

Designing and building a **distribution network** is one method of ensuring successful product delivery. Again, there is typically a trade-off between the cost of the distribution network's design and customer service. For example, a firm may utilize a large number of regional or local warehouses in order to deliver products quickly to customers. The transportation cost from factory to warehouse, the inventory holding cost, and the cost to build and operate warehouses would be quite high, but the payoff would be better customer service. On the other hand, a firm may choose to operate only a few highly dispersed warehouses, saving money on the inbound transportation costs from factories (since they would be delivering larger quantities at one time) and the warehouse construction and operating costs but then having to be content with limited customer service capabilities as the warehouses would be located farther from most customers. Today, the use of massive, efficient warehouses to serve large market areas is growing, as described in the nearby SCM Profile of Skechers USA.

SCM Profile | Skechers Achieves Warehousing Efficiencies

One of the largest buildings in California sets a new standard for automated, energy-efficient warehousing. The 1.82 million square feet structure enables footwear retailer Skechers USA to consolidate operations from six warehouses to a single distribution hub serving the U.S. and Canada. "This building has the most advanced building-automation robotics coupled with being the largest green building of its kind in the United States, and probably in the world," says Iddo Benzeevi, president and CEO of Highland Fairview Properties, the project's developer.

The building stretches more than a half mile from one end to the other and is 700 feet wide. Yet it is technology as much as size that makes Skechers' new facility remarkable. Lighting can be switched on and off by activity sensors and is powered in part by on-site solar panels covering much of the roof. Energy efficiency was a necessity; with 81 million cubic feet of enclosed space, it would require millions of dollars in electricity costs to circulate air through the building's interior. Instead, fresh air is drawn through louvers facing the prevailing winds, eliminating the need for energy-intensive climate control systems in the majority of the space. "The design is a paradigm shift, a technological breakthrough that gave us the ability to get the building to that size and still be green," says Benzeevi.

Human hands will seldom touch merchandise from the time it enters the center until it emerges for pickup at one of 270 truck bays. An automated storage and retrieval system of conveyor belts and robotic lifts will whisk shoes to and from densely packed storage racks that stretch to a height of 50 feet. The automated system will enable Skechers to move as many as 20,000 pairs of shoes in an hour.

The Skechers project epitomizes a trend toward massive distribution centers. Since the end of the recession, companies have increasingly consolidated multiple warehouses into single, large distribution centers to achieve greater economies of scale.[23]

When firms operate globally, their supply chains are more complex, making global location decisions, the topic of Chapter 11, a necessary aspect of supply chain management. The increasing demand for products in emerging global markets like Russia, India, and China combined with growing foreign competition in domestic markets, along with low labor costs in many Asian countries, have made overseas business commonplace for many companies. Firms must understand both the risks and advantages of operating in foreign locations and the impact this may have on their **global supply chains**. Some of the advantages include a larger market for products, economies of scale in purchasing and production, lower labor costs, a supply base of potentially cheaper, higher-quality suppliers, and the generation of new product ideas from foreign suppliers and employees. Some of the risks include fluctuating exchange rates affecting production, warehousing, and purchasing and selling prices; government intervention or political instabilities causing supply disruptions; security concerns; and potential changes in subsidies, tariffs, and taxes.

Companies react to these problems by building flexibility into their global supply chains. This is accomplished by using a number of suppliers as well as manufacturing and storage facilities in various foreign locations. As product demand and economic conditions change, the supply chain can react to take advantage of opportunities or cost changes to maximize profits. "Obviously, those with production capability in multiple regions and/or countries present a lower risk than a single location or a cluster of facilities in a single region or country," says Mark Taylor, vice president at North Carolina-based Risk

International Services. "Even if you source 90 percent from the primary, by maintaining a second or third qualified (supplier), you've substantially shortened your lead time in making a change."[24]

For service products, the physical distribution issue is typically much less complex. Making sure services are delivered in a timely fashion is the topic of Chapter 12. Services are, for the most part, delivered by a server when customers request service. For instance, consider an example in which a customer walks into an auto repair facility in search of service for her automobile. She may talk to two or three facility employees during this service but eventually will complete a repair form, wait for the service to be completed, and then receive her repaired automobile. She will leave, satisfied with the service she received provided that a number of things occurred: she got what she came for (the repair job), she got the type of service she expected to get (a reasonable waiting period, knowledgeable servers, and a repaired auto), and she got the service at a reasonable price. Otherwise, she will most likely be dissatisfied.

Successful service delivery depends on service location (service providers must be close to the customers they are trying to serve), service capacity (customers will leave if the wait is too long), and service capability (customers must be able to trust what servers are telling them or doing for them). The final requirement of successful service is knowing what customers want. Residence Inn now has a guarantee of family-friendly amenities. They know that about one-third of their customers remove minibar items to chill food and drink items, and about half of families will want to wash items in the sink. Their suites come equipped to handle these needs.[25] Goods producers must also be concerned with the delivery of services to their customers, such as providing warranty repairs and information, financing, insurance, and equipment troubleshooting and operating information.

Integration Elements

Thus far, three of the foundations of supply chain management have been discussed: supply, operations, and logistics activities occurring among the firm and its tiers of customers and suppliers. The final foundation topic—and certainly the most difficult one—is to integrate these processes among the focal firm and its key supply chain trading partners. Supply chain **process integration** is discussed in the final two chapters of the text.

Processes in a supply chain are said to be integrated when members of the supply chain work together to make purchasing, inventory, production, quality, logistics, and other decisions that impact the overall profits of the supply chain. If one key process activity fails or is performed poorly, then the flow of goods moving along the supply chain is disrupted, jeopardizing the effectiveness of the entire supply chain. Successful supply chain process integration occurs when the participants realize that effective supply chain management must become part of each member's strategic planning process, where objectives and policies are jointly determined based on the end consumers' needs and what the supply chain as a whole can do for them.

Ultimately, firms act together to maximize total supply chain profits by determining optimal purchase quantities, product availabilities, service levels, lead times, production quantities, use of technology, and product support at each tier within the supply chain. This integration process also requires high levels of internal functional integration of activities within each of the participating firms, such that the supply chain acts as one entity. This idea of supply chain integration can run contrary to the notion among many potential supply chain participants of their firm's independent profit-maximizing objectives, making supply chain integration a very tough sell in many supplier–buyer–customer situations. Thus, continued efforts are required to break down obstacles, change cultural norms and adversarial relationships, knock down silos, reduce conflict, and bridge functional barriers within and between companies if supply chain integration is to become a reality. When John Bradshaw, for instance, was hired by Belgium-based Godiva Chocolatier as vice president of global procurement, his changes had everything to do with integration. "Each function was doing its work in isolation and throwing the results over the wall for the next function," remarked Bill Kornegay, senior vice president of global supply chain for Godiva. "He had everyone work through touch points in the process, such as who should be communicating with whom and when, helping tear down walls that built up over time," he added. Bradshaw's strategies were projected to save the company over $10 million per year.[26]

One additional integration topic is the use of a **supply chain performance measurement** system. Performance measurements must be utilized along supply chains to help firms keep track of their supply chain management efforts. It is crucial for firms to know whether certain strategies are working as expected—or not—before they become financial drains on the organizations. Firms work together to develop long-term supply chain management strategies and then devise tactics to implement these strategies. Performance measurements help firms decide the value of these tactics and should be developed to highlight performance within the areas of purchasing, operations, logistics, and integration.

Performance measures should be designed around each important supply chain activity and should be detailed performance descriptors instead of merely sales or cost figures. High levels of supply chain performance occur when the strategies at each of the firms fit well with overall supply chain strategies. Thus, each firm must understand its role in the supply chain, the needs of the supply chain's end customer, the needs of the firm's immediate customers, and how these needs translate into internal operations requirements and the requirements being placed on suppliers. Once these needs and the products and services themselves can be communicated and transported through the supply chain effectively, successful supply chain management and its associated benefits will be realized.

CURRENT TRENDS IN SUPPLY CHAIN MANAGEMENT

The practice of supply chain management is a fairly recent phenomenon, and many organizations are beginning to realize both the benefits and problems accompanying integrated supply chains. Supply chain management is a complex and time-consuming undertaking, involving cultural change among most or all of the participants, investment and training in new software and communication systems, the building of trust between supply chain members, and a change or realignment of the competitive strategies employed among at least some of the participating firms. Further, as competitors, products, technologies, economic conditions, and customers change, the priorities for supply chains also change. A look at the most recent surveys and interviews of executives in a number of industries reveals a number of supply chain issues that companies are addressing today, including the contraction of the supply chain, managing supply chain risk, and increasing supply chain visibility.[27] While these and other supply chain management issues are discussed in numerous places in this text, these newest trends are discussed below to give the reader a better sense of some of the issues facing executives and their companies' supply chains today.

Shrinking the Supply Chain

A number of concerns have many company executives considering moving their foreign production back home or close to home, referred to as **back-shoring**, **near-shoring**, or **right-shoring**. Volatile fuel costs, a desire to reduce delivery times and hence improve on-time capabilities, and the deceasing labor cost differentials when comparing labor costs in China, India, and the U.S. have all contributed to this trend. Some of these firms have also found that demand in their foreign markets is contracting or their foreign suppliers have gone out of business. Further, security concerns are growing in many foreign markets, prompting a concern that it might be time to concentrate on doing what the firm does best, back in its domestic market.

Mexico is once again looking good as a production location to U.S. organizations. A survey by global business advisory firm AlixPartners found that the geographical proximity of Mexico and recent improvements in its transport services have encouraged 63 percent of U.S.-based senior executives to choose Mexico as the most attractive location for near-shoring manufacturing operations. "As companies think about near-shoring production that was previously off-shored to respond to rising labor costs overseas and exchange rate changes, Mexico is obviously high on their lists," says Foster Finley, managing director of AlixPartners.[28]

While a few years ago China was the preferred destination for U.S. offshore manufacturing, this trend appears to be ending. A 2011 analysis by the Boston Consulting Group (BCG), a global business adviser, concluded, "By sometime around 2015, for many goods destined for North American consumers, manufacturing in some parts of the U.S. will be just as economical as manufacturing in China." The report also described how Chinese wages were rising by 17 percent annually while the value of their currency was continuing to increase. Consequently, the gap between U.S. and Chinese wages is narrowing rapidly. In another BCG report, they surveyed manufacturers with offshore operations in 2011 and found that 40 percent were investigating bringing that work back to the U.S. within the year.[29]

Managing Supply Chain Risk

Supply chain risk can be defined as the likelihood of an internal or external event that causes a disruption or failure of supply chain operations, causing potential reductions in service levels, product quality, and sales, with an increase in costs. In recent years, some companies have been subjected to severe internal events while having no contingency plans to adequately manage these risks—Mattel's recall in 2007 of millions of Chinese-made toys that had been coated with lead paint; Toyota's sticking gas pedals in 2009/2010 vehicles, causing recalls and huge liability problems; and BP's 2010 Gulf of Mexico oil well blowout that killed eleven people and thousands of animals while disrupting commerce along the Gulf Coast, are a few such events. In other cases, external events have caused supply chain failures for many organizations—for example, when Hurricane Katrina slammed into New Orleans, Louisiana, and the surrounding area in 2005; the Eyjafjallajökull volcano in Iceland erupted in 2010, causing disruption to air travel across Europe; the Haiti earthquake in 2010 flattened cities and killed 200,000; and the 2011 Japanese tsunami engulfed many communities in Japan, killing 28,000 people. Even small events such as weather and traffic problems that can impact deliveries are a part of supply chain risk. Finally, security problems such as freight thefts, product tampering, intentional property damage, and terrorism all constitute potential risks to supply chains. In other words, supply chain risk can be the result of economic volatility, environmental crises, natural disasters, work stoppages, supply shortages, quality breakdowns, and many other unpleasant surprises. When one of these unanticipated events involves supply chains, the consequences can range from unpleasant to catastrophic; from increased costs and delays to a complete market collapse.

Supply chain disruptions, for example, were not on the minds of Astella Pharma executives on the night of June 17, 2009. Thieves stole a trailer containing $10 million of the company's pharmaceutical products from a truck stop in Tennessee. The cost of the stolen product, though, was a fraction of the losses eventually suffered by Astella. Acting on advice from the U.S. Food & Drug Administration, the company contacted every party in its supply chain to warn them of the stolen drugs. As a preventive measure, Astella withdrew from the marketplace all drugs with the same lot numbers as those that were stolen. The theft eventually cost the company $47 million, a figure equivalent to 10 percent of its North American sales for that quarter.[30]

Unfortunately, a recent study has shown that for firms with annual revenues of less than $500 million, only 25 percent take a proactive approach to risk management, even though most executives agree that supply chain risk levels are higher today than in 2005.[31] Managing risk involves identifying and understanding potential risks, determining the likelihood and consequences of each risk, ranking the risks according to their weighted costs, and then finally implementing risk mitigation plans for the risks deemed unacceptable.[32]

SCM Profile: Boeing's New Supply Chain Visibility

After decades of amassing gargantuan amounts of raw materials in warehouses and then accessing them as needed to build airliners at its Seattle facility, Boeing Co. desired a new approach for its new passenger liner, the 787. Instead of keeping its manufacturing in house, Boeing took a more global approach to sourcing components for the 787. Major portions of the aircraft were built in Australia, Canada, Korea, Japan, Italy, the UK, and Tulsa, Oklahoma. What's more, Boeing not only wanted to source components differently, it wanted them assembled at two different locations—Seattle and Charleston, South Carolina, all the while maintaining a high level of supply chain visibility.

"There's no question that Boeing, with its 787 program, has done probably the most unique and complicated deployment of our specific platform solution," says Doug Russell, vice president, Supply Chain Solutions at Virginia-based Exostar. "They're doing both single- and multi-tier visibility and have really pushed the edge of the envelope to leverage the capabilities of our solution to establish that visibility well down into their supply chain," Russell says. "It extends, in some cases, all the way to the raw materials like titanium and other exotic metals that are part of the 787, and it definitely represents a new approach in the aerospace and defense industry."

Boeing calls the five or six tiers of managed supply and demand, "Partner Managed Inventory". In practice, it means the company buys its raw materials and, figuratively speaking, places that raw material in a warehouse at the beginning of the supply chain. Then, when the need arises, it will order a titanium hinge from supplier A, who orders the machined part from supplier B, who orders the forging from supplier C, who orders the raw material out of the stock Boeing has already acquired. This way Boeing can watch the entire supply chain and have visibility into inventory at each step along the way.[33]

Increasing Supply Chain Visibility

Supply chain visibility can be defined as the ability of suppliers, manufacturers, business partners, and customers to know exactly where products are, at any point in the supply chain. This inventory visibility is obviously made easier by technology and can prove very advantageous when dealing with the types of disruptive events discussed above in the risk segment. UPS and Fedex tracking methods are good examples of visibility—shipments are tracked and monitored using technology and alerts are sent to shippers as the item is in transit and then delivered. Today, more sophisticated software applications are being developed and offered to organizations for tracking orders, inventories, deliveries, returned goods, and even employee attendance.[34]

Automaker Renault is using a cloud platform to allow tracking of its spare parts to all export markets around the world. The company expects that its cloud platform will help it to better serve its international markets and customers while reducing inventory and transportation costs.[35] In another example, Boeing has begun using a new system to provide visibility into its supply chain for manufactured parts for its new 787 jetliner as described in the nearby SCM Profile.

SUMMARY

Supply chain management is the integration of key business processes from initial raw material extraction to the final or end customer, including all intermediate processing, transportation, and storage activities and final sale to the end-product customer. It is working together to provide benefits to all stakeholders. Today, the practice of supply chain management is becoming extremely important to reduce costs and improve quality and customer service, with the end objective of improving competitiveness. Many firms are just now becoming adept at managing at least some part of their supply chains. Supply chain management is an outgrowth and expansion of lean and Six Sigma activities and has grown in popularity since the 1980s. The foundations of supply chain management can be found in the areas of purchasing, production, logistics, and collaboration between trading partners. Finally, as markets, political forces, technology, and economic conditions change around the world, the practice of supply chain management must also change and grow. This chapter serves as an opening discussion of the topic of supply chain management and describes what the remaining chapters will cover.

KEY TERMS

back-shoring, 21
bullwhip effect, 10
business process reengineering (BPR), 12
customer relationship management, 17
demand management, 16
distribution network, 17
enterprise resource planning (ERP), 16
ethical and sustainable sourcing, 15
global supply chains, 18
inventory visibility, 16
lean production system, 16
material requirements planning (MRP), 16
near-shoring, 21
process integration, 19
right-shoring, 21
second-tier customers, 8
second-tier suppliers, 8
Six Sigma quality management, 16
strategic partnerships, 15
supplier certification, 15
supplier evaluation, 15
supplier management, 14
supply chain, 5
supply chain management (SCM), 7
supply chain performance measurement, 20
supply management, 14
third-party logistics providers (3PLs), 13
third-party logistics services, 17

DISCUSSION QUESTIONS

1. Define the term *supply chain management* in your own words, and list its most important activities.
2. Can a small business like a local sandwich or bicycle shop benefit from practicing supply chain management? What would they most likely concentrate on?
3. Describe and draw a supply chain for a bicycle repair shop, and list the important supply chain members.
4. What roles do "collaboration" and "trust" play in the practice of supply chain management?
5. What types of organizations would benefit the most from practicing supply chain management? What sorts of improvements could be expected?
6. What is the bullwhip effect and what causes it? How would you try to reduce the bullwhip effect?

7. What are the benefits of supply chain management?
8. Can nonprofit, educational, or government organizations benefit from supply chain management? How?
9. What does the term, "third-tier supplier" mean? What about "third-tier customer"? What about the "focal firm"? Provide examples.
10. Could a firm have more than one supply chain? Explain.
11. When did the idea and term "supply chain management" first begin to be thought about and discussed? Which two operations management practices became the origin of supply chain management?
12. Do you think supply chain management is simply the latest trend in management thinking and will die out in a few years? Why or why not?
13. How has technology impacted supply chain management?
14. What are the four foundation elements of supply chain management? Describe some activities within each element.
15. Is the use of a large number of suppliers a good idea? Why?
16. Do you think the proper way to choose a supplier is to always find the one that will give you the lowest price? When might this not be a good idea?
17. What is supplier management? What are some of the activities of supplier management?
18. Why don't firms just buy out their suppliers and industrial customers, forming conglomerates, instead of practicing supply chain management?
19. What is demand management, and why is this an important part of supply chain management?
20. What is the difference between and MRP system and an ERP system?
21. What role do information systems play in supply chain management? Give some examples.
22. Briefly describe the terms *lean production* and *Six Sigma systems.*
23. What are 3PLs, and what role do they play in SCM?
24. What is logistics? What is the objective of logistics?
25. What trade-offs must be considered in designing a distribution system?
26. What are the advantages and risks involved with global supply chains?
27. What does process integration mean? Can supply chain management succeed without it? Why, or why not?
28. Why are performance measurement systems important when trying to manage supply chains?
29. What is back-shoring or near-shoring, and why is this happening today?
30. How would you define supply chain risk? Provide an example not listed in the textbook.
31. Describe supply chain visibility, and why supply chain managers like it.

ESSAY/PROJECT QUESTIONS

1. Visit the Web sites of companies like Wal-Mart, Dell, and Home Depot and see if you can find discussions of their supply chain management activities. List information you can find on purchasing/supplier, logistics, information system, inventory management, quality, and customer service issues.
2. Search on the term *supply chain management.* How many hits did you get? Describe five of the Web sites found in your search.
3. Go to http://www.agrichain-centre.com/ (or a similar website found when searching on *New Zealand supply chain management*), and discuss the current state of supply chain (or value chain) management in New Zealand.
4. Search on the term "bullwhip effect," and write a paper on the impacts of the bullwhip effect and the companies profiled in the papers you find.
5. Search on the term "supply chain management software applications," and write a paper about how companies use these to improve their financial performance.
6. Search on "green supply chains," and write a paper regarding the global regulatory status of environmental legislation and how it is impacting supply chain management.

ADDITIONAL RESOURCES

Burgess, R., "Avoiding Supply Chain Management Failure: Lessons from Business Process Reengineering," *The International Journal of Logistics Management* 9(1), 1998: 15–24.

Chopra, S., and P. Meindl, *Supply Chain Management: Strategy, Planning, and Operation.* Upper Saddle River, NJ: Prentice Hall, 2001.

Frazelle, E., *Supply Chain Strategy: The Logistics of Supply Chain Management.* New York: McGraw-Hill, 2002.

Hammer, M., and J. Champy, *Reengineering the Corporation.* London: Nicholas Brealey, 1993.

Handfield, R. B., and E. L. Nichols, *Introduction to Supply Chain Management.* Upper Saddle River, NJ: Prentice Hall, 1999.

Lambert, D. M., M. C. Cooper, and J. D. Pagh, "Supply Chain Management: Implementation Issues and Research Opportunities," *The International Journal of Logistics Management* 9(2), 1998: 1–19.

Lee, H. L., V. Padmanabhan, and S. Whang. "Information Distortion in a Supply Chain: The Bullwhip Effect," *Management Science* 43(4), 1997: 546–558.

Simchi-Levi, D., P. Kaminsky, and E. Simchi-Levi, *Designing and Managing the Supply Chain.* New York: McGraw-Hill, 2000.

Stevens, G. C., "Integrating the Supply Chain," *International Journal of Physical Distribution and Logistics Management* 19(8), 1989: 3–8.

Tan, K. C., "A Framework of Supply Chain Management Literature," *European Journal of Purchasing and Supply Management* 7(1): 39–48.

Webster, S., *Principles & Tools for Supply Chain Management.* New York: McGraw-Hill/Irwin, 2008.

ENDNOTES

1. Terreri, A., "Supply Chain Trends to Watch," *World Trade* 23(7), 2010: 16–21.
2. Anonymous, "Supply Chain Efficiency Can Lead to Bottom Line Success," *Logistics Management* 51(11), 2012: 16.

3. Hannon, D., "Supply Chain Chief Drives Collaboration," *Purchasing* 139(4), 2010: 52–53.
4. Carbone, J., "Supply Chain Manager of the Year: Steve Darendinger Champion of Change," *Purchasing*, 135(13), 2006: 37.
5. Listed in the CSCMP Terms and Glossary at www.cscmp.org
6. Found in the ISM Glossary of Key Supply Management Terms at www.ism.ws
7. Found in the APICS dictionary at www.apics.org
8. Zieger, A., "Don't Choose the Wrong Supply Chain Partner," *Frontline Solutions* 4(6), 2003: 10–14.
9. Tan, K., S. Lyman, and J. Wisner, "Supply Chain Management: A Strategic Perspective," *International Journal of Operations and Production Management* 2(6), 2002: 614–631.
10. Found at http://www.gartner.com/technology/supply-chain/top25.jsp
11. Hannon, D., "Supply Chain Chief Drives Collaboration," *Purchasing* 139(4), 2010: 52–53.
12. U.S. Census Bureau information found at http://www.census.gov/manufacturing/asm/index.html
13. Johnson, R., C. Poirier, M. Swink, and F. Quinn, "Eighth Annual Global Supply Chain Survey: Surviving Tough Economic Times," *Supply Chain Management Review* 14(6), 2010: 12–19.
14. Keith, O., and M. Webber, "Supply-Chain Management: Logistics Catches Up with Strategy," *Outlook*, 1982, cit. Christopher, M. G., *Logistics: The Strategic Issue*. London: Chapman and Hall, 1992.
15. Shaw, A., *Some Problems in Market Distribution*. Cambridge, MA: Harvard University Press, 1915.
16. Dutton, G., "Is Your Supply Chain Safe?" *World Trade* 26(1), 2013: 35–40.
17. Cable, J., "What You Can't See Can Hurt You," *Industry Week* 259(1), 2010: 44.
18. Anonymous, "InnerWorkings Earns Recognition as a John Deere 'Partner-Level Supplier,'" *Marketing Weekly News*, April 13, 2013: 126.
19. Weiss, M., and J. Drewry, "Making Partnerships Matter," *CIO* 25(3), 2011: 1.
20. Shea, M., and B. Gilleon, "The Powerful Potential of Demand Management," *Supply Chain Management Review* 15(3), 2011: 18–27.
21. Anonymous, "Lean Prevents Brain Damage," *Industrial Engineer* 44(12), 2012: 18.
22. Walz, M., "Trends to Watch in 2012," *World Trade* 25(1), 2012: 24–28.
23. Hannon, D., "Supply Chain Chief Drives Collaboration," *Purchasing* 139(4), 2010: 52–53.
24. Phillips, Z., "Outsourcing Overseas Cuts Costs, Raises Risks," *Business Insurance* 44(31), 2010: 11–12.
25. Anonymous, "Lodging Companies: Residence Inn Helps Families," *Marketing Weekly News*, May 19, 2012: 1358.

26. Ramirez, S., "The Art and Science of Supply Management," *World Trade* 23(4), 2010: 26–30.

27. See, for example, Dittman, J., "WT100 and the University of Tennessee: Supply Chain Survey," *World Trade* 24(7), 2011: 42–46; Zalud, B., "Don't Unchain that Supply Chain 'Melody,'" *Security* 48(9), 2011: 52–58; Burnson, P., "Global Trends Roundtable: What's on the Supply Chain Horizon," *Supply Chain Management Review* 16(2), 2012: 20–26; Trunick, P., "Cost vs. Risk in the Supply Chain," *World Trade* 25(10), 2012: 43; and Walz, M., "Trends to Watch in 2012," *World Trade* 25(1), 2012: 24–28.

28. Atkins, W., "Sectors: Logistics–Rethinking Logistics," *Foreign Direct Investment* June/July 2011: 1.

29. Anonymous, "The Re-Shoring Movement: Why Manufacturing Is Returning to America," *Agency Sales* 42(8), 2012: 48–52.

30. Schlegel, G., "Risk Management: Welcome to the New," *Logistics Management* 51(2), 2012: 42–45.

31. Ibid.

32. Tummala, R., and T. Schoenherr, "Assessing and Managing Risks Using the Supply Chain Risk Management Process (SCRMP)," *Supply Chain Management* 16(6), 2011: 474–483.

33. McCue, D., "High Flying: Supply Chain Visibility," *World Trade* 26(1), 2013: 24–29.

34. McCrea, B., "Supply Chain and Logistics Technology: Defining Visibility," *LogisticsManagement.com*, September 1, 2011: 1.

35. Anonymous, "Renault Expects Better Supply Chain Visibility from Cloud," *Material Handling & Logistics*, December 5, 2012: 1.

36. Copyright © 1994 President and Fellows of Harvard College (the Beer Game board version) and © 2002 The MIT Forum for Supply Chain Innovation (the Beer Game computerized version).

Appendix 1.1

The Beer Game

The Beer Game has become a very popular game played in operations management and supply chain management courses since being developed by MIT in the 1960s.[36] The game simulates the flow of product and information in a simple supply chain consisting of a retailer, a wholesaler, a distributor, and a manufacturer. One person takes the role of each supply chain partner in a typical game. The objective is to minimize total supply chain inventory and back-order costs. In this way, a class can be separated into any number of four-person supply chains—each supply chain competing against the others. The game is used to illustrate the bullwhip effect and the importance of timely and accurate communications and information with respect to purchases along the supply chain (in this game, no one is allowed to share any information other than current order quantities, as might be found in unmanaged or unlinked supply chains).

Each supply chain participant follows the same set of activities:

1. Each participant fills customer orders from current inventory and creates back orders if demand cannot be met.
2. Participants forecast customer demand and then order beer from their supplier (or schedule beer production if the participant is the manufacturer), which then takes several weeks to arrive.
3. Each participant attempts to manage inventories in order to minimize back order costs (stockouts) and inventory carrying costs.

Figure A1.1 illustrates the beer supply chain, showing the transportation and information delays. There is no product transportation or order delay between the retailer and the end customers. For the other supply chain members, there is a one-week delay between customer order and supplier acceptance, and a two-week transportation delay from the time a customer's order is received until that order reaches the customer. It also takes two weeks to complete a production order at the factory, such that beer will be ready to fill customer orders.

Here is how the game progresses:

Starting conditions. At the start of the game (Week 0), each supply chain member (except the manufacturer) has twelve cases of beer in ending inventory (see Table A1.1), four cases in the second week of inbound transportation delay, four cases in the first week (updated) of inbound transportation delay, and four cases in the beginning of the first week of inbound transportation delay. The manufacturer has twelve cases of beer in ending inventory, four cases of beer in the second week of production leadtime, four cases in the first week of production leadtime, and four cases at the beginning of the first week of production leadtime. Each player also has an *outgoing order* of four cases sitting in their outgoing order box (or production order box). The retailer must begin with twenty weeks of customer demand information provided by the game

Figure A1.1 The Beer Game Supply Chain

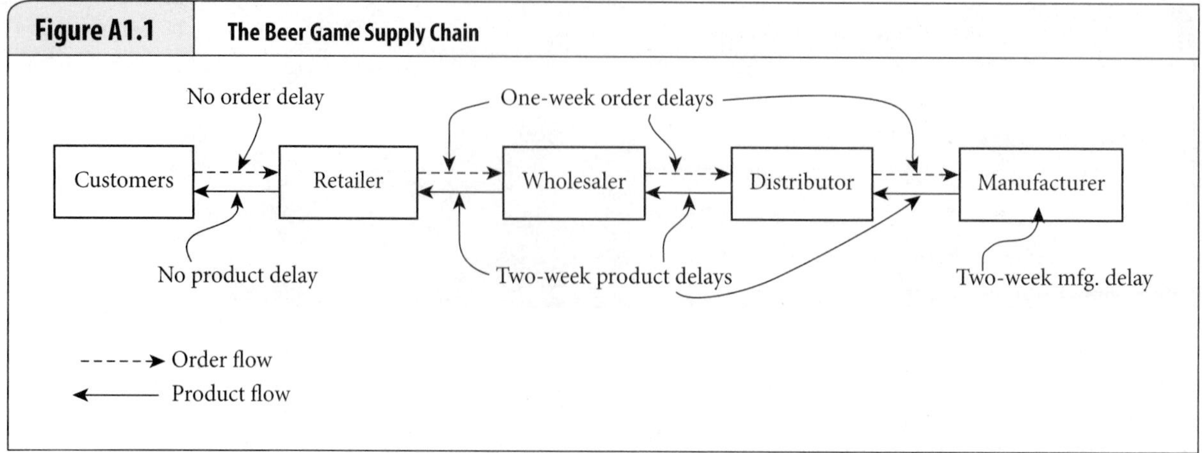

coordinator or instructor, such that the retailer can only view one week's demand at a time (these can be written on the underneath side of 20 sticky notepads for each retailer, for example).

Step 1. Each member *updates his or her beer inventories.*

- Move the cases of beer from the second week of inbound delay for the previous period and add to the ending inventory of the previous period, putting the total in the beginning inventory column of the current period (see Week 0/Week 1 of Table A1.1). For the manufacturer, this is a production delay.
- Move inventory from the first week of inbound delay (updated column) to the second week of delay (see Table A1.1).
- Move inventory from the first week of inbound delay (beginning column) to the first week of inbound delay (updated column) (see Table A1.1).

Step 2. Each member *fills his or her customer orders.*

- The retailer uncovers and reads the current week's customer demand slip, and then places the slip face down in the discard area, *such that it cannot be seen by the wholesaler.*
- The retailer then fills this order (after first satisfying any back orders) and subtracts demand from beginning inventory. This amount then becomes the ending inventory amount. If ending inventory is negative, then a back order of this amount is created, and ending inventory becomes zero.
- Next, the retailer places last week's outgoing order on the wholesaler's incoming demand order box.
- Finally, the retailer forecasts future demand and orders beer from the wholesaler by writing an order on the slip provided and places it face down in the retailer's outgoing order box, *such that it cannot be seen by the wholesaler.* (This order will go to the wholesaler next week—remember the one-week delay).

The wholesaler follows the same steps as above: it reads the incoming demand order slip, discards it, satisfies any back orders, and fills as much of the incoming order as possible from beginning inventory. At this point, the wholesaler must tell the retailer how much of the order it can satisfy, and the retailer records this amount in the first week beginning delay for the current period. The wholesaler then updates its ending inventory and back

Table A1.1 Inventory Record Sheet

Your supply chain role:

Your name:

Team name:

Incoming demand from supply chain customer

Discard area

Outgoing orders to supply chain supplier, OR production orders for manufacturer

Week	Ending Inventory	Beginning Inventory	Back Orders	Second Week Inbound Delay	First Week Inbound Delay	
					Updated	Beginning
0	12		0	4	4	4
1		16		4	4	
2						
3						
4						
5						
6						
7						
8						
9						
10						
11						
12						
13						
14						
15						
16						
17						
18						
19						
20						
Totals						

Amount of outgoing order received

Note: Ending inventories must be zero when you have a back order. If ending inventory is greater than zero, back orders must equal zero. Back orders equal previous period back orders plus incoming order minus current inventory. At end of game: Sum *ending inventory* column and *back orders* column and determine total cost as—[Total ending inventories × \$1] + [Total back orders × \$2] = \$________. Then sum total costs for all supply chain members. Total supply chain costs = \$________.

order quantities, it sends last week's outgoing order to the distributor's incoming demand, and then it decides how much to order and places the order sheet face down in the wholesaler's outgoing order box, *such that it cannot be seen by the distributor.*

The distributor goes through the same steps as the wholesaler when it gets an incoming order from the wholesaler.

The manufacturer follows the same steps also, except instead of sending last week's outgoing order somewhere, it reads the outgoing order and fills the production request by transferring that number of cases from its raw materials storage area to the first week's beginning production delay (it simply creates the cases needed for the order).

Step 3. Repeat Steps 1 and 2 until the game limit is reached. Calculate total costs at game's end.

A typical game progresses in this fashion for twenty weeks (this is usually sufficient to introduce the bullwhip effect into the game). The game is played with sticky notepads for beer orders, using Table A1.1 to keep track of inventories, orders, and back orders. Players must take care *not to talk* to the other players during the game *or to show what orders they are receiving or planning* for the next week. The retailer must *not look at future customer demand data,* provided by the instructor. Remember, this game is meant to illustrate what happens when *no communication* about future orders or order strategies occurs between supply chain members.

At the end of twenty weeks (or shorter if time does not permit), players determine the total cost of their inventories and back orders on the inventory record sheet (back orders cost $2 per unit per week, and inventories cost $1 per unit per week). Given these costs, the basic strategy should be to attempt to avoid stockouts or back orders, while also somewhat trying to minimize total inventory carrying costs. This requires attempting to forecast future demand accurately (as time progresses, firms should use their inventory record sheet demand information for forecasting purposes). The winning team is the team with the lowest total supply chain costs.

BEER GAME QUESTIONS AND EXERCISES

1. All players but the retailer should answer this question—what do you think the retailer's customer demand pattern looked like? How did your customer orders vary throughout the game?

2. What happened to the current inventory levels, looking back up the supply chain from retailer to manufacturer? Why?

3. How could the supply chain members reduce total inventory and back order costs in the future?

4. Go to http://www.beergame.lim.ethz.ch/, and try playing this Internet version of the game. Report on your experiences playing the game.

PART 2

Supply Issues in Supply Chain Management

Chapter **2**

PURCHASING MANAGEMENT

Improving environmental sustainability performance has become a competitive priority for many organizations. The greenness of their products, services and operations is assuming a more important role in customers' sourcing decisions and consumers' purchasing decisions.

— CAPS Research Team.[1]

I don't want to be talking to CEOs about terms and conditions. I want to be talking to them about technology and quality and driving waste from the system.

— Grace Lieblein, General Motors Purchasing Chief.[2]

General Motors, Ford Motor Co. and Chrysler Group have all chosen purchasing chiefs with engineering backgrounds, and those executives are edging away from their companies' former focus on the lowest possible "piece price."

— David Sedgwick, Automotive News.[3]

Learning Objectives

After completing this chapter, you should be able to

- Understand the role of purchasing and its strategic impact on an organization's competitive advantage.
- Understand the traditional purchasing process, e-procurement, public procurement, and green purchasing.
- Understand and know how to handle small value purchase orders.
- Understand sourcing decisions and the factors impacting supplier selection.
- Understand and be able to compute total cost of ownership.
- Understand the pros and cons of single sourcing versus multiple sourcing.
- Understand centralized, decentralized, and hybrid purchasing organizations.
- Describe the opportunities and challenges of global sourcing.

Chapter Outline

Introduction

A Brief History of Purchasing Terms

The Role of Supply Management in an Organization

The Purchasing Process

Sourcing Decisions: The Make-or-Buy Decision

Roles of the Supply Base

SCM Profile: Mayo Retools Medical Equipment Procurement Strategies, Tactics

In 1864, Dr. William Worrall Mayo opened a medical practice in Rochester, Minnesota, that evolved into the world's largest nonprofit medical practice and research group, known as the Mayo Clinic. In 2014, the clinic marks 150 years of continuous service to more than a million patients annually. The Mayo Clinic employs more than 4,000 physicians and scientists and 50,000 allied health staff. In addition to its significant presence in Rochester, Minnesota, Jacksonville, Florida, and Phoenix, Arizona, the Mayo Clinic operates several medical colleges and dozens of healthcare facilities in other states in the U.S.

The Mayo Clinic supply chain (MCSC) supports an enormous $3 billion annual expense stream of which 20 percent is budgeted for purchasing and servicing capital medical equipment. MCSC recently revamped its purchasing strategy to better align its information technology, processes, and human resources to support the clinic's mission to provide high-quality and cost-effective healthcare. The goal of MCSC is not to purchase equipment at the lowest cost but to focus on the total cost over the life of an asset. To implement the new purchasing strategy, MCSC embraced category management and reformed its information systems and organizational structure.

Category management is a purchasing concept to break down an organization's purchases into discrete groups of related products called product categories. Each product category is managed as a strategic business unit with its own strategy and turnover. Instead of renewing traditional master agreements that focused on basic purchasing terms and conditions, MCSC purchases service contracts to cover its asset base, negotiates discounts for routine purchases, establishes group buy periods, and streamlines the purchase-to-pay process with a single monthly invoice and payment.

To improve its information systems, the Mayo Clinic adopted Novation's standard to organize its assets. Novation is a leading healthcare supply chain analytics and contracting company. With a standardized data system, the Mayo Clinic integrated its asset management system and customized budget system with its enterprise resource planning system. While the change is in its infancy stage, the MCSC team is confident that this initiative will result in an integrated data warehouse and reporting system.

The Mayo Clinic also relocated resources within its purchasing team and realigned contracting staff to related categories such as hospital, outpatient, imaging, and surgery. Since purchasing medical equipment requires specialized medical knowledge and expertise, MCSC redesigned its purchasing process to establish a physician-led committee that oversees and coordinates the capital equipment purchasing process.

The Mayo Clinic is hopeful that its new purchasing strategy will provide a solid foundation for future collaboration and a higher level of innovation across the organization and healthcare industry.[4]

INTRODUCTION

In the context of supply chain management (SCM), purchasing can be defined as the act of obtaining merchandise; capital equipment; raw materials; services; or maintenance, repair, and operating (MRO) supplies in exchange for money or its equivalent. Purchasing can be broadly classified into two categories: **merchant** and **industrial buyers**. The first category, merchant buyers, includes the wholesalers and retailers who primarily purchase for resale purposes. Generally, merchants purchase their merchandise in volume to take advantage of quantity discounts and other incentives such as transportation economy and storage efficiency. They create value by consolidating merchandise, breaking bulk, and providing the essential logistical services. The second category is the industrial buyers, whose primary task is to purchase raw materials for conversion purposes. Industrial buyers also purchase services, capital equipment, and MRO supplies. The typical industrial buyers are the manufacturers, although some service firms such as restaurants, landscape gardeners, and florists also purchase raw materials for conversion purposes.

An effective and efficient purchasing system is crucial to the success of a business. Indeed, the *Annual Survey of Manufactures*[5] consistently shows that the total cost of materials exceeds value added through manufacturing in the U.S. Thus, it is not surprising that purchasing concepts and theories that evolved over the last two decades focused on industrial buyers' purchases of raw materials and how purchasing can be exploited to improve competitive success.

The primary focus of this chapter is the industrial buyer. The chapter describes the role of purchasing in an organization, the processes of a traditional purchasing system and the common documents used, how an electronic purchasing system works, various strategies for handling small order problems, the advantages and disadvantages of centralized versus decentralized purchasing systems, purchasing for nonprofits and government agencies, sourcing issues including supplier selection, and other important topics affecting the role of purchasing and supply management in supply chain management.

A BRIEF HISTORY OF PURCHASING TERMS

Purchasing is a key business function that is responsible for acquisition of required materials, services, and equipment. However, acquisition of services is widely called *contracting*. The increased strategic role of purchasing in today's business setting has brought a need for higher levels of skill and responsibility on the part of purchasing professionals. Consequently, the term **supply management** is increasingly being used in place of purchasing to describe the expanded set of responsibilities of purchasing professionals. The traditional purchasing function of receiving requisitions and issuing purchase orders is no longer adequate; instead, a holistic and comprehensive acquisition strategy is required to meet the organization's strategic objectives.

The Institute of Supply Management (ISM) defines supply management as the "identification, acquisition, access, positioning, management of resources and related capabilities the organization needs or potentially needs in the attainment of its strategic objectives."[6] Key activities of supply management have expanded beyond the basic purchasing function to include negotiations, logistics, contract development and administration, inventory control and management, supplier management, and other activities. However, purchasing remains the core activity of supply management. Although *procurement* is frequently used in place of *purchasing*, procurement typically includes the added activities of specifications development, value analysis, negotiation, expediting, contract administration, supplier quality control, and some logistics activities; hence, it is widely used by government agencies due to the type of purchases and frequent service contracting they made with government suppliers. However, it is difficult to clearly distinguish where purchasing activities end and the supply management function begins. Moreover, many organizations use these terms interchangeably. In many parts of this book, we have retained the traditional term purchasing in place of supply management to emphasize the term's original meaning.

THE ROLE OF SUPPLY MANAGEMENT IN AN ORGANIZATION

Traditionally, purchasing was regarded as being a service to production, and corporate executives paid limited attention to issues concerned with purchasing. However, as global competition intensified in the 1980s, executives realized the impact of large quantities of purchased material and work-in-process inventories on manufacturing cost, quality, new product development, and delivery lead time. Savvy managers adopted new supply chain management concepts that emphasized purchasing as a key strategic business process rather than a narrow specialized supporting function to overall business strategy.

The *Annual Survey of Manufactures* (as shown in Table 2.1), conducted by the U.S. Census Bureau, shows that manufacturers spend more than 50 percent of each sales dollar (shown as "value of shipments") on raw materials (shown as "cost of materials") from 1981 to 2011. Purchases of raw materials actually exceeded value added through manufacturing (shown as "manufacture"), which accounted for less than 50 percent of sales. Purchases as a percent of sales dollars for merchants are expected to be much higher since merchandise is primarily bought for resale purposes. Unfortunately, aggregate statistics for merchants are not readily available.

However, individual information can easily be obtained from the annual report, Form 10K, of publicly traded companies, either directly or from the U.S. Securities and Exchange Commission (SEC). For example, Wal-Mart reported that its cost of sales ranged from 75.2 to 75.7 percent of its net sales for the four most recent fiscal years ending January 31, 2011 to 2014. This ratio shows the potential impact of purchasing on a company's profits. Therefore, it is obvious that many successful businesses are treating purchasing as a key strategic process.

The primary goals of purchasing are to ensure uninterrupted flows of raw materials at the lowest total cost, to improve quality of the finished goods produced, and to maximize customer satisfaction. Purchasing can contribute to these objectives by actively seeking better materials and reliable suppliers, working closely with and exploiting the expertise of strategic suppliers to improve the quality of raw materials, and involving suppliers and purchasing personnel in product design and development efforts. Purchasing is the crucial link between the sources of supply and the organization itself, with support coming from overlapping activities to enhance manufacturability for both the customer and the supplier. The involvement of purchasing and strategic suppliers in concurrent engineering activities is essential for selecting components and raw materials that ensure that requisite quality is designed into the product and to aid in collapsing design-to-production cycle time.

Table 2.1 Cost of Materials as a Percentage of the Value of Shipments

	VALUE OF SHIPMENTS	COST OF MATERIALS		MANUFACTURE		CAPITAL EXPENDITURES	
YEAR	$ MILLIONS	$ MILLIONS	%	$ MILLIONS	%	$ MILLIONS	%
2011	$5,481,368	$3,237,468	59.1%	$2,281,046	41.6%	$146,319	2.7%
2010	$4,916,647	$2,763,128	56.2%	$2,185,326	44.4%	$127,952	2.6%
2009	$4,436,196	$2,438,427	55.0%	$1,978,017	44.6%	$130,081	2.9%
2008	$5,486,266	$3,213,708	58.6%	$2,274,367	41.5%	$168,505	3.1%
2007	$5,338,307	$2,975,906	55.7%	$2,390,643	44.8%	$159,422	3.0%
2006	$5,015,553	$2,752,904	54.9%	$2,285,929	45.6%	$135,801	2.7%
2005	$4,742,077	$2,557,601	53.9%	$2,210,349	46.6%	$128,292	2.7%
2004	$4,308,971	$2,283,144	53.0%	$2,041,434	47.4%	$113,793	2.6%
2003	$4,015,387	$2,095,279	52.2%	$1,923,415	47.9%	$112,176	2.8%
2002	$3,914,719	$2,022,158	51.7%	$1,889,291	48.3%	$123,067	3.1%
2001	$3,967,698	$2,105,338	53.1%	$1,850,709	46.6%	$142,985	3.6%
2000	$4,208,582	$2,245,839	53.4%	$1,973,622	46.9%	$154,479	3.7%
1999	$4,031,885	$2,084,316	51.7%	$1,954,498	48.5%	$150,325	3.7%
1998	$3,899,810	$2,018,055	51.7%	$1,891,266	48.5%	$152,708	3.9%
1997	$3,834,701	$2,015,425	52.6%	$1,825,688	47.6%	$151,510	4.0%
1996	$3,715,428	$1,975,362	53.2%	$1,749,662	47.1%	$146,468	3.9%
1995	$3,594,360	$1,897,571	52.8%	$1,711,442	47.6%	$134,318	3.7%
1994	$3,348,019	$1,752,735	52.4%	$1,605,980	48.0%	$118,665	3.5%
1993	$3,127,620	$1,647,493	52.7%	$1,483,054	47.4%	$108,629	3.5%
1992	$3,004,723	$1,571,774	52.3%	$1,424,700	47.4%	$110,644	3.7%
1991	$2,878,165	$1,531,221	53.2%	$1,341,386	46.6%	$103,153	3.6%
1990	$2,912,227	$1,574,617	54.1%	$1,348,970	46.3%	$106,463	3.7%
1989	$2,840,376	$1,532,330	53.9%	$1,325,434	46.7%	$101,894	3.6%
1988	$2,695,432	$1,444,501	53.6%	$1,269,313	47.1%	$84,706	3.1%
1987	$2,475,939	$1,319,845	53.3%	$1,165,741	47.1%	$85,662	3.5%
1986	$2,260,315	$1,217,609	53.9%	$1,035,437	45.8%	$80,795	3.6%
1985	$2,280,184	$1,276,010	56.0%	$1,000,142	43.9%	$91,245	4.0%
1984	$2,253,429	$1,288,414	57.2%	$983,228	43.6%	$80,660	3.6%
1983	$2,045,853	$1,170,238	57.2%	$882,015	43.1%	$67,480	3.3%
1982	$1,960,206	$1,130,143	57.7%	$824,118	42.0%	$77,046	3.9%
1981	$2,017,543	$1,193,970	59.2%	$837,507	41.5%	$83,767	4.2%

Source: Annual Survey of Manufactures, 1981–2011, U.S. Census Bureau.

The Financial Significance of Supply Management

Undoubtedly, purchasing has become more global and gained strategic corporate focus over the last two decades. The increasing use of outsourcing (discussed later in the chapter) of noncore activities has further elevated the role of purchasing in a firm. In addition to affecting the competitiveness of a firm, purchasing also directly affects profitability. Next, we discuss the financial significance of purchasing on a firm.

Profit-Leverage Effect

Purchase spend is the money a firm spends on goods and services. The **profit-leverage effect** of purchasing measures the impact of a change in purchase spend on a firm's profit before taxes, assuming gross sales and other expenses remain unchanged. The measure is commonly used to demonstrate that a decrease in purchase spend directly increases profits before taxes by the same amount. However, it is important to remember that a decrease in purchase spend must be achieved through better purchasing strategy, thus enabling the firm to acquire materials of similar or better quality and yield at a lower total acquisition cost. The profit-leverage effect example in Table 2.2 shows that if a firm manages to lower its purchase spend on materials by \$20,000, profits before taxes increase by \$20,000 because purchase spend on materials is a part of the cost of goods sold. Indeed, the reduction in purchase spend has an identical impact on gross profits. Table 2.2 shows that gross profits also increased by \$20,000 from \$500,000 to \$520,000. The direct effect of purchasing on a firm's profitability is a key reason that drives business executives to continually refine the sourcing function. Boosting sales and cutting costs are not the only ways to increase profits. An often overlooked but very efficient means of improving profits is through smarter purchasing.

Return on Assets Effect

Return on assets (ROA) is a financial ratio of a firm's net income in relation to its total assets. The ratio is also referred to as **return on investment (ROI)**. In the context of accounting, total assets consist of current and fixed assets. Current assets include cash, accounts receivable, and inventory, whereas fixed assets include equipment, buildings, and real estate. ROA indicates how efficiently management is using its total assets to generate profits. A high ROA suggests that management is capable of generating large profits with relatively small investments. The formula for ROA is:

$$\text{Return on assets (ROA)} = \frac{\textit{net income}}{\textit{total assets}}$$

Assuming the firm in Table 2.2 has total assets of \$500,000, its ROA is then 10 percent (\$50,000 ÷ \$500,000). If the firm reduces its purchase spend on materials by \$20,000 through a more effective purchasing strategy, its ROA then increases to 14 percent (\$70,000 ÷ \$500,000). The \$20,000 reduction in purchase spend on materials is also likely to result in a lower raw material inventory (and thus lower total assets). However, the effect on ROA from this potential change in inventory is difficult to quantify because the ratio of a firm's raw material inventory to its total assets, and the ratio of raw materials cost to its total cost of goods sold, vary widely depending on the firm and industry.

Table 2.2 Profit-Leverage Effect

	SIMPLIFIED PROFIT & LOSS STATEMENT	REDUCE MATERIAL COSTS BY $20,000
Gross Sales/Net Revenue	$1,000,000	$1,000,000
– Cost of Goods Sold (Materials + Manufacturing Cost)	$500,000	$480,000
Gross Profits	$500,000	$520,000
– General & Administrative Expenses (45% of Gross Sales)	$450,000	$450,000
Profits Before Taxes	$50,000	$70,000

Inventory Turnover Effect

Inventory turnover shows how many times a firm's inventory is utilized and replaced over an accounting period, such as a year. There are numerous ways to compute the inventory turnover ratio, but a widely used formula is the ratio of the cost of goods sold to average inventory at cost. To compute a monthly ratio, it is a common practice to use the mean of beginning and ending monthly inventory as the average inventory. This monthly inventory average is a good measure for computing the annual inventory turnover ratio. In general, low inventory turnover indicates poor sales, overstocking, and/or obsolete inventories. A firm must compare its inventory turnover ratio against the industry standard to judge how well the company is doing compared to competitors. We will discuss some company-specific examples of inventory turnover ratios in Chapter 7. Through a more effective sourcing strategy, purchasing can help to reduce inventory investment, and thus improve the firm's inventory turnover. Several inventory turnover formulas are shown here:

$$\text{Inventory turnover ratio} = \frac{\textit{Cost of goods sold}}{\textit{Average inventory}}$$

$$\text{Monthly inventory turnover ratio} = \frac{\textit{Cost of goods sold for the month}}{\dfrac{\textit{Beginning inventory} + \textit{Ending inventory}}{2}}$$

$$\text{Annual inventory turnover ratio} = \frac{\textit{Cost of goods sold for the year}}{\textit{Average monthly inventory}}$$

Consider a hypothetical example in which a firm has an ending inventory of $125,000 as of December 31, 2012 and the following accounting information. The monthly and annual inventory turnover ratios can be computed as follows:

MONTH (2013)	ENDING INVENTORY	COST OF GOODS SOLD	MONTHLY INVENTORY TURNOVER RATIO
January	$52,000	$85,000	$\frac{\$85{,}000}{\left[\frac{\$125{,}000 + \$52{,}000}{2}\right]} = 0.96$
February	$88,000	$1,250,000	$\frac{\$1{,}250{,}000}{\left[\frac{\$52{,}000 + \$88{,}000}{2}\right]} = 17.86$
March	$85,000	$950,000	$\frac{\$950{,}000}{\left[\frac{\$88{,}000 + \$85{,}000}{2}\right]} = 10.98$
April	$55,000	$750,000	$\frac{\$750{,}000}{\left[\frac{\$85{,}000 + \$55{,}000}{2}\right]} = 10.71$
May	$75,000	$950,000	$\frac{\$950{,}000}{\left[\frac{\$55{,}000 + \$75{,}000}{2}\right]} = 14.62$

June	$85,000	$850,000	$\frac{\$850{,}000}{\left[\frac{\$75{,}000 + \$85{,}000}{2}\right]} = 10.63$
July	$156,000	$555,000	$\frac{\$550{,}000}{\left[\frac{\$85{,}000 + \$156{,}000}{2}\right]} = 4.61$
August	$215,000	$1,325,000	$\frac{\$1{,}325{,}000}{\left[\frac{\$156{,}000 + \$215{,}000}{2}\right]} = 7.14$
September	$65,000	$985,000	$\frac{\$985{,}000}{\left[\frac{\$215{,}000 + \$65{,}000}{2}\right]} = 7.04$
October	$100,000	$850,000	$\frac{\$850{,}000}{\left[\frac{\$65{,}000 + \$100{,}000}{2}\right]} = 10.30$
November	$165,000	$1,250,000	$\frac{\$1{,}250{,}000}{\left[\frac{\$100{,}000 + \$165{,}000}{2}\right]} = 9.43$
December	$105,000	$1,050,000	$\frac{\$1{,}050{,}000}{\left[\frac{\$165{,}000 + \$105{,}000}{2}\right]} = 7.78$

Total cost of goods sold for the year = $85,000 + $1,250,000 + $950,000 + $750,000 + $950,000 + $850,000 + $555,000 + $1,325,000 + $985,000 + $850,000 + $1,250,000 + $1,050,000 = $10,850,000

Average monthly inventory = [($125,000 + $52,000)/2 + ($52,000 + $88,000)/2 + ($88,000 + $85,000)/2 + ($85,000 + $55,000)/2 + ($55,000 + $75,000)/2 + ($75,000 + $85,000)/2 + ($85,000 + $156,000)/2 + ($156,000 + $215,000)/2 + ($215,000 + $65,000)/2 + ($65,000 + $100,000)/2 + ($100,000 + $165,000)/2 + ($165,000 + $105,000)/2]/12 = $104,667

Thus, the annual inventory turnover ratio for 2013 is $\frac{\$10{,}850{,}000}{\$104{,}667} = 103.66$.

THE PURCHASING PROCESS

The traditional purchasing process is a manual, paper-based system. However, with the advent of information technology, personal computers, local area networks, and the Internet, many companies are moving toward a more automated, electronic-based system. The goal of a proper purchasing system is to ensure the efficient transmission of information from the users to the purchasing personnel and, ultimately, to the suppliers. Once the information is transmitted to the appropriate suppliers, the system must also ensure the efficient flows of the purchased materials from the suppliers to the users and the flow of invoices from the suppliers to the accounting department. Finally, the system must have adequate operational or **internal control** to prevent abuse of purchasing funds. For example, purchase orders (POs) should be prenumbered and issued in duplicate, and buyers should not be authorized to pay invoices. Prenumbered purchase orders make it easier to trace any missing or unaccounted-for purchase orders. A duplicate purchase order should be issued to the accounting department for internal control purposes and to inform the department of a future payment or commitment of resources. The

SCM Profile: Reducing the Risk of Purchasing Fraud

Though purchasing is a key strategic process affecting the core competency of a firm, the average business loses about 5 percent of its revenues to purchasing fraud such as theft, bribery, kickbacks, bid rigging, collusion, and charging for products or services not rendered.[7] For example, in 2012, the former CEO of the Hospital for Special Surgery in New York, New York, was arrested and charged in a $1.4 million kickback scheme, and the former CFO of St. Vincent Hospital in Santa Fe, New Mexico, pleaded guilty to fraud and conspiracy that involved more than $3 million in suspicious payments.

Purchasing fraud not only causes monetary losses, it also tarnishes an organization's reputation. While purchasing fraud can be very difficult to prevent and detect, developing an effective purchasing process coupled with rigorous internal controls are great deterrents against purchasing fraud.

A documented code of conduct and ethical expectation of the firm provide valuable guidelines for employees to grasp what is acceptable or unacceptable. Consequences of violating the code of conduct should be clearly addressed. Similarly, the firm should have a written vendor code of conduct to address topics such as legal compliance, gratuities, kickbacks, gifts, fair competition, and reporting of misconduct, among others. The firm should also establish a gift policy to address what gifts are acceptable. Gifts in the form of cash, including gift cards should be prohibited.

An effective internal control system should ensure that purchasing duties are segregated appropriately. For example, large purchase orders should go through multiple levels of review and approval. It is imperative that the system be designed to prevent any one person from processing and approving large purchases, and authorizing payments for the invoices. There should be a clearly defined policy documenting the purchasing process for different levels of purchases. For instance, purchases in excess of $25,000 should require a bidding process. Also, bidding exceeding a designated amount should involve multiple buyers. An internal audit team should be used to audit the purchasing process and transactions to assess fraud risk.

As firms continue to expand their supply chains, they continue to expose themselves to more purchasing fraud. Having an effective purchasing process and internal control system will help to minimize fraud.[8]

authority to approve payments should be different from the authority to approve purchase orders. The nearby SCM Profile discusses the prevention of purchasing fraud in greater detail.

The Manual Purchasing System

Figure 2.1 shows a simplified traditional manual purchasing system. While some manual systems may look slightly different than what is shown in Figure 2.1, it captures the essential elements of a good purchasing system that is easy to use and yet exerts adequate internal control of the process. The manual purchasing system is slow and prone to errors due to duplication of data entries during various stages of the purchasing process. For example, similar information on the material requisition, such as the product description, is reproduced on the purchase order.

Figure 2.1 **Traditional Manual Purchasing System**

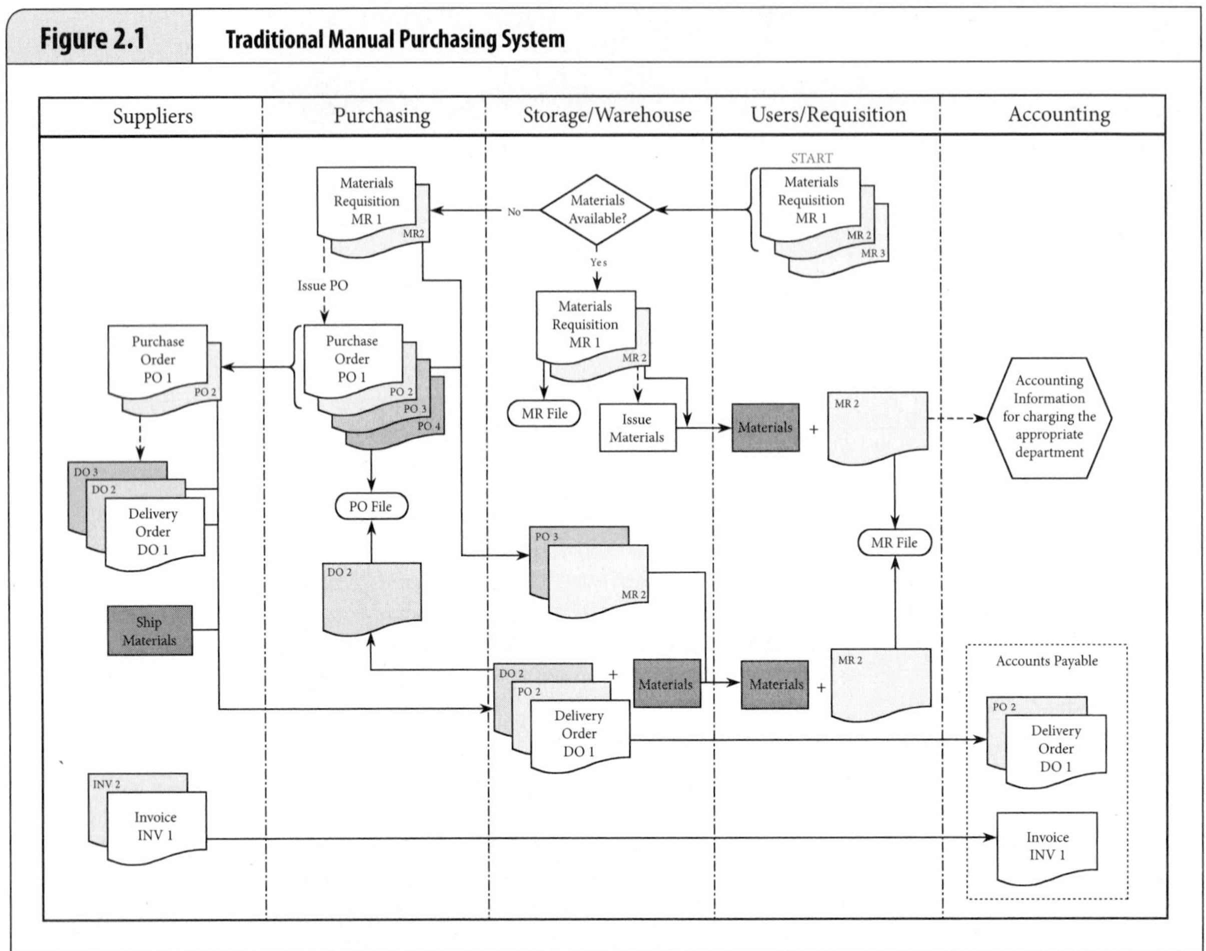

The Material Requisition

The purchasing process starts when the material user initiates a request for material by issuing a **material requisition (MR)** in duplicate. A **purchase requisition**, instead of a material requisition, is used in some firms. The product, quantity, and delivery due date are clearly described on the material requisition. The number of duplicates issued depends on the internal control system of the organization. Generally, the issuer retains a copy and the warehouse receives the original plus a duplicate. The duplicate accompanies the material as it moves from the warehouse to the user. This copy also provides the essential information for the accounting department to charge the appropriate user or department for the material.

While most requisitions are transmitted through the generic material requisition, a **traveling requisition** is used for materials and standard parts that are requested on a recurring basis. Instead of describing the product on the generic material requisition, the product description and other pertinent information, such as delivery lead time and lot size, are preprinted on the traveling requisition. When a resupply is needed, the user simply enters the quantity and date needed and submits it to the warehouse. Once the resupply information is recorded, the traveling requisition is returned to the user for future requests.

Planned order releases from the material requirements planning (MRP) system or a bill of materials (BOM) can also be used to release requisitions or to place orders directly with the suppliers. This approach is suitable for firms that use the same components to make standard goods over a relatively long period of time.

If the requested material is available in the warehouse, the material is issued to the user without going through the purchasing department. Otherwise, the requisition is assigned to a buyer who is responsible for the material. If there is a better substitute for the material, purchasing recommends and works with the user to explore whether it is a viable substitute. However, purchasing personnel should not change the specifications of the materials or parts without the user's knowledge and agreement. While it is the right and responsibility of purchasing personnel to select the appropriate supplier, the user in many cases may suggest a list of potential suppliers when requesting new material. A sample material requisition is shown in Figure 2.2.

Figure 2.2 **Sample Purchase Requisition**

BabiHutan Inc.
523 Las Vegas Blvd
Las Vegas, NV89154
Tel: 702-123-4567

Purchase Requisition

RX #: 6334554

Requestor: ______________ Department: ______________

Phone #: __________ Account #: __________ Date: __________

Suggested Vendor: ______________________________

Address: ______________________ Phone: __________

No.	Description	Price	Quantity

Special instructions: ______________________________

Approval Authority: ______________________ Date: __________

Distribution: White-Purchasing/Yellow-Purchasing (return to requestor)/Pink-Department

The Request for Quotation and the Request for Proposal

If the material is not available in the warehouse, the material requisition is routed to the purchasing department. If there is no current supplier for the item, the buyer must identify a pool of qualified suppliers and issue a **request for quotation (RFQ)**. A **request for proposal (RFP)** may be issued instead for a complicated and highly technical component part, especially if the complete specification of the part is unknown. An RFP allows suppliers to propose new material and technology, thus enabling the firm to exploit the technology and expertise of suppliers.

A growing trend among firms that practice supply chain management is **supplier development**. When there is a lack of suitable suppliers, firms may assist existing or new suppliers to improve their processing capabilities, quality, delivery, and cost performance by providing the needed technical and financial assistance. Developing suppliers in this manner allows firms to focus more on core competencies, while **outsourcing** noncore activities to suppliers.

The Purchase Order

When a suitable supplier is identified, or a qualified supplier is on file, the buyer issues a **purchase order (PO)** in duplicate to the selected supplier. Generally, the original purchase order and a duplicate are sent to the supplier. An important feature of the purchase order is the terms and conditions of the purchase, which is typically preprinted on the back. The purchase order is the buyer's offer and becomes a legally binding contract when accepted by the supplier. Therefore, firms should require the supplier to acknowledge and return a copy of the purchase order to indicate acceptance of the order. A sample purchase order is shown in Figure 2.3.

The supplier may offer the goods at its own terms and conditions, especially if it is the sole producer or holds the patent to the product. Then a supplier's **sales order** will be used. The sales order is the supplier's offer and becomes a legally binding contract when accepted by the buyer.

Once an order is accepted, purchasing personnel need to ensure on-time delivery of the purchased material by using a **follow-up** or by **expediting** the order. A follow-up is considered a proactive approach to prevent late delivery, whereas expediting is considered a reactive approach that is used to speed up an overdue shipment.

The **Uniform Commercial Code (UCC)** governs the purchase and sale of goods in the U.S, except in the state of Louisiana. Louisiana has a legal system that is based on the Napoleonic Code.

Electronic Procurement Systems (e-Procurement)

Electronic data interchange (EDI) was developed in the 1970s to improve the purchasing process. However, its proprietary nature required significant up-front investments. The rapid advent of Internet technologies in the 1990s spurred the growth of more flexible Internet-based e-procurement systems. Proponents of e-commerce argued that Internet-based systems would quickly replace the manual system, and many e-commerce service providers surfaced in the late 1990s. Since then, there has been a shake-up among these companies as they have struggled to find a sustainable market. A large number of e-commerce firms saw their share values plummet in the early 2000s, and many are no longer in business after the dot-com bubble burst in 2000. Critics argued that growth in

Figure 2.3 Sample Purchase Order

BabiHutan Inc.
523 LasVegas Blvd
Las Vegas, NV89154
Tel: 702-123-4567

Purchase Order

PO#: 885729

Date: ________

Vendor:	Required Delivery Date: ______ Payment Terms: ______ FOB Terms: ______ Price Agreement No.: ______
Ship To:	Include PO # in all packages, invoice, shipping papers & correspondence. Mail original and one copy of invoice attached to second copy of Purchase Order for payment.

No.	Description	Unit Price	Quantity	Total Price
		Total $ of Order		

Buyer: ________ Phone: ______ Fax: ______

Buyer Signature: ________ Requisition No.: ______

SEE REVERSE FOR TERMS & CONDITIONS

Distribution: White-Vendor/Yellow-Vendor(return with invoice)/Pink & Blue-Purchasing/Green-Fixed Assets

e-commerce had been overinflated, and the savings for users were inadequate to justify their time and investment. Today, though, many well-managed e-commerce firms are beginning to thrive as users realize the benefits of their services.

Figure 2.4 describes the Internet-based electronic purchasing system used by the University of Nevada, Las Vegas. The database that drives the e-procurement system resides on a server, but the software is installed on workstations. The e-procurement system is also accessible via the Internet. The e-procurement system allows users to submit their purchase requisitions to the purchasing department electronically and enables buyers to transmit purchase orders to suppliers over the Internet, fax, e-mail, or snail mail.

Figure 2.4 Internet-Based Electronic Purchasing System

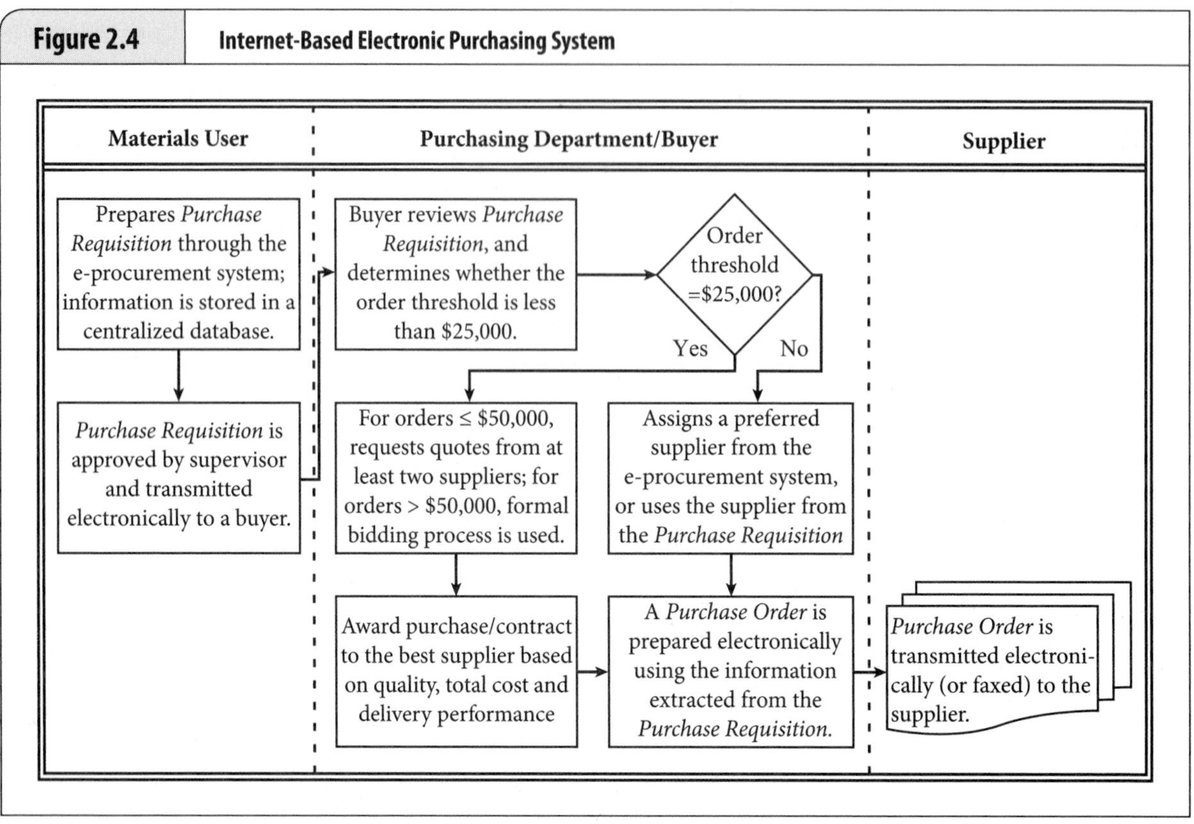
Materials User
Purchasing Department/Buyer
Supplier
Prepares Purchase Requisition through the e-procurement system; information is stored in a centralized database.
Purchase Requisition is approved by supervisor and transmitted electronically to a buyer.
Buyer reviews Purchase Requisition, and determines whether the order threshold is less than $25,000.
Order threshold =$25,000?
Yes
No
For orders ≤ $50,000, requests quotes from at least two suppliers; for orders > $50,000, formal bidding process is used.
Assigns a preferred supplier from the e-procurement system, or uses the supplier from the Purchase Requisition
Award purchase/contract to the best supplier based on quality, total cost and delivery performance
A Purchase Order is prepared electronically using the information extracted from the Purchase Requisition.
Purchase Order is transmitted electronically (or faxed) to the supplier.

The material user initiates the e-procurement process by entering a purchase request and other pertinent information, such as quantity and date needed, into the purchase requisition module. The material user may recommend suppliers or potential sources for the requisition. Next, the purchase requisition is approved and transmitted electronically to a buyer at the purchasing department. The buyer reviews the purchase requisition for accuracy and appropriate approval level and determines the value of the requisition. If the amount is below $25,000, the buyer extracts details of the purchase requisition stored in the database to prepare an electronic purchase order. Next, the buyer assigns a preferred supplier from the e-procurement database, or uses a supplier from the purchase requisition. If the amount of the purchase requisition is between $25,000 and $50,000, two formal requests for quotation are needed before a purchase order can be released. However, if the amount exceeds $50,000, a supplier must be chosen by means of a formal bidding process. At the specified time and place, bids are opened publicly. The purchase is awarded to the lowest responsible bidder whose bid conforms to all requirements of the solicitation. Then an electronic purchase order (or formal contract for purchase of services) is prepared and transmitted (or mailed) to the selected supplier.

Advantages of the e-Procurement System

The traditional manual purchasing system is a tedious and labor-intensive task of issuing material requisitions and purchase orders. Although EDI solved some of these problems, its proprietary nature requires a high start-up cost, making it inaccessible to small firms with limited budgets. Internet-based e-procurement systems have changed the infrastructure requirement, making it readily affordable to most firms. Benefits derived from implementing an e-procurement system include:

1. *Time savings*: E-procurement is more efficient when (a) selecting and maintaining a list of potential suppliers, (b) processing requests for quotation and purchase orders, and (c) making repeat purchases. Individual buyers can create preferred supplier lists for each category of products and services. For example, a small tools supplier group may consist of fifteen suppliers. The buyer uses this group to purchase small tools. The list can be edited and shared with all buyers in the firm. Supplier performance data can be updated quickly and made available online in real time. Collecting, sorting, reviewing, and comparing RFQs are labor-intensive and time-consuming processes. Using the manual purchasing system, a typical firm may have to sort and match hundreds of bids on a daily basis. E-procurement eliminates these non-value-adding activities. Duplicate data entry on the purchase order is eliminated since the information can be extracted from the RFQ, originally entered by the user. Also, an e-procurement system minimizes the need for interdepartmental routing of paper purchase requisitions, streamlines the approval process, and automates purchase order issuance.

   Some e-procurement systems can be programmed to handle automatic bidding of frequently ordered items on a fixed interval, such as daily or weekly—a commonly used practice. The ability to submit automatic bidding is invaluable for handling perishable goods, which must be ordered in small lot sizes, and other frequently purchased items where the specifications are known.

2. *Cost savings*: Buyers can handle more purchases, and the manual task of matching bids to purchase requisitions is reduced. Other cost savings include lower prices of goods and services (since more suppliers can be contacted), reduced inventory costs (due to the ability to purchase on a more frequent basis), use of fewer buyers, lower administrative costs, elimination of the need for preprinted purchase requisition forms, and faster order fulfillment.
3. *Accuracy*: The system eliminates double-key inputs—once by the material users and then once again by the buyers. The system also enhances the accuracy of communications between buyers and suppliers. More up-to-date information on suppliers, with goods and services readily available online, allows users to assess their options before preparing a purchase requisition.
4. *Real-time use*: Buyers have real-time access to the purchase requisition once it is prepared. Once the purchase requisition is processed, the buyer can post the bid instantly, instead of waiting to contact all the suppliers individually to alert them of the bids. The system enables buyers to initiate bids and suppliers to respond in real time on a 24/7 basis.
5. *Mobility*: The buyer can submit, process, and check the status of bids, as well as communicate with suppliers regardless of the buyer's geographical location and time of day. Thus, the e-procurement system is highly flexible.
6. *Trackability*: The e-procurement system allows submitters and buyers to track each purchase requisition electronically through the process—from submission, to approval, and finally conversion to a purchase order. Moreover, audit trails can be maintained for all transactions in electronic form. Tracing an electronic bid and transaction is much easier and faster than tracking paper trails. Buyers and suppliers can ask for additional information online, leave comments, or indicate whether they are interested in bidding.

7. *Management benefits*: The system can be designed to store important supplier information, including whether suppliers are minority or locally owned, thus allowing the buyers to support such businesses. Summary statistics and supplier performance reports can be generated for management to review and utilize for future planning.
8. *Supplier benefits*: Benefits include lower barriers to entry and transaction costs, access to more buyers, and the ability to instantly adjust to market conditions, thus making e-procurement attractive to most suppliers.

Small Value Purchase Orders

The administrative costs to process an order can be quite substantial. It has been estimated that the cost of placing an order using the manual purchasing system can be as high as $175.[9] The figure could be higher when we consider the salary of senior purchasing personnel and other indirect costs incurred by purchasing personnel. It is not uncommon to find that the cost to process a purchase order exceeds the total dollar value of the order itself. While *small dollar value* is a relative term depending on the size of the firm, $500 to $1,000 can be considered a reasonable cutoff point.

Small value purchases, particularly in a manual purchasing system, should be minimized to ensure that buyers are not overburdened with trivial purchases that may prevent them from focusing on more crucial purchases. Due to the efficiency of the e-procurement system, buyers are less likely to be overburdened by small value purchases. Nevertheless, all firms should have a system in place to handle small value purchases. To control unnecessary administrative costs and reduce order cycle time, purchasing managers have various alternatives to deal with small value purchases. Generally, the alternatives are used for purchases of office supplies and other indirect materials. Let us review the alternatives.

Procurement Credit Card/Corporate Purchasing Card

Procurement credit cards or **corporate purchasing cards** (P-cards) are credit cards with a predetermined credit limit, usually not more than $5,000 depending on the organization, issued to authorized personnel of the buying organization to make low-dollar purchases. It is not uncommon that in many companies, more than half of their purchases are less than $500. American Express, Diners Club, MasterCard, and Visa are commonly used for this purpose. The P-card allows the material user to purchase the material directly from the supplier without going through purchasing. Usually, the user must purchase the needed materials from a list of authorized suppliers. Procurement credit cards have gained popularity over the last decade, especially among government agencies, because of their ease of use and flexibility. In a 2012 P-card study, it was reported that P-card transactions for small value purchases under $2,500 have exceeded paper checks since 2009. The percentage of P-card transactions between $2,500 and $10,000 has increased steadily since 2003, from 9 percent to 31 percent by 2011.[10]

When authorized, P-cards can also be used to pay for meals, lodging, and other traveling expenses, thus eliminating the need to process travel expenses in advance for the user. At the end of the month, an itemized statement is sent to the purchasing department, the cardholder's department, or directly to the accounting department. Generally, the purchasing department is responsible for managing the overall program, but the individual unit is responsible for managing its cardholder accounts. To ensure appropriate internal control of the procurement credit card system, a supervisor should be assigned to review the monthly statement of each cardholder to prevent unauthorized use of the procurement card. Cardholders should maintain proper supporting documents and records for each purchase.

Despite the success of the P-card program, there are unique challenges in expanding the program globally. P-card programs are more common in English-speaking regions, such as the U.K., the U.S., and Australia, and less common in France, Germany, and Italy, where automatic transfers are more common. In some Asian markets where employee turnover is high, employers are concerned about card fraud. Card-issuing banks may not have coverage in all countries to enable a corporation to expand its P-card program globally. There are also country-specific challenges. Germany, for instance, has complicated data protection laws, and new programs must be reviewed by each company's Workers Council. The same issues with data protection laws are also found in France, where direct debit is preferred. In Eastern Europe, the commercial card market is still in its infancy, and P-card programs are virtually nonexistent.[11]

Blanket or Open-End Purchase Orders

A **blanket purchase order** covers a variety of items and is negotiated for repeated supply over a fixed time period, such as quarterly or yearly. The subtle difference of an **open-end purchase order** is that additional items and expiration dates can be renegotiated. Price and estimated quantity for each item, as well as delivery terms and conditions, are usually negotiated and incorporated in the order. A variety of mechanisms, such as a **blanket order release** or production schedule, may be used to release a specific quantity against the order. Blanket or open-end purchase orders are suitable for buying MRO supplies and office supplies. At a fixed time interval, usually monthly, the supplier sends a detailed statement of all releases against the order to the buying firm for payment.

While blanket purchase orders are frequently used to handle small value purchases, when used in conjunction with blanket order releases, cooperative supplier relationships, and single sourcing, blanket purchase orders are a formidable tool for handling the complex purchasing needs of a large, multidivision corporation.

Blank Check Purchase Orders

A **blank check purchase order** is a special purchase order with a signed blank check attached, usually at the bottom of the purchase order. Due to the potential for misuse, it is usually printed on the check that it is not valid for over a certain amount (usually $500 or $1,000). If the exact amount of the purchase is known, the buyer enters the amount on the check before passing it to the supplier. Otherwise, the supplier enters the amount due on the check and cashes it after the material is shipped. Nevertheless, purchasing managers are embracing the use of procurement credit cards and phasing out blank check purchase orders.

Stockless Buying or System Contracting

Stockless buying or **system contracting** is an extension of the blanket purchase order. It requires the supplier to maintain a minimum inventory level to ensure that the required items are readily available for the buyer. It is stockless buying on the buyer's perspective because the burden of keeping the inventory is on the supplier. Some firms require suppliers to keep inventory at the buyer's facilities to minimize order cycle time.

Petty Cash

Petty cash is a small cash reserve maintained by a midlevel manager or clerk. Material users buy the needed materials and then claim the purchase against the petty cash by submitting the receipt to the petty cashier. A benefit of this system is that the exact reimbursement is supported by receipts.

Standardization and Simplification of Materials and Components

Where appropriate, purchasing should work with design, engineering, and operations to seek opportunities to standardize materials, components, and supplies to increase the usage of standardized items. For example, a car manufacturer could design different models of automobiles to use the same starter mechanism, thus increasing its usage and reducing storage space requirements while allowing for large quantity price discounts. This will also reduce the number of small value purchases for less frequently used items.

Simplification refers to reduction of the number of components, supplies, or standard materials used in a product or process. For example, a computer manufacturer could integrate the video card directly onto the motherboard instead of using different video card modules for different models. Thus, simplification can further reduce the number of small value purchases while reducing storage space requirements, as well as allowing for quantity purchase discounts.

Accumulating Small Orders to Create a Large Order

Numerous small orders can be accumulated and mixed into a large order, especially if the material request is not urgent. Otherwise, purchasing can simply increase the order quantity if the ordering cost exceeds the inventory holding cost. Larger orders also reduce the purchase price and unit transportation cost.

Using a Fixed Order Interval for a Specific Category of Materials or Supplies

Another effective way to control small orders is to group materials and supplies into categories and then set fixed order intervals for each category. Order intervals can be set to biweekly or monthly depending on usage. Instead of requesting individual materials or supplies, users request the appropriate quantity of each item in the category on a single requisition to be purchased from a supplier. This increases the dollar value and decreases the number of small orders.

SOURCING DECISIONS: THE MAKE-OR-BUY DECISION

The term **outsourcing** is commonly used to refer to buying materials or components from suppliers instead of making them in-house. In recent years, the trend has been moving toward outsourcing combined with the creation of supply chain relationships to replace the practice of backward or forward vertical integration. **Backward vertical integration** refers to acquiring upstream suppliers, whereas **forward vertical integration** refers to acquiring downstream customers. For example, an end-product manufacturer acquiring a supplier's operations that supplied component parts is an example of backward integration. Acquiring a distributor or other outbound logistics providers would be an example of forward integration.

The **make or buy decision** is a strategic one that can impact an organization's competitive position. It is obvious that most organizations buy their MRO and office supplies rather than make the items themselves. Similarly, seafood restaurants usually buy their fresh seafood from fish markets. However, the decision on whether to make or buy technically advanced engineering parts that impact the firm's competitive position is a complex one. For example, do you think the Honda Motor Company would rather make or buy the engines for its automobile manufacturing facilities? Why?

Traditionally, cost has been the major driver when making sourcing decisions. However, organizations today focus more on the strategic impact of the sourcing decision on the firm's competitive advantage. For example, the Honda Motor Company would not outsource the making of its engines because it considers engines to be a vital part of its automobiles' performance and reputation. However, Honda may outsource the production of brake drums to a high-quality, low-cost supplier that specializes in brake drums. Generally, firms outsource noncore activities while focusing on core competencies. Finally, the make-or-buy decision is not an exclusive either-or option. Firms can always choose to make some components or services in-house while buying the rest from suppliers.

Reasons for Buying or Outsourcing

Organizations buy or outsource materials, components, and/or services from suppliers for many reasons. Let us review these now:

1. *Cost advantage*: For many firms, cost is an important reason for buying or outsourcing, especially for supplies and components that are nonvital to the organization's operations and competitive advantage. This is usually true for standardized or generic supplies and materials for which suppliers may have the advantage of **economies of scale** because they supply large quantities of the same item to multiple users. In most outsourcing cases, the quantity needed is so small that it does not justify the investment in capital equipment to make the item. Some foreign suppliers may also offer a cost advantage because of lower labor and/or materials costs.
2. *Insufficient capacity:* A firm may be running at or near capacity, making it unable to produce the components in-house. This can happen when demand grows faster than anticipated or when expansion strategies fail to meet demand. The firm buys parts or components to free up capacity in the short term to focus on vital operations. Firms may even subcontract vital components and/or operations under very strict terms and conditions in order to meet demand. When managed properly, **subcontracting** instead of buying is a more effective means to expand short-term capacity because the buying firm can exert better control over the manufacturing process and other requirements of the components or end products.
3. *Lack of expertise:* The firm may not have the necessary technology and expertise to manufacture the item. Maintaining long-term technological and economical viability for noncore activities may be affecting the firm's ability to focus on core competencies. Suppliers may hold the patent to the process or product in question, thus precluding the make option, or the firm may not be able to meet environmental and safety standards to manufacture the item.
4. *Quality:* Purchased components may be superior in quality because suppliers have better technologies, processes, skilled labor, and the advantage of economies of scale. Suppliers' superior quality may help firms stay on top of product and process technologies, especially in high-technology industries with rapid innovation and short product life cycles.

Reasons for Making

An organization also makes its own materials, components, services, and/or equipment in-house for many reasons. Let us briefly review them:

1. *Protect proprietary technology*: A major reason for the make option is to protect proprietary technology. A firm may have developed an equipment, product, or process that needs to be protected for the sake of competitive advantage. Firms may

choose not to reveal the technology by asking suppliers to make it, even if it is patented. An advantage of not revealing the technology is to be able to surprise competitors and bring new products to market ahead of competition, allowing the firm to charge a price premium.

2. *No competent supplier*: If existing suppliers do not have the technology or capability to produce a component, the firm may be forced to make an item in-house, at least for the short term. The firm may use supplier development strategies to work with a new or existing supplier to produce the component in the future as a long-term strategy.
3. *Better quality control*: If the firm is capable, the make option allows for the most direct control over the design, manufacturing process, labor, and other inputs to ensure that high-quality components are built. The firm may be so experienced and efficient in manufacturing the component that suppliers are unable to meet its exact specifications and requirements. On the other hand, suppliers may have better technologies and processes to produce better-quality components. Thus, the sourcing option ensuring a higher quality level is a debatable question and must be investigated thoroughly.
4. *Use existing idle capacity*: A short-term solution for a firm with excess idle capacity is to use the excess capacity to make some of its components. This strategy is valuable for firms that produce seasonal products. It avoids layoff of skilled workers and, when business picks up, the capacity is readily available to meet demand.
5. *Control of lead time, transportation, and warehousing costs:* The make option provides better control of lead time and logistical costs since management controls all phases of the design, manufacturing, and delivery processes. Although raw materials may have to be transported, finished goods can be produced near the point of use, for instance, to minimize holding cost.
6. *Lower cost:* If technology, capacity, and managerial and labor skills are available, the make option may be more economical if large quantities of the component are needed on a continuing basis. Although the make option has a higher fixed cost due to initial capital investment, it has a lower variable cost per unit because it does not include suppliers' profit margins.

Make-or-Buy Break-Even Analysis

The current sourcing trend is to buy equipment, materials, and services unless self-manufacture provides a major benefit such as protecting proprietary technologies, achieving superior characteristics, or ensuring adequate supplies. However, buying or outsourcing has its own shortcomings, such as loss of control and exposure to supplier risks. While cost is rarely the sole criterion in strategic sourcing decisions, **break-even analysis** is a handy tool for computing the cost-effectiveness of sourcing decisions when cost is the most important criterion. Several assumptions underlie the analysis: (1) all costs involved can be classified as either fixed or variable cost, (2) fixed cost remains the same within the range of analysis, (3) a linear variable cost relationship exists, (4) fixed cost of the make option is higher because of initial capital investment in equipment, and (5) variable cost of the buy option is higher because of supplier profits.

Consider a hypothetical situation (shown below) in which a firm has the option to make or buy a part. Its annual requirement is 15,000 units. A supplier is able to supply the part at \$7 per unit. The firm estimates that it costs \$500 to prepare the contract with the supplier. To make the part, the firm must invest \$25,000 in equipment, and the firm estimates that it costs \$5 per unit to make the part.

Figure 2.5 Break-even Analysis

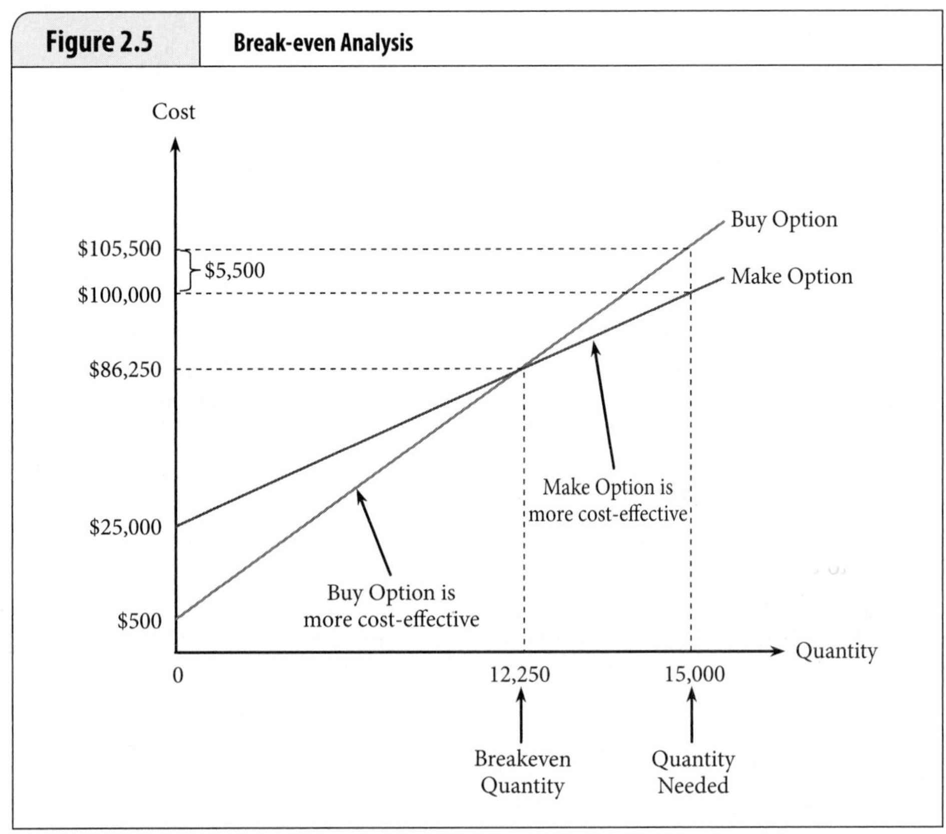

COSTS	MAKE OPTION	BUY OPTION
Fixed Cost	$25,000	$500
Variable Cost	$5	$7
Annual Requirement = 15,000 units		

Break-even Point

The break-even point, Q, is found by setting the total cost of the two options equal to one another and solving for Q (see Figure 2.5):

Total Cost to Make	= Total Cost to Buy
$\Rightarrow$ \$25,000 + \$5Q	= \$500 + \$7Q
$\Rightarrow$ 7Q – 5Q	= 25,000 – 500
$\Rightarrow$ 2Q	= 24,500 units
$\Rightarrow$ Break-even point, Q	= 12,250 units

The Total Cost for both options at the Break-even Point is:

$$TC_{BE} = \$25{,}000 + (\$5 \times 12{,}250) = \$86{,}250$$

For the annual requirement of 15,000 units:

The Total Cost for the Make Option is:

$$TC_{Make} = \$25{,}000 + (\$5 \times 15{,}000) = \$100{,}000$$

The Total Cost for the Buy Option is:

$$TC_{Buy} = \$500 + (\$7 \times 15{,}000) = \$105{,}500$$

The Cost Difference is:

$$TC_{Buy} - TC_{Make} = \$105{,}500 - \$100{,}000 = \$5{,}500$$

The analysis shows that the break-even point is 12,250 units. The total cost at the break-even point is $86,250. If the requirement is less than 12,250 units, it is cheaper to buy. It is cheaper to make the part if the firm needs more than 12,250 units. With small purchase requirements (less than 12,250 units), the low fixed cost of the buy option makes it attractive. With higher purchase requirements (greater than 12,250 units), the low variable cost of the make option makes it more attractive. The analysis shows that the firm should make the item since the quantity is large enough to warrant the capital investment.

ROLES OF THE SUPPLY BASE

The **supply base** or **supplier base** refers to the list of suppliers that a firm uses to acquire its materials, services, supplies, and equipment. Firms engaging in supply chain management emphasize long-term strategic supplier alliances by reducing the variety of purchased items and consolidating volume into one or fewer suppliers, resulting in a smaller supply base. For example, both Xerox and Chrysler reduced their supply bases by about 90 percent in the 1980s. An effective supply base that complements and contributes to a firm's competitive advantage is critical to its success. Savvy purchasing managers develop a sound supply base to support the firm's overall business and supply chain strategies, based on an expanded role for suppliers. It is thus vital to understand the strategic role of suppliers.

Besides supplying the obvious purchased items, key or preferred suppliers also supply:

1. product and process technology and expertise to support the buyer's operations, particularly in new product design and value analysis;
2. information on the latest trends in materials, processes, or designs;
3. information on the supply market, such as shortages, price increases, or political situations that may threaten supplies of vital materials;
4. capacity for meeting unexpected demand; and
5. cost efficiency due to economies of scale, since the supplier is likely to produce the same item for multiple buyers.

When developing and managing the supply chain, preferred suppliers are found or developed to provide these services and play a very important role in the success of the supply chain.

SUPPLIER SELECTION

The decision to select a supplier for office supplies or other noncritical materials is likely to be an easy one. However, the process of selecting a group of competent suppliers for important materials, which can potentially impact the firm's competitive advantage, is a complex one and should be based on multiple criteria. In addition to cost and delivery performance, firms should also consider how suppliers can contribute to product and process technology. Factors that firms should consider while selecting suppliers include:

1. *Process and product technologies*: Suppliers should have competent process technologies to produce superior products at a reasonable cost to enhance the buyer's competitive edge.
2. *Willingness to share technologies and information*: With the current trend that favors outsourcing to exploit suppliers' capabilities and to focus on core competencies, it is vital that firms seek suppliers that are willing to share their technologies and information. Suppliers can assist in new product design and development through **early supplier involvement (ESI)** to ensure cost-effective design choices, develop alternative conceptual solutions, select the best components and technologies, and help in design assessment. By increasing the involvement of the supplier in the design process, the buyer is free to focus more attention on core competencies.
3. *Quality*: Quality levels of the purchased item should be a very important factor in supplier selection. Product quality should be high and consistent since it can directly affect the quality of the finished goods.
4. *Cost*: While the unit cost of an item is not typically the sole criterion in supplier selection, total cost of ownership is an important factor. **Total cost of ownership** or **total cost of acquisition** includes the unit cost of the item, payment terms, cash discount, ordering cost, carrying cost, logistical costs, maintenance costs, and other more qualitative costs that may not be easy to assess. An example of a total cost of ownership analysis is provided in the following section. The total cost analysis demonstrates how other costs besides the unit cost can affect purchase decisions.
5. *Reliability*: Aside from a reliable product quality level, reliability can refer to other supplier characteristics. For example, is the supplier financially stable? Otherwise, it may not be able to invest in research and development or stay in business. Is the supplier's delivery lead time reliable? Otherwise, production may have to be interrupted due to a shortage of material.
6. *Order system and cycle time*: How easy to use is a supplier's ordering system, and what is the normal order cycle time? Placing orders with a supplier should be easy, quick, and effective. Delivery lead time should be short, so that small lot sizes can be ordered on a frequent basis to reduce inventory holding costs.
7. *Capacity*: The firm should also consider whether the supplier has the capacity to fill orders to meet requirements and the ability to fill large orders if needed.
8. *Communication capability*: Suppliers should possess a communication capability that facilitates communication between the parties.
9. *Location*: Geographical location is another important factor in supplier selection, as it impacts delivery lead-time, transportation, and logistical costs. Some firms require their suppliers to be located within a certain distance from their facilities.
10. *Service*: Suppliers must be able to back up their products by providing good services when needed. For example, when product information or warranty service is needed, suppliers must respond on a timely basis.

There are numerous other factors—some strategic, others tactical—that a firm ust consider when choosing suppliers. The days of using competitive bidding to identify the cheapest supplier for strategic items are long gone. The ability to select competent strategic suppliers directly affects a firm's competitive success. Strategic suppliers are trusted partners and become an integral part of the firm's design and production efforts.

The Total Cost of Ownership Concept

The total cost of ownership concept extends the traditional break-even analysis beyond considering only the original purchase cost and capital equipment cost; other qualitative and quantitative factors, including freight and inventory costs, tooling, tariffs and duties, currency exchange fees, payment terms, maintenance, and nonperformance costs should be considered. Firms can use a total cost analysis to select the most cost-effective supplier or as a negotiation tool to inform suppliers regarding areas where they need to improve. Example 2.1 demonstrates a total cost of ownership analysis.

Example 2.1 Kuantan ATV Inc.: A Total Cost of Ownership Analysis

Kuantan ATV, Inc. assembles five different models of all-terrain vehicles (ATVs) from various ready-made components to serve the Las Vegas, Nevada, market. The company uses the same engine for all its ATVs. The purchasing manager, Ms. Jane Kim, needs to choose a supplier for engines for the coming year. Due to the size of the warehouse and other administrative restrictions, she must order the engines in lot sizes of 1,000 each. The unique characteristics of the standardized engine require special tooling to be used during the manufacturing process. Kuantan ATV agrees to reimburse the supplier for the tooling. This is a critical purchase, since late delivery of engines would disrupt production and cause 50 percent lost sales and 50 percent back orders of the ATVs. Jane has obtained quotes from two reliable suppliers but needs to know which supplier is more cost-effective. She has the following information:

Requirements (annual forecast)	12,000 units
Weight per engine	22 pounds
Order processing cost	$125 per order
Inventory carrying rate	20% per year
Cost of working capital	10% per year
Profit margin	18%
Price of finished ATV	$4,500
Back-order cost	$15 per unit backordered

Two qualified suppliers have submitted the following quotations:

UNIT PRICE	SUPPLIER 1	SUPPLIER 2
1 to 999 units/order	$510.00	$505.00
1,000 to 2,999 units/order	$500.00	$498.00
3,000+ units/order	$490.00	$488.00
Tooling Cost	$22,000	$20,000
Terms	2/10 net 30	1/10 net 30
Distance	125 miles	100 miles
Supplier Quality Rating (defects)	2%	3%
Supplier Delivery Rating (late delivery)	1%	2%

Jane also obtained the following freight rates from her carrier:

Truckload (TL ≥ 40,000 lbs): $0.80 per ton-mile
Less-than-truckload (LTL): $1.20 per ton-mile
Note: per ton-mile = 2,000 lbs per mile; number of days per year = 365

TOTAL COST OF OWNERSHIP COMPUTATION—SUPPLIER 1

Note that due to the size of the warehouse, order lot size, Q, is limited to 1,000 units. The total cost of ownership for supplier 1 can be computed as follows (see Figure 2.6):

(1) Total Engine Cost = Annual requirement × Unit cost
= 12,000 units × $500/unit = $6,000,000.00

(2) Cash Discount (based on 365 days per year)
A cash discount of *2/10 net 30* means the invoice must be paid within 30 days, but a 2% discount is given if the invoice is paid within 10 days of the invoice date. The calculation of the cash discount is done in two parts—whether the buyer pays the invoice on the 10th day (receives a 2% discount) or 30th day (pays the full amount). It is assumed that the buyer will take advantage of the largest discount.
(A) Net 30 = Saving on the cost of capital by paying invoices on the 30th day
= Total engine cost × cost of capital × 30/365
= $6,000,000.00 × 10% × 30/365 = $49,315.07
(B) 2/10 cash discount = Saving on the cost of capital and 2% discount by paying invoices on the 10th day
= Total engine cost × (cost of capital + 2% discount)
= $6,000,000.00 × (10% ×10/365 + 2%)
= $136,438.36
Hence, the buyer should pay invoices on the 10th day to take advantage of the $136,438.36 cash discount provided by the 2/10 term.

(3) Tooling Cost = $22,000.00

(4) Transportation Cost
Since the order size is 1,000 units, the total weight of each shipment is 22,000 pounds (1,000 units × 22 lbs/unit). Since it is less than 40,000 pounds, the buyer must use less-than-truckload shipment at $1.20 per ton-mile.
Total Transportation Cost = distance × quantity × weight/unit × rate/ton-mile
= 125 miles × 12,000 units × 22 lbs/unit × $1.20/2,000 lbs-mile
= $19,800.00

(5) Since the number of orders = annual requirement /order size, Ordering Cost
= number of orders × order processing cost
= (12,000 units/1,000 units) × $125 = $1,500.00

(6) Since average inventory = order size/2,
Carrying Cost = Average inventory × price per unit × inventory carrying rate
= (order size/2) × price per unit × inventory carrying rate
= (1,000 units/2) × $500/unit × 20% = $50,000.00

(7) Quality Cost = Total engine cost × defect rate
= $6,000,000.00 × 2% = $120,000.00

(8) Delivery Rating
(A) Backorder Cost (50%) = Total quantity × late delivery rate × back order percentage × unit back order cost
= 12,000 units ×1% × 50% × $15/unit = $900.00
(B) Lost Sales (50%) = Total quantity × late delivery rate × lost sales percentage × price of ATV × profit margin
= 12,000 units ×1% × 50% × $4,500/unit × 18%
= $48,600.00

(9) Total Cost of Supplier 1 = $6,000,000.00 – $136,438.36 + $22,000.00 + $19,800.00 + $1,500.00 + $50,000.00 + $120,000.00 + $900.00 + $48,600.00
= $6,126,361.64

The total cost of ownership for supplier 2 can be computed using the same logic. The total cost analysis (see Figure 2.6) shows that Supplier 1 is more cost-effective, although its unit price and tooling costs are slightly higher than those of Supplier 2. The cash discount, quality cost, and delivery performance set Supplier 1 apart from Supplier 2. Using unit cost as the sole criterion to select a supplier would have ultimately cost the company $138,925.75 ($6,265,287.40 – $6,126,361.64).

Figure 2.6 **Total Cost of Ownership Analysis**

Description	Supplier 1			Supplier 2		
1. Total Engine Cost	12,000 units × $500		$6,000,000.00	12,000 units × $498		$5,976,000.00
2. Cash Discount						
n/30	$6,000,000 × 10% × 30/365	$49,315.07		$5,976,000 × 10% × 30/365	$49,117.81	
1/10	N/A			$5,976,000 (10% × 10/365 + 1%)	$76,132.60	
2/10	$6,000,000 (10% × 10/365 + 2%)	$136,438.36		N/A		
Largest discount			$(136,438.36)			$(76,132.60)
3. Tooling Cost			$22,000.00			$20,000.00
4. Transportation Cost (22,000 lb LTL)	125 miles × 12,000 units × 22 lb × $1.20/2000		$19,800.00	100 miles × 12,000 units × 22 lb × $1.20/2000		$15,840.00
5. Ordering Cost	(12,000/1000) × $125		$1,500.00	(12,000/1000) × $125		$1,500.00
6. Carrying Cost	(1000/2) × $500 × 20%		$50,000.00	(1000/2) × $498 × 20%		$49,800.00
7. Quality Cost	$6,000,000 × 2%		$120,000.00	$5,976,000 × 3%		$179,280.00
8. Delivery Rating						
Backorder (50%)	12,000 × 1% × 50% × $15		$900.00	12,000 × 2% × 50% × $15		$1,800.00
Lost Sales (50%)	12,000 × 1% × 50% × $4500 × 18%		$48,600.00	12,000 × 2% × 50% × $4500 × 18%		$97,200.00
TOTAL COST			$6,126,361.64			$6,265,287.40

HOW MANY SUPPLIERS TO USE

The issue of how many suppliers to use for each purchased item is a complex one. While numerous references propose the use of a single source for core materials and supplies to facilitate cooperative buyer–supplier partnerships, single sourcing can be a very risky proposition. Although Xerox and Chrysler had substantially reduced their supply base in the 1980s, it was not documented that they resorted to single sourcing for their vital materials and components. The current trends in sourcing favor using fewer sources, although not necessarily a single source. Theoretically, firms should use single or a few sources, whenever possible, to enable the development of close relationships with the best suppliers. However, by increasing reliance on one supplier, the firm increases its risk that poor supplier performance will result in plant shutdowns or poor-quality finished products. Although **sole sourcing** and **single sourcing** are sometimes used interchangeably, sole sourcing typically refers to the situation when the supplier is the only available source, whereas single sourcing refers to the deliberate practice of concentrating purchases of an item with one source from a pool of viable suppliers. A comparison follows of some of the reasons favoring the use of a single supplier versus using two or more suppliers for a purchased item.

Reasons Favoring a Single Supplier

1. *To establish a good relationship*: Using a single supplier makes it easier for the firm to establish a mutually beneficial strategic alliance relationship with the supplier, as with well-managed supply chains, especially when the firm can benefit from the supplier's technologies and capabilities.
2. *Less quality variability*: Since the same technologies and processes are used to produce the parts when using a single source, variability in the quality levels is less than if the parts are purchased from multiple suppliers.

3. *Lower cost*: Buying from a single source concentrates purchase volume with the supplier, typically lowering the purchase cost per unit. Due to the large purchase volume, the supplier is more likely to ensure that it meets all of its performance goals to keep the business. Single sourcing also avoids duplicate fixed costs, especially if the part requires special tooling or expensive setups.
4. *Transportation economies*: Because single sourcing concentrates volume, the firm can take advantage of truckload (TL) shipments, which are cheaper per unit than the less-than-truckload (LTL) rate. By moving up to full truckloads, the firm has the option of using both rail and motor carriers. Rail carriers are more efficient for hauling heavy loads over long distances.
5. *Proprietary product or process purchases*: If it is a proprietary product or process, or if the supplier holds the patents to the product or process, the firm has no choice but to buy from the sole source.
6. *Volume too small to split*: If the requirement is too small, it is not worthwhile to split the order among many suppliers. Single sourcing is a good approach for acquiring supplies and services that do not contribute to the firm's core competencies.

Reasons Favoring Multiple Suppliers

1. *Need capacity*: When demand exceeds the capacity of a single supplier, the firm has no choice but to use multiple sources.
2. *Spread the risk of supply interruption*: Multiple sources allow the firm to spread the risk of supply interruptions due to a strike, quality problem, political instability, and other supplier problems.
3. *Create competition*: Using multiple sources encourages competition among suppliers in terms of price and quality. While modern supplier management philosophy opposes the use of multiple sources simply to create competition, this may still be the preferred approach for sourcing nonvital items that do not affect the firm's competitive advantage. Using a single source to develop alliances for these types of purchases may not be cost-effective.
4. *Information*: Multiple suppliers usually have more information about market conditions, new product developments, and new process technologies. This is particularly important if the product has a short product life cycle.
5. *Dealing with special kinds of businesses*: The firms, particularly government contractors, may need to give portions of their purchases to small, local, or women- or minority-owned businesses, either voluntarily or as required by law.

The number of suppliers to use for one type of purchase has changed from the traditional multiple suppliers to the use of fewer, more reliable suppliers and even to the extent of using a single, highly rated, and trusted supplier. Relationships between buyers and suppliers traditionally were short-term, adversarial, and based primarily on cost, resulting in a mutual lack of trust. Buyer–supplier relationships, particularly in integrated supply chain settings, have evolved today into trusting, cooperative, and mutually beneficial long-term relationships. Firms today reduce their supply base to only the best suppliers.

PURCHASING ORGANIZATION

Purchasing's organization within the firm has evolved over the years as the responsibilities of the purchasing function of firms changed from a clerical, supporting role to an integral part of corporate strategy that directly affects the competitiveness of the firms. In addition to the actual buying process, purchasing personnel are now involved in product design, production decisions, supplier relationship management, and other aspects of a firm's operations. The decision of how to organize purchasing to best serve its purpose is firm and industry-specific and dependent on many factors, such as market conditions and the types of parts and materials required. Purchasing structure can be viewed as a continuum, with centralization at one extreme and decentralization at the other. While there are few firms that adopt a pure centralized or decentralized structure, the benefits of each are worth a closer examination. The current trend is toward purchasing centralization for the vital materials where firms can take advantage of economies of scale and other benefits.

Centralized purchasing is where a single purchasing department, usually located at the firm's corporate office, makes all the purchasing decisions, including order quantity, pricing policy, contracting, negotiations, and supplier selection and evaluation. **Decentralized purchasing** is where individual, local purchasing departments, such as at the plant level, make their own purchasing decisions. A discussion of advantages and disadvantages to each of these purchasing structures follows.

Advantages of Centralization

1. *Concentrated volume*: An obvious benefit is the concentration of purchase volume to create quantity discounts, less-costly volume shipments, and other more favorable purchase terms. This is often referred to as **leveraging purchase volume**. A centralized system also provides the buying firm more clout and bargaining power. Suppliers generally are more willing to negotiate, give better terms, and share technology due to the higher volume.
2. *Avoid duplication*: Centralized purchasing eliminates the duplication of job functions. A corporate buyer can research and issue a large purchase order to cover the same material requested by all units, thus eliminating duplication of activities. This also results in fewer buyers, reducing labor costs.
3. *Specialization*: Centralization allows buyers to specialize in a particular product or group of items instead of being responsible for all purchased materials and services. It allows buyers to spend more time and resources to research items for which they are responsible, thus becoming specialized buyers.
4. *Lower transportation costs*: Centralization allows larger shipments to be made to take advantage of truckload or railcar shipments, and yet smaller shipments still can be arranged for delivery directly from suppliers to the points of use.
5. *No competition between units*: Under the decentralized system, when different units purchase the same material, a situation may be created in which units are competing among themselves, especially when scarce materials are purchased from the same supplier. Centralization minimizes this problem.
6. *Common supply base*: A common supply base is used, thus making it easier to manage and negotiate contracts.

Advantages of Decentralization

1. *Better knowledge of unit requirements*: A buyer at the individual unit is more likely to know its exact needs better than a central buyer at the home office.

2. *Local sourcing*: If the firm desires to support local businesses, it is more likely that a local buyer will know more about local suppliers. The proximity of local suppliers allows materials to be shipped more frequently in small lot sizes and is conducive to the creation of closer supplier relationships.
3. *Less bureaucracy*: Decentralization allows quicker response due to less bureaucracy and closer contact between the user and the buyer. Coordination and communication with operations and other divisions are more efficient.

Thus, while centralized purchasing may result in lower costs and better negotiating power, the centralized system may also be too rigid and even infeasible for large, multiunit organizations consisting of several unrelated business operations. For these reasons, a **hybrid purchasing organization** may be warranted. Large multiunit organizations may use a **decentralized/centralized purchasing structure** to decentralize purchasing at the corporate level, while centralizing the procurement function at the business unit level. Conversely, a firm may utilize a **centralized/decentralized purchasing structure** to negotiate national contracts at the corporate level, while decentralizing buying at the business unit level. These hybrid purchasing organizations allow firms to exploit the advantages of both the centralized and decentralized systems.

GLOBAL SOURCING

International agreements aimed at relaxing trade barriers and promoting free trade have provided opportunities for firms to expand their supply bases to participate in **global sourcing** (also occasionally referred to as international purchasing). Indeed, world merchandise exports and commercial services trade reached $17.93 trillion and $4.35 trillion, respectively in 2012.[12] In 2012, the U.S. was the world's largest importer ($2.34 trillion) and second largest exporter for merchandise trade ($1.55 trillion). In the same year, the U.S. was the world's largest importer and exporter for commercial services (imports were $411 billion; exports were $621 billion). The world's top three merchandise trade exporters were China ($2.05 trillion), the U.S. ($1.55 trillion), and Germany ($1.41 trillion). While global sourcing provides opportunities to improve quality, cost, and delivery performance, it also poses unique challenges for purchasing personnel. Engaging in global sourcing requires additional skills and knowledge to deal with international suppliers, logistics, communication, political, cultural, and other issues not usually encountered in domestic sourcing. The total cost of ownership example shown previously in Example 2.1 can also be used to compare the cost-effectiveness of domestic versus global sourcing.

Various methods are employed for global sourcing. It is not merely limited to setting up an international purchasing office or using existing purchasing personnel to handle the transactions in-house. An **import broker** or **sales agent**, who performs transactions for a fee, can be used. Import brokers and sales agents do not take title to the goods. Instead, title passes directly from the seller to the buyer. International purchasers can also buy foreign goods from an **import merchant**, who buys and takes title to the goods and then resells them to the buyer. Purchasing from a **trading company**, which carries a wide variety of goods, is another option.

There are numerous international trade organizations designed to reduce tariff and nontariff barriers among member countries. A **tariff** is an official list or schedule showing the duties, taxes, or customs imposed by the host country on imports or exports. **Nontariff barriers** are import quotas, licensing agreements, embargoes, laws, and other regulations imposed on imports and exports. A discussion of major international trade organizations follows.

1. The *World Trade Organization* (WTO) is the largest and most visible international trade organization dealing with the global rules of trade between nations. It replaced the General Agreement on Tariffs and Trade (GATT) on January 1, 1995. Its primary goal is to ensure that international trade flows smoothly, predictably, and freely among member countries. The WTO Secretariat is based in Geneva, Switzerland. It has 159 member countries as of March 2013.
2. The *North American Free Trade Agreement* (NAFTA) was implemented on January 1, 1994. Its goal is to remove trade and investment barriers among the U.S, Canada, and Mexico. Under NAFTA, all nontariff agricultural trade barriers between the U.S and Mexico were eliminated. Most tariffs affecting agricultural trade between the U.S. and Canada were removed by 1998. NAFTA was fully implemented as of January 1, 2008. Ten years after its implementation (from 1994 to 2004), studies showed that NAFTA had only a modest positive effect on the U.S. and Mexican economies.[13] In 2014, twenty years after its implementation, though NAFTA has helped boost trade among its member countries, the trade agreement has fallen short of generating the jobs and economic growth its advocates promised decades ago.
3. The *European Union* (EU) was set up on May 9, 1950, and was comprised of Belgium, France, Luxembourg, Italy, the Netherlands, and Germany. The U.K., Denmark, and Ireland joined the EU in 1973. As of July 2013, the EU has twenty-eight member countries. One of the primary goals of the EU is to create a single market without internal borders for goods and services, allowing member countries to better compete with markets like the U.S. The EU's economy, measured by the combined gross domestic product (GDP) of its member countries exceeded the GDP of the U.S. in 2012.

Reasons for Global Sourcing

Firms expand their supply bases to include foreign suppliers for many reasons. These can include lower price, better quality, an overseas supplier holding the patent to the product, faster delivery to foreign units, better services, and better process or product technologies.

A primary reason that many firms purchase from foreign suppliers is to lower the price of materials. As stated earlier, price generally is an important factor when purchasing standard materials and supplies that do not impact the competitive position of the firm. Many factors can contribute to cheaper materials from overseas suppliers—for example, cheaper labor costs and raw materials, favorable exchange rates, more efficient processes, or intentional dumping of products by foreign suppliers in overseas markets.

Additionally, the quality of overseas products may be better due to newer and better product and process technologies. Further, while foreign suppliers may be located farther away, they may be able to deliver goods faster than domestic suppliers due to more efficient transportation and logistical systems. Foreign suppliers may even maintain inventory and set up support offices in the host country to compete with domestic sources and to provide better services.

Firms may buy from foreign suppliers to support the local economy where they have subsidiaries, or they may be involved in **countertrade**, in which the contract calls for the exchange of goods or services for raw materials from local suppliers. While foreign purchasing may provide a number of benefits to the buyer, some problems may also be encountered.

Potential Challenges for Global Sourcing

Over the last few decades, global sourcing has surged due to many factors, such as the improvement of communication and transportation technologies, the reduction of international trade barriers, and deregulation of the transportation industry. However, global sourcing poses additional challenges that purchasing must know how to handle effectively. For example, the complexity and costs involved in selecting foreign suppliers and dealing with duties; tariffs; custom clearance; currency exchange; and political, cultural, labor, and legal problems present sizable challenges for the international buyer.

Unlike dealing with domestic suppliers, the costs involved in identifying, selecting, and evaluating foreign suppliers can be prohibitive. A foreign supplier in a distant location, customs clearance, transportation, and other logistical issues may render delivery lead time unacceptable, especially for perishable goods. While many multinational corporations

SCM Profile | **Multinational Problems with Supplies in China**

As multinational corporations expand their operations globally, a number of problems can surface such as the recent scandals in China—from melamine-tainted baby milk to donkey meat sold in some of Wal-Mart's Chinese stores. While most countries, including China, have stringent food safety rules, not all suppliers understand and follow rules and regulations. Ineffective government oversight has forced many Western multinational corporations in China to tighten their inspections of suppliers. In China, attempts to foster reliable buyer–supplier relationships require additional efforts. Some recent examples of challenges faced by Western companies doing business in China include:

1. Fonterra Co-operative Group owned almost half of China's Sanlu Group. In 2008, Sanlu was implicated in a scandal involving the addition of melamine to make watered-down milk appear to contain more protein. Sadly, six children died and 300,000 infants became ill from the tainted product. Fonterra wrote off its $113 million investment in Sanlu when the latter went bankrupt.
2. In 2012, Chinese chicken suppliers to Yum! Brands KFC were caught feeding birds with excessive antibiotics and hormones to boost their weight. Yum! KFC apologized to consumers for these lapses, but sales dropped significantly in 2013. Additionally, in 2013, Yum! Little Sheep Mongolian Hot Pot restaurants, the largest hot pot restaurant chain in China, was forced to take a $258 million write down when its competitors were found to serve fox and rat meat as lamb, even though Yum! Little Sheep Mongolian Hot Pot restaurants were never accused.
3. In 2013, an investigation by a television network claimed that Tesco, the big British retailer, sold mislabeled duck as mutton in China. Tesco swiftly removed the meat from store shelves and investigated its suppliers.
4. In 2013, the French supermarket operator Carrefour, was accused of selling beefless "juicy beef balls" in its store in Beijing. Carrefour quickly removed all their beef balls from their 200 outlets in China and promised to investigate its suppliers. Carrefour never revealed what was in their "juicy beef balls."
5. In 2014, Wal-Mart recalled all its Five Spice donkey meat from its Chinese stores after the meat tested positive for fox DNA. Wal-Mart recalled the products, apologized to customers, and promised to investigate its suppliers.[14]

source globally for better quality materials and component parts, the opposite can also be true. It is not uncommon for multinational corporations to suffer irreparable damage to their reputations and incur expensive legal liabilities for unknowingly purchased tainted raw materials or faulty component parts from overseas suppliers. The nearby SCM Profile discusses some of these issues.

In addition to the Uniform Commercial Code (UCC), which governs the purchase and sale of goods in the U.S. (except the state of Louisiana), global purchasers must also know the United Nations' **Contracts for the International Sale of Goods (CISG)**. The CISG applies to international purchases and sales of goods, unless both parties elect to opt out. The UCC allows either party to modify the terms of acceptance for the purchase contract; however, the terms of acceptance cannot be modified under the CISG.

Global purchasers must also deal with more complex shipping terms than domestic buyers. The International Chamber of Commerce created a uniform set of rules, called **incoterms** (which is the commonly used term referring to the **International Commercial Terms**), to simplify international transactions of goods with respect to shipping costs, risks, and responsibilities of buyer, seller, and shipper. However, incoterms do not deal with transfer of title of the goods. Incoterms are often used in conjunction with a geographical location. *Incoterms 2010* revised the thirteen incoterms adopted in 2000, which were divided into four categories, to eleven rules. These eleven Incoterms 2010 are divided into two categories based on method of delivery. Seven of these eleven rules are applicable to sales that involve all method of delivery, whereas the remaining four rules are applicable to sales that involve transportation over water.

Countertrade

Global sourcing may involve countertrade, in which goods and/or services of domestic firms are exchanged for goods and/or services of equal value or in combination with currency from foreign firms. This type of arrangement is sometimes used by countries where there is a shortage of hard currency or as a means to acquire technologies. Countertrade transactions are more complicated than currency transactions because goods are exchanged for goods.

The various forms of countertrade include barter, offset, and counterpurchase. **Barter** is the complete exchange of goods or services of equal value without the exchange of currency. The seller can either consume the goods or services or resell the items. **Offset** is an exchange agreement for industrial goods or services as a condition of military-related export. It is also commonly used in the aerospace and defense sectors. Most of the offset packages are divided into direct and indirect offsets. **Direct offset** usually involves coproduction, or a joint venture and exchange of related goods or services; whereas **indirect offset** involves exchange of goods or services unrelated to the initial purchase. **Counterpurchase** is an arrangement whereby the original exporter agrees to sell goods or services to a foreign importer and simultaneously agrees to buy specific goods or services from the foreign importer. Many developing countries mandate the transfer of technology as part of a countertrade or offset arrangement.

PROCUREMENT IN GOVERNMENT AND NONPROFIT AGENCIES

Public procurement or **public purchasing** refers to the management of the purchasing and supply management function in the government and nonprofit sectors, such as educational institutions; hospitals; and federal, state, and local governments. Although public procurement is subjected to political pressure and public scrutiny, its goals are similar to the private sector. However, public procurement is subjected to special rules and regulations that are established by the federal, state, and local governments. For example, all U.S. federal government purchases must comply with the **Federal Acquisition Regulation (FAR)**. Consequently, the procedures for public procurement differ from the private sector—in addition to ensuring that purchases for goods and services are in strict compliance with statutes and policies, public procurement procedures are generally designed to **maximize competition**. The e-procurement system described in Figure 2.4 is an example of a public procurement system. In addition to the typical operations control, the e-procurement system in Figure 2.4 requires additional treatments of purchases exceeding $25,000.

In the U.S., the **General Services Administration (GSA)**, passed by the 81st Congress and signed into law by President Harry Truman in 1949, is responsible for most federal purchases. The GSA, based in Washington, D.C., has eleven regional offices in Boston, New York, Philadelphia, Atlanta, Chicago, Kansas City, Fort Worth, Denver, San Francisco, Auburn (Washington), and Washington, D.C. It is one of the world's largest purchasing entities. The **Department of Defense (DOD)** is the other major public procurement entity in the U.S.

Characteristics of Public Procurement

A unique characteristic of public procurement is the preference to use competitive bidding to encourage competition among suppliers. For example, a government agency may implement procurement procedures that require a written quote for purchases that are more than $2,500 but less than $10,000, two written quotes for purchases that are less than $25,000, three written quotes for purchases less than $100,000, and competitive bids for purchases over $100,000.

In competitive bidding, the contract is usually awarded to the *lowest-priced bidder* determined to be *responsive* and *responsible* by the buyer. A responsive bid is one that conforms to the invitation to bid, and a responsible bid is one that is capable and willing to perform the work as specified.

The bidding process is usually very time-consuming and not cost-efficient for small purchases. On October 13, 1994, U.S. President Bill Clinton signed the **Federal Acquisition Streamlining Act (FASA)** to remove many restrictions on government purchases below $100,000. Instead of using full and open competitive bidding, government agencies can now use simplified procedures that require fewer administrative details, lower approval levels, and less documentation for soliciting and evaluating bids up to $100,000. **Micro-purchases**, government purchases of $2,500 and below, can now be made without obtaining competitive quotes. Additionally, all federal purchases between $2,500 and $100,000 are now reserved for small businesses, unless the buyer cannot obtain offers from two or more small businesses that are competitive on price, quality, and delivery. In the U.S., a small business is defined as one with fewer than 100 employees.

U.S. government agencies are required to advertise all planned purchases over $25,000. When the requirements are clear, accurate, and complete, the government agency usually uses an **invitation for bid (IFB)** to solicit **sealed bids**. The specifications for the proposed purchase; instructions for preparation of bids; and the conditions of purchase, delivery, and payment schedule are usually included with the IFB. The IFB also designates the date and time of bid opening. Sealed bids are opened in public at the purchasing office at the time designated in the invitation, and facts about each bid are read aloud and recorded. A contract is then awarded to the lowest responsible and responsive bidder.

Generally, bidders are also required to furnish bid bonds to ensure that the successful bidder will fulfill the contract as stated. There are three basic types of bid bond: **bid** or **surety bonds** guarantee the successful bidder will accept the contract; **performance bonds** guarantee the work of the successful bidder meets specifications and in the time stated; and **payment bonds** protect the buyer against any third-party liens not fulfilled by the bidder.

Another characteristic of public procurement is the **Buy American Act** that mandates U.S. government purchases and third-party purchases that utilize federal funds to buy domestically produced goods, if the price differential between the domestic product and an identical foreign-sourced product does not exceed a certain percentage amount. However, the U.S. president has the authority to waive the Buy American Act.

While **green purchasing** is not a new sourcing concept, there is a push to expand green purchasing requirements in the public sector. There are at least five federal statutes and more than a dozen presidential executive orders requiring federal purchasing officials to include environmental considerations and human health when making purchasing decisions.[15] Public procurement advocates the purchase of more energy-efficient products, bio-based products, recycled content products, non-ozone-depleting substances, green power, and other environmentally friendly products. The term **green power** refers to electricity products that include large proportions of electricity generated from renewable and environmentally preferable energy resources, such as wind and solar energy.[16]

SUMMARY

Over the last decade, the purchasing function has evolved into an integral part of supply chain management. Purchasing is an important strategic contributor to overall business competitiveness. It is the largest single function in most organizations, controlling activities and transactions valued at more than 50 percent of sales. Every dollar saved due to better purchasing impacts business operations and profits directly. Purchasing personnel talk to customers; users; suppliers; and internal design, finance, marketing, and operations personnel, in addition to top management. The information they gain from all this exposure can be used to help the firm to provide better, cheaper, and more timely products and services to both internal and external customers. Savvy executives are thus turning to purchasing to improve business and supply chain performance.

KEY TERMS

backward vertical integration, 52
barter, 66
bid, 68
blank check purchase order, 51
blanket order release, 51
blanket purchase order, 51
break-even analysis, 54
Buy American Act, 68
centralized purchasing, 62
centralized/decentralized purchasing structure, 63
Contracts for the International Sale of Goods (CISG), 66
corporate purchasing cards, 50
counterpurchase, 64
countertrade, 62
decentralized purchasing, 62
decentralized/centralized purchasing structure, 63
Department of Defense (DOD), 67
direct offset, 66
early supplier involvement (ESI), 57
economies of scale, 53
expediting, 46
Federal Acquisition Regulation (FAR), 67
Federal Acquisition Streamlining Act (FASA), 67
follow-up, 46
forward vertical integration, 52
General Services Administration (GSA), 67
global sourcing, 63
green power, 68
green purchasing, 68
hybrid purchasing organization, 63
import broker, 63
import merchant, 63
incoterms, 66
indirect offset, 66
industrial buyers, 37
internal control, 42
International Commercial Terms, 66
inventory turnover, 41
invitation for bid (IFB), 67
leveraging purchase volume, 62
make or buy decision, 52
material requisition (MR), 44
maximize competition, 67
merchant, 37
micro-purchases, 67
nontariff barriers, 63
offset, 66
open-end purchase order, 51
outsourcing, 46
payment bonds, 68
performance bonds, 68
petty cash, 51
planned order releases, 44
procurement credit cards, 50
profit-leverage effect, 40
public procurement, 66
public purchasing, 66
purchase order (PO), 46
purchase requisition, 44
purchase spend, 40
request for proposal (RFP), 46
request for quotation (RFQ), 46
return on assets (ROA), 40
return on investment (ROI), 40
sales agent, 63
sales order, 46
sealed bids, 67
simplification, 52
single sourcing, 60
sole sourcing, 60
stockless buying, 51
subcontracting, 53
supplier base, 56
supplier development, 46
supply base, 56
supply management, 37
surety bonds, 68
system contracting, 51
tariff, 63
total cost of acquisition, 57
total cost of ownership, 57
trading company, 63
traveling requisition, 44
Uniform Commercial Code (UCC), 46

DISCUSSION QUESTIONS

1. Describe the steps in a traditional manual purchasing system.
2. Describe the e-procurement system and its advantages over the manual system. Are there any disadvantages to the electronic system? Do you think the e-procurement system will ultimately replace the manual system? Why or why not?
3. How can purchasing help to improve the competitive edge of an organization?
4. What is the profit-leverage effect of purchasing? What is the return-on-assets effect of purchasing?
5. How does a merchant differ from an industrial buyer?
6. Describe the purpose of a material requisition, a purchase order, a request for quotation, and a request for proposal. Does the material requisition serve the same purpose as the purchase order?
7. Why are small value purchase orders problematic? How can purchasing more effectively deal with this problem?
8. Should unit price be used as the sole criterion for selecting suppliers? Why?
9. Explain backward vertical integration. What are the advantages of outsourcing compared to backward vertical integration?
10. When should a firm outsource instead of making the items in-house?
11. What factors should be considered while choosing suppliers?
12. Describe the difference between sole source and single source.
13. What are the reasons to use a single supplier? Is this the most efficient way to purchase materials in general?
14. Describe centralized and decentralized purchasing and their advantages.
15. Describe how the hybrid purchasing organization works.
16. Describe how blanket orders and blanket order releases can be used to manage the procurement system of a business that owns a dozen large restaurants in a city.
17. How does public procurement differ from corporate purchasing?
18. Describe the different types of bid bonds.
19. What are micro-purchases? How can they be used to improve public procurement?
20. Why do firms purchase from foreign suppliers? What are the risks involved in global sourcing?
21. What is countertrade? Describe the various types of countertrade.
22. Describe how a typical government bidding process is conducted.
23. How can global sourcing enhance a firm's competitiveness?
24. Describe the disadvantages of global sourcing and how it can adversely affect a firm's competitiveness.

ESSAY/PROJECT QUESTIONS

1. Go to the World Trade Organization's website, and use the information to write a report that includes (a) the functions of the WTO, (b) the latest number of membership countries, (c) its relationship with GATT, (d) the number of countries that had originally signed the GATT by 1994, and (e) the last five countries that became members of the WTO.

2. Utilize the Internet to search for "incoterms 2010." Write a report to (a) summarize the incoterms into two groups, and (b) describe each of the eleven terms.

3. Go to the General Services Administration's website, and use the information to write a brief report to summarize the roles of GSA. Additionally, discuss the roles of the Federal Acquisition Regulation (FAR), Federal Management Regulation (FMR), and the Federal Travel Regulation (FTR).

SPREADSHEET PROBLEMS

1. If a firm's net income (profits before taxes) is $120,000 and it has total assets of $1.5 million, what is its return on assets?

2. If a firm's total assets is $2.5 million and its return on assets is 12 percent, what is its net income?

3. If a firm is able to sustain the same level of operations in terms of sales and administrative expenses but reduces its materials cost by $50,000 through smarter purchases, what is the profit-leverage effect on gross profits? What is the profit-leverage effect on profits before taxes?

4. If a firm's cost of goods sold is $2.5 million and its average inventory is $500,000, what is the inventory turnover?

5. If a firm's cost of goods sold is $5 million and its inventory turnover is ten times, what is the average inventory?

6. If a firm's inventory turnover is eight times and its average inventory is $160,000, what is the cost of goods sold?

7. A retailer in Las Vegas has an ending inventory of $250,000 as of December 31, 2012, and the following accounting information.

Month	Ending Inventory	Cost of Goods Sold
January	$225,000	$1,200,000
February	$325,000	$1,250,000
March	$240,000	$1,350,000
April	$325,000	$1,500,000
May	$460,000	$950,000
June	$220,000	$850,000
July	$85,000	$1,650,000
August	$156,000	$1,325,000
September	$220,000	$1,750,000
October	$265,000	$850,000
November	$100,000	$2,200,000
December	$350,000	$3,500,000

a. Compute the monthly inventory turnover ratio for each of the twelve months.
b. What are the annual cost of goods sold and the average inventory for the year?
c. Compute the annual inventory turnover ratio. How is the retailer's performance compare to the industry standard, assuming its business is similar to Wal-Mart's?

8. A small firm has an ending inventory of $52,000 as of December 31, 2012, and the following accounting information.

Month	Ending Inventory	Cost of Goods Sold
January	$75,000	$225,000
February	$56,000	$325,000
March	$25,000	$240,000
April	$85,000	$325,000
May	$125,000	$460,000
June	$95,000	$220,000
July	$72,000	$85,000
August	$45,000	$156,000
September	$52,500	$220,000
October	$120,000	$265,000
November	$162,500	$100,000
December	$255,000	$350,000

a. Compute the monthly inventory turnover ratio for each of the twelve months.
b. What are the annual cost of goods sold and the average inventory for the year?
c. Compute the annual inventory turnover ratio. What can the purchasing department do to improve the firm's performance?

9. You are given the following information:

COSTS	MAKE OPTION	BUY OPTION
Fixed Cost	$125,000	$5,000
Variable Cost	$15	$17

a. Find the break-even quantity and the total cost at the break-even point.
b. If the requirement is 150,000 units, is it more cost-effective for the firm to buy or make the components? What is the cost savings for choosing the cheaper option?

10. You are given the following information:

COSTS	MAKE OPTION	BUY OPTION
Fixed Cost	$25,000	$3,000
Variable Cost	$8	$12

a. Find the break-even quantity and the total cost at the break-even point.
b. If the requirement is 4,500 units, is it more cost-effective for the firm to buy or make the components? What is the cost savings for choosing the cheaper option?
c. If the requirement is 6,000 units, is it more cost-effective for the firm to buy or make the components? What is the cost savings for choosing the cheaper option?

11. Ms. Jane Kim, Purchasing Manager of Kuantan ATV, Inc., is negotiating a contract to buy 20,000 units of a common component part from a supplier. Ms. Kim has done a preliminary cost analysis on manufacturing the part in-house and concluded that she would need to invest $50,000 in capital equipment and incur a variable cost of $25 per unit to manufacture the part in-house. Assuming the total fixed cost to draft a contract with her supplier is $1,000, what is the maximum purchase price that she should negotiate with her supplier? What other factors should she negotiate with the suppliers?

12. A Las Vegas, Nevada, manufacturer has the option to make or buy one of its component parts. The annual requirement is 20,000 units. A supplier is able to supply the parts for $10 each. The firm estimates that it costs $600 to prepare the contract with the supplier. To make the parts in-house, the firm must invest $50,000 in capital equipment and estimates that the parts cost $8 each.

- **a.** Assuming that cost is the only criterion, use break-even analysis to determine whether the firm should make or buy the item. What is the break-even quantity, and what is the total cost at the break-even point?
- **b.** Calculate the total costs for both options at 20,000 units. What is the cost savings for choosing the cheaper option?

13. Given the following information, use total cost analysis to determine which supplier is more cost-effective. Late delivery of raw material results in 60 percent lost sales and 40 percent back orders of finished goods.

Order lot size	1,000
Requirements (annual forecast)	120,000 units
Weight per engine	22 pounds
Order processing cost	$125/order
Inventory carrying rate	20% per year
Cost of working capital	10% per year
Profit margin	15%
Price of finished goods	$4,500
Back order cost	$15 per unit

UNIT PRICE	SUPPLIER 1	SUPPLIER 2
1 to 999 units/order	$50.00	$49.50
1000 to 2,999 units/order	$49.00	$48.50
3,000+ units/order	$48.00	$48.00
Tooling cost	$12,000	$10,000
Terms	2/10, net 30	1/10, net 30
Distance	125 miles	100 miles
Supplier Quality Rating	2%	2%
Supplier Delivery Rating	1%	2%

Truckload (TL $\geq$ 40,000 lbs): $0.85 per ton-mile

Less-than-truckload (LTL): $1.10 per ton-mile

Note: per ton-mile = 2,000 lbs per mile; number of days per year = 365

14. A buyer received bids from three suppliers for a vital component part for its latest product. Given the following information, use total cost analysis to determine which supplier should be chosen. Late delivery of the component results in 70 percent lost sales and 30 percent back orders of finished goods.

Order lot size	2,000
Requirements (annual forecast)	240,000 units
Weight per engine	40 pounds
Order processing cost	$200/order
Inventory carrying rate	20% per year
Cost of working capital	10% per year
Profit margin	15%
Price of finished goods	$10,500
Back order cost	$120 per unit

UNIT PRICE	SUPPLIER 1	SUPPLIER 2	SUPPLIER 3
1 to 999 units/order	$200.00	$205.00	$198.00
1,000 to 2,999 units/order	$195.00	$190.00	$192.00
3,000 + units/order	$190.00	$185.00	$190.00
Tooling Cost	$12,000	$10,000	$15,000
Terms	2/10, net 30	1/15, net 30	1/10, net 20
Distance	120 miles	100 miles	150 miles
Supplier Quality Rating	2%	1%	2%
Supplier Delivery Rating	1%	1%	2%

Truckload (TL ≥ 40,000 lbs): $0.95 per ton-mile

Less-than-truckload (LTL): $1.20 per ton-mile

Note: per ton-mile = 2,000 lbs per mile; number of days per year = 365

ADDITIONAL RESOURCES

Johnson, P. F., M. R. Leenders, and A. E. Flynn, *Purchasing and Supply Management*, 14th ed. New York: McGraw-Hill Irwin, 2010.

Monczka, R., R. Handfield, L. C. Giunipero, and J. L. Patterson, *Purchasing and Supply Chain Management*, 5th ed. Florence, KY: Cengage Learning, 2011.

Prahalad, C. K., and G. Hamel, "The Core Competence of the Corporation," *Harvard Business Review* 68(3), 1990: 79–91.

Tan, K. C., "A Framework of Supply Chain Management Literature," *European Journal of Purchasing & Supply Management* 7(1), 2001: 38–48.

Tan, K. C., V. R. Kannan, and R. B. Handfield, "Supply Chain Management: Supplier Performance and Firm Performance," *International Journal of Purchasing and Materials Management* 34(3), 1998: 2–9.

Wisner, J. D., and K. C. Tan, "Supply Chain Management and Its Impact on Purchasing," *Journal of Supply Chain Management* 36(4), 2000: 33–42.

ENDNOTES

1. CAPS Research Team, "Justifying Environmental Sustainability Activities," *Inside Supply Management* 25(1), January/February 2014: 36–37.
2. Sedgwick, D., "Suppliers in the Driver's Seat," *Automotive News* 88(6608), February 17, 2014: 1, 8.
3. Sedgwick, D., "Engineers Steer Detroit 3 Purchasing," *Automotive News* 87(6582), August 19, 2013: 3, 44.
4. Dudas, J. M., "Mayo Retools Medical Equipment Procurement Strategies, Tactics," *Healthcare Purchasing News* 37(11), November 2013: 62–63.
5. "2011 Statistics for All Manufacturing by State," *Annual Survey of Manufactures*, U.S. Census Bureau, December 17, 2013.
6. ISM Glossary of Key Supply Management Terms, www.ism.ws/glossary, accessed March 17, 2014.
7. Rendon, J. M., and R. G. Rendon, "Fighting Procurement Fraud," *Inside Supply Management* 25(1), January/February 2014: 38, 40.
8. Mann, L., "How to Reduce the Risk of Purchasing Fraud," *Healthcare Financial Management* 67(7), July 2013: 78–82.

9. Tan, K. C., and R. Dajalos., "Purchasing Strategy in the 21st Century: E-Procurement," *Practix: Best Practices in Purchasing & Supply Chain Management* 4(3), 2001: 7–12.
10. Palmer, R., and M. Gupta, "2012 Purchasing Card Benchmark Survey Results," RPMG Research Corporation.
11. Hannon, D., "P-Card Program Expansion Is a Global Challenge," *Purchasing* 138(12), December 19, 2009: 53–55.
12. World Trade Organization, "International Trade Statistics 2013," Geneva: WTO Publications.
13. Hornbeck, J. F., "CRS Report for Congress—NAFTA at Ten: Lessons from Recent Studies," February 13, 2004.
14. Lin, L., "Keeping the Mystery Out of China's Meat," *Bloomberg Businessweek,* March 24–April 6, 2014: 27–28.
15. Case, S., and D. Arnold, "Greening Federal Purchasing," *Government Procurement,* August 2005: 18–26.
16. U.S. Department of Energy, "Guide to Purchasing Green Power, Renewable Electricity, Renewable Energy Certificates and On-Site Renewable Generation," EPA430-K-04-015, September 2004.

Chapter 3

CREATING AND MANAGING SUPPLIER RELATIONSHIPS

Coming together is a beginning, staying together is progress, working together is success.

— ***Henry Ford***[1]

"We knew that driving supplier performance and improving the total value of acquisition would require a greater level of supplier integration. Over the past three years, Cessna has been driving a collaborative approach linked to our supplier relationship management process with a vision to be the customer of choice. We firmly believe that having world-class suppliers requires being a good customer to them. This vision has been driven by various collaborative strategies, with the supply base working together for the betterment of the supply chain. Trust between Cessna and its suppliers is the cornerstone of these collaborative strategies. It really comes down to this: Do what you say you will, and work to address suppliers' interests."

— ***Brent E. Edmisten, Director, Strategic Sourcing, Cessna Aircraft Company***[2]

Learning Objectives

After completing this chapter, you should be able to

- Explain the importance of supplier partnerships.
- Understand the key factors for developing successful partnerships.
- Develop a supplier evaluation and certification program.
- Explain the importance of supplier development.
- Explain the importance of a supplier recognition program.
- Understand the capabilities of supplier relationship management.
- Explain the benefits of using SRM software to manage suppliers.

Chapter Outline

SCM Profile: Supplier Relationship Management at Jaguar Land Rover[3]

In 2008, the JD Power automotive quality survey put Jaguar in ninth place and Land Rover in thirty-fourth place. This was clearly not a satisfactory situation for Jaguar Land Rover (JLR), a company selling premium-brand automobiles. The survey results prompted changes in how their suppliers were managed. The quality of supplier parts was one of the key problems, with the proportion of rejected parts for some suppliers as high as 65 percent. The poor-quality components caused costly production line stoppages and repairs to assembled cars prior to delivery to customers. The resulting delivery delays to dealers were also causing poor customer satisfaction. JLR realized it had to improve the quality of its products through innovative partnerships with its key suppliers.

JLR addressed the poor quality issues by appointing a quality director who was responsible for launching an Inbound Materials Project to review quality across its supply chains and make improvements to the inspection of inbound supplier components. Initially, there were sixteen quality containment suppliers doing rework on JLR components. This caused inconsistent quality control and difficulty in data sharing across the company. To resolve these issues, JLR decided to select Gobel & Partner (G&P) as the sole quality control provider. This allowed G&P to invest £2 million in the QTrak Quality Management System to provide real-time data through tablets and smartphones to customers.[4] Qtrak enables component suppliers causing the most problems to be identified so that the quality processes at these high-risk suppliers could be reviewed. G&P's objective was to ensure that no bad components were delivered to JLR assembly plants. The traditional adversarial relationship has been transformed to one where G&P is now considered a critical partner in JLR's goal of delivering premium quality brands. Wolfram Leidtke, JLR board quality director, said: "JLR is a premium brand and accordingly needs to have premium quality vehicles. Procurement has aligned with this objective. G&P has been able to transfer their global knowledge and work with JLR to develop a new approach to incoming material quality and the results are starting to speak for themselves."[5]

These improvements in supplier quality resulted in JLR grabbing the top spot in the 2012 JD Power Survey for customer satisfaction. In 2013, G&P won the CIPS (Chartered Institute of Purchasing and Supply) "Best Supplier Relationship Management Award." The shortlist for the CIPS award also includes Balfour Beatty and Reconomy, EE and Capita Travel and Events, F. Hoffmann-La Roche and Partners, and Northumbrian Water & Aqua Consultants.[6]

INTRODUCTION

In today's competitive environment, as companies focus on their core competencies, the level of outsourcing will continue to rise. Increasingly, companies are requiring their suppliers to deliver innovative and quality products not only in just-in-time (JIT) fashion but also at a competitive price. In the last few decades, we have learned that good supplier relations can provide many benefits such as delivery flexibility, better quality, better information, and faster material flows between buyers and suppliers. Many companies believe strongly that better supplier partnerships are important to achieving competitive corporate performance. As such, companies are realizing the importance of developing win–win, long-term relationships with suppliers. It is critical that customers and suppliers develop stronger relationships and partnerships based on a strategic rather than a tactical perspective and then manage these relationships to create value for all participants. Successful partnerships with key suppliers can contribute to innovations and have the potential to create a competitive advantage for the firm. Selecting the right supply partners and successfully managing these relationships over time is thus strategically important; it is often stated that "a firm is only as good as its worst suppliers." As presented in the chapter opening SCM Profile feature, Jaguar Land Rover Limited was able to enhance the quality of its products through an innovative partnership with a key supplier, Gobel & Partner.

According to the Institute for Supply Management's glossary of terms, a supplier partnership is defined as:

> A commitment over an extended time to work together to the mutual benefit of both parties, sharing relevant information and the risks and rewards of the relationship. These relationships require a clear understanding of expectations, open communication and information exchange, mutual trust and a common direction for the future. Such arrangements are a collaborative business activity that does not involve the formation of a legal partnership. The term strategic alliance is used in many organizations to mean the same thing as a supplier partnership. In some organizations, however, the term strategic alliance is used to describe a more inclusive relationship involving the planned and mutually advantageous joint utilization of additional operating resources of both organizations.[7]

Ford Motor Company uses its Aligned Business Framework (ABF) program to provide "regular communication between the OEM and its global suppliers about technology developments that can enhance Ford vehicles and set them apart from competitors. It also encourages collaboration in product development, provides opportunities for supplier growth, develops trust, and encourages long-term relationships with its vendors."[8] This rigorous framework is beneficial to Ford since it enables the company to reduce costs and obtain suppliers' innovative technologies. At the same time, this arrangement also benefits the suppliers, who get a long-term commitment that will significantly improve their forecasting and planning. According to Ford, "... the ABF program has improved the perception suppliers have of the company. There are 104 ABF-certified suppliers, 76 of which are in manufacturing (the rest are in non-production areas). The OEM sources 65 percent of global production from these suppliers, almost twice as much as in 2005. That number will soon be at least 70 percent, since Ford is consolidating its supply chain to 750 this year from 1,150."[9] Good supplier relationships are just one ingredient necessary for developing an end-to-end integrated supply chain.

DEVELOPING SUPPLIER RELATIONSHIPS

According to Kenichi Ohmae, global management consultant, and known as "Mr. Strategy" worldwide, "Companies are just beginning to learn what nations have always known: in a complex, uncertain world filled with dangerous opponents, it is best not to go it alone."[10] Building strong supplier partnerships requires a lot of hard work and commitment by both buyers and sellers. Developing true partnerships is not easily achieved, and much has to be done to get the partnership to work. Several key ingredients for developing successful partnerships are discussed below.

Building Trust

Trust is critical for any partnership or alliance to work. It must be built not just at the senior management level but at all levels of the organization. Trust enables organizations to share valuable information, devote time and resources to understand each other's business, and achieve results beyond what could have been done individually. Jordan Lewis, in his book *Trusted Partners*, points out that "Trust does not imply easy harmony. Obviously, business is too complex to expect ready agreement on all issues. However, in a trusting relationship conflicts motivate you to probe for deeper understandings and search for constructive solutions. Trust creates goodwill, which sustains the relationship when one firm does something the other dislikes."[11] With trust, partners are more willing to work together; find compromise solutions to problems; work toward achieving long-term benefits for both parties; and in short, go the extra mile. In addition, there is goodwill developed over time between the partners. This can be beneficial when one partner gets into a difficult situation and the other partner is willing to help out.

Shared Vision and Objectives

All partnerships should state the expectations of the buyer and supplier, reasons and objectives of the partnership, and plans for the dissolution of the relationship. According to Lenwood Grant, sourcing expert with Bristol-Myers-Squibb, "You don't want a partnership that is based on necessity. If you don't think that the partnership is a good mix, but you do it because you have to—possibly because that supplier is the only provider of that material in the market, because you've signed an exclusive contract in the past, or for some other reason—it's not a true partnership and is likely to fail."[12] Both partners must share the same vision and have objectives that are not only clear but mutually agreeable. Many alliances and partnerships have failed because objectives are not well aligned or are overly optimistic. The focus must move beyond tactical issues and toward a more strategic path to corporate success. When partners have equal decision-making control, the partnership has a higher chance of success.

Personal Relationships

Interpersonal relationships in buyer–supplier partnerships are important since it is people who communicate and make things happen. According to Leonard Greenhalgh, author of *Managing Strategic Relationships*, "An alliance or partnership isn't really a relationship between companies, it's a relationship between specific individuals. When you are considering strategic alliances of any kind, the only time the company matters is in the status associated with it [strategic alliance]. Whoever is interfacing with the other company, they are the company."[13]

Mutual Benefits and Needs

Partnering should result in a win–win situation, which can only be achieved if both companies have compatible needs. Mutual needs not only create an environment conducive for collaboration but opportunities for increased innovation. When both parties share in the benefits of the partnership, the relationship will be productive and long lasting. An alliance is much like a marriage: if only one party is happy, the marriage is not likely to last. For example, Toyota's performance improvement programs with suppliers are supported by highly qualified Toyota engineers who work as consultants on the projects. Any cost savings arising from this program are shared with the suppliers. Toyota also ensures that their suppliers earn a reasonable return. An important recipe for success is when the buyer is respectful, fair, and trustworthy in its dealings with the supplier.

Commitment and Top Management Support

First, it takes a lot of time and hard work to find the right partner. Having done so, both parties must dedicate their time, best people, and resources to make the partnership succeed. According to author Stephen R. Covey, "Without involvement, there is no commitment. Mark it down, asterisk it, circle it, underline it. No involvement, no commitment."[14] Commitment must start at the highest management level. Partnerships tend to be successful when top executives are actively supporting the partnership. The level of cooperation and involvement shown by the organization's top leaders is likely to set the tone for joint problem solving further down the line.

Successful partners are committed to continuously looking for opportunities to grow their businesses together. Management must create the right kind of internal attitude needed for alliances to flourish. Since partnerships are likely to encounter bumps along the way, it is critical that management adopt a collaborative approach to conflict resolution instead of assigning blame.

Change Management

With change comes stress, which can lead to a loss of focus. As such, companies must avoid distractions from their core businesses as a result of the changes brought about by the partnership. Companies must be prepared to manage change that comes with the formation of new partnerships. According to author Stephen Covey, "The key to successful change management is remaining focused on a set of core principles that do not change, regardless of the circumstances."[15] In a study of Hewlett-Packard's global procurement and strategic supplier relationships, HP identified several key steps to ensure successful relationships:[16]

- Identify internal champions
- Secure executive buy-in
- Coordinate internal communication and support teams
- Train and survey hiring managers
- Conduct business reviews with key client groups

HP realized that being proactive and prepared enabled better change management.

Information Sharing and Lines of Communication

Both formal and informal lines of communication should be set up to facilitate free flows of information. When there is high degree of trust, information systems can be customized to serve each other more effectively. Confidentiality of sensitive financial, product, and process information must be maintained. Any conflict that occurs can be resolved if the channels of communication are open. For instance, early communication to suppliers of specification changes and new product introductions are contributing factors to the success of purchasing partnerships. Buyers and sellers should meet regularly to discuss any change of plans, evaluate results, and address issues critical to the success of the partnerships. Since there is free exchange of information, nondisclosure agreements are often used to protect proprietary information and other sensitive data from leaking out. It is not the quantity but rather the quality and accuracy of the information exchanged that indicates the success of information sharing.

While collaboration has many positives, there is also the fear of the loss of trade secrets when sensitive information is shared between partners. According to the U.S. Economic Espionage Act of 1996, the definition of trade secrets is: "All forms and types of financial, business, scientific, technical, economic, or engineering information, including patterns, plans, compilations, programmed devices, formulas, designs, prototypes, methods, techniques, processes, procedures, programs, or codes, whether tangible or intangible, and whether or how stored, compiled, or memorialized physically, electronically, graphically, photographically, or in writing."[17] Trade secrets tend to be more critical in the high-technology sector where the unique technique or process used in the company's business can provide it with tremendous competitive advantage. Vendors have been known to steal or misappropriate trade secrets, terminate the partnership, and become competitors. One of the most basic and successful approaches for protecting trade secrets is to require employees and vendors to sign a nondisclosure agreement.

Relationship Capabilities

Organizations must develop the right capabilities for creating long-term relationships with their suppliers. In a study on world-class procurement organizations, the Hackett Group found that one of the two best practices for top-performing companies is using cross-functional teams to achieve common objectives.[18] Thus, companies aspiring to be world class must develop cross-functional team capabilities. In addition, the employees must not only be able to collaborate successfully within the company in a cross-functional team setting but have the skills to do so externally. Key suppliers must have the right technology and capabilities to meet cost, quality, and delivery requirements. In addition, suppliers must be sufficiently flexible to respond quickly to changing customer requirements. Before entering into any partnership, it is imperative for an organization to conduct a thorough investigation of its suppliers' capabilities and core competencies. Organizations prefer working with suppliers who have the technology and technical expertise to assist in the development of new products or services that would lead to a competitive advantage in the marketplace. A survey carried out by global management consulting company Accenture "demonstrates that leaders in SRM [Supplier Relationship Management] have turned their investment in more sophisticated collaboration capabilities into hard dollars—achieving an average of $79 million savings from post-contract award activities—far in excess of the survey average of $22 million. Many believe they can increase those savings by as much as 20 percent in the near term."[19]

Performance Metrics

The old adage "You can't improve what you can't measure" is particularly true for buyer–supplier alliances. Measures related to quality, cost, delivery, and flexibility have traditionally been used to evaluate how well suppliers are doing. Information provided by supplier performance will be used to improve the entire supply chain. Thus, the goal of any good performance evaluation system is to provide metrics that are understandable, easy to measure, and focused on real value-added results for both the buyer and supplier.

By evaluating supplier performance, organizations hope to identify suppliers with exceptional performance or developmental needs, improve supplier communication, reduce risk, and manage the partnership based on an analysis of reported data. FedEx not only has performance scorecards for its suppliers but has also developed a Web-based "reverse scorecard" that allows suppliers to provide constructive performance feedback to the company to enhance the customer–supplier relationship.[20] After all, it is not unusual that the best customers want to work with the best suppliers. Additionally, the best suppliers are commonly rewarded and recognized for their achievements. Supplier awards will be discussed later in this chapter.

Although price or cost is an important factor when selecting suppliers, other criteria such as technical expertise, lead times, environmental awareness, and market knowledge must also be considered. In the electronics industry, which pioneered the Six Sigma revolution, quality is the prime supplier selection criteria due to its strategic importance. Thus quality and the ability of suppliers to bring new technologies and innovations to the table, rather than cost, are often the key selection drivers. A multicriteria approach is therefore needed to measure supplier performance. Examples of broad performance metrics are shown in Table 3.1.

Over the past several years, **total cost of ownership (TCO),** a broad-based performance metric, has been widely discussed in the supply chain literature. As mentioned in Chapter 2, TCO is defined as "the combination of the purchase or acquisition price of a good or service and additional costs incurred before or after product or service delivery."

Table 3.1 Examples of Supplier Performance Metrics

1. Cost/Price

- Competitive price
- Availability of cost breakdowns
- Productivity improvement/cost reduction programs
- Willingness to negotiate price
- Inventory cost
- Information cost
- Transportation cost
- Actual cost compared to: historical (standard) cost, target cost, cost-reduction goal, benchmark cost
- Extent of cooperation leading to improved cost

2. Quality

- Zero defects
- Statistical process controls
- Continuous process improvement
- Fit for use
- Corrective action program
- Documented quality program such as ISO 9000
- Warranty
- Actual quality compared to: historical quality, specification quality, target quality
- Quality improvement compared to: historical quality, quality-improvement goal
- Extent of cooperation leading to improved quality

3. Delivery

- Fast
- Reliable/on-time
- Defect-free deliveries
- Actual delivery compared to promised delivery window (i.e., two days early to zero days late)
- Extent of cooperation leading to improved delivery

Table 3.1 Examples of Supplier Performance Metrics (Continued)

4. Responsiveness and Flexibility
- Responsiveness to customers
- Accuracy of record keeping
- Ability to work effectively with teams
- Responsiveness to changing situations
- Participation/success of supplier certification program
- Short-cycle changes in demand/flexible capacity
- Changes in delivery schedules
- Participation in new product development
- Solving problems
- Willingness of supplier to seek inputs regarding product/service changes
- Advance notification given by supplier as a result of product/service changes
- Receptiveness to partnering or teaming

5. Environment
- Environmentally responsible
- Environmental management system such as ISO 14000
- Extent of cooperation leading to improved environmental issues

6. Technology
- Proactive improvement using proven manufacturing/service technology
- Superior product/service design
- Extent of cooperation leading to improved technology

7. Business Metrics
- Reputation of supplier/leadership in the field
- Long-term relationship
- Quality of information sharing
- Financial strength such as Dun & Bradstreet's credit rating
- Strong customer support group
- Total cash flow
- Rate of return on investment
- Extent of cooperation leading to improved business processes and performance

8. Total Cost of Ownership
- Purchased products shipped cost-effectively
- Cost of special handling
- Additional supplier costs as the result of the buyer's scheduling and shipment needs
- Cost of defects, rework, and problem solving associated with purchases

Costs are often grouped into **pretransaction, transaction**, and **posttransaction costs**.[21] These three major cost categories are described as follows:

- *Pretransaction costs:* These costs are incurred prior to order and receipt of the purchased goods. Examples are the cost of certifying and training suppliers, investigating alternative sources of supply, and delivery options for new suppliers.
- *Transaction costs:* These costs include the cost of the goods/services and cost associated with placing and receiving the order. Examples are purchase price, preparation of orders, and delivery costs.

- *Posttransaction costs:* These costs are incurred after the goods are in the possession of the company, agents, or customers. Examples are field failures, company's goodwill/reputation, maintenance costs, and warranty costs.

TCO provides a proactive approach for understanding costs and supplier performance leading to reduced costs. However, the challenge is to effectively identify the key cost drivers needed to determine the total cost of ownership.

Continuous Improvement

The process of evaluating suppliers based on a set of mutually agreed performance measures provides opportunities for continuous improvement. As discussed in Chapter 8, continuous improvement involves continuously making a series of small improvements over time, resulting in the elimination of waste in a system. Both buyers and suppliers must be willing to continuously improve their capabilities in meeting customer requirements of cost, quality, delivery, sustainability, and technology. Partners should not focus on merely correcting mistakes, but work proactively toward eliminating them completely. For continuous improvement to work, employees must first identify areas that are working to understand the improvements made. These improvements provide the basis for implementing improvements in other processes, which in turn will lead to even more success. In today's dynamic environment, staying ahead of change means that you have to practice continuous improvement. Companies must work with suppliers on continuous improvement programs to ensure that products and services are meeting customer requirements.

Monitoring Supplier Relationships

Unless an organization has a firm grasp of the key issues surrounding supplier relationships, it cannot reap the benefits of such relationships. An assessment of how the relationships with an organization's suppliers are doing will enable these relationships to be managed better. In a study of the food industry, five key performance indicators were identified to objectively measure supply chain relationship performance:[22]

- Creativity—promoting quality, innovation, and a long-term approach by encouraging high performance.
- Stability—investment, synchronization of objectives, and confidence building.
- Communication—frequent, open dialogue and information sharing.
- Reliability—concentrating on service and product delivery, lowering joint costs.
- Value—creating a win-win relationship in which each side is delighted to be a part.

In the same study, several intrinsic characteristics of relationship performance were also identified as follows:[23]

- Long-term Orientation—encouraging stability, continuity, predictability, and long-term, joint gains.
- Interdependence—loss in autonomy is compensated through the expected gains.
- C^3 Behavior—Collaboration, Co-operation, Coordination, jointly resourcing to achieve effective operations.
- Trust—richer interaction between parties to create goodwill and the incentive to go the extra mile.

- Commitment—the relationship is so important that it warrants maximum effort to maintain it.
- Adaption—willingness to adapt products, procedures, inventory, management, attitudes, values, and goals to the needs of the relationship.
- Personal Relationships—generating trust and openness through personal interaction.

The assessment of key performance indicators should create a clear understanding of where the issues are so that the problems can be resolved to further improve the relationship.

Key Points

It must be noted that developing supplier partnerships is not easy. All the factors mentioned above have to be in place for the supplier relationship to be successful. While there are numerous instances where supplier partnerships work well, there are also examples where the relationship did not turn out as expected. In 2007, Mattel pulled more than 18 million toys off the shelves due to product safety concerns.[24] A failure on the part of Mattel to properly monitor the quality of the goods it purchased from Chinese suppliers created a "moral hazard" within its supply chain. In China, production costs are increasing, and intense pressures to reduce prices are making it more difficult for suppliers to

SCM Profile | Fraud in the Supply Chain—The 2013 Horse Meat Scandal

One of the biggest food scandals involved finding horse meat in beef products, starting in January 2013. The Food Safety Authority of Ireland (FSAI) found that beef patties sold at a Tesco supermarket had 29 percent horse DNA. The meat supplier was Silvercrest Foods, an Irish frozen meat processor owned by the ABP Food Group. Tesco immediately stopped buying from Silvercrest. Shortly after that, Aldi and Burger King found similar contaminated patties and dropped Silvercrest as well. FSAI also found that meat labeled as beef sold to Rangeland Foods and Freeza Meats had contained 75 to 80 percent horse meat.[25] Following that revelation, Ireland initiated a recall, which was followed shortly by Britain, France, and Sweden. It was estimated that 10 million burgers were withdrawn from sale by Tesco, Lidl, Iceland, Aldi, Dunnes Stores, and other supermarkets.[26] The scandal shows the inability of food manufacturers to guarantee what goes into processed meat products. The UK government has also been criticized for a lack of oversight.

Although several brands were affected by the horse meat scandal, Tesco suffered far more because it became the official face of the scandal in the media.[27] Sales losses at Tesco were more than a £1 million following the scandal, and the new DNA testing on processed beef products could cost Tesco between £1 and £2 million a year. Tesco withdrew four products affected by the horse meat contamination but reformulated and relaunched with new suppliers to ensure that their "market-leading technical processes and specifications can enable customers to place a renewed level of trust in the company's entire product range."[28]

The results of more than 7,000 tests in twenty-seven EU countries indicated that 5 percent of the samples had horse DNA and phenylbutazone, a banned equine painkiller. A European Commission concluded that it was "a matter of food fraud and not of food safety."[29]

maintain their profit margins. As a result, without a good quality verification program, it is easy for suppliers to compromise on quality and to deliver substandard products. The importance of supplier relationships cannot be overstated, and cultivating these relationships is an essential part of doing business in China.

The recent horse meat supplier scandal is considered to be the biggest food fraud of the twenty-first century and caused the recall of millions of burgers and beef products across Europe. It was discovered that burgers at Tesco, Burger King, Co-op, and Aldi in Britain, which had tested positive for horse DNA, were made by the Silvercrest factory of the ABP Group in Ireland (see the nearby SCM Profile). Consequently, sales of frozen burgers over a two-month period in 2013 declined sharply, by as much as 41 percent.[30] The frozen ready-meals market also took a hit since shoppers were suspicious about the quality of these meals after the horse meat scandal broke. According to Ryan Finstad, director of operations at California-based supply chain solutions provider Cathay Solutions, "Companies that have long-standing relationships with their manufacturers have naturally become more lax over time. As these firms searched for ways to cut costs, they may have reduced or eliminated monitoring of manufacturers that had historically performed well."[31] These problems can be avoided if companies have better two-way communications, a quality assurance program in place, sound performance metrics, and trust built into the relationship.

SUPPLIER EVALUATION AND CERTIFICATION

Only the best suppliers are targeted as partners. Companies want to develop partnerships with the best suppliers to leverage their expertise and technologies to create a competitive advantage. Learning more about how an organization's key suppliers are performing can lead to greater visibility, which can provide opportunities for further collaborative involvement in value-added activities. Many organizations are tracking product and service quality, on-time deliveries, customer service efforts, and cost-control programs as part of the supplier rating system. This information can be used to develop supplier programs that will help eliminate problems or improve supply chain performance.

A supplier evaluation and certification process must be in place so that organizations can identify their best and most reliable suppliers. In addition, sourcing decisions are made based on facts and not perception of a supplier's capabilities. Providing frequent feedback on supplier performance can help organizations avoid major surprises and maintain good relationships. For example, Honeywell has developed a Supplier Portal Web site, which allows "Honeywell's internal Integrated Supply Chain professionals to share information, interact/collaborate, and ultimately form closer relationships with Honeywell's external supply base."[32] In addition, the company has the Honeywell Supplier Scorecard Training module. The purpose of the scorecard is to communicate to Honeywell the supplier's overall performance in terms of quality (parts per million defective) and on-time delivery for the last month, last three months, and last twelve months.[33] The Web site also enhances supplier relationships since the Web-based technology has resulted in improvements in efficiency and productivity for Honeywell and the suppliers because faster decisions can be made as a result of speedier transmission of information.

One of the goals of evaluating suppliers is to determine if the supplier is performing according to the buyer's requirements. An extension of supplier evaluation is **supplier certification**, defined by the Institute of Supply Management as "an organization's process for evaluating the quality systems of key suppliers in an effort to eliminate incoming inspections."[34] The certification process implies a willingness on the part of customers and suppliers to share goals, commitments, and risks to improve their relationships. This would involve making visits to observe the operations at the supplier organizations. For example, dirty bathrooms and messy shop floors could indicate that an emphasis on quality is lacking in the production facility. A supplier certification program also indicates long-term mutual commitment. For example, a certification program might provide incentives for suppliers to deliver parts directly to the point of use in the buyer firm, thus reducing costs associated with incoming inspection and storage of inventory.

Implementing an effective supplier certification program is critical to reducing the supplier base, building long-term relationships, reducing time spent on incoming inspections, improving delivery and responsiveness, recognizing excellence, developing a commitment to continuous improvement, and improving overall performance. Supplier certification allows organizations to identify the suppliers who are most committed to creating and maintaining a partnership and who have the best capabilities. Listed below are several criteria generally found in certification programs:

- No incoming product lot rejections (e.g., less than 0.5 percent defective) for a specified time period
- No incoming nonproduct rejections (e.g., late delivery) for a specified time period
- No significant supplier production-related negative incidents for a specified time period
- ISO 9001/Q9000 certified or successfully passing a recent, on-site quality system evaluation
- ISO 14001 certified
- Mutually agreed upon set of clearly specified quality performance measures
- Fully documented process and quality system with cost controls and continuous improvement capabilities
- Supplier's processes are stable and in control

The Weighted Criteria Evaluation System

One approach toward evaluating and certifying suppliers is to use the weighted criteria evaluation system described below:

1. Select the key dimensions of performance mutually acceptable to both customer and supplier.
2. Monitor and collect performance data.
3. Assign weights to each of the dimensions of performance based on their relative importance to the company's objectives. The weights for all dimensions must sum to one.
4. Evaluate each of the performance measures on a rating between 0 (fails to meet any intended purpose or performance) and 100 (exceptional in meeting intended purpose or performance).
5. Multiply the dimension ratings by their respective importance weights and then sum to get an overall weighted score.
6. Classify vendors based on their overall scores, for example:
    - Unacceptable (less than 50)—supplier dropped from further business

Example 3.1 Supplier Scorecard Used for the XYZ Company

PERFORMANCE MEASURE	RATING	×	WEIGHT	=	FINAL VALUE
Technology	80		0.10		8.00
Quality	90		0.25		22.50
Responsiveness	95		0.15		14.25
Delivery	90		0.15		13.50
Cost	80		0.15		12.00
Environmental	90		0.05		4.50
Business	90		0.15		13.50
Total score			1.00		88.25

Note: Based on the total score of 88.25, the XYZ Company is considered a certified supplier.

- Conditional (between 50 and 70)—supplier needs development work to improve performance but may be dropped if performance continues to lag
- Certified (between 70 and 90)—supplier meets intended purpose or performance
- Preferred (greater than 90)—supplier will be considered for involvement in new product development and opportunities for more business

7. Audit and ongoing certification review.

An example of the above evaluation and certification process is shown in Example 3.1.

Federal-Mogul is an example of a company that uses a weighted scorecard to evaluate its suppliers. The company has a SupplyNet Scorecard Web site[35] that provides its Supplier Rating Qualifications and rates suppliers on three main categories, with the weights shown in parentheses: delivery (40 percent), quality (40 percent), and supplier cost-saving suggestions (SCSS) (20 percent). The quality score is based on two equally weighted components: parts per million (ppm) defective and quantity of supplier corrective action requests (SCARs) issued. The on-time delivery score is computed as "the average percentage across using plants for the current month. On-time delivery percentage has a window of one day early and zero days late to the due date and +/− 5 percent of order quantity. The on-time delivery percentage is determined by line items received on time divided by the number of line items due by the supplier for the month." The *Overall Rating Weighted Point Score* ranges from 0 to 100. Suppliers are considered "preferred" if they score between 90 and 100. Preferred suppliers are those that Federal-Mogul will work with on new product development, approve for new business, and assist in maintaining a competitive position. An "acceptable" supplier rating is between 70 and 89. In this category, the supplier is required to provide a plan to Federal-Mogul on how to achieve preferred status. A score of 0 to 69 means that the supplier has a "developmental" supplier rating. Here, Federal-Mogul requires the vendor to take corrective action if the supplier is rated at this level for three consecutive months during the calendar year.

External Certifications

Today, external certifications such as ISO 9000 and ISO 14000 have gained popularity globally as natural extensions of an organization's internal supplier evaluation and certification program. These evaluation criteria are frequently used to evaluate suppliers and are briefly discussed next.

ISO 9000

In 1987, the global network of national standards institutes called the International Organization for Standardization (ISO) developed **ISO 9000**, a series of management and quality assurance standards in design, development, production, installation, and service. There are many standards in the ISO 9000 family, including:[36]

- ISO 9001:2008—sets out the criteria for a quality management system and is the only standard in the family that can be certified to;
- ISO 9000:2005—covers the basic concepts and language of a quality management system;
- ISO 9004:2009—focuses on how to make a quality management system more efficient and effective;
- ISO 19011:2011—sets out guidance on internal and external audits of quality management systems.

The European Union in 1992 adopted a plan that recognized ISO 9001 as a third-party certification; the result is that many European companies (as well as companies outside Europe) prefer suppliers with ISO 9001 certifications. Thus, companies wanting to sell in the global marketplace are compelled to seek ISO 9001 certifications.

To date, more than 1.1 million ISO 9001 certificates have been awarded.[37] In the U.S., 26,177 certificates were issued in 2012, representing 2.4 percent of the worldwide total. Not surprising, China had the largest number of ISO 9001 certificates in 2012—334,032, representing 30.3 percent of total certificates issued. Obtaining the ISO 9001 certification provides further verification that the supplier has an established quality management system in place. ISO certification will lead organizations to consistently deliver products that meet customer and applicable statutory and regulatory requirements. In addition, organizations seek to enhance customer satisfaction by continual improvement of their quality management system. A recent survey clearly showed that the primary reason for seeking ISO 9001 certification is improved customer satisfaction. The ISO 9000 standards are discussed further in Chapter 8.[38]

ISO 14000

In 1996, **ISO 14000**, a family of international standards for environmental management, was first introduced. In 2004, it was revised to make the standards easier to understand and emphasized compliance and compatibility with ISO 9000 for businesses that wanted to combine their environmental and quality management systems. There are many standards in the ISO 14000 family and these are covered in ISO's publication, "Environmental management—The ISO 14000 family of International Standards."[39] Organizations can only be certified to ISO 14001:2004, which sets the criteria and framework for an organization to develop an effective environmental management system but does not state requirements for environmental performance.

The benefits of investing in an **Environmental Management System (EMS)** based on ISO14000 standards include reduced cost of waste management, savings in energy consumption and materials, lower distribution costs, and improved corporate image among regulators, customers, and community.[40] As of 2012, there were 5,699 ISO 14001 certificates issued in the U.S., representing 2 percent of the 285,844 certificates issued globally in 155 countries.[41] China and Japan are the top two countries with ISO 14001 certificates. Given the interest in sustainability, investments in environmental management systems and ISO 14001 are likely to increase in the future. Additionally, as more organizations are certified in ISO 14001, they are likely to pass this requirement on to their suppliers. ISO 14001 enables an organization's management, employees, and external stakeholders to measure and improve environmental impact.

SUPPLIER DEVELOPMENT

Supplier development is defined as "any activity that a buyer undertakes to improve a supplier's performance and/or capabilities to meet the buyer's short- and/or long-term supply needs."[42] Supplier development requires financial and human resource investments by both partners and includes a wide range of activities such as training of the supplier's personnel, investing in the supplier's operations, and ongoing performance assessment. As companies outsource more and more parts, a larger portion of costs lies outside the company in a supply chain, and it becomes increasingly difficult to achieve further cost savings internally. One way out of this dilemma is for companies to work with their suppliers to lower the total cost of materials purchased. Companies that are able to leverage their supply base to impact their total cost structure will have a competitive advantage in their markets.

A seven-step approach to supplier development is outlined below:[43]

1. *Identify critical goods and services.* Assess the relative importance of the goods and services from a strategic perspective. Goods and services that are purchased in high volume, do not have good substitutes, or have limited sources of supply are considered strategic supplies.
2. *Identify critical suppliers not meeting performance requirements.* Suppliers of strategic supplies not currently meeting minimum performance in quality, on-time delivery, cost, technology, or cycle time are targets for supplier development initiatives.
3. *Form a cross-functional supplier development team.* Next, the buyer must develop an internal cross-functional team and arrive at a clear agreement for the supplier development initiatives.
4. *Meet with the top management of suppliers.* The buyer's cross-functional team meets with the suppliers' top management to discuss details of strategic alignment, supplier performance expectations and measurement, a time frame for improvement, and ongoing professionalism.
5. *Rank supplier development projects.* After the supplier development opportunities have been identified, they are evaluated in terms of feasibility, resource and time requirements, supply base alternatives, and expected return on investment. The most promising development projects are selected.
6. *Define the details of the buyer–supplier agreement.* After consensus has been reached on the development project rankings, the buyer and supplier representatives jointly decide on the performance metrics to be monitored such as percent improvement in quality, delivery, and cycle time.
7. *Monitor project status and modify strategies.* To ensure continued success, management must actively monitor progress, promote exchange of information, and revise the development strategies as conditions warrant.

Intel's Supplier Continuous Quality Improvement (SCQI) program is a "corporate wide program that utilizes critical Intel supplier management tools and processes to drive continuous improvements in a supplier's overall performance and business."[44] Their SCQI program was started in the 1980s with the objective of improving supplier quality and minimizing the time needed to inspect incoming products. According to Intel, the SCQI program accomplishes the following:[45]

- Establishes aligned goals, indicators, and metrics
- Enables benchmarking of supplier performance
- Identifies potential quality issues before they impact Intel
- Drives supplier agility and ability to provide leading-edge products and services
- Matures critical Intel–supplier relationships
- Encourages collaborative agreements, team problem resolution, and two-way continuous learning
- Encourages continuous improvement throughout the year
- Provides data to support supplier recognition

With the SCQI program, Intel was able to reap valuable benefits from their suppliers. Additionally, as the quality of the suppliers' products improves, greater opportunities exist for making further improvements.

By tracking supplier performance over time, Honeywell is able to observe trends and to catch problems early. Honeywell has implemented its Six Sigma Plus program aimed at eliminating variations in processes to meet required specifications with no more than 3.4 parts per million defective (99.9997 percent error free) and to apply lean manufacturing techniques to eliminate waste and to synchronize suppliers' activities. At Honeywell, Six Sigma Plus is an "overall strategy to accelerate improvements in all Honeywell products, processes, services, and reduce the punitive cost of poor quality through elimination of waste and reduction of defects and variations."[46] The ultimate aim of the Six Sigma Plus strategy is to provide maximum value to customers through a logical and structured approach to all business processes.

In summary, it is critical that an organization has an active supplier development program. The program should be managed such that it can meet both current and future needs. With a proactive supplier development program, suppliers are forced to stay on top of today's dynamic environment so that customers are not stuck with products or services that are not leading edge.

SUPPLIER RECOGNITION PROGRAMS

While a large percentage of companies track supplier performance, only about half recognize excellent performance with supplier awards and appreciation banquets. Today, it is not sufficient just to reward your best suppliers with more business; companies need to recognize and celebrate the achievements of their best suppliers. As award-winning suppliers, they serve as role models for a firm's other suppliers. Boeing understands that *supplier performance excellence is critical to its success.* The company's Supplier of the Year Award is based on "meeting or exceeding quality, on-time delivery, post-delivery support and affordability goals, and demonstrating the ability to anticipate and respond to changing requirements."[47] Boeing realizes that they need excellent suppliers to keep the company at the leading edge of technology and innovation. "These partners are critical to helping Boeing provide our customers the most affordable, highest-quality products and services possible," said Jack House, leader of Boeing's Supplier Management program. He added, "Boeing must have a global supply chain that is capable of recognizing and reducing risk, while demonstrating a strong commitment to customer service and consistent performance excellence."[48]

As part of Intel's SCQI Program (see discussion in the preceding section), there are three recognition awards: Certified Supplier Award (CSA), Preferred Quality Supplier (PQS) Award, and Supplier Continuous Quality Improvement (SCQI) Award. The CSA is given to suppliers who consistently meet Intel's expectations and have a proven commitment to continuous improvement. Intel's PQS award is for outstanding commitment to quality, excellent performance, and excellence at meeting and exceeding high expectations and tough performance goals. The SCQI Award, which is the most prestigious of Intel's three recognition awards, is given to suppliers who have a score of at least 95 percent on performance and the capability to meet cost, quality, availability, delivery, technology and environmental, social, and governance goals. In addition, "suppliers must also achieve 90 percent or greater on a challenging improvement plan and demonstrate solid quality and business systems." William Holt, Executive Vice President and General Manager of Intel's Technology and Manufacturing Group, said, "We are pleased to recognize these world-class suppliers for their exceptional performance and commitment to excellence. Delivering a sustained pace of innovation requires continuously improving and we are delighted to work with such nimble and distinguished companies."[49] Hitachi Kokusai Electric (HiKE) is one of the eight suppliers honored by Intel with the Supplier Continuous Quality Improvement Award. Manabu Shinomoto, President and Chief Executive Officer, HiKE, said, "Our winning this award demonstrates our continuous commitment to quality and our important role in supporting Intel as they respond to the fast changing needs of the mobile, PC, and consumer electronics markets."[50]

Hormel Food Corporation's No. 1 Award program differs from other programs because they only give this award once every five years. Hormel gave out its first award in 1996, with the last award presented in 2011. To qualify for the No. 1 Award, a supplier must have met the following criteria:[51]

- Have a supplier rating index of 96 percent or better in the fourth calendar quarter of the reporting year.
- The average of the five-year supplier rating index must be equal to or greater than 96 percent.
- Must be a recipient of the Spirit of Excellence Award—an annual award given by Hormel Foods—for a minimum of four times over the last five consecutive years.
- Meet additional requirements in the areas of number of products sold by the supplier to Hormel Foods, dollars of exposure and deliveries to Hormel Foods, number of Hormel Foods locations serviced, and participation in continuous improvement processes.

Hormel also has a yearly Spirit of Excellence Award given to suppliers achieving a minimum Supplier Rating Index score of 92 over a twelve-month period. The criteria for the Supplier Rating Index include an ability to meet requirements, make timely deliveries, provide accurate administrative support, and maintain inventories. Additional criteria such as customer support, awareness of environmental concerns, and sales representative performance are considered but are not a requirement for the award. "The Hormel Foods Spirit of Excellence Award program recognizes the suppliers that truly go above and beyond, making an impact on our business," said Melanie A. Faust, director of purchasing at Hormel Foods. "We're honored to partner with these distinguished suppliers."[52] The Spirit of Excellence Award also recognizes the role these suppliers play in Hormel's continuous improvement process throughout the year.

SUPPLIER RELATIONSHIP MANAGEMENT

Supplier relationship management (SRM) has garnered increasing attention among firms actively practicing supply chain management. According to global consultant Accenture, SRM "encompasses a broad suite of capabilities that facilitate collaboration, sourcing, transaction execution and performance monitoring between an organization and its trading partners. SRM leverages the latest technology capabilities to integrate and enhance supplier oriented processes along the supply chain such as design-to-source, source-to-contract and procure-to-pay."[53] In a nutshell, SRM involves streamlining the processes and communication between the buyer and supplier and using software applications that enable these processes to be managed more efficiently and effectively.

The success of e-procurement, which has a predominantly internal focus, created the need for SRM solutions for managing the supply side of an organization's supply chain. SRM software automates the exchange of information among several layers of relationships that are complex and too time-consuming to manage manually and results in improved procurement efficiency, lower business costs, real-time visibility, faster communication between buyer and seller, and enhanced supply chain collaboration. A list of some of the SRM software vendors is shown in Table 3.2.

Many organizations are investing in SRM software modules due to the wealth of information that can be derived from these systems. SRM software can organize supplier information and provide answers to questions such as:

- Who are our current suppliers? Are they the right set of suppliers?
- Who are our best suppliers, and what are their competitive rankings?
- What are our suppliers' performances with respect to on-time delivery, quality, and costs?
- Can we consolidate our buying to achieve greater scale economies?

Table 3.2	Examples of Companies Offering SRM Software
EcVision (www.ecvision.com)	
Customers:	Li & Fung Trading, Gap Inc., Coach, Jimlar, Timberland, Limited Brands, Falabella, BonTon Stores, JCPenney, Brown Shoe Company, Kilin Trading, Max Smart, Nordstrom, New Balance, Phillips-Van Heusen, Abercrombie & Fitch
JDA Software Group, Inc. (www.jda.com)	
Customers:	Airbus SAS, Finmeccanica SpA, Galileo Avionica SpA, GES International Limited, Honeywell International Inc., Lockheed Martin Integrated Systems & Solutions, Northrop Grumman Information Systems, Rafael Advanced Defense Systems Ltd., Rockwell Collins, Inc., Samsung SDS Co., Ltd., Sandia National Laboratories, Schneider Electric SA, The Tokyo Electric Power Company, Inc., Toshiba Semiconductor Company
(Acquisition of Manugistics in July 2006; i2 Technologies in January 2010)	
Oracle (www.oracle.com)	
Customers:	Dartmouth-Hitchcock Medical Center, Commonwealth Bank, Duke Energy, Foxwoods, City of Los Angeles
(Acquisition of PeopleSoft in 2005)	
SAP (www.sap.com/)	
Customers:	British American Tobacco, Capgemini Procurement Services, Consol Energy Inc., Deloitte, Johnson Controls, Pitney Bowes Inc., Newell-Rubbermaid, envia Mitteldeutsche Energie AG, Swisscom

- Do we have consistency in suppliers and performance across different locations and facilities?
- What goods/services do we purchase?
- What purchased parts can be reused in new designs?

An SRM software suite can "automate, simplify, and accelerate the business' procure-to-pay processes for goods and services" as well as:[54]

- Reduce procurement costs by closing the loop from source to pay
- Streamline the purchase of goods and services
- Automate operational processes to reduce purchasing errors, eliminate manual tasks, and avoid maverick buying
- Build collaborative supplier relationships and integrate suppliers into the procurement processes
- Accelerate procurement order and invoicing cycle times

In general, SRM software varies by vendors in terms of capabilities offered. AMR Research has identified five key tenets of an SRM system:[55]

- **Automation** of transactional processes between an organization and its suppliers.
- **Integration** that provides a view of the supply chain that spans multiple departments, processes, and software applications for internal users and external partners.
- **Visibility** of information and process flows in and between organizations. Views are customized by role and aggregated via a single portal.
- **Collaboration** through information sharing and suppliers' ability to input information directly into an organization's supply chain information system.
- **Optimization** of processes and decision-making through enhanced analytical tools such as data warehousing and online analytical processing (OLAP) tools with the migration toward more dynamic optimization tools in the future.

There are two types of SRM: transactional and analytic. **Transactional SRM** enables an organization to track supplier interactions such as order planning, order payment, and returns. The volume of transactions involved may result in independent systems maintained by geographic region or business lines. Transactional SRM tends to focus on short-term reporting and is event driven, focusing on such questions as: What did we buy yesterday? What supplier did we use? What was the cost of the purchase? On the other hand, **analytic SRM** allows the company to analyze the complete supplier base. The analysis provides answers to questions such as: Which suppliers should the company develop long-term relationships with? Which suppliers would make the company more profitable? Analytic SRM enables more difficult and important questions about supplier relationships. Thus, we can see that transactional SRM addresses tactical issues such as order size, whereas analytic SRM focuses on long-term procurement strategies. With analytic SRM, an organization can assess where it was yesterday, where it stands today, and where it wants to go in the future to meet its strategic purchasing goals.

The challenges in any SRM software implementation are assembling all the data needed for an SRM application to work and employee training. For example, analysis of supplier information requires access to applications containing data about suppliers, as well as enterprise resource planning (ERP) and accounting and existing supplier information

SCM Profile | Online Supplier Collaboration at Toshiba Semiconductor Company[56]

Toshiba Semiconductor Company, headquartered in Japan, is a global manufacturer of semiconductor products with more than twenty manufacturing and assembly locations and thirty sales offices worldwide. JDA® Software Group, a leading global provider of innovative supply chain management, merchandising, and pricing excellence solutions, provided Toshiba with the JDA Strategic Sourcing business solution, which enabled procurement professionals to evaluate global demand and spend allocation, inventory, supplier capability, and performance to derive a supply base with the optimal number of well-managed supplier partners.[57] The reduced supply base will lead to smaller transactions that will result in the best price, quality, and delivery performance. The outcome is a significantly increased level of purchasing quality.

According to Seijiro Suzuki, Chief Information Officer, "JDA solutions are optimizing Toshiba's business processes by enabling us to conduct purchasing activities more efficiently, with greater speed due to the Web and with more reliable suppliers. Our implementation also is enabling us to handle a large volume of RFQs—between 7,000 and 8,000 per site at six of our major factories in Japan. Since the price of semiconductor products is changing every minute, we have to be able to adjust the price of our materials accordingly. The speed with which we can collect information from suppliers and make decisions affects our bottom line. JDA solutions help Toshiba achieve this competitive advantage."[58]

JDA solutions will also allow Toshiba to be more strategic by enabling product designers to collaborate in the design stage where 80 percent of a product's cost is controlled. According to Suzuki, "Toshiba's purchasing people will turn their attention from paperwork and checking supplier quotes to playing an active role in the product design process. Purchasers and developers can collaboratively use the database to select the best suppliers."[59]

databases. Before SRM implementation, buyers typically spend 10 percent of their time on supplier relationship development, 40 percent on expediting, and 50 percent on order processing/tracking. After SRM implementation, the buyer's time allocation is estimated to be 50 percent on collaborative planning, 30 percent on supplier relationship development, 10 percent on expediting, and 10 percent on exception management.

Until recent years, purchasing professionals did not have the right technologies to help them accomplish their jobs effectively. Automating procurement activities can lead to significant cost savings as buyers move toward managing processes by exception. This effectively frees buyers to focus on more strategic and value-added activities such as collaborative planning. In addition, purchasing professionals can work effectively on maximizing the return on their relationships with suppliers. Greater procurement visibility from using SRM software also translates into smoother processes, faster cycle times, reduced new product development, improved time to market, streamlined purchasing, and reduced inventory costs. The Toshiba Semiconductor Company (see the nearby SCM Profile) used JDA's SRM software to reduce its list of suppliers to the most valuable suppliers only. In the process, Toshiba was able to get the best price, quality, and delivery performance from its suppliers.

SUMMARY

Over the past few decades, we have seen the buyer–supplier relationship evolve from an arms-length/adversarial approach to one favoring the development of long-term partnerships. Significant competitive advantage can be achieved by organizations working closely with their suppliers. Without a shared vision, mutual benefits, and top management commitment, partnerships are likely to be short-lived. Other ingredients necessary for developing and managing lasting supplier relationships are trust, creating personal relationships, effective change management, sharing of information, and using performance metrics to create superior capabilities. Mutually agreeable measures to monitor supplier performance provide the basis for continuous improvement to enhance supplier quality, cost, and delivery. Supplier certification ensures that buyers continue to work with their best suppliers to improve cost, quality, delivery, and new product development to gain a competitive advantage. Finally, supplier relationship management software automates the exchange of information and allows for improved efficiency and effectiveness in managing supplier relationships and improving performance. Organizations that successfully implement supplier relationship management can improve quality, reduce cost, access new technologies from their suppliers, increase speed to market, reduce risk, and achieve high performance.

KEY TERMS

analytic SRM, 95
automation, 95
collaboration, 95
Environmental Management System (EMS), 90
integration, 95
ISO 14000, 90
ISO 9000, 90
optimization, 95
posttransaction costs, 84
pretransaction, 84
supplier certification, 87
supplier development, 91
Supplier relationship management (SRM), 94
Total Cost of Ownership (TCO), 83
transaction, 84
transactional SRM, 95
visibility, 95

DISCUSSION QUESTIONS

1. Why should an organization be concerned with supplier relationships?
2. Compare and contrast the arm's-length or adversarial approach to the partnership approach to building customer–supplier relationships.
3. How can an organization manage its suppliers effectively?
4. What are the key factors that contribute to a lasting buyer–supplier partnership?
5. It has often been pointed out that 60 percent of strategic alliances fail. What are the reasons for this?
6. What are the criteria used in evaluating a supplier?
7. Discuss how an organization develops a supplier evaluation and certification program.
8. Why should an organization invest in supplier development programs? What are the challenges of supplier development activities?
9. What are the benefits of ISO 9000 certification?

10. Are environmental concerns impacting purchasing decisions? What are the benefits of ISO 14000 certification?

11. Research ISO's Web site (www.iso.ch), and discuss the growth of ISO 9000 and 14000 certifications by regions of the world such as Africa/West Asia, Central and South America, North America, Europe, Far East, and Australia/New Zealand.

12. What are the key capabilities of supplier relationship management software?

13. Why do organizations have supplier awards programs?

14. Why do organizations use supplier certification? What are its benefits?

15. Product fraud and recalls are damaging to an organization's reputation and profitability. How can supplier development and relationships help in avoiding such scandals?

16. What are the similarities and differences in capabilities of SRM software offered by ecVision, JDA, Oracle, and SAP?

17. What are the advantages of using SRM solutions to manage suppliers?

18. What are the differences between transactional and analytic SRM?

19. **Discussion Problem:** The Margo Manufacturing Company is performing an annual evaluation of one of its suppliers, the Mimi Company. Bo, purchasing manager of the Margo Manufacturing Company, has collected the following information.

PERFORMANCE CRITERIA	SCORE	WEIGHT
Technology	85	0.10
Quality	95	0.25
Responsive	90	0.15
Delivery	80	0.15
Cost	90	0.20
Environment	75	0.05
Business	95	0.10
Total score		1.00

A score based on a scale of 0 (unsatisfactory) to 100 (excellent) has been assigned for each performance category considered critical in assessing the supplier. A weight is assigned to each of the performance criteria based on its relative importance. Vendors are classified based on their overall scores as follows:

- Unacceptable (less than 50)—supplier dropped from further business
- Conditional (between 50 and 70)—supplier needs development work to improve performance but may be dropped if performance continues to lag
- Certified (between 70 and 90)—supplier meets intended purpose or performance
- Preferred (greater than 90)—supplier will be considered for involvement in new product development and opportunities for more business

How would you evaluate the Mimi Company's performance as a supplier?

20. **Discussion Problem.** The Michelle Equipment Company is in the process of ranking its suppliers for one of its key components. To assist in the evaluation process, the information on the three suppliers is shown in the table below.

PERFORMANCE CRITERIA	WEIGHT	SCORE		
		SUN DEVILS	GAMECOCKS	SPARTANS
Price	0.10	85	90	80
Payment terms	0.20	90	95	85
Quality	0.10	90	95	95
Delivery	0.10	95	90	85
Suggestions for quality improvement	0.20	80	90	95
Reputation	0.20	85	90	90
Sustainability	0.10	85	85	90
Total score	1.00			

Each performance category is scored on a scale from 0 (unsatisfactory) to 100 (excellent) and assigned a weight based on its relative importance. Suppliers are considered "preferred" if they score between 90 and 100. Preferred suppliers are those that Michelle Equipment will work with on new product development, approve for new business, and assist in maintaining a competitive position. An "acceptable" supplier rating is between 70 and 89. In this category, the supplier is required to provide a plan to Michelle Equipment on how to achieve preferred status. A score of 0 to 69 means that the supplier has a "developmental" supplier rating. How would you evaluate each of the suppliers? Which supplier would you pick?

ESSAY/PROJECT QUESTIONS

1. Go to the Institute for Supply Management website (www.ism.ws), and find the listing for the latest ISM Annual International Supply Management Conference. Then find the conference proceedings, and report on a paper that was presented regarding a topic covered in this chapter.
2. Find a company online that is using a development program to improve a supplier's performance and/or capabilities and report on its experiences.
3. Find a company online that has successfully implemented a supplier certification program and write an essay on this company and its experiences.
4. Pick a company online that is using SRM, and report on its success and/or challenges with the software solution.
5. Many organizations find it necessary to recognize and celebrate the achievements of their best suppliers. Go online, and identify a company that has used a supplier recognition program and report on its experiences.

ENDNOTES

1. Brainy Quote, http://www.brainyquote.com/quotes/quotes/h/henryford121997.html
2. Edmisten, B. E., "Collaboration Counts," *Inside Supply Management* 20(10), October 2009: 10.
3. "Best Supplier Relationship Management: Jaguar Land Rover and Gobel & Partner," *Supply Management*, October 8, 2013; http://www.supplymanagement.com/analysis/features/2013/best-supplier-relationship-management-jaguar-land-rover-and-gobel-partner
4. "Quality First for Goebel & Partner," *Insights Magazine*; http://www.eef.org.uk/insights/members/Quality-first-for-GP.htm

5. "Best Supplier Relationship Management: Jaguar Land Rover and Gobel & Partner"
6. Wilkes, J., "CIPS Supply Management Awards in September," *Supplychain-digital.com*, August 23, 2013; http://www.supplychaindigital.com/procurement/cips-supply-management-awards-in-september
7. "ISM Glossary of Key Supply Management Terms: Supplier Partnership," Institute of Supply Management website.
8. Toensmeier, P., "How Ford Keeps Its Global Suppliers Close," *Procurement Journal*, August 16, 2013; http://www.thomasnet.com/journals/procurement/how-ford-keeps-its-global-suppliers-close/
9. Ibid.
10. Ohmae, K., "The Global Logic of Strategic Alliances," *Harvard Business Review*, March–April 1989: 143–152.
11. Lewis, Jordan D., *Trusted Partners: How Companies Build Mutual Trust and Win Together*. New York: The Free Press, 1999: 7.
12. "Buyers Target Strategic Partners," *Purchasing*, April 5, 2001; www.manufacturing.net/pur/
13. "Supplier Selection & Management Report," March 2002, Institute of Management and Administration (IOMA).
14. Covey, S. R., "Covey Quotations," Stephen R. Covey Sayings; http://www.goodreads.com/author/quotes/1538.Stephen_R_Covey
15. MacDonald, M., "Managing Change: A Matter of Principle," *Supply Chain Management Review*, January/February 2002.
16. "Delivering Value Through Strategic Supplier Relationships: HP Global Procurement Case Study," October 2013; http://www.procurementandsupply.com/resource/2a.%20Delivering%20value%20through%20strategic%20supplier%20relationships%20-%20Debbie%20Johnstone.pdf
17. Drab, D., "Economic Espionage and Trade Secret Theft: Defending Against the Pickpockets of the New Millennium," August 2003, Xerox Corporation; http://www.xerox.com/downloads/wpaper/x/xgs_business_insight_economic_espionage.pdf
18. Hannon, D., "Best Practices: Hackett Group Outlines the World-Class Procurement Organization," *Purchasing*, December 8, 2006.
19. "Accenture Builds High Performance in Supplier Relationship Management with mySAP SRM Solutions"; http://www.accenture.com/SiteCollectionDocuments/PDF/SRM_BuildingHighPerformace6.pdf
20. Babineaux, F. M., "Measuring Supplier Performance (How to Get What You Measure and Other Intentional Consequences)," 87th Annual International Supply Management Conference, 2002 International Conference Proceedings, May 2002; http://www.ism.ws/pubs/Proceedings/YearProceedingsIndex.cfm?navItemNumber=23078&LISTITEMID=509&View=1
21. "ISM Glossary of Key Supply Management Terms: Total Cost of Ownership," Institute of Supply Management website.
22. Humphries, A. S., and L. McComie, "Managing and Measuring for Supply Chain Relationships Performance"; http://www.sccindex.com/Documents/Food Supply Chains CH2.pdf

23. Ibid.

24. Kelly, K. M., "Lessons from the Toy Aisle," *Automotive Design & Production* 119(10), October 2007: 8.

25. Suddath, C., "The Irish Horse Meat Mystery," *Bloomberg Businessweek*, February 14, 2013; http://www.businessweek.com/articles/2013-02-14/the-irish-horse-meat-mystery

26. Tasker, J., "Review of the Year: Horsemeat Scandal," *Farmers Weekly*, December 29, 2013; http://www.fwi.co.uk/articles/29/12/2013/142318/review-of-the-year-horse-meat-scandal.htm

27. Doubrin, D., "The impact of the Horsemeat Scandal," *YouGov*, May 3, 2013; http://yougov.co.uk/news/2013/05/03/impact-horsemeat-scandal/

28. Wall, M., "Horsemeat Scandal: The Business Impact," *BBC News*, February 8, 2013; http://www.bbc.com/news/business-21379587

29. Castle, S., "Europe Says Tests Show Horse Meat Scandal Is 'Food Fraud,'" *The New York Times*, April 16, 2013; http://www.nytimes.com/2013/04/17/business/global/european-study-affirms-role-of-fraud-in-horsemeat-scandal.html?_r=0

30. Morris, B., "Horsemeat Scandal: How Tastes Changed," January 13, 2014; http://www.bbc.co.uk/news/business-25715666

31. Finstad, R., "Total Recall: A Flawed System of Trade," *Far Eastern Economic Review* 70(9), November 2007: 46–50.

32. Honeywell Supplier Portal; https://www.supplier.honeywell.com/servlet/com.honeywell.supplier.MainServlet

33. Honeywell Supplier Scorecard Training Module; https://www.supplier.honeywell.com/docs/ssc/help/scorecard_viewlet_swf.html

34. "Glossary of Key Supply Management Terms: Supplier Certification," Institute of Supply Management website.

35. See www.federalmogul.com/en-US/Suppliers/Pages/SupplyNet-Scorecard.aspx#.UuqR4bTDXlc

36. ISO 9000—Quality Management; http://www.iso.org/iso/iso_9000

37. The ISO Survey of Management System Standard Certifications—2012 Executive Summary; http://www.iso.org/iso/iso_survey_executive-summary.pdf

38. Jarvis, A., and C. MacNee, "Improved Customer Satisfaction—Key Result of ISO 9000 User Survey," December 2, 2011; http://www.iso.org/iso/home/news_index/news_archive/news.htm?refid=Ref1543

39. "ISO 14000—Environmental Management—The ISO 14000 Family of International Standards"; http://www.iso.org/iso/theiso14000family_2009.pdf

40. "ISO 14000—Environmental Management"; http://www.iso.org/iso/iso14000

41. "The ISO Survey of Management System Standard Certifications—2012"; http://www.iso.org/iso/home/standards/certification/iso-survey.htm

42. Handfield, R. B., D. R. Krause, T. V. Scannell, and R. M. Monzka, "Avoid the Pitfalls in Supplier Development," *Sloan Management Review*, Winter 2000: 37–49.

43. Ibid.

44. "Supplier Continuous Quality Improvement (SCQI) Program"; https://supplier.intel.com/static/quality/scqi.htm

45. "Supplier Continuous Quality Improvement (SCQI) Program"; https://supplier-preview.intel.com/static/quality/SCQI_Program_Brochure_2008.pdf

46. Honeywell Six Sigma Plus; http://www.honeywell.com/sites/htsl/processn3_CC41WY2LZW40WXRU3AAO1BOS1YFDKUN5Y_HCT8SSRWCE3JP6RLFT5UK00X6IBWN-J9HF.htm

47. "Media: Boeing Honors 17 Suppliers for Exceptional Performance"; http://boeing.mediaroom.com/index.php?s=20295&item=128662

48. Ibid.

49. "Supplier Continuous Quality Improvement (SCQI) Program"; https://supplier.intel.com/static/quality/scqi.htm

50. "Hitachi Kokusai Electric, Inc. Receives Intel's Prestigious Supplier Continuous Quality Improvement Award"; http://www.ksec.com/Docs/SCQI 2012 Press Release.pdf

51. Wichita, K., "Hormel Foods Announces Recipients of Prestigious Supplier Award," May 12, 2011; http://www.hormelfoods.com/Newsroom/Press-Releases/2011/05/20110512-1

52. "Hormel Foods Honors Suppliers with Spirit of Excellence Awards," April 18, 2013; http://www.hormelfoods.com/Newsroom/Press-Releases/2013/04/20130418.

53. "Accenture Builds High Performance," op. cit.

54. "SAP Supplier Relationship Management"; http://www.sap.com/solution/lob/procurement/software/srm/index.html

55. Barling, B., "The Five Tenets of SRM," *AMR Research*, June 10, 2002.

56. "Successful Sourcing Strategies: Toshiba," *JDA Case Study*; http://www.jda.com/company/display-collateral/pid/943/

57. JDA Strategic Sourcing; http://www.jda.com/company/display-collateral/pid/1871/

58. "Successful Sourcing Strategies: Toshiba," *JDA Case Study*; http://www.jda.com/company/display-collateral/pid/943/

59. Ibid.

Chapter 4
ETHICAL AND SUSTAINABLE SOURCING

During my trip to Colombia, I didn't just meet the coffee farmers, I met their children and their families. Fair trade has truly brought a better quality of life to farming communities, from access to education to community development, and meeting with these people really opened my eyes to the impact fair trade has had on their lives.

— Grace Potter, musician and spokesperson for Green Mountain Coffee[1]

We think green is not just good for the environment, we think it's good for the economy. If it can be viable both financially and environmentally, it can be a huge game changer for the city.

— Rina Cutler, Philadelphia's Deputy Mayor of Transportation and Utilities[2]

Learning Objectives

After completing this chapter, you should be able to

- Understand and appreciate the trends in ethical and sustainable sourcing.
- Define and describe the terms used in ethical and sustainable sourcing.
- Describe the differences in ethical and sustainable sourcing.
- Understand how ethical and sustainable strategies are developed and implemented.
- Understand the use of environmental supplier certifications.
- Discuss the benefits of strategic supplier alliances.
- Describe how and why sourcing practices are benchmarked.
- Discuss why firms would want to assess their sourcing capabilities.

Chapter Outline

Introduction

Ethical and Sustainable Sourcing Defined

Developing Ethical and Sustainable Sourcing Strategies

Ethical and Sustainable Sourcing Initiatives

Early Supplier Involvement

Strategic Alliance Development

Rewarding Supplier Performance

Benchmarking Successful Sourcing Practices

Assessing and Improving the Firm's Sourcing Function

SCM Profile | Ethical and Sustainable Practices at Infinity Foods

South of London along the coast sits the famous seaside resort of Brighton. In this city of 160,000 is North Laine, a patchwork of quirky cafes and shops selling antiques, vintage clothing, handmade jewelry, and vegetarian food. On one corner sits Infinity Foods. Its casually dressed staff and its shelves of organic veggies, gluten-free bread, and eco-friendly liquid soap might tempt some to dismiss Infinity Foods as faddish and unviable, catering to only to sandal-wearing hippies.

Although some of Infinity's staff do wear sandals, Infinity is far from unviable. The shop has been around since 1973, and in 2011 Infinity marked its 40th anniversary. For most of those years, Infinity Foods has been a workers' co-operative, owned and managed entirely by its nearly 100 staff. Apart from pay increments based on length of service, everyone earns the same basic wage. Additionally, all staff earn variable bonuses making up about 40 percent of their pay. There is no traditional organizational hierarchy: managers also stack shelves and work the checkouts. "We, who own the business, are face-to-face with our customers and in touch with their ethical concerns," says Dexter Bailey, one of the managers.

Ethical concerns mean that only organic, fair trade, vegetarian, and locally grown products make it onto Infinity's shelves. There is also a bias against multinational suppliers. Since Green & Black's chocolate, for instance, was taken over by global conglomerate Kraft, Infinity replaced G&B with local producer Montezuma. Such decisions are debated by Infinity's annually elected steering committee and then voted on by all members.

Infinity Foods' shop and café are their most visible faces, but the bulk of its business is its wholesale operation, based at three adjoining warehouses in Portslade, just outside Brighton. Although only half of Infinity's staff work there, it accounts for 80 percent of sales, supplying health food stores, restaurants, and cafés across southern England.

This ethically driven co-operative, though, does have a place in its vocabulary for terms such as "profit," "expansion," and "investment." Infinity's profit is spread equitably among staff, paying them a proper living wage. The expansion of the wholesale operation and Infinity's rising revenues came thanks to an upsurge in sales of organic food from the 1990s onwards, says Scott Muir, their wholesale buyer. In many ways, the wholesale site is a normal place of work. There are forklift trucks, safety notices at every turn, and a busy office juggling orders and invoices. The one thing that distinguishes it from an ordinary warehouse, however, is the selection of fair trade and organic herbal teas that are available for all warehouse workers.[3]

INTRODUCTION

As discussed in Chapters 2 and 3, purchasing, sourcing, or supply management departments are increasingly seen as highly valued, strategic contributors to their organizations because of their ability to impact product design and quality, cost of goods sold, manufacturing cycle time, and the firm's overall profitability. Another area of concern has slowly been coming into play for purchasing departments over the past five to ten years, and this is the use of ethical and sustainable sourcing practices. Global population growth, the increasing awareness of environmental issues, and consumers' desires for better corporate responsibility have combined to place unprecedented pressures on company personnel to effectively manage firms' supply chains. Additionally, as world economies floundered recently, firms began squeezing as many costs out of their operations as possible to survive. Thus, as never before, purchasing personnel are in a position to have a tremendous impact on their companies' and their supply chains' costs and reputations through use of ethical and sustainable sourcing practices. These and other strategic purchasing activities are discussed in this chapter.

The influence of the purchasing, sourcing, or supply management department both within the organization and outside its boundaries is quite unique in that it interacts with customers and suppliers; internal design, production, finance, marketing, and accounting personnel; and also the firm's executive managers. As companies move toward taking a more proactive role in managing their supply chains, purchasing departments are then seen as one of the primary designers and facilitators of important inward- and outward-facing sourcing policies. These policies might include various ethical practices such as those described in the chapter opening SCM Profile of Infinity Foods.

The global recession hastened many organizations' plans to institute supply chain management strategies to reduce costs, delivery cycle times, and carbon footprints, while improving quality, customer service, and ethical reputations, with the ultimate goals of improving competitiveness, market share, and profits. Indeed, the increasing number of global competitors; demands by customers for companies to become more ethically and environmentally focused; and rising costs of fuel and materials have combined to place added pressures on firms to improve their performance in supply chain management.

Today, these trends have become the drivers of strategic sourcing and supply chain management initiatives. Taking the notion of sourcing one step further, **strategic sourcing** can be thought of as managing the firm's external resources in ways that support the long-term goals of the firm. This includes the development of ethical and sustainable sourcing initiatives (which are also tied to the make-or-buy decision), managing and improving supplier relationships and capabilities, identification and selection of environmentally and socially conscious suppliers, and monitoring and rewarding supplier performance. Some of these topics have been introduced in earlier chapters and will only be lightly touched upon here, while others particularly related to ethical and sustainable sourcing will be covered in greater detail in this chapter.

Developing socially responsible and environmentally friendly sourcing strategies that also create a competitive advantage is no easy task. Creating and implementing strategies to support ethical and green purchasing might provide some benefits for the firms involved but can ultimately fail, because of misaligned strategies, lack of commitment, unrealized goals, and loss of trust in buyer–supplier relationships. Purchasing managers proactively managing their firms' supply chains must also come to understand that some sourcing strategies are better suited to some supply chains than to others. Indeed, firms may have dozens of supply chains associated with their most important inbound purchased items and outbound finished products. Some of these supply chains may be driven by a low-cost overall strategy, while others may have the environment, quality, or customer service as the overriding objective. Even different parts and components used in one product may have diverging supply chain strategies. In the following sections, the development of successful ethical and sustainable sourcing strategies is discussed.

ETHICAL AND SUSTAINABLE SOURCING DEFINED

Ethical Sourcing

To establish a common ground for further discussion, it is necessary to first define and describe the origins of the terms *ethical* and *sustainable* sourcing. To start with, **business ethics** is the application of ethical principles to business situations, and has been very widely studied. A library search, for instance, would reveal over 250 books dedicated solely to the topic of business ethics. Generally speaking, there are two approaches to deciding whether or not an action is ethical. The first approach is known as **utilitarianism**. It maintains that an ethical act creates the greatest good for the greatest number of people. The second approach is known as **rights and duties** and states that some actions are right in themselves without regard for the consequences. This approach maintains that ethical actions recognize the rights of others and the duties those rights impose on the ones performing the actions.

The practice of business ethics is also referred to as **corporate social responsibility (CSR)**. Much of the discussion to date of corporate social responsibility assumes that a corporation can act ethically just as an individual can. Many companies, for instance, have formal CSR initiatives that include ethical sourcing. The majority of S&P 500 companies now publicly state a commitment to act as a responsible corporation and do some type of CSR reporting. CSR initiatives and reporting are also growing globally. For instance, the consulting group KPMG reported that 79 percent of the largest 250 global companies produce CSR reports. Overall, this trend is growing in all industries and countries.[4]

Extending from business ethics then, the term **ethical sourcing** can be defined as:

> *That which takes into account the public consequences of organizational buying, or bringing about positive social change through organizational buying behavior.*[5]

Ethical sourcing practices include promoting diversity by intentionally buying from small firms, ethnic minority businesses, and women-owned enterprises; discontinuing purchases from firms that use child labor or other unacceptable labor practices; or sourcing from firms in underdeveloped nations.

Purchasing managers and other corporate executives play a central role in promoting ethical sourcing by creating a supportive organizational culture, developing policies that outline the firm's desire to practice ethical sourcing, communicating these policies to supply chain trading partners, and then developing tactics that specifically describe how ethical sourcing will be implemented. Massachusetts-based athletic footwear retailer Reebok launched its ethical sourcing program in the early 1990s. It emphasizes the roles played by supplier factory managers in maintaining ethical workplace conditions. Reebok also tries to collaborate with its competitors in establishing common human rights guidelines, since they all may be buying merchandise from the same suppliers. In 2002, Reebok unveiled an Internet-based human rights compliance-monitoring software application, generating considerable interest from other firms about buying the application. In response, Reebok established a not-for-profit organization built around the technology and in 2004 launched the Fair Factories Clearinghouse with the backing of the National Retail Federation.[6]

Purchasing goods from suppliers in developing countries can be risky in that if human rights, animal rights, safety, or environmental abuses become associated with the firm's suppliers or foreign manufacturing facilities, this could lead to negative publicity for the buyer, along with product boycotts, a tarnished company image, brand degradation, lower employee morale, and ultimately lower sales, profits, and stock prices. This very thing happened to running gear manufacturer Nike in the mid-1990s when it contracted with

Pakistani suppliers to make footballs. Unfortunately, the work was subcontracted to local villagers, where children as young as ten were used in the production processes. Similar problems for Nike also cropped up in Cambodia and Malaysia at about the same time. In 1998, CEO Phil Knight acknowledged that, "Nike product has become synonymous with slave wages, forced overtime, and arbitrary abuse." Nike then pledged to reform this company image. In Malaysia, for example, Nike reimbursed workers, paid to relocate them, and then met with representatives of its 30 contract Malaysian factories about enforcing labor standards.[7]

As companies seek lower production costs, exposures to these types of risks increase. To minimize these risks, ethical sourcing policies should include:

- Determining where all purchased goods come from and how they are made;
- Knowing if suppliers promote basic workplace principles (such as the right to equal opportunity and to earn a decent wage; the prohibition of bonded, prison, or child labor; and the right to join a union);
- Use of ethical ratings for suppliers alongside the other standard performance criteria;
- Use of independent verification of vendor compliance;
- Reporting of supplier compliance performance to shareholders; and
- Providing detailed ethical sourcing expectations to vendors.[8]

Use of ethical supply chain sourcing practices can be fraught with difficulties. Modern supply chains can encompass many countries, each with its own set of labor issues, wages, and working and living conditions. Many companies may not even be aware of their supply chains beyond their immediate or first-tier suppliers and customers. Nike's global supply chain, for instance, employs some 800,000 workers in fifty-two countries. The **Ethical Trading Initiative (ETI)** is an alliance of organizations seeking to take responsibility for improving working conditions and agreeing to implement the ETI Base Code, a standard for ethical practices for the firm and its suppliers. The ETI Base Code is shown in Table 4.1.

The purchase of **fair trade products** is an activity that is becoming increasingly popular as firms seek to demonstrate a more ethical approach to purchasing. A fair trade product refers to one that is manufactured or grown by a disadvantaged producer in a developing country that receives a fair price for its goods. Mostly, the term refers to farming products such as coffee, cocoa, bananas, sugar, tea, and cotton which are produced in developing countries and exported to large firms in developed countries.

Agencies such as the Fairtrade Foundation, Fairtrade Labelling Organizations International, and the World Fair Trade Organization seek out and certify products as being fair trade products.[9] In 2006, the rock musician Bono launched the fashion label Red to sell ethically sourced and fair trade certified products. A portion of Red's revenues is used to fight AIDS, tuberculosis, and malaria in Africa.[10] Leading retailers offer items for sale that are designated as fair trade products. Fair Trade USA, the certifier of fair trade products in the U.S., reports that consumers are increasing their commitment to fair trade faster than ever before. In the U.S. today, there are over 700 companies offering fair trade products.[11]

In the U.K., for example, consumers can purchase fair trade rubber gloves with the knowledge that Sri Lankan rubber farmers are benefitting from a fair price, technical support, and help in buying farming equipment. Many consumers are willing to pay more for these items too. Recently, Cadbury pledged to spend £1.5 billion to ensure its Dairy Milk bars sold in the U.K. are certified as fair trade products.[12] Worldwide, fair trade certified

Table 4.1 The Ethical Trading Initiative's Base Code

CLAUSES	ABBREVIATED EXPLANATIONS
1. Employment is freely chosen	No forced, bonded, or involuntary prison labor. Workers are not required to pay "deposits" to their employer and are free to leave after reasonable notice.
2. Freedom of association and the right to collective bargaining are respected	Workers have the right to join trade unions and to bargain collectively. Employers adopt an open attitude toward the activities of trade unions. Worker representatives are not discriminated against. Where the right to collective bargaining is restricted under law, employers facilitate the development of parallel means for bargaining.
3. Working conditions are safe and hygienic	A safe and hygienic work environment shall be provided. Adequate steps shall be taken to minimize the causes of hazards in the workplace. Workers shall receive regular health and safety training. Accommodations shall be clean, safe, and meet the basic needs of workers. The company shall assign responsibility for health and safety to a senior management representative.
4. Child labor shall not be used	There shall be no new recruitment of child labor. Persons under 18 shall not be employed at night or in hazardous conditions. Policies and procedures shall conform to the provisions of the relevant International Labor Organization standards.
5. Living wages are paid	Wages and benefits for a standard work week meet national legal or industry standards, whichever is higher. Wages should be enough to meet basic needs. All workers shall be provided with written and understandable information about their employment conditions before they enter employment and about the particulars of their wages each time that they are paid.
6. Working hours are not excessive	Working hours comply with national laws and benchmark industry standards, whichever affords greater protection. Workers shall not on a regular basis be required to work in excess of 48 hours per week and shall be provided with at least one day off for every 7 day period. Overtime shall be voluntary, shall not exceed 12 hours per week, and shall always be compensated at a premium rate.
7. No discrimination is practiced	There is no discrimination in hiring, compensation, access to training, promotion, termination, or retirement based on race, caste, national origin, religion, age, disability, gender, marital status, sexual orientation, union membership, or political affiliation.
8. Regular employment is provided	Work performed must be on the basis of recognized employment relationships established through national law and practice. Obligations to employees under labor or social security laws shall not be avoided through the use of labor-only contracting, subcontracting, or apprenticeship schemes.
9. No harsh or inhumane treatment is allowed	Physical abuse or discipline, the threat of physical abuse, sexual or other harassment, or other forms of intimidation shall be prohibited.

Source: Ethical Trading Initiative website: www.ethicaltrade.org

product sales amounted to about $6.6 billion in 2011, a 12 percent increase from 2010. Most recent records indicate that fair trade products are produced by over 1.2 million farmers and workers at 991 fair trade certified organizations in sixty-six countries.[13]

Sustainable Sourcing

While the notion of protecting the earth's environment has been a topic of concern for many years, it has more recently become a popular topic of debate as politicians and voters have made global warming a political issue. Former U.S. Vice President and longtime environmentalist Al Gore, for example, starred in the award-winning 2006 global warming documentary *An Inconvenient Truth* (he won the Nobel Peace Prize in 2007 for his environmental work). Additionally, awards such as the Goldman Environmental Prize have served as a support mechanism for environmental reform, providing global publicity for specific environmental problems.

The Goldman Prize began in 1990 and awards $150,000 to each prize recipient. Winners are announced every April to coincide with Earth Day. As of April 2013, there have been

157 prize winners, including the 1991 prize winner, Dr. Wangari Maathai from Kenya. In the 1970s, Maathai founded the Green Belt Movement, an environmental organization concentrating on the planting of trees, environmental conservation, and women's rights in Africa. In 2004, she also became the first African woman to receive the Nobel Peace Prize for "her contribution to sustainable development, democracy and peace."[14] Others such as David Brower, the former executive director of the Sierra Club; Eileen O'Neill, head of Discovery Channel and proponent of their Planet Green multimedia initiative; Patrick Moore, Director and cofounder of Greenpeace International; and many others have played major roles in championing the modern environmental movement.[15]

Growing out of this environmental awareness was the idea of **green purchasing**. Green purchasing is a practice aimed at ensuring that purchased products or materials meet environmental objectives of the organization such as waste reduction, hazardous material elimination, recycling, remanufacturing, and material reuse. According to the globally recognized Institute for Supply Management, green purchasing is defined as *making environmentally conscious decisions throughout the purchasing process, beginning with product and process design, and through product disposal.*[16] Companies such as California-based healthcare provider Kaiser Permanente and beer producer Anheuser-Busch have been recognized as corporate trailblazers in green purchasing. In 2001, Kaiser Permanente formed an environmental stewardship council focusing on green buildings, green purchasing, and environmentally sustainable operations. Anheuser-Busch, for example, worked with its suppliers to reduce the lid diameter of four types of cans, saving millions of pounds of aluminum each year as well as reducing the energy needed to produce and transport the cans.[17]

Walmart at 50—More Sustainable than Ever

Over the years, the one thing that has won Walmart the most accolades has been its commitment to the planet. As the Arkansas-based retailer marks the big 5-0, its culture is committed to identifying, developing, and expanding sustainable practices that will improve quality of life the world over while also helping its own bottom line. "We've done all of this because it is the right thing to do for the generations that will follow us. But sustainability is also the right thing to do for our business. Every time we cut back on packaging or fuel or electricity, we save money. Every penny we save adds up for our customers, our shareholders and our future," says Walmart president and CEO Mike Duke.

In 2011, Walmart-driven renewable projects provided more than 1.1 billion kilowatt hours of Walmart's electricity needs, earning Walmart the EPA's recognition as the second-largest on-site green-power generator in the U.S. Walmart diverted 80 percent of its waste away from landfills in the U.S. and diverted 52 percent of its waste from landfills in both China and Brazil. Walmart also completed its 100th solar energy installation in the U.S. and installed its first rooftop solar systems in Canada and China.

Walmart has pledged to reduce greenhouse gases from its supply chain and is striving to take 20 million metric tons out from 2010 to 2015. In 2011, Walmart, which operates a fleet of more than 6,000 trucks, achieved nearly a 69 percent improvement in fleet efficiency compared to a 2005 baseline. Through better route management and increased pallets per trailer, Walmart delivered 65 million more cases while driving 28 million fewer miles. In terms of the overall impact relative to CO_2 emissions, the fleet efficiencies were comparable with taking roughly 7,900 cars off the road.[18]

The term **sustainability** as applied to supply chains is a broad term that includes green purchasing as well as some aspects of social responsibility as well as financial performance. It can be defined as *the ability to meet the needs of current supply chain members without hindering the ability to meet the needs of future generations in terms of economic, environmental and social challenges*. The idea of sustainability is certainly not new as evidenced by the way early Native Americans thought and lived and as Gifford Pinchot, the first Chief Forester of the U.S. Forest Service, wrote in an article in 1908:

> *Are we going to protect our springs of prosperity, our raw material of industry and commerce and employer of capital and labor combined; or are we going to dissipate them? According as we accept or ignore our responsibility as trustees of the nation's welfare, our children and our children's children for uncounted generations will call us blessed, or will lay their suffering at our doors.*[19]

For businesses and their trading partners, sustainability is seen today as doing the right things in ways that make economic sense. Some have begun referring to sustainability in terms of supporting the **three P's**, which refers to *people*, *planet*, and *profit*. The objectives then are not only to sustain the world we live in, but to sustain employees and the balance sheet as well. For years, Walmart's sustainability efforts have been well documented, as shown in the nearby SCM Profile.

Office supply retailer Staples began using fifty-three all-electric battery-powered trucks in 2011. This program helped Staples save millions of gallons of diesel fuel and their cost annually. Food retailer Safeway is focusing on locally grown products to cut transportation-related costs and emissions simply by reducing the number of delivery miles traveled. The company sees local food sources as an opportunity for reducing greenhouse gas emissions while also supporting regional farms.[20] Matt Kissler, vice president of package and product innovation at Walmart's membership warehouse affiliate Sam's Club, may have gotten to the heart of the matter when he said, "Sustainability is not just about the environment. No matter how good we do things for the environment, if they are not sustainable for our business, sustainability will not work. If what we are doing is not sustainable financially for our business entities, we should not be doing it."[21]

Sustainable sourcing is one activity within the larger umbrella term of sustainability—it includes green purchasing, some form of financial benefit, as well as aspects of ethical sourcing. Very simply, it has been defined as

> *A process of purchasing goods and services that takes into account the long-term impact on people, profits, and the planet.*[22]

Leading companies practicing sustainable sourcing seek to:

- *Grow revenues* by introducing new and differentiated sustainable products and services;
- *Reduce costs* by increasing resource efficiencies, avoiding use of noncompliant suppliers, and rethinking transportation and distribution systems;
- *Manage risk* by managing brand and reputation, and developing approaches for meeting regulations and capturing sustainability-conscious customers; and
- *Build intangible assets* by further enhancing brand and reputation through social and environmental responsibility.[23]

To accomplish these goals, companies must develop collaborative relationships with their key suppliers and customers to make sustainable sourcing a beneficial reality.

The Hershey Co., for example, decided in 2012 that all of its chocolate will come from certified sustainable cocoa sources, thus joining the strategies of other big chocolate producers such as Mars and Nestlé. Kip Walk, director of cocoa for Blommer Chocolate Co., points out, "Up to now most of the focus for sustainable products has been in Europe, Australia and Canada. Hershey's announcement brings sustainability into focus for the United States." All the major chocolate brands are looking to have a 100 percent sustainable supply by 2020.[24]

Local and national governments are now getting involved to set some clear targets for organizations to achieve. China's approach to sustainability can be found in its goals for energy use per unit of GDP, water use per unit of value-added industrial output, and sulfur dioxide emissions. When a surge of manufacturing output in 2010 resulted in greenhouse gas emissions in excess of what China's five-year plan called for, the government cut off power to heavy industrial districts, forcing many plants to close temporarily. This dramatic move (unthinkable in most industrialized countries) demonstrated that, in China, sustainability goals are no less important than economic goals.[25] The city of Yellowknife, Canada,

SCM Profile | Yellowknife Canada Named Most Sustainable Small City

The city of Yellowknife is recognized as the most sustainable small city in Canada, an honor it achieved through years of planning. Yellowknife developed three initiatives to guide planning for the city: the Integrated Parks, Trails, and Open Space Development Study; the Community Energy Program; and the Smart Growth Development Program. These are described below.

INTEGRATED PARKS, TRAILS, AND OPEN SPACE DEVELOPMENT STUDY

Yellowknife's park system preserves environmentally sensitive areas, protects lands for active transportation, and helps active residents year-round. The study presents a ten-year vision to protect green spaces, develop gathering spaces, and integrate park and trail planning.

COMMUNITY ENERGY PROGRAM

The Community Energy Planning Committee establishes targets for emission reductions and the use of alternative energy sources. Its current goals are to reduce emissions by 20 percent and reduce energy use by 10 percent by 2014. The city has incorporated sustainable planning guidelines for energy-efficient building standards. The conventional heating systems at some existing facilities have been replaced with biomass heating systems. The city has also developed a heat recovery system for its primary arena facility, and that system is sharing heat with a neighboring recreation facility. Finally, the city is developing a geothermal resource to heat buildings in the downtown core.

SMART GROWTH DEVELOPMENT PROGRAM

This program considers the impacts of decisions related to land use mix, density, urban design, transportation, the natural environment, and the economy. The smart growth principles include solutions that fit with the community's vision of how and where it wants to grow; protection of natural features, minimizing environmental impacts, and making natural areas easily accessible; the revitalization of built-up areas through redevelopment and adaptive reuse of existing buildings; increasing transportation options by providing infrastructure for walking, bicycling, carpooling, and public transit; and reduction of greenhouse gases through conservation, local renewable energy opportunities, and green building design.[27]

has recently been named the most sustainable small city in Canada, as described in the nearby SCM Profile. Seattle, Washington, has been practicing sustainable purchasing for years. Its Green Purchasing Program promotes use of goods, materials, and services that help to reduce greenhouse gas emissions. Purchasing contracts also mandate 100 percent recycled paper for city work, duplex document production, and toxin-free chemicals in products the city buys.[26]

From the supplier's perspective, there are tools available to help determine what buyers want, in terms of environmentally friendly goods. In its 2013 Consumer Recycling and Sustainability Survey, for example, tire maker Bridgestone Americas surveyed consumers in twenty cities and found that:

- Most consumers are holding companies accountable for the sustainability of their products;
- The top three ways companies can show they are environmentally responsible are—(1) creating products that minimize energy and water use, (2) generating less waste, and (3) minimizing carbon emissions;
- More than 86 percent of respondents said they recycle, while 36 percent regarded themselves as serious recyclers.[28]

Companies and government agencies alike are coming to realize that every purchase has a global environmental impact, and with careful sourcing, money can be saved. Collection, transport, manufacturing, and scrapping of raw materials and finished products require the use of fossil fuels; products purchased from distant suppliers require greater amounts of fuel for transportation; products transported via ship or rail use less fuel than trucks or airlines; plant-based products generally have a smaller environmental impact than petroleum-based products; factories powered by solar or wind energy have a smaller environmental impact than factories powered by oil or coal; and energy-efficient products consume less energy.

DEVELOPING ETHICAL AND SUSTAINABLE SOURCING STRATEGIES

To achieve the objectives described thus far in this chapter, a number of sourcing strategies must be considered and implemented. Care must be taken, though, when developing these plans. Failure to align sourcing strategies with overall supply chain objectives, for example, may result in considerable resources being expended to design and manage a set of sourcing activities, only to find that the resulting impact on the firm and its supply chains is something much less than ultimately desired.

In one of the more important papers written on this topic, Martin Fisher uses two types of supply chains as examples—those for **functional products** and those for **innovative products**.[29] Functional products are maintenance, repair, and operating (MRO) materials and other commonly purchased items and supplies. These items are characterized by low profit margins, relatively stable demands, and high levels of competition. Thus, companies purchasing functional products most likely concentrate on finding a dependable supplier selling at a low price. Factory maintenance and cleaning products, for example, might fall into this category.

Examples of innovative consumer goods are the Amazon Kindle and GM's Volt; in factory settings, innovative products might be new types of control mechanisms, new software applications, or new robotics systems. Innovative products are characterized by short product life cycles, volatile demand, high profit margins, and relatively less competition. Consequently, the sourcing criteria for these products may be more closely aligned with a supplier's quality reputation, delivery speed and flexibility, and communication capabilities. Many of California-based Apple's purchases, for example, might fall into the innovative product category. Overlaying both of these types of purchases is whether or not to invoke an ethical or sustainable sourcing strategy. This adds yet another layer of complexity to the sourcing decision.

Many of the commonly used sourcing strategies of thirty years ago do not work well today. For instance, "squeezing" or hard-bargaining suppliers to generate a lower annual **purchasing spend** (or expense) may ultimately prove harmful to buyer–supplier relationships, eventually leading to deteriorations in quality, ethical reputation, sustainability performance, and customer service as suppliers seek ways to cut corners in order to keep their profit margins at desired levels. If long-term sourcing plans are to be successful, they must support the firm's long-term strategies; and suppliers must also see some benefit from the initiatives implemented. A framework for ethical and sustainable sourcing strategy development is shown in Table 4.2.

In Step 1 in Table 4.2, the firm formalizes its ethical and sustainable sourcing policies. Obviously, these policies will vary based on use of foreign suppliers, types of items purchased, and the firm's experiences with this type of sourcing. Ethical sourcing policies should include the importance placed on fair working conditions; use of minority, women-owned, and small businesses; guidelines on human rights and use of child labor; use of subcontracting; and supplier reporting and verification procedures. Sustainable sourcing policies should include supplier compliance issues in terms of waste reduction, energy conservation, use of renewable energy, hazardous material elimination, recycling, remanufacturing, and material reuse.

In Step 2, training and communication of the policies occurs. It is all well and good to develop ethical and/or sustainable sourcing policies, but the firm must also do an adequate job of implementing these policies. In early 2000, for instance, Canadian retailer Hudson Bay had begun developing proactive sustainable sourcing plans, but in 2002 they

Table 4.2 Ethical and Sustainable Sourcing Strategy Framework

STEPS	DESCRIPTION
1. Establish corporate ethical and sustainable sourcing policies.	Establishes a vision and direction and enforces the importance of ethical and sustainable sourcing.
2. Train purchasing staff; communicate policies to suppliers and customers.	Ensures that buyers are skilled in environmental and social considerations in sourcing and that suppliers and customers understand why and how purchasing decisions are made.
3. Prioritize items based on ethical and sustainability opportunities and ease of implementation. Get started.	Allows buyers to "pick low hanging fruit" to provide evidence for successful strategy implementation.
4. Develop a performance measurement system.	Measurement provides accountability and a way to improve over time. Should be reviewed periodically.
5. Monitor progress, make improvements. Increase use of certified fair trade and green products and services.	Use performance measures to identify weaknesses. Step up efforts to develop better capabilities in the firm and its supply base.
6. Expand focus to include other departments and customers. Increase brand value.	Use the purchasing department's success and influence to grow awareness in the firm and among customers. Communicate successes and programs to stakeholders.

Source: Based in part on Newman, D., "Steps You Can Take to 'Green' Your Procurement," *Summit* 9(4), 2006: 10; and "Buying a Better World," found at www.forumforthefuture.org

were accused of using sweatshops for manufacturing. As it turned out, they had not properly communicated their new vendor codes of conduct to their suppliers. Additionally, the shareholders and general public had no idea of their social compliance programs. This caused a number of actual and perceived problems for Hudson Bay to overcome. Today, their social compliance programs are formalized and widely communicated, and they audit all supplier facilities for compliance to their codes of conduct.[30]

Step 3 is all about getting started. It is important to keep efforts simple early on, find successes quickly, and then build on these successes. If companies cannot show some financial benefit from ethical and sustainable sourcing policies, then ultimately these efforts will fail. Buyers might consider concentrating on products where the market for fair trade and green products is mature, as with office supplies, cleaning supplies, and some apparel.

Step 4 calls for the design of performance metrics to gauge the success of the firm's efforts. Measures can be qualitative or quantitative and in the general areas of cost, quality, time, flexibility, and innovativeness. In managed supply chains, performance indicators should be standardized across trading partners. Metrics for sustainability can be used in the areas of packaging, energy use, hazardous materials, and recycling. Metrics could include the number of fair trade certified products purchased, the number of ethical standards adopted by suppliers, the number of suppliers adopting the Ethical Trading Initiative's Base Code, and the number of small and minority suppliers used. As products, suppliers, and markets change, these metrics should be revisited and potentially revised. More on performance measurement can be found in Chapters 13 and 14.

Step 5 is to monitor performance and outcomes, while adjusting the work plans, priorities, policies, and use of suppliers to more adequately meet the ethical and sustainability goals of the firm. It may be that certain elements in the various programs or conduct codes need to be revised as the firm and its operating environments change. Over time as the firm and its suppliers adjust to these policies, improvements can be made, more fair trade products and green products will be identified, and further initiatives will be developed.

Finally, Step 6 addresses the impact of ethical and sustainable sourcing on other facets of the organization, its trading partners, and ultimately the firm's brand. As successes are realized, it will become easier for the firm to operate more ethically and sustainably. Eventually, other divisions and trading partners will become interested. Consumers will start expecting it. Increasingly, companies are taking their ethical and sustainable factors and leveraging them for greater brand value. Even during the recent global recession, consumers preferred organizations that addressed various ethical and sustainable issues. According to Christopher Satterthwaite, CEO of U.K.-based Chime Communications, "The big message for brands that want to get ahead of the game is that there is a sustainable advantage to be had if they do their homework, find the right sustainability 'fit', and tell their story in an open and honest way."[31]

As personnel in design, marketing, production, and other departments begin working with purchasing personnel to develop these and other sourcing strategies, a number of initiatives, some of which have already been introduced in earlier chapters, may be used separately or in some combination to support the organization's long-term goals. These proactive sourcing initiatives, when combined with internal operations and customer relationship initiatives, form the foundation for successful supply chain management and, ultimately, competitive advantage for the firm. The following section discusses a number of ethical and sustainable sourcing initiatives.

ETHICAL AND SUSTAINABLE SOURCING INITIATIVES

Ethical and Sustainable Supplier Certification Programs

Proactively seeking and creating **strategic supplier alliances** have become important objectives of firms actively managing their supply chains. Strategic alliances are a more formalized type of collaborative relationship, involving commitments to long-term cooperation, shared benefits and costs, joint problem solving, continuous improvement, and information sharing. Because of these relationships, suppliers are able to invest more of their resources toward becoming specialized in areas required by the buyer, to establish production and/or storage facilities close to the buyer's facilities, to purchase compatible communication and information systems, and to invest in better technologies that will ultimately improve supplier performance.

Ethical and sustainable supplier certifications are one way to identify strategic alliance candidates or to further develop existing alliances. In many cases, certification programs are simply based on internationally recognized certifications such as the Switzerland-based International Organization for Standardization's ISO 9000 quality certification and ISO 14000 environmental certification.[32] For the organization actively managing its supply chains, these types of certification requirements are good, but may not be specific enough in areas of importance to the firm. In these cases, firms develop their own formal certification programs, which may include ISO certification as one element of the certification process. Other certification requirements might include, for example, the Forest Stewardship Council (FSC) certification for recycled paper, Energy Star certification for various environmental standards, or fair trade certifications for social and ethical performance.

The use of **ethical and environmental certifications** for suppliers is increasing. The New York-based Rainforest Alliance and California-based Trans-Fair USA certifies billions of dollars in coffee, bananas, and cocoa each year from suppliers in dozens of countries, and, in exchange, suppliers work to preserve the environment and improve conditions for farm workers.[33] Massachusetts-based Integrity Interactive Corp. offers a Web-based service that allows a firm to communicate a code of ethics to its supply chain members. The website delivers the company's code of ethics to suppliers, collects certifications, and reports results back to the initiating company. The certification website allows companies to identify rogue suppliers before they can cause problems or disruptions in their supply chains. Suppliers who fail to certify according to the ethical requirements can then face various consequences. World-class companies such as Ryder Systems and H.J. Heinz are busy using the system to certify their suppliers.[34]

Supply Base Rationalization Programs

As first mentioned in Chapter 2, firms taking an active role in supply chain management seek to reduce purchases from marginal or poor-performing suppliers while increasing and concentrating purchases among their more desirable, top-performing suppliers. Firms doing this are practicing **supply base rationalization**, also referred to as **supply base reduction** or **supply base optimization**; this has been a common occurrence since the late 1980s. Indeed, activities aimed at fostering buyer–supplier partnerships and increasing the performance and value of suppliers are simply easier when fewer suppliers are involved. Thus, supply base rationalization programs have the benefits of reduced purchase prices due to quantity discounts, fewer supplier management problems, closer and more frequent collaborations between buyer and supplier, and greater overall levels of quality and delivery reliability (since only the best suppliers remain in the supply base).

Companies can design supply base rationalization initiatives based in part on ethical and sustainable performance requirements—in this way, firms will interact more frequently and closely with suppliers exhibiting preferred ethical and sustainable habits. Building relationships with suppliers that are leaders in these areas can bring many benefits to the firm, including those mentioned above, along with brand enhancement and better environmental and ethical performance. Two international standards by the World Resources Institute (WRI) and the World Business Council on Sustainable Development (WBCSD), known as the GHG Protocol standards, cover individual product footprints and for the first time allow buyers to measure and question their suppliers' greenhouse gas emissions.[35]

Outsourcing Products and Services

Purchasing spend as a percentage of sales has been increasing over the years, in part because firms have opted to **outsource** the production of materials, parts, services, and assembled components to concentrate more resources and time on the firm's core business activities. As first described in Chapter 2, many organizations are outsourcing more, while making fewer parts. In managed supply chains where a higher level of trust permeates buyer–supplier relationships, the use of outsourcing is also growing. Aside from outsourcing noncore products and service functions such as maintenance items and janitorial services, firms are also outsourcing to suppliers with outstanding ethical and sustainable credentials, due in part to brand enhancement and the lower potential costs of sustainability. Georgia-based Metcam, for example, a sheet metal component manufacturer, is a supplier to a number of companies seeking to outsource for sustainability reasons. Michigan-based Steelcase outsourced to Metcam to help it reach its sustainability goals. The company has its suppliers track information on recycled content, materials used, and transportation costs. Metcam's ISO 14000 environmental certification has helped it get this type of business.[36]

Outsourcing solely based on low cost can be quite dangerous, as witnessed by the devastating loss of 1,100 workers after the collapse of the Rena Plaza in Dhaka, Bangladesh, in April 2013. The facility housed a number of clothing manufacturers that were being used by several large clothing suppliers. The Supplier Ethical Data Exchange (Sedex) focuses on responsible and ethical business practices and provides reports to industrial buyers to help avoid these and other outsourcing risks. Over 22 percent of independent audits, for example, revealed fire safety noncompliance in Bangladesh (the leading problem area) followed by 18 percent in China and 17 percent in Pakistan. "Fire safety concerns are at the top of risk issues. If a building is vulnerable in any way, it provides big risks to suppliers, companies, and investors," says Mark Robertson, a spokesperson at Sedex. "Companies and their investors ignore these risks at their peril," he adds.[37]

Ron Kifer, CIO at California-based Applied Materials Inc., tries to ensure that the outsourcing his company does is aligned with the company's social and ethical objectives. "We just got into IT outsourcing within the past couple of years, and we're trying to apply the same ideas: giving back to community, supporting the economies in which we live and work, and green initiatives. We need to make sure that our suppliers are operating to the same high standards as the company," he says.[38] A number of other strategic sourcing initiatives are discussed in the following sections.

EARLY SUPPLIER INVOLVEMENT

As relationships with suppliers become more trusted, reliable, and long-term in nature, key suppliers often become more heavily involved in the internal operations of their industrial customers, including managing inventories of their own products at their customers' points of use and participating in their customers' new product and process design processes. Key supplier representatives might participate in making decisions on product part and assembly design, new product materials usage, and even the design of the processes to be used in manufacturing new products. Thus, strategic suppliers play a greater role in their customers' decision-making processes as trading relationships mature, which in turn further solidifies the supply chain. California-based semiconductor company Novellus has a long history of getting suppliers involved in the product design process. It has allowed them to reduce production lead times and time to market while reducing costs and thus producing better profit margins. Before, Novellus experienced production delays and higher costs as a result of suppliers having problems manufacturing their parts. Now, since the suppliers are part of the design process from the start, these problems do not occur.[39]

While serving on a customer's new product development team, a supplier representative's input can help the firm to reduce material cost, improve product quality and innovation, and reduce product development time. Cost reductions occur with use of more standardized parts, fewer parts, and less expensive materials. Cost, quality, innovation, and delivery timing improvements all come about when suppliers use the information gained through **early supplier involvement** to design parts and processes at their own facilities to match a buyer's specifications. Additionally, since they have been involved in the buyer's new product design process, these part and process changes can be timed to be in place and available when first needed by the buyer. Use of these **value engineering** techniques with help from the supplier allows firms to design better quality and cost savings into the products from the time a product first hits the shelves. Over the product's life, this can generate significant savings and revenues while reducing the need for cost-savings initiatives later on.

Early supplier involvement is perhaps one of the most effective supply chain integrative techniques. Buyers and suppliers working together—sharing proprietary design and manufacturing information that their competitors would love to see—establishes a level of trust and cooperation that results in many future collaborative and potentially successful projects. Discussions of several other early supplier involvement activities follow.

Vendor Managed Inventories

Vendor managed inventory (VMI) services for key customers is perhaps one of the more value-enhancing activities performed by trusted suppliers. When past performance allows customers to develop trust in a supplier's ability to manage inventories at the customer sites, carrying costs can be reduced and stockouts avoided. From the customer's perspective, allowing a supplier to track and manage purchased inventories, while determining delivery schedules and order quantities, saves time and money. For the supplier, it means avoiding ill-advised orders from buyers, deciding how and where inventories are set up, when to ship, and how to ship. Further, they have the opportunity to educate their customers about other products. VMI programs have become very popular. According to data from the American Productivity and Quality Center's 2013 Open Standards Benchmarking report, more than half of participating organizations have implemented VMI programs at customer sites.[40]

Ideally, these valued suppliers manage their customers' inventories using real-time visibility of inventory movements in customers' storage areas or at the point of assembly or sale. This can be accomplished with bar code labels and scanners that instantly update computer counts of inventories as the items are used or sold, or using radio frequency identification systems (discussed in Chapter 7). This data is then made available to trusted suppliers using compatible inventory management systems or a secured website. This allows a supplier to profile demand, determine an accurate forecast, and then ship an order quantity when the inventory levels become low enough.

Walmart is generally given credit for popularizing the use of VMI in the mid-1990s when it initiated a relationship with Procter & Gamble to manage its diaper inventories. A similar arrangement with Rubbermaid soon followed.[41] Ohio-based Datalliance, the leading VMI service provider, sees the concept exploding. According to Carl Hall, Datalliance President, "More and more, retailers are looking to their product suppliers to help streamline their supply chains all the way to the individual store and shelf. Now a growing number of retailers are asking suppliers to also take on the job of store level replenishment planning in order to further improve product availability while at the same time reducing administrative costs. Done on a collaborative basis, direct store replenishment can increase sales and margins while reducing costs for both the retailer and the supplier. That's why we're putting even more emphasis on providing solutions for this growing practice."[42]

A shared form of VMI is termed **co-managed inventories**. In this case, the buyer and supplier reach an agreement regarding how information is shared, order quantities, when an order is generated, and the delivery timing and location. This type of controlled VMI may be preferable for very high-value, strategic item purchases, where the customer desires more input into the day-to-day supply activities, or perhaps when the customer is still assessing a supplier's ability to take full responsibility for the order fulfillment process.

Supplier Co-location

A more advanced and dedicated extension of the vendor managed inventory concept is **supplier co-location**. The concept refers to a situation wherein a supplier's employee is permanently housed in the purchasing department of the buyer's organization, acting as both buyer and supplier representative. This person is given all the rights and duties of an employee for the buyer organization—forecasting demand, monitoring inventory levels, and placing purchase orders, with access to all the files and records of the buyer organization. This special arrangement requires high levels of trust from both organizations and occurs only with long-term buyer–supplier relationships and in large organizations.

By the mid-1990s, many firms had adopted a supplier co-location strategy, including Harley-Davidson, Honeywell, IBM, Intel, DuPont, Ford, Motorola, and AT&T. Back then, it was sometimes referred to as JIT II. "One of the real bangs for the buck of JIT II is that suppliers, who have more expertise on the parts they supply than their customers do, can suggest modifications during the design phase that customers would not know about on their own," says Bill Grimes, a former vice president of global supply for Honeywell.[43] When Chrysler planned a $1 billion Jeep plant in Toledo, Ohio, in 2004, they partnered with three suppliers who would manage body, paint, and chassis operations. They termed it the most advanced use of supplier co-location yet in North America.[44]

Several advantages exist for both partners using supplier co-location. The purchasing organization gets the service of a cost-free employee who understands its particular problems and requirements and can easily communicate these needs to the supplier. The supplier gets the security of future purchases and the "first mover" advantage of having someone on-site when new items need to be purchased. Communication between both firms also improves with this arrangement. The supplier representative learns very quickly about new products and design changes occurring at the customer's firm that are going to impact the supplier. This person also learns about production problems, product returns, and warranty repair issues potentially caused by the supplier's products and can help to more quickly alleviate these problems. Additionally, the co-located representative can assist the company to optimize its transportation network and sustainability strategy—the use of cross-docking locations, other distribution points, backhaul alternatives, and use of third-party logistics services. The arrangement benefits both sides and creates an even closer working relationship between the two companies.

STRATEGIC ALLIANCE DEVELOPMENT

As the growth of supply chain management continues, firms become more adept at managing their suppliers and more willing to assist them in improving their production and service capabilities. Simply put, **strategic alliance development**, an extension of supplier development (covered in Chapter 3), refers to increasing the firm's key or strategic suppliers' capabilities. As supply bases become smaller, more opportunities for creating collaborative relationships with these suppliers also occur. As a whole then, supply bases become more manageable. The more basic supplier management activities tend to become somewhat less time-consuming as strategic supplier alliances begin to constitute more and more of the supply base. Consequently, strategic alliance development starts to occupy more of the purchasing function's time and resources.

Business owners and executives are beginning to realize that strategic supplier alliances, if successful, can result in better market penetration, access to new technologies and knowledge, and higher returns on investment than competitors with no such alliances. Rayovac, for example, is a strategic alliance partner with Six Flags theme parks. Both companies benefit from the alliance, as described in the nearby SCM Profile.

Supplier development activities become more vital to companies as they come to depend more and more on a smaller group of high-performance suppliers. Alliance development will eventually even extend to a firm's second-tier suppliers, as the firm's key suppliers begin to form their own alliance development activities. Alliance development among the firm and its key suppliers tends to be much more of a collaborative activity, requiring both sides to commit time, people, communication, and monetary resources to achieving goals that will benefit both parties. The company and its strategic suppliers jointly decide on improvement activities, resources required, and the means to measure progress. As the improvements take place, suppliers eventually become capable of passing these same capabilities on to their key suppliers, thus extending these capabilities up the supply chain.

Strategic alliance development requires companies to improve relationship value systems within their organizations' cultures, learn from their mistakes and from the successes of other alliances, and make investments to enable collaborative problem solving. Many firms are hiring strategic relationship managers, whose job is to build trust, commitment, and mutual value with alliance partners. These relationship managers work on negotiating win–win collaborations resulting mutual benefits, such that alliances become the norm among the various business units in the organization. Strategic supplier alliances, like products, have their own life cycles, requiring ongoing management, development, and negotiating activities to monitor success, manage conflict, evaluate the current fit with partners, revisit the ground rules for working together, and make adjustments through mutual problem solving and information sharing. Organizing and managing a successful alliance

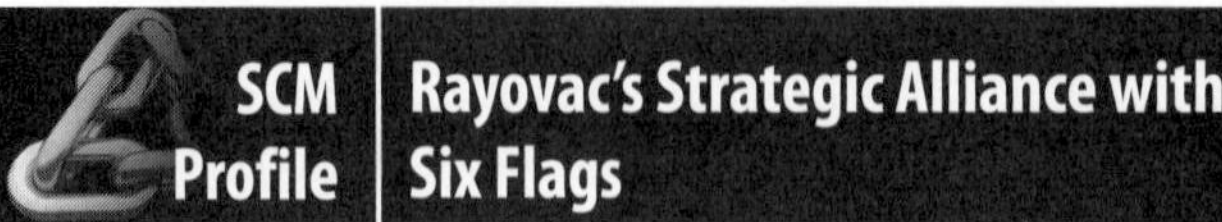

SCM Profile: Rayovac's Strategic Alliance with Six Flags

Rayovac, the consumer battery brand of Spectrum Brand Holding's, Inc., is in a strategic alliance with Six Flags Entertainment Corporation, the world's largest regional theme park company with nineteen parks across the U.S., Mexico, and Canada. Consequently, the companies collaborate on a large number of marketing initiatives. "Six Flags shares our passion for powering fun so this partnership is an ideal fit for the brand," said Kent Klagos, Division Vice President for Rayovac Marketing.

Rayovac is the exclusive supplier of batteries sold at the theme parks. Its alliance includes a wide assortment of advertising for Rayovac on the Six Flags television network, digital menu boards, jumbotron, online media outlets, and ticket jackets throughout the parks. Additionally, a car race powered by Rayovac will be included in ad rotations at a variety of the parks' top attractions. In-park marketing activities such as couponing days and a host of other creative tie-ins are also part of the partnership.

Rayovac will headline Six Flags' special events such as the popular Fright Fest and Holiday in the Park with increased media exposure. The multidimensional partnership also uniquely empowers the Rayovac brand to capitalize on the sponsorship to create customized account-specific retail sales promotions and ticket offers. "We're excited to add Rayovac's legendary battery brand to our roster of blue chip brand partners. In turn, Six Flags' portfolio of strategic media platforms will seamlessly allow Rayovac's core brand messaging of value and fun to engage the varied demographic audience that populates our theme parks across the country," said Lou Koskovolis, EVP, Corporate Alliances, Six Flags Media Networks.[45]

program is thus very important to a firm's competitiveness. Table 4.3 describes the strategic alliance organization process.

To make strategic alliance programs successful, firms must determine how to organize a program that can cut across functional boundaries; disseminate program information quickly and effectively throughout the organization; acquire the necessary resources; create program acceptance by the line managers and their employees; achieve concrete, measurable success; and reward supplier performance. Some firms have chosen to organize

Table 4.3 Maintaining a Successful Strategic Alliance Program

STEPS	DISCUSSION
1. Determine the key strategic parameters to organize around.	Can be based on business units, geographic areas, industries, key alliance partners, or combinations of these.
2. Facilitate the dissemination of information.	Alliance management and development information should be centrally controlled and available through internal websites, pamphlets, and workshops.
3. Elevate the importance of the strategic alliance program.	Assign a director or vice president of alliance programs, reporting to top management. Establish consistent procedures for alliance programs throughout the organization.
4. Provide continuous evaluation of alliance performance, visibility, and support.	Management can increase the value and acceptance of alliance programs when successes are made visible to the firm's lower level managers and employees. Alliance management requires resources and ongoing reevaluation.
5. Reward suppliers as performance merits.	Rewards typically include increased business and other nonmonetary awards.

Source: Adapted from Dyer, J., P. Kale, and H. Singh, "How to Make Strategic Alliances Work," *Sloan Management Review* 42(4), 2001: 37–43.

around their key alliance partners by assigning alliance managers to each of these partners. Others have decided to create an alliance board to oversee alliances and coordinate alliance managers in various divisions within the organization or in different geographic regions of the world.

The alliance management function can act as a clearinghouse for information regarding all types of alliance needs, from negotiation strategies to problem-solving assistance to outreach programs and workshops. To give the alliance management function credibility, the program director should report to the organization's top management. This facilitates the use of company resources as well as provides internal visibility to the function. Alliance strategies, goals, policies, and procedures can then be generated and communicated across the entire organization. Finally, since alliance goals change over time, they must be evaluated periodically. Performance evaluation metrics must be established; and, as alliances show signs of success, strategies can be shared across the various alliance boundaries. As briefly mentioned earlier, continued alliance success depends on both the supplier and the buyer getting value from the alliance. The topic of negotiations with strategic alliance partners follows.

Negotiating Win–Win Strategic Alliance Agreements

When negotiating with strategic alliances, the most advantageous outcome occurs when both parties utilize **collaborative negotiations**. This is sometimes also referred to as **integrative** or **win–win negotiations**. In other words, both sides work together to maximize the joint outcome or to create a joint optimal result. The belief is that there is more to gain from collaborating rather than trying to seek an outcome that favors primarily one side's interests (referred to as **distributive negotiations**). For collaborative negotiations to succeed, members from both parties must trust each other, believe in the validity of each other's perspective, and be committed to working together. From the perspective of key supply chain trading partners, these requirements should already be present, so collaborative negotiations may be easier to achieve in actively managed supply chains.

Successful collaborative negotiations require open discussions and a free flow of information between parties, preferably in face-to-face meetings. This is particularly important when the goal is to improve ethical or sustainable performance.

In contrast, distributive negotiation is adversarial and usually means that some information will be withheld, distorted, delayed, or completely misrepresented. The likelihood that one or the other or some combination of the two methods occurs depends on the nature of the trading relationship, the strategic nature of the item(s) being negotiated, and potentially the balance of power in the relationship. In the automotive sector, particularly at Toyota, collaborative negotiations are described to be part of a *lean thinking* approach to supplier relationships, although automobile manufacturers typically enjoy high levels of buyer dominance that may tilt the negotiating scales somewhat in the buyer's favor.

To maximize the likelihood of achieving equitable collaborative negotiations, supply chain partners should first develop a collaborative negotiation infrastructure and then facilitate a negotiating approach that supports win–win outcomes. Table 4.4 describes the steps in developing a collaboration infrastructure. Over time, purchasing representatives will get better at collaborative negotiations as they become more familiar with their trading partners' interests, learn from previous negotiations, and determine how best to work with each trading partner. Managers or negotiating team leaders can also aid in this process by encouraging exchanges of information, dealing fairly with negotiating problems, and brainstorming options for achieving mutual gains.

Table 4.4 Developing a Collaborative Negotiation Infrastructure

STEPS	DESCRIPTION
1. Build a preparation process	Gain an understanding of both parties' interests; brainstorm value-maximizing solutions and terms; identify objective criteria wherein both sides evaluate fairness of an agreement.
2. Develop a negotiation database	Review previous negotiations to catalogue standards, practices, precedents, metrics, creative solutions used, and lessons learned.
3. Design a negotiation launch process	Create an environment allowing parties to first focus on how they will work together to create a shared vocabulary, build working relationships, and map out a shared decision-making process.
4. Institute a feedback mechanism	Create a debriefing process to provide feedback to negotiating teams and capture lessons learned.

Source: Adapted from Kliman, S., "Enabling Win-Win," *Executive Excellence* 17(4), 2000: 9–11.

REWARDING SUPPLIER PERFORMANCE

Rewarding suppliers for improving or maintaining high levels of performance accomplishes several objectives: it provides an incentive to suppliers to meet and surpass specific performance goals; it provides an incentive for marginal suppliers to achieve a level of performance that will allow their supplier status to be upgraded, potentially resulting in rewards; and, finally, it gives suppliers an incentive to create and share rewards, in turn, with *their* suppliers. Sharing the benefits of good performance in this way is one of the central foundations of building effective supply chains. As mentioned at the start of the chapter, both suppliers and buyers must be able to realize benefits from supply chain relationships. Without this incentive, suppliers may keep any improvements realized within their operations quiet while keeping the benefits as well. With time, this lack of information and benefit sharing stunts the growth of relationships within the supply chain and results in lower overall supply chain performance.

More and more, companies are beginning to reward suppliers for their ethical and environmental performance. Companies such as Nike, Unilever, and Nestlé understand the role suppliers play in reducing carbon footprints and enhancing their brands. Nike, at one time, was targeted by ethical activists but today is a leader in managing conditions within the factories making its products. It is one of a growing group of companies going beyond requirements for social audits of factories to look at how its practices can put pressure on other companies to act in a similar fashion.[46] Lately, Walmart has been working to redefine itself as a green company, and doing so has raised its bottom line. Due to its size and retail dominance, Walmart has tremendous influence on its suppliers and is rewarding them with more business based on carbon emission reductions, water conservation, and renewable energy performance.[47]

As many may remember from their childhoods, performance motivation can come in several forms, including punishment and various reward mechanisms. Motivational tools can be used as an integral part of supplier management and supplier development programs. Punishment may take the form of a reduction or elimination of future business, a downgrade of the supplier's status from key to marginal, or a **billback penalty** equal to the costs resulting from a late delivery or poor material quality, for example. On the other hand, when performance meets or exceeds expectations, suppliers can be rewarded in some way.

Many formal strategic supplier agreements allow suppliers to benefit in the following ways:

- A share of the cost reductions resulting from supplier improvements;
- A share of the cost savings resulting from a supplier's suggestions made to the focal firm;

- More business and/or longer contracts for high performance;
- Access to in-house training seminars and other resources; and
- Company and public recognition in the form of awards.

These benefits tend to stimulate further capital investment among suppliers to improve their operating capabilities, leading to even greater levels of quality, service, and environmental, ethical, or cost performance. The U.S. healthcare industry is a good case in point. Hospital costs tend to be escalating rapidly, so hospital managers are beginning to offer incentives to suppliers to keep costs down. The Nebraska Medical Center (NMC) in Omaha, for example, partnered with Cardinal Health, a health-system consulting firm, to explore out-of-the-box options for supply cost reductions. The agreement with NMC provided an incentive of 30 percent of any savings they generated. They created a just-in-time inventory system that improved control and reduced inventory carrying costs. They also assigned several of their employees to work at the NMC facility (recall from the earlier chapter discussion that this is known as supplier co-location). These and other supply strategies saved NMC millions of dollars while allowing them to maintain a 99 percent in-stock performance.[48]

BENCHMARKING SUCCESSFUL SOURCING PRACTICES

Benchmarking, the practice of copying what other businesses do best, is a very effective way to quickly improve sourcing practices and supply chain performance. Without benchmarking, firms must learn through their own experiences the methods and tools that work the best. Benchmarking allows firms to potentially leapfrog the experience-gaining stage by trying things that have worked well for other companies. Meaningful benchmarking data regarding sourcing practices can be obtained in any number of ways, both formal and informal—from using evaluation surveys distributed to a firm's customers and suppliers regarding *their* sourcing and supplier management practices, to discussing sourcing strategies with colleagues at business association meetings or conferences, to collecting published trade information on benchmarking studies.

A large number of resources are available for firms seeking to learn about and implement successful sourcing practices. The Center for Advanced Purchasing Studies (CAPS), an Arizona-based, nonprofit, independent research organization, helps firms achieve competitive advantage by providing leading-edge research information regarding strategic purchasing. For instance, CAPS provides research studies, benchmarking reports, and best practices case studies, along with organizing purchasing symposiums and roundtable discussions for purchasing professionals and academics.[49]

Another organization, the Supply-Chain Council headquartered in Washington, D.C., helps practitioners reduce their supply chain costs and improve customer service by providing their Supply Chain Operations Reference (SCORE) model as a framework for supply chain improvement. They also provide case studies and bring together practitioners to discuss best practices in periodic business conferences around the world.[50]

The Arizona-based Institute for Supply Management (ISM), established in 1915, provides a wide variety of resources to supply management professionals worldwide, including a monthly publication featuring the latest supply management trends and information and the globally recognized Certified Purchasing Manager (CPM), Certified Professional in Supply Management (CPSM), and Accredited Purchasing Practitioner (APP) programs. They also publish the globally recognized *Journal of Supply Chain Management*, organize several annual global supply management conferences, and support many seminars and Web conferences for supply management professionals.[51]

The issue of best purchasing practices has been the subject of a number of research studies over the years, and these findings have proven very beneficial for firms seeking to benchmark best sourcing practices.[52] Some of the research has found a positive relationship between purchasing benchmarking and firm performance. Some of the successful sourcing practices found to be common among the companies studied were:

- use of a central database to access information on parts, suppliers, lead times, and other purchasing information;
- software applications for sharing information with suppliers;
- use of the Internet for supplier searches;
- alliances with key suppliers for specific components;
- supplier certification and the elimination of incoming quality checks for key supplier deliveries;
- involving suppliers in the research and development processes of new products;
- reducing the firm's supply base;
- continuous measurement of supplier performance, and establishing supplier improvement targets; and most recently
- creating an ethical and sustainable supply chain.

ASSESSING AND IMPROVING THE FIRM'S SOURCING FUNCTION

As stated throughout this textbook so far, the sourcing function is one of the most value-enhancing functions in an organization. Today, as purchasing staff members are expected to generate cost savings and service and quality enhancements for the organization, they must be viewed as strategic internal suppliers of the organization. Bearing this in mind, it may then be preferable to periodically monitor the purchasing or sourcing function's performance against set standards, goals, and/or industry benchmarks. Thus, as the firm strives to continuously improve its products and processes, purchasing can also gauge its success in improving its own value-enhancing contributions to the firm and its varied supply chains.

As stated earlier, criteria can be utilized to provide feedback to the purchasing staff regarding their contributions to the strategic goals of the firm. Surveys or audits can be administered as self-assessments among buyers as part of the annual evaluation process, and assessments can also include feedback from internal customers of the supply management or sourcing function, such as engineering, sales, marketing, and finance personnel. Feedback may even be included from supplier representatives. Assessment criteria to evaluate the purchasing department's performance should include some or all of the following:

- participating in and leading multifunctional teams;
- participating in value engineering/value analysis efforts;
- finding and evaluating ethical and sustainable suppliers;
- optimizing the supply base;

- managing and developing local, regional, and global suppliers;
- creating early supplier involvement initiatives;
- creating strategic supplier alliances;
- furthering the integration and development of existing key suppliers;
- contributing to new product development efforts;
- initiating supplier cost reduction programs;
- contributing to the improvement of purchased product and service quality;
- improving time to market; and
- maintaining and improving internal cooperative relationships.

Since these criteria require both qualitative and quantitative assessments, the performance evaluation tool recommended here would be some form of weighted-factor rating method, as covered in Chapter 3. Because of the tremendous potential value of these activities, supply management staff members should be continuously auditing their capabilities and successes in these areas.

Thus, the skill set requirements of purchasing professionals have been changing as purchasing, sourcing, or supply management has evolved from the tactical, clerical function it was about thirty years ago to the highly demanding strategic function it is today. To achieve the type of world-class performance suggested by the preceding assessment criteria, sourcing personnel must today exhibit world-class skills. One recent survey of procurement professionals conducted by *Purchasing* magazine found that their top three responsibilities were negotiating contracts, selecting suppliers, and managing supplier relationships. Given the recent economic downturn, controlling costs is also seen as a very important activity of purchasing personnel. Important cost-controlling activities include reducing the supply base, negotiating global agreements with suppliers, and adopting new technologies suited to purchasing activities.[53]

SUMMARY

Achieving supply chain management success often starts with the sourcing activity. We hope we have provided, in this and previous chapters, evidence of the strategic role played by the sourcing function and the impact of sourcing on the management of the supply chain. Firms that fail to recognize this importance will simply not experience the same level of success in the long run. Two relatively new sourcing topics, ethical and sustainable sourcing, are quickly gaining importance with regards to how firms are choosing to operate. Sourcing personnel are playing an important role today in helping the firm to achieve success in these two areas while maintaining cost, quality, and customer service objectives. The sourcing process is thus comprised of a number of related activities that, when taken together, provide competitive advantage to the firm. Firms can maximize this advantage by developing effective supply chain strategies and then assessing and revising these strategies periodically as missions, markets, competitors, and technologies change. As we head into the internal operations segment of this text, we hope you will continue to consider the sourcing issues discussed and how they interact with other processes as materials, services, and information move down the supply chain toward the immediate customers and, eventually, the end users.

KEY TERMS

benchmarking, 123
billback penalty, 122
business ethics, 106
collaborative negotiations, 121
co-managed inventories, 118
corporate social responsibility (CSR), 106
distributive negotiations, 121
early supplier involvement, 117
ethical and environmental certifications, 115
ethical sourcing, 106
Ethical Trading Initiative (ETI), 107
fair trade products, 107
functional products, 112
green purchasing, 109
innovative products, 112
integrative or win–win negotiations, 121
outsource, 116
purchasing spend, 113
rewarding suppliers, 122
rights and duties, 106
strategic alliance development, 119
strategic sourcing, 105
strategic supplier alliances, 115
supplier co-location, 118
supply base optimization, 115
supply base rationalization, 115
supply base reduction, 115
sustainability, 110
sustainable sourcing, 110
three P's, 110
utilitarianism, 106
value engineering, 117
vendor managed inventory (VMI), 117

DISCUSSION QUESTIONS

1. What is the difference between purchasing and strategic sourcing?
2. What is ethical sourcing, and why would firms do it?
3. What are some common practices or activities of ethical sourcing?
4. What are some of the risks of ethical sourcing? How about the potential advantages? Do you think ethical sourcing is a good practice?
5. What is a fair trade product? Could farmers in the U.S. make fair trade products?
6. What is sustainable sourcing, and how does it differ from ethical sourcing? From green purchasing?

7. What are the benefits of sustainable sourcing? Can firms actually make money from sustainable sourcing? Do you think it is a good practice?
8. What are the three P's? What do they have to do with sustainability?
9. Describe some sustainable and ethical things your university is doing.
10. Where do ethical and sustainable sourcing policies come from in an organization?
11. What are innovative and functional products? Can firms buy functional products in an ethical way? A sustainable way? What about innovative products?
12. What are the benefits of obtaining ethical and sustainable certifications? Why would a buyer want its suppliers to have these certifications?
13. What advantages do company-designed supplier certification programs have over industry certifications like ISO 9000?
14. What is supply base rationalization, and what are its advantages and disadvantages?
15. What is outsourcing? How is it different from plain ol' purchasing? Would a firm ever want to outsource a core product or process? Why or why not?
16. When would firms want to insource a product or process?
17. Do companies outsource for ethical or sustainable reasons? If so, provide some examples.
18. What is sourcing's role in value engineering, and what benefits does this give to the firm?
19. Why is early supplier involvement a good way to integrate the supply chain?
20. Describe the differences between vendor-managed inventories and co-managed inventories, and when it might be advisable to do either of them.
21. Discuss the advantages and risks of supplier co-location.
22. What is the difference between supplier management and strategic alliance development?
23. What makes supplier alliances fail? How can firms reduce the failure rate?
24. Describe the differences between integrative and distributive negotiations, and when each should be used.
25. Why are second- and third-tier suppliers important to the focal firm?
26. What is a common method for developing second-tier suppliers?
27. **Discussion Problem:** If your firm had 500 suppliers and they each had 100 suppliers, how many second-tier suppliers would your firm have? What if your firm reduced its supply base to twenty?
28. What are some typical supplier rewards and punishments that a buyer could use? If you work for a company, describe how it rewards and punishes its suppliers. Do you think appropriate methods are being used? Why or why not?
29. What is benchmarking? What are some different ways you could use benchmarking to improve your performance at school?

30. Why would a firm want to monitor its own purchasing performance?

31. How could a company use benchmarking and performance measurement to improve its ethical and sustainable purchasing practices?

ESSAY/PROJECT QUESTIONS

1. Go to the International Organization for Standardization website (www.iso.ch), and write a short description and history of the organization, including the various certifications that can be obtained.

2. Go to the CAPS website (www.capsresearch.org), and find the latest cross-industry benchmarking report and determine the overall purchase dollars as a percentage of sales in the U.S. What benchmarking research is CAPS doing now?

3. Go to the Fair Factories Clearinghouse website (www.fairfactories.org), and describe the organization, along with some of the current events underway.

4. Go to the Goldman Environmental Prize website, and describe the most recent award winners.

5. What is an ASP? Find some on the Internet that are not listed in the chapter, and describe what they do.

6. Gather information on business ethics and ethical purchasing, and report on several of the most current news items and controversies.

ADDITIONAL READINGS

Anderson, M., and P. Katz. "Strategic Sourcing," *International Journal of Logistics Management* 9(1), 1998: 1–13.

Burt, D., D. Dobler, and S. Starling. *World Class Supply Management: The Key to Supply Chain Management*. 7th ed. New York: McGraw-Hill/Irwin, 2003.

Kaplan, N., and J. Hurd. "Realizing the Promise of Partnerships." *Journal of Business Strategy* 23(3), 2002: 38–42.

Lummus, R., R. Vokurka, and K. Alber. "Strategic Supply Chain Planning." *Production and Inventory Management Journal* 39(3), 1998: 49–58.

Simchi-Levi, D., P. Kaminsky, and E. Simchi-Levi. *Designing and Managing the Supply Chain: Concepts, Strategies, and Case Studies*. 2nd ed. New York: McGraw-Hill/Irwin, 2003.

Vonderembse, M. "The Impact of Supplier Selection Criteria and Supplier Involvement on Manufacturing," *Journal of Supply Chain Management* 35(3), 1999: 33–39.

ENDNOTES

1. Anonymous, "Green Mountain Coffee Roasters, Inc.—Great Coffee, Good Vibes, Pass It On," *Economics Week*, October 19, 2012: 532.

2. Sullivan, D., "Philadelphia Strives for Green Initiatives," *BioCycle* 52(2), 2011: 22–28.

3. Hannon, D. "Supply Chain Chief Drives Collaboration," *Purchasing* 139(4), 2010: 52–53.

4. Smith, T., "Two Sides of the Coin," *Journal of Investing* 20(3), 2011: 103–107.

5. Worthington, I., M. Ram, H. Boyal, and M. Shah, "Researching the Drivers of Socially Responsible Purchasing: A Cross-National Study of Supplier Diversity Initiatives," *Journal of Business Ethics* 79(3), 2008: 319–331.

6. Berthiaume, D., "Reebok's Sourcing Strategy Places Ethics First," *Chain Store Age*, January 2006: 32A.

7. Boggan, S., "Nike Admits Mistakes Over Child Labor," *Independent/UK*, October 20, 2001: found online at www.independent.co.uk; Levenson, E., "Citizen Nike," *CNNMoney.com*, November 17, 2008: found online at www.cnnmoney.com/2008

8. Coleman, F., "In Search of Ethical Sourcing," *Directorship* 33(2), 2007: 38–39; Cooper, B., "Perspectives on the Ethical Sourcing Debate in the Clothing Industry," *Just-Style*, November 2007: 21.

9. Murray, S., "Confusion Reigns over Labeling Fair Trade Products," *Financial Times*, June 13, 2006: 2. Also see http://www.fairtrade.net, http://www.wfto.com

10. Allen, B., "In Pursuit of Responsible Procurement," *Summit* 9(4), 2006: 7.

11. Anonymous, "Fair Trade USA—Mainstream Consumers Drive Fair Trade Certified Sales Up 24 Percent," *Economics Week*, March 25, 2011: 658.

12. Tighe, C., "Rubber Gloves Form Next Fair Trade," *Financial Times*, April 13, 2009: 17.

13. "Global Fairtrade Certified Sales Grow by 12% to $6.6 Billion in 2011," July 18, 2012. Found at www.fairtraderesource.org/2012/07/18/global-fairtrade-certified-sales-grow-12-to-6-6b-in-2011/

14. For more information, see the Goldman Environmental Prize webpage: www.goldmanprize.org and also www.nobelprize.org

15. See, for example, Androich, A., "Get Your Green On," *RealScreen*, July/August 2007: 14; Watson, T., "Environmental Pioneer Dies," *USA Today*, November 7, 2000: 24A.

16. To visit the Institute for Supply Management website, go to www.ism.ws

17. Turner, M., and P. Houston, "Going Green? Start with Sourcing," *Supply Chain Management Review* 13(2), 2009: 14–20.

18. Bird, C., "Making Sustainability Happen," *Government Finance Review* 27(5), 2011: 55–57.

19. Pinchot, G., *The Conservation of Natural Resources*. Washington DC: U.S. Dept. of Agriculture, 1908. (Farmers' Bulletin, 327) NAL Call no.: 1 Ag84F no.327; also see Beatley, T., "Sustainability 3.0 Building Tomorrow's Earth-Friendly Communities," *Planning* 75(5), 2009: 16–22.

20. Gelinas, T., "Sustainability on the Retail Level," *Fleet Equipment* 38(4), 2012: 4.

21. Anonymous, "Getting Leaner—Ahead of the Pack: Suppliers Adjust to New Packaging Priorities," *Retailing Today*, Fourth Quarter 2006: 16.

22. Mulani, N., "Sustainable Sourcing: Do Good While Doing Well," *Logistics Management* 47(7), 2008: 25–26.

23. Ibid.

24. Anonymous, "Brave New Chocolate," *Candy Industry* 178(1), 2013: 50–55.

25. Anonymous, "China Treats Sustainability and Economic Growth as Complementary, not Conflicting, Goals," *Economics Week*, March 2, 2012: 585.

26. Kuranko, C., "The Green Standard," *The American City & County* 123(9), 2008: 40–43.

27. Bird, C., "Making Sustainability Happen," *Government Finance Review* 27(5), 2011: 55–57.

28. Bridgestone Americas Media Center, "Bridgestone Releases Earth Day 2013 Consumer Recycling and Sustainability Survey Findings," found at http://www.bridgestoneamericasmedia.com/2013-04-22-Bridgestone-Releases-Earth-Day-2013-Consumer-Recycling-and-Sustainability-Survey-Findings

29. Fisher, M. "What Is the Right Supply Chain for Your Product?" *Harvard Business Review* 75(2), 1997: 105–116.

30. Reeve, T., and J. Steinhausen, "Sustainable Suppliers, Sustainable Markets," *CMA Management* 81(2), 2007: 30–33.

31. Murphy, A., C. Satterthwaite, D. Grounsell, and M. Chandra, "As the Recession Eases Should Sustainability Become a Priority?" *Marketing*, October 14, 2009: 24.

32. The interested reader is invited to navigate the ISO website: www.iso.org

33. Alpert, B., "Do-Gooders Who Could Do Better," *Barron's* 87(46), 2007: 40–41.

34. Anonymous, "Integrity Interactive Corporation, New Integrity Interactive Service," *Business & Finance Week*, April 14, 2008: 195.

35. Jeffries, E., "Setting Standards on Carbon," *Supply Management* 17(3), 2012: 44–46.

36. Andel, T., "Sustainability's Chain Reaction," *Material Handling & Logistics*, April 15, 2013: 1.

37. Sulliovan, R., "The Devastating Cost of Cheap Outsourcing," *FT.com*, June 16, 2013: 1.

38. Pratt, M., "Ethical Outsourcing," *Computerworld* 42(17), 2008: 32–33.

39. Atkinson, W., "Novellus Realizes Benefits of Early Supplier Involvement," *Purchasing* 137(4), 2008: 15.

40. Partida, B., "Should You Manage Customer Inventory?" *Supply Chain Management Review* 17(3), 2013: 70–72.

41. Shister, N., "Applying the Ideas of the Wal-Marts of the World to Smaller Companies," *World Trade* 19(3), 2006: 26–29.

42. Anonymous, "Computers, Software: Datalliance Expands Staff to Support Growth in VMI," *Marketing Weekly News*, May 19, 2012: 509.

43. Atkinson, W., "Does JIT II Still Work in the Internet Age?" *Purchasing* 130(17), 2001: 41–42.

44. "Chrysler Embarks on 'Most Advanced Supplier Colocation Project,'" *MSI* 22(11), 2004: 48; Kelly, K., and B. Visnic, "A New Relationship," *Ward's Auto World* 40(9), 2004: 37–38.

45. Anonymous, "Rayovac and Six Flags Announce Strategic Alliance," *Marketing Weekly News*, September 11, 2010: 805.

46. Murray, S., "Commercial Approach Can Help Fill the Gap," *FT.com*, June 19, 2012: 1.

47. Anonymous, "Social Sciences," *Library Journal* 136(7), 2011: 1.

48. Fosdick, G., and M. Uphoff, "Adopting Cross-Industry Best Practices for Measurable Results," *Healthcare Executive* 22(3), 2007: 14–19.

49. See http://www.capsresearch.org for more information.

50. See http://supply-chain.org for more information.

51. See http://www.ism.ws for more information.

52. See, for instance, Andersen, B., T. Fagerhaug, S. Randmael, J. Schuldmaier, and J. Prenninger, "Benchmarking Supply Chain Management: Finding Best Practices," *Journal of Business and Industrial Marketing* 14(5/6), 1999: 378–389; Carr, A., and L. Smeltzer, "The Relationship Among Purchasing Benchmarking, Strategic Purchasing, Firm Performance, and Firm Size," *Journal of Supply Chain Management* 35(4), 1999: 51–60; Ellram, L., G. Zsidisin, S. Siferd, and M. Stanly, "The Impact of Purchasing and Supply Management on Corporate Success," *Journal of Supply Chain Management* 38(1), 2002: 4–17; and Krause, D., S. Vachon, and R. Klassen, "Special Topic Forum on Sustainable Supply Chain Management," *Journal of Supply Chain Management* 45(4), 2009: 18–25.

53. Avery, S., "Today's Travel Procurement Professional Knows How to Manage Supplier Relationships," *Purchasing* 138(2), 2009: 54.

PART 3

Operations Issues in Supply Chain Management

Chapter 5
DEMAND FORECASTING

The key to making a good forecast is not in limiting yourself to quantitative information.

— ***Nate Silver, statistician and founder of the*** **New York Times** ***political blog FiveThirtyEight.com***[1]

Leading organizations widely acknowledge that forecasting is at the heart of the performance management process, and is potentially a significant driver of business value and investor confidence—a view this research confirms.

— ***Scott Parker, Head of Financial Management, KPMG International***[2]

Learning Objectives

After completing this chapter, you should be able to

- Explain the role of demand forecasting in a supply chain.
- Identify the components of a forecast.
- Compare and contrast qualitative and quantitative forecasting techniques.
- Calculate and apply the quantitative forecasting techniques.
- Assess the accuracy and interpret the results of forecasts.
- Explain collaborative planning, forecasting, and replenishment.

Chapter Outline

The ISM Report on Business

The Institute of Supply Management (ISM), formerly known as the National Association of Purchasing Management (NAPM), surveys supply management professionals participating on the Business Survey Committee comprised of more than 300 purchasing and supply executives, seeking information on "changes in production, new orders, new export orders, imports, employment, inventories, prices, lead times, and the timeliness of supplier deliveries in their companies, comparing the current month to the previous month." The *ISM Report on Business*, available the first business day of each month, is considered to be an accurate indicator of the overall direction of the economy and the health of the manufacturing and nonmanufacturing sectors. Three quotes regarding the value of the report follow:[3]

> *I find the surveys conducted by the purchasing and supply managers to be an excellent supplement to the data supplied by various departments and agencies of the government.*
>
> —Alan Greenspan, former Chairman of the Federal Reserve Board

> *The ISM Manufacturing Report on Business has one of the shortest reporting lags of any macro-economic series and gives an important early look at the economy. It also measures some concepts (such as lead times and delivery lags) that can be found nowhere else. It makes an important contribution to the American statistical system and to economic policy.*
>
> —Joseph E. Stiglitz, former Chairman of President Clinton's Council of Economic Advisors

> *The ISM Manufacturing Report on Business is extremely useful. The PMI, the Report's composite index, gives the earliest indication each month of the health of the manufacturing sector. It is an essential component for assessing the state of the economy.*
>
> —Michael J. Boskin, Hoover Institute Senior Fellow

The ISM report provides several indices for the manufacturing sector: New Orders, Production, Employment, Supplier Deliveries, Inventories, Customers' Inventories, Prices, Backlog of Orders, Exports, and Imports. The most important index is the Purchasing Managers Index (PMI) developed by Theodore Torda, Senior Economist of the U.S. Department of Commerce, and introduced in 1982. The PMI is a composite of five weighted seasonally adjusted indices (weights are shown in parentheses): New Orders (0.20), Production (0.20), Employment (0.20), Supplier Deliveries (0.20), and Inventories (0.20). A reading below 50 represents contraction, and a reading over 50 indicates growth or expansion in the manufacturing sector of the economy compared to the previous month. The purchasing surveys provide comprehensive information for tracking the economy and developing business forecasts. In January 2008, ISM started computing a composite index for the nonmanufacturing sector. The NMI (Non-Manufacturing Index) is based on four equally weighted indicators: Business Activity (seasonally adjusted), New Orders (seasonally adjusted), Employment (Seasonally adjusted), and Inventories. A NMI index over 50 represents growth or expansion for the nonmanufacturing sector of the economy compared with the previous month, and a reading under 50 indicates contraction.[4] Purchasing and supply executives use the report in a variety of ways. For example, the Customers' Inventories Index is a strong indicator of future new orders and production and is used to measure changes in supply chain activity.

INTRODUCTION

Much has been written about demand-driven supply chains. In today's competitive environment, organizations are moving to a more effective demand-driven supply chain to enable them to respond quickly to shifting demand. Consumers are now more demanding and discriminating. The market has evolved into a "pull" environment with customers dictating to the supplier what products they desire and when they need them delivered. If a retailer cannot get the product it wants at the right quantity, price, and time from one supplier, it will look for another company that can meet its demands. Any temporary stockout has a tremendous potential downside on sales, profitability, and customer relationships.

There are several ways to closely match supply and demand. One way is for a supplier to hold plenty of stock available for delivery at any time. While this approach maximizes sales revenues, it is also expensive because of the cost of carrying inventory and the possibility of write-downs at the end of the selling season. Use of flexible pricing is another approach. During heavy demand periods, prices can be raised to reduce peak demand. Price discounts can then be used to increase sales during periods with excess inventory or slow demand. This strategy can still result in lost sales, though, as well as stockouts, and thus cannot be considered an ideal or partnership-friendly approach to satisfying demand. In the short term, companies can also use overtime, subcontracting, or temporary workers to increase capacity to meet demand for their products and services. In the interim, however, firms will lose sales as they train workers, and quality may also tend to suffer.

Managing demand is challenging because of the difficulty in forecasting future consumer requirements accurately. In order for supply chain integration to be successful, suppliers must be able to accurately forecast demand so they can produce and deliver the right quantities demanded by their customers in a timely and cost-effective fashion. Thus, it is imperative that suppliers along the supply chain find ways to better match supply and demand to achieve optimal levels of cost, quality, and customer service to enable them to compete with other supply chains. Any problems that adversely affect the timely delivery of products demanded by consumers will have ramifications throughout the supply chain.

Zara Espana, S.A., a Spanish clothing and accessories retailer, is a giant player in the fashion industry with a major advantage over its competitors due to its fast response time. The typical lead time in the fashion industry from new product design to availability at the store is six months but Zara is able to do it in two weeks.[5] Product life cycles in the fashion industry are short and so is the selling season. Their tight integration of design, planning, and production enables Zara to respond quickly to market needs. Since its lead time for new product introduction is only two weeks, Zara in effect has to be able to forecast demand just two weeks in advance. The flow of current information among customers, store managers, market specialists, designers, and production staff also mitigates the bullwhip effect (which tends to result in higher safety stock levels). Zara is thus able to avoid overproduction and heavy discounting common in the fast fashion industry.

THE IMPORTANCE OF DEMAND FORECASTING

Forecasting is an important element of demand management. It provides an estimate of future demand and the basis for planning and sound business decisions. Since all organizations deal with an unknown future, some error between a forecast and actual demand is to be expected. Thus, the goal of a good forecasting technique is to minimize the deviation between actual demand and the forecast. Since a forecast is a prediction of the future, factors that influence demand, the impact of these factors, and whether they will continue to influence future demand must be considered in developing an accurate forecast. In addition, buyers and sellers should share all relevant information to generate a single consensus forecast so that the correct decisions on supply and demand can be made. Improved forecasts benefit not only the focal company but also the trading partners in the supply chain. Having accurate demand forecasts allows the purchasing department to order the right amount of parts and materials, the operations department to produce the right amount of products, and the logistics department to deliver a correctly sized order. Thus, timely and accurate demand information is a critical component of an effective supply chain. Inaccurate forecasts would lead to imbalances in supply and demand. In today's competitive business environment, collaboration (or cooperation and information sharing) between buyers and sellers is the rule rather than the exception. The benefits of better forecasts are lower inventories, reduced stockouts, smoother production plans, reduced costs, and improved customer service.

As discussed in the chapter-opening SCM Profile, the Institute of Supply Management (ISM) has been publishing monthly the Manufacturing ISM *Report on Business* since 1931, except for a four-year interruption during World War II. The indices for the manufacturing sector include New Orders, Production, Manufacturing Employment, Supplier Deliveries, Inventories, Customers' Inventories, Prices, Backlog of Orders, Exports, and Imports. Many business executives use these indices to forecast the overall direction of the economy and the health of the manufacturing sector. For example, purchasing and supply managers utilize the Customers' Inventories Index to help forecast future new orders and make production decisions and to measure changes in supply chain activity. The *Wall Street Journal* publishes the *ISM Report on Business*, which includes both the manufacturing and nonmanufacturing sectors.

Many have argued that demand forecasting is both an art and a science. Since there are no accurate crystal balls available, it is impossible to expect 100 percent forecast accuracy at all times. The impact of poor communication and inaccurate forecasts resonates all along the supply chain and results in the *bullwhip effect* (described in Chapter 1) causing stockouts, lost sales, high costs of inventory and obsolescence, material shortages, poor responsiveness to market dynamics, and poor profitability. Numerous examples exist showing the problems that companies faced when their sales forecasts did not match customer demands during new product introductions. For instance, Nintendo's Wii, which was introduced at about the same time as Sony's PlayStation 3 (PS3), had exceeded all expectations and outsold Sony by a huge margin. Nintendo consequently struggled to meet the unexpectedly high demand for Wiis. Another example is Apple, which for the first time had introduced two iPhone models simultaneously (the high-end 5s and the plastic 5c), in September 2013. In the first three days of the product launch in eleven countries including China, Apple sold 9 million new iPhones. Due to the high order rate, Apple ran out of stock and was forced to delay the delivery of the phones by a month.[6] Analysts had previously forecasted sales of approximately 6 million units. This indicates the challenge faced by companies in forecasting sales, ramping up production to meet the demand for their products, and defending their market position.

FORECASTING TECHNIQUES

Understanding that a forecast is very often inaccurate does not mean that nothing can be done to improve the forecast. Both quantitative and qualitative forecasts can be improved by seeking inputs from trading partners. **Qualitative forecasting methods** are based on opinions and intuition, whereas **quantitative forecasting methods** use mathematical models and relevant historical data to generate forecasts. The quantitative methods can be divided into two groups: time series and associative models.

Qualitative Methods

Qualitative forecasting methods are based on intuition or judgmental evaluation and are generally used when data is limited, unavailable, or not currently relevant. This approach can vary widely in cost, and accuracies depend to a large extent on the skill and experience of the forecaster(s) and the amount of relevant information, time, and money available. Specifically, qualitative techniques are used to develop long-range projections when current data is no longer very reliable, and for new product introductions when current data simply does not exist. Discussions of four common qualitative forecasting models follow.

Jury of Executive Opinion

A group of the firm's senior management executives who are knowledgeable about their markets, their competitors, and the business environment collectively develop the forecast. This technique has the advantage of several individuals with considerable experience working together, but if one member's views dominate the discussion, then the value and reliability of the outcome can be diminished. This technique is applicable for long-range planning and new product introductions, but is also commonly used for general demand forecasting. A survey of commercial banks in the U.S., for example, found that most banks preferred this type of forecasting, for medium-term forecasts.[7]

Delphi Method

The Delphi method was first developed by Project RAND in the late 1950s and can be used for a wide range of applications, including forecasting. A group of internal and external experts are surveyed during several rounds in terms of future events and long-term forecasts of demand, in hopes of converging on a consensus forecast. Group members do not physically meet and thus avoid the scenario where one or a few experts could dominate a discussion. The answers from the experts are accumulated after each round of the survey and summarized. The summary of responses is then sent out to all the experts in the next round, wherein individual experts can modify their responses based on the group's response summary. This iterative process continues until a consensus is reached. The process can be both time-consuming and very expensive. This approach is applicable for high-risk technology forecasting; large, expensive projects; or major new product introductions. Ultimately, the value of a Delphi forecast is dependent upon the qualifications of the expert participants. Additionally, studies of Delphi technique usage have found that the number of experts can vary widely, depending on the circumstances, the available time, and the number of experts available.[8]

Sales Force Composite

The sales force represents a good source of market information. This type of forecast is generated based on the sales force's knowledge of the market and estimates of customer needs. Due to the proximity of the sales personnel to the consumers, the forecast tends to be reliable, but individual biases could negatively impact the effectiveness of this approach. For example, if bonuses are paid when actual sales exceed the forecast, there is a tendency for the sales force to under-forecast.

Customer Surveys

A forecasting questionnaire can be developed that uses inputs from customers on important issues such as future purchasing needs, new product ideas, and opinions about existing or new products. The survey can be administered through telephone, mail, Internet, or personal interviews. The data collected from these surveys is then analyzed, and forecasts are developed from the results. When Google, for example, wanted to partner in 2010 with Sony, Logitech, and Intel to produce a set-top box version of Google TV, it needed an idea of how much it could potentially charge for the device. Dish Network performed a customer survey to find out the potential price, and they forecasted a price of between $200 and $300.[9]

Quantitative Methods

Quantitative forecasting models use mathematical techniques that are based on historical data and can include causal variables to forecast demand. **Time series forecasting** is based on the assumption that the future is an extension of the past; thus, historical data can be used to predict future demand. **Cause-and-effect forecasting** assumes that one or more factors (independent variables) are related to demand and, therefore, can be used to predict future demand.

Since these forecasts rely solely on past demand data, all quantitative methods become less accurate as the forecast's time horizon increases. Thus, for long-time horizon forecasts, it is generally recommended to utilize a combination of both quantitative and qualitative techniques.

Components of a Time Series

A time series typically has four components: trend, cyclical, seasonal, and random variations:

- *Trend Variations*: Trends represent either increasing or decreasing movements over many years and are due to factors such as population growth, population shifts, cultural changes, and income shifts. Common trend lines are linear, S-curve, exponential, or asymptotic.
- *Cyclical Variations*: Cyclical variations are wavelike movements that are longer than a year and are influenced by macroeconomic and political factors. One example is the **business cycle** (recessions or expansions that tend to occur every eight or ten years). Recent business cycles in the U.S. have been affected by global events such as the 1991 Mexican financial crisis; the 1997 Asian economic crisis; the September 11, 2001, terrorist attacks in the U.S.; hurricanes Katrina and Rita in 2005; and the 2011 Japanese Tohoku earthquake and tsunami.
- *Seasonal Variations*: Seasonal variations show peaks and valleys that repeat over a consistent interval such as hours, days, weeks, months, years, or seasons. Due to seasonality, many companies do well in certain months and not so well in other months. For example, snow blower sales tend to be higher in the fall and winter but taper off in the spring and summer. A fast-food restaurant will see higher sales during the day around breakfast, lunch, and dinner. U.S. hotels experience large crowds during traditional holidays such as July 4, Labor Day, Thanksgiving, Christmas, and New Years.
- *Random Variations*: Random variations are due to unexpected or unpredictable events such as natural disasters (hurricanes, tornadoes, fire), strikes, and wars. An example is the recent eruption at Iceland's Eyjafjallajökull volcano, which caused ash clouds to reach mainland Europe. Numerous flights to England and Europe were shut down, which led to the highest air travel disruption since the World War II.[10] Another natural disaster is the earthquake of magnitude

7.0 that hit Haiti in 2010. The Haitian government reported that 250,000 residences and 30,000 commercial buildings were badly damaged; 230,000 people died, 300,000 were injured, and 1,000,000 were made homeless as a result of the earthquake.[11]

Time Series Forecasting Models

As discussed earlier, time series forecasts are dependent on the availability of historical data. Forecasts are estimated by extrapolating the past data into the future. A survey[12] of forecasting models used shows that time series models are the most widely used (72 percent), and judgmental models are the least used (11 percent). The study also finds that within the time series models, the ones most commonly used are the simple models (averages and simple trend) and exponential smoothing. In general, demand forecasts are used in planning for procurement, supply, replenishment, and corporate revenue.

Some of the more common time series approaches such as naïve forecast, simple moving average, weighted moving average, and exponential smoothing are discussed next.

Naïve Forecast

Using the **naïve forecast**, the estimate for the next period is equal to the actual demand for the immediate past period. The formula is:

$$F_{t+1} = A_t$$

where F_{t+1} = forecast for period $t + 1$

A_t = actual demand for period t.

For example, if the current period's actual demand is 100 units, then the next period's forecast is 100 units. This method is inexpensive to understand, develop, store data for, and operate. However, there is no consideration of causal relationships, and the method may not generate accurate forecasts. Many economic and business series are considered good candidates for using the naïve forecast because the series behave like random walks.

Simple Moving Average Forecast

The **simple moving average forecast** uses historical data to generate a forecast and works well when the demand is fairly stable over time. The formula for the n-period moving average forecast is shown below:

$$F_{t+1} = \frac{\sum_{i=t-n+1}^{t} A_i}{n}$$

where F_{t+1} = forecast for period $t + 1$

n = number of periods used to calculate moving average

A_i = actual demand in period i

When n equals 1, the simple moving average forecast is the naïve forecast. The average tends to be more responsive if fewer data points are used to compute the average. However, random events can also impact the average adversely. Thus, the decision maker must balance the cost of responding slowly to changes versus the cost of responding to random variations. The advantage of this technique is that it is simple to use and easy to understand. A weakness of the simple moving average method is its inability to respond to trend changes quickly. Example 5.1 illustrates the simple moving average forecast.

Example 5.1 Simple Moving Average Forecasting

PERIOD	ACTUAL DEMAND
1	1600
2	2200
3	2000
4	1600
5	2500
6	3500
7	3300
8	3200
9	3900
10	4700
11	4300
12	4400

Using the data provided, calculate the forecast for period 5 using a four-period simple moving average.

SOLUTION

$$F_5 = \text{forecast for period 5} = \frac{1600 + 2200 + 2000 + 1600}{4} = 1850$$

An Excel spreadsheet solution is shown in Figure 5.1.

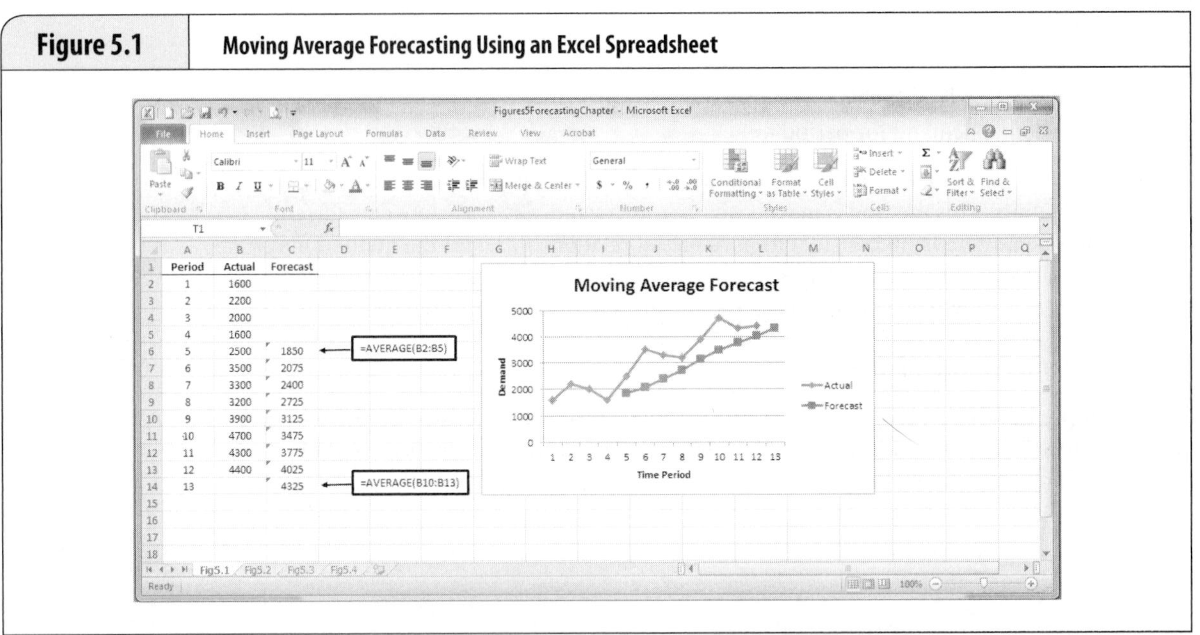

Figure 5.1 Moving Average Forecasting Using an Excel Spreadsheet

Weighted Moving Average Forecast

The simple moving average forecast places equal weights $(1/n)$ on each of the n-period observations. Under some circumstances, a forecaster may decide that equal weighting is undesirable. An n-period weighted moving average forecast is the weighted average of the n-period observations, using unequal weights. The only restriction is that the weights should be nonnegative and sum to 1. The formula for the n-period weighted moving average forecast is shown below:

$$F_{t+1} = \sum_{i=t-n+1}^{t} w_i A_i$$

where F_{t+1} = forecast for period $t+1$;

n = number of periods used in determining the moving average;

A_i = actual demand in period i;

w_i = weight assigned to period i; $\Sigma w_i = 1$.

For example, the three-period weighted moving average forecast with weights (0.5, 0.3, 0.2) is

$$F_t = 0.5\,A_{t-1} + 0.3\,A_{t-2} + 0.2\,A_{t-3}.$$

Note that generally a greater emphasis (and thus the highest weight) is placed on the most recent observation and, hence, the forecast would react more rapidly than the three-period simple moving average forecast. However, the forecaster may instead wish to apply the smallest weight to the most recent data such that the forecast would be less affected by abrupt changes in recent data. The weights used thus tend to be based on the experience of the forecaster, and this is one of the advantages of this forecasting method. Although the forecast is more responsive to underlying changes in demand, it still lags demand because of the averaging effect. As such, the weighted moving average method does not do a good job of tracking trend changes in the data. Example 5.2 illustrates the weighted moving average forecast.

Example 5.2 Weighted Moving Average Forecasting

Based on data provided in Example 5.1, calculate the forecast for period 5 using a four-period weighted moving average. The weights of 0.4, 0.3, 0.2, and 0.1 are assigned to the most recent, second most recent, third most recent, and fourth most recent periods, respectively.

SOLUTION

$$F_5 = 0.1(1600) + 0.2(2200) + 0.3(2000) + 0.4(1600) = 1840$$

An Excel spreadsheet solution is shown in Figure 5.2.

Figure 5.2 Weighted Moving Average Forecasting Using an Excel Spreadsheet

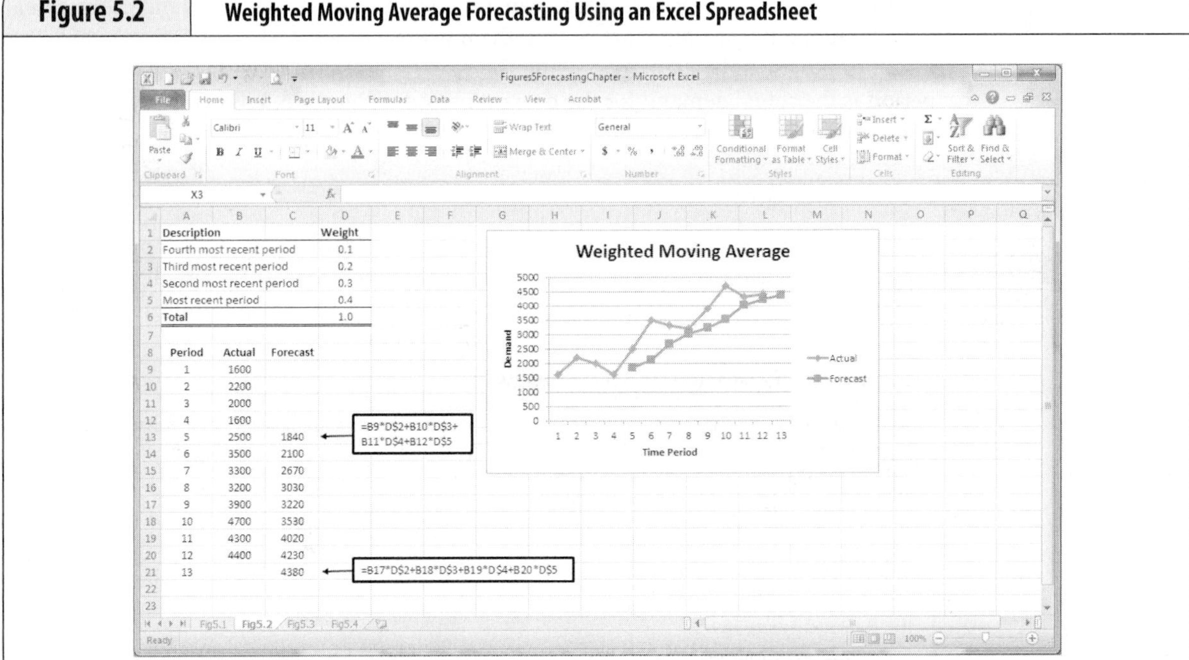

Exponential Smoothing Forecast

Exponential smoothing is a sophisticated weighted moving average forecasting technique in which the forecast for the next period's demand is the current period's forecast adjusted by a fraction of the difference between the current period's actual demand and forecast. This approach requires less data than the weighted moving average method because only two data points are needed. Due to its simplicity and minimal data requirement, exponential smoothing is one of the more widely used forecasting techniques. This model, like the other time series models, is suitable for data that shows little trend or seasonal patterns. Other higher-order exponential smoothing models (which are not covered here) can be used for data exhibiting trend and seasonality. The exponential smoothing forecasting formula is:

$$F_{t+1} = F_t + \alpha (A_t - F_t)$$

or

$$F_{t+1} = \alpha A_t + (1 - \alpha)F_t$$

where F_{t+1} = forecast for period $t + 1$;
F_t = forecast for period t;
A_t = actual demand for period t;
α = smoothing constant $(0 \leq \alpha \leq 1)$

The exponential smoothing forecast is equivalent to the naïve forecast when α is equal to 1. With an α value closer to 1, there is a greater emphasis on recent data resulting in a major adjustment of the error in the last period's forecast. Thus with a high α value, the model is more responsive to changes in the recent demand. When α has a low value, more weight is placed on past demand (which is contained in the previous forecast), and the model responds slower to changes in demand. The impact of using a small or large value of α is similar to the effect of using a large or small number of observations in calculating the moving average. In general, the forecast will lag any trend in the actual data because only partial adjustment to the most recent forecast error can be made. The initial forecast can be estimated using the naïve method, that is, the forecast for next period is the actual demand for the current period. Example 5.3 illustrates the exponential smoothing forecast.

Linear Trend Forecast

A **linear trend forecast** can be estimated using simple linear regression to fit a line to a series of data occurring over time. This model is also referred to as the simple trend model. The trend line is determined using the least squares method, which minimizes the sum of

Example 5.3 Exponential Smoothing Forecasting

Based on data provided in Example 5.1, calculate the forecast for period 3 using the exponential smoothing method. Assume the forecast for period 2 is 1600. Use a smoothing constant (α) value of 0.3.

SOLUTION

Given: $F_2 = 1600$, $\alpha = 0.3$

$$F_{t+1} = F_t + \alpha(A_t - F_t)$$

$$F_3 = F_2 + \alpha(A_2 - F_2) = 1600 + 0.3(2200 - 1600) = 1780$$

Thus, the forecast for week 3 is 1780.

An Excel spreadsheet solution is shown in Figure 5.3.

Figure 5.3 **Exponential Smoothing Forecasting Using an Excel Spreadsheet**

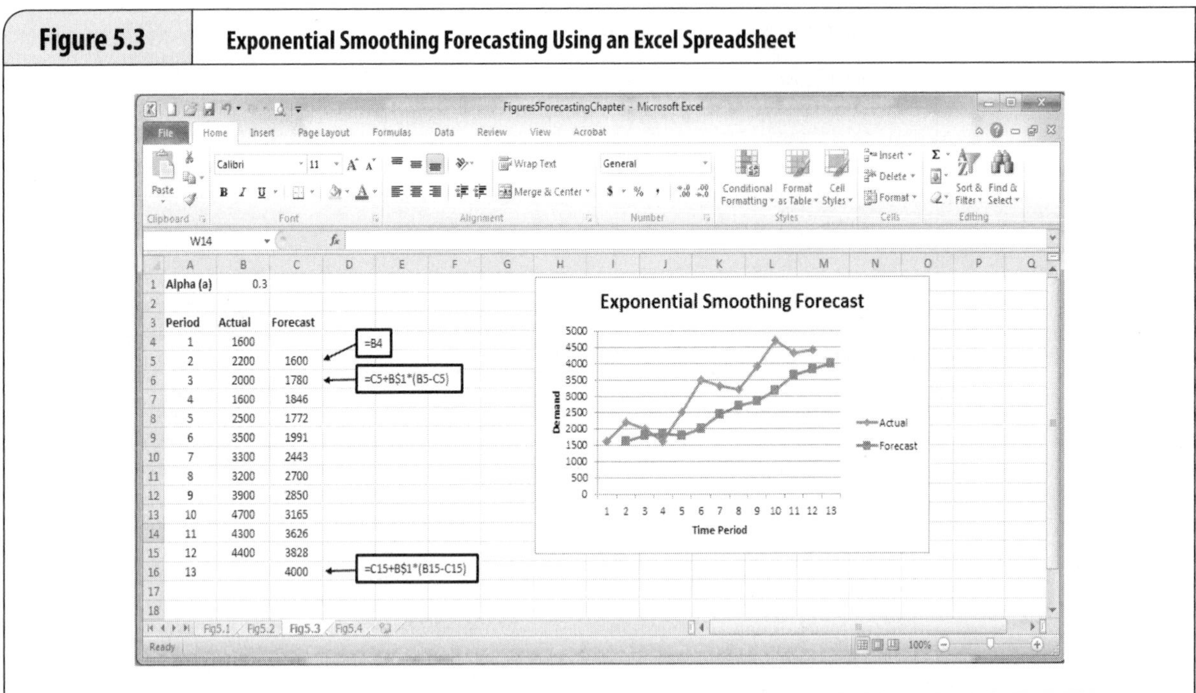

the squared deviations to determine the characteristics of the linear equation. The trend line equation is expressed as:

$$\hat{Y} = b_0 + b_1 x$$

Where $\hat{Y}$ = forecast or dependent variable

x = time variable

b_0 = intercept of the vertical axis

b_1 = slope of the trend line

The coefficients b_0 and b_1 are calculated as follows:

$$b_1 = \frac{n\sum(xy) - \sum x \sum y}{n\sum x^2 - (\sum x)^2}$$

$$b_0 = \frac{\sum y - b_1 \sum x}{n}$$

where x = independent variable values

y = dependent variable values

n = number of observations

Example 5.4 illustrates the linear trend forecast.

Cause-and-Effect Models

The cause-and-effect models have a cause (independent variable or variables) and an effect (dependent variable). One of the more common models used is regression analysis. In demand forecasting, the external variables that are related to demand are first identified.

Example 5.4 Linear Trend Forecast

The demand for toys produced by the Miki Manufacturing Company is shown in the table below.

PERIOD	DEMAND	PERIOD	DEMAND	PERIOD	DEMAND
1	1600	5	2500	9	3900
2	2200	6	3500	10	4700
3	2000	7	3300	11	4300
4	1600	8	3200	12	4400

The company desires to know the trend line and the forecast for period 13.

SOLUTION

PERIOD (*X*)	DEMAND (*Y*)	X^2	*XY*
1	1600	1	1600
2	2200	4	4400
3	2000	9	6000
4	1600	16	6400
5	2500	25	12500
6	3500	36	21000
7	3300	49	23100
8	3200	64	25600
9	3900	81	35100
10	4700	100	47000
11	4300	121	47300
12	4400	144	52800
$\Sigma x = 78$	$\Sigma y = 37200$	$\Sigma x^2 = 650$	$\Sigma xy = 282800$

$$b_1 = \frac{n\Sigma(xy) - \Sigma x \Sigma y}{n\Sigma x^2 - (\Sigma x)^2} = \frac{12(282800) - 78(37200)}{12(650) - 78^2} = 286.71$$

$$b_0 = \frac{\Sigma y - b_1 \Sigma x}{n} = \frac{37200 - 286.71(78)}{12} = 1236.4$$

The trend line is then $\hat{Y} = 1236.4 + 286.7x$

To forecast the demand for period 13, we substitute $x = 13$ into the trend equation above.

The linear trend forecast for period 13 $= 1236.4 + 286.7(13) = 4963.5 = 4964$ toys.

An Excel spreadsheet solution is shown in Figure 5.4.

Once the relationship between the external variable and demand is determined, it can be used as a forecasting tool. Let's review several cause-and-effect models.

Simple Linear Regression Forecast

When there is only one explanatory variable, we have a simple regression model equivalent to the linear trend model described earlier. The difference is that the *x* variable is no longer time but instead an explanatory variable of demand. For example, demand could be dependent on the size of the advertising budget. The regression equation is expressed as:

$$\hat{Y} = b_0 + b_1 x$$

Where $\hat{Y}$ = forecast or dependent variable

x = explanatory or independent variable

b_0 = intercept of the vertical axis

b_1 = slope of the regression line

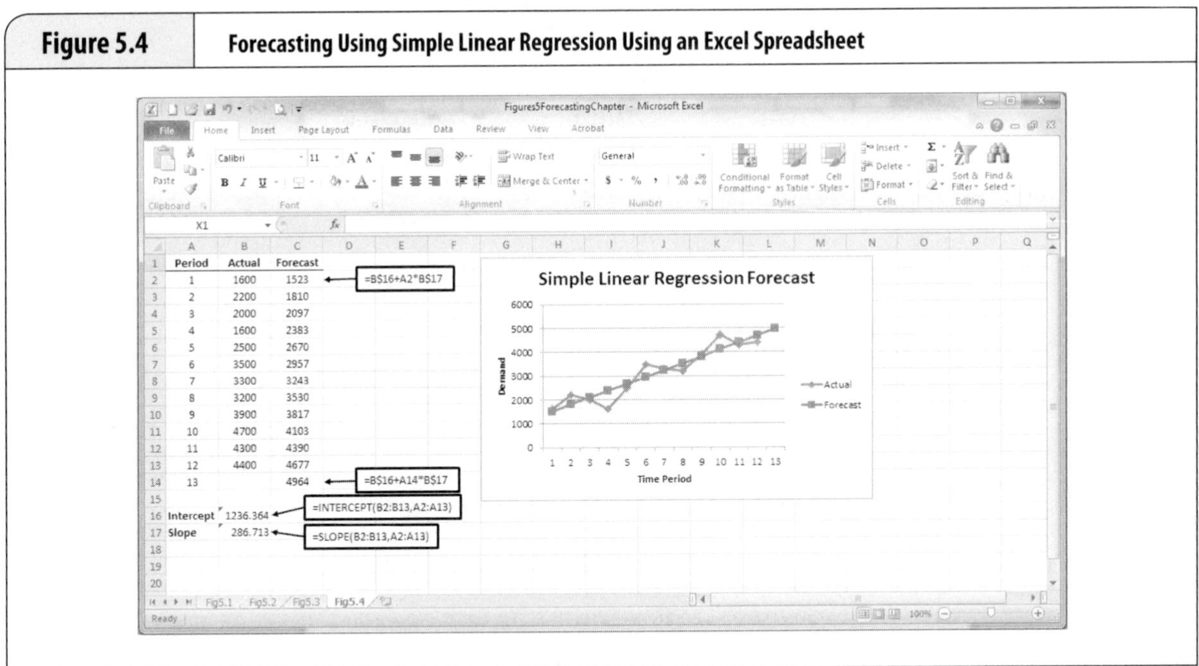

Figure 5.4 Forecasting Using Simple Linear Regression Using an Excel Spreadsheet

Example 5.5 illustrates the simple linear regression forecast.

The linear regression results indicate that a one-dollar increase in advertising will increase sales by $48.44. Further, a planned monthly advertising expenditure of $4000 would yield a sales forecast of $196,349.

Multiple Regression Forecast

When several explanatory variables are used to predict the dependent variable, a **multiple regression forecast** is applicable. Multiple regression analysis works well when the relationships between demand (dependent variable) and several other factors (independent or explanatory variables) impacting demand are strong and stable over time. The multiple regression equation is expressed as:

$$\hat{Y} = b_0 + b_1x_1 + b_2x_2 + \ldots + b_kx_k$$

Where $\hat{Y}$ = forecast or dependent variable

x_k = k^{th} explanatory or independent variable

b_0 = constant

b_k = regression coefficient of the independent variable x_k

Although the mathematics involved in determining the parameters of the equation is complex, numerous software programs such as Excel, SAS, and SPSS statistical packages can be used to solve the equation. Any statistics textbook should provide the formula for calculating the regression coefficient values and discussion of the assumptions and challenges of using multiple regression techniques. Multiple regression forecasting requires much more data than any of the other techniques discussed earlier, and the additional cost must be balanced against possible improvement in the level of forecast accuracy.

Example 5.5 Simple Linear Regression Forecasting

Data on sales and advertising dollars for the past six months are shown below.

$ SALES (Y)	$ ADVERTISING (X)
100,000	2000
150,000	3000
125,000	2500
50,000	1000
170,000	3500
135,000	2750

Determine the linear relationship between sales and advertising dollars.

SOLUTION

$ SALES (Y)	$ ADVERTISING (X)	X^2	XY
100,000	2000	4,000,000	200,000,000
150,000	3000	9,000,000	450,000,000
125,000	2500	6,250,000	312,500,000
50,000	1000	1,000,000	50,000,000
170,000	3500	12,250,000	595,000,000
135,000	2750	756,2500	371,250,000
$\Sigma y = 730{,}000$	$\Sigma x = 14{,}750$	$\Sigma x^2 = 40{,}062{,}500$	$\Sigma xy = 1{,}978{,}750{,}000$

$$\hat{Y} = b_0 + b_1 x$$

$$b_1 = \frac{n\Sigma(xy) - \Sigma x \Sigma y}{n\Sigma x^2 - (\Sigma x)^2} = \frac{6(1978750000) - 14750(730000)}{6(40062500) - 14750^2} = 48.43836$$

$$b_0 = \frac{\Sigma y - b_1 \Sigma x}{n} = \frac{730000 - 48.43836(14750)}{6} = 2589.041$$

$$b_0 = 2589.041$$

$$\hat{Y} = 2589.04 + 48.44x$$

FORECAST ACCURACY

The ultimate goal of any forecasting endeavor is to have an accurate and unbiased forecast. The cost associated with prediction error can be substantial and include the costs of lost sales, safety stock, unsatisfied customers, and loss of goodwill. Companies must strive to do a good job of tracking forecast error and taking the necessary steps to improve their forecasting techniques. Typically, forecast error at the disaggregated (stock keeping unit) level is higher than at the aggregated (company as a whole) level. For example, actual demand had exceeded Apple's aggregate demand forecasts for its new iPhone 5S and 5C; whereas individually, the demand for the iPhone 5C was low, sales of the top-of-the-line iPhone 5S exceeded projections.[13] **Forecast error** is the difference between the actual quantity and the forecast. Forecast error can be expressed as:

$$e_t = A_t - F_t$$

where e_t = forecast error for period t
A_t = actual demand for period t
F_t = forecast for period t

Several measures of forecasting accuracy are shown below:

$$\textbf{Mean absolute deviation (MAD)} = \frac{\sum_{t=1}^{n} |e_t|}{n}$$

$$\textbf{Mean absolute percentage error (MAPE)} = \frac{100}{n} \sum_{t=1}^{n} \left| \frac{e_t}{A_t} \right|$$

$$\textbf{Mean square error (MSE)} = \frac{\sum_{t=1}^{n} e_t^2}{n}$$

$$\textbf{Running sum of forecast errors (RSFE)} = \sum_{t=1}^{n} e_t$$

where e_t = forecast error for period t

A_t = actual demand for period t

n = number of periods of evaluation

The RSFE is an indicator of bias in the forecasts. **Forecast bias** measures the tendency of a forecast to be consistently higher or lower than the actual demand, over time. A positive RSFE indicates that the forecasts are generally lower than actual demand, which can lead to stockouts. A negative RSFE shows that the forecasts are generally higher than actual demand, which can result in excess inventory carrying costs.

The **tracking signal** is used to determine if the forecast bias is within the acceptable control limits. It is expressed as:

$$\text{Tracking signal} = \frac{RSFE}{MAD}$$

If the tracking signal falls outside preset control limits, there is a bias problem with the forecasting method, and an evaluation of the way forecasts are generated is warranted. A biased forecast will lead to excessive inventories or stockouts. Some inventory experts suggest using a tracking signal of ± 4 for high-volume items and ± 8 for lower-volume items. Over time when the quality of forecasts improved, it is recommended that the control limits be reduced to ± 3. As tighter limits are instituted, there is a greater probability of finding exceptions that actually require no action, but it also means catching changes in demand earlier, which could lead to further improvement in forecasts. Example 5.6 illustrates the use of these forecast accuracy measures.

In one study, researchers found that bias in the forecast could be intentional, driven by organizational issues such as motivation of staff and satisfaction of customer demands, influencing the generation of forecasts.[14] For example, sales personnel tend to favor under-forecasting so they can meet or exceed sales quotas, and production people tend to over-forecast because having too much inventory presents less of a problem than the alternative. The key to generating accurate forecasts is collaborative forecasting with different partners inside and outside the company working together to eliminate forecasting error. A collaborative planning, forecasting, and replenishment system, discussed later in the chapter, provides for free exchange of forecasting data, point-of-sale data, promotions, and other relevant information between trading partners; this collaborative effort, rather than more sophisticated and expensive forecasting algorithms, can account for significant improvements in forecasting accuracy.

Example 5.6 Forecast Accuracy Measures

The demand and forecast information for the XYZ Company over a twelve-month period is shown in the table below.

PERIOD	DEMAND	FORECAST	PERIOD	DEMAND	FORECAST
1	1600	1523	7	3300	3243
2	2200	1810	8	3200	3530
3	2000	2097	9	3900	3817
4	1600	2383	10	4700	4103
5	2500	2670	11	4300	4390
6	3500	2957	12	4400	4677

Calculate the MAD, MSE, MAPE, RSFE, and tracking signal. Assume that the control limit for the tracking signal is ±3. What can be concluded about the quality of the forecasts?

SOLUTION

PERIOD	DEMAND	FORECAST	ERROR (e)	ABSOLUTE ERROR	e^2	ABSOLUTE % ERROR
1	1600	1523	77	77	5929	4.8
2	2200	1810	390	390	152,100	17.7
3	2000	2097	−97	97	9409	4.9
4	1600	2383	−783	783	613,089	48.9
5	2500	2670	−170	170	28,900	6.8
6	3500	2957	543	543	294,849	15.5
7	3300	3243	57	57	3249	1.7
8	3200	3530	−330	330	108,900	10.3
9	3900	3817	83	83	6889	2.1
10	4700	4103	597	597	356,409	12.7
11	4300	4390	−90	90	8100	2.1
12	4400	4677	−277	277	76,729	6.3
Total			0	3494	1,664,552	133.9
Average				291.17	138,712.7	11.16
			RSFE	MAD	MSE	MAPE

MAD = 291.2

MSE = 138,712.7

MAPE = 11.2%

RSFE = 0

$$\text{Tracking signal} = \frac{RSFE}{MAD} = 0$$

The results indicate no bias in the forecasts, and that the tracking signal is well within the control limits of ±3. However, the forecasts are on average 291 units or 11.2 percent off from actual demand. This situation might require attention to determine the underlying causes of the variation.

COLLABORATIVE PLANNING, FORECASTING, AND REPLENISHMENT

Collaborative planning, forecasting, and replenishment (CPFR) is a concept first developed by the Voluntary Interindustry Commerce Solutions (VICS) Association, which merged with GS1 US in 2012. According to the Council of Supply Chain Management Professionals, CPFR is:

> *A concept that aims to enhance supply chain integration by supporting and assisting joint practices. CPFR seeks cooperative management of inventory through joint visibility and replenishment of products throughout the supply*

SCM Profile | Terra Technology 2013 Forecasting Benchmark Study[15]

Terra Technology, a Connecticut-based business planning advisor, is in its fourth year of a study of demand planning performance. The 2013 study encompasses 500 distribution centers, 450,000 item locations, nearly 5 billion physical cases, and more than $130 billion in combined company annual sales. Overall, the study finds that the average weekly forecast error decreased slightly from 53 percent in 2011 to 51 percent in 2012. However, the difference between the top-performing companies and the average narrowed for both forecast value-added and error, indicating a growing challenge to forecast demand in fast-moving markets. Bias for the group stayed the same at 7 percent, with the consumer packaged goods industry consistently over-forecasting for every year in the study. Sales increases relied more on promotions and new products introductions, but caused forecasting to be more challenging, with increased errors and bias four to five times higher than regular sales.

The following are detailed findings from its study:

- In 2012, the slight upward trend in forecast error observed in previous years appears to have been halted. Error was down from 53 percent the year before to 51 percent. The difference between the top performers and the average shrank by two percentage points. Monthly error decreased from 38 percent to 36 percent.
- The slowest-moving products, which represent 79 percent of all items, showed errors that were two-thirds more than top sellers. These slow-moving products needed 60 percent more safety stock to satisfy the fill rates.
- Bias for the slowest-moving products continues to be a problem, resulting in an unusually high inventory burden on the industry.
- Promotional activities often drive revenue but they also add more supply chain complexity resulting in more challenging forecasting. As a group, errors tended to be higher for products on promotion at 56 percent, compared to 49 percent without promotion. Forecast error for nonpromotional products during the year was 46 percent.
- When items are on promotion, bias jumped more than five times. Top performers had an eight times bias advantage compared to the average.
- Demand planning was better than the naïve forecast by 24 percent for the highest-velocity products but by only 4 percent for slow-moving items.
- Demand sensing performs consistently across all business activities, emphasizing the value of new mathematics that automatically adjusts to the dynamic market conditions whether in a recession or recovery.

chain. Information shared between suppliers and retailers aids in planning and satisfying customer demands through a supportive system of shared information. This allows for continuous updating of inventory and upcoming requirements, essentially making the end-to-end supply chain process more efficient. Efficiency is also created through the decrease expenditures for merchandising, inventory, logistics, and transportation across all trading partners.[16]

The objective of CPFR is to optimize the supply chain by improving demand forecast accuracy, delivering the right product at the right time to the right location, reducing inventories across the supply chain, avoiding stockouts and improving customer service. This can be achieved only if the trading partners are working closely together and are willing to share information and risk through a common set of processes. The real value of CPFR comes from an exchange of forecasting information rather than from more sophisticated forecasting algorithms to improve forecasting accuracy. The fact is that forecasts developed solely by the firm tend to be inaccurate. When both the buyer and seller collaborate to develop a single forecast, incorporating knowledge of base sales, promotions, store openings or closings, and new product introductions, it is possible to synchronize buyer needs with supplier production plans, thus ensuring efficient replenishment. The jointly managed forecasts can be adjusted in the event that demand or promotions have changed, thus avoiding costly corrections after the fact.

On the surface, when decisions are made with incomplete, one-sided information, it may appear that companies have optimized their internal processes when, in reality, inventory has merely shifted along the supply chain. Without supply chain trading partners collaborating and exchanging information, the supply chain will always be suboptimal and contain excess inventories, resulting in less-than-maximum supply chain profits.

CPFR is an approach that addresses the requirements for good demand management. The benefits of CPFR include the following:

- Strengthens partner relationships
- Provides analysis of sales and order forecasts
- Uses point-of-sale data, seasonal activity, promotions, new product introductions, and store openings or closings to improve forecast accuracy
- Manages the demand chain and proactively eliminates problems before they appear
- Allows collaboration on future requirements and plans
- Uses joint planning and promotions management
- Integrates planning, forecasting, and logistics activities
- Provides efficient category management and understanding of consumer purchasing patterns
- Provides analysis of key performance metrics (e.g., forecast accuracy, forecast exceptions, product lead times, inventory turnover, percentage stockouts) to reduce supply chain inefficiencies, improve customer service, and increase revenues and profitability.

California boating supply retailer West Marine, an early adopter of CPFR, has benefited greatly from its implementation. Within a few years of the start of its CPFR program, West Marine had developed relationships with 200 suppliers and achieved 85 percent forecast accuracy, 80 percent on-time shipments, and 96 percent in-stock deliveries during its peak season. West Marine had to address both business processes and cultural issues. The company worked with its suppliers to match supply and demand. While collaboration with external constituents is critical for CPFR success, it is equally important that effective collaboration within the company is emphasized. For example, logistics, planning, and replenishment associates must work closely together. West Marine identified the following ten performance improvement steps in its successful implementation of CPFR:[17]

1. Seek long-term, holistic solutions, not quick or myopic fixes.
2. Reconcile conflicting goals and metrics.
3. Pursue inclusive problem solving; do not depend upon "experts" who don't have accountability for the business.
4. Instill collaborative processes that encourage idea creation, shared problem solving, and high adoption rates across organizational boundaries.

5. Use a disciplined and iterative set of methodologies such as CPFR, SCOR, or Six Sigma to help teams define issues, root causes, and solutions.
6. Develop a culture of continuous improvement, particularly at the customer-facing associate level, because those employees are most likely to know what is needed.
7. Create clear accountabilities and assign authority with a focus on core business processes rather than on traditional organizational "silos" or loyalties.
8. Commit to technology enablement for execution, communication, exception management, and root-cause analysis.
9. Reduce decision cycle times.
10. Implement rapidly.

As part of their CPFR initiative, the company worked closely with suppliers to match supply and demand. The CPFR program has been extended to West Marine's supplier network. Other early adopters of CPFR are Procter & Gamble and Walmart.

The top three challenges for CPFR implementation are the difficulty of making internal changes, cost, and trust. As with any major implementation, internal resistance to change must be addressed by top management. Change is always difficult; however, if top management is committed to the project, then the project is much more likely to succeed. Companies will need to educate their employees on the benefits of the process changes and the disadvantages of maintaining the status quo. There is also the question of reducing the scale of CPFR and, therefore, the cost of implementation for smaller trading partners. While cost is an important factor, companies with no plans for adopting CPFR should determine if they are at a competitive disadvantage. Trust, a major cultural issue, is considered a big hurdle to widespread implementation of CPFR because many retailers are reluctant to share the type of proprietary information required by CPFR. While the suppliers of Walmart such as Procter & Gamble, for instance, may be willing to share sensitive data with Walmart, they do not want other suppliers to obtain this information. However, other experts do not believe that trust is the stumbling block for mass adoption of CPFR. Jim Uchneat of Benchmarking Partners, Inc., says, "Trust may be a catch-all phrase that covers a host of other problems, but I have never found trust between people to be the issue. CPFR won't shift the power dynamics in a retailer/buyer relationship. If people are hoping that this is the case and refer to this as 'trust,' then they are fooling themselves. Lack of trust is more often related to the unreliable data in systems and the lack of integration internal to retailers and manufacturers."[18]

USEFUL FORECASTING WEBSITES

Several forecasting websites that provide a wealth of information on the subject are shown here:

1. Institute for Business Forecasting & Planning (https://ibf.org/)

   The Institute of Business Forecasting & Planning (IBF), established in 1982, is a membership organization recognized worldwide for fostering the growth of demand planning, forecasting, and sales and operations Planning (S&OP), as its mission.

   The IBF provides education, benchmarking research, training, certification, conferences, and advisory services on a global scale. IBF is instrumental in helping businesses increase cash flow, market share, and growth by improving forecasting and planning performance. Learning, sharing, and advancing are the foundational cycle that IBF members and their companies experience. No other organization has as much depth and experience in providing educational content for demand planning and forecasting as IBF.[19]

2. International Institute of Forecasters (www.forecasters.org/)

   The International Institute of Forecasters (IIF), a nonprofit organization founded in 1981, is dedicated to developing and furthering the generation, distribution, and use of knowledge on forecasting through the following objectives:[20]

   - Develop and unify forecasting as a multidisciplinary field of research drawing on management, behavioral sciences, social sciences, engineering, and other fields.
   - Contribute to the professional development of analysts, managers, and policy makers with responsibilities for making and using forecasts in business and government.
   - Bridge the gap between theory and practice, with practice helping to set the research agenda and research providing useful results.
   - Bring together decision makers, forecasters, and researchers from all nations to improve the quality and usefulness of forecasting.

   The Institute also publishes the *International Journal of Forecasting, Foresight: The International Journal of Applied Forecasting*, and *The Oracle*.

3. Forecasting Principles: Evidence-based Forecasting (www.forecastingprinciples.com/)

   The Forecasting Principles site summarizes all useful knowledge about forecasting so that it can be used by researchers, practitioners, and educators. (Those who might want to challenge this are invited to submit missing information.) This knowledge is provided as principles (guidelines, prescriptions, rules, conditions, action statements, or advice about what to do in given situations). This site describes all evidenced-based principles on forecasting and provides sources to support the principles. The primary source is *Principles of Forecasting*, a comprehensive summary of forecasting knowledge involving 40 authors and 123 reviewers.[21]

4. Stata (Data Analysis and Statistical Software): Statistical Software Providers (www.stata.com)

   This website provides links to a large number of statistical and forecasting software providers. Additionally, visitors can access information on worldwide forecasting seminars and short courses, user groups, a bookstore, the *Stata Journal*, and user manuals.

FORECASTING SOFTWARE

Forecasts are seldom calculated manually. If a forecaster uses a quantitative method, then a software solution can be used to simplify the process and save the time required to generate a forecast. Several leading forecasting software providers and their products are shown below.

1. *Business Forecast Systems, Inc.* (www.forecastpro.com/)

   Founded in 1986, Business Forecast Systems, Inc. (BFS), is the maker of Forecast Pro, the leading software solution for business forecasting, and is a premier provider of forecasting education. With more than 35,000 users worldwide, Forecast Pro helps thousands of companies improve planning, cut inventory costs, and decrease stockouts by improving the accuracy of their forecasts.

   The company offers three editions of Forecast Pro to address the different needs of its customers: Forecast Pro Unlimited, Forecast Pro TRAC, and Forecast Pro XE. Several of the forecasting approaches discussed in this chapter such as moving average, trend, and exponential smoothing models are included in the software. Washington-based shoe designer Brooks Sports, Inc., is an example of one of the company's customers that has benefited greatly from use of Forecast Pro software. Their experience with Forecast Pro is discussed in the SCM Profile on Brooks Sports.

2. *John Galt* (www.johngalt.com/)

   Founded in 1996, Chicago-based John Galt Solutions has a proven track record of delivering affordable forecasting and inventory management solutions for supply chains. With its ForecastX Wizard and Atlas Planning Suite, it provides a wide range of affordable, easy-to-implement supply chain planning solutions for mid-market companies.

   The company's basic forecasting software, ForecastX Wizard, combines a statistical forecasting engine with Microsoft Excel, giving forecasters a blend of accuracy, ease of use, and flexibility. The ForecastX Wizard Premium has more interactive features, enhanced inventory planning, closed-loop collaboration, and streamlined reporting. The *Supply & Demand Chain Executive* magazine selected John Galt Solutions based on its track record for delivering supply chain solutions. Over 5,000 customers today use solutions from John Galt to increase forecast accuracy, optimize inventory levels, and maximize supply chain performance.[22]

SCM Profile

Improved Forecasting at Brooks Sports[23]

Brooks Sports, Inc., is a U.S. high-performance running shoes designer and retailer, with apparel and accessories in more than eighty countries. In 2001, the company decided to shift from a broad product line to one focusing on delivering products for the serious runner. Brooks has nine principles that define who it is:[24]

1. We do one thing and we do it better than anyone on the planet.
2. The answer is the run.
3. We make essential gears for runners not consumers.
4. We relate to our audience runner-to-runner not corporation-to-consumer.
5. We run to compete and win, as a team
6. When we celebrate the run, good things happen.
7. In all things, we seek the balance between art and science.
8. Big success is determined by the smallest of details.
9. At the end of the day, we will succeed because of our culture.

A revised strategic focus brought new challenges such as inconsistent style growth, a long production planning horizon and short product life, and an inability to share sales data with vendors. Brooks needed more accurate and timely forecasts and it turned to Forecast Pro for assistance. "Forecast Pro has been a great solution for Brooks," says Tom Ross, Financial Analyst. "Implementing Forecast Pro's event modeling is very simple, which is an essential feature for us because of our moving product launches. We also use event models to address the challenge of forecasting events that don't occur on a regular basis—such as races—which can have a dramatic impact on the sales of specific products. Another powerful feature of Forecast Pro is the ability to forecast a product hierarchy. This helps us to serve our multiple constituents within Brooks—we review higher-level forecasts with management and easily generate detailed forecasts at the SKU level for demand planning. We now can systematically track changes, giving us a better understanding of our forecasting performance."

The result is that Brooks has improved its forecast accuracy by 40 percent, decreased unfulfilled demand from 20 percent to 5 percent, and reduced closeouts by 60 percent. In addition, improved forecasting has resulted in smoother production, lower cost, and better profit.

3. *JustEnough* (www.justenough.com/)

   JustEnough solves complex demand problems without overcomplicating things. While other companies might focus on the science side of demand management with solutions using complex metrics, JustEnough software allows planning decisions to be executed based on the company's expertise.[25]

   McPherson Companies is a large, independent lubricant distributor in the southeastern United States and used JustEnough Sales Forecasting and Inventory Planning Solutions. "Some of the software makers offered Citrix-like forecasting spreadsheets, but JustEnough stood out because its dashboards offered flexibility and easy, visual interpretations of sales patterns and inventory changes. The others regurgitated the data for you but required additional software to allow you to both interpret what the raw data revealed and to create still more management reports. We will turn inventory nine times in one year with the help of JustEnough versus just 6.5 times the previous year. Faster turns improve cash flow. As an inventory-heavy company, that's significant," Bright explained.[26]

   Another JustEnough customer is Ackermans, one of the oldest consumer retailers in South Africa selling baby ware, baby furniture, consumer goods, apparel, and financial services products. The company has more than 450 stores located across Southern Africa. "We needed something that wasn't too complicated or so overly sophisticated that it was going to make users run for the hills," said Bouwer Strydom, Ackermans' planning manager. "It also couldn't be too complex or expensive for us to maintain. It had to fit in with our ongoing business processes without us having to re-engineer anything to fit replenishment. We determined that the demand forecasting solution from JustEnough would be able to grow with us, as opposed to us having to grow into it."[27]

4. Avercast, LLC (http://www.avercast.com/)

   Avercast, LLC's enterprise level inventory forecasting and demand planning software solutions are the "world's first easy-to-use tools for companies that want to optimize inventories based on true demand. Avercast's proprietary forecasting technology includes an industry leading 185 forecasting algorithms to handle product trending, sales seasonality, new product introductions, mature and aging products, intermittent product demand, low volume and slow moving products, product promotions, and much more."[28]

   S. Bacher, one of South Africa's oldest distributors and wholesalers, uses Avercast Business Forecasting software. "Historically we were looking at each brand as an overall category with little regard for item-level decisions," said Justin Seef, S. Bacher's procurement director. "Now we can easily drill down to the item level using Avercast and consider purchasing strategies that leverage the pace of sales. After using Avercast Business Forecasting for six months our stock was reduced by 23 percent while simultaneously increasing our stock of more popular items."[29]

5. *SAS* (www.sas.com/)

   According to its online brochure, "SAS Forecast Server generates large quantities of high-quality forecasts quickly and automatically, allowing organizations to plan more effectively for the future. The unsurpassed scalability of SAS Forecast Server enables your business to operate more efficiently at all levels by quickly and automatically producing statistically based forecasts you can trust. SAS Forecast Server bundles the SAS High-Performance Forecasting engine with the SAS Forecast Studio GUI."

Amway China is an example of a global company that has managed its forecasting function well with SAS Forecast Server and SAS Inventory Optimization solutions (see the nearby SCM Profile on the company).

Cloud-Based Forecasting

Instead of investing in the software described above, many companies are choosing instead to use cloud services to track and forecast demand. **Cloud-based forecasting** can be described as using supplier-hosted or software-as-a-service (SaaS) advanced forecasting applications that are provided to companies on a subscription basis. Today, cloud-based forecasting is accomplished with state-of-the-art time series forecasting algorithms using seasonal and cyclical adjusting models. Some also utilize artificial intelligence-based expert systems to select the forecasting method best suited for a customer's environment.

With cloud-based forecasting, organizations can easily detour around outdated in-house applications, instantly increase data storage and data analysis capabilities as needed, and provide workers with new capabilities without devoting time and resources to software, hardware, and extensive training. Users need only a browser and can be up and running in one day. Firms can reduce their IT costs significantly, improve employee productivity, and improve forecast accuracy, which also reduces stockout costs and inventory carrying costs. Many of these applications are provided as part of larger cloud-based enterprise

SCM Profile | Amway China Improves Replenishment Time Through Better Forecasts

When the Chinese government outlawed direct selling in 1998, Amway had to decide if it wanted to pull out or come up with a new way to sell consumer products in China. Amway had already invested in a large-scale factory and decided to revise its sales model to meet the new regulations. In 2006, Amway received a new license, and China is currently its largest market, representing more than one-third of its worldwide sales.[30] A lesson learned by Amway is that it needs to have a true understanding of the marketplace, culture, and political environment. As the business grew, Amway lacked the visibility within its supply chain and struggled to improve its inventory accuracy and replenishment to its retailers.

Today, Amway China delivers more than 1,000 products to 229 stores, 29 home delivery centers, 22 warehouses, and a 40,000 square meter logistics center in Guangzhou. The logistics planner schedules shipments, destinations, amount of goods, and warehouse space using past experience. Originally, the outcome was increased logistics costs due to numerous mistakes made. Amway China turned to SAS to find a solution to its problems.[31] Using SAS Forecast Server and SAS Inventory Optimization, Amway China was able to predict the optimum inventory based on the specified service levels, delivery times, and costs. SAS used 70 million orders from its last three years as inputs to the time series forecasting model to derive the predicted demand. "With SAS predictive analysis and inventory optimization, we can keep inventory at the right level at the right time. When business or customer demands change, we can quickly adjust via the flexible inventory optimization system. With the IOS (Inventory Optimization System), Amway China cannot only reduce logistics costs, but also enhance customer satisfaction and improve its competitive edge," says Raymond Hui, Distribution Vice President. Using SAS, Amway increased customer satisfaction to 97 percent, reduced inventory, minimized late deliveries, and decreased total costs.

management applications such as transportation management, customer relationship management, and sales force management systems. A few examples are provided here.

Arizona-based AFS Technologies provides on-demand trade promotion management and other software solutions to the consumer packaged goods industry.[32] Its easy-to-use tools allow users to get a clear-cut picture of sales, from warehouse to customer, and perform sales forecasting along with a number of other applications. Canada-based Angoss Software offers KnowledgeSCORE on-demand predictive sales analytics as part of firms' CRM strategies.[33] Their cloud-based data analysis capabilities combine best-of-breed predictive analytics technologies for big data needs and can improve field sales productivity and sales forecasting. Mailplus, an Australian mail courier service, began using a cloud-based integrated business management system from NetSuite because its in-house system could no longer handle Mailplus's rapid growth. "The more franchises we added to our system, the greater the system stress—to point that it was crashing almost daily and costing us thousands of dollars a month to maintain and service," says Chris Burgess, Mailplus CEO. It uses the NetSuite SuiteCloud system for a wide range of applications including sales and financial forecasting.[34]

SUMMARY

Forecasting is an integral part of demand management since it provides an estimate of future demand and the basis for planning and making sound business decisions. A mismatch in supply and demand could result in excessive inventories and stockouts and loss of profits and goodwill. Proper demand forecasting enables better planning and utilization of resources for businesses to be competitive. Both qualitative and quantitative methods are available to help companies forecast demand better. The qualitative methods are based on judgment and intuition, whereas the quantitative methods use mathematical techniques and historical data to predict future demand. The quantitative forecasting methods can be divided into time series and cause-and-effect models. Since forecasts are seldom completely accurate, management must monitor forecast errors and make the necessary improvements to the forecasting process.

Forecasts made in isolation tend to be inaccurate. Collaborative planning, forecasting, and replenishment (CPFR) is an approach in which companies work together to develop mutually agreeable plans while taking responsibility for their actions. The objective of CPFR is to optimize the supply chain by generating a consensus demand forecast, delivering the right product at the right time to the right location, reducing inventories, avoiding stockouts, and improving customer service. Major corporations such as Walmart, West Marine, and Procter & Gamble are early adopters of CPFR.

The computation involved in generating a forecast is seldom done manually. Forecasting software solutions such as Forecast Pro, SAS, and Microsoft Excel are readily available. More recently, cloud-based forecasting solutions have made it possible to have forecasting and other supply chain software on-demand on the Internet.

KEY TERMS

business cycle, 140

cause-and-effect forecasting, 140

cloud-based forecasting, 157

collaborative planning, forecasting, and replenishment (CPFR), 150

forecast bias, 149

forecast error, 148

linear trend forecast, 144

mean absolute deviation (MAD), 149

mean absolute percentage error (MAPE), 149

mean square error (MSE), 149

multiple regression forecast, 147

naïve forecast, 141

qualitative forecasting methods, 138

quantitative forecasting methods, 138

running sum of forecast errors (RSFE), 149

simple moving average forecast, 141

time series forecasting, 140

tracking signal, 149

DISCUSSION QUESTIONS

1. What is demand management?
2. What is demand forecasting?
3. Why is demand forecasting important for effective supply chain management?
4. Explain the impact of a mismatch in supply and demand. What strategies can companies adopt to influence demand?
5. What are qualitative forecasting techniques? When are these methods more suitable?
6. What are the main components of a time series?

7. Explain the difference between a time series model and an associative model. Under what conditions would one model be preferred to the other?
8. What is the impact of the smoothing constant value on the simple exponential smoothing forecast?
9. Compare and contrast the jury of executive opinion and the Delphi techniques.
10. Explain the key differences between the weighted moving average and the simple exponential smoothing forecasting methods.
11. What are three measures of forecasting accuracy?
12. How could the MAD be used to generate a better smoothing constant for an exponential smoothing forecast?
13. What is a tracking signal? What information does the tracking signal provide that managers can use to improve the quality of forecasts?
14. What are the key features of CPFR? Why would a company consider adopting CPFR?
15. West Marine identified the ten performance improvement steps in its successful implementation of CPFR. Is West Marine's approach unique, or can its experience be duplicated at another company? What are the key challenges that other companies will face in implementing CPFR?
16. Why is widespread adoption of CPFR below expectations?
17. What is cloud-based forecasting, and why do companies use this in solving their supply chain forecasting problems?

PROBLEMS

1. Ms. Winnie Lin's company sells computers. Monthly sales for a six-month period are as follows:

MONTH	SALES
Jan	18,000
Feb	22,000
Mar	16,000
Apr	18,000
May	20,000
Jun	24,000

   a. Plot the monthly data on a sheet of graph paper.
   b. Compute the sales forecast for July using the following approaches: (1) a three-month moving average; (2) a weighted three-month moving average using .50 for June, .30 for May, and .20 for April; (3) a linear trend equation; (4) exponential smoothing with α (smoothing constant) equal to .40, assuming a February forecast of 18,000.
   c. Which method do you think is the least appropriate? Why?
   d. Calculate the MAD for each of the four techniques in part b. Which is the best? Why?

2. The owner of the Chocolate Outlet Store wants to forecast chocolate demand. Demand for the preceding four years is shown in the following table:

YEAR	DEMAND (POUNDS)
1	68,800
2	71,000
3	75,500
4	71,200

Forecast demand for Year 5 using the following approaches: (1) a three-year moving average; (2) a three-year weighted moving average using .40 for Year 4, .20 for Year 3, and .40 for Year 2; (3) exponential smoothing with $\alpha = .30$, and assuming the forecast for Period 1 = 68,000.

3. The forecasts generated by two forecasting methods and actual sales are as follows:

MONTH	SALES	FORECAST 1	FORECAST 2
1	269	275	268
2	289	266	287
3	294	290	292
4	278	284	298
5	268	270	274
6	269	268	270
7	260	261	259
8	275	271	275

Compute the MSE, the MAD, the MAPE, the RSFE, and the tracking signal for each forecasting method. Which method is better? Why?

ESSAY/PROJECT QUESTIONS

1. Find a software company online providing forecasting solutions, and provide a description of the experience of one of its customers' use of the product.
2. Find a company online that is using collaborative planning, forecasting, and replenishment, and report on its experiences.
3. Find a software company online providing forecasting solutions, and list the different forecasting techniques that are included in its software.
4. Write a report comparing Apple's demand forecasts of their iPhones and actual sales for each generation of iPhone models since the phone was first introduced in 2007.

ENDNOTES

1. Brainy Quotes; http://www.brainyquote.com/quotes/keywords/forecast.html
2. "Forecasting with Confidence," KMPG; http://www.kpmg.com/dutchcaribbean/en/services/Advisory/Documents/forecasting-with-confidence.pdf
3. The Institute for Supply Management's *Manufacturing and Non-Manufacturing Report on Business* is available at www.ism.ws/ISMReport/content.cfm?ItemNumber=10743&navItemNumber=12944
4. "ISM *Report On Business*® Frequently Asked Questions;" http://www.ism.ws/ISMReport/content.cfm?ItemNumber=10706&navItemNumber=12957

5. Loeb, W., "Zara's Secret to Success: The New Science of Retailing," *Forbes*, October 14, 2013; http://www.forbes.com/sites/walterloeb/2013/10/14/zaras-secret-to-success-the-new-science-of-retailing-a-must-read/

6. "Apple report blowout sales of iPhone 5S and 5C," *Reuters*, September 23, 2013; http://www.reuters.com/article/2013/09/23/us-apple-iphone-idUSBRE98J0LD20130923

7. Jun, M., and R. Peterson, "Forecasting Methods and Uses for Demand Deposits of U.S. Commercial Banks," *Journal of Commercial Banking and Finance* 2(1), 2003: 53–64.

8. Gordon, L., and D. Kung, "Corporate Compliance Issues in Managing Supply Chains in the Environmental-Friendly 21st Century," *Journal of International Technology and Information Management* 21(4), 2012: 81–104.

9. Schiller, K., "Five Trends Shaking Up the Internet," *Information Today* 27(9), 2010: 1–54.

10. "2010 Eruptions of Eyjafjallajökull"; http://en.wikipedia.org/wiki/2010_eruptions_of_Eyjafjallajökull

11. "2010 Haitian Earthquake"; http://en.wikipedia.org/wiki/2010_Haiti_earthquake

12. Chaman, L. Jain, "Benchmarking Forecasting Models," *The Journal of Business Forecasting* 25(4), Winter 2006/2007: 14–17.

13. "iPhone 5s Demand Higher Than Expected, Took Time to 'Build the Mix' Customers Wanted"; http://www.macrumors.com/2014/01/27/iphone-5s-5c-demand/

14. Lawrence, M., M. O'Conner, and B. Edmundson, "A Field Study of Forecasting Accuracy and Processes," *European Journal of Operational Research* 22(1), April 1, 2000: 151–160.

15. "2013 Forecasting Benchmark Study," Terra Technology; http://www.terratechnology.com/key-findings-2013/

16. "Supply Chain Management Terms and Glossary," Council of Supply Chain Management Professionals; http://cscmp.org/sites/default/files/user_uploads/resources/downloads/glossary-2013.pdf

17. Smith, L., "West Marine: A CPFR Success Story"; http://www.lomag-man.org/cpfr_industrie_achat_distribution/documentation_cpfr/WestMarineA_CPFRSuccStorySupChManReManNet_an.pdf

18. Uchneat J., "CPFR's Woes Not Related to Trust," *Computerworld*, July 22, 2002; www.computerworld.com/news/2002/story/0,11280,72834,00.html

19. "What Is the IBF? The Institute of Business Forecasting & Planning," Institute of Business Forecasting & Planning; https://ibf.org/index.cfm?fuseaction=showObjects&objectTypeID=4

20. "About the IIF," International Institute of Forecasting; http://forecasters.org/about/

21. "About ForPrin," *Forecasting Principles*; http://www.forecastingprinciples.com/index.php?option=com_content&view=article&id=34&Itemid=234#Objectives

22. "John Galt Solutions Selected as Top Innovator by Supply & Demand Chain Executive Magazine"; www.johngalt.com/News_&_Events/pr_Demand_Inventory_Management_SDC.shtml

23. "Collaborative Forecasting Running Smoothly at Brooks Sports," Forecast Pro; http://www.forecastpro.com/customers/success/brooks.htm

24. Brooks Running Company; http://www.brooksrunning.com/on/demandware.store/Sites-BrooksRunning-Site/default/MeetBrooks-WhatMakesUsTick

25. "About Us," JustEnough; http://www.justenough.com/about-us/

26. "JustEnough Helps McPherson Oil Leapfrog Its Average Annual Inventory Turns by 38%," JustEnough; http://www.justenough.com/resources/case-studies/mcpherson-oil/

27. "Ackermans: JustEnough Provides Visibility into Premier Retailer's Stock Mix," JustEnough; http://www.justenough.com/resources/case-studies/ackermans/

28. http://www.avercast.com/2010SupplyDemandChainExecutiveTop100.php

29. "Request a Product Demonstration," Avercast; http://www.avercast.com/SBacherAndCompany.php

30. "Amway's President on Reinventing the Business to Succeed in China," *Harvard Business Review*, April 2013; http://hbr.org/2013/04/amways-president-on-reinventing-the-business-to-succeed-in-china/ar/1

31. "The Right Inventory at the Right Time," SAS; http://www.sas.com/en_us/customers/amway-china.html

32. See afsi.com for more information.

33. Anonymous, "Angoss Software Corporation," *Marketing Weekly News*, July 14, 2012: 149.

34. Anonymous, "Computer Software—NetSuite Cloud Helps Accelerate Mailplus' Growth by 24 Percent," *Marketing Weekly News*, December 1, 2012: 208.

Chapter 6

RESOURCE PLANNING SYSTEMS

What we have done in the past is in the rear view. It is all about innovation going forward.

— Satya Nadella, CEO, Microsoft[1]

We had a blank sheet to create new systems for the business.

— Dave Sharrat, Product Lifecycle Management System Senior Manager, Jaguar Land Rover[2]

A fool with a tool is still a fool.

— Grady Booch, co-developer of the Unified Modeling Language and Chief Scientist in Software Engineering at IBM Research.[3]

Learning Objectives

After completing this chapter, you should be able to

- Understand the chase, level, and mixed aggregate production strategies.
- Describe the hierarchical operations planning process in terms of materials planning (APP, MPS, MRP) and capacity planning (RRP, RCCP, CRP).
- Know how to compute available-to-promise quantities, MRP explosion, and DRP implosion.
- Understand the limitations of legacy MRP systems, and why organizations are migrating to integrated ERP systems.
- Describe an ERP system, and understand its advantages and disadvantages.
- Understand best-of-breed versus single integrator ERP implementations.

Chapter Outline

SCM Profile: The Resurgence of Manufacturing in the U.S.

Advances in transportation, technology, and telecommunications infrastructure accelerated globalization when China opened its borders to foreign businesses in the early 1990s. Multinational corporations, especially manufacturing firms, saw opportunities with the enormous labor cost differential in China compared to developed markets. Despite the low productivity and skill levels of Chinese labor, manufacturers in developed nations found that the labor cost differential still justified the offshoring of manufacturing to China. By 2009, China had become the world's largest merchandise exporter, while the U.S. remained the world's leading merchandise importer.[4]

Recently, numerous trade reports and economic indicators show that there is a resurgence of manufacturing in the U.S. The Manufacturing Report On Business by the Institute for Supply Management (ISM) reported that U.S. economic activity in the manufacturing sector expanded in March 2014 for the tenth consecutive month. It also stated that the overall U.S. economy and employment grew for the fifty-eighth and ninth consecutive months, respectively.[5]

There are numerous factors that foster the recent resurgence of manufacturing in the U.S. First, the lack of skilled labor and rising wages in China are driving American manufacturers to reshore to the U.S. In the last few years, China labor costs have risen roughly 20 percent per year, while labor costs in the U.S. have risen only 3 percent. In some U.S. industries, labor costs have remained relatively flat. In addition to experiencing significant wage inflation, China is also facing severe labor shortages, especially on the eastern seaboard where most of China's manufacturing takes place. For example, Hon Hai Precision Industry Co., the world's largest provider of electronics manufacturing services, has begun to relocate its operations progressively from its eastern seaboard facility in Shenzhen to inland China (Guizhou) in pursuit of cheaper labor costs. Although the U.S. labor costs are still comparatively high, its labor force is unrivaled in productivity in terms of manufacturing value added per employee or per hour worked.

Second, natural gas and oil prices have reached an unsustainable, exceptionally high level. Additionally, use of hydraulic fracturing technology has opened new reserves of natural gas and oil in the U.S. with significantly reduced production costs. Indeed, the U.S. is now the world's leader and fastest growing producer of oil and natural gas. This new, inexpensive energy source gives American manufacturers a unique and potent cost advantage for reshoring manufacturing to the U.S. The Boston Consulting Group reported that cheap natural gas will have a crucial effect on U.S. manufacturing over the next few years. Cheap domestic natural gas allows American manufacturers to replace high transportation and logistics costs with lower domestic manufacturing costs.

Third, American manufacturers have learned that it is crucial to keep research and development (R&D) close to manufacturing. The risks of intellectual property loss and nationalization, dealing with unethical suppliers selling illegal raw materials, and the need to respond quickly to changes in the market place have forced American manufacturers to reconsider their R&D and overseas operations. These risks outweigh many assumptions made a decade ago. In many cases, most of these risks can be eliminated by simply reshoring to the U.S.[6]

Over the last two decades, American manufactures have transitioned from made-in-America to outsourcing most manufacturing activities. Whether the resurgence of manufacturing or reshoring in the U.S. is sustainable will be more apparent in the next few years. Manufacturing executives must reexamine their strategic directions to focus on product innovation and new process technology to increase productivity. Reshoring also dramatically reduces delivery lead times and cycle inventories.

INTRODUCTION

Resource planning is the process of determining the production capacity required to meet demand. In the context of resource planning, *capacity* refers to the maximum workload that an organization is capable of completing in a given period of time. A discrepancy between an organization's capacity and demand results in inefficiencies, either in underutilized resources or unfulfilled orders. The goal of resource planning is to minimize this discrepancy.

One of the most critical activities of an organization is to balance the production plan with capacity; this directly impacts how effectively the organization deploys its resources in producing goods and services. Developing feasible operations schedules and capacity plans to meet delivery due dates and minimize waste in manufacturing or service organizations is a complex problem. The need for better operations scheduling continues to challenge operations managers, especially in today's intensely competitive global marketplace. In an environment fostering collaborative buyer–supplier relationships, the challenge of scheduling operations to meet delivery due dates and eliminating waste is becoming more complex. The problem is compounded in an integrated supply chain, where a missed due date or stockout cascades downstream, magnifying the bullwhip effect and adversely affecting the entire supply chain.

Operations managers are continuously involved in resource and operations planning to balance capacity and output. Capacity may be stated in terms of labor, materials, or equipment. With too much excess capacity, production cost per unit is high due to idle workers and machinery. However, if workers and machinery are stressed due to too little capacity, quality levels are likely to deteriorate. Firms generally run their operations at about 85 percent of capacity to allow time for scheduled repairs and maintenance and to meet unexpected increases in demand.

This chapter describes the hierarchical operations planning process in terms of materials and capacity planning. A hypothetical industrial example is used to demonstrate the hierarchical planning process. This chapter also discusses the evolution of the manufacturing planning and control system from the material requirements planning to the enterprise resource planning system.

OPERATIONS PLANNING

Operations planning is usually hierarchical and can be divided into three broad categories: (1) **long-range**, (2) **intermediate** or **medium-range**, and (3) **short-range planning horizons**. While the distinctions among the three can be vague, long-range plans usually cover a year or more, tend to be more general, and specify resources and outputs in terms of aggregate hours and units. Medium-range plans normally span six to eighteen months, whereas short-range plans usually cover a few days to a few weeks depending on the type and size of the firm. Long-range plans are established first and are then used to guide the medium-range plans, which are subsequently used to guide the short-range plans. Long-range plans usually involve major, strategic decisions in capacity, such as the construction of new facilities and purchase of capital equipment, whereas medium-range plans involve minor changes in capacity such as changes in employment levels. Short-range plans are the most detailed and specify the exact end items and quantities to make on a weekly, daily, or hourly basis.

Figure 6.1 shows the planning horizons and how a business plan cascades into the various hierarchical materials and capacity plans. The **aggregate production plan (APP)** is a long-range materials plan. Since capacity expansion involves the construction of a new

Figure 6.1 Manufacturing Planning and Control System

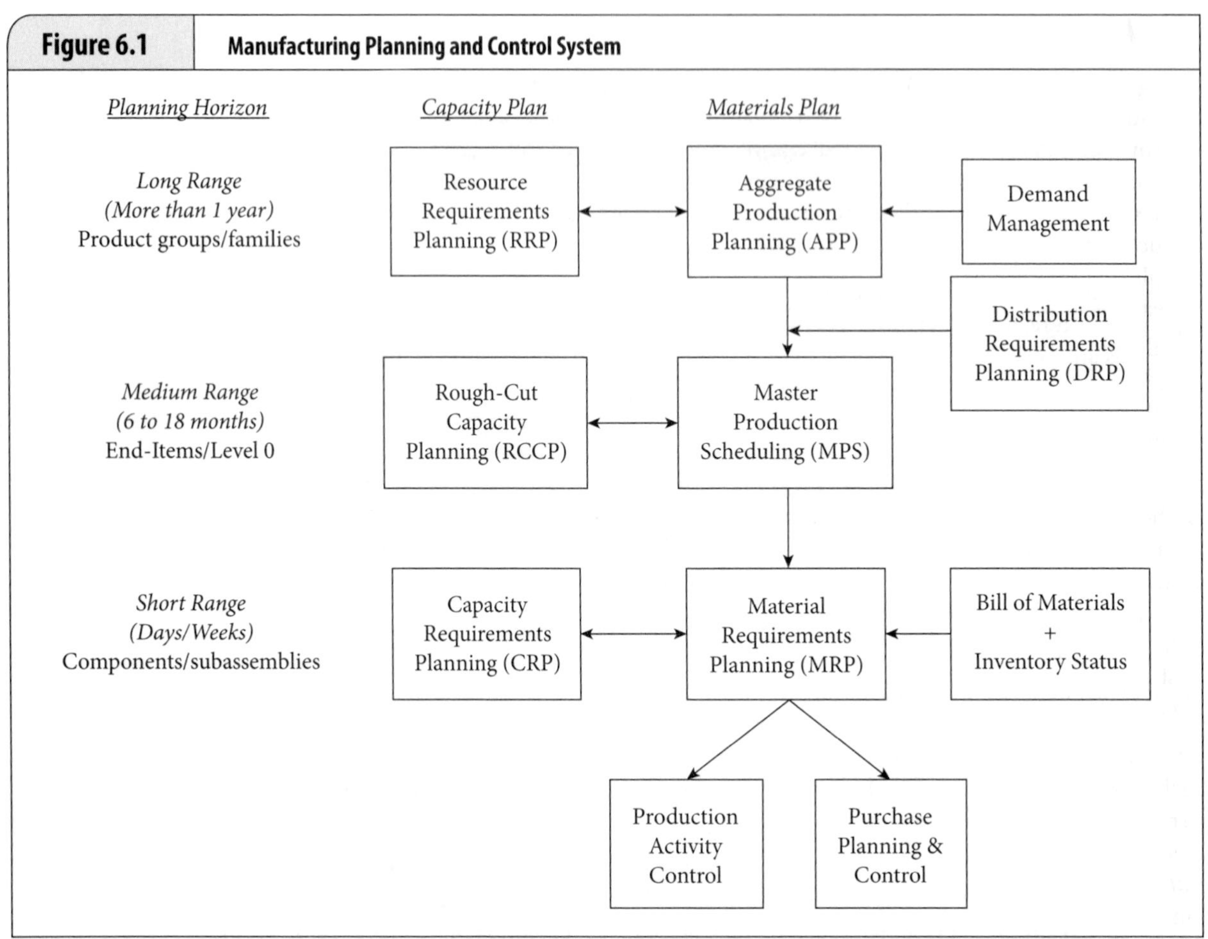

facility and major equipment purchases, the aggregate production plan's capacity is usually considered fixed during the planning horizon. The aggregate production plan sets the aggregate output rate, workforce size, utilization and inventory, and backlog levels for an entire facility. The **master production schedule (MPS)** is a medium-range plan and is more detailed than the aggregate production plan. It shows the quantity and timing of the end items that will be produced. The **material requirements plan (MRP)** is a short-range materials plan. MRP is the detailed planning process for the required component parts to support the master production schedule. It is a system of converting the end items from the master production schedule into a set of time-phased component part requirements.

Material requirements planning was first developed in the 1960s. As it gained popularity among manufacturers in the 1980s and as computing technologies emerged, MRP grew in scope into **manufacturing resource planning (MRP-II)**. MRP-II combined MRP with master production scheduling, rough-cut capacity planning, capacity requirement planning, and other operations planning software modules. Eventually, the MRP-II system evolved into **enterprise resource planning (ERP)** in the 1990s.

Distribution requirements planning (DRP) describes the time-phased net requirements from central supply warehouses and distribution centers. It links production with distribution planning by providing aggregate time-phased net requirements information to the master production schedule.

THE AGGREGATE PRODUCTION PLAN

Aggregate production planning is a hierarchical planning process that translates annual business plans and demand forecasts into a production plan for all products. As shown in Figure 6.1, *demand management* includes determining the aggregate demand based on forecasts of future demand, customer orders, special promotions, and safety stock requirements. This forecast of demand then sets the aggregate utilization, production rate, workforce levels, and inventory balances or backlogs. Aggregate production plans are typically stated in terms of product families or groups. A **product family** consists of different products that share similar characteristics, components, or manufacturing processes. For example, an all-terrain vehicle (ATV) manufacturer who produces both automatic and manual drive options may group the two different types of ATVs together, since the only difference between them is the drive option. Production processes and material requirements for the two ATVs can be expected to be very similar and, thus, can be grouped into a family.

The planning horizon covered by the APP is normally at least one year and is usually extended or rolled forward by three months every quarter. This allows the firm to see its capacity requirements at least one year ahead on a continuous basis. The APP *disaggregates* the demand forecast information it receives and links the long-range business plan to the medium-range master production schedule. The objective is to provide sufficient finished goods in each period to meet the sales plan while meeting financial and production constraints.

Costs relevant to the aggregate planning decision include inventory cost, setup cost, machine operating cost, hiring cost, firing cost, training cost, overtime cost, and costs incurred for hiring part-time and temporary workers to meet peak demand. There are three basic production strategies that firms use for completing the aggregate plan: (1) the *chase strategy*, (2) the *level strategy*, and (3) the *mixed strategy*. Example 6.1 provides an illustration of an APP.

The Chase Production Strategy

The pure **chase production strategy** adjusts capacity to match the demand pattern. Using this strategy, the firm will hire and lay off workers to match its production rate to demand. The workforce fluctuates from month to month, but finished goods inventory remains constant. Using Example 6.1, the ATV Corporation will use six workers to make 120 units in January, and then lay off a worker in February to produce 100 units, as shown

Example 6.1 An Aggregate Production Plan for the ATV Corporation

The ATV Corporation makes three models of all-terrain vehicles: Model A, Model B, and Model C. Model A uses a 0.4-liter engine, Model B uses a 0.5-liter engine, and Model C uses a 0.6-liter engine. The aggregate production plan is the twelve-month plan that combines all three models together in total monthly production. The planning horizon is twelve months. The APP determines the size of the workforce, which is the constrained resource. Table 6.1 shows the annual aggregate production plan from January to December, assuming the beginning inventory for January is 100 units (30 units each of Model A and Model B, and 40 units of Model C), and the firm desires to have an ending inventory of 140 units at the end of the year. On average, one unit of ATV requires eight labor hours to produce, and a worker contributes 160 hours (8 hours × 5 days × 4 weeks) per month. Note that the 1,120 labor hours needed in December as shown in Table 6.1 excludes the labor hours (8 hours × 40 units = 320 hours) required to produce the additional 40 units, which is the difference between the January beginning inventory of 100 units and the desired December ending inventory of 140 units.

The final column in Table 6.1 (Planned Capacity) refers to a typical manufacturing workforce situation wherein the firm desires to maintain a minimum core workforce of ten workers while also relying on overtime and subcontracting to handle the forecasted high seasonal demands.

Table 6.1 ATV Corporation's Aggregate Production Plan

PERIOD	FORECAST DEMAND (UNITS)	CAPACITY (LABOR HOURS)	
		NEEDED (HOURS)	PLANNED
January	120	960	10 workers
February	100	800	10 workers
March	300	2,400	12 workers + overtime
April	460	3,680	18 workers + overtime
May	600	4,800	25 workers + overtime
June	700	5,600	25 workers + overtime + subcontracting
July	760	6,080	25 workers + overtime + subcontracting
August	640	5,120	25 workers + overtime
September	580	4,640	25 workers + overtime
October	400	3,200	20 workers
November	200	1,600	10 workers
December	140	1,120	10 workers
	5,000	40,000	

Table 6.2 An Example of the Chase Production Strategy

PERIOD	FORECAST DEMAND (UNITS)	PRODUCTION (UNITS)	CAPACITY NEEDED (LABOR)		ENDING INVENTORY (UNITS)
			HOURS	WORKERS	
January	120	120	960	6	100
February	100	100	800	5	100
March	300	300	2,400	15	100
April	460	460	3,680	23	100
May	600	600	4,800	30	100
June	700	700	5,600	35	100
July	760	760	6,080	38	100
August	640	640	5,120	32	100
September	580	580	4,640	29	100
October	400	400	3,200	20	100
November	200	200	1,600	10	100
December	140 + 40	180	1,120 + 320	9	140
	5,040	5,040	40,320	252	

in Table 6.2. In March, the firm must hire ten additional workers so that it has enough labor to produce 300 units. An additional eight workers must be hired in April. The firm continues its hiring and layoff policy to ensure its workforce and production capacity matches demand. In December, 180 units will be produced (although the demand is 140) because of the firm's desire to increase its ending inventory by 40 units in December.

The pure chase strategy obviously has a negative motivational impact on the workers, and it assumes that workers can be hired and trained easily to perform the job. In this strategy, the finished goods inventories always remain constant, but the workforce fluctuates

Figure 6.2 Constant Inventory Level under the Chase Production Strategy

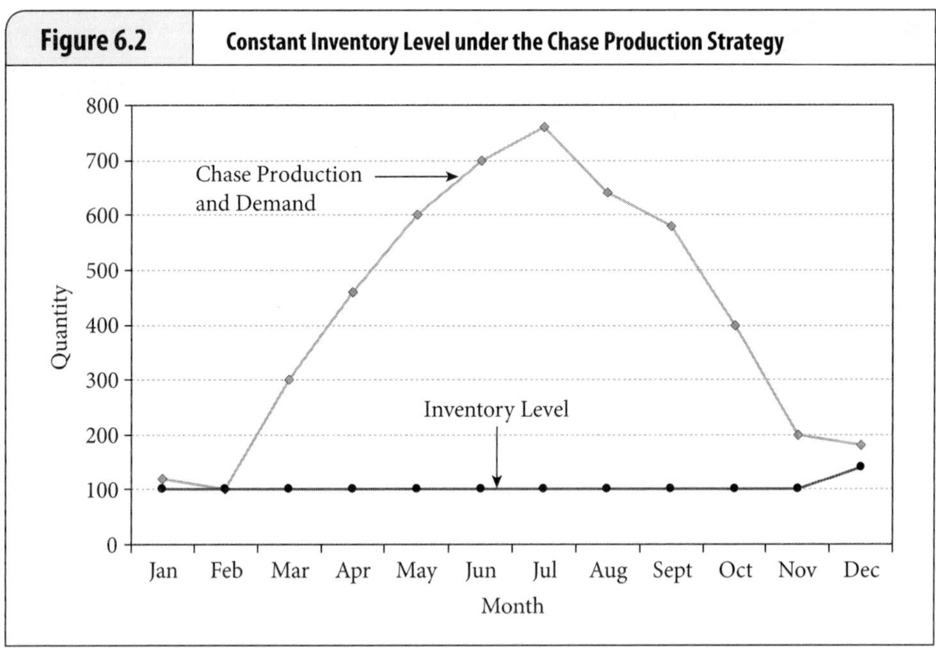

in response to the demand pattern. Figure 6.2 shows that the chase production curve perfectly overlaps on the demand curve. The inventory level remains constant at 100 units until December, when it increases by 40 units. Hiring, training, and termination costs are significant cost components in the chase production strategy.

This strategy works well for **make-to-order manufacturing firms** since they cannot rely on finished goods inventory to satisfy the fluctuating demand pattern. Make-to-order firms generally produce one-of-a-kind, specialty products based on customer specifications. Make-to-order firms cannot build ahead of orders since they do not know the actual specifications of the finished goods. However, make-to-order products generally require highly skilled labor, capable of producing unique products using general-purpose equipment. Although a chase production strategy works well when unskilled labor is required, the strategy can be problematic when highly skilled workers are needed, especially in a tight labor market.

The Level Production Strategy

A pure **level production strategy** relies on a constant output rate and capacity while varying inventory and backlog levels to handle the fluctuating demand pattern. Using this strategy, the firm keeps its workforce levels constant and relies on fluctuating finished goods inventories and backlogs to meet demand. Since the level production strategy keeps a constant output rate and capacity, it is more suited for firms that require highly skilled labor. The workforce is likely to be more effective and its morale higher when compared to the chase strategy. Again using the Example 6.1 forecast information, a pure level production strategy calls for a monthly production rate of 420 units ([5,000 units annual demand + 40 units additional ending inventory] ÷ 12 months). Thus, this strategy requires a constant workforce of twenty-one workers, as shown in Table 6.3.

The firm allows finished goods inventories to accrue while cumulative demand remains less than cumulative production, and then relies on a series of backlogs to handle the demand from August through November. Figure 6.3 shows that level production is

Table 6.3 An Example of Level Production Strategy

PERIOD	FORECAST DEMAND (UNITS)	PRODUCTION (UNITS)	CAPACITY NEEDED (LABOR)		ENDING INV/ (BACKLOG) (UNITS)
			HOURS	WORKERS	
January	120	420	3,360	21	400
February	100	420	3,360	21	720
March	300	420	3,360	21	840
April	460	420	3,360	21	800
May	600	420	3,360	21	620
June	700	420	3,360	21	340
July	760	420	3,360	21	0
August	640	420	3,360	21	(220)
September	580	420	3,360	21	(380)
October	400	420	3,360	21	(360)
November	200	420	3,360	21	(140)
December	140 + 40	420	3,360	21	140
	5,040	5,040	40,320	252	

Figure 6.3 Fluctuating Inventory/Backlog Level under the Level Production Strategy

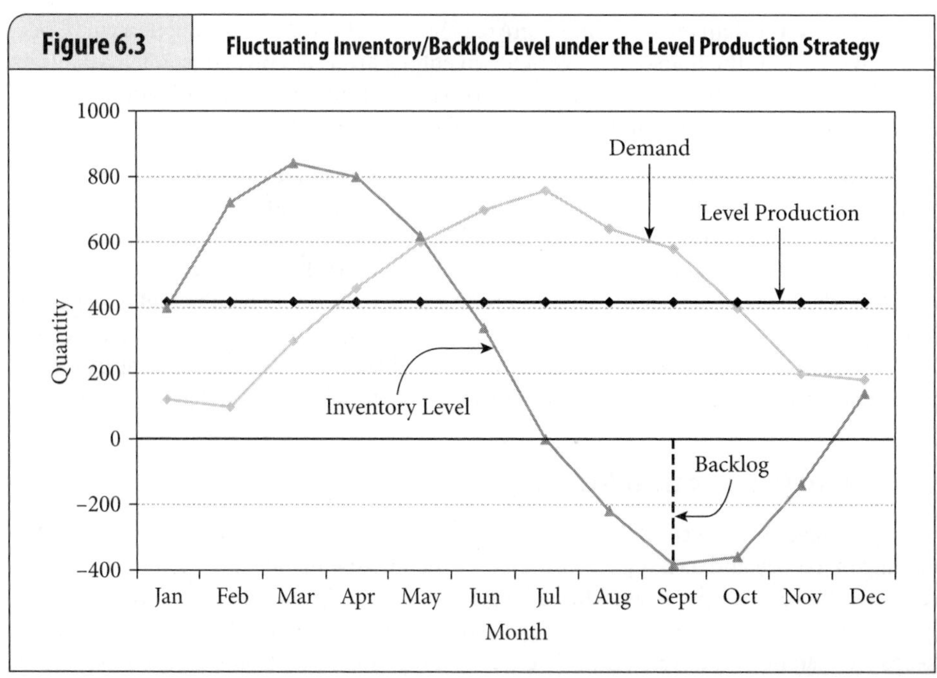

characterized by the fluctuating inventory/backlog level while the workforce and production capacity remain constant. Inventory carrying and stockout costs are major cost concerns in the level production strategy. This strategy works well for **make-to-stock** manufacturing firms, which typically emphasize immediate delivery of off-the-shelf, standard goods at relatively low prices. Firms whose trading partners seek the lowest prices of stock items might select the level production strategy. Additionally, this strategy works well in a situation where highly skilled workers are needed in a tight labor market.

The Mixed Production Strategy

Instead of using either the pure chase or level production strategy, many firms use a mixed production strategy that strives to maintain a stable core workforce while using other short-term means such as overtime, an additional shift, subcontracting, or the hiring of part-time and temporary workers to manage short-term high demand. Usually, these firms will then schedule preventive maintenance, produce complementary products that require similar resources but different demand cycles, or continue to produce the end items, holding these as finished goods inventory during the off-peak demand periods.

For example, all-terrain-vehicle manufacturers can produce snowmobiles to smooth out the seasonal effect of the two products. Table 6.1 shows the mixed strategy (shown in the table as the Planned Capacity column) in which the firm strives to maintain a minimum core workforce of ten workers while avoiding hiring above twenty-five workers during the peak or high demand season. Hiring above twenty-five workers may strain other capacities, such as machine capacity and the availability of component parts. Instead, the mixed strategy uses overtime and subcontracting to cope with the high demand periods. If labor is the only constrained capacity, it may hire enough workers to run an additional shift to cope with the high demand. We can see here that firms with multiple products and with customers seeking both low-cost and make-to-order items may opt for this type of production strategy to minimize stockouts and cycle time.

THE MASTER PRODUCTION SCHEDULE

The master production schedule (MPS) is a time-phased, detailed disaggregation of the aggregate production plan, listing the exact end items to be produced. It is more detailed than the aggregate production plan. The MPS planning horizon is shorter than the aggregate production plan's but must be longer than a firm's production lead time to ensure the end item can be completed within the planning horizon.

For example, disaggregating ATV Corporation's January and February aggregate production plans may yield the master production schedule shown in Table 6.4. The plan results in time-phased production requirements of the specific model of ATV to produce for every week in January and February. The sum of the weekly MPS matches the quantity of the APP for that same month. For example, the MPS quantities for January and February

Table 6.4 ATV's Master Production Schedule for January and February

PERIOD	APP QUANTITY (UNITS)	MPS QUANTITY (UNITS)		
		MODEL A	MODEL B	MODEL C
January—week 1	120	10	10	10
January—week 2		10	10	10
January—week 3		20	0	10
January—week 4		0	20	10
February—week 1	100	20	0	0
February—week 2		0	20	0
February—week 3		0	0	20
February—week 4		20	20	0
Total	220	80	80	60

in Table 6.4 (80, 80, and 60 units for the three models) equal the monthly APP quantities of 120 and 100 units, respectively. The master production schedule provides more detail by breaking down the aggregate production plan into specific weekly demand for Model A, Model B, and Model C.

For the service industry, the master production schedule may just be the appointment book or scheduling software, which is created to ensure that capacity in the form of skilled labor matches demand. Master production schedules in the form of appointments are not overbooked to ensure capacity is not strained. The firm continues to revise and add appointments to the MPS until it obtains the best possible schedule. An example is to schedule patients' appointments in a hospital by means of a medical appointment scheduling software application.

Master Production Schedule Time Fence

The master production schedule is the production quantity required to meet demand from all sources and is the basis for computing the requirements of all time-phased end items. The material requirements plan uses the MPS to compute component part and subassembly requirements. Frequent changes to the MPS can be costly and may create system nervousness.

System nervousness can be defined as a situation wherein a small change in the upper-level production plan causes a major change in the lower-level production plan. For example, in the case of the clinic booking new appointments, it is very difficult for the clinic to book additional appointments for the current period because it is very likely that the appointment book is already fully booked. If a patient insists that she must see the doctor immediately, it is likely that another patient's appointment may have to be delayed or the clinic would need to work overtime to see an additional patient. However, it is much easier for the clinic to book new appointments farther into the future.

System nervousness can create serious problems for manufacturing firms. For example, if the January production plan for the ATV Corporation is suddenly doubled during the second week of January, the firm would be forced to quickly revise purchase orders, component assembly orders, and end-item production orders, causing a ripple effect of change within the firm and up its supply chain to its suppliers. The change would also likely cause missed delivery due dates. The firm needs sufficient lead time to purchase items and manufacture the end items, especially if manufacturing lead times and lot sizes are large.

Many firms use a **time fence system** to deal with this problem. The time fence system separates the planning horizon into two segments: a *firmed* and a *tentative segment*. A firmed segment is also known as a **demand time fence**, and it usually stretches from the current period to a period several weeks into the future. A firmed segment stipulates that the production plan or MPS cannot be altered except with the authorization of senior management. The tentative segment is also known as the **planning time fence**, and it typically stretches from the end of the firmed segment to several weeks farther into the future. It usually covers a longer period than the firmed segment, and the master scheduler can change production to meet changing conditions. Beyond the planning time fence, the computer can schedule the MPS quantities automatically, based on existing ordering and scheduling policies.

Available-to-Promise Quantities

In addition to providing time-phased production quantities of specific end items, the MPS also provides vital information on whether additional orders can be accepted for

Table 6.5 Discrete ATP Calculation for January and February

		WEEK							
		1	2	3	4	5	6	7	8
Model A—0.4-liter Engine									
MPS	BI = 30	10	10	20	0	20	0	0	20
Committed Customer Orders		10	0	28	0	0	20	0	10
ATP:D		30	2	0	0	0	0	0	10
Model B—0.5-liter Engine									
MPS	BI = 30	10	10	0	20	0	20	0	20
Committed Customer Orders		20	10	7	0	0	20	18	0
ATP:D		13	0	0	2	0	0	0	20
Model C—0.6-liter Engine									
MPS	BI = 40	10	10	10	10	0	0	20	0
Committed Customer Orders		20	10	0	0	0	10	0	15
ATP:D		30	0	10	0	0	0	5	0

delivery in specific periods. This information is particularly important when customers are relying on the firm to deliver the right quantity of products purchased on the desired delivery date. This information is the **available-to-promise (ATP) quantity**, or the uncommitted portion of the firm's planned production (or scheduled MPS). It is the difference between confirmed customer orders and the quantity the firm planned to produce, based on the MPS. The available-to-promise quantity provides a mechanism to allow the master scheduler or sales personnel to quickly negotiate new orders and delivery due dates with customers or to quickly respond to customers' changing demands. The three basic methods of calculating the available-to-promise quantities are: (1) *discrete available-to-promise*, (2) *cumulative available-to-promise without look ahead*, and (3) *cumulative available-to-promise with look ahead*. The discrete available-to-promise (ATP:D) computation is discussed next. Readers who are interested in the other two methods are referred to Fogarty, Blackstone, and Hoffmann (1991).[7]

The ATV Corporation's January and February master production schedule for Model A, Model B, and Model C is used in Table 6.5 to demonstrate the ATP:D method for computing the ATP quantities. Let us assume there are four weeks each in January and February, which are shown in the first row and are labeled Week 1 to Week 8. The MPS row indicates the time-phased production quantities derived from the master production schedule in Table 6.4. These are the quantities to be produced by manufacturing firms as planned. The number labeled "BI" is the beginning inventory heading into the first week of January. Committed customer orders are orders that have already been booked for specific customers. Finally, the ATP:D quantities are the remaining unbooked or unpromised units.

Calculating Discrete Available-to-Promise Quantities

The discrete available-to-promise (ATP:D) is computed as follows:

1. The ATP for the first period is the sum of the beginning inventory and the MPS, minus the sum of all the committed customer orders (CCOs) from the first period up to but not including the period of the next scheduled MPS.

2. For all subsequent periods, there are two possibilities:
   a. If no MPS has been scheduled for the period, the ATP is zero.
   b. If an MPS has been scheduled for the period, the ATP is the MPS quantity minus the sum of all CCOs from that period up to but not including the period of the next scheduled MPS.
3. If an ATP for any period is negative, the deficit must be subtracted from the most recent positive ATP, and the quantities must be revised to reflect these changes.

As a check, the sum of the BI and MPS quantities for all periods must equal the sum of all CCOs and ATPs. Using these guidelines, the ATP:D quantities in Table 6.5 are computed as follows:

Model A

1. $ATP_1 = BI + MPS_1 - CCO_1 = 30 + 10 - 10 = 30$
2. $ATP_2 = MPS_2 - CCO_2 = 10 - 0 = 10$
3. $ATP_3 = MPS_3 - CCO_3 - CCO_4 = 20 - 28 - 0 = -8$ (need to use 8 units from ATP_2)
   Revising: $ATP_2 = 10 - 8 = 2$ and $ATP_3 = -8 + 8 = 0$
4. $ATP_4 = 0$ (no scheduled MPS)
5. $ATP_5 = MPS_5 - CCO_5 - CCO_6 - CCO_7 = 20 - 0 - 20 - 0 = 0$
6. $ATP_6 = 0$ (no scheduled MPS)
7. $ATP_7 = 0$ (no scheduled MPS)
8. $ATP_8 = MPS_8 - CCO_8 = 20 - 10 = 10$

Checking the calculations, the sum of the BI and MPS quantities for the eight periods equals 110 units, which is also the sum of the CCOs and the ATPs for the same periods. Further, the calculation shows that 30 units of the Model A ATV can be promised for delivery in the first week of January or later, 2 units can be promised in the second week or later, and another 10 units can be promised for delivery in the eighth week or later. The eight-period total ATP of 42 units is the difference between the sum of the beginning inventory and MPS (110 units), and the sum of the committed customer orders (68 units) for the eight weeks. Also note that although no MPS has been scheduled for the sixth week, the committed customer orders of 20 units are still possible, since the units can come from the uncommitted MPS of the previous weeks.

Model B

1. $ATP_1 = BI + MPS_1 - CCO_1 = 30 + 10 - 20 = 20$
2. $ATP_2 = MPS_2 - CCO_2 - CCO_3 = 10 - 10 - 7 = -7$ (need to use 7 units from ATP_1)
   Revising: $ATP_1 = 20 - 7 = 13$ and $ATP_2 = -7 + 7 = 0$
3. $ATP_3 = 0$ (no scheduled MPS)
4. $ATP_4 = MPS_4 - CCO_4 - CCO_5 = 20 - 0 - 0 = 20$
5. $ATP_5 = 0$ (no scheduled MPS)
6. $ATP_6 = MPS_6 - CCO_6 - CCO_7 = 20 - 20 - 18 = -18$ (need to use 18 units from ATP_4 since $ATP_5 = 0$)
   Revising: $ATP_4 = 20 - 18 = 2$ and $ATP_6 = -18 + 18 = 0$
7. $ATP_7 = 0$ (no scheduled MPS)
8. $ATP_8 = MPS_8 - CCO_8 = 20 - 0 = 20$

Checking, the BI plus the eight MPS weekly quantities equals 110 units and the CCOs plus the ATPs for the eight periods also equals 110 units. The calculation shows that 13 units of the Model B ATV can be promised for delivery in the first week or later, 2 units can be promised for delivery in the fourth week or later, and another 20 units can be promised for delivery in the eighth week or later. The eight-period total ATP of 35 units is the difference between the sum of the beginning inventory and MPS (110 units), and the sum of the committed customer orders (75 units) for the eight-week period. Note that although no MPS has been scheduled for the seventh week, the CCO of 18 units came from the uncommitted MPS quantities of the previous weeks.

Model C

1. $ATP_1 = BI + MPS_1 - CCO_1 = 40 + 10 - 20 = 30$
2. $ATP_2 = MPS_2 - CCO_2 = 10 - 10 = 0$
3. $ATP_3 = MPS_3 - CCO_3 = 10 - 0 = 10$
4. $ATP_4 = MPS_4 - CCO_4 - CCO_5 - CCO_6 = 10 - 0 - 0 - 10 = 0$
5. $ATP_5 = 0$ (no scheduled MPS)
6. $ATP_6 = 0$ (no scheduled MPS)
7. $ATP_7 = MPS_7 - CCO_7 - CCO_8 = 20 - 0 - 15 = 5$
8. $ATP_8 = 0$ (no scheduled MPS)

Checking, the total BI and eight-period MPS is 100 units, and the total CCOs and ATPs for the eight periods is also 100 units. The calculation shows that 30 units of Model C ATV can be promised for delivery in the first week of January or later, 10 units can be promised in the third week or later, and another 5 units can be promised for delivery in the seventh week or later. The total of eight-period ATP of 45 units is the difference between the sum of the BI and MPS (100 units), and the sum of the committed customer orders (55 units) for the eight-week period.

Note that while the total uncommitted production quantity can easily be computed by subtracting all CCOs from the scheduled MPS, it lacks time-phased information. For this reason, the ATP quantities must be determined as shown. This enables the master scheduler or salesperson to quickly book or confirm new sales to be delivered on specific due dates. Reacting quickly to demand changes and delivering orders on time are necessities in high-performing supply chains, and the tools discussed here enable firms to effectively meet customer needs. In supply chain relationships, using the MPS and ATP information effectively is essential to maintaining speed and flexibility (which impacts customer service) throughout the supply chain as products make their way to end users.

THE BILL OF MATERIALS

The **bill of materials (BOM)** is an engineering document that shows an inclusive listing of all component parts and subassemblies making up the end item. Figure 6.4 is an example of a *multilevel bill of materials* for the ATV Corporation's all-terrain vehicles. It shows the parent–component relationships and the exact quantity of each component, known as the **planning factor**, required for making a higher-level part or assembly. For example, "engine assembly" is the immediate *parent* of "engine block," and conversely "engine block" is an immediate *component* of "engine assembly." The "24-inch solid steel bar" is a *common component part*, because it is a component of the "6-inch steel bar" and the "12-inch steel bar." The *planning factor* of "connecting rods" shows that four connecting rods are needed

Figure 6.4 Bill of Materials for the ATV

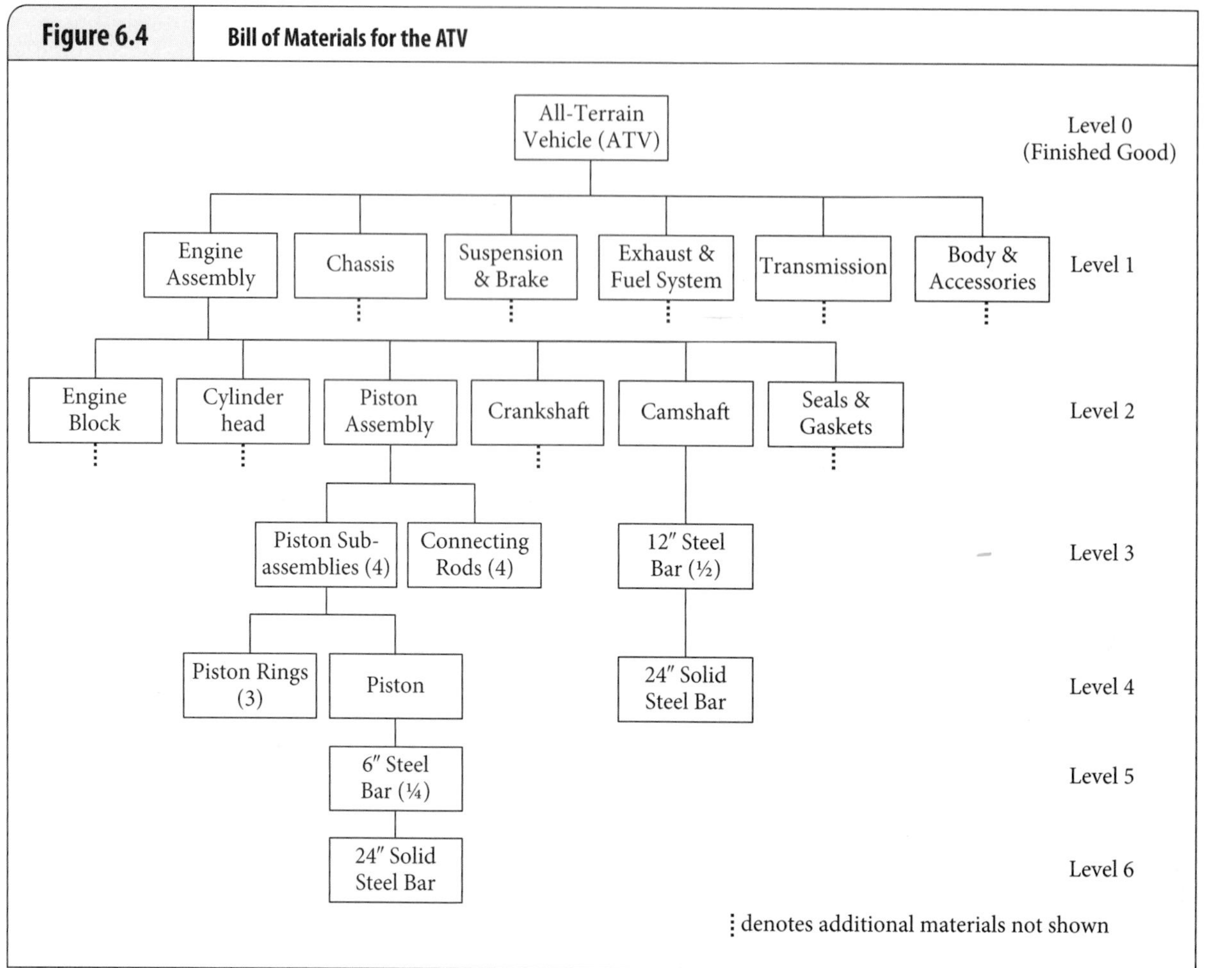

to make one "piston assembly." Note that twelve "piston rings" (3 × 4) are needed to assemble one ATV since there are three "piston rings" in each "piston subassembly," and there are four "piston subassemblies" in each "piston assembly."

The BOM is shown in various levels, starting from Level 0. The level numbers increase as one moves down on the BOM. Level 0 is the final product, which is the **independent demand** item. In this case, it is the ATV. It has a demand pattern that is subject to trends and seasonal variations, and to general market conditions. Gross requirements of Level 0 items come from the master production schedule (i.e., Table 6.4 in the ATV Corporation example). The next level in the BOM is Level 1, which consists of all components and subassemblies required for the final assembly of one unit of an ATV. The gross requirements of Level 1 components and subassemblies are computed based on the demand for ATVs as specified in Level 0. Therefore, the requirements for all the items in Level 1 and below are called **dependent demand** items. For example, the engine assembly, chassis, suspension and brake, and transmission used to assemble the ATV are dependent demand items. However, if the components or subassemblies are sold as *service parts* to customers for repairing their ATVs, then they are independent demand items.

Correspondingly, the multilevel bill of materials can also be presented as an **indented bill of materials** as shown in Table 6.6. At each level of indentation, the level number

Table 6.6 Indented Bill of Materials—All-Terrain Vehicles

PART DESCRIPTION	LEVEL	PLANNING FACTOR
Engine Assembly	1	1
Engine Block (components not shown)	2	1
Cylinder Head (components not shown)	2	1
Piston Assembly	2	1
Piston Subassembly	3	4
Piston Rings	4	3
Pistons	4	1
6" Steel Bar	5	¼
24" Solid Steel Bar	6	1
Connecting Rods	3	4
Crankshaft (components not shown)	2	1
Camshaft	2	1
12" Steel Bar	3	½
24" Solid Steel Bar	4	1
Seals & Gaskets (components not shown)	2	1
Chassis (components not shown)	1	1
Suspension & Brake (components not shown)	1	1
Exhaust & Fuel System (components not shown)	1	1
Transmission (components not shown)	1	1
Body & Accessories (components not shown)	1	1

increases by one. The indented bill of materials in Table 6.6 can be seen as an illustration of the multilevel bill of materials (Figure 6.4) rotated 90 degrees counterclockwise.

Another type of bill of materials is the **super bill of materials**, which is useful for planning purposes. It is also referred to as a *planning bill of materials, pseudo bill of materials, phantom bill of materials*, or *family bill of materials*. Using the ATV Corporation's BOM in Figure 6.4 as an example, a simplified product structure diagram can be created for the family of ATVs that consists of different engine sizes (i.e., models) and transmission options. Instead of stating the planning factor, the percentage of each option is used. Figure 6.5 shows that 33⅓ percent of the ATVs are Model A, Model B, and Model C, respectively. Similarly, 75 percent of the ATVs use automatic transmissions and the remaining 25 percent use manual transmissions. Therefore, the ATV Corporation's January planned production (120 units) consists of 40 units each of Model A, Model B, and Model C (see Table 6.4). Similarly, 90 (75 percent × 120) units of the ATVs will be manufactured with automatic transmissions, and the remaining 30 (25 percent × 120) units will be manufactured with manual transmissions.

The super bill of materials enables the firm to forecast the total demand of ATVs and then break down the forecast into different models and transmission options using the correct percentage instead of forecasting the demand for each option individually. It provides quick information on the quantity of components for each option needed for the scheduled production. In addition, it also reduces the number of master production schedules. For the ATV Corporation example, the number of master production schedules was reduced from six (3 models × 2 transmission options) to one.

Figure 6.5 Super Bill of Materials for the ATV

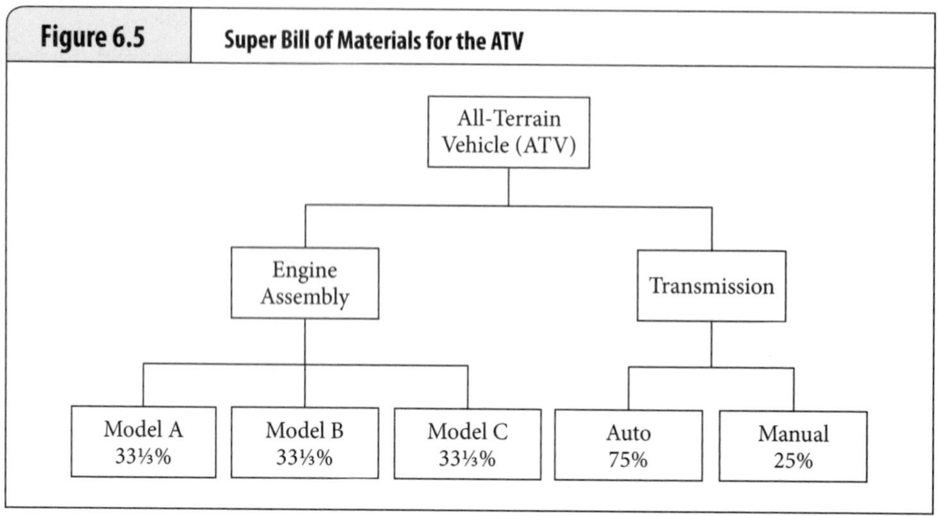

When the exact proportion of each option is uncertain, the percentage can be increased slightly to cover the uncertainty. For example, the ATV Corporation may increase its automatic transmission option to 78 percent and manual option to 27 percent, for a total of 105 percent. The firm raises its total planned production by 5 percent to cover uncertainty. This is known as **option overplanning**.

THE MATERIAL REQUIREMENTS PLAN

As illustrated in the ATV bill of materials in Figure 6.4, **dependent demand** is a term used to describe the internal demand for parts based on the **independent demand** of the final product, for which the parts are used. Subassemblies, components, and raw materials are examples of dependent demand items. Dependent demand may have a pattern of abrupt and dramatic changes because of its dependency on the demand of the final product, especially if the final product is produced in large lot sizes. Once the independent demand of the final product is known or forecasted, the dependent demand item requirements can be exactly calculated using material requirements planning (MRP) software, along with when the items should be assembled or purchased.

For example, the ATV Corporation's MPS (Table 6.4) shows that 120 ATVs will be produced in January. The firm thus knows that 120 handlebars and 480 wheel rims will be needed. The demand for handlebars, wheel rims, and all of the other dependent demand items can be calculated using the MRP, based on the bill of materials (BOM) and the demand of the final product as stated on the MPS.

Material requirements planning is a software-based production planning and inventory control system that has been used widely by manufacturing firms for computing dependent demand and timing requirements. With the advent of computer and information technologies, the span of MRP evolved to include aggregate production planning, master production scheduling, and capacity requirements planning to become **closed-loop MRP**. It further evolved into manufacturing resource planning (MRP-II) by including other aspects of materials and resource planning. A complete MRP-II system consists of many modules that enable the firm to book orders, schedule production, control inventory, manage distribution, and perform accounting and financial analyses.

While there are hundreds of suppliers still selling and supporting their original MRP systems, some suppliers have expanded their systems to enable the users to perform more sophisticated analyses and integrate organization-wide activities, including operations and facilities that are located in different countries from the head office. This new generation of MRP system is known as the enterprise resource planning (ERP) system.

Material requirements planning is used to calculate the exact quantities, need dates, and planned order releases for components and subassemblies needed to manufacture the final products listed on the MPS. MRP begins the computation process by first obtaining the requirements of the final product (the Level 0 item on the BOM) from the MPS to calculate the requirements of Level 1 components and then working its way down to the lowest level components, taking into account existing inventories and the time required for each processing step. While these manufacturing and delivery lead times are disregarded in the MPS, they are considered in the MRP computation process. For example, if a parent item requires an immediate component with a three-week lead time, the component must be ordered three weeks ahead of the need date.

For MRP, a dependent demand management system, to work effectively, it requires: (1) the independent demand information (the demand for the final product or service part) from the MPS; (2) parent–component relationships from the bill of materials, including the planning factor and lead time information; and (3) the inventory status of the final product and all of its components. The MRP takes this information to compute the *net requirements* of the final product and components, and then offsets the net requirements with appropriate lead times to ensure orders are released on time for fabricating the higher level components or purchasing the lower level components. This information, called **planned order releases**, is the most important output of the MRP. For items manufactured in-house, planned order releases are transmitted to the shop floor, but for purchased items, planned order releases are transmitted to suppliers directly or via the purchasing department.

A key benefit of MRP is that production information—such as scheduled receipts, on-hand inventories, net requirements, and planned order releases—is available for the entire planning horizon; thus, it provides *visibility* for schedulers to plan ahead. However, the need for offsetting net requirements by the lead time to obtain planned order releases causes a *loss of visibility* in the planning horizon of components. This problem is especially acute for products with a deep bill of materials. Another drawback of the MRP is that it ignores capacity and shop floor conditions.

Terms Used in Material Requirements Planning

Prior to examining how the MRP logic works, let us look at some terms as they apply to the MRP:

- *Parent*: The item generating the demand for lower level components. Level 0 is the final product. It is the parent of all Level 1 components. Similarly, each Level 1 item becomes the parent of the Level 2 components used to make that item. For example, Figure 6.4 shows that "piston assembly" is a parent of "piston subassemblies" and "connecting rods."
- *Components*: The parts demanded by a parent. For example, Figure 6.4 shows that "piston assembly" is a component of "engine assembly."
- *Gross requirement*: A time-phased requirement prior to considering on-hand inventory and lead time to obtain the item. The gross requirement is satisfied from inventory and production.

- *Net requirement*: The unsatisfied item requirement for a specific time period. It equals the gross requirement for that period minus the current on-hand inventory and any scheduled receipts.
- *Scheduled receipt*: A committed order awaiting delivery for a specific period. It is an order released in a past period and due to be received in a specific later period. This information is updated automatically by the MRP software logic system once an order has been placed. For example, an item with a two-week lead time ordered on the first week of the month becomes a scheduled receipt on the third week.
- *Projected on-hand inventory*: The projected inventory at the end of the period. It equals the beginning inventory minus the gross requirement, plus the scheduled receipt and any planned receipt from an earlier planned order release.
- *Planned order release*: A specific order to be released to the shop (if the component is made in-house) or to the supplier (if the component is purchased) to ensure that it is available on the need date. A key consideration here is that the *planned order releases of the parent determine the gross requirements of the components.*
- *Time bucket*: The time period used on the MRP. It is usually expressed in days or weeks. The current period is the *action time bucket.*
- *Explosion*: The common term used to describe the process of converting a parent item's planned order releases into component gross requirements.
- *Planning factor*: The number of components needed to produce one unit of the parent item. For example, Figure 6.4 shows that three "piston rings" are needed to produce one "piston subassembly."
- *Firmed planned order*: A planned order that the MRP software logic system cannot automatically change when conditions change. The primary purpose of a firmed planned order is to prevent *system nervousness*, similar to the time fence system explained earlier in the master production schedule discussion.
- *Pegging*: Relates gross requirements for a component to the planned order releases that created the requirements.
- *Low-level coding*: Assigns the lowest level on the bill of materials to all common components to avoid duplicate MRP computations. For example, Figure 6.4 shows that "24-inch solid steel bar" is a common component in Level 4 and Level 6. Instead of computing its planned order releases at Level 4 and Level 6 separately, a low-level code of 6 is assigned to the item. Its net requirements at Level 4 are added to those at Level 6, and the MRP explosion logic is performed at Level 6 only.
- *Lot size*: The order size for MRP logic. Lot size may be determined by various lot-sizing techniques, such as the EOQ (a fixed order quantity) or lot-for-lot (order whatever amount is needed each period). A lot size of 50 calls for orders to be placed in multiples of 50. With a net requirement of 85 units, using lot-for-lot (LFL) order sizing will result in an order of 85 units; however, an order of 100 units would be placed when using a fixed order quantity of 50 (order sizes are multiples of 50).
- *Safety stock*: Protects against uncertainties in demand, supply, quality, and lead time. Its implication in MRP logic is that the minimum projected on-hand inventory should not fall below the safety stock level.

An MRP example is provided in Example 6.2.

Example 6.2 An MRP Example at the ATV Corporation

Model A's production schedule for the ATV Corporation is used to illustrate the MRP logic. Its gross requirements are first obtained from the master production schedule in Table 6.4, and the inventory status shows that 30 units of Model A are available at the start of the year. The parent–component relationships and planning factors are available from the BOM in Figure 6.4. Assuming the following lot sizes (Q), lead times (LT), and safety stocks (SS) are used, the MRP computations of the Model A ATV and some of its components are as follows:

MODEL A ATV—LEVEL 0		1	2	3	4	5	6	7	8
Gross Requirements		10	10	20	0	20	0	0	20
Scheduled Receipts			10						
Projected On-hand Inventory	30	20	20	20	20	20	20	20	20
Planned Order Releases		20		20			20		

Q = 10; LT = 2; SS = 15

×1 ×1 ×1

ENGINE ASSEMBLY—LEVEL 1		1	2	3	4	5	6	7	8
Gross Requirements		20		20			20		
Scheduled Receipts		20							
Projected On-hand Inventory	2	2	2	0	0	0	0	0	0
Planned Order Releases		18			20				

Q = LFL; LT = 2; SS = 0

×1 ×1

PISTON ASSEMBLY—LEVEL 2		1	2	3	4	5	6	7	8
Gross Requirements		18			20				
Scheduled Receipts		20							
Projected On-hand Inventory	10	12	12	12	22	22	22	22	22
Planned Order Releases				30					

Q = 30; LT = 1; SS = 10

×4

CONNECTING RODS—LEVEL 3		1	2	3	4	5	6	7	8
Gross Requirements				120					
Scheduled Receipts									
Projected On-hand Inventory	22	22	22	52	52	52	52	52	52
Planned Order Releases			150						

Q = 50; LT = 1; SS = 20

Level 0 MRP Computation—Model A ATV

The first row is the planning horizon for the eight weeks in January and February. The gross requirements are derived directly from the MPS. The scheduled receipt of 10 units in Week 2 is due to an order placed last week, or earlier but scheduled to be delivered in Week 2. The order size for the Model A ATV is in multiples of 10 units, the lead time is two weeks, and the desired safety stock is 15 units. The projected on-hand inventory of

20 units for the first week is computed by taking the beginning inventory of 30 units and subtracting the gross requirement of 10 units in that week. The projected on-hand inventory of 20 units in Week 2 is computed by taking the previous balance of 20 units, adding the scheduled receipt of 10 units, and subtracting the gross requirement of 10 units.

During Week 3, additional Model A ATVs must be completed to ensure the on-hand balance is above the safety stock level of 15 units. Since the opening inventory of 20 units is entirely consumed to meet the Week 3 gross requirement, the net requirement here is 15 units (the safety stock). Given that orders must be in multiples of 10, 20 units must be ordered in Week 1 to satisfy both the lead time and the safety stock requirements. Simply stated, if 20 units are needed in Week 3, the two-week lead time requires the order to be placed two weeks earlier, which explains why there is a planned order release of 20 units in the Week 1. The on-hand inventory balance of 20 units at the end of Week 3 is computed by taking the previous balance of 20 units, adding the planned order receipt of 20 units (due to the planned order release in Week 1), and subtracting the gross requirement of 20 units.

Similarly, the gross requirements of 20 units each in Week 5 and Week 8 consumed the beginning of period inventory, triggering a net requirement of 15 units for those periods and a planned order release of 20 units each during Week 3 and Week 6 respectively.

Level 1 MRP Computation—Engine Assembly

The BOM in Figure 6.4 indicates that the gross requirements for the engine assembly are derived from the planned order releases of the Model A ATV. Since the planning factor is 1 unit, the Model A ATV's planned order releases translate directly into gross requirements for engine assembly in the Weeks 1, 3, and 6 (as indicated by the arrows in Example 6.2). The scheduled receipt of 20 units in Week 1 is due to a committed order placed previously. The gross requirements of 20 units each for Weeks 3 and 6 triggered net requirements of 18 and 20 units, which turn into planned order releases for Weeks 1 and 4, respectively (note here that no safety stock is required and the lot size is LFL, thus order sizes vary according to whatever quantities are needed to have end-of-period inventories of 0).

Level 2 MRP Computation—Piston Assembly

The gross requirements for the piston assembly are derived directly from the planned order releases of engine assembly (recall that based on the BOM in Figure 6.4, the engine assembly is the immediate parent of the piston assembly and the planning factor is 1). Therefore, the gross requirements of piston assembly are eighteen and 20 units, respectively, for Weeks 1 and 4. Computations of its projected on-hand balances and planned order releases are similar to earlier examples (note here that inventories must not drop below the safety stock requirement of 10, and order quantities must be made in multiples of 30).

Level 3 MRP Computation—Connecting Rods

The BOM in Figure 6.4 indicates that four connecting rods are required for each piston assembly. Thus, the gross requirement for connecting rods in Week 3 is obtained by multiplying the planned order releases for piston assemblies by 4. Due to the requirement to offset the lead times in each MRP computation, the planned order release for connecting rods can be determined only up to the second period, although the gross requirements of the Model A ATV are known for the first eight weeks. This is known as *loss of visibility*, as discussed earlier.

Since there are no lower-level components shown for the connecting rods, we can assume that the ATV Corporation purchases this component. Thus, the planned order releases would be used by the purchasing department (as shown by the purchase planning and control function in Figure 6.1) to communicate order quantities and delivery requirements to its connecting rod supplier. Production activity control involves all aspects of shop floor scheduling, dispatching, routing, and other control activities. In supply chain settings, manufacturing firms share their planned order release information with their strategic suppliers through electronic data interchange (EDI), their ERP system, or other forms of communication. Since the firm manufactures its own piston assemblies, the planned order release information for this part is communicated to shop floor operators and used to trigger production in that week. We can see, then, that planned order releases for purchased items eventually become the independent demand gross requirements for the firm's suppliers. Communicating this information accurately and quickly to strategic suppliers is a necessary element in an effective supply chain information system.

CAPACITY PLANNING

The material plans (the aggregate production plan, the master production schedule, and the material requirements plan) discussed so far have focused exclusively on production and materials management, but organizations must also address capacity constraints. Excess capacity wastes valuable resources such as idle labor, equipment, and facilities, while insufficient capacity adversely affects quality levels and customer service. Thus, a set of capacity plans is used in conjunction with the materials plan to ensure capacity is not over- or underutilized.

In the context of capacity planning, **capacity** refers to a firm's labor and machine resources. It is the maximum amount of output that an organization is capable of completing in a given period of time. Capacity planning follows the basic hierarchy of the materials planning system as shown in Figure 6.1. At the aggregate level, **resource requirements planning (RRP)**, a long-range capacity planning module, is used to check whether aggregate resources are capable of satisfying the aggregate production plan. Typical resources considered at this stage include gross labor hours and machine hours. Generally, capacity expansion decisions at this level involve a long-range commitment, such as new machines or facilities. If existing resources are unable to meet the aggregate production plan, then the plan must be revised. The revised APP is reevaluated using the resource requirements plan until a feasible production plan is obtained.

Once the aggregate production plan is determined to be feasible, the aggregate production information is disaggregated into a more detailed medium-range production plan, the master production schedule. Although RRP has already determined that aggregate capacity is sufficient to satisfy the APP, medium-range capacity may not be able to satisfy the MPS. For example, the master production schedule may call for normal production quantities when much of the workforce typically takes vacation. Therefore, the medium-range capacity plan, or **rough-cut capacity plan (RCCP)**, is used to check the feasibility of the master production schedule.

The RCCP takes the master production schedule and converts it from production to capacity required, then compares it to capacity available during each production period. If the medium-range capacity and production schedule are feasible, the master production schedule is firmed up. Otherwise, it is revised, or the capacity is adjusted accordingly. Options for increasing medium-range capacity include overtime, subcontracting, adding resources, and an alternate routing of the production sequence.

Capacity requirements planning (CRP) is a short-range capacity planning technique that is used to check the feasibility of the material requirements plan. The time-phased material requirements plan is used to compute the detailed capacity requirements for each workstation during specific periods to manufacture the items specified in the MRP. Although the RCCP may show that sufficient capacity exists to execute the master production schedule, the CRP may indicate that production capacity is inadequate during specific periods.

Capacity Strategies

Capacity expansion or contraction is an integral part of an organization's manufacturing strategy. Effectively balancing capacity with demand is an intricate management decision as it directly affects a firm's competitiveness. Short- to medium-term capacity can be increased through the use of overtime, additional shifts, and subcontracting, whereas long-term capacity can be increased by introducing new manufacturing techniques, hiring additional workers, and adding new machines and facilities. Conversely, capacity contraction can be attained by reducing the workforce and disposing idle machines and facilities.

The three commonly recognized capacity strategies are lead, lag, and match capacity strategies. A **lead capacity strategy** is a proactive approach that adds or subtracts capacity in anticipation of future market conditions and demand, whereas a **lag capacity strategy** is a reactive approach that adjusts its capacity in response to demand. In favorable market conditions, the lag strategy generally does not add capacity until the firm is operating at full capacity. The lag capacity strategy is a conservative approach that may result in a lost opportunity when demand increases rapidly, whereas the lead strategy is more aggressive and can often result in excess inventory and idle capacity. Leaders in the electronics industry usually favor the lead capacity strategy because of the short product life cycles. A **match** or **tracking capacity strategy** is a moderate strategy that adjusts capacity in small amounts in response to demand and changing market conditions.

THE DISTRIBUTION REQUIREMENTS PLAN

The **distribution requirements plan (DRP)** is a time-phased finished-goods inventory replenishment plan in a distribution network. Distribution requirements planning is a logical extension of the MRP system, and its logic is analogous to MRP. Distribution requirements planning ties the physical distribution system to the manufacturing planning and control system by determining the aggregate time-phased net requirements of the finished goods, and provides demand information for adjusting the MPS. A major difference between MRP and DRP is that while MRP is driven by the production schedule specified in the MPS to compute the time-phased requirements of components, the DRP is driven by customer demand for the finished goods. Hence, the MRP operates in a dependent demand situation, whereas the DRP operates in an independent demand setting. The result of MRP execution is the production of finished-goods inventory at the manufacturing site, whereas DRP time-phases the movements of finished goods inventory from the manufacturing site to the central supply warehouse and distribution centers.

An obvious advantage of the DRP system is that it extends manufacturing planning and control visibility into the distribution system, thus allowing the firm to adjust its production plans and to avoid stocking excessive finished goods inventory. By now, it should be clear that excessive inventory is a major cause of the bullwhip effect. Distribution requirements planning provides time-phased demand information needed for the manufacturing and distribution systems to effectively allocate finished goods inventory and production capacity to improve customer service and inventory investment. A distribution requirements planning example is provided in Example 6.3.

Example 6.3 A DRP Example at the ATV Corporation

The ATV Corporation's January and February distribution schedule for its Model A ATV is used to illustrate the DRP replenishment schedules from the firm's central supply warehouse to its two distribution centers. The time buckets used in the DRP are the same weekly time buckets used in the MRP system. DRP uses the order quantity, delivery lead time, on-hand balance, and safety stock information to determine the planned order releases necessary to meet anticipated market demand.

Gross requirements from the two distribution centers in Las Vegas and East Lansing are first obtained from the demand management system. The same MRP logic is used to compute the planned order releases of the two distribution centers. The gross requirements of the central supply warehouse reflect the cascading demand of Las Vegas and East Lansing distribution centers. The gross requirements of 14 units in the first week for the central supply warehouse are the sum of the planned order releases of the two distribution centers. The planned order releases of the central supply warehouse are passed on to the manufacturing facility, where they are absorbed into the MPS. This process is commonly referred to as **implosion**, where demand information is gathered from a number of field distribution centers and aggregated in the central warehouse, and eventually passed onto the manufacturing facility. While both the processes are similar, the *implosion* DRP logic is different from the *explosion* notion in MRP, where a Level 0 finished good is broken into its component requirements.

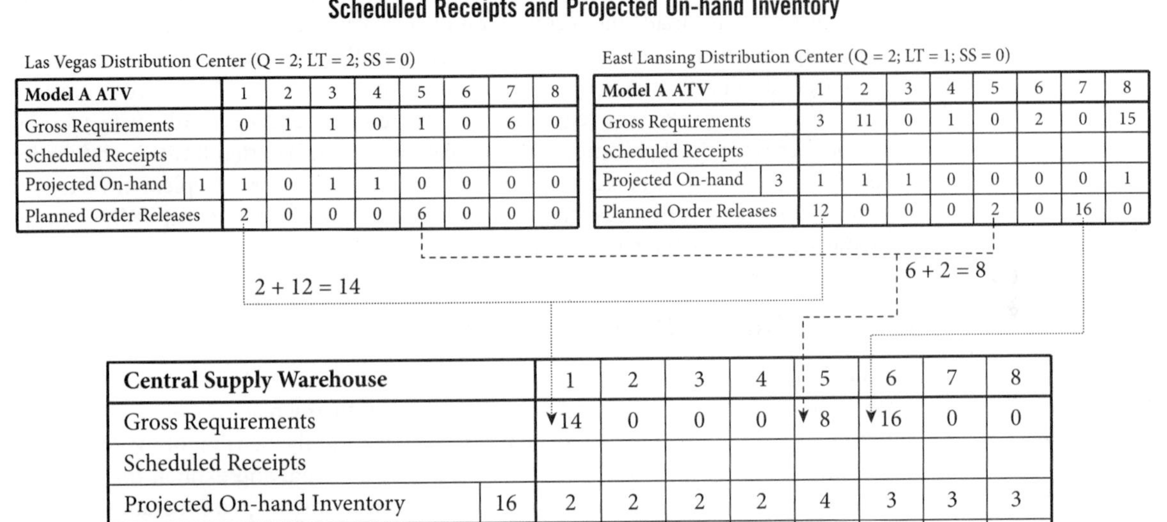

Scheduled Receipts and Projected On-hand Inventory

Las Vegas Distribution Center (Q = 2; LT = 2; SS = 0)

Model A ATV		1	2	3	4	5	6	7	8
Gross Requirements		0	1	1	0	1	0	6	0
Scheduled Receipts									
Projected On-hand	1	1	0	1	1	0	0	0	0
Planned Order Releases		2	0	0	0	6	0	0	0

East Lansing Distribution Center (Q = 2; LT = 1; SS = 0)

Model A ATV		1	2	3	4	5	6	7	8
Gross Requirements		3	11	0	1	0	2	0	15
Scheduled Receipts									
Projected On-hand	3	1	1	1	0	0	0	0	1
Planned Order Releases		12	0	0	0	2	0	16	0

2 + 12 = 14

6 + 2 = 8

Central Supply Warehouse		1	2	3	4	5	6	7	8
Gross Requirements		14	0	0	0	8	16	0	0
Scheduled Receipts									
Projected On-hand Inventory	16	2	2	2	2	4	3	3	3
Planned Order Releases		0	0	10	15	0	0	0	0

Q = 5; LT = 2; SS = 2

THE LEGACY MATERIAL REQUIREMENTS PLANNING SYSTEMS

For over four decades, an MRP system was the first choice among manufacturing firms in the U.S. for planning and managing their purchasing, production, and inventories. To improve the efficiency and effectiveness of the manufacturing planning and control system, many manufacturers have utilized an **electronic data interchange (EDI)** to relay planned order releases to their suppliers. This information system has worked well for coordinating internal production, as well as purchasing.

By the end of the twentieth century, however, the global business environment was rapidly changing. Many savvy manufacturers and service providers were building multi-plant international sites, either to take advantage of cheaper raw materials and labor or to expand their markets. Business executives found themselves spending more time dealing with international subcontractors using different currencies and languages among varying political environments. The need to access real-time information on customers' requirements, production levels and available capacities, company-wide inventory levels, and plants capable of meeting current order requirements increased. The existing MRP systems simply could not handle these added tasks.

To fully coordinate the information requirements for purchasing, planning, scheduling, and distribution of an organization operating in a complex multiunit global environment, an enterprise-wide information system was needed. Thus, ERP systems that operated from a single, centralized database were engineered to replace the older legacy MRP systems.

The term **legacy MRP system** is a broad label used to describe an older information system that usually works at an operational level to schedule production within an organization. Many legacy systems were implemented in the 1960s, 1970s, and 1980s and subjected to extensive modifications as requirements changed over the years. Today, these systems have lasted beyond their originally intended life spans. The continuous modifications of these systems made them complex and cumbersome to work with, especially when considering they were not designed to be user-friendly in the first place. Legacy systems were designed to perform a very specific operational function and were programmed as independent entities with little regard for meeting requirements or coordinating with other functional areas. Communication between legacy systems is often limited, and visibility across functional areas is severely restricted. Legacy systems were implemented to gather data for transactional purposes and, thus, lacked any of the analytical capabilities required for today's complex global environment.

Manufacturing Resource Planning

The development of the legacy system can be traced back to the evolution of the MRP system, the closed-loop MRP system, and the **manufacturing resource planning (MRP-II)** system. The development of closed-loop MRP was a natural extension of the MRP system. It was an attempt to further develop the MRP into a formal and explicit manufacturing planning and control system by adding capacity requirements planning and feedback to describe the progress of orders being manufactured. The originally developed MRP is a part of the closed-loop MRP system.

Manufacturing resource planning was an outgrowth of the closed-loop MRP system. Business and sales plans were incorporated, and a financial function was added to link financial management to operations, marketing, and other functional areas. The concept of manufacturing resource planning was that the information system should link internal operations to the financial function to provide management with current data, including sales, purchasing, production, inventory, and cash flow. It should also be able to perform "what-if" analyses as internal and external conditions change. For example, MRP-II enables the firm to determine the impact on profit and cash flow if the firm is only able to fill 85 percent of its orders due to late deliveries of raw materials. MRP-II is an explicit and formal manufacturing information system that integrates the internal functions of an organization, enabling it to coordinate manufacturing plans with sales, while providing management with essential accounting and financial information.

Today, manufacturing resource planning has further evolved to include other functional areas of the organization. Although it synchronizes an organization's information systems and provides insight into the implications of aggregate production plans, master production schedules, capacities, materials plans, and sales, it primarily focuses on one unit's internal operations. It lacks the capability to link the many operations of an organization's foreign branches with its headquarters. It also lacks the capability to directly interface with external supply chain members. For this reason, enterprise-wide information systems began to be developed.

THE DEVELOPMENT OF ENTERPRISE RESOURCE PLANNING SYSTEMS

While traditional or legacy MRP systems continue to be used and modified to include other functional areas of an organization, the emergence and growth of supply chain management, e-commerce, and global operations have created the need to exchange information directly with suppliers, customers, and foreign branches of organizations. The concept of the manufacturing information system thus evolved to directly connect all functional areas and operations of an organization and, in some cases, its suppliers and customers via a common software infrastructure and database. This type of manufacturing information system is referred to as an enterprise resource planning (ERP) system.

The typical ERP system is an umbrella system that ties together a variety of specialized systems, such as production and inventory planning, purchasing, logistics and warehousing, finance and accounting, human resource management, customer relationship management, and supplier relationship management using a common, shared, centralized database. However, exactly what is tied together varies on a case-by-case basis, based on the ERP system capabilities and the needs of the organization. Figure 6.6 illustrates a generic ERP system, where a centralized database and software application infrastructure are used to drive a firm's information systems and to link the operations of its branches, key suppliers, and key customers with the firm's headquarters.

Enterprise resource planning is a broadly used industrial term to describe the multimodule application software for managing an enterprise's internal functional activities, as well as its suppliers and customers. Initially, ERP software focused on integrating the

Figure 6.6 A Generic ERP System

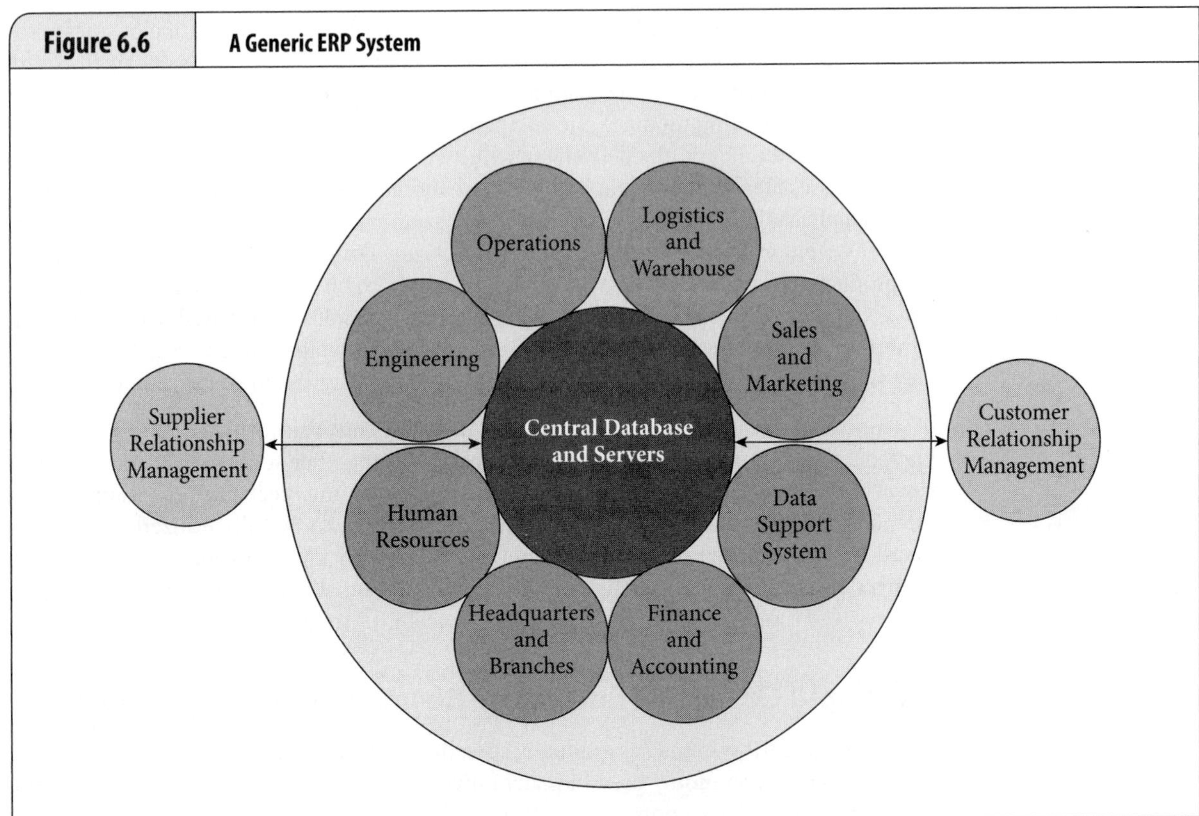

internal business activities of a multifacility organization or enterprise to ensure that it was operating under the same information system. With the onset of supply chain management, ERP vendors today are designing their products to include modules for managing suppliers and customers. For example, ERP enables an organization to deal directly with key suppliers to assess the availability of their resources, as if they are an extended unit of the firm. Similarly, ERP also allows key customers to directly access the firm's inventory information and manufacturing and delivery schedules.

ERP utilizes the idea of a centralized and shared database system to tie the entire organization together, as opposed to the traditional legacy MRP system that uses multiple databases and interfaces that frequently result in duplicate and inconsistent information across different branches or even departments within an organization. With ERP, information is entered once at the source and made available to all users. It eliminates the inconsistency and incompatibility created when different functional areas use different systems with overlapping data.

The legacy MRP system typically utilizes multiple software packages and databases for different functional areas. Usually, each functional area implements its own information system based on its unique needs, with very little input or coordination from the other functional areas. The different packages within an organization often are incompatible with each other and prevent transactions from taking place directly between systems. The multiple databases also cause the same information to be stored in multiple locations; thus, multiple entries of the same data are required. This need to enter the same data repeatedly is a major cause of inconsistency in database management. For example, a customer, ATV Inc., may be entered as ATV Inc. in one database and ATV Incorporated in another database. From an information system's perspective, ATV Inc. and ATV Incorporated are two distinct customers.

With a shared, centralized database system, ERP is capable of automating business processes rapidly and accurately. For example, when taking a sales order, a sales agent has all the necessary information of the customer (e.g., the credit history, rating, and limit from the finance and accounting module), the company's production and inventory levels (from the operations module), and the delivery schedule (from the sales and marketing module) to complete the sale. After the sale is confirmed and entered into the centralized database, other supply chain partners affected by the transaction can directly utilize the same information system to take appropriate proactive actions. For example, suppliers can find out the production schedules planned by upstream supply chain members so that raw materials and components can be produced accordingly to support sales. Similarly, downstream companies can also utilize the same information system and database to access delivery schedules of raw materials and components ordered from their upstream supply chain members.

Thus, ERP integrates the internal operations of an enterprise with a common software platform and centralized database system. It also ties together supply chain member processes using the same information system. ERP provides the mechanism for supply chain members to share information so that scarce resources can be fully utilized to meet demand, while minimizing the bullwhip effect and supply chain inventories. Production changes and other modifications can also be executed quickly and efficiently to minimize delivery lead times. Example 6.4 illustrates a typical ERP transaction.

The Rapid Growth of Enterprise Resource Planning Systems

The use of ERP systems has gradually spread from manufacturing to the service sector and has become commonly used in many university classrooms. Many universities in the U.S., for instance, have cooperated with major ERP software providers to integrate ERP

Example 6.4 A Hypothetical ERP Transaction

The following example demonstrates a hypothetical ERP transaction for the ATV Corporation. The ATV Corporation makes three models of all-terrain vehicles: Model A, Model B, and Model C. The corporation is headquartered in the U.S. with manufacturing facilities in the U.S. and Mexico. ATV sells its products in the U.S., Canada, and Mexico. Its sales representatives make quarterly visits to customers to take sales orders and provide necessary customer services. The following steps describe a sales transaction by a sales representative during a typical visit to a retail customer in Canada.

We assume here that a dealer ordered 100 units of Model A and 150 units of Model B, to be delivered within thirty days.

1. *Ordering* The field sales representative takes the order of 100 units of Model A and 150 units of Model B. Using the Internet, the sales rep accesses the sales and marketing module of the ERP system at the ATV Corporation headquarters in the U.S. to check the price and other related information, such as quantity discounts, guarantees, and rebates. The sales rep also accesses the customer's credit history and rating from the finance and accounting module.
2. *Availability* Simultaneously, the ERP system checks the inventory status and the available-to-promise quantities of its manufacturing facilities in the U.S. and Mexico and notifies the sales rep whether or not the order can be filled on time. The sales rep finds that the Mexico factory has sufficient inventory to fill the Model A order immediately, while the Model B order can be manufactured in ten days from the U.S. factory. Logistics information shows that shipping from Mexico to Canada takes two weeks, and delivery time from the U.S. factory takes one week. Thus, the entire order is accepted, and the factory in Mexico receives instructions to ship 100 units of Model A to Canada immediately. The inventory status is updated accordingly. An invoice in English will be printed, and the finance and accounting module will be updated to reflect the partial delivery upon shipment of the goods from Mexico.
3. *Manufacturing* The operations module immediately schedules the production of 150 units of Model B at the U.S. factory. All dependent demand items and labor necessary to produce 150 units of Model B are scheduled to meet the due date. For components manufactured in-house, planned order releases are transmitted to the shop floor. For purchased items, the information is sent to the suppliers.

   The human resource module checks to ensure that there are sufficient workers in the U.S. factory to complete the order. If not, the personnel manager will be notified and additional workers may be employed.
4. *Order Tracking* An advance shipping notice (ASN) that provides delivery information to the dealer's receiving operations is transmitted. The customer relationship management module allows the customer to track the status of its order.

training into their business curricula. There are many reasons, some of which are discussed in the following paragraph, for the rapid growth of ERP since the early 1990s.

At the turn of the twenty-first century, many firms were uncertain as to how the Year 2000 Millennium Bug or Y2K bug (conversion of the year from 1999 to 2000) would affect their information systems. Most information systems installed were programmed to use the last two digits of the year (e.g., the year 1998 would be shown as 98). Using the same logic, the year 2000 would be recorded as 00, which might also be interpreted as the year 1900, or 98 years prior to 1998. This could adversely affect time-sensitive programming logic (e.g., interest calculations). In addition, the legacy MRP systems had been modified so extensively over the years that the many layers of program codes made it too complex and redundant to correctly assess the true impact of Y2K. The extensive modifications to the legacy systems had also made them too expensive to maintain. Thus, many savvy business managers took a proactive approach to set aside sufficient budgetary funds to replace their legacy MRP systems with the more efficient ERP systems to reduce costs and deal with the Y2K problem as well.

The rapid development of computer and information technology over the last two decades has also contributed positively to the growth of ERP. Tasks that were previously limited to mainframe computers are today easily implemented on servers and desktop computers that cost only a fraction of the capital investment previously needed. Information systems that were previously off-limits are now accessible to many smaller organizations. ERP is expected to remain the key building block of global business management information systems. As the global business environment continues to change, ERP is expected to evolve to become more flexible to adapt to mergers and acquisitions and to provide more real-time monitoring and response.

A somewhat recent development in ERP is **cloud computing**. Software vendors such as Oracle Cloud and Microsoft Azure have begun to offer cloud-based services where end users can simply log on to remote servers without installing any software or storing data on local hard drives. The cloud is a metaphor for the Internet. In its simplest terms, cloud computing means accessing programs or storing data over the Internet (on some other company's server) instead of the user's local hard drive. With a high-speed online connection, cloud computing can be done anywhere and anytime. The popular Microsoft Office product, for example, is now available for a monthly fee in the cloud called Microsoft 365.

Cloud computing can also be done by accessing the application software from a local computer and storing the data in the cloud. The data in the cloud can be synchronized on one or more local hard drives. This allows data to be accessed offline via the local hard drive when Internet connection is unavailable. However, the downside is that the user

SCM Profile | **Moving IBM's Smarter Supply Chain to the Cloud**

IBM, a Fortune 500 company, delivers information technology hardware, software, and services in more than 170 countries. The company generated almost $100 billion in revenues with a net income of $18 billion in 2013. IBM faces fierce competition for market share. Every opportunity to cut costs and gain efficiency matters to the long-term survival and performance of the company. IBM is not a stranger in the cloud computing arena. Indeed, IBM has been a leading proponent in cloud computing. It reported overall cloud revenues of $4 billion in 2013.

In 2012, IBM's Integrated Supply Chain (ISC) team began moving its Quality Early Warning System (QEWS) to the cloud. QEWS is IBM's innovative solution to identify potential quality defects in its end-to-end hardware supply chain processes. IBM's ISC organization manages IBM's supply chain processes, employs more than 20,000 workers in seventy countries, and manages more than $33 billion in annual spend. By the end of 2013, the ISC team had also begun to move other applications to the cloud.

ISC's cloud initiative saved the company an estimated $50 million in warranty costs, and marked IBM's shift from reactive to predictive analytics that encompasses a variety of statistical techniques that analyze historical data to identify risks and opportunities, and make data-driven predictions about future events. The initiative notably increased ISC's agility to realign its strategy with IBM's overall corporate strategy, which was already closely tied to cloud computing. Moving QEWS to the cloud reduces lead time for existing clients to adopt cloud computing, and reduces ISC's lead time to setup new clients on the system. ISC is now more agile and able to collaborate better with key suppliers and strategic partners at a lower technological cost.

ISC's successful endeavor revealed that cloud computing is an agile and powerful technology that can overcome the limitations of traditional computing. Cloud computing allows users to access huge volumes of computing power and data over the Internet, anywhere and anytime. Also, cloud deployment is surprisingly low cost.[8]

Cloud computing is very real in the business world. It is also quickly spreading in academia, affecting how students utilize common application software (such as Microsoft Word, Excel, and PowerPoint) and store data. Technologically savvy students should begin to explore the various free options to store data in the cloud—OneDrive, Google Drive, and Dropbox are some of the widely used free options available.

must ensure the latest data is synchronized in the cloud and local hard drive before accessing it. Also, storing, accessing, and synchronizing data in the cloud causes a noticeable delay in the storage and retrieval process compared to using a local hard drive. Despite these minor drawbacks, it is hard to imagine any technologically savvy business or student not utilizing the cloud to store, retrieve, and share data in this digital age. The following SCM Profile describes IBM's experience in moving its Quality Early Warning System to the cloud.

IMPLEMENTING ENTERPRISE RESOURCE PLANNING SYSTEMS

ERP systems have continued to evolve, and integration of e-commerce, customer relationship management (CRM), and supplier relationship management (SRM) applications are now considered ERP requirements by most organizations. While many firms believe a well-designed and implemented ERP system can translate into a substantial competitive advantage, research analysts and industrial practitioners are still debating the usefulness of ERP, and the advantages and disadvantages of using a **best-of-breed solution** versus a **single integrator solution**. It is important to understand that ERP is not a panacea for poor business decisions, but in the right hands it can be a valuable tool to enhance competitiveness. (Recall the chapter opening quote by Mr. Grady Booch.)

The *best-of-breed* solution picks the best application or module for each individual function required for the supply chain (thus, best of breed). The resulting system can include several different applications that must be integrated to work as a single coordinated system to achieve the global scope required of the ERP. A major criticism of the best-of-breed solution is that multiple software infrastructures and databases may have to be used to link the multiple applications obtained from different vendors. This may severely affect the ability of the system to update the databases rapidly and efficiently—a similar problem of the legacy MRP systems.

The *single integrator* approach picks all the desired applications from a single vendor for the ERP system. The obvious advantages are that all of the applications should work well together, and getting the system up and running should be easier. As companies become more global, and as firms desire to expand their systems with other compatible modules later on, the notion of using a single integrator solution becomes more attractive. On the other hand, as information technology continues to evolve and as competition increases in the ERP software market, ERP vendors are designing their products to be more compatible with each other. Therefore, implementing an ERP system using the best-of-breed solution approach is becoming easier. Best-of-breed vendors will continue to fill a void in the ERP market with specialized applications that mainstream ERP vendors may not provide.

Choosing whether to utilize a single integrator ERP solution or combine niche software is a challenge facing many companies today. If the firm's IT department has its way, the company will choose a single integrator solution for its ERP implementation; if people overseeing other business processes have their way, a company is more likely to choose the best-of-breed solution.[9]

The emergence of the single integrator ERP solution over the last decade does not signal the extinction of best-of-breed software vendors. While it is rare now, to find major companies using best-of-breed ERP packages, best-of-breed vendors will continue to fill the niches left by the large ERP vendors. Some businesses require unique best-of-breed software to do advanced or big data analytical decision making. Businesses are often interested in tasks that extend beyond core ERP functions, into areas such as sales and operations planning or analyses using ERP data. Many best-of-breed ERP vendors have thrived by creating early software innovations around the edges of ERP, exploiting gaps left by ERP product suites. Many of these surviving vendors, for example, are in inventory management systems.[10] Finally, businesses often turn to best-of-breed system vendors when the cost savings expected from their ERP implementations fail to materialize. In general, best-of-breeds are better suited to more intricate workplaces, while single integrator ERP solutions fit the less complex business environments.[11]

Implementing an ERP system has proven to be a real challenge for many companies. Most ERP systems are written based on the best practices of selected firms. Thus, a condition required for implementation of the system is that the user's business processes must conform to the approaches used in the software logic. These processes can be significantly different from those currently used within the company. Having to adapt a company's business processes to conform to a software program is a radical departure from the conventional business practice of requiring the software to be designed around the business processes.

Two primary requirements of successful implementation of ERP are computer support and accurate, realistic inputs. Instead of implementing the entire system at once, some organizations choose to implement only those applications or modules that are absolutely critical to operations at that time. New modules are then added in later phases. This ensures that the system can be implemented as quickly as possible while minimizing interruption of the existing system. However, many implementations have failed due to a variety of reasons, as follows:

- *Lack of top management commitment*: While management may be willing to set aside sufficient funds to implement a new ERP system, it may not take an active role in the implementation process. Often, this leads users to revert to the old processes or systems because of their lack of knowledge or interest in learning the capabilities of the new ERP system.
- *Lack of adequate resources*: Implementing a new ERP system is a long-term commitment requiring substantial capital investment. Although the cost has become more affordable due to the rapid advent of computer technology, full implementation may still be out of reach for many small organizations. In addition, small firms may not have the necessary workforce and expertise to implement the complex system.
- *Lack of proper training*: Many employees may already be familiar with their legacy MRP systems. Thus, when a new ERP system is implemented, top management may assume that users are already adequately prepared and underestimate the training required to get the new system up and running. Lack of financial resources can also reduce the amount of training available for its workforce.
- *Lack of communication*: Lack of communication within an organization, or between the firm and its ERP software provider, can also be a major hindrance for successful implementation. Lack of communication usually results in the wrong specifications and requirements being implemented.
- *Incompatible system environment*: In certain cases, the firm's environment does not give ERP a distinct advantage over other systems. For example, there is no advantage for a small, family-owned used-car dealer in a small town to implement an expensive new ERP system.

Advantages and Disadvantages of Enterprise Resource Planning Systems

When properly installed and operating, an ERP system can provide a firm and its supply chain partners with a significant competitive advantage, which can fully justify the investments of time and money in ERP. A fully functional ERP system is capable of enhancing the firm's capability to fully utilize capacity, accurately schedule production, reduce inventory, meet delivery due dates, and enhance the efficiency and effectiveness of the supply chain. Let us look at some specific advantages and disadvantages.

Enterprise Resource Planning System Advantages

As mentioned earlier, the primary advantage of ERP over the legacy MRP systems is that ERP uses a single database and a common software infrastructure to provide a broader scope and up-to-date information, enabling management to make better decisions that can benefit the entire supply chain. ERP is also fairly robust in providing real-time information and, thus, is able to communicate information about operational changes to supply chain members with little delay. ERP systems are also designed to take advantage of Internet technology. Thus, users are able to access the system via the Internet.

ERP helps organizations reduce supply chain inventories due to the added visibility throughout the supply chain. It enables the supply, manufacturing, and logistics processes to flow smoothly by providing visibility of the order fulfillment process throughout the supply chain. Supply chain visibility leads to reductions of the bullwhip effect and helps supply chain members to better plan production and end-product deliveries to customers.

ERP systems also help organizations to standardize manufacturing processes. Manufacturing firms often find that multiple business units across the company make the same product using different processes and information systems. ERP systems enable the firm to automate some of the steps of a manufacturing process. Process standardization eliminates redundant resources and increases productivity.

ERP enables an organization, especially a multi-business-unit enterprise, to efficiently track employees' time and performance and to communicate with them via a standardized method. Performance can be monitored across the entire organization using the same measurements and standards. The use of a single software platform and database also allows the ERP system to integrate financial, production, supply, and customer order information. By having this information in one software system rather than scattered among many different systems that cannot communicate with one another, companies can keep track of materials, orders, and financial status efficiently and coordinate manufacturing, inventory, and shipping among many different locations and business units at the same time.

Enterprise Resource Planning System Disadvantages

While the benefits of ERP systems can be impressive, ERP is not without shortcomings. For example, a substantial capital investment is needed to purchase and implement the system. Considerable time and money must be set aside to evaluate the available ERP software applications, to purchase the necessary hardware and software, and then to train employees to operate the new system. Total cost of ERP ownership includes hardware, software, professional and software customization services, training, and other internal staff costs. ERP systems are very complex and have proven difficult to implement, particularly in large multi-business-unit organizations.

However, the primary criticism of ERP is that the software is designed around a specific business model based on specific business processes. Although business processes are usually adopted based on best practices in the industry, the adopting firm must change its business model and associated processes to fit the built-in business model designed into the ERP system. Thus as mentioned earlier, the adopting firm must restructure its processes to be compatible with the new ERP system. This has resulted in a very unusual situation where a software system determines the business practices and processes a firm should implement, instead of designing the software to support existing business practices and processes.

Despite the widespread adoption of costly ERP systems by large firms since the Y2K scramble, many implementation challenges remain unsolved, and scores of ERP systems today are grossly underutilized.[12] Intricate business process reengineering challenges arise when business processes are adapted to the software. Consequently, firms struggle to justify

Profile Trends in ERP Software

Enterprise resource planning (ERP) software continued to evolve over the last several years with notable rapid developments in mobility and business intelligence, the increased adoption of software as a service (SaaS), and cloud solutions. SaaS is a popular ERP software delivery platform in which applications and the associated data are hosted in the cloud by independent software vendors.

As we enter a new phase of ERP adoption, the last couple of years have witnessed ERP offerings that provide greater flexibility in ERP solutions to drive businesses in new ways. While there are numerous predicted trends in ERP software, the two prominent developments are mobile revolution and cloud-based ERP. Knowing the emerging ERP trends allows managers to better understand the developing technology and options available to achieve the desired results from an ERP implementation.

The mobile revolution is likely a key priority as organizations seek to get the most out of their ERP investment. With the advent of mobile devices such as smartphones, tablets, and portable computers, ERP users and key personnel can access information from these devices anytime and anywhere. In the past, key ERP personnel would receive alerts on their mobile device, and then call someone in the office to input corrective actions into the ERP system. With mobility, executive ERP users can take necessary corrective actions via their mobile devices. Also, managers are able to approve workflows, manage customers and inventory, and monitor customer service and performance of their businesses in real time, regardless of where they are. Mobile ERP will continue to gain popularity as businesses and resources become more dispersed.

The second major ERP trend is cloud-based ERP solutions. Many ERP software providers will expand their SaaS models to release cloud-based versions of their ERP software solutions. The option of accessing part or all of their ERP software and data in the cloud reduces capital cost as businesses no longer need to make upfront investments in expensive hardware and system maintenance. Instead, businesses can emphasize implementing the best cloud-based systems that best deliver a competitive advantage for the company. Besides cost savings, cloud-based ERP enhances collaboration with suppliers and customers because the software solution and data reside in the cloud. The controlled processes allow all users to access real-time information. The seller no longer has to call customers back to tell them when a product has shipped.[13]

their investment and find ways to better utilize their ERP systems. This raises the question of whether large firms can effectively manage their operations and supply chain activities without sophisticated information technology. The following SCM Profile describes two prominent trends of ERP software.

ENTERPRISE RESOURCE PLANNING SOFTWARE APPLICATIONS

ERP systems typically consist of many modules that are linked together to access and share a common database. Each module performs different functions within the organization and is designed so that it can be installed on its own or with a combination of other modules. Most ERP software providers design their products to be compatible with their competitors' products so that modules from different providers can be combined. Integration of customer relationship management, supplier relationship management, and e-procurement modules into the ERP system is now becoming relatively commonplace.

Today, there are hundreds of ERP software providers, each targeting a specific market segment and industry type. SAP and Oracle are the two prominent ERP providers in terms of market share. Although each software company configures its products differently from its competitors, some common modules of ERP systems are described here:

- *Accounting and finance*: This module assists an organization in maintaining financial control and accountability. It tracks accounting and financial information such as revenues, costs, assets, liabilities, and other accounting and financial information of the company. It is also capable of generating routine and advanced accounting and financial reports, product costing, budgeting, and analyses.
- *Customer relationship management*: This module provides the capability to manage customers. It enables collaboration between the organization and its customers by providing relevant, personalized, and up-to-date information. It also enables customers to track sales orders. The customer relationship management module allows the user to communicate effectively with existing customers and acquire new customers through sales automation and partner relationship management. Finally, it allows the firm to segment customers and track their purchase activities, and then design customized promotions appealing to each customer segment.
- *Human resource management*: It helps an organization plan, develop, manage, and control its human resources. It allows the firm to deploy the right people to support its overall strategic goals and to plan the optimal workforce levels based on production levels.
- *Manufacturing*: It schedules materials and tracks production, capacity, and the flow of goods through the manufacturing process. It may even include the capability for quality planning, inspection, and certifications.
- *Supplier relationship management*: This module allows the firm to manage its suppliers. It automates processes and enables the firm to more effectively collaborate with all its suppliers corporation-wide. It also monitors supplier performance and tracks deliveries of goods purchased. It enables the user to effectively manage business processes through real-time collaboration during design, production, and distribution planning with suppliers.

- *Supply chain management*: This module handles the planning, execution, and control of activities involved in a supply chain. It assists the firm in strengthening its supply chain networks to improve delivery performance. It may also cover various logistics functions, including transportation, warehousing, and inventory management. The supply chain management module creates value by allowing the user to optimize its internal and external supply chains.

ERP systems have continued to evolve in the twenty-first century. One of the latest developments is the integration of e-business capabilities to use the Internet to conduct business transactions, such as sales, purchasing, inventory management, and customer service. Customers and suppliers are demanding access to certain information, such as order status, inventory levels, and invoice reconciliation through the ERP system. As information technology continues to become more sophisticated, ERP software providers will continue to add new functions and capabilities to their systems.

SUMMARY

While both manufacturing and service organizations rely on effective production and capacity planning to balance demand and capacity, manufacturers have the added advantage of being able to build up inventory as stored capacity. Service firms are unable to inventory their services, so they rely upon backlogs or reservations, cross-training, or queues to match supply with demand. However, excess capacity results in underutilized equipment and workforce and eventually leads to unnecessary cost, adversely impacting all firms along the supply chain.

This chapter covers materials planning, capacity planning, and enterprise resource planning, which are all widely used for balancing demand with supply. An example was used to demonstrate how the aggregate production plan, master production schedule, material requirements plan, and distribution requirements plan are related to each other. This chapter also briefly discusses how the various materials plans are related to the capacity plans. A central piece of the materials plan is the material requirements plan, which takes information from the master production schedule, the bill of materials, and inventory status to compute planned order releases. For items that are produced in-house, planned order releases are released to the shop floor to trigger production. For purchased items, planned order releases are released to suppliers.

Finally, this chapter discusses the enterprise resource planning system, including its relationships with the traditional MRP and MRP-II systems, its advantages and disadvantages, implementation issues, and ERP modules. The goal of ERP development was to build a single software application that runs off a common shared database to serve the needs of an entire organization, regardless of its units' geographical locations and the currency used. Despite its complexity and considerable costs, ERP provides a way to integrate different business functions of different businesses, on different continents. The integrated approach can have a tremendous payback if companies select the right applications and implement the software correctly. Unfortunately, many companies that have installed these systems have failed to realize all of the benefits expected.

Implementing ERP should be viewed as a long-term, ongoing project. No matter what resources a firm has initially committed to replacing legacy systems, selecting and implementing ERP applications and training users, ERP requires ongoing management commitment and resources. As needs and technologies change and new applications are designed, new functionality and business processes will need to be continuously revisited and improved.

KEY TERMS

aggregate production plan (APP), 167

available-to-promise (ATP) quantity, 175

best-of-breed solution, 193

bill of materials (BOM), 177

capacity, 185

capacity requirements planning (CRP), 185

chase production strategy, 169

closed-loop MRP, 180

cloud computing, 192

demand time fence, 174

dependent demand, 178

distribution requirements planning (DRP), 168

electronic data interchange (EDI), 187

enterprise resource planning (ERP), 168

implosion, 187

indented bill of materials, 178

independent demand, 178

intermediate or medium-range planning horizon, 167

lag capacity strategy, 186

lead capacity strategy, 186

legacy MRP system, 188

level production strategy, 171

long-range, 167

make-to-order manufacturing firms, 171

make-to-stock, 172

DISCUSSION QUESTIONS

1. Why is it important to balance production capacity with market demand?
2. Describe long-range, medium-range, and short-range planning in the context of materials plan and capacity plan. How are they related?
3. Describe aggregate production planning, master production planning, material requirements planning, and distribution requirements planning. How are these plans related?
4. Describe how MRP evolved into closed-loop MRP, MRP-II, and eventually into ERP.
5. Compare and contrast chase versus level production strategies. Which is more appropriate for an industry where highly skilled laborers are needed? Why?
6. Is a level production strategy suitable for a pure service industry, such as professional accounting and tax services or law firms? Can these firms inventory their outputs?
7. What is the purpose of low-level coding?
8. What is the purpose of available-to-promise quantity, and how is it different from on-hand inventory?
9. What is system nervousness? Discuss how it can be minimized or avoided.
10. What are the crucial inputs for material requirements planning?
11. What is a BOM, and how is it different from the super BOM?
12. Are manufacturing or purchasing lead times considered in the MPS and the MRP?
13. What is the difference between scheduled receipts and planned order releases?
14. In MRP computation, do the gross requirements of level 3 items come from the gross requirements or planned order releases of the level 2 items? Explain how this works.
15. What is the difference between an MRP explosion and a DRP implosion?
16. Briefly describe resource requirements planning, rough-cut capacity planning, and capacity requirements planning. How are these plans related?
17. How are the various capacity plans (ERP, RCCP, CRP) related to the material plans (APP, MPS, MRP)?
18. Why are production planning and capacity planning important to SCM?
19. Why have so many firms rushed to implement ERP systems over the past ten years?
20. Describe the limitations of a legacy MRP system.

21. Why is it important to learn the fundamentals of the traditional MRP system, even if it is considered an outdated, legacy system?

22. What are the advantages of an ERP system over the legacy MRP system?

23. Explain best-of-breed and single integrator ERP implementations. What are the advantages and disadvantages of the best-of-breed implementation?

24. Explain why many ERP implementations have failed to yield the expected benefits over the last ten years.

25. Describe how a cloud-based ERP system works. When might a firm use a cloud-based ERP?

ESSAY/PROJECT QUESTIONS

1. It is inevitable that cloud computing will significantly affect how businesses and students use information technology in the next few years. If you have not done so, search on the Internet to sign up for free cloud storage on OneDrive, Google Drive, and/or Dropbox. Do not forget to sync your files to your local hard drives.

2. Visit the websites of SAP, Oracle, and Microsoft, and use the information to write a brief report of each company and its ERP software. Do their products offer the same configurations or functionalities?

3. Use the Internet to search for relevant information to prepare a brief report on how SAP and Oracle expanded their product lines. Which of the two firms is known for its aggressive strategy of acquiring smaller best-of-breed providers?

4. Use the Internet to search for information to write a report on whether the trend is toward a single integrator or best-of-breed ERP implementation.

5. Use resources available on the Internet to prepare a report on the current and projected ERP market total revenue and the rate of growth over the next five years.

6. Use resources available on the Internet to prepare a story about a firm that has successfully implemented an ERP system.

7. Use resources available on the Internet to prepare a report that describes a failed ERP implementation. What can be learned from this company?

8. Explore the websites of SAP and Oracle, and use the information to write a report to discuss their (a) supply chain management, (b) supplier relationship management, and (c) customer relationship management software applications.

9. Use resources on the Internet to write a report describing Microsoft's strategy and competitive position in the ERP market.

10. Use resources on the Internet to write a report on the current stage of ERP implementation in the U.S., Europe, and China.

SPREADSHEET PROBLEMS

1. Given the following production plan, use a (a) chase production strategy and (b) level production strategy to compute the monthly production, ending inventory or backlog, and workforce levels. A worker is capable of producing 100 units per month. Assume the beginning inventory as of January is zero, and the firm desires to have zero inventory at the end of June.

MONTH	JAN	FEB	MAR	APR	MAY	JUN
Demand	2000	3000	5000	6000	6000	2000
Production						
Ending Inventory						
Workforce						

2. Given the following production plan, use a (a) chase production strategy and (b) level production strategy to compute the monthly production, ending inventory or backlog, and workforce levels. A worker can produce 50 units per month. Assume that the beginning inventory in January is 500 units, and the firm desires to have 200 units of inventory at the end of June.

MONTH	JAN	FEB	MAR	APR	MAY	JUN
Demand	2000	3000	5000	6000	6000	2000
Production						
Ending Inventory						
Workforce						

3. Given the following production schedule, compute the available-to-promise quantities.

WEEK		1	2	3	4	5	6	7	8
Model A									
MPS	BI = 60	20	30	20	20	20	50	0	20
Committed Customer Orders		50	10	30	10	20	20	10	0
ATP:D									

4. Given the following production schedule, compute the available-to-promise quantities.

WEEK		1	2	3	4	5	6	7	8
Model B									
MPS	BI = 20	20	0	20	20	0	20	20	20
Committed Customer Orders		10	10	10	10	10	0	0	10
ATP:D									

5. The bill of materials for product A with the associated component parts and planning factors (in parenthesis) are showed below. How many units of the following components are required to make one unit of the product A?

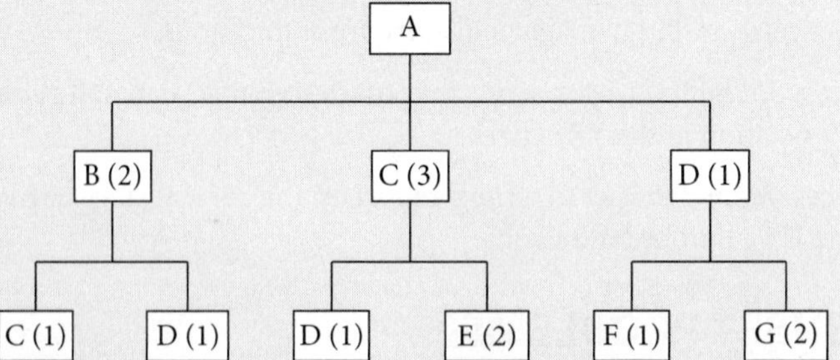

a. Component B
b. Component C
c. Component D
d. Component E

e. Component F

f. Component G

6. Given the following information, complete the planned order releases and projected on-hand balances for component part X.

PART X		WEEK 1	WEEK 2	WEEK 3	WEEK 4	WEEK 5
Gross Requirements		80	0	90	0	90
Scheduled Receipts		60				
Projected Balance	120					
Planned Order Releases						

Q = 60; LT = 3 weeks; Safety Stock = 5

7. Given the following information, complete the planned order releases and projected on-hand balances for component part Y.

PART Y		WEEK 1	WEEK 2	WEEK 3	WEEK 4	WEEK 5
Gross Requirements		80	50	90	0	80
Scheduled Receipts		160				
Projected Balance	120					
Planned Order Releases						

Q = 20; LT = 2 weeks; Safety Stock = 10

8. The bills of materials for two finished products (D and E), inventory status, and other relevant information are given below. Compute the planned order releases and projected on-hand balances for parts D, E, and F.

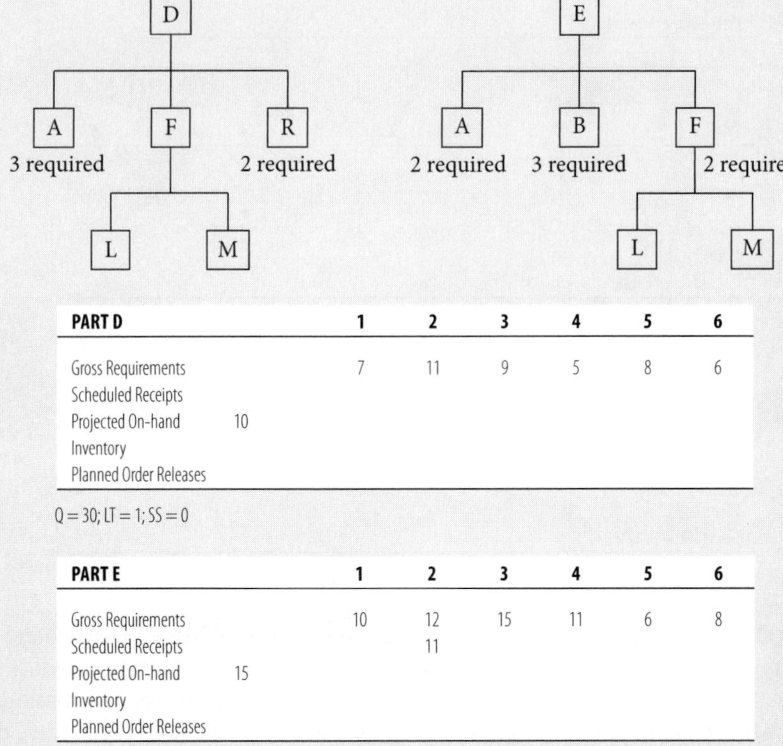

PART D		1	2	3	4	5	6
Gross Requirements		7	11	9	5	8	6
Scheduled Receipts							
Projected On-hand Inventory	10						
Planned Order Releases							

Q = 30; LT = 1; SS = 0

PART E		1	2	3	4	5	6
Gross Requirements		10	12	15	11	6	8
Scheduled Receipts			11				
Projected On-hand Inventory	15						
Planned Order Releases							

Q = LFL; LT = 2; SS = 3

PART F		1	2	3	4	5	6
Gross Requirements							
Scheduled Receipts		60					
Projected On-hand Inventory	20						
Planned Order Releases							

Q = 60; LT = 1; SS = 0

9. The bill of materials for a finished product E, inventory status, and other relevant information are given below. Compute the planned order releases and projected on-hand balances for parts E, F, and M.

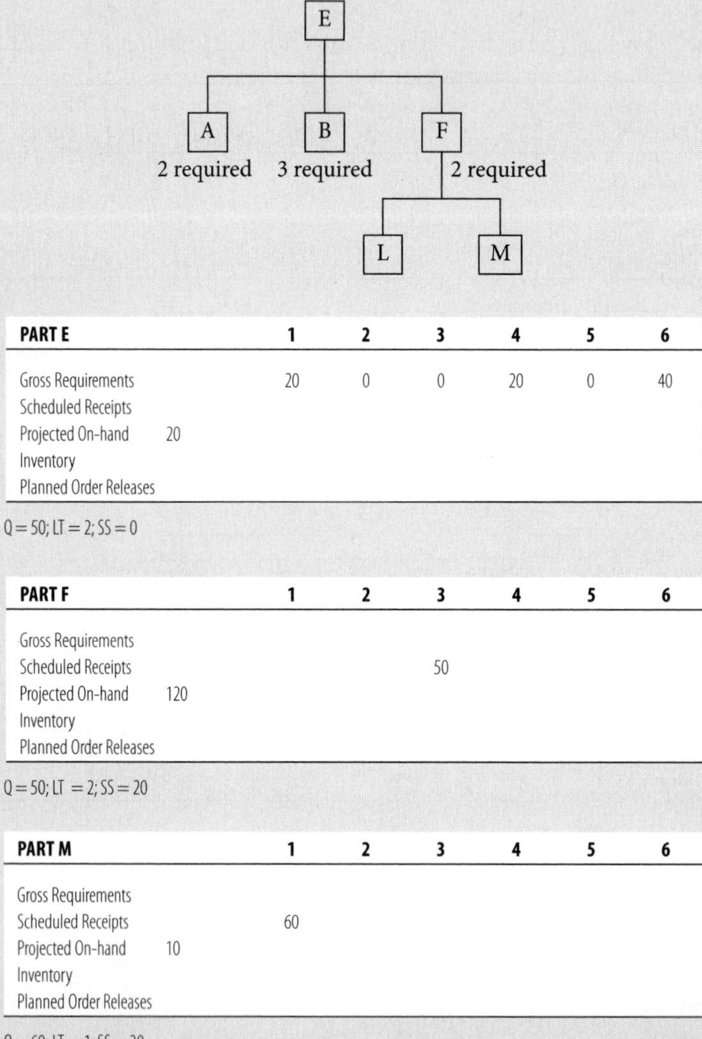

PART E		1	2	3	4	5	6
Gross Requirements		20	0	0	20	0	40
Scheduled Receipts							
Projected On-hand Inventory	20						
Planned Order Releases							

Q = 50; LT = 2; SS = 0

PART F		1	2	3	4	5	6
Gross Requirements							
Scheduled Receipts				50			
Projected On-hand Inventory	120						
Planned Order Releases							

Q = 50; LT = 2; SS = 20

PART M		1	2	3	4	5	6
Gross Requirements							
Scheduled Receipts		60					
Projected On-hand Inventory	10						
Planned Order Releases							

Q = 60; LT = 1; SS = 30

10. Crop-Quick Inc. replenishes its three distribution centers in Boston, Denver, and Houston from its Las Vegas central supply warehouse. The distribution schedule for one of its products for the next six weeks is shown below. Use proper distribution requirements planning logic to complete the replenishment schedules of the three distribution centers and the central supply warehouse.

BOSTON DISTRIBUTION CENTER		1	2	3	4	5	6
Gross Requirements		0	20	0	55	0	0
Scheduled Receipts							
Projected On-hand Inventory	10						
Planned Order Releases							

Q = 30; LT = 1; SS = 5

DENVER DISTRIBUTION CENTER		1	2	3	4	5	6
Gross Requirements		0	20	10	0	0	20
Scheduled Receipts			11				
Projected On-hand Inventory	15						
Planned Order Releases							

Q = LFL; LT = 2; SS = 2

HOUSTON DISTRIBUTION CENTER		1	2	3	4	5	6
Gross Requirements		50	0	0	45	0	0
Scheduled Receipts							
Projected On-hand Inventory	20						
Planned Order Releases							

Q = 60; LT = 1; SS = 0

LAS VEGAS CENTRAL WAREHOUSE		1	2	3	4	5	6
Gross Requirements							
Scheduled Receipts							
Projected On-hand Inventory	50						
Planned Order Releases							

Q = 20; LT = 1; SS = 0

ADDITIONAL RESOURCES

Chopra, S., and P. Meindl, *Supply Chain Management*, 5th ed. Upper Saddle River, NJ: Pearson, 2013.

Duffy, R. J., and M. Gorsage, "Facing SRM and CRM," *Inside Supply Management* 13(8), August 2002: 30–37.

Fogarty, D. W., J. H. Blackstone, and T. R. Hoffmann, *Production and Inventory Management*, 2nd ed. Cincinnati: South-Western Publishing, 1991.

Hopp, W. J., and M. L. Spearman, "To Pull or Not to Pull: What Is the Question?" *Manufacturing & Service Operations Management* 6(2), 2004: 133–148.

Jacobs, F. R., and R. B. Chase, *Operations and Supply Chain Management*, 14th ed. Boston: McGraw-Hill, 2014.

Orlicky, J., *Material Requirements Planning: The New Way of Life in Production and Inventory Management*. New York: McGraw-Hill, 1975.

Simchi-Levi, D., P. Kaminsky, and E. Simchi-Levi, *Designing and Managing the Supply Chain*, 3rd ed. Boston: McGraw-Hill Irwin, 2008.

Vollmann, T. E., W. L. Berry, D. C. Whybark, and F. R. Jacobs, *Manufacturing Planning and Control for Supply Chain Management*, 6th ed. Boston: McGraw-Hill Irwin, 2011.

Monk, E. F., and B. J. Wagner, *Concepts in Enterprise Resource Planning*, 4th ed. Boston: Cengage Learning, 2013.

ENDNOTES

1. Saran, C., "New Microsoft Chief Satya Nadella States Commitment to Software," *Computer Weekly*, February 11, 2014: 4–5.
2. Saran, C., "Jaguar Land Rover Streamlines Car Design with Integrated IT Systems," *Computer Weekly*, February 11, 2014: 9–10.
3. See, for example, http://fearnoproject.com/2010/04/29/%E2%80%9Ca-fool-with-a-tool-is-still-a-fool%E2%80%9D/
4. World Trade Organization, "International Trade Statistics 2010," Geneva: WTO Publications.
5. Holcomb, B. J., "ISM Report on Business," *Inside Supply Management Magazine* 25(2), March 2014: 14–15.
6. Shih, W., "The Resurgence of Manufacturing in America," *Inside Supply Management* 24(5), June 2013: 30–33.
7. Fogarty, D. W., J. H. Blackstone, and T. R. Hoffmann, *Production & Inventory Management*, 2nd ed. Cincinnati: South-Western, 1991.
8. Ward, T., and V. Gopal, "How They Did It: Moving IBM's Smarter Supply Chain to the Cloud," *Supply Chain Management Review* 18(2), March/April 2014: 26–31.
9. Field, A. M., "Stretching the Limits of ERP," *The Journal of Commerce* 8, January 2007: 76–78.
10. Roberto, M., "ERP Enters Age of Infrastructure," *Manufacturing Business Technology* 25(7), July 2007: 24–25.
11. Curt, B., "The ERP Edge," *Multichannel Merchant* 3(7), July 2007: 50–54.
12. Jutras, C., "The ERP in Manufacturing Benchmark Report," *Aberdeen Group, Inc.*, August 2006: 1–31.
13. Johnson, G., "Trends in ERP Software," *Quality* 53(3), March 2014: 30–33.

Chapter 7

INVENTORY MANAGEMENT

Our storage systems feed our assembly stations just like a heart pumps blood through your arteries. If they're not pumping, we only maintain enough material in the assembly area for about one shift. Then, we have to shut down.

— Philipp Hossfeld, Global Assembly Manager, ODU GmbH & Co. KG.[1]

When you're small retail, your real business is inventory management, just having the right things at the right time.

— Warren Shoulberg, Editorial Director, Gifts & Decorative Accessories magazine.[2]

The issue is that most midsize wholesaler-distributors aren't using information to make better business decisions. They need to stop worrying about what happened yesterday and start looking at what will happen tomorrow.

— Jack Phillips, CEO and Co-founder, International Institute for Analytics.[3]

Learning Objectives

After completing this chapter, you should be able to

- Distinguish dependent from independent demand inventories.
- Describe the four basic types of inventories and their functions.
- Understand the costs of inventory and inventory turnovers.
- Understand ABC classification, the ABC inventory matrix, and cycle counting.
- Understand RFID and how it can be used in inventory management.
- Understand the EOQ model and its underlying assumptions.
- Understand the quantity discount and the EMQ models and their relationships with the basic EOQ model.
- Understand and be able to distinguish among the various statistical ROP models.
- Understand the continuous review and periodic review systems.

Chapter Outline

SCM Profile — The Myths and Truths About Inventory Optimization

For supply chain managers charged with inventory management, especially in the manufacturing or retail industry, the objective is to have the right inventory at the right place, in the right quantity, and at the right time to meet the demands of their customers. Although many supply chain managers rely on expensive and sophisticated forecasting tools to optimize inventory across their organizations, they can reduce their inventory by simply changing the flow of inventory from source to consumption. Nonetheless, inventory management remains one of the most challenging tasks for manufacturers, distributors, and retailers. This supply chain profile highlights some common myths and truths about inventory management.

The first myth is that forecasting alone can help retailers to effectively and efficiently service their customers. However, the truth is that firms should reduce cycle times and minimize variabilities between supply and demand points prior to implementing any forecasting solution. The accuracy of a forecast depends heavily on the total cycle times and variables used in the forecast. Large fluctuations in the variables and long cycle times adversely affect the accuracy of forecast. Thus, it is necessary to reduce cycle times and variabilities before forecasting.

Many retailers believe that inventory should be positioned as far forward in their supply chains (i.e., retail stores) as possible. However, the truth is that overallocating inventory to retail stores adversely affects gross margin because retailers routinely slash prices to quickly dispose of overstocked, perishable merchandise. Also, forward placement of inventory in stores increases interstore transfers and inventory levels because safety stock is spread out in the retail stores rather than concentrated in the central warehouse. Instead of positioning inventory at the front end of the supply chain, retailers should align stock replenishment to match seasonal and promotional demands to improve cycle time and speed to market.

A third myth is that extra inventory equals better service. For most distributors and retailers, inventory is the largest component of working capital. The truth is that extra inventory ties up unnecessary working capital and requires additional storage space. Besides, perishable inventory expires quickly and must be disposed. A better solution is to adopt just-in-time replenishment that emphasizes frequent delivery in small lot sizes, though this can increase inbound shipping cost. Through effective inventory management, it is possible to lower inventory levels while simultaneously improving service. Inventory positioning has a huge impact on a firm's inventory performance. Distributors and retailers must carefully consider where, when, and how much inventory to deploy at each distribution center, warehouse, and retail store. Wrong replenishment timing, incorrect stock positioning, or erroneous quantity will affect customer service and performance.

Supply chain managers must be knowledgeable and understand inventory management to differentiate the myths from the truths. To meet mounting consumer expectations and challenges of a global economy, business students must learn to understand the concepts and tools of inventory management.[4]

INTRODUCTION

Inventory can be one of the most expensive assets of an organization. It may account for more than 10 percent of total revenue or total assets for some organizations. Although companies in the manufacturing sector usually carry more inventory than service firms, effective inventory management is nonetheless important to both manufacturers and

Table 7.1 Inventory Investment Compared to Total Revenue and Total Assets

COMPANY	FINANCIAL YEAR END	TOTAL REVENUE ($)	TOTAL ASSETS ($)	YEAR END INVENTORY ($)	INVENTORY/ TOTAL REVENUE (%)	INVENTORY/ TOTAL ASSETS (%)
Las Vegas Sands Corp.	Dec 31, 13	13,770	22,724	42	0.31	0.18
MGM Mirage	Dec 31, 13	9,810	26,110	108	1.10	0.41
Microsoft Corp.	Jun 30, 13	77,849	142,431	1,938	2.49	1.36
Ford Motor Co.*	Dec 31, 13	139,369	202,206	7,708	5.53	3.81
General Motors Company*	Dec 31, 13	152,092	166,344	14,039	9.23	8.44
Toyota Motor Corp.*	Mar 31, 13	222,373	377,281	18,243	8.20	4.84
Wal-Mart Stores, Inc.	Jan 31, 14	476,294	204,751	44,858	9.42	21.91
Target Corp.	Feb 1, 14	72,596	44,553	8,766	12.08	19.68
Pfizer, Inc.	Dec 31, 13	51,584	172,101	6,166	11.95	3.58
Intel Corp.	Dec 28, 13	52,708	92,358	4,172	7.92	4.52
Advanced Micro Devices, Inc.	Dec 28, 13	5,299	4,337	884	16.68	20.38

Note: All numbers in millions, except ratios (*Source:* Annual Reports on Form 10-K)
* automotive division only; excludes financing services

service organizations. Table 7.1 shows the amount of inventory, and the ratio of inventory to total revenue and total assets, of a few large, globally recognized manufacturing and service firms. While the inventory to total assets ratio for service organizations (such as the first two casino hotel companies shown in Table 7.1) is relatively low compared to most manufacturers, inventory management for service firms poses a different challenge. Casino hotels, for example, carry a wide range of perishable food items to stock the diverse restaurants operating within their properties. Managing perishable inventory presents a unique challenge to operations managers.

Inventory management policy affects how efficiently a firm deploys its assets in producing goods and services. Developing effective inventory control systems to reduce waste and stockouts in manufacturing or service organizations is a complex problem. The right amount of inventory supports manufacturing, logistics, and other functions, but excessive inventory is a sign of poor inventory management that creates an unnecessary waste of scarce resources. In addition, excessive inventory adversely affects financial performance. The need for better inventory management systems continues to challenge operations managers.

This chapter first explains the difference between dependent demand and independent demand items. Then it focuses on the independent demand items to describe the basic concepts and tools of inventory management, including the ABC inventory control system, inventory costs, and radio frequency identification. The chapter also discusses the three fundamental deterministic inventory models and the two major types of stochastic inventory models.

DEPENDENT DEMAND AND INDEPENDENT DEMAND

Inventory management models are generally separated by the nature and types of the inventory being considered and can be classified as dependent demand and independent demand models.

Dependent demand is the internal demand for parts based on the demand of the final product in which the parts are used. Subassemblies, components, and raw materials are examples of dependent demand items. Dependent demand may have a pattern of abrupt and dramatic change because of its dependency on the demand of the final product, particularly if the final product is produced in large lot sizes. Dependent demand can be calculated once the demand of the final product is known. Hence, material requirements planning (MRP) software is often used to compute exact material requirements.

The dependent demand inventory system was discussed in Chapter 6. For example, the ATV Corporation's master production schedule discussed in Table 6.4 in Chapter 6 shows that 120 all-terrain vehicles will be produced in January. The firm thus knows that 120 handlebars and 480 wheel rims will be needed. The demand for handlebars, wheel rims, and other dependent demand items can be calculated based on the bill of materials and the demand of the final product as stated on the master production schedule.

Independent demand is the demand for a firm's end products and has a demand pattern affected by trends, seasonal patterns, and general market conditions. For example, the customer demand for all-terrain vehicles is independent demand. Batteries, headlights, seals, and gaskets originally used in assembling the all-terrain vehicles are dependent demands; however, the replacement batteries, headlights, seals, and gaskets sold as *service parts* to the repair shops or end users are independent demand items. Similarly, the original battery used in assembling your new car is a dependent demand item for the automobile manufacturer, but the new battery that you bought to replace the original battery is an independent demand item. Independent demand items cannot be derived using the material requirements planning logic from the demand for other items and, thus, must be forecasted based on market conditions.

CONCEPTS AND TOOLS OF INVENTORY MANAGEMENT

Savvy operations managers are concerned with controlling inventories not only within their organizations but also throughout their many supply chains. An effective independent demand inventory system ensures smooth operations and allows manufacturing firms to store up production capacity in the form of work-in-process and finished goods inventories. While some service firms are unable to inventory their output, such organizations may rely on appointment backlogs, labor scheduling, and cross-training to balance supply and demand.

All manufacturing and service organizations are concerned with effective inventory planning and control. Inventory requires capital investment, handling, and storage space, and it is also subject to deterioration and shrinkage. Although a firm's operating costs and financial performance can be improved by reducing inventory, the risk of stockouts can be devastating to customer service. Therefore, companies must strike a delicate balance between inventory investment and customer service. This section discusses some important concepts and tools of inventory management. Vendor-managed inventory and comanaged inventory, discussed in Chapter 4, will not be explored here.

The Functions and Basic Types of Inventory

Inventory includes all the materials and goods that are purchased, partially completed materials and component parts, and the finished goods produced. The primary functions of inventory are to *buffer* uncertainty in the marketplace and to *decouple*, or break, the dependencies between stages in the supply chain. For example, an appropriate amount of inventory, known as *safety stock* or *buffer stock*, can be used to cushion uncertainties due to fluctuations in supply, demand, and/or delivery lead time. Similarly, the right amount of inventory enables a work center to operate without interruption when other work centers in the same production process are off-line for maintenance or repair. Keeping the correct amount of inventory at each work center also allows a faster work center to operate smoothly when it is constrained by slower upstream work centers.

In the increasingly global business environment, it is not unusual that organizations use the concept of *geographical specialization* to manufacture their products in developing countries. In this scenario, the developing countries specialize in cheap labor and abundant raw materials, whereas the manufacturing firms provide the technology and capital to produce the goods. The ability to geographically separate the consumption of the finished goods from production is a key function of inventory. For manufacturers, inventory also acts as *stored capacity*. For instance, snowmobile manufacturers can build up inventory by producing snowmobiles year-round in anticipation of peak demand during the busy winter season.

There are four broad categories of inventories: raw materials; work-in-process; finished goods; and maintenance, repair, and operating (MRO) supplies.

- *Raw materials* are unprocessed purchased inputs or materials for manufacturing the finished goods. Raw materials become part of finished goods after the manufacturing process is completed. There are many reasons for keeping raw material inventories, including volume purchases to create transportation economies or take advantage of quantity discounts; stockpiling in anticipation of future price increases or to avoid a potential short supply; or keeping safety stock to guard against supplier delivery or quality problems.
- *Work-in-process* (WIP) describes materials that are partially processed but not yet ready for sales. One reason to keep WIP inventories is to decouple processing stages or to break the dependencies between work centers.
- *Finished goods* are completed products ready for shipment. Finished goods inventories are often kept to buffer against unexpected demand changes and in anticipation of production process downtime; to ensure production economies when the setup cost is very high; or to stabilize production rates, especially for seasonal products.
- *Maintenance, repair, and operating (MRO) supplies* are materials and supplies used when producing the products but are not parts of the products. Solvents, cutting tools, and lubricants for machines are examples of MRO supplies. The two main reasons for storing MRO supplies are to gain purchase economies and to avoid material shortages that may shut down production.

Inventory Costs

The bottom line of effective inventory management is to control inventory costs and minimize stockouts. Inventory costs can be categorized in many ways: as direct and indirect costs; fixed and variable costs; and order (or setup) and holding (or carrying) costs.

Direct costs are those that are directly traceable to the unit produced, such as the amount of materials and labor used to produce a unit of the finished good. **Indirect costs** are those that cannot be traced directly to the unit produced, and they are synonymous with manufacturing overhead. Maintenance, repair, and operating supplies; heating; lighting; buildings; equipment; and plant security are examples of indirect costs. **Fixed costs** are independent of the output quantity, but **variable costs** change as a function of the output level. Buildings, equipment, plant security, heating, and lighting are examples of fixed costs, whereas direct materials and labor costs are variable costs. A key focus of inventory management is to control variable costs since fixed costs are generally considered *sunk costs*. Sunk costs are costs that have already been incurred and cannot be recovered or reversed.

Order costs are the direct variable costs associated with placing an order with the supplier, whereas **holding or carrying costs** are the costs incurred for holding inventory in storage. Order costs include managerial and clerical costs for preparing the purchase, as well as other incidental expenses that can be traced directly to the purchase. Examples of holding costs include handling charges, warehousing expenses, insurance, pilferage, shrinkage, taxes, and the cost of capital. In a manufacturing context, **setup costs** are used in place of order costs to describe the costs associated with setting up machines and equipment to produce a batch of product. However, in inventory management discussions, *order costs* and *setup costs* are often used interchangeably.

Inventory Investment

Inventory serves many important functions for manufacturing and service firms; however, excessive inventory is detrimental to a firm's financial health and competitive edge. Whether inventory is an asset that contributes to organizational objectives or a liability depends on its management.

Inventory is expensive, and it ties up a firm's working capital. Moreover, inventory requires storage space and incurs other carrying costs. Some products such as perishable food items and hazardous materials require special handling and storage that add to the cost of holding inventory. Inventory can also deteriorate quickly while it is in storage. In addition, inventory can become obsolete very quickly as new materials and technologies are introduced. Most importantly, large piles of inventory delay a firm's ability to respond swiftly to production problems and changes in technologies and market conditions.

Inventory investment can be measured in various ways. The typical annual physical stock counts to determine the total dollars invested in inventory provides an absolute measure of inventory investment. The inventory value is then reported in a firm's balance sheet. This value can be compared to the budget and past inventory investments. However, the absolute dollars invested in inventory does not provide sufficient evidence about whether the company is using its inventory wisely. A widely used measure to determine how efficiently a firm is using its inventory to generate revenue is the **inventory turnover ratio** or **inventory turnovers**. This ratio shows how many times a company turns over its inventory in an accounting period. Higher turnovers are generally viewed as a positive trend because it indicates the company is able to generate more revenue per dollar in inventory investment. Moreover, higher turnovers allow the company to increase cash flow and reduce warehousing and carrying costs. Conversely, a low inventory turnover may point to overstocking or deficiencies in the product line or marketing effort. Table 7.2 shows recent inventory turnover ratios for the same eleven firms shown in Table 7.1.

The formula for the inventory turnover ratio can be stated as:

$$\text{Inventory turnover ratio} = \frac{\text{Cost of Revenue}}{\text{Average Inventory}}$$

Inventory turnover ratio can be computed for any accounting period—monthly, quarterly, or annually. Cost of revenue is also the cost of goods sold, which is readily available

Table 7.2 Inventory Turnover Ratios

COMPANY	FINANCIAL YEAR END	TOTAL REVENUE ($)	COST OF REVENUE ($)	YEAR END INVENTORY ($)	INVENTORY TURNOVER RATIO
Las Vegas Sands Corp.	Dec 31, 13	13,770	10,362	42	246.71
MGM Mirage	Dec 31, 13	9,810	8,741	108	80.94
Microsoft Corp.	Jun 30, 13	77,849	20,249	1,938	10.45
Ford Motor Co.*	Dec 31, 13	139,369	125,234	7,708	16.25
General Motors Company*	Dec 31, 13	152,092	134,925	14,039	9.61
Toyota Motor Corp.*	Mar 31, 13	222,373	191,500	18,243	10.50
Wal-Mart Stores, Inc.	Jan 31, 14	476,294	358,069	44,858	7.98
Target Corp.	Feb 1, 14	72,596	51,160	8,766	5.84
Pfizer, Inc.	Dec 31, 13	51,584	9,586	6,166	1.55
Intel Corp.	Dec 28, 13	52,708	21,187	4,172	5.08
Advanced Micro Devices, Inc.	Dec 28, 13	5,299	3,321	884	3.76

All numbers in millions, except ratios (*Source:* Annual Reports on Form 10-K)
* automotive division only; excludes financing services

from a firm's income statement. The average inventory is the mean of the beginning and ending inventory for a period. However, a firm's inventory may fluctuate widely in a financial year; thus, the average of the beginning and ending inventory may be a poor indicator of the firm's actual average inventory for the year. In this case, the average of the twelve monthly ending inventories can be used as the average inventory when computing the annual inventory turnover ratio. In Table 7.2, since the average of the monthly inventories was not available in the *annual reports*, the financial year-end closing inventory was used to compute the ratio.

In 2013, for instance, Las Vegas Sands Corp. (LVS) turned over its inventory a staggering 247 times. However, the nature of LVS's business may suggest that a major portion of its revenue came from hotel room and gaming sales, with the inventory consisting mostly of goods for the restaurants. Therefore, the revenue generated by hotel room and gaming sales could be excluded from the calculation of the turnover ratio. Firms put a significant emphasis on improving their turnovers. In 2014, Goodwill Denver worked with Decision-Point Systems to design a mobile warehouse management system to process donations that helped to increase their inventory turnover, allowing them to reduce costs while better serving their community.[5]

The ABC Inventory Control System

A common problem with many inventory management systems is the challenge to maintain accurate inventory records. Many organizations use **cycle counting** to reconcile discrepancies between their physical inventory and inventory record on a monthly or quarterly basis. Cycle counting, or physically counting inventory on a periodic basis, also helps to identify obsolete stocks and inventory problems so that remedial action can be taken in a reasonable amount of time. However, cycle counting can be costly and time-consuming and can disrupt operations.

The **ABC inventory control system** is a useful technique for determining which inventories should be counted more frequently and managed more closely and which others

Table 7.3 ABC Inventory Classification

CLASSIFICATIONS	PERCENT OF TOTAL ANNUAL DOLLAR USAGE	PERCENT OF TOTAL INVENTORY ITEMS
A Items	80	20
B Items	15	40
C Items	5	40

should not. ABC analysis is often combined with the **80/20 rule** or **Pareto analysis**. The 80/20 rule suggests that 80 percent of the objective can be achieved by doing 20 percent of the tasks, but the remaining 20 percent of the objective will take up 80 percent of the tasks. The Pareto analysis recommends that tasks falling into the first category be assigned the highest priority and managed closely.

The ABC inventory control system prioritizes inventory items into Groups A, B, and C. However, it is not uncommon that some firms choose to use more than three categories. The *A items* are given the highest priority, while *C items* have the lowest priority and are typically the most numerous (the *B items* fall somewhere in between). Greater attention, safety stocks, and resources are devoted to the high-priority or *A items*. The priority is most often determined by annual dollar usage. However, priority may also be determined by product shelf life, sales volume, whether the materials are critical components, or some other criteria. A summary of the classification is provided in Table 7.3.

When prioritizing inventories by annual dollar usage, the ABC system suggests that approximately 20 percent of the items make up about 80 percent of the total annual dollar usage, and these items are classified as the *A items*. The *B items* make up roughly 40 percent of the items and account for about 15 percent of the total annual dollar usage, while the *C items* are the remaining 40 percent of the items, making up about 5 percent of the total annual dollar usage of inventory. Since the *A items* are the highest annual dollar usage items, they should be monitored more frequently and may have higher safety stock levels to guard against stockouts, particularly if these items are used in products sold to supply chain trading partners. The *C items* would then be counted less frequently, and stockouts may be allowed to save inventory space and carrying costs. For example, St. Onge, a Pennsylvania-based engineering and logistics firm, migrated to an ABC inventory classification system to allow it to allocate more resources to its more profitable A items.[6]

ABC inventory classification can be done monthly, quarterly, annually, or any fixed period. For the fast-moving consumer market, an *A item* may become a *C item* within months or even weeks. For these cases, the ABC inventory classification based on annual dollar usage might not be useful to management. An illustration of an ABC inventory classification using annual dollar usage is shown in Example 7.1.

The nearby SCM Profile demonstrates the importance of ABC analysis or the 80/20 rule and other inventory management techniques in the retailing industry.

The ABC Inventory Matrix

The ABC Inventory analysis can be expanded to assist in identifying obsolete stocks and to analyze whether a company is stocking the correct inventory by comparing two ABC analyses. First, an ABC analysis is done based on annual inventory dollar usage (as shown in Example 7.1) to classify inventories into A, B, and C groups. Next, a second ABC analysis is done based on current or on-hand inventory dollar value (as shown in Example 7.2) to

Example 7.1 ABC Inventory Classification Based on Annual Dollar Usage

Note that in this example, the *A items* only account for about 67 percent of the total annual dollar volume, while the *B items* account for about 28 percent. This illustrates that judgment must also be applied when using the ABC classification method, and the 80/20 rule should only be used as a general guideline.

INVENTORY ITEM NUMBER	ITEM COST ($)	ANNUAL USAGE (UNITS)	ANNUAL USAGE ($)	PERCENT OF TOTAL ANNUAL DOLLAR USAGE	CLASSIFICATION BY ANNUAL DOLLAR USAGE
A246	1.00	22,000	22,000	35.2	A
N376	0.50	40,000	20,000	32.0	A
C024	4.25	1,468	6,239	10.0	B
R221	12.00	410	4,920	7.8	B
P112	2.25	1,600	3,600	5.8	B
R116	0.12	25,000	3,000	4.8	B
T049	8.50	124	1,054	1.7	C
B615	0.25	3,500	875	1.4	C
L227	1.25	440	550	0.9	C
T519	26.00	10	260	0.4	C
Total Annual Dollar Usage:			$62,498	100%	

SCM Profile: Guidelines for Improving Inventory Management

In the March 2013 issue of the *Logistics Management* trade magazine, a panel of inventory management experts reviewed current inventory strategies and developed some useful guidelines for improving inventory management. Several of these guidelines are presented below.

The panel recommended exploiting inventory optimization software using real-time data from warehouse management and ERP systems. These software optimization tools, loosely referred to as business analytics or big data, take into account demand and supply variability, real-time data, and other replenishment parameters to determine optimum inventory decisions. These optimization tools provide users powerful real-time information to allow fast inventory movements. Companies can thus treat ocean carriers as mobile warehouses, allocating inventory before it arrives at the port.

Next, inventory managers should not treat all stock items the same. ABC analysis should be used to categorize inventories. Inventory managers should focus on the 20 percent of the inventory that typically make up 80 percent of the volume. The A items should be managed closely to maximize sales and profits. Some companies might have different targeted fill rates for each group. For example, one panel member used 99 percent fill rates for fast-moving A items, 98 percent fill rates for B items, and 95 percent fill rates for C items. The goal is to allocate more resources to the more profitable A items. Inventory managers also must not ignore their slow-moving inventory as these items occupy store space, utilize resources, and run the risk of obsolescence. Slow-moving items should be pulled back from retail locations and field warehouses to central distribution centers to aggregate demand variability, which reduces safety stock.

Monitoring suppliers' performance and tracking products as they move along the supply chains are important aspects of inventory management. To reduce safety stock, unreliable suppliers must be identified and corrective steps must be taken to resolve problems because safety stock is required to cushion suppliers' delivery time and quality variabilities.

Last but not least, inventory managers should leverage mobile devices and slotting. Mobile technology such as smartphones and tablets are valuable devices that allow quick access to accurate real-time information on the shop floor or anywhere with a high-speed Internet wireless connection. Slotting refers to the placement of merchandise on a store's shelves or warehouses. Proper slotting to keep the fastest moving items closer to docks and more accessible locations helps maximize throughput and productivity.[7]

classify inventories again into A, B, and C groups. Finally, the two ABC analyses are combined to form an **ABC inventory matrix** as shown in Figure 7.1. The *A items* based on current inventory value should match the *A items* based on annual inventory dollar usage, falling within the unshaded diagonal region of the figure. Similarly, the B and C items should match when comparing the two ABC analyses. Otherwise, the company is stocking the wrong items. The ABC inventory matrix also suggests that some overlaps are expected between two borderline classifications (as indicated by the wide diagonal region). For instance, some marginal *B items* based on annual inventory dollar usage might appear as *C items* based on the current inventory value classification and vice versa.

Referring to Figure 7.1, plots in the upper-left shaded triangle of the ABC inventory matrix indicate that some *A items* based on annual inventory dollar usage are showing up as *B* or *C items* based on the current inventory value classification and that some *B items* have similarly been classified as *C items*. This suggests that the company has current inventories for its *A* and *B items* that are too low and is risking stockouts of its higher dollar usage items. Conversely, plots in the lower-right shaded triangle show that some *C items*

Figure 7.1 Generic ABC Inventory Matrix

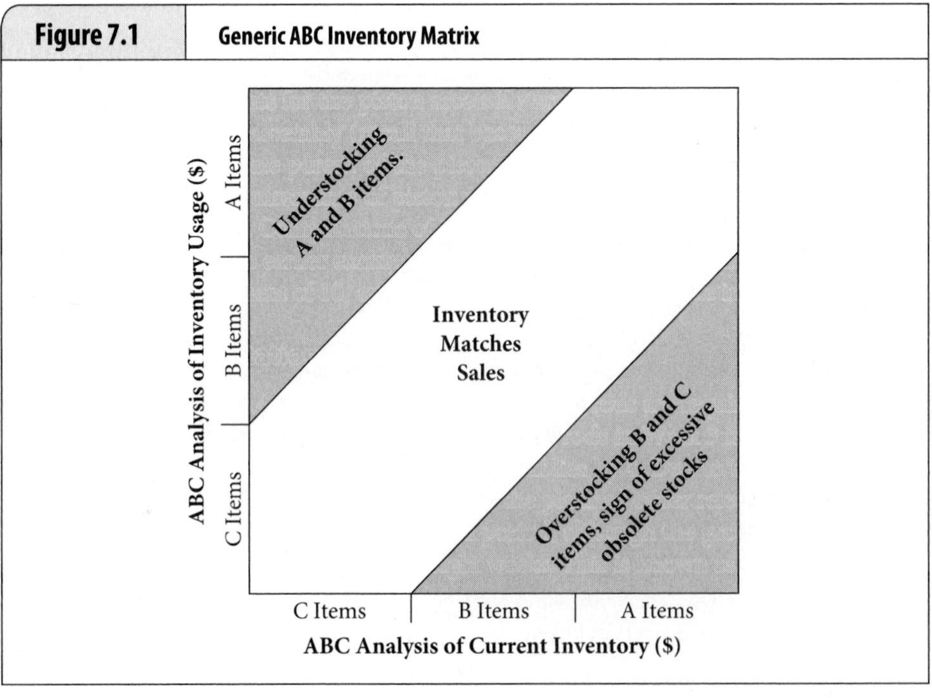

Example 7.2 ABC Inventory Classification Based on Current Inventory Value

					CLASSIFICATION BY	
INVENTORY ITEM NUMBER	ITEM COST ($)	CURRENT INVENTORY (UNITS)	CURRENT INVENTORY VALUE ($)	PERCENT OF TOTAL CURRENT INVENTORY	CURRENT INVENTORY VALUE	ANNUAL DOLLAR USAGE
T519	26.00	300	7,800	40.5	A	C
A246	1.00	5,600	5,600	29.1	A	A
L227	1.25	1,200	1,500	7.8	B	C
C024	4.25	348	1,479	7.7	B	B
R221	12.00	80	960	5.0	B	B
P112	2.25	352	792	4.1	B	B
T049	8.50	50	425	2.2	C	C
N376	0.50	800	400	2.1	C	A
R116	0.12	2,100	252	1.3	C	B
B615	0.25	120	30	0.2	C	C
Total Physical Inventory ($):			$19,238	100%		

based on annual inventory dollar usage are showing up as *A* and *B items* based on current inventory value, and some *B items* are similarly showing up as *A items*, thus indicating that the company has current inventories for its *B* and *C items* that are too high, and is incurring excess inventory carrying costs. This may also point to the presence of excessive *obsolete stock* if the inventory turnover ratios are very low. Obsolete stocks should be disposed of so that valuable inventory investment and warehouse space can be used for productive inventory. When used in conjunction with inventory turnovers, the ABC inventory matrix is a powerful tool for managing inventory investment. Example 7.2 shows the classifications based on current inventory value for the same ten items shown in Example 7.1, and it also shows the annual dollar usage classifications.

The two ABC analyses from Examples 7.1 and 7.2 are combined and plotted on the ABC inventory matrix shown in Figure 7.2. Each inventory item is plotted on the matrix using the "percent of total current inventory" on the horizontal axis and the "percent of total annual dollar usage" on the vertical axis. For instance, the coordinate of the item "T519" would be (40.5, 0.4). The vertical axis ranges from 0.4 percent to 35.2 percent, and the horizontal axis ranges from 0.2 percent to 40.5 percent; thus "T519" falls on the extreme lower-right corner of the matrix. The plots in Figure 7.2 show that six of the inventory items fell along the diagonal, suggesting the appropriate stocking levels. The company has probably overstocked items "T519" and "L227" and understocked "N376" and possibly "R116." It is important, however, that the inventory turnover ratios for each item be used in conjunction with the ABC inventory matrix to get a sense of how fast or slow inventories are turning over.

Radio Frequency Identification

The barcode has been used to identify the manufacturer and content of a package or container for decades. However, it cannot store enough information to differentiate goods at the item level. Direct line of sight is required to read a barcode, and the information stored on it is static and not updatable. **Radio frequency identification (RFID)** has been used as an eventual successor to the barcode for tracking an individual unit of goods. RFID

Figure 7.2 ABC Inventory Matrix for Example 7.2

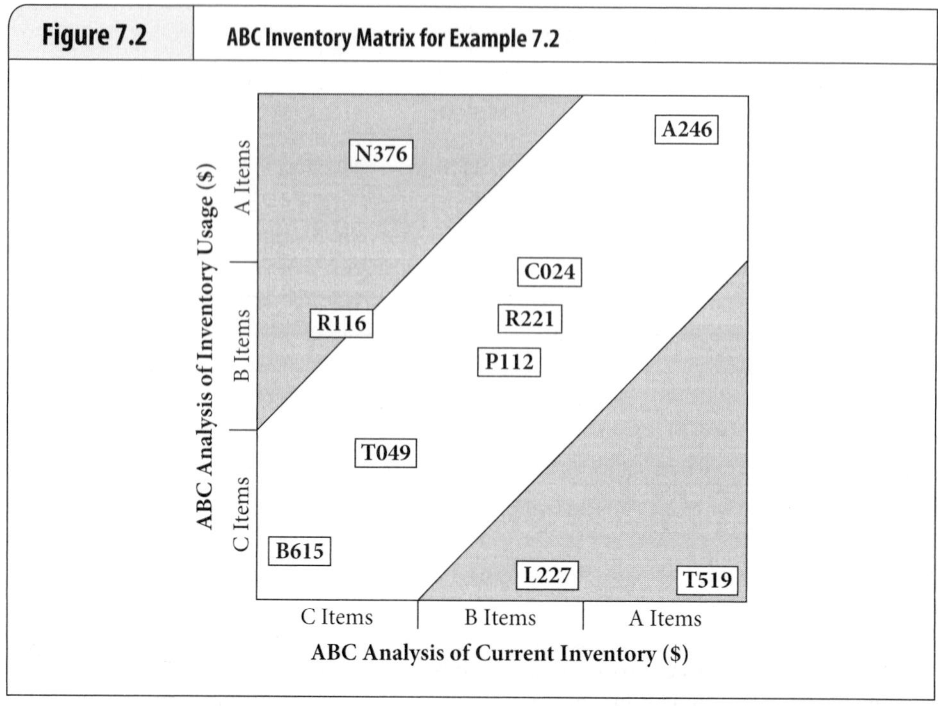

tags do not require direct line of sight to be read, and information on the tag is updatable. RFID technology is used in libraries; for passport identification, animal tracking, medical disciplines, toll payments; and in many other fields.

There are two major RFID standards: the **electronic product code (EPC)** standard, managed by the EPCglobal, Inc.,[8] a subsidiary of GS1 that created the UPC barcode, and the 18000 standard of the International Standards Organization (ISO). Wal-Mart Stores, Inc., and the Department of Defense are the two largest adopters of RFID to date. By 2005, both organizations had issued mandates for their top suppliers to use RFID technology to identify their products.[9] Wal-Mart Stores adopted the EPC standard, whereas the Department of Defense chose the EPC standard for general purpose applications and the ISO standard for air interface communications between the readers and the tags. The EPC standard is more widely adopted, especially in the commercial sector.

Similar to barcode technology, a reader is used to read the information stored in RFID tags. However, the reader does not have to be placed directly in line of sight of the tag to read the radio signal—a significant advantage of RFID over barcode. The EPC standards call for six classes of tags as shown in Table 7.4. Class 0 tags are read-only tags, but class 1 tags can be programmed once to update the information stored on the tags. Similar to a rewritable CD, class 2 tags are enhanced Generation 2 class 1 tags that can be rewritten multiple times. Classes 0, 1, and 2 are **passive RFID tags** that do not store power on the tags, and classes 3 and 4 are **active RFID tags** that contain a power source to boost their range. Class 5 tags can communicate with other class 5 tags and other devices.

The current EPC standard is the 96-bit ultra-high-frequency (UHF) Class 1, General 2 write-once-read-many (WORM) tag. The management board of GS1, which oversees EPCglobal standards, ratified the new EPC Gen2v2 standard in 2013. Gen2v2, a fully backward-compatible EPC standard operating in the 860–960 MHz UHF range, is a major update since 2008. This generation of tags is expected to pave the way to the Class 2 high

Table 7.4 EPCglobal's Tag Classes

EPC CLASS TYPE	FEATURES	TAG TYPE
Class 0	Read only	Passive (64 bits only)
Class 1*	Write once, read many	Passive (minimum 96 bits)
Class 2	Read/write	Passive (minimum 96 bits)
Class 3	Read/write with battery power to enhance range	Semi-active
Class 4	Read/write active transmitter	Active
Class 5	Read/write active transmitter	Active tag that can communicate with other class 5 tags

* current EPCglobal standard is Gen2v2, ratified in 2013

memory full read/write tags. A 256-bit version of the tag is being created at this writing, but full details are not yet available. Class 3 tags have not yet been fully defined, whereas class 4 and 5 tags are still in the early definition stage.

The current 96-bit EPC is a number made up of a header and three sets of data as shown in Figure 7.3. The 8-bit *header* identifies the version of the EPC being used; the 28-bit *EPC manager* identifies the manufacturer (and even plant) of the product; the 24-bit *object class* identifies the unique product family; and the 36-bit *serial number* uniquely identifies the individual physical item being read. The 8-bit header can identify 256 (2^8) versions of EPC; the 28-bit EPC manager can classify 268,435,456 (2^{28}) companies; the 24-bit object class can identify 16,777,216 (2^{24}) product families per company; and the 36-bit serial number can differentiate 68,719,476,736 (2^{36}) specific items per product family. Using this mammoth combination (which is unmatched by the barcode), it is not difficult to envisage that RFID can revolutionize inventory management in the supply chain.

Components of a Radio Frequency Identification System

An RFID solution consists of four parts: the tag, reader, communication network, and RFID software. The tag consists of a computer chip and an antenna for wireless communication with the handheld or fixed-position RFID reader, and the communication network connects the readers to transmit inventory information to the enterprise information system. The RFID software manages the collection, synchronization, and communication of the data with warehouse management, ERP and supply chain planning systems, and stores the information in a database. Figure 7.4 shows a generic RFID system.

Figure 7.3 Structure of the Electronic Product Code

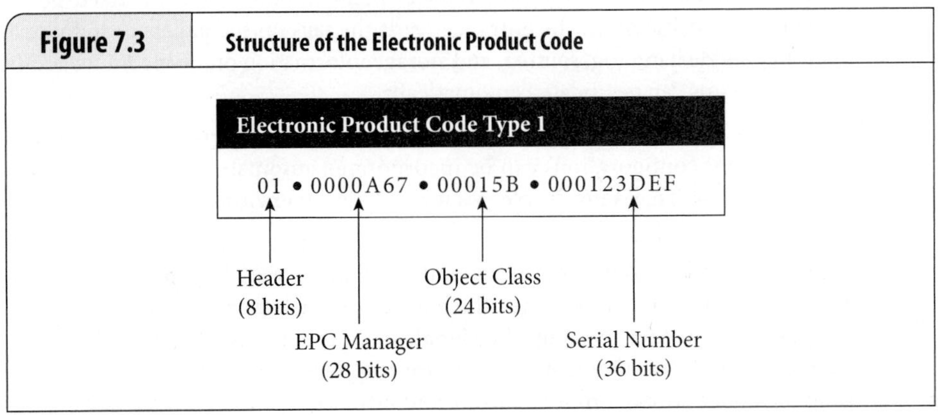

Figure 7.4 RFID System

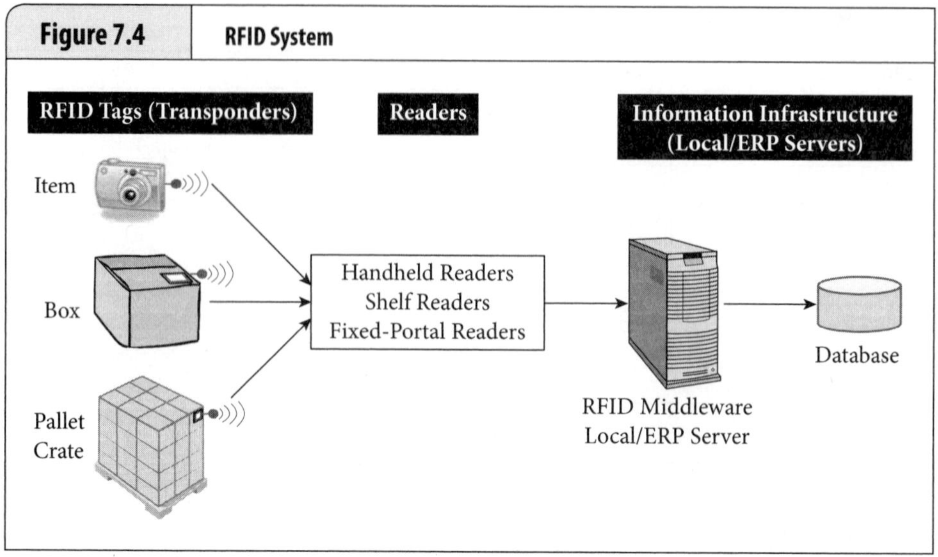

Though RFID was designed for use at the item level to identify individual items, current implementation focuses at the aggregate level where tags are placed on cases, crates, pallets, or containers due to the high cost of the tags. A passive 96-bit RFID tag costs approximately 7–15 cents today compared to $2 in 1999,[10,11] but it is still not financially feasible to tag individual low-ticket items. Thus, the existing focus is at the aggregate level focusing on cases or pallets of items, although some retailers have started to place RFID tags on individual high-ticket items like cameras and electronic products to prevent theft and closely manage the expensive inventory.

How Radio Frequency Identification Automates the Supply Chain

RFID is a valuable technology for tracking inventory in the supply chain. It can synchronize information and physical flow of goods across the supply chain from manufacturers to retail outlets and to the consumers at the right place at the right time. Likewise, RFID can track returned goods through the supply chain and prevent counterfeiting. It also helps to reduce out-of-stock items. There is no doubt that RFID is an invaluable tool for improving inventory management and supply chain efficiencies. The steps by which the RFID can automate the supply chain follow.

1. *Materials Management*: As a supply vehicle enters the warehouse, the fixed-portal RFID reader positioned at the entrance reads the tags on the pallets or individual items to provide handling, routing, and storage information of the incoming goods. Inventory status can be updated automatically.
2. *Manufacturing*: An RFID tag can be placed on the unit being produced so that specific customer configurations can be incorporated automatically during the production process. This is invaluable in a make-to-order environment.
3. *Distribution Center*: As the logistics vehicle arrives at the loading dock, the fixed-portal RFID reader communicates with the tag on the vehicle to confirm that it is approved to pick up goods. When the loaded vehicle leaves the dock and crosses the portal, the reader picks up the signals from the tags to alert the RFID software and ERP system to update the inventory automatically and initiate an advance shipping notice (ASN), proof of pickup, and invoices.

4. *Retail Store*: As the delivery vehicle enters the unloading dock, the fixed-portal reader picks up the signals from the tags, and the RFID software application processes the signals to provide specific handling instructions and initiate automatic routing of the goods. The RFID reader can also be placed on the store shelf to trigger automatic replenishments when an item reaches its reorder point. Moreover, inventory status can be updated in real time automatically at any stage of the supply chain, and handheld readers can be used to assist in cycle counting. Item-level tagging can be used to recommend complementary products. For instance, a computer screen and a reader can be placed in the changing room, so when a consumer tests a tagged suit in the changing room, the reader picks up the signal to suggest matching shirts and shoes on an LCD screen. When RFID is fully implemented at the item level, it is not difficult to envisage that instead of waiting for a cashier, a consumer could simply walk out the door of a store with the purchase. A reader built into the door would be able to recognize the items in the consumer's cart and charge the consumer's preapproved credit card automatically.

Global RFID Implementation and Challenges[12,13,14]

Radio frequency identification is one of the latest developments in inventory management. RFID technology has also been adopted by major retailers worldwide, including Marks & Spencer and Tesco in the U.K. and Metro Group in Germany. In the U.S., Wal-Mart mandated its top 1,000 suppliers to ship RFID-tagged pallets and cases to its warehouses by the end of 2007. The U.S. Department of Defense has also required that pallets delivered to its warehouses from its largest suppliers be tagged with RFID.

Tagging strategies differ considerably by region. In the U.S., the focus is on case- or pallet-level tagging, whereas European retailers focus on item-level tagging. U.S. retailers focus on case- and pallet-level tagging for inventory management to help reduce inventory and stockouts while simultaneously improving customer service. Consumer privacy issues and high implementation costs for hardware and tags deter American retailers from moving into item-level tagging. In Europe, the cultural climate has made it easier to deploy RFID, and retailers are using the technology at the item level for category management and garment sorting and are looking at RFID for smart shelves such as automatic replenishment. While most retailers in Asia expect to gain from integrating RFID technology along their supply chains, China is skeptical about sharing potentially confidential information with foreign businesses and lags behind other nations in RFID technology use. In Japan, the RFID market focuses on government applications, logistics usage, and asset tagging.

However, rapid industry adoption has proved more challenging than initially believed and, as in the case of Wal-Mart, has had mixed success. Tag and RFID system costs are among the major impediments to a faster adoption of the technology. RFID tags can cost ten to twenty times more than simple barcodes. Globally, the RFID industry still does not have its own UHF spectrum allocation; though the new Gen2v2 standard uses 860–960 MHz. Differences between radio frequencies in different parts of the world are another major hurdle to broader adoption. While the U.S. favors the 915 MHz UHF, the Europeans prefer the 868 MHz UHF. The Chinese use frequencies from 840.25–844.75 MHz to 920.25–924.75 MHz; while in Japan, 125–134 kHz, 13.56 MHz, 2.4–2.5 GHz, and 5.8 GHz are used, with the 950–956 MHz UHF allocated for unlicensed, low-power use. Another challenge of RFID is that UHF signals are reflected by metal and absorbed by water. Finally, with limited benefit information from a few RFID pilot projects, it is difficult for a company to calculate returns.

While considerable progress has been made on code standardization over the last few years, much work remains to be done. The U.S. and Europe have jointly worked on a common standard based on the modified EPCglobal UHF Gen-2 standard, but China and Japan have decided to develop their own. China supports its own EPC classification system for domestic product labeling, whereas Japan uses its Ubiquitous ID standard. Using competing RFID standards is likely to eventually lead to the need for costly multiprotocol readers that can handle tags that comply with the different standards. Despite all the challenges, RFID is ultimately likely to replace barcode technology in inventory management.

Big Data Decision-Making

Another recent development that may change inventory management and combine with RFID to enable better business decision making is big data. **Big data** broadly refers to collections of data sets that are too large and complex to be processed by traditional

SCM Profile | **Use of Big Data**

Google is famous for its search engine. Its core business is targeted marketing and advertising. To excel in this business, Google captures and exploits two types of big data—a comprehensive index and library of all the contents on the web and the behavior of Google users worldwide as they interact with its products and services. Google stores and indexes all the information on the web. On a big data perspective, Google processes about 12 billion searches each month. The company estimated that the web consists of 60 trillion pages that are stored in an index that exceeds 100 million gigabytes. Having a comprehensive index of the web and consumer behavior in real time allows Google to serve highly relevant searches and ads that closely mirror the user's intent.

Some organizations use big data to help create effective employee training with target results. From the target results, the firms work backward to identify leading indicators of results and then extend further back to track employee behaviors that affect the leading indicators. For example, Accenture, the global consulting and technology giant, analyzed almost 1,000 of its largest client projects over three years to determine important people-related factors that contribute to the success of their projects. Their analyses of big data revealed that employee training during or within 12 months prior to the project positively affects the success of projects. Also, they found that the more recently trained the team members, the higher the likelihood of success. These analytics convinced Accenture's top management to employ data-driven predictive training programs that include soft skill training in the 12 months prior to the project and functioning training during the project.

Jiffy Lube exploits big data to enhance the quality of its services. Jiffy Lube operates more than 2,000 fast lube stores that hire more than 20,000 employees to offer dozens of services. Technical certifications are a crucial factor to Jiffy Lube's success because staff must be certified to perform a service. The lack of reliable certification tracking hindered Jiffy Lube's ability to ensure adherence to this standard. In 2008, the company began to track employees' certifications using big data technology. A simple color-coded, real-time online report by individual, store, franchisee, and region was used to report employees' certification status. Certification at or above target level was shown in green, 50 to 99 percent in yellow, and below 50 percent was shown in red. Making the certification information online throughout the organization has helped to create awareness. In three years, total training has doubled. By early 2014, 76 percent of stores were at 80 to 100 percent certification.[15]

database management tools or data processing software applications. Instead, massive parallel software running on hundreds or even thousands of servers simultaneously is often required to store and process the data. RFID generates a huge amount of data as inventory moves through the supply chain. Big data technology helps to process the data in real time to take advantage of the information captured by RFID. The nearby SCM Profile demonstrates how big data is being used by some large corporations.

INVENTORY MODELS

A variety of inventory models for independent demand items are reviewed in this section by classifying the models into two broad categories. First, the deterministic inventory models are discussed that assume demand, delivery lead time, and other parameters are deterministic. These models use fixed parameters to derive the optimum *order quantity* to minimize *total inventory costs*. Thus, these models are also known as the **fixed order quantity models**. The economic order quantity, quantity discount, and economic manufacturing quantity models are the three most widely used fixed order quantity models. Following this, the statistical reorder point is discussed, where demand and/or lead time are not constant but can be estimated by means of a normal distribution. Finally, the continuous review and periodic review systems are briefly discussed.

The Economic Order Quantity Model

The **economic order quantity (EOQ) model** is a classic independent demand inventory system that provides many useful ordering decisions. The basic order decision is to determine the optimal order size that minimizes total annual inventory costs—that is, the sum of the annual order cost and the annual inventory holding cost. The issue revolves around the trade-off between annual inventory holding cost and annual order cost: when the order size for an item is small, orders have to be placed on a frequent basis, causing high annual order costs; however, the firm then has a low average inventory level for this item, resulting in low annual inventory holding costs. When the order size for an item is large, orders are placed less frequently, causing lower annual order costs, but high average inventory levels for this item, resulting in higher annual expenses to hold the inventory. The EOQ model thus seeks to find an optimal order size that minimizes the sum of the two annual costs. In EOQ computations, the term *carrying cost* is often used in place of holding cost and *setup cost* is used in place of order cost.

Assumptions of the Economic Order Quantity Model

Users must carefully consider the following assumptions when determining the economic order quantity:

1. *The demand is known and constant.* For example, if there are 365 days per year and the annual demand is known to be 730 units, then daily usage must be exactly 2 units throughout the entire year.
2. *Order lead time is known and constant.* For example, if the delivery lead time is known to be ten days, every delivery will arrive exactly ten days after the order is placed.
3. *Replenishment is instantaneous.* The entire order is delivered at one time and partial shipments are not allowed.
4. *Price is constant.* Quantity or price discounts are not allowed.

5. *The holding cost is known and constant.* The cost or rate to hold inventory must be known and constant.
6. *Order cost is known and constant.* The cost of placing an order must be known and remains constant for all orders.
7. *Stockouts are not allowed.* Inventory must be available at all times.

Deriving the Economic Order Quantity

The economic order quantity can be derived easily from the total annual inventory cost formula using basic calculus. The total annual inventory cost is the sum of the annual purchase cost, the annual holding cost, and the annual order cost. The formula can be shown as:

$$TAIC = \text{Annual purchase cost} + \text{Annual holding cost} + \text{Annual order cost}$$
$$TAIC = APC + AHC + AOC = (R \times C) + (Q/2 \times k \times C) + (R/Q \times S)$$

where

$TAIC$ = total annual inventory cost
APC = annual purchase cost
AHC = annual holding cost
AOC = annual order cost
R = annual requirement or demand
C = purchase cost per unit
S = cost of placing one order
k = holding rate, where annual holding cost per unit = $k \times C$
Q = order quantity

Since R, C, k, and S are deterministic (i.e., assumed to be constant terms), Q is the only unknown variable in the $TAIC$ equation. The optimum Q (the EOQ) can be obtained by taking the first derivative of $TAIC$ with respect to Q and then setting it equal to zero. A second derivative of $TAIC$ can also be taken with respect to Q to prove that the $TAIC$ is a concave function, and thus $\frac{dTAIC}{dQ} = 0$ is at the lowest point (i.e., minimum) of the total annual inventory cost curve. Thus:

$$\frac{dTAIC}{dQ} = 0 + (½ \times k \times C) + (-1 \times R \times S \times 1/Q^2)$$
$$= \frac{kC}{2} - \frac{RS}{Q^2}$$

Then setting $\frac{dTAIC}{dQ}$ equal to zero,

$$\frac{kC}{2} - \frac{RS}{Q^2} = 0$$
$$\Rightarrow \frac{kC}{2} = \frac{RS}{Q^2}$$
$$\Rightarrow Q^2 = \frac{2RS}{kC}$$
$$\Rightarrow \text{EOQ} = \sqrt{\frac{2RS}{kC}}$$

The second derivative of *TAIC* is

$$\frac{d^2TAIC}{dQ^2} = 0 - \left(-2 \times \frac{RS}{Q^3}\right) = \left(\frac{2RS}{Q^3}\right) \geq 0,$$

implying that the *TAIC* is at its minimum when $\frac{dTAIC}{dQ} = 0$.

The annual purchase cost drops off after the first derivative is taken. The managerial implication here is that purchase cost does not affect the order decision if there is no quantity discount (the annual purchase cost remains constant regardless of the order size, as long as the same annual quantity is purchased). Thus, the annual purchase cost is ignored in the classic EOQ model. Example 7.3 provides an illustration of calculating the EOQ. It should be noted that all demand must be converted to the annual requirement, and holding cost is the product of holding rate and unit cost of the item. For example, if the annual holding rate, k, is 12 percent and the item cost, C, is \$10 per unit, the holding cost, kC, is \$1.20 per unit per year.

Figure 7.5 shows the relationships between annual holding cost, annual order cost, and total annual holding plus order cost. Using the data in Example 7.3, at the EOQ (600 units), annual holding cost (\$1,200) equals annual order cost (\$1,200). At or close to the EOQ, the annual total cost curve is rather flat, indicating that it is not very sensitive to small variations in the economic order quantity. Therefore, the classic EOQ model is said to be very *robust* to minor errors in estimating cost parameters, such as holding rate, order cost, or annual usage. Table 7.5, for example, compares the annual total cost at an EOQ of 600 units and at 10 percent below and above the EOQ. The analysis shows that the cost variations range from only 0.01 percent to 0.56 percent above the minimum total cost.

Figure 7.5 and Table 7.5 show that if the order size is smaller than the EOQ, the annual holding cost is slightly lower, whereas the annual order cost is slightly higher. The net

Example 7.3 Calculating the EOQ at the Las Vegas Corporation

The Las Vegas Corporation purchases a critical component from one of its key suppliers. The operations manager wants to determine the economic order quantity, along with when to reorder, to ensure the annual inventory cost is minimized. The following information was obtained from historical data.

Annual requirements (R)	=	7,200 units
Setup cost (S)	=	\$100 per order
Holding rate (k)	=	20%
Unit cost (C)	=	\$20 per unit
Order lead time (LT)	=	6 days
Number of days per year	=	360 days

Thus,

$$EOQ = \sqrt{\frac{2RS}{kC}} = \sqrt{\frac{2 \times 7{,}200 \text{ units} \times \$100}{0.20 \times \$20}} = 600 \text{ units}$$

1. The annual purchase cost = $R \times C$ = 7,200 units × \$20 = \$144,000.
2. The annual holding cost = $Q/2 \times k \times C$ = (600/2) × 0.20 × \$20 = \$1,200.
3. The annual order cost = $R/Q \times S$ = (7,200/600) × \$100 = \$1,200.
   (Note that when using the EOQ, the annual holding cost equals the annual order cost.)
4. The total annual inventory cost = \$144,000 + \$1,200 + \$1,200 = \$146,400.
5. For an order lead time of six days, the **reorder point (ROP)** would be:
   ROP = (7,200/360) × 6 = 120 units
   Thus, the purchasing manager should reorder the component from the supplier whenever the physical or on-hand stock is down to 120 units, and 600 units should be ordered each time. The order cycle can also be computed as follows:
6. Number of orders placed per year = 7,200/600 = 12 orders.
7. Time between orders = 360/12 = 30 days.

Figure 7.5 The Economic Order Quantity and Total Costs

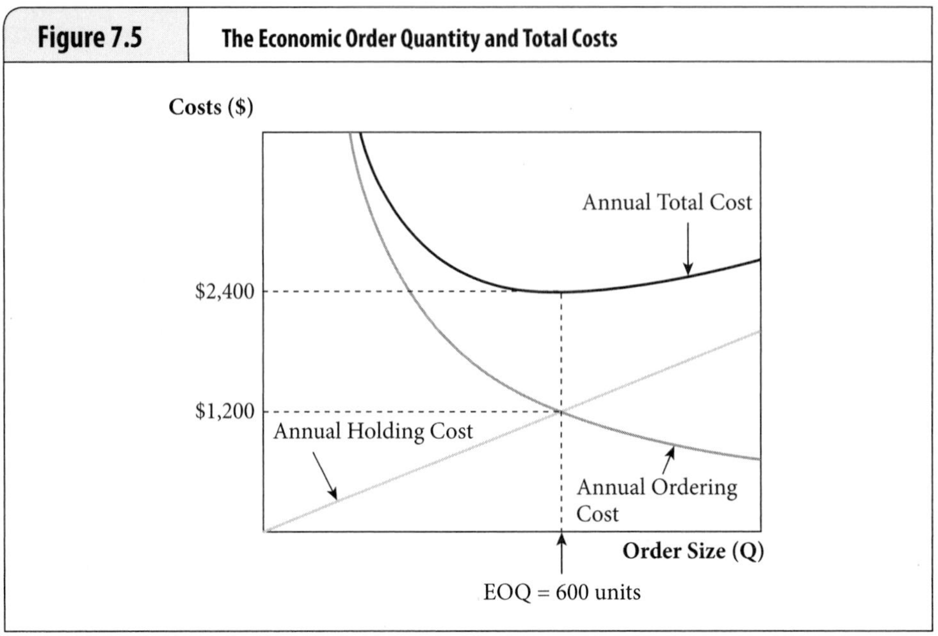

effect is a slightly higher annual total cost. Similarly, if the order quantity is slightly larger than the EOQ, the annual holding cost is slightly higher, whereas the annual order cost is slightly lower. The net effect is again a slightly higher annual total cost.

Figure 7.6 shows the movement of physical inventory and the relationships of the EOQ, average inventory, lead time, reorder point, and order cycle. Continuing with the use of the data in Example 7.3, at Time 0, the firm is assumed to start with a complete order of 600 units. The inventory is consumed at a steady rate of 20 units per day. On

Table 7.5 Percent Variation in Total Annual Cost

Q (UNITS)	AHC ($)	AOC ($)	ATC ($)	VARIATION (%)
540	1,080.00	1,333.33	2,413.33	0.56
550	1,100.00	1,309.09	2,409.09	0.38
560	1,120.00	1,285.71	2,405.71	0.24
570	1,140.00	1,263.16	2,403.16	0.13
580	1,160.00	1,241.38	2,401.38	0.06
590	1,180.00	1,220.34	2,400.34	0.01
EOQ = 600	1,200.00	1,200.00	2,400.00*	0.00
610	1,220.00	1,180.33	2,400.33	0.01
620	1,240.00	1,161.29	2,401.29	0.05
630	1,260.00	1,142.86	2,402.86	0.12
640	1,280.00	1,125.00	2,405.00	0.21
650	1,300.00	1,107.69	2,407.69	0.32
660	1,320.00	1,090.91	2,410.91	0.45

* indicates minimum total cost at the EOQ

Figure 7.6 Physical Inventory with the EOQ Model

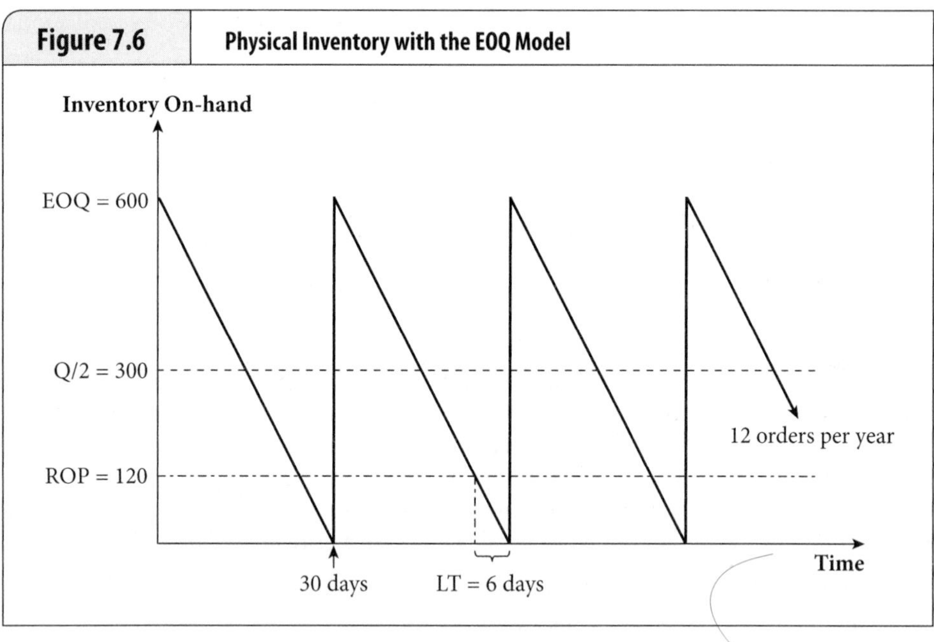

the twenty-fourth day, the ROP of 120 is reached and the firm places its first order of 600 units. It arrives six days later (on the thirtieth day). The 120 units of inventory will be totally consumed immediately prior to the arrival of the first order. The vertical line on the thirtieth day shows that all 600 units are received (this is the instantaneous replenishment assumption of the EOQ model). A total of twelve orders (including the initial 600 units) will be placed during the year to satisfy the annual requirement of 7,200 units.

The Quantity Discount Model

The **quantity discount model** or **price-break model** is one variation of the classic EOQ model. It relaxes the constant unit price assumption by allowing purchase quantity discounts. In this case, the unit price of an item is allowed to vary with the order size. For example, a supplier may offer a price of $5 per unit for orders up to 200 units, $4.50 per unit for orders between 201 and 500 units, and $4 per unit for orders of more than 500 units. This creates an incentive for the buyer to purchase in larger quantities to take advantage of the quantity discount, provided the savings is greater than the extra cost of holding larger inventory levels. Unlike the EOQ model, the annual purchase cost now becomes an important factor in determining the optimal order size and the corresponding total annual inventory cost. The quantity discount model must consider the trade-off between purchasing in larger quantities to take advantage of the price discount (while also reducing the number of orders required per year) and the higher costs of holding inventory. With the quantity discount model, there are thus two variables in the *TAIC* equation (the purchase price *C* and the order quantity *Q*). Hence a new approach is needed to find the optimal order quantity.

The purchase price per unit, *C*, is no longer fixed, as assumed in the classical EOQ model derivations. Consequently, the total annual inventory cost must now include the annual purchase cost, which varies depending on the order quantity. The new total annual inventory cost formula can now be stated as:

$$\text{Total annual inventory cost} = \text{Annual purchase cost} + \text{Annual holding cost} + \text{Annual order cost},$$

or

$$TAIC = APC + AHC + AOC = (R \times C) + (Q/2) \times (k \times C) + (R/Q) \times S$$

The quantity discount model yields a total annual inventory cost curve for each price level; hence, no single curve is relevant to all purchase quantities. The relevant total annual inventory cost curve is a combination of the cost curves for each price level, starting with the top curve where the price is the highest, and dropping down curve by curve at the price break point. A **price break point** is the minimum quantity required to get a price discount. There is an EOQ associated with each price level; however, the EOQ may not be *feasible* at that particular price level because the order quantity may not lie in the given quantity range for that unit price. Due to the stepwise shape of the total inventory cost curve, the optimal order quantity lies at either a *feasible EOQ* or at a *price break point.*

A fairly straightforward two-step procedure can be used to solve the quantity discount problem. Briefly, the two steps can be stated as follows:

1. Starting with the lowest purchase price, compute the EOQ for each price level until a feasible EOQ is found. If the feasible EOQ found is for the lowest purchase price, this is the optimal order quantity. The reason is that the EOQ for the lowest price level is the lowest point on the total annual inventory cost curve (see Figure 7.7). If the feasible EOQ is not associated with the lowest price level, proceed to step 2.
2. Compute the total annual inventory cost for the feasible EOQ found in step 1, and for all the price break points at each *lower* price level. Price break points *above* the feasible EOQ will result in higher total annual inventory cost, thus need not be evaluated. The order quantity that yields the lowest total annual inventory cost is the optimal order quantity.

Examples 7.4 and 7.5 illustrate the quantity discount model.

The Economic Manufacturing Quantity Model

The **economic manufacturing quantity (EMQ)** or **production order quantity (POQ) model** is another variation of the classic EOQ model. It relaxes the *instantaneous replenishment* assumption by allowing usage or partial delivery during production. The EMQ model is especially appropriate for a manufacturing environment where items are being manufactured and consumed simultaneously; hence the name economic manufacturing quantity. Inventory builds up gradually during the production period rather than at once as in the EOQ model.

For instance, let us assume that the production lot size for a manufactured product is 600 units, the manufacturer's production rate is 100 units per day, and its demand is 40 units per day. The manufacturer thus needs six days (600/100) to produce a batch of 600 units. While being produced, the items are also consumed simultaneously; hence, inventory builds up at the rate of 60 units (100 – 40) per day for six days. The maximum inventory is 360 units (60 × 6 days), which is less than the lot size of 600 units as would have been in the case of the classic EOQ model. The lower inventory level implies that the holding cost of the EMQ model is less than the EOQ model given the same cost parameters.

Figure 7.7 **Total Annual Inventory Cost Where the EOQ at the Lowest Price Level Is the Optimal Order Quantity**

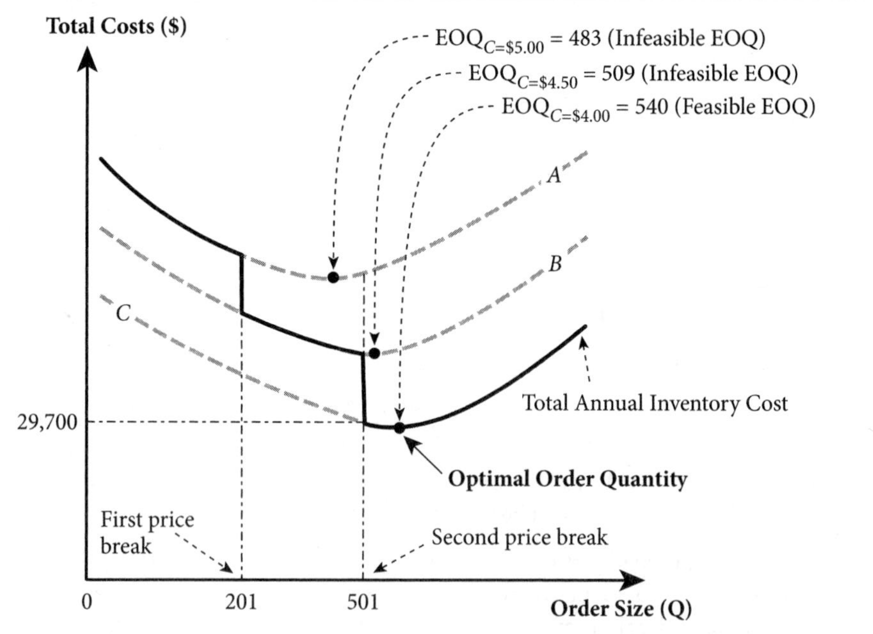

Example 7.4 Finding the Optimal Order Quantity with Quantity Discounts at the Kuantan Corporation

The Kuantan Corporation purchases a component from a supplier who offers quantity discounts to encourage larger order quantities. The supply chain manager of the company wants to determine the optimal order quantity to ensure the total annual inventory cost is minimized. The company's annual demand forecast for the item is 7,290 units, the order cost is $20 per order, and the annual holding rate is 25 percent. The price schedule for the item is:

ORDER QUANTITY	PRICE PER UNIT ($)
1–200	5.00
201–500	4.50
501 and above	4.00

The two questions of interest here are: (1) what is the optimal order quantity that will minimize the total annual inventory cost for this component? And (2) what is the minimum total annual inventory cost?

SOLUTION:

Step 1: Find the first feasible EOQ starting with the lowest price level:

$$EOQ_{C=\$4.00} = \sqrt{\frac{2 \times 7{,}290 \text{ units} \times \$20}{0.25 \times \$4}} = 540 \text{ units}$$

This is a *feasible* EOQ because order size of 540 units falls within the order quantity range for the price level of $4.00 per unit. Thus, 540 units is the optimal order quantity. In this case, the optimal order size falls on a feasible EOQ.

Step 2: The minimum total annual inventory cost is then:

$$\begin{aligned} TAIC &= APC + AHC + AOC = (R \times C) + (Q/2 \times k \times C) + (R/Q \times S) \\ &= (7{,}290 \times \$4) + (540/2 \times 0.25 \times \$4) + (7{,}290/540 \times \$20) \\ &= \$\,29{,}160 + \$270 + \$270 = \$29{,}700 \end{aligned}$$

The annual holding cost equals the annual order cost because the optimal order quantity falls on an EOQ.

Cost curves A, B, and C in Figure 7.7 are the annual inventory costs at price levels of $5, $4.50, and $4, respectively. Since each cost curve is only applicable for its price range, the relevant total annual inventory cost is the combination of these three cost curves where the total cost drops vertically at each price break point, curve by curve, to the next lower cost curve. Figure 7.7 shows that the feasible EOQ for the lowest price level is the lowest point on the total annual inventory cost curve; thus, it is the optimal order quantity. The two infeasible EOQs for the price levels of $4.50 and $5 are also shown in Figure 7.7 to reiterate that if an EOQ falls outside of its price range, it is irrelevant to the total annual inventory cost.

Example 7.5 Finding the Optimal Order Quantity with Quantity Discounts at the Soon Corporation

The Soon Corporation is a multinational company that purchases one of its crucial components from a supplier who offers quantity discounts to encourage larger order quantities. The supply chain manager of the company wants to determine the optimal order quantity to minimize the total annual inventory cost. The company's annual demand forecast for the item is 1,000 units, its order cost is \$20 per order, and its annual holding rate is 25 percent. The price schedule is:

ORDER QUANTITY	PRICE PER UNIT (\$)
1–200	5.00
201–500	4.50
501 and above	4.00

The first price break point is 201 units and the second is 501 units. What is the optimal order quantity that will minimize the total annual inventory cost for this component, and what is the total annual inventory cost?

SOLUTION:

Step 1: Find the first feasible EOQ starting with the lowest price level:

$$\text{A. } EOQ_{C=\$4.00} = \sqrt{\frac{2 \times 1{,}000 \text{ units} \times \$20}{0.25 \times \$4}} = 200 \text{ units}$$

This quantity is *infeasible* because an order quantity of 200 units does not fall within the required order quantity range to qualify for the \$4 price level (the unit price for an order quantity of 200 units is \$5). Next, we evaluate the EOQ at the next higher price level of \$4.50:

$$\text{B. } EOQ_{C=\$4.50} = \sqrt{\frac{2 \times 1{,}000 \text{ units} \times \$20}{0.25 \times \$4.50}} = 189 \text{ units}$$

This quantity is also *infeasible* because it fails to qualify for the \$4.50 price level. Moving on to the next higher price level of \$5:

$$\text{C. } EOQ_{C=\$5.00} = \sqrt{\frac{2 \times 1{,}000 \text{ units} \times \$20}{0.25 \times \$5}} = 179 \text{ units}$$

This order quantity is the *first feasible EOQ* because a 179-unit order quantity corresponds to the correct price level of \$5 per unit.

Step 2: Find the total annual inventory costs for the first feasible EOQ found in step 1 and for the price break points at each lower price level (201 units at \$4.50 and 501 units at \$4).

$$TAIC = APC + AHC + AOC + (R \times C) + (Q/2 \times k \times C) + (R/Q \times S)$$

A) $TAIC_{EOQ=179, C=\$5} = (1{,}000 \times \$5) = (179/2 \times 0.25 \times \$5) + (1{,}000/179 \times \$20) = \$5{,}000 + \$111.88 + \$111.73 = \$5{,}223.61$

B) $TAIC_{Q=201, C=\$4.50} = (1{,}000 \times \$4.50) + (201/2 \times 0.25 \times \$4.50) + (1{,}000/201 \times \$20) = \$41{,}500 + \$113.06 + \$99.50 = \$4{,}712.56$

C) $TAIC_{Q=501, C=\$4} = (1{,}000 \times \$4) + (501/2 \times 0.25 \times \$4) + (1{,}000/501 \times \$20) = \$4{,}000 + \$250.50 + \$39.92 = \$4{,}290.42$

Comparing the total annual inventory costs in A, B, and C, the optimal order quantity is 501 units, which qualifies for the deepest discount. In this case, the optimal order size falls on a *price break point*; hence, the annual holding cost (\$250.50) does not equal the annual order cost (\$39.92). When the quantity discount is large compared to the holding cost, it makes sense to purchase in large quantities and hold more inventory. However, this ignores the fact that excessive inventory hides production problems and can become obsolete very quickly. In the attempt to find the optimal order quantity to minimize inventory cost, a manager should also consider the impact of excessive inventory on firm performance. Figure 7.8 demonstrates the characteristics of the cost curves for this example. Cost curves A, B, and C are the annual inventory costs at price levels of \$5, \$4.50, and \$4, respectively. The relevant total annual inventory cost is derived from these three cost curves by joining the relevant portion of each cost curve vertically at the price break points.

It is also clear that the production rate must be greater than the demand rate; otherwise, there would not be any inventory buildups. On the seventh day, the production of the first batch stops and the inventory starts to deplete at the demand rate of 40 units for the next nine days (360/40). The first production lot and the subsequent usage of the inventory take fifteen days (6 + 9) to complete, and then the second cycle repeats.

Figure 7.9 depicts the inventory versus time for the EMQ model. The item is produced in lot size of Q, at the production rate of P, and consumed at the demand rate of D. Hence, inventory builds up at the rate of $(P–D)$ during the production period, T_P. At the end of the production period (T_P), inventory begins to deplete at the demand rate of D until it is exhausted at the end of the inventory cycle, T_C.

Figure 7.8 **Total Annual Inventory Cost Where the Optimal Order Quantity Is at the Price Break Point**

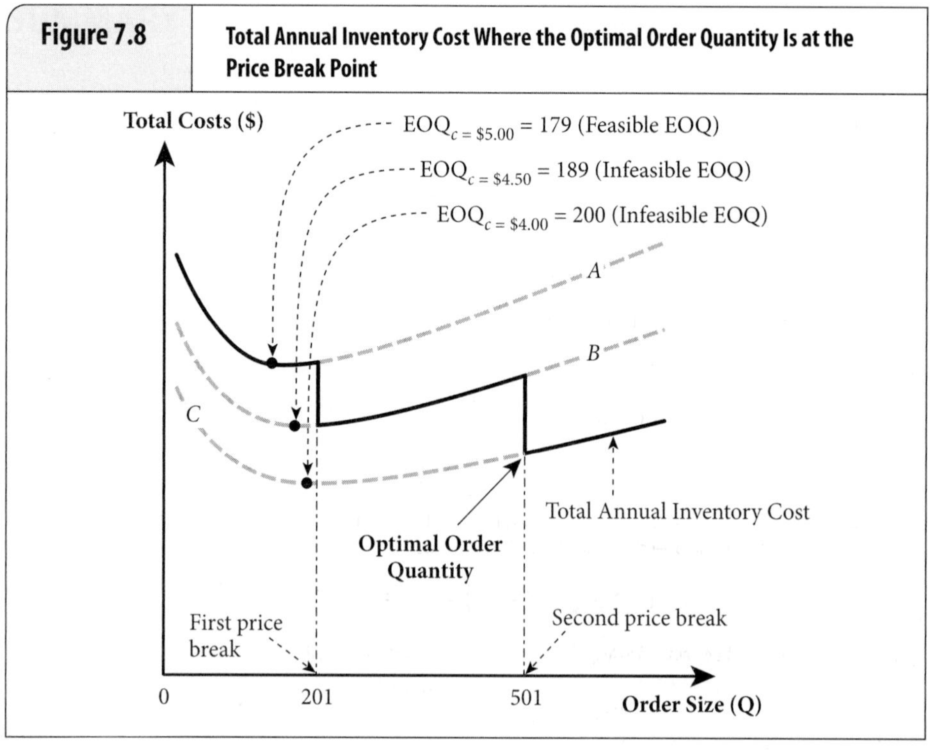

Figure 7.9 **Physical Inventory with the Economic Manufacturing Quantity Model**

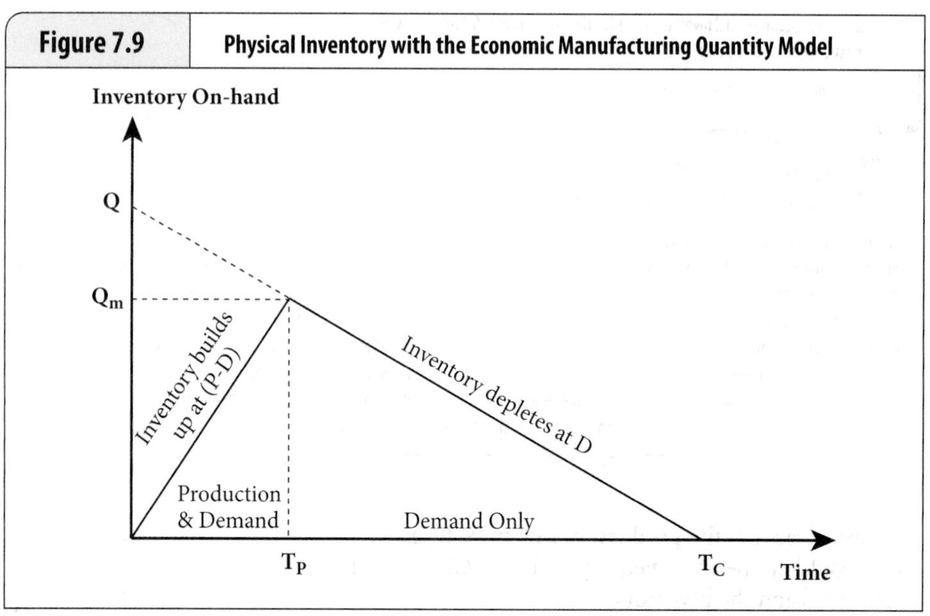

The production rate, P, which can be expressed as Q/T_p, is the production lot size divided by the time required to produce the lot. The maximum inventory, Q_M, can be obtained by multiplying the inventory build-up rate with the production period, and can be expressed as $(P-D) \times T_p$. These relationships can be stated as:

$$P = \frac{Q}{T_p} \quad \text{and} \quad Q_M = (P - D) \times T_p.$$

Therefore, $T_P = \frac{Q}{P}$ and substituting $\frac{Q}{P}$ for T_P in Q_M gives,

$$Q_M = (P - D) \times \frac{Q}{P}$$
$$= \frac{PQ}{P} - \frac{DQ}{P}$$
$$= Q\left(1 - \frac{Q}{P}\right)$$

Hence, the average inventory, $\frac{Q_M}{2} = \frac{Q}{2}(1 - \frac{D}{P})$.

The total annual inventory cost can be stated as:

Total annual inventory cost = Annual product cost + Annual holding cost + Annual setup cost,

or

$$TAIC = APC + AHC + ASC = (R \times C) + \left[\frac{Q}{2}\left(1 - \frac{D}{P}\right) \times k \times C\right] + [R/Q \times S]$$

where

$TAIC$ = total annual inventory cost
APC = annual product cost
AHC = annual holding cost
ASC = annual setup cost
R = annual requirement or demand
C = total cost of one unit of the finished product
S = cost of setting up the equipment to process one batch of the product
k = holding rate, where annual holding cost per unit = $k \times C$
Q = order quantity

Like the EOQ model where Q is the only unknown variable in the $TAIC$ equation, the optimum Q (the EMQ) can be obtained by taking the first derivative of $TAIC$ with respect to Q and then setting it equal to zero. A second derivative of $TAIC$ can also be taken with respect to Q to prove that the $TAIC$ is a concave function, and thus $\frac{dTAIC}{dQ} = 0$ is at the lowest point of the cost curve. Thus:

$$\frac{dTAIC}{dQ} = 0 + \left[½\left(1 - \frac{D}{P}\right) \times k \times C\right] + [-1 \times R \times S \times 1/Q^2]$$
$$= \left[\frac{kC}{2}\left(1 - \frac{D}{P}\right)\right] - \frac{RS}{Q^2}.$$

Then setting $\frac{dTAIC}{dQ}$ equal to zero and solving for the EMQ,

$$\left[\frac{kC}{2}\left(1 - \frac{D}{P}\right)\right] - \frac{RS}{Q^2} = 0$$
$$\Rightarrow \left[\frac{kC}{2}\left(1 - \frac{D}{P}\right)\right] - \frac{RS}{Q^2}$$
$$\Rightarrow Q^2 = \frac{2RS}{kC\left(1 - \frac{D}{P}\right)} = \frac{2RS}{kC\left(\frac{P - D}{P}\right)} = \frac{2RS}{kC}\left(\frac{P}{P - D}\right)$$

And the

$$EMQ = \sqrt{\left(\frac{2RS}{kC}\right)\left(\frac{P}{P-D}\right)}$$

The second derivative of the *TAIC* is:

$$\frac{d^2TAIC}{dQ^2} = 0 - \left(-2 \times \frac{RS}{Q^3}\right) = \left(\frac{2RS}{Q^3}\right) \geq 0,$$

implying that the *TAIC* is at its minimum when $\frac{dTAIC}{dQ} = 0$.

Similar to the EOQ model, the annual product cost drops off after the first derivative is taken, indicating that product cost does not affect the order decision if the unit cost of each product produced is constant; thus, the annual product cost is also ignored in the EMQ model. Example 7.6 provides an illustration of calculating the EMQ for a manufacturing company.

The Statistical Reorder Point

The two major inventory management decisions are to determine (1) the right order quantity or lot size and (2) when to release an order. Three basic independent demand lot-sizing techniques have been discussed, but as of yet, the question of when to order has not been fully discussed. The **reorder point (ROP)** is the lowest inventory level at which a new order must be placed to avoid a stockout. In a deterministic setting where both the demand and delivery lead time are known and constant, Example 7.3 showed that the reorder point was

Example 7.6 Calculating the EMQ at the Lone Wild Boar Corporation

The Lone Wild Boar Corporation manufactures a crucial component internally using the most advanced technology. The operations manager wants to determine the economic manufacturing quantity to ensure that the total annual inventory cost is minimized. The daily production rate (P) for the component is 200 units, annual demand (R) is 18,000 units, setup cost (S) is \$100 per setup, and the annual holding rate (k) is 25 percent. The manager estimates that the total cost (C) of a finished component is \$120. It is assumed that the plant operates year-round and there are 360 days per year.

SOLUTION:

1. The daily demand rate, $D = 18{,}000/360 = 50$ units per day.
2. $EMQ = \sqrt{\left(\frac{2RS}{kC}\right)\left(\frac{P}{P-D}\right)} = \sqrt{\left(\frac{2 \times 18{,}000 \times 100}{0.25 \times 120}\right)\left(\frac{200}{200-50}\right)} = 400$ units.
3. The highest inventory level, $Q_M = Q\left(1 - \frac{D}{P}\right) = 400\left(1 - \frac{50}{200}\right) = 300$ units.
4. The annual product cost $= R \times C = 18{,}000$ units $\times \$120 = \$2{,}160{,}000$.
5. The annual holding cost $= \frac{Q_M}{2} \times k \times C = \frac{300}{2} \times 0.25 \times 120 = 4{,}500$.
6. The annual setup cost $= R/Q \times S = (18{,}000/400) \times \$100 = \$4{,}500$.
   (Note that at the EMQ, the annual holding cost equals the annual setup cost.)
7. The $TAIC = \$2{,}160{,}000 + \$4{,}500 + \$4{,}500 = \$2{,}169{,}000$.
8. The length of a production period, $T_p = \frac{EMQ}{P} = 400/200 = 2$ days.
9. The length of each inventory cycle, $T_c = \frac{EMQ}{D} = 400/50 = 8$ days.
10. The rate of inventory buildup during production, $(P - D) = 200 - 50 = 150$ units per day.
11. The number of inventory cycles per year = 360 days/8 days = 45 cycles.

Figure 7.10 illustrates the EMQ model for the Lone Wild Boar Corporation. A unique observation regarding the classic EOQ, quantity discount, and the EMQ models is that when ordering at the EOQ or EMQ, the annual order or setup cost equals the annual holding cost, except in the quantity discount model when the optimal order quantity falls on a price break point.

Figure 7.10 Lone Wild Boar Corporation's EMQ Model

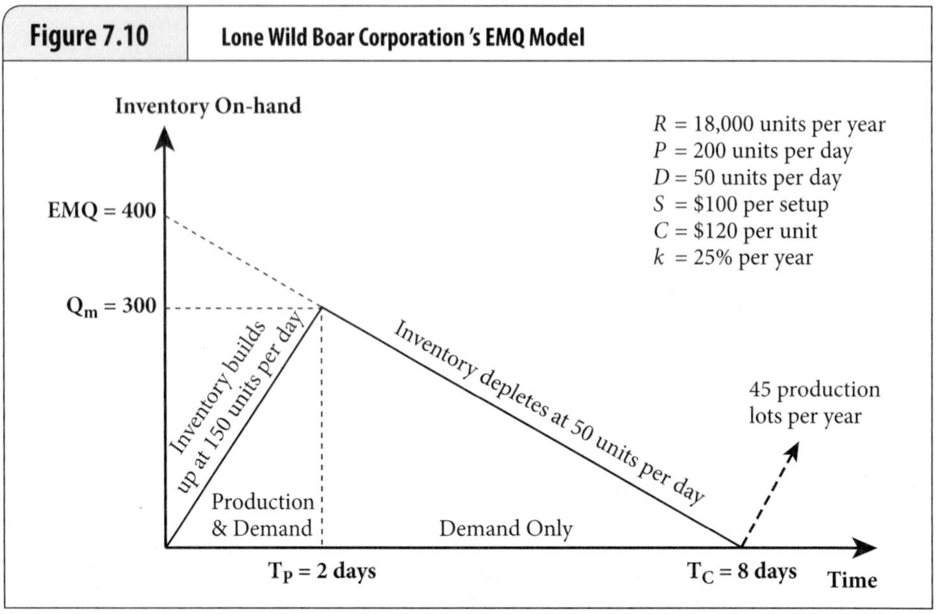

equal to the demand during the order's delivery lead time. In reality, the demand and delivery lead time tend to vary. Uncertain demand or lead time raises the possibility of stockouts, thus requiring *safety stock* to be held to safeguard against variations in demand or lead time. Next, we discuss how the probabilistic demand pattern and lead time affect the ROP.

The Statistical Reorder Point with Probabilistic Demand and Constant Lead Time

This model assumes the lead time of a product is constant while the demand during the delivery lead time is unknown but can be specified using a normal distribution. Since the statistical reorder point is to determine the lowest inventory level at which a new order should be placed, demand prior to a purchase order does not directly affect the ROP. Figure 7.11 illustrates the relationship between safety stock and the probability of a stockout. If the average demand during the lead time is represented by μ, and the ROP is represented by x, then the safety stock is $(x - \mu)$, which can be derived from the standard deviation formula $\left(Z = \frac{x-\mu}{\sigma}\right)$. Then, if the probability of stockout is represented by α, the probability that inventory is sufficient to cover demand or the *in-stock probability* is (1– α). The in-stock probability is commonly referred to as the **service level** (actually, the calculation of the true service level requires use of a loss function for a stockout, which is beyond the scope of this text). Next, the Z-value can be determined from the standardized normal

Figure 7.11 The Relationship of Safety Stock to the Probability of a Stockout

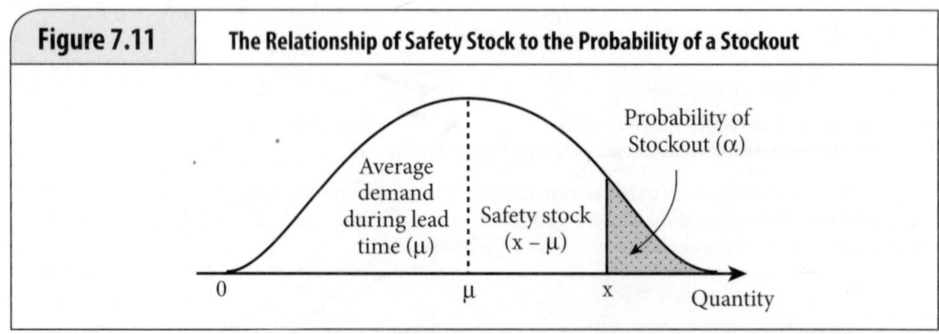

curve and a desire to achieve a specific service level (see the Z-Table in the Appendix). For example, a 97.5 percent service level ($\alpha = 2.5$ percent) corresponds to the Z-value of 1.96. Note that at the middle of the normal curve, where the reorder point equals the average demand, the required safety stock is zero and the probability of stockout would be 50 percent.

The statistical reorder point (x) can be calculated as the average demand during the order's delivery lead time plus the desired safety stock, or:

$$\text{ROP} = \bar{d}_{\text{LT}} + Z\sigma_{\text{dLT}}$$

The safety stock $Z\sigma_{\text{dLT}}$ or $(x-\mu)$ can be derived from the standard deviation formula of the normal curve as shown earlier, and σ_{dLT} is the standard deviation of demand during the delivery lead time. Example 7.7 illustrates the calculation of the ROP with probabilistic demand and constant delivery lead time.

The safety stock computation as shown in Example 7.7 needs to be modified if the standard deviation is available for daily demand and not lead time demand. In this situation, if the delivery lead time is greater than one day, the standard deviation of daily demand (σ_{d}) must be converted to the standard deviation of lead time demand (σ_{dLT}). If the daily demand is identically distributed, we can use the statistical premise that the variance of a series of independent occurrences is equal to the sum of the variances. That is, the variance of demand during the lead time equals the sum of the variances of all the identical daily demand that covers the lead time period. This can be expressed as:

$$\sigma^2_{\text{dLT}} = \sigma^2_{\text{d}} + \sigma^2_{\text{d}} + \sigma^2_{\text{d}} + \ldots = \sigma^2_{\text{d}}\,(LT)$$

where

σ^2_{dLT} = variance of demand during the lead time

σ^2_{d} = variance of the identically and independently distributed daily demand

LT = lead time in days

Thus, the standard deviation of demand during the lead time is $\sigma_{\text{dLT}} = \sigma_{\text{d}}\sqrt{LT}$. Hence the safety stock and the statistical reorder point can be stated as:

$$\text{Safety stock} = Z\sigma_{\text{d}}\sqrt{LT}$$

$$\text{and ROP} = \bar{d}_{\text{LT}} + Z\sigma_{\text{d}}\sqrt{LT}.$$

Example 7.8 illustrates this calculation.

Example 7.7 Calculating the Statistical Reorder Point Using Probabilistic Demand and Constant Delivery Lead Times at London, Inc.

London, Inc., stocks a crucial part that has a normally distributed demand pattern during the reorder period. Past demand shows that the average demand during lead time (μ) for the part is 550 units, and the standard deviation of demand during lead time (σ_{dLT}) is 40 units. The supply chain manager wants to determine the safety stock and statistical reorder point that result in 5 percent stockouts or a service level of 95 percent. Alternately, the manager wants to know the additional safety stock required to attain a 99 percent service level.

SOLUTION:

The normal distribution Z-table in the Appendix shows that a 95 percent service level (5 percent stockouts allowed) corresponds to a Z-value of 1.65 standard deviations above the mean.

The required safety stock is

$$(x - \mu) = Z\sigma_{\text{dLT}} = 1.65 \times 40 = 66 \text{ units.}$$

The ROP $= \bar{d}_{\text{LT}} + Z\sigma_{\text{dLT}} = 550 + 66$ units $= 616$ units. This means the manager must reorder the part from their supplier when their current stock level reaches 616 units.

Alternately, the required safety stock at a 99 percent service level $= Z\sigma_{\text{dLT}} = 2.33 \times 40 \times 93$ units. The additional safety stock compared to the 95 percent service level is 27 units.

Example 7.8 Calculating the Statistical Reorder Point at Brussels, Inc., Using the Standard Deviation of Daily Demand and Constant Delivery Lead Times

Brussels, Inc., is a local liquor retailer specializing in selling beer at big discounts. Historical data shows that the demand for beer has a normal distribution. The average daily demand for beer at Brussels is 150 cases, and its standard deviation for daily demand is 30 cases. Brussels' supplier maintains a very reliable and constant lead time of six days. The manager desires to determine the standard deviation of demand during lead time, the safety stock and statistical reorder point that results in a 97.5 percent service level and the safety stock reduction if the manager decides to attain a 90 percent service level.

SOLUTION:

Average daily demand, $\bar{d} = 150$ cases

Standard deviation of daily demand, $\sigma_d = 30$ cases

Lead time, $LT = 6$ days

$$\text{The standard deviation of demand during lead time, } \sigma_{dLT} = \sigma_d\sqrt{LT}$$
$$= 30\sqrt{6} \text{ cases} = 73.5 \text{ cases}$$

The Z-Table shows that a 97.5 percent service level (2.5 percent stockouts allowed) corresponds to the Z-value of 1.96 standard deviations above the mean.

The corresponding safety stock, $Z\sigma_d\sqrt{LT} = 1.96 \times 30\sqrt{6} = 144$ cases.

The ROP $= \bar{d}_{LT} + Z\sigma_d\sqrt{LT} = (150 \times 6) + 144 = 1{,}044$ cases. Thus ordering more beer when they have a current inventory of 1,044 cases will result in a 97.5 percent service level.

For the lower service level of 90 percent, safety stock $= Z\sigma_d\sqrt{LT} = 1.28 \times 30\sqrt{6} = 94$ cases. The safety stock reduction would be 50 cases.

The Statistical Reorder Point with Constant Demand and Probabilistic Lead Time

When the demand of a product is constant and the lead time is unknown but can be specified by means of a normal distribution, the safety stock is used to buffer against variations in the lead time instead of demand. The safety stock is then (daily demand $Z \times \sigma_{LT}$), and the reorder point is:

$$\text{ROP} = (\text{daily demand } \times \text{ average lead time in days}) + (\text{daily demand } \times Z\sigma_{LT})$$

where

σ_{LT} = the standard deviation of lead time in days.

The calculation is demonstrated in Example 7.9.

Example 7.9 Calculating the Statistical Reorder Point at the Harpert Store Using Constant Demand and Probabilistic Lead Time

The Harpert Store has an exclusive contract with Brussums Electronics to sell its most popular mp3 player. The demand of this mp3 player is very stable at 120 units per day. However, the delivery lead times vary and can be specified by a normal distribution with a mean lead time of eight days and a standard deviation of two days. The supply chain manager at Brussums desires to calculate the safety stock and reorder point for a 95 percent service level (in-stock probability).

SOLUTION:

Daily demand $(d) = 120$ units.

Mean lead time $(\overline{LT}) = 8$ days.

Standard deviation of lead time $(\sigma_{LT}) = 2$ days.

A service level of 95 percent yields a $Z = 1.65$ from the Z-Table.

$$\text{Required safety stock} = (d \times Z\sigma_{LT}) = 120 \text{ units} \times 1.65 \times 2 = 396 \text{ units.}$$
$$\text{ROP} = (d \times \overline{LT}) + (d \times Z\sigma_{LT}) = (120 \times 8) + 396 = 1{,}356 \text{ units.}$$

Brussums must order more mp3 players from Harpert when its current inventory reaches 1,356 units.

The Statistical Reorder Point with Probabilistic Demand and Lead Time

When both the demand and lead time of a product are unknown but can be specified by means of a normal distribution, safety stock must be held to cover the variations in both demand and lead time, resulting in higher safety stocks when compared to variations in the demand or lead time only. The reorder point can be computed as follows:[16]

$$\text{ROP} = (\bar{d} \times \overline{LT}) + Z\sigma_{\text{dLT}}$$

Where

$$\sigma_{\text{dLT}} = \text{Standard deviation of demand during the lead time}$$
$$= \sqrt{\sigma_{\text{LT}}^2(\bar{d})^2 + \sigma_{\text{d}}^2(\overline{LT})}$$

and where

σ_{LT} = Standard deviation of lead time days, and

σ_{d} = Standard deviation of daily demand.

Note that this standard deviation formula (σ_{dLT}) can be applied to all the previous reorder point examples by observing the following fact: "constant" or "no variation" means zero standard deviation. Therefore:

1. When the lead time and demand are constant, then σ_{LT} and σ_{d} are zero, and the average daily demand and average lead time would be the deterministic demand and lead time. Thus, the reorder point is the demand during lead time period.
2. When the daily demand is probabilistic and lead time is constant, then σ_{LT} is zero and the average lead time would be the deterministic lead time. Using this guideline, the reorder point in Example 7.8 can also be computed as:

   $$\text{ROP} = (150 \times 6) + 1.96\sqrt{0^2(150)^2 + 30^2(6)} = 900 + 1.96 \times 30\sqrt{6} = 1{,}044 \text{ cases.}$$
3. When the daily demand is constant and the lead time is probabilistic, then σ_{d} is zero and the average daily demand would be the deterministic daily demand. Using this guideline, the reorder point in Example 7.9 can also be computed as:

   $$\text{ROP} = (120 \times 8) + 1.65\sqrt{2^2(120)^2 + 0^2(8)} = 960 + 1.65 \times 2 \times 120 = 1{,}356 \text{ units.}$$

Example 7.10 demonstrates the safety stock and reorder point computation when both the daily demand and lead time are probabilistic.

The Continuous Review and the Periodic Review Inventory Systems

The order quantity and reorder point inventory models discussed thus far assume that the physical inventory levels are precisely known at every point in time. This implies that stock movements must be updated in real time and that there are no discrepancies between physical inventory and the stock record. In other words, a *continuous review* of the physical inventory is required to make sure that orders are initiated when physical inventories reaches their reorder points. In practice, a **continuous review system** can be difficult to achieve and very expensive to implement. Inventory review costs can be lowered by using a **periodic review system** instead, where physical inventory is reviewed at regular intervals, such as weekly or monthly. However, more safety stock would be required for the periodic review system to buffer the added variation due to the longer review period.

Example 7.10 Calculating the Statistical Reorder Point at the Dosseldorf Store Using Probabilistic Demand and Delivery Lead Time

The Dosseldorf Store is the sole distributor of a popular cell phone. The demand for this cell phone is normally distributed with an average daily demand of 120 units and a standard deviation of 18 units per day. The cell phones are ordered and shipped directly from the manufacturer. Past delivery records for the manufacturer show that delivery lead times are normally distributed with an average of eight days and a standard deviation of two days. The supply chain manager at Dosseldorf desires to determine the safety stock required and the reorder point for a 95 percent service level.

SOLUTION:

Average daily demand, $\bar{d} = 120$ units.
Standard deviation of daily demand, $\sigma_d = 18$ units.
Average lead time, $\overline{LT} = 8$ days.
Standard deviation of lead time, $\sigma_{LT} = 2$ days.
A desired service level of 95 percent yields $Z = 1.65$ from the Z-Table.

$$\begin{aligned}\text{The required safety stock} &= Z\sigma_{dLT}\\ &= 1.65 \times \sqrt{\sigma_{LT}^2(\bar{d})^2 + \sigma_d^2(\overline{LT})}\\ &= 1.65 \times \sqrt{2^2(120)^2 + 18^2(8)} = 1.65 \times 245.34 = 405 \text{ units.}\\ \text{The ROP} &= (\bar{d} \times \overline{LT}) + Z\sigma_{dLT} = (120 \times 8) + 405 = 1{,}365 \text{ units.}\end{aligned}$$

Dosseldorf must order more cell phones from its supplier when its current stock reaches 1,365 units to achieve a 95 percent service level.

When analyzing the continuous review and the periodic review systems, the following symbols are used:

s = order point
S = maximum inventory level
Q = order quantity
R = periodic review
$n = 1, 2, 3 \ldots$

The Continuous Review System

The continuous review system implies that physical inventory is known at all times, so it is more expensive to administer. However, the only uncertainty is the magnitude of demand during the delivery lead time; thus, the only safety stock required is for potential stockouts during this time period. There are two continuous review systems, described below.

1. *(s, Q) continuous review policy*: This policy orders the same quantity, Q, when physical inventory reaches the reorder point, *s*. The quantity, Q, can be determined by one of the fixed order quantity methods (such as the EOQ). This policy works properly only if the quantity demanded is one unit at a time. Otherwise, the inventory level may fall below the reorder point, s.
2. *(s, S) continuous review policy*: When current inventory reaches or falls below the reorder point, *s*, sufficient units are ordered to bring the inventory up to a predetermined level, S. If the quantity demanded is one unit at a time, this system is similar to the (*s*, Q) policy. However, if the quantity demand is larger than one unit and when physical inventory falls below the reorder point, then the order size is larger than Q. For instance, suppose $s = 10$, $S = 120$, and current inventory is 11 units. If the next demand is 3 units, then on-hand inventory will be reduced to 8 units. Consequently, an order size of 112 units would be released.

The Periodic Review System

The periodic review system reviews physical inventory at specific intervals of time. Although this system is cheaper to administer, a higher level of safety stock is needed to buffer against uncertainty in demand over a longer planning horizon. There are three periodic review systems, described below.

1. *(nQ, s, R) periodic review policy*: If at the time of inventory review, the physical inventory is equal to or less than the reorder point, s, the quantity, nQ, is ordered to bring the inventory up to the level between s and $(s + Q)$. Recall that $n = 1, 2, 3, \ldots,$ and the order size is then some multiple of Q. No order is placed if the current inventory is higher than the reorder point. For example, let $s = 100$ and $Q = 50$. If the current inventory is 20 units at the time of the review, then $2Q$ quantities $(2 \times 50 = 100)$ are ordered to bring the inventory level up to 120 units.
2. *(S, R) periodic review policy*: At each review time, a sufficient quantity is ordered to bring the inventory up to a predetermined maximum inventory level, S. This policy places a variable sized order as long as the physical inventory is less than the maximum inventory level, S. If order cost is high, this is obviously not a preferred system. However, it may work well if a large variety of items are ordered from the same supplier.
3. *(s, S, R) policy*: If at the time of inventory review, the physical inventory is equal to or less than the reorder point, s, a sufficient quantity is ordered to bring the inventory level up to the maximum inventory level, S. However, if the physical inventory is higher than the reorder point s, no order is placed. This policy addresses the major deficiency of the (S, R) policy.

SUMMARY

Organizations rely on inventory to balance supply and demand, and to buffer uncertainties in the supply chain. However, inventory can be one of the most expensive assets of an organization; hence it must be managed closely. The right amount of inventory supports business operations, but too little of it can adversely affect customer service. Conversely, excess inventory not only leads to unnecessary inventory carrying cost but hides production problems and other flaws in a company.

This chapter covered the crucial roles of inventory and various inventory management techniques that are widely used for balancing demand with supply. The classic ABC inventory classification was discussed along with the ABC inventory matrix as a means to monitor if a firm is stocking the right inventories. Ample examples were used to demonstrate the order size and order period inventory models. This chapter also covered two of the latest developments in inventory management—RFID and big data. Radio frequency identification certainly has the potential to drastically change the way inventories are managed in the future, and big data analysis allows firms to gain a competitive advantage through better decision making.

KEY TERMS

ABC inventory control system, 213
ABC inventory matrix, 216
active RFID tags, 218
big data, 222
carrying costs, 212
continuous review system, 237
cycle counting, 213
dependent demand, 209
direct costs, 211
economic manufacturing quantity (EMQ), 228
economic order quantity (EOQ) model, 223
electronic product code (EPC), 218
fixed costs, 211
fixed order quantity models, 223
holding or carrying costs, 212
independent demand, 210
indirect costs, 211
inventory turnover ratio, 212
inventory turnovers, 212
order costs, 212
Pareto analysis, 214
passive RFID tags, 218
periodic review system, 237
price break point, 228
price-break model, 227
production order quantity (POQ) model, 228
quantity discount model, 227
radio frequency identification (RFID), 217
reorder point (ROP), 233
service level, 234
setup costs, 212
variable costs, 212
80/20 rule, 214

DISCUSSION QUESTIONS

1. Describe and provide examples of dependent and independent demand.
2. Describe the four basic types of inventory.
3. What is the ABC inventory system, and how is it used to manage inventory?
4. What is the ABC inventory matrix, and how is it used to manage inventory?
5. Describe inventory turnover and how it can be used to manage inventory.
6. Why is it important to conduct cycle counting?
7. What is the electronic product code (EPC)?
8. Briefly describe how RFID can be used to manage inventory.

9. Explain why item-level tagging is more expensive than case-level tagging in RFID.
10. What is big data?
11. How can firms use big data to make better decisions?
12. What is the purpose of the EOQ and the ROP? How can they be used together?
13. What are the assumptions of the EOQ model?
14. What are the two major costs considered in the EOQ model? Why is the total purchase price not a factor affecting the order quantity?
15. How is the quantity discount model related to the EOQ model?
16. How is the EMQ model related to the EOQ model?
17. Discuss whether the EOQ model is still useful if a small error was made while estimating one of the cost parameters used in the EOQ computation.
18. Assume that you used the EOQ model to compute the order quantity for an item, and the answer was 20 units. Unfortunately, the minimum lot size for the item is 24 units. Discuss how this is going to impact your annual holding cost, annual order cost, and annual total inventory cost.
19. Explain whether the continuous review or periodic review inventory system is likely to result in higher safety stock. Which is likely to require more time and effort to administer? Why?
20. Use the inventory turnover ratios in Table 7.2 to comment on which firm is the most efficient in deploying its inventory to generate sales.
21. What is the order quantity when the annual order or setup cost equals the annual holding cost in the (a) EOQ model, (b) quantity discount model, and (c) EMQ model?
22. Why is inventory management important to SCM?

ESSAY/PROJECT QUESTIONS

1. Visit the website of EPCglobal, Inc., and use the information to write a brief report on RFID technology and the state of RFID implementation.
2. Use the Internet to search for relevant information to prepare a brief report on the state of RFID implementation in North America, Europe, and Asia.
3. Use resources available on the Internet to prepare a report on the RFID implementation at Wal-Mart Stores, Inc.
4. Use resources available on the Internet to prepare a brief report on big data and business analytics.
5. Use resources available on the Internet (e.g., http://finance.yahoo.com/) to access the annual reports (financial statements and balance sheets) of three of your favorite listed companies to (a) extract their latest total revenue, cost of revenue, total assets, and year-end or average inventory, and use these numbers to (b) prepare their inventory/total revenue ratio, inventory/total assets ratio, and the inventory turnover ratio. Comment on how they performed based on these ratios. (Hint: See Tables 7.1 and 7.2.)

SPREADSHEET PROBLEMS

1. The revenue for a firm is $2,500,000. Its cost of revenue is $850,000, and its average inventory for the year is $62,000. What is their inventory turnover?

2. Given the following information, what is the annual inventory turnover ratio?

Revenue	$2,2000,000
Cost of Revenue	$1,250,000
Quarter 1 Ending Inventory	$85,000
Quarter 2 Ending Inventory	$98,000
Quarter 3 Ending Inventory	$125,000
Quarter 4 Ending Inventory	$68,000

3. Given the following information, compute the economic order quantity, annual holding cost, annual order cost, and annual total inventory cost.

Annual requirements (*R*)	= 50,000 units
Order cost (*S*)	= $150 per order
Holding rate (*k*)	= 15%
Unit cost (*c*)	= $100 per unit

4. The annual requirement of a part is 360,000 units. The order cost is $120 per order, the holding rate is 12 percent, and the part cost is $2,500 per unit. What are the (a) EOQ, (b) annual holding cost, (c) annual order cost, and (d) annual total inventory cost?

5. The weekly requirement of a part is 950 units. The order cost is $85 per order, the holding cost is $5 per unit per year, and the part cost is $250 per unit. The firm operates fifty-two weeks per year. Compute the (a) EOQ, (b) annual holding cost, (c) annual order cost, and (d) annual total inventory cost.

6. The monthly demand for a part is 1,500 units. The order cost is $285 per order, the holding cost is $56 per unit per year, and the part cost is $850 per unit. The firm operates twelve months per year. Compute the (a) EOQ, (b) annual holding cost, (c) annual order cost, and (d) annual total inventory cost.

7. Icy Snowmobile, Inc., has an annual demand for 1,200 snowmobiles. Their purchase cost for each snowmobile is $2,500. It costs about $250 to place an order, and the holding rate is 35 percent of the unit cost. Compute the (a) EOQ, (b) annual holding cost, (c) annual order cost, and (d) total annual inventory cost.

8. Steamy Speedboats has an annual demand for 1,500 speedboats. Its supplier offers quantity discounts to promote larger order quantities. The cost to place an order is $300, and the holding rate is 32 percent of the purchase cost. The purchase cost for each speedboat is based on the price schedule given below. Compute the (a) optimal order quantity, (b) annual purchase cost, (c) annual holding cost, (d) annual order cost, and (e) total annual inventory cost.

ORDER QUANTITY	PRICE PER UNIT ($)
1–50	18,500
51–100	18,000
101–150	17,400
151 and above	16,800

9. Using the Steamy Speedboats problem above, assume that the order cost has dropped from $300 to $50. What are the (a) optimal order quantity, (b) annual

purchase cost, (c) annual holding cost, (d) annual order cost, and (e) total annual inventory cost?

10. Using the Steamy Speedboats problem above, assume that the holding rate has dropped from 32 percent to 15 percent. What are the (a) optimal order quantity, (b) annual purchase cost, (c) annual holding cost, (d) annual order cost, and (e) total annual inventory cost?

11. Frankfurt Electronics produces a component internally using a state-of-the-art technology. The operations manager wants to determine the optimal lot size to ensure that the total annual inventory cost is minimized. The daily production rate for the component is 500 units, annual demand is 36,000 units, setup cost is $150 per setup, and the annual holding rate is 30 percent. The manager estimates that the total cost of a finished component is $80. If we assume that the plant operates year-round, and there are 360 days per year, what are the (a) daily demand, (b) optimal lot size, (c) highest inventory, (d) annual product cost, (e) annual holding cost, (f) annual setup cost, (g) total annual inventory cost, (h) length of a production period, (i) length of each inventory cycle, (j) rate of inventory buildup during the production cycle, and (k) number of inventory cycles per year? Plot the movement of the inventory during one production cycle using time on the horizontal axis and on-hand inventory on the vertical axis (see Figure 7.10).

12. Paris Store stocks a part that has a normal distribution demand pattern during the reorder period. Its average demand during lead time is 650 units, and the standard deviation of demand during lead time is 60 units. What are the safety stock and statistical reorder point that result in a 97.5 percent service level?

13. Lindner Congress Bookstore sells a unique calculator to college students. The demand for this calculator has a normal distribution with an average daily demand of 15 units and a standard deviation of 4 units per day. The lead time for this calculator is very stable at five days. Compute the standard deviation of demand during lead time, and determine the safety stock and statistical reorder point that result in 5 percent stockouts.

14. The daily demand of a product is very stable at 250 units per day. However, its delivery lead time varies and can be specified by a normal distribution with a mean lead time of twelve days and standard deviation of three days. What are the safety stock and reorder point for a 97.5 percent service level?

15. The daily demand of a product can be specified by a normal distribution. Its average daily demand is 250 units with a standard deviation of 40 units. The delivery lead time of this product is also normally distributed with an average of ten days and a standard deviation of three days. What are the safety stock and reorder point for a 95 percent service level?

16. Given the following inventory information, perform an ABC analysis.

ITEM NUMBER	UNIT COST ($)	ANNUAL USAGE (UNITS)
B8867	6.00	100
J1252	5.25	6,500
K9667	0.25	4,000
L2425	1.00	1,500
M4554	5.50	2,000
T6334	70.00	500
W9856	0.75	800
X2215	1.50	8,000
Y3214	32.00	1,000
Y6339	4.00	3,500

17. Given the following inventory information, construct an (a) ABC analysis by annual dollar usage, (b) ABC analysis by current inventory value, and (c) ABC inventory matrix. Is the firm stocking the correct inventories?

ITEM NUMBER	UNIT COST ($)	ANNUAL USAGE (UNITS)	CURRENT INVENTORY (UNITS)
B8867	6.00	100	8,000
J1252	5.25	6,500	120
K9667	0.25	4,000	1,000
L2425	1.00	1,500	375
M4554	5.50	2,000	500
T6334	70.00	500	800
W9856	0.75	800	20,000
X2215	1.50	8,000	2,000
Y3214	32.00	1,000	500
Y6339	4.00	3,500	125

18. Given the following inventory information, construct an (a) ABC analysis by annual dollar usage, (b) ABC analysis by current inventory value, and (c) an ABC inventory matrix. Is the firm stocking the correct inventories?

ITEM NUMBER	UNIT COST ($)	ANNUAL USAGE (UNITS)	CURRENT INVENTORY (UNITS)
A967	32.00	1	4,500
B886	6.00	100	8,000
C314	5.25	32	115
D879	12.50	54	254
E536	0.05	125	120
F876	0.07	423	500
G112	0.12	500	1008
H098	1.22	235	750
J125	5.25	6,500	120
K966	0.25	4,000	1,000
L242	1.00	1,500	375
M455	5.50	2,000	500
N007	7.21	54	525
P231	5.25	32	300
Q954	3.25	25	240
T633	70.00	500	800
W985	0.75	800	20,000
X221	1.50	8,000	2,000
Y321	32.00	1,000	500
Z633	4.00	3,500	125

19. Given the following information for an important purchased part, compute the (a) EOQ, (b) total purchase cost, (c) annual holding cost, (d) annual order cost, (e) annual total cost, (f) reorder point, (g) number of orders placed per year, and (h) time between orders. Use Microsoft Excel to plot the cost curves (annual holding cost, annual order cost, and annual total cost) on the vertical axis, and the order quantity on the horizontal axis.

Annual requirements (*R*)	= 5,000 units
Order cost (*S*)	= $100 per order
Holding rate (*k*)	= 20%
Unit cost (*C*)	= $20 per unit
Lead time (*LT*)	= 6 days
Number of days per year	= 360 days

20. Given the following information for a purchased part, compute the (a) EOQ, (b) total purchase cost, (c) annual holding cost, (d) annual order cost, (e) annual total cost, (f) reorder point, (g) number of orders placed per year, and (h) time between orders. Use Microsoft Excel to plot the cost curves (annual holding cost, annual order cost, and annual total cost) on the vertical axis, and the order quantity on the horizontal axis.

Monthly demand	= 3,500 units
Order cost (S)	= \$250 per order
Holding cost (kC)	= \$8.65 per unit per year
Unit cost (C)	= \$85 per unit
Lead time (LT)	= 12 days
Number of days per year	= 365 days

ADDITIONAL READINGS

Jacobs, F. R., and R. B. Chase, *Operations and Supply Chain Management,* 14th ed. Boston: McGraw-Hill/Irwin, 2014.

EPCglobal, "EPCglobal Tag Data Standards Version 1.3 Ratified Specification," EPCglobal Inc., March 8, 2006.

EPCglobal, "The EPCglobal Architecture Framework EPCglobal Final Version 1.2," EPCglobal Inc., September 10, 2007.

EPCglobal, "EPC Radio-Frequency Identity Protocols Generation-2 UHF RFID," EPCglobal Inc., 2013.

Fogarty, D. W., J. H. Blackstone, and T. R. Hoffmann, *Production & Inventory Management*, 2nd ed. Cincinnati: South-Western, 1991.

Hax, A., and D. Candea, *Production and Inventory Management.* Englewood Cliffs, NJ: Prentice Hall, 1984.

Krajewski, L. J., L. P. Ritzman and M. J. Malhorta. *Operations Management: Processes and Supply Chains*, 10th ed. Reading, MA: Prentice Hall, 2013.

Vollmann, T. E., W. L. Berry, D. C. Whybark, and F. R. Jacobs, *Manufacturing Planning and Control for Supply Chain Management*, 5th ed. Boston: McGraw-Hill/Irwin, 2005.

ENDNOTES

1. Trebilcock, B., "The Heart of Production at ODU," *Modern Materials Handling* 69(4), April 20, 2014: 20–24.
2. Shoulberg, W., "The Lessons from Winter '13-'14," *Gifts & Decorative Accessories* 115(3), March/April 2014: 12.
3. Stevens-Huffman, L., "Profit from Big Data," *Smart Business Philadelphia* 8(3), November 2013: 12–15.
4. Barnes, J., "The Myths and Truths About Inventory Optimization," *Supply Chain Management Review* 18(2), March/April 2014: 10–19.
5. Andel, T., "Goodwill's WMS Enables Business and Mission Success," *Material Handling & Logistics*, April 14, 2014: 32.
6. Napolitano, M., "Top 8 Guidelines to Improve Inventory Management," *Logistics Management* 57(3), March 2013: 40–43.
7. Ibid.
8. http://www.epcglobalinc.org/home, accessed May 30, 2010.

9. Anonymous, "Wal-Mart, DOD Start Massive RFID Rollout; Is Everybody Ready?" *Inventory Management Report* 05(01), January 2005: 1, 10–12.

10. Songini, M. L., "Procter & Gamble: Wal-Mart RFID Effort Effective," *ComputerWorld* 41(9), February 26, 2007: 14.

11. RFID Frequently Asked Question, RFID Journal; http://www.rfidjournal.com/faq/show?85, accessed May 11, 2014.

12. Fish, L. A., and W. C. Forrest, "A Worldwide Look at RFID," *Supply Chain Management Review* 11(3), April 1, 2007: 48–55.

13. Hoffman, W., "Wave of the Future: Changes in Technology, Industry Consolidation, Global Standards Begin to Raise RFID's Profile," *Journal of Commerce* 9(35), September 8, 2008: 44.

14. Wu, N., H. H. Tsai, Y. S. Chang, and H. C. Yu, "The Radio Frequency Identification Industry Development Strategies of Asian Countries," *Technology Analysis & Strategic Management* 22(4), May 2010: 417–431.

15. Dearborn, J., "BIG Data: A Quick-Start Guide for Learning Practitioners," *T+D* 68(5), May 2014: 52–57.

16. Narsimhan, S., D. W. McLeavey, and P. Billington, *Production Planning and Inventory Control*, 2nd ed. Saddle River, NJ: Prentice Hall, 1995.

Chapter 8

PROCESS MANAGEMENT—LEAN AND SIX SIGMA IN THE SUPPLY CHAIN

Open communication is essential. Everyone needs to understand the challenges that our industry is facing from a competitive viewpoint and realize that lean is an essential tool to enable success.

— ***David Pulman, President, Global Mfg. and Supply, GlaxoSmithKline***[1]

Caterpillar views Six Sigma as part of our values in action—who we are and how we live, work and better serve our customers. We demonstrate our value of excellence through Six Sigma. Six Sigma is the foundation of how we plan and execute our strategy, ensuring our resources are focused on the right projects that will deliver on our company's goals and help our customers win.

— ***Rob Grove, manager of strategic support services, Caterpillar***[2]

Learning Objectives

After completing this chapter, you should be able to

- Discuss and compare the major elements of lean and Six Sigma.
- Describe why lean and Six Sigma are integral parts of SCM.
- Discuss the Toyota Production System and its association with lean production.
- Discuss the linkage between lean programs and environmental protection.
- Describe the historical developments of lean and Six Sigma.
- Describe and use the various tools of Six Sigma.
- Understand the importance of statistical process control for improving quality.

Chapter Outline

SCM Profile: The Adoption of Lean Six Sigma at the City of Irving, Texas

Irving, Texas, a city with more than 215,000, has witnessed improvements since 2007, thanks to its adoption of lean Six Sigma. The city was recently recognized for its efforts with the Texas Award for Performance Excellence, and in 2012 the city won the U.S. Malcolm Baldrige Quality Award. And, while he considers it an honor for Irving to receive these awards, City Manager Tommy Gonzalez says the government's eyes are set not on awards but on metrics. Gonzalez directs a workforce made up of knowledgeable Six Sigma belts—four black belts, thirty green belts, twenty-eight yellow belts, and about 1,000 white belts.

As the economy began to weaken in 2008, Irving had to assess strategies for staying viable. "We found the lean Six Sigma model to correlate with the way we thought about being efficient while still focusing on the delivery of service to the public and optimizing those service levels and reducing the time that it took to get that product to them, whether it is a direct service or delivery of information, or if it was a matter of picking up someone's trash as quickly as possible," says Gonzales. One example of Irving's use of lean thinking is its community pool. About 9,700 people were visiting three small pools around the city each year. Each facility was over 40 years old and costly to maintain. So Irving built one large community pool, designed to be energy efficient, and the number of visits rose to 110,000 each year. According to Gonzales, "When you have three facilities that hardly have anyone walking through, the fixed costs are high. So we were able to go in, reduce costs and give the people what they want. We're thinking that's a pretty good result."

Since October 2007, city employees have saved more than 30,000 hours and $38 million. The maximum plan review time for the city's commercial permit review process went from ninety days to six days. A citywide inventory of traffic signs led to the removal of more than 300 redundant signs and a cost avoidance of $103,121. Redesigned trucks have saved 990 hours per truck crew per year. And a health insurance audit led to the removal of 151 ineligible dependents, resulting in annual savings of $590,000. Lean Six Sigma has also lead to a drop in the crime rate, a vibrant local economy, the opening of a new convention center, and the creation of 3,000 new jobs. "We found a way to put processes and systems in place while at the same time changing the culture and motivating our folks to be the best they can be in terms of the best representation of themselves. If you focus on that, then you'll always know what the vision is, and you'll always know how to use the processes and systems we have in place. And that's something that has worked well for us so far," says Gonzales.[3]

INTRODUCTION

As discussed in earlier chapters, supply chain management goals are concerned with achieving low cost along with high levels of quality and responsiveness throughout the supply chain. Customer expectations make it necessary for firms to adopt strategic initiatives emphasizing speed, innovation, cooperation, quality, and efficiencies. Lean thinking and Six Sigma quality, two important operating philosophies that are central to the success of supply chain management, seek to achieve these strategic initiatives, while at the same time resolve the trade-offs that can exist when simultaneously pursuing the goals of high quality, fast response, and low cost.

In the 1990s, supply chain management emerged as a strategy combining several practices already in use—**quick response (QR)**, **efficient consumer response (ECR)**, just-in-time (JIT), and Japanese **keiretsu relationships**. The first two are concerned with speed and flexibility, while keiretsu involves partnership arrangements. The QR program was developed by the

U.S. textile industry in the mid-1980s as an offshoot of JIT and was based on merchandisers and suppliers working together to respond more quickly to consumer needs by sharing information, resulting in better customer service and less inventory and waste. In the early 1990s, ECR was developed by a U.S. grocery industry task force charged with making grocery supply chains more competitive. In this case, point-of-purchase transactions at grocery stores were forwarded via computer to distributors and manufacturers, allowing the stores to keep stocks replenished while minimizing the need for safety stock inventories. Keiretsu networks are cooperative coalitions between Japanese manufacturing firms and their suppliers. In many cases, keiretsus are formed as the result of financial support given to suppliers by a manufacturing firm.

Supply chain management is thus closely associated with JIT. While many argue that Henry Ford and his company essentially invented JIT practices, the term **just-in-time** was originally associated with Toyota managers like Mr. Taiichi Ohno along with his kanban system, encompassing continuous problem solving in order to eliminate waste. Use of the term *lean* has today largely replaced use of the term JIT, and is associated with the Toyota Production System. Lean thinking is broader, although closely related to JIT, and describes a philosophy incorporating tools that seek to economically optimize time, human resources, assets, and productivity, while improving product and service quality. In the early 1980s, these practices started making their way to the Western world, first as JIT and then today, as **lean production**, **lean manufacturing**, or simply **lean thinking**. Lean thinking has evolved into a way of doing business for many organizations.

Quality assessment and improvement is a necessary element of lean production. First, as the process of waste elimination begins to shrink inventories, problems with human resource requirements, queues, lead times, quality, and timing are typically uncovered both in production and with inbound and outbound materials. Eventually, these problems are remedied, resulting in higher levels of quality and customer service. Second, as the drive to continuously reduce throughput times continues, the need for a continuing emphasis on improving quality throughout the productive system results in the need for an overall quality improvement or Six Sigma program. **Six Sigma** stresses a commitment by the firm's top management to help the firm identify customer expectations and excel in meeting and exceeding those expectations. Since global economic changes (such as the most recent global recession) along with changes in technology and competition cause customer expectations to change, firms must then commit to a program of continual reassessment and improvement; this, too, is an integral part of Six Sigma. Thus, to achieve the primary objectives of low cost, high quality, and fast response, supply chain management requires the use of lean and Six Sigma thinking throughout the supply chain. These topics are discussed in this chapter.

LEAN PRODUCTION AND THE TOYOTA PRODUCTION SYSTEM

The term *lean production* essentially refers to the **Toyota Production System** in its entirety, which was created and refined by several of Toyota's key executives over a number of decades. In 2010, Toyota came under fire for a number of recalls involving over 8 million vehicles worldwide for several quality and safety problems. While these problems were indeed serious, they do not diminish the value of lean production or the Toyota Production System. In fact, in 2010, Toyota promised a return to its "customer first" principles.[4] Several of the important events in the creation of the Toyota Production System are described next.

Mr. Sakichi Toyoda invented the power loom in 1902 and in 1926 founded the Toyoda Automatic Loom Works. In 1937, he sold his loom patents to finance an automobile manufacturing plant to compete with Ford and General Motors, which accounted for over

90 percent of the vehicles sold in Japan at the time. Sakichi's son Kiichiro Toyoda was named managing director of the new facility.[5]

Kiichiro spent a year in Detroit studying Ford's manufacturing system and others, and then returned to Japan, where he adapted what he learned to the production of small quantities of automobiles, using smaller, more frequently delivered batches of materials. This later was referred to as the just-in-time system within Toyoda. At Ford, their system was designed such that parts were fabricated, delivered directly to the assembly line, and then assembled onto a vehicle within just a few minutes. Henry Ford had called this *flow production*, the precursor to JIT.[6]

Mr. Eiji Toyoda, nephew of Sakichi, began working at Toyoda in 1936 and was named managing director of the renamed and reorganized Toyoda Automotive Works in 1950. Eiji, too, traveled to Detroit to study Ford's automobile manufacturing system and was particularly impressed with its quality improvement activities, most notably its employee suggestion system. He was also impressed with Ford's daily automobile output of 7,000 cars, compared to Toyoda's cumulative thirteen-year output of just 2,700 cars. Back in Japan, he implemented the concepts he had seen in the U.S. and this became the foundation of what was later referred to as the Toyota Production System.

In 1957, the company was again renamed, and became the Toyota Company. It introduced its first U.S. car that year—the Toyopet Crown. While popular in Japan, the car's quality, speed, and styling problems resulted in sales of only 288 units in fourteen months in the U.S. Consequently, Toyota withdrew from the U.S. market to better analyze U.S. consumers and their demands for reliability. "No detail was unimportant, and they paid very close attention to customers," says Dave Cole, chairman of Michigan-based Centre for Automotive Research. In 1965, the Corona was introduced in the U.S. and by 1972 U.S. sales had reached 1 million units.[7] In 1982, Eiji established Toyota Motor Sales USA, and finally in 1983, Eiji renamed the firm the Toyota Motor Corporation.

Taiichi Ohno began his career at the Toyoda Automatic Loom Works in 1932. He eventually expanded on the concepts established by Kiichiro and Eiji, by developing and refining methods to produce items only as they were needed for assembly. He visited Detroit several times to observe auto manufacturing techniques. After World War II, the Toyoda production facilities were rebuilt, with Taiichi playing a major role in establishing the low-batch production principles he developed earlier. These principles proved very valuable at the time, since postwar Japan was experiencing severe materials shortages. What Taiichi and Eiji had both realized during their trips to the U.S. was the tremendous waste everywhere (referred to as **muda** in Japan). These wastes of labor, inventories, space, time, and processing were certainly things Toyoda could not afford. From this realization came the idea that parts should be produced only as needed by the next step in an entire production process. When a type of signal or card (called a **kanban**) was used, the system became much more effective. This began to be called the kanban or JIT system within Toyoda.

Refinements to the JIT concepts continued under Taiichi's tutelage, and he later attributed the system to two things—Henry Ford's autobiography wherein he explained the Ford manufacturing system, and U.S. supermarket operations characterized by daily supply deliveries, which Ohno observed during a visit to the U.S. in 1956. The final two notable people in the development of the Toyota Production System were Shigeo Shingo, a quality consultant hired by Toyota, and W. Edwards Deming who happened to be in Japan after the war, helping to conduct the census. He became known to Ohno and others at Toyota when he began attending professional manufacturing meetings to discuss statistical quality control techniques. By the 1950s in Japan, Deming had created and was discussing his fourteen-point quality management guideline and ideas for continuous improvement with many Japanese manufacturing engineers and managers.

Shingo developed the concept of **poka-yoke** in 1961, when he was employed at Toyota. Poka-yoke means error- or mistake-proofing. The idea is to design processes such that mistakes or defects are prevented from occurring in the first place, and if they do occur, further errors are also prevented. These fail-safe mechanisms can be electrical, mechanical, visual, procedural, or any other method that prevents problems, errors, or defects, and they can be implemented anywhere in the organization. Poka-yoke thus leads to higher levels of quality and customer service.[8]

By 1959, Toyota was making 100,000 cars per year. In the latter part of the 1950s though, as mentioned earlier, it was experiencing quality problems that were impacting potential sales in the U.S. To remedy this, Toyota implemented what it referred to as total quality control (TQC) in concert with its JIT system. This then became the final piece of the Toyota Production System, and was later refined and renamed total quality management (TQM). Interestingly, in the first quarter of 2007, Toyota sold more vehicles worldwide than General Motors, ending GM's 76-year reign as the world's largest auto maker.[9] (As another side note, GM regained its global leadership position in 2011).[10]

Actually, the term *lean production* did not originate at Toyota. It was first used in a benchmarking study conducted by the International Motor Vehicle Program (IMVP) at the Massachusetts Institute of Technology. The IMVP conducted a global automobile quality and productivity benchmarking study that culminated in the book, *The Machine that Changed the World* wherein the elements of lean production and the benchmarking results were presented.[11] The word "lean" was suggested because the Japanese facilities in the benchmarking study, when compared to their U.S. counterparts, used half the manufacturing labor, half the space, and half the engineering hours to produce a new automobile model in half the time. They also used much less than half the average inventory levels to produce the same number of vehicles, and had far fewer defects.

SCM Profile

Mitsubishi Caterpillar's Lean Story

In 2003, Mitsubishi Caterpillar Forklift America Inc. (MCFA) began implementing lean manufacturing. Planting the seed and managing the lean process was difficult at first. After the company's initiation of lean, it took three to five years to see visible bottom-line results such as millions saved in parts and labor costs, an 80 percent reduction in internal manufacturing lead time, a 75 percent reduction in manufacturers' warranty claims, and increasingly fewer safety incidents. Today, the lean legacy is so engrained at MCFA that long after current management leaves, the processes will continue.

At MCFA, the dealer inventory pool is a small strategic stock of products stored at the plant. With this, dealers have a selection of premade products to choose from, allowing a fast turn for their customers if needed. The reorganization of their production system to a "one-piece flow" exponentially increased efficiency, cutting the manufacturing time of a lift truck from 10 days to 48 hours. In 2009, MCFA averaged fewer than two incidents of injury per month, while the Occupational Safety and Health Administration (OSHA) national average is over five. In the first four months of 2010, MCFA reported zero incidents. MCFA also received more than 75 percent fewer manufacturing warranty claims, meaning the product is being manufactured correctly the first time. This practice is reinforced through an internal initiative deemed "quality focus," where the company emphasizes driving quality back to the source.[12]

The use of lean thinking has spread rapidly over the years among many manufacturers, services, and small businesses in numerous industries. Mitsubishi Caterpillar's lean story is briefly explained in the nearby SCM Profile. Pennsylvania-based Industrial Scientific Corp., a gas detection instrument manufacturer, has been working with lean for about five years—today there are one-third fewer people on the manufacturing floor while output is up by 30 percent and order lead times have gone from two weeks to less than three days. Texas-based Photo Etch, an aerospace manufacturer, implemented lean and reduced its manufacturing lead times by half, while defects plummeted. It now uses 30 percent less floor space, which is allowing it to explore other business opportunities.[13] Elkhart General Hospital used lean thinking in 2009 to address medication management. It was using IV carts that were refilled every 24 hours; this meant that about half of the prefilled IVs were thrown out because medications changed or patients were discharged. So it changed to a two-hour fill system—this reduced IV waste so much that pharmacists were redeployed to other activities, and money was saved on medications. Overall, this one change saved the hospital $1 million annually.[14] Mike Shanahan, co-owner of Connecticut-based small manufacturer Cadco Ltd., used lean thinking to speed up the production of warming trays and revise the layout of its facility. According to Mr. Shanahan, "The concept of lean is nothing like we thought it would be. It doesn't have to be complicated, unruly or expensive. In my eyes, it's all about finding the simplest way to accomplish a task or an operation. And its success can be measured in either small increments, astounding results, or something in between. Either way, it can be applied to almost any operation or any size."[15]

LEAN THINKING AND SUPPLY CHAIN MANAGEMENT

Simply put, the objective of supply chain management is to balance the flow of materials with customer requirements throughout the supply chain, such that costs, quality, and customer service are at optimal levels. Lean production emphasizes reduction of waste, continuous improvement, and the synchronization of material flows from within the organization and eventually including the organization's first-tier suppliers and customers. In many respects, then, supply chain management seeks to incorporate lean thinking across entire supply chains. Supply chain management encourages cross-training, satisfying internal customer demand, moving products or people through the production system quickly, and communicating end-customer demand forecasts and production schedules up the supply chains. In addition, it seeks to optimize inventory levels across entire supply chains. Thus, when implemented within the focal firm as well as its trading partners, the realized benefits of lean are much more significant.

Firms are increasingly implementing lean strategies along their supply chains. As a matter of fact, one of the newest terms in the lean lexicon is **yokoten**. Yokoten is a Japanese term meaning "across everywhere." In lean terminology, it is used to mean the sharing of best practices. Lean firms are using yokoten to reach out to closely linked suppliers and customers to make the supply chain leaner. For manufacturers, most of their costs derive from supply chains. Consequently, supply chains represent the best opportunity for seeing results from lean implementations. When *Logistics Management* magazine conducted a lean survey among hundreds of its subscribers, it found that use of lean improvements to supply chains had grown significantly—from just 30 percent in 2007 to 46 percent in 2011, a growth of over 50 percent. "The lean movement is largely process improvements that don't cost anything for the most part," says Norm Saenz, senior VP of TranSystems, a supply chain consulting firm. "These kinds of process improvements are generally smart and eliminate wastes, without necessarily investing in technology, equipment, and software," he says.[16]

Many firms successfully implement a few lean activities at a time, based on resources, product characteristics, customer needs, and supplier capabilities. Coffeehouse giant Starbucks has a VP of lean thinking who travels from region to region with his lean team, looking for ways to reduce the wasted movements of its baristas. This in turn gives baristas more time to interact with customers and improve the Starbucks experience. The results are streamlined operations, happier customers, and a better bottom line.[17] Noted lecturer and author of many books on lean and associated topics, Norman Bodek, suggests that maybe half of U.S. manufacturing companies are into some aspect of lean. "Many do run kaizen blitzes, but only a fraction are truly committed to using all of the aspects of lean," he suggests. "As an example, I feel that only one percent have the person 'pull the cord' [to] stop the process when they discover a problem."[18] The following section is a discussion of the lean elements.

THE ELEMENTS OF LEAN

Table 8.1 presents the major lean elements that are discussed in this section of the chapter, along with a short description of each element. As noted above, lean programs can vary significantly, based on a company's resource capabilities, product and process orientation, and past failures or successes with other improvement projects. Firms with a mature lean program will most likely be practicing a significant number of these elements.

Table 8.1 The Elements of Lean

ELEMENTS	DESCRIPTIONS
1. Waste reduction	Eliminating waste is the primary concern of lean thinking. This includes reducing excess inventories, material movements, production steps, scrap losses, rejects, and rework.
2. Lean supply chain relationships	Firms work with suppliers and customers with the mutual goal of eliminating waste, improving speed, and improving quality. Key suppliers and customers are considered partners.
3. Lean layouts	WIP inventories are positioned close to each process, and layouts are designed to reduce movements of people and materials. Processes are positioned to allow smooth flow of work through the facility.
4. Inventory and setup time reduction	Inventories are reduced by reducing production batch sizes, setup times, and safety stocks. This tends to create or uncover processing problems that are then controlled.
5. Small batch scheduling	Firms produce frequent small batches of product, with frequent product changes, to enable a level production schedule. Smaller, more frequent purchase orders are communicated to suppliers, and more frequent deliveries are offered to customers. Kanbans are used to pull WIP through the system.
6. Continuous improvement	As queues and lead times are reduced, problems surface more quickly, causing the need for continual attention to problem solving and process improvement. With lower safety stocks, quality levels must be high to avoid process shutdowns. Attention to supplier, WIP, and finished goods quality levels are high.
7. Workforce empowerment	Employees are cross-trained to add processing flexibility and to increase the workforce's ability to solve problems. Employees are trained to provide quality inspections as parts enter a process area. Employee roles are expanded and they are given top management support and resources to identify and fix problems.

Sources: Lamming, R. *Beyond Partnership: Strategies for Innovation and Lean Supply*. London: Prentice Hall, 1993; Ohno, T. *The Toyota Production System: Beyond Large-Scale Production*. Portland, OR: Productivity Press, 1988; Schonberger, R. J. *Japanese Manufacturing Techniques*. New York, NY: The Free Press, 1982; Womack, J. and D. Jones. *Lean Thinking: Banish Waste and Create Wealth for Your Corporation*. New York, NY: Simon and Schuster, 1996.

Waste Reduction

One of the primary and long-term goals of all lean endeavors is **waste reduction**. The desired outcome of waste reduction is value enhancement. Firms reduce costs and add value to their products and services by eliminating waste from their productive systems. Scott Sedam, president of TrueNorth Development, a global provider of lean methods to the construction industry, sums up the importance of waste reduction in construction: "In the end, what our industry needs is a culture change, a 'hair on fire' attitude that every penny counts and every associate, whether manager, direct employee, supplier or trade, feels responsible. That's the challenge, and that's the goal. Getting there is not easy, but it has been done in many other industries. Now it's home building's turn at the plate, and not a moment too soon."[19]

Waste is a catch-all term encompassing things such as excess wait times, inventories, material and people movements, processing steps, processing variabilities, and *any other nonvalue-adding activity*. Taiichi Ohno of Toyota, described what he called the **seven wastes**, which have since been applied across many industries around the world, to identify and reduce waste. The seven wastes are shown and described in Table 8.2. The common term across the seven wastes is *excess*. Obviously, firms require some level of inventories, material and worker movements, and processing times, but the idea is to determine the *right* levels of these things and then decide how best to achieve them.

Table 8.2 The Seven Wastes

WASTES	DESCRIPTION
Overproducing	Production of unnecessary items to maintain high utilization.
Waiting	Excess idle machine and operator time; materials experiencing excess wait time for processing.
Transportation	Excess movement of materials between processing steps; transporting items long distances using multiple handling steps.
Overprocessing	Nonvalue-adding manufacturing, handling, packaging, or inspection activities.
Excess inventory	Storage of excess raw materials, work-in-process, and finished goods.
Excess movement	Unnecessary movements of employees to complete a task.
Scrap and rework	Scrap materials and product rework activities due to poor-quality materials or processing.

Source: Ohno, T. *Toyota Production System*. Portland, OR: Productivity Press, 1988.

Unfortunately, many companies and their trading partners view waste as simply a cost of doing business. To identify and eliminate waste, workers and managers must be continually assessing processes, methods, and materials for their value contributions to the firm's salable products and services. This is accomplished through worker–management interactions and commitment to the continued elimination of waste, and frequent solicitation of feedback from customers. Significant waste reduction results in a number of positive outcomes including lower costs, shorter lead times, better quality, and greater competitiveness. During the recent economic downturn, eliminating waste enabled firms to stay profitable while sales levels were declining. The use of lean programs increased in popularity during those years.

Using the Five-Ss to Reduce Waste

Another method used for waste reduction has been termed the **Five-Ss**. The original Five-Ss came from Toyota and were Japanese words relating to industrial housekeeping.

The idea is that by implementing the Five-Ss, the workplace will be cleaner, more organized, and safer, thereby reducing processing waste and injury accidents, and improving productivity. Food retailer and processor, Safeway, for example, uses a Five-S system in its Bellevue, Washington ice cream plant. Each production station includes a bulletin board containing proper start-up and shut-down procedures, a list of ingredients, results of the latest Five-S audit, and a photo of what a clean station should look like. Following the Five-Ss allows Safeway to avoid what it terms the 6th S—surprises.[20] Table 8.3 lists and describes each of these terms, and presents the equivalent S-terms used in the English version of the Five-S system.

Table 8.3 **The Five-Ss**

JAPANESE S-TERM	ENGLISH TRANSLATION	ENGLISH S-TERM IN USE
1. Seiri	Organization	Sort
2. Seiton	Tidiness	Set in order
3. Seiso	Purity	Sweep or shine
4. Seiketsu	Cleanliness	Standardize
5. Shitsuke	Discipline	Self-discipline or Sustain

Sources: Becker, J. "Implementing 5S: To Promote Safety & Housekeeping," *Professional Safety* 46(8), 2001: 29–31; Rooney, S. and J. Rooney. "Lean Glossary," *Quality Progress* 38(6), 2005: 41–47.

The goals of the first two (sorting and setting in order) are to eliminate searching for parts and tools, avoid unnecessary movements, and avoid using the wrong tools or parts. Work area tools and materials are evaluated for their appropriateness, and approved items are arranged and stored near their place of use. Seiso/sweep refers to proper workplace cleaning and maintenance, while Seiketsu/standardize seeks to reduce processing variabilities by eliminating nonstandard activities and resources. Shitsuke/self-discipline or sustain means using effective work habits through use of the first four terms.

The Five-S system can be employed in any service or manufacturing environment. Many lean efforts begin with implementation of the Five-Ss. Firms can conduct a "waste hunt" using the Five-Ss, and then follow up with a "red-tag event" to remove or further evaluate all nonessential, red-tagged items. Some companies have also added their own "sixth-S", for surprises, as described in the Safeway example earlier, or safety, for assessing the safety of work conditions.[21]

Lean Supply Chain Relationships

Quite commonly, firms must hold safety stocks of purchased products because their suppliers' delivery times are inconsistent or the quality of the purchased goods does not always meet specifications. Internally, extra work-in-process (WIP) inventories are stored as a way to deal with temperamental processing equipment or other variabilities causing processing problems. On the distribution side, firms hold stocks of finished goods in warehouses prior to shipment to customers, in some cases for months at a time, to avoid stockouts and maintain high customer service levels. Holding high levels of these inbound, internal, and outbound inventories costs the firm money while not adding much, if any value to the products or the firm; thus, they are considered wastes.

When the focal firm, its suppliers, and its customers begin to work together to identify customer requirements, remove wastes, and reduce costs, while improving quality and customer service, it marks the beginning of lean supply chain relationships. Companies like

Kansas-based Cox Machine, an aerospace component manufacturer, have been doing this successfully for years. Cox uses mutually beneficial shipping methods, advance shipping notices, and barcoding to help its customers reduce their leadtimes and inventories. Cox shares its forecasts with its suppliers so it can deliver just when the materials are needed. When materials arrive, they are delivered directly to the machine cell, which reduces inventories.[22]

Using lean thinking with suppliers includes having them deliver smaller quantities, more frequently, to the point of use at the focal firm. While this reduces inventories, it also means higher inbound transportation costs—to reduce these costs, suppliers might consider locating warehouses or production facilities near the buyer. To entice suppliers to make these investments, buyers use fewer suppliers in order to give them a greater share of their purchasing needs.

Making small, frequent purchases from just a few suppliers puts the focal firm in a position of greater dependence on these suppliers. It is therefore extremely important that deliveries always be on time, delivered to the right location, in the right quantities, and be of high quality, since existing inventories will be lower. To encourage closer relationships and better collaboration with its best suppliers, consumer products company Procter & Gamble holds an annual "Goldmine Day" for instance, where suppliers can meet with each other and with Procter & Gamble to share ideas and information. "I like that P&G was telling us of its plans and that the company would not be able to get where it wants to go without the collective ideas of its partners," said one participant. "The event probably got a lot of the strategic partners talking to one another more than they were prior to the event," he added.[23]

Firms can also use lean thinking with their key customers. As these relationships develop, the focal firm reserves more of its capacity for these large, steady customers. They locate production or warehousing facilities close to these customers and make frequent small deliveries of finished products to their customers' points of use, thus reducing transportation times and average inventory levels. Lean thinking with customers means determining how to give them exactly what they want when they want it, while minimizing waste as much as possible. New York-based printed circuit board manufacturer, IEC Electronics, uses a new product introduction ambassador to hand-deliver prototypes to customers and answer any questions they might have, to build better customer relationships.[24]

It can be seen, then, that mutual dependencies and mutual benefits occur among all of these **lean supply chain relationships**, resulting in increased product value and competitiveness for the trading partners.

Lean Layouts

The primary design objective with **lean layouts** is to reduce wasted movements of workers, customers, and/or WIP inventories, while achieving smooth product flow through the facility. Moving parts and people around a facility does not add value. Lean layouts allow people and materials to move only when and where they are needed, as quickly as possible. Thus, whenever possible, processing centers, offices, or departments that frequently transfer parts, customers, or workers between them should be located close together, to minimize the times for these movements.

Lean layouts are very visual, meaning that lines of visibility are unobstructed, making it easy for operators at one processing center to monitor work occurring at other centers. In manufacturing facilities, all purchased and WIP inventories are located on the production floor at their points of use, and the good visibility makes it easy to spot inventory buildups and potential bottlenecks. When these and other production problems occur, they are spotted and rectified quickly. The relative closeness of the processing centers facilitates teamwork and joint problem solving and requires less floor space than conventional production layouts.

Lean layouts allow problems to be tracked to their source more quickly as well. As processed components flow from one processing center to the next, a quality problem, when found, can generally be traced to the previous work center, provided inspections are performed at each processing stage. Physio-Control, a Washington-based manufacturer of medical devices, created a lean layout that brought most parts within arms reach for the operators. This allowed operators to work more consistently and make fewer assembly errors. The need for quality checks was reduced, which led to leadtime reductions. Additionally, the new layout required 10 percent less floor space and eliminated a significant amount of operator walking time to retrieve parts.[25]

Manufacturing Cells

Manufacturing cells or **work cells** are designed to process any parts, components, or jobs requiring the same or similar processing steps, saving duplication of equipment and labor. These similarly processed parts are termed **part families**. In many cases, these manufacturing cells are U-shaped to facilitate easier operator and material movements within the cell, as shown in Figure 8.1. In assembly line facilities, manufacturing cells are positioned close to the line, feeding finished components directly to the line instead of delivering them to a stock area where they would be brought back out when needed. Manufacturing cells are themselves actually small assembly lines and are designed to be flexible, allowing machine configurations to change as processing requirements dictate.

Figure 8.1 A U-Shaped Work Cell Layout

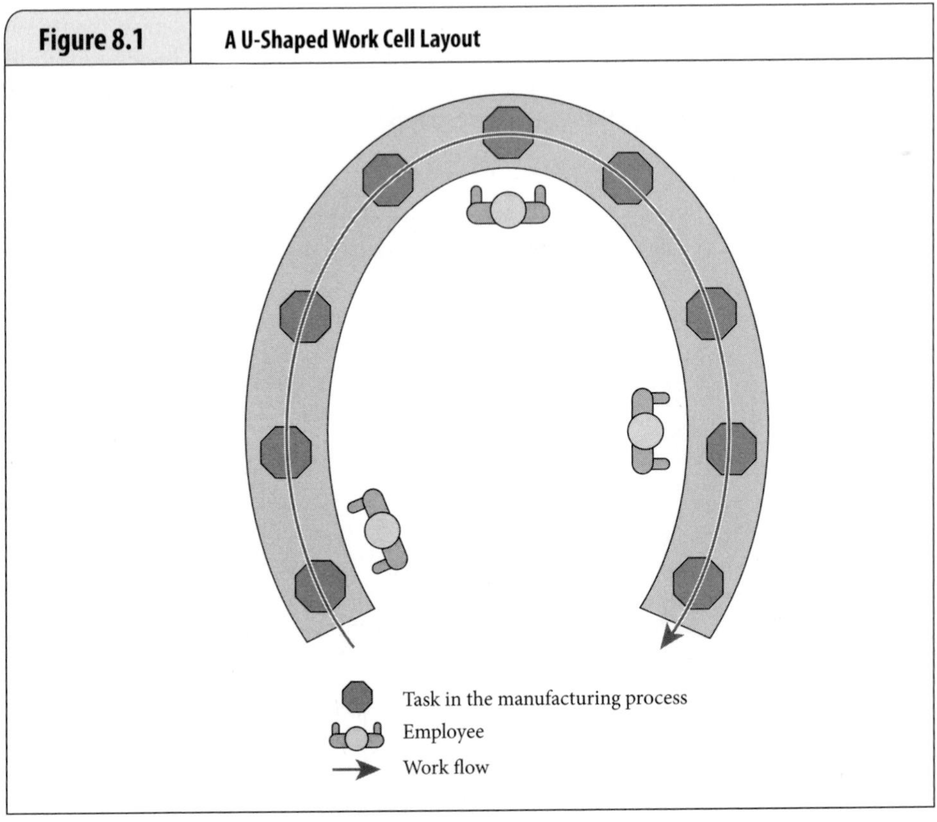

Inventory and Setup Time Reduction

In lean thinking, excess inventories are considered a waste, since they can hide a number of purchasing, production, and distribution problems within the organization. Just as water in a lake hides boat-damaging rocks beneath its surface, so excess inventories hide value-damaging problems along the supply chain. And, just as reducing the water levels causes rocks to become detectable, so too the reduction of inventory levels causes problems to surface in the organization and among its trading partners. Once these problems are detected, they can be solved, improving product value and allowing the system to run more effectively with lower inventory investment. For example, reducing safety stocks of purchased materials will cause stockouts and potential manufacturing disruptions when late supplier deliveries occur. Firms must then either find a way to resolve the supplier delivery problem or find a more reliable supplier. Either way, the end result is a smoother running supply chain with less inventory investment. The same story can be applied to production machinery. Properly maintained equipment breaks down less often, so less safety stock is needed to keep downstream processing areas fed with parts to be further processed.

Another way to reduce inventory levels is to reduce purchase order quantities and production lot sizes. Figure 8.2 illustrates this point. When order quantities and lot sizes are cut in half, average inventories are also cut in half, assuming usage remains constant. Unfortunately, this means that the firm must make more purchase orders (potentially increasing annual order costs). Thus, ordering costs must be reduced and this can be accomplished by automating or simplifying the purchasing process as discussed in Chapter 2.

Since reducing manufacturing lot sizes means increasing the number of **equipment setups**, and since setting up production equipment for the next production run takes valuable time, increasing the number of setups means the firm must find ways to reduce setup times. Setup times can be reduced in a number of ways including doing setup preparation work while the previous production lot is still being processed, moving machine tools closer to the machines, improving tooling or die couplings, standardizing setup procedures, practicing various methods to reduce setup times, and purchasing machines that require less setup time.

Figure 8.2 **Relationship between Order Quantity, Lot Size, and Average Inventory**

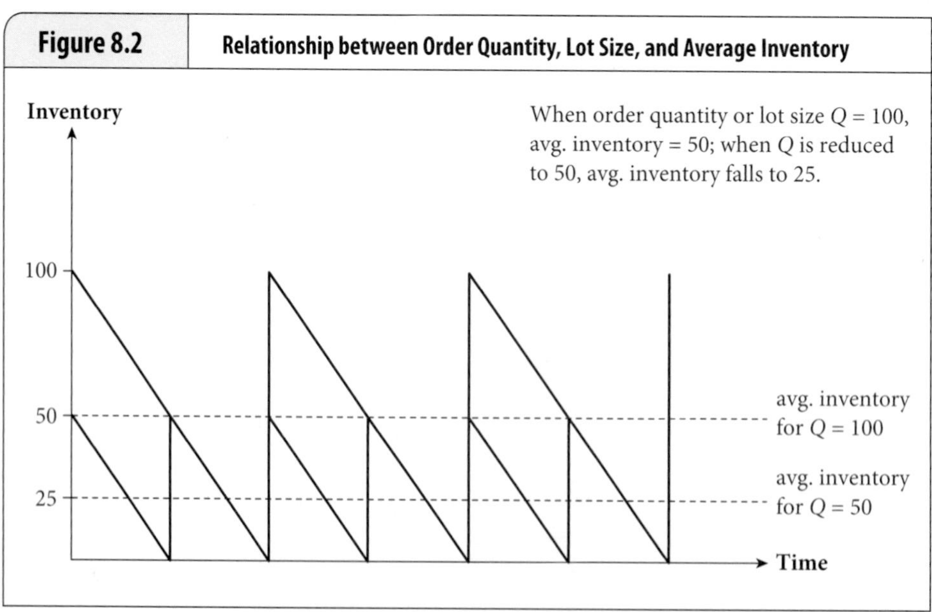

Finally, once inventories have been reduced and the flow problems uncovered and solved, the firm can reduce inventories still further, uncovering yet another set of problems to be solved. With each inventory reduction iteration, the firm runs leaner, cheaper, faster, and with higher levels of product quality.

Small Batch Scheduling

Continuing with the elements of lean, saying that a manufacturer should purchase small quantities more frequently, and produce items using small lot sizes with more setups is one thing, but actually accomplishing this feat is something else. Many firms have tried and failed, eventually returning to carrying high levels of inventory and producing with large lot sizes, rather than dealing with the many problems accompanying lean production. Use of level schedules of small batches though, communicated throughout the production processes and to outside suppliers, is a primary requirement of lean production.

Small batch scheduling drives down costs by reducing purchased, WIP, and finished goods inventories, and it also makes the firm more flexible to meet varying customer demand. Figure 8.3 illustrates this point. In the same period of time, the firm with small lot sizes and short setup times can change products nine times, while the firm with large lot sizes and long setup times can only change products three times (and has yet to produce product D). Maintaining a set, level, small batch production schedule will allow suppliers to anticipate and schedule deliveries also, resulting in fewer late deliveries. Texas-based National Coupling Co. has been using lean manufacturing since 2002 and today can produce about 1,500 coupling assemblies per week, with setups involving 60 to 80 product families. This equates to about six assemblies every ten minutes on its assembly line. "With setups reduced to less than five minutes, we can maintain a high-velocity, high variability production line," says Ken Oberholz, vice president of operations. This flexibility allows National Coupling to always make the right assemblies at the right time, with everything driven by customer requirements. "In an emergency we can drop a coupling order in the front of the line and 90 minutes later they're in assembly, and that's without interrupting production," adds Oberholz.[26]

Moving small production batches through a lean production facility is often accomplished with the use of **kanbans**. The Japanese word "kanban" has several meanings in Japan—it can refer to a billboard, as in "The Donut Shoppe," or more historically, to a uniform worn by servants of the samurai to indicate they acted on the authority of their clan or lord. Mr. Chihiro

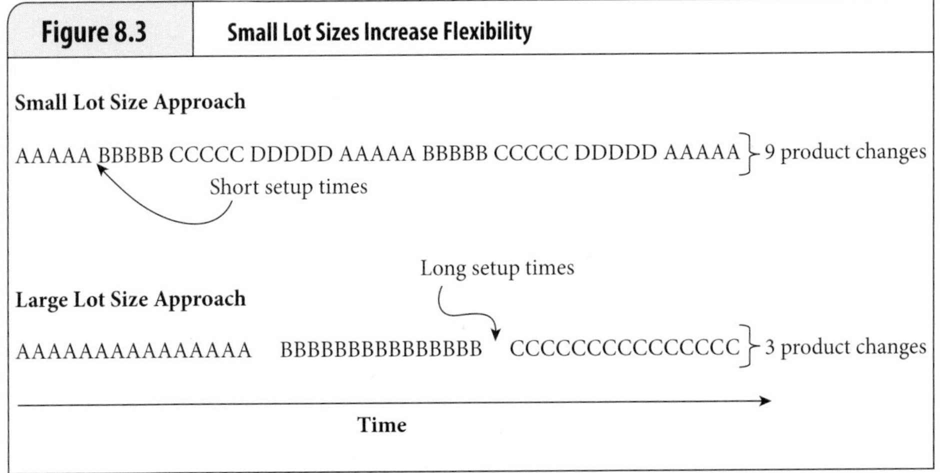

Nakao, a former Toyota manager who worked directly with Taiichi Ohno recalls a story about the origins of the word kanban at Toyota—Mr. Ohno supposedly caught a worker trying to pull materials early from an upstream workcenter and he yelled, "Who are you and where did you come from?! What makes you think you have any right to this material?! Show me your kanban!"[27] Thus, the origin of the more modern "permission slip" or "authority" definition of the word *kanban*. In lean facilities, it has come to simply refer to a signal.

When manufacturing cells need parts or materials, they use a kanban to signal their need for items from the upstream manufacturing cell, processing unit, or external supplier providing the needed material. In this way, nothing is provided until a downstream demand occurs. That is why a lean system is also known as a **pull system**. Ideally, parts are placed in standardized containers, and kanbans exist for each container. Figure 8.4 illustrates how a kanban pull system works. When finished components are moved from Work cell B to the final assembly line, the following things occur:

1. The container holding finished parts in Work cell B's output area is emptied and a **production kanban** (a light, flag, or sign) is used to tell Work cell B to begin processing more components to restock the empty container in its output area.
2. During this stage, when parts are moved from Work cell B's input area to its processing area, the container holding these parts is emptied and a withdrawal kanban (a light, flag, or sign) is used to indicate to Work cell A that more parts are needed. This authorizes a full container of parts to move from Work cell A's output area to Work cell B's input area, and the empty container is moved to Work cell A's output area.
3. As this movement occurs, a production kanban is used to authorize Work cell A to begin processing parts to restock its empty container in the output area.
4. Finally, as full containers of parts are emptied and used in Work cell A's processing area, the emptied containers in Work cell A's input area create a withdrawal kanban seen by the external supplier who then restocks Work cell A's empty containers in the input area.

Figure 8.4 A Kanban Pull System

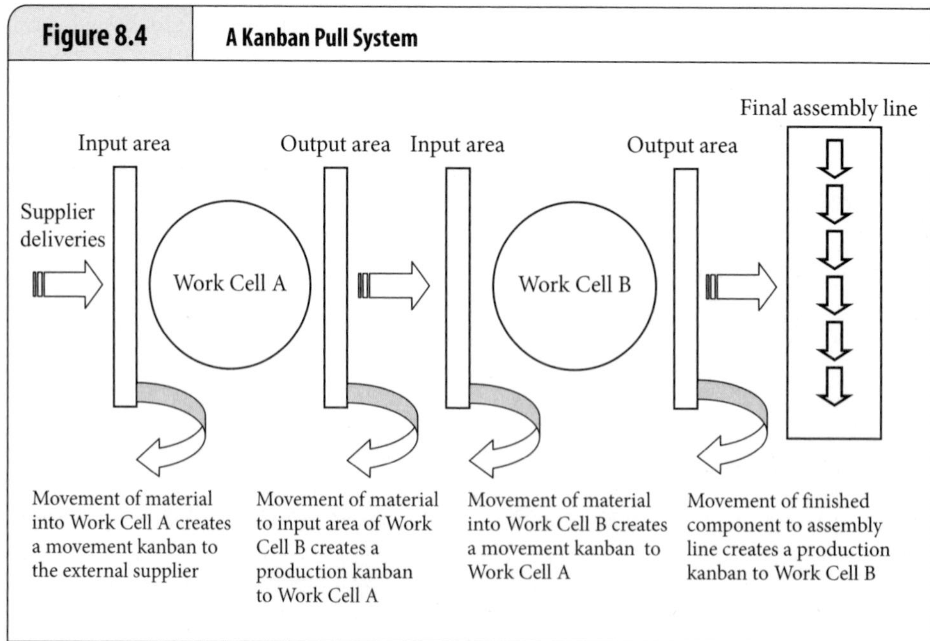
Final assembly line
Input area
Output area
Input area
Output area
Supplier deliveries
Work Cell A
Work Cell B
Movement of material into Work Cell A creates a movement kanban to the external supplier
Movement of material to input area of Work Cell B creates a production kanban to Work Cell A
Movement of material into Work Cell B creates a movement kanban to Work Cell A
Movement of finished component to assembly line creates a production kanban to Work Cell B

Thus, it can be seen that kanbans are used to control the flow of inventory through the facility. Inventories are not allowed to accumulate beyond the size of each container and the number of containers in the system. When containers are full, production stops until an output area container is emptied, which generates another production kanban.

A simple relationship can be used to determine the number of containers or kanban card sets for a lean production system:

$$\text{No. of containers} = \frac{DT\,(1+S)}{C},$$

where

D = the demand rate of the assembly line;

T = the time for a container to make an entire circuit through the system, from being filled, moved, being emptied, and returned to be filled again;

C = the container size, in number of parts; and

S = the safety stock factor, from 0 to 100 percent.

Example 8.1 illustrates the container calculation.

Referring to Example 8.1, reducing inventory in the kanban system (one of the objectives of lean production) occurs when the number of containers used is reduced. When this happens, the circuit time for each container would also have to be reduced to enable the demand to be met. This can be done by reducing setup time, processing time, wait time, move time, or some combination of these.

Example 8.1 Calculating the Number of Containers in a Kanban System

Mejza Manufacturing has an assembly line with a demand of twenty Part 1's per hour at Work cell B. The container used for this part holds five Part 1's. If it takes two hours for a container to make a circuit from Work cell B to the next assembly area and back again, and if it is desired to carry 10 percent excess of Part 1 in the system, then the number of containers needed in the system is:

$$\text{No. of containers} = \frac{DT(1+S)}{C} = \frac{20\frac{Pts}{hr}(2\,hr)(1+0.1)}{5\,Pts} = 8.8 \rightarrow 9$$

The maximum Part 1 inventory for this system would then be the total number of containers times the container size, or $9 \times 5 = 45$ units.

Continuous Improvement

As alluded to already, lean systems are never-ending works in progress. Compact layouts are designed to allow work to flow sequentially and quickly through the facility. Inventory is moved from supplier delivery vehicles to the shop floor and placed in containers in designated work cell storage areas.

Purchase orders and production batches are small. In this system, problems often will surface, at least initially, as suppliers struggle to deliver frequently and on time, and as workers strive to maintain output levels while spending more time during the day setting up machines for small production runs. To make the lean system work better, employees continuously seek ways to reduce supplier delivery and quality problems, and in the production area they solve movement problems, visibility problems, machine breakdown problems, machine setup problems, and internal quality problems. In Japanese manufacturing facilities, this is known as **kaizen**. A literal translation of kaizen is "good change."

SCM Profile: Kaizen Events at E-ONE

Florida-based E-ONE Inc., a custom manufacturer of rescue equipment, has been using kaizen events since 2008. The company uses two types of kaizen events—major events, when a full, cross-functional team is selected for process improvement, and minor kaizen events, which are driven on a department level and may need only limited resources. Highlights from twelve major kaizen events occurring over a recent one-year period include:

- Reducing the amount of walking required by operators by 56.9 miles per year.
- Reducing consumables by several thousand per year.
- Identifying and eliminating 13,886 SKU items in materials and supplies.
- Eye injuries down by 97 percent.
- Back injuries down by 90 percent.
- Finger injuries down by 77 percent.
- Repetitive trauma injuries down by 87 percent.
- Obstacles on shop floors that could create a fall hazard down by 90 percent.
- Ergonomically poor work methods down by 89 percent.
- Poor housekeeping and disorderly work cells were reduced by 84 percent.
- Instances of employees not wearing the proper gear were reduced by 90 percent.
- Instances of the wrong tool/equipment being used for a job task were reduced by 90 percent.
- Improper material handling was reduced by 88 percent.
- Standards, policies, or administrative controls needing improvement were reduced by 92 percent.[29]

Some firms embrace what is known as a **kaizen blitz**, which is a rapid improvement event or workshop, aimed at finding big improvements. Most kaizen improvements, though, are small individual events, emphasizing creativity. In Indianapolis, for example, Franciscan St. Francis Health System implemented over 4,200 kaizen improvements in 2011 alone, for an average of about two improvements per employee.[28] The nearby SCM Profile describes the results of some of E-ONE's kaizen events.

Quality improvement is certainly part of the ongoing continuous improvement effort in lean systems. For example, receiving a batch of goods from an external supplier or an internal work cell that does not satisfy production requirements is like not getting a batch at all. Because of low safety stock levels, processing areas needing these supplies will very quickly be out of stock and unable to operate. High quality levels are then necessary throughout the production system to meet demand. Further discussions of quality and continuous improvement can be found in later segments of this chapter.

Workforce Commitment

Since lean systems depend so much on waste reduction and continuous improvement for their success, dedicated employees must play a significant role in this process. Managers must show strong support for lean production efforts by providing subordinates with the skills, tools, time, and other necessary resources to identify process problems and implement solutions. Managers must create a culture in which workers are encouraged to speak out when problems are found. At the Scania engine plant in Sweden, the facility is idled every Wednesday at 8 a.m. for twenty-six minutes so that every work team can hold an improvement meeting based on ideas on a whiteboard. Workers check the progress of each open idea, remove those that have been completed, and discuss new ones that were posted during the week. If additional resources or approvals are required, ideas move up to the whiteboard of the next level of management. All boards are public. Top management's whiteboard is placed in the middle of the plant where everyone can see the continuing problem solving.[30]

In lean manufacturing systems, employees are cross-trained on many of the various production processes to enable capacities to be adjusted as needed when machines break down or workers are absent. Employees are given time during their day to work on reducing machine setup times as well as to solve other production problems as they occur. They are also expected to perform a number of quality checks on processed items coming into the work cell. When quality problems are found, workers are empowered to shut down the production process until the source of the problem can be found and corrected. Most employees who work for lean companies enjoy their jobs; they are given a number of responsibilities and are considered one of the most important parts of a successful lean organization.

LEAN SYSTEMS AND THE ENVIRONMENT

In Chapter 4, the topics of ethical and sustainable procurement were introduced and their importance to supply chain management was discussed. Since lean systems are ultimately concerned with waste reduction throughout the firm and its supply chains, the linkage between lean and environmental sustainability should seem clear.

Many organizations have realized the positive impact lean systems can have on the environment—adopting lean practices reduces waste and the cost of environmental management, which leads to improved environmental performance. Further, lean systems increase the possibility that firms will adopt more advanced environmental management systems, leading to yet further performance improvements. Professors King and Lennox analyzed thousands of companies in the early 1990s and found ample evidence of this linkage between the concept of lean and environmental sustainability. They found that firms minimizing inventories and adopting quality standards were more likely to practice pollution prevention.[31]

Other examples abound. At automaker Ford, its lean program has resulted, for example, in more than 800 parts made from recycled materials to be used in production, which diverts 70,000 tons of waste per year from landfills. Additionally, more than 10 million pounds of rubber from used tires are reused in auto parts, saving Ford $5 million each year. California-based specialty packaging company, Emerald Packaging, has a number of what it calls "green lean" initiatives including batch size reductions that has reduced plastics use by 5 percent, and use of a preventive maintenance program that has reduced defective parts, scrap losses, and excess plastics use.[32]

As discussed in this first portion of the chapter, creating lean processes is a necessary element in successful supply chain management. A second, equally necessary element is the practice of continuous quality improvement—one of the best examples of this is Six Sigma quality. A discussion of Six Sigma quality and its relationship to lean thinking and supply chain management follows.

THE ORIGINS OF SIX SIGMA QUALITY

Six Sigma quality, many times simply referred to as Six Sigma, was pioneered by global communications leader Motorola in 1987, and is a statistics-based decision-making framework designed to make significant quality improvements in value-adding processes.

Six Sigma (with capital Ss) is a registered trademark of Motorola. In the 1980s, a senior staff engineer at Motorola named Mikel Harry formed a team of engineers to experiment with problem solving using statistical analyses, and this became the foundation for Six Sigma. Richard Schroeder, vice president of customer service at Motorola, heard about Harry's work and applied the methodology to his work at Motorola. Soon, both groups were announcing large reductions in errors and related costs. Ultimately, both men left Motorola and formed the Six Sigma Academy. Today, the firm has been renamed SSA & Company and is based in New York City.[33]

Since Six Sigma is all about pleasing the customer, a very straightforward customer-oriented definition of quality can be employed—*the ability to satisfy customer expectations.* This definition is echoed by the American Society for Quality when it states: "Quality is defined by the customer through his/her satisfaction." In this sense, both a fast-food hamburger and a steakhouse chopped sirloin sandwich can be considered to possess equally high quality, if they meet or exceed the expectations of their customers.

Quality perfection is represented by the term Six Sigma, which refers to the statistical likelihood that 99.99966 percent of the time, a process sample average will fall below a control limit placed 4.5 standard deviations (or sigmas) above the true process mean, assuming the process is in control. This represents the goal of having a defect occur in a process only 0.00034 percent of the time, or 3.4 times out of every million measurement opportunities—very close to perfection. This description makes it sound like the methodology should be called 4½ sigma. The 1½ sigma difference is the subject of much debate, explained by a somewhat confusing term called **sigma drift**.[34] Sigma drift refers to the idea that process variations will grow over time, as process measurements drift off target. In truth, any process exhibiting a change in process variation of 1.5 standard deviations would be detected using quality control charts, instigating an improvement effort to get the process back on target. Table 8.4 shows the **defects per million opportunities (DPMO)** to be expected for various sigmas, using the Six Sigma methodology.

The Six Sigma concept, though, is not just concerned with statistics. It is a broad improvement strategy that includes the concepts and tools of **total quality management (TQM)**, a focus on the customer, performance measurement, and formal training in quality control methods. Six Sigma embodies an organizational culture wherein everyone from CEO, to production worker, to frontline service employee is involved in quality assessment and improvement. Six Sigma is proactive in nature and seeks to permanently fix the root

Table 8.4 Six Sigma DPMO Metrics

NO. STANDARD DEVIATIONS ABOVE THE MEAN	PERCENT OF DEFECT-FREE OUTPUT	DEFECTS PER MILLION OPPORTUNITIES (DPMO)
2	69.15	308,537
2.5	84.13	158,686
3	93.32	66,807
3.5	97.73	22,750
4	99.38	6,210
4.5	99.865	1,350
5	99.977	233
5.5	99.9968	32
6	99.99966	3.4

Note: Standard deviations include a 1.5 sigma "drift."

causes of problems, instead of repeatedly spending time and money tinkering with and patching-up processes as problems occur in the business. In Six Sigma, sources of process variation are sought out and remedied prior to the time these variations can cause production and customer satisfaction problems.

Today, many organizations practice Six Sigma, including early adopters Honeywell, General Electric, and Dow Chemical. In 1999, Ford Motor Company became the first U.S. automaker to adopt a Six Sigma strategy. Automobile manufacturing provides a great example of the need for Six Sigma. Since automobiles have roughly 20,000 **opportunities for a defect to occur (OFD)**, and assuming an automobile company operates at an impressive 5½ sigma level (32 DPMO from Table 8.4), this would equate to about one defect for every two cars produced. Improving to the Six Sigma level would mean about one defect for every 15 automobiles produced. Calculating the DPMO can be accomplished using the following formula:

$$\text{DPMO} = \frac{\text{number of defects}}{(\text{OFD per unit})\ (\text{number of units})} \times 1{,}000{,}000$$

Example 8.2 illustrates the calculation of DPMO and the use of Table 8.4.

Example 8.2 Calculating the DPMO for Blakester's Speedy Pizza

Blake Roberts, owner of Blakester's Speedy Pizza, keeps track of customer complaints. For each pizza delivery, there are three possible causes of complaints: a late delivery, a cold pizza, or an incorrect pizza. Each week, Blake tracks the delivery "defects" for pizza deliveries, and then uses this information to determine his company's Six Sigma quality level. During the past week, his company delivered 620 pizzas. His drivers received sixteen late delivery complaints, nineteen cold pizza complaints, and five incorrect pizza complaints. Blake's defects per million opportunities is:

$$\text{DPMO} = \frac{\text{number of defects}}{(\text{OFD per unit})\ (\text{number of units})} \times 1{,}000{,}000$$

$$= \frac{40}{(3)(620)} \times 1{,}000{,}000 = 21{,}505 \text{ defective pizza deliveries per million.}$$

From Table 8.4, it can be concluded that Blakester's is operating at slightly better than 3.5 Sigma.

Increasingly, companies are using Six Sigma programs to generate cost savings or increased sales through process improvements. In fact, Motorola reported savings of $16 billion from 1986 to 2001, GE saved $4.4 billion from 1996 to 1999, and Honeywell saved $1.8 billion from 1998 to 2000.[35] These types of outcomes are possible as firms identify customer requirements, uncover all of the opportunities for errors or defects to occur, review performance against Six Sigma performance standards, and then take the actions necessary to achieve those standards. The most successful projects meet strategic business objectives, reduce product and service variations to optimal levels, and produce a product or service that satisfies the customer.

In countries such as China and India, where competitive advantage has largely been due to the low cost of labor, many Chinese and Indian companies are today looking to quality management as a way to help them better compete in global markets. The China National Institute for Standards, for example, the national standardization body for China, is currently developing standards for Six Sigma practices.[36] Further, Vestas Wind Energy India, a wind power company based in Chennai, India, saved $10 million since its recent Six Sigma implementation.[37] And, finally, a survey conducted in 2012 of manufacturing companies in Germany, France, Scandinavia, the U.S., Canada, India, and China found that 47 percent had launched Six Sigma programs, 43 percent had started zero defect programs, 83 percent had implemented continuous improvement programs, and 73 percent had launched lean manufacturing programs. A majority in each case were either satisfied or very satisfied with the results.[38]

Like any other improvement strategy or program, however, Six Sigma cannot guarantee continued or even initial business success. Poor management decisions and investments or a company culture not conducive to change can undermine even the best Six Sigma program. Ironically, Six Sigma originator Motorola struggled financially for a number of years; in 2009, after losing billions over a three-year period, Motorola was split into two independent companies—Motorola Mobility and Motorola Solutions. In 2012, Google acquired Motorola Mobility.[39] Camera and film maker, Polaroid, another early user of Six Sigma, filed for Chapter 11 bankruptcy protection in 2001, and the following year, it sold its name and all of its assets to a subsidiary of Illinois-based Bank One Corp.[40]

COMPARING SIX SIGMA AND LEAN

Six Sigma and lean actually have many similarities. For lean practices to be successful, purchased parts and assemblies, work-in-process, and finished goods must all meet or exceed quality requirements. Also, recall that one of the elements of lean is continuous improvement, and these are the areas where the practice of Six Sigma can be put to good use in a lean system. Evidence points to the growing use of both of these initiatives simultaneously. The Avery Point Group, an executive search firm headquartered in Connecticut, did a sampling of Internet job board postings and found that over half of the companies seeking candidates with Six Sigma knowledge also wanted capabilities in lean thinking.[41]

Successful manufacturing companies over the long term must ultimately offer high-quality goods at reasonable prices, while providing a high level of customer service. Rearranging factory floor layouts and reducing batch sizes and setup times will reduce manufacturing lead times and inventory levels, providing better delivery performance and lower cost. These are lean production activities. Reducing waste uncovers process problems. Solving these process problems requires performance monitoring, use of statistical quality control techniques, and creating long-term relationships with high-quality suppliers; these activities fall under the purview of Six Sigma. This short explanation describes how the two concepts can work together to achieve better overall firm performance. Lean production is all about reducing waste, while Six Sigma is all about solving problems and improving quality. The melding of these methods is called lean Six Sigma, discussed next.

Lean Six Sigma

A term is now being used to describe the combining of lean thinking and Six Sigma quality practices—**Lean Six Sigma**, or simply **Lean Six**. In 2009, for example, the U.S. Navy commissioned the nuclear aircraft carrier U.S.S. George H.W. Bush, built by global security company Northrop Grumman using lean manufacturing and Six Sigma extensively, to improve quality, reduce costs, and shorten cycle time. Since 2007, the U.S. Defense Department's Lean Six Sigma office has completed more than 330 projects and trained more than 1,000 officials on the techniques of Lean Six, allowing them to take on new projects themselves. Further, more than 30,000 department employees have been trained in Lean Six. After posting financial losses in 2008, Swiss chemical company Clariant replaced its CEO, who began a multiyear restructuring program to generate cash and reduce spending. Lean Six is being used to supplement these efforts.[42] And, finally, the nearby SCM Profile describes the key role Lean Six Sigma played in the production of armored personnel carriers used in Iraq.

SCM Profile — Saving Lives with Lean Six Sigma

The mine-resistant ambush protected (MRAP) vehicle is a huge, heavily armored personnel carrier used to protect U.S. soldiers from attacks by improvised explosive devices (IEDs), which at one time were responsible for 70 percent of U.S. casualties. The MRAP was first used in 2006 and was an immediate success. In 2007, production of this vehicle was one of the highest priority goals within the U.S. Department of Defense. To meet a massive production goal, the process efficiency and quality improvement method of Lean Six Sigma (LSS) was used.

The first action taken was to develop a value steam map. Its purpose was to create a picture of the entire MRAP production enterprise, to identify gaps in process, relationships, and other key dimensions. Once these gaps were identified, their effects on the overall enterprise were assessed. One key finding of the map was that it identified the Charleston production facility as the most significant choke point.

Charleston required immediate attention. The group moved to implement solutions for improving the MRAP operation at Charleston. Charleston formed a process improvement team fully devoted to LSS activities. The team worked under a master black belt coach. Four key LSS events were focused on: the 5S's, navigation and communications equipment deliveries, implementing cycle time boards to monitor output, and communicating and standardizing quality assurance inspections. In all, fifty-seven projects were identified and completed.

The results of the LSS activities were profound. The MRAP production lines were transformed from messy and disorganized to neat and fast. The team was able to ramp up production from the original five per day to fifty vehicles per day by the end of 2008, using the original production lines and workforce. Much more importantly, the increased quantities of MRAP vehicles saved American lives. In June 2008, fatalities were down by almost 90 percent, due in large part to the MRAPs.[43]

SIX SIGMA AND SUPPLY CHAIN MANAGEMENT

By now, the supply chain management objectives of better customer service, lower costs, and higher quality should be starting to sound familiar. To sustain and improve competitiveness, firms must perform better in these areas than their competitors. Through better process integration and communication, trading partners along the supply chain realize how poor-quality products and services can cause negative reactions to occur, such as greater levels of safety stock throughout the supply chain, lost time and productivity due to product and component repairs, the increased costs of customer returns and warranty repairs, and, finally, loss of customers and damage to reputations.

The impact of poor quality on the supply chain and potential damage to a firm's reputation can be illustrated by the problems toy-maker Mattel had to deal with regarding the Chinese-made toys it was selling in many of its global markets in 2007. Mattel announced it was pulling 9 million Chinese-made Barbies, Polly Pockets, and other toys off store shelves, due to quality and safety problems. Some of the toys had high levels of lead paint while others had tiny magnets that could be swallowed. Some of the magnets were in fact swallowed, causing physical harm to the children involved. Obviously, the cost to Mattel and its suppliers, the toy retailers, and the children who played with these toys was very high.[44] Thus, the impacts of poor quality (and conversely high quality as well) can be felt throughout the supply chain and ultimately by end customers.

Six Sigma is an enterprise-wide philosophy, encompassing suppliers, employees, and customers. It emphasizes a commitment by the organization to strive toward excellence in the production of goods and services that customers want. Firms implementing a Six Sigma program have made a decision to understand, meet, and then strive to exceed customer expectations; and this spills over to their trading partners as well. Florida-based Jabil Circuits is a good example—it is an electronics manufacturer with about 150 strategic suppliers. "We use Six Sigma criteria and push our suppliers to have zero defects," says Erich Hoch, chief supply chain officer at Jabil. It has a dedicated team that works with suppliers on any quality issues. They help to identify the sources of quality problems and the procedures to correct them. Ultimately, suppliers with quality problems that fail to correct them in a timely fashion will lose Jabil's business.[45]

Good supply chain trading partners use Six Sigma methods to assure that their suppliers are performing well and that their customers' needs are being met. Ultimately, this translates into end consumers getting what they want, when they want it, for a price they are willing to pay. While Six Sigma programs tend to vary somewhat in the details from one organization to another, all tend to employ a mix of qualitative and quantitative elements aimed at achieving customer satisfaction. The most common elements addressed in most Six Sigma programs are discussed in the following section.

THE ELEMENTS OF SIX SIGMA

The philosophy and tools of Six Sigma are borrowed from a number of resources including quality professionals such as W. Edwards Deming, Philip Crosby, and Joseph Juran; the Malcolm Baldrige National Quality Award and the International Organization for Standardization's ISO 9000 and 14000 families of standards; the Motorola and General Electric practices relating to Six Sigma; and statistical process control techniques originally developed by Walter Shewhart. From these resources, a number of commonly used elements emerge that are collectively known today as Six Sigma. A few of the quality resources are discussed next, followed by a brief look at the qualitative and quantitative elements of Six Sigma.

Deming's Contributions

W. Edwards Deming's Theory of Management as explained in his book *Out of the Crisis* essentially states that since managers are responsible for creating the systems that make organizations work, they must also be held responsible for the organization's problems (not the workers). Thus, only management can fix problems, through application of the right tools, resources, encouragement, commitment, and cultural change. Deming's Theory of Management was the centerpiece of his teachings around the world (Deming died in 1993) and includes his Fourteen Points for Management, shown in Table 8.5.[46]

Deming's Fourteen Points are all related to Six Sigma principles, covering the qualitative as well as quantitative aspects of quality management. He was convinced that high quality was the outcome of a philosophy geared toward personal and organizational growth. He argued that growth occurred through top management vision, support, and value placed on all employees and suppliers. Value is demonstrated through investments in training, equipment, continuing education, support for finding and fixing problems, and teamwork both within the firm and with suppliers. Use of statistical methods, elimination of inspected-in quality, and elimination of quotas are also required to improve quality. Today, Deming's work lives on through the Deming Institute, a nonprofit organization he founded to foster

Table 8.5 Deming's Fourteen Points for Management

1. Create a constancy of purpose for improvement of product and service.	Define values, mission, and vision to provide direction for management and employees. Invest in innovation, training, and research.
2. Adopt the new philosophy.	Adversarial management–worker relationships and quota work systems no longer work. Management must work toward cooperative relationships aimed at increasing quality and customer satisfaction.
3. Cease dependence on mass inspection.	Inspecting products does not create value or prevent poor quality. Workers must use statistical process control to improve quality.
4. End the practice of awarding business on the basis of price tag alone.	Purchases should not be based on low cost; buyers should develop long-term relationships with a few good suppliers.
5. Constantly improve the production and service system.	Significant quality improvement comes from continual incremental improvements that reduce variation and eliminate common causes.
6. Institute training.	Managers need to learn how the company works. Employees should receive adequate job training and statistical process control training.
7. Adopt and institute leadership.	Managers are leaders, not supervisors. They help, coach, encourage, and provide guidance to employees.
8. Drive out fear.	A supportive organization will drive out fear of reprisal, failure, change, and loss of control. Fear causes short-term thinking.
9. Break down barriers between departments.	Cross-functional teams focus workers, break down departmental barriers, and allow workers to see the big picture.
10. Eliminate slogans, exhortations, and targets for the workforce.	Slogans and motivational programs are aimed at the wrong people. They don't help workers do a better job. These cause worker frustration and resentment.
11. Eliminate numerical quotas for workers and managers.	Quotas are short-term thinking and cause fear. Numerical goals have no value unless methods are in place to allow them to be achieved.
12. Remove barriers that rob people of pride of workmanship.	Barriers are performance and merit ratings. Workers have become a commodity. Workers are given boring tasks with no proper tools, and performance is appraised by supervisors who know nothing about the job. Managers won't act on worker suggestions. This must change.
13. Encourage education and self-improvement for everyone.	All employees should be encouraged to further broaden their skills and improve through continuing education.
14. Take action to accomplish the transformation.	Management must have the courage to break with tradition and explain to a critical mass of people that the changes will involve everyone. Management must speak with one voice.

a greater understanding of Deming's principles and vision. The institute provides conferences, seminars, and training materials to managers seeking to make use of the Deming operating philosophy.[47]

Crosby's Contributions

Philip Crosby, a former vice president of quality at the New York-based manufacturer ITT Corporation, was a highly sought-after quality consultant during the latter part of his life and wrote several books concerning quality and striving for zero defects, most notably *Quality Is Free* and *Quality Without Tears* (he died in 2001)[48]. His findings about quality improvement programs as discussed in *Quality Is Free* were that these programs invariably more than paid for themselves. In *Quality Without Tears*, Crosby discussed his four Absolutes of Quality, shown in Table 8.6. Industrial giants such as IBM and General Motors have benefited greatly

Table 8.6 Crosby's Four Absolutes of Quality

1. The definition of quality is conformance to requirements.	Adopt a do-it-right-the-first-time attitude. Never sell a faulty product to a customer.
2. The system of quality is prevention.	Use SPC as part of the prevention system. Make corrective changes when problems occur. Take preventative action.
3. The performance standard is zero defects.	Insist on zero defects from suppliers and workers. Education, training, and commitment will eliminate defects.
4. The measure of quality is the price of nonconformance.	The price of nonconformance is the cost of poor quality. Implementing a prevention program will eliminate this.

from implementing Crosby's ideas. Crosby emphasized a commitment to quality improvement by top management, development of a prevention system, employee education and training, and continuous assessment—all very similar to the teachings of Deming.

Juran's Contributions

Joseph Juran, founder of the Juran Institute, helped to write and develop the *Quality Handbook* (now in its sixth edition[49]) and wrote a number of other books on quality as well. Born in 1904, Juran remained an active lecturer right up until his death in 2008 at the age of 103. He also remained active by writing and by overseeing his Juran Foundation in New York. "My job of contributing to the welfare of my fellow man," Juran wrote, "is the great unfinished business."[50]

Like Deming, Juran helped to engineer the Japanese quality revolution starting in the 1950s. Juran, similar to both Crosby and Deming, strived to introduce new types of thinking about quality to business managers and employees, but Juran's recommendations did vary somewhat from those of Crosby and Deming. He is recognized as the person who brought the human element to the practice of quality improvement. Juran did not seek cultural change but sought to work within the system to instigate change. He felt that to get managers to listen, your message had to be spoken in dollars. To get workers to listen, you had to speak about specific things. So, he advocated the determination of the costs of poor quality to get the attention of managers, and the use of statistical control methods for workers.

Juran's recommendations were focused on his Quality Trilogy, shown in Table 8.7. He found in his dealings with companies that most had given priority to quality control but paid little attention to quality planning and improvement. Thus, while both Japan and the

Table 8.7 Juran's Quality Trilogy

1. Quality planning	The process of preparing to meet quality goals. Identify internal and external customers, determine their needs, and develop products that satisfy those needs. Managers set short- and long-term goals, establish priorities, and compare results to previous plans.
2. Quality control	The process of meeting quality goals during operations. Determine what to control, establish measurements and standards of performance, measure performance, interpret the difference between the actual measure and the standard, and take action if necessary.
3. Quality improvement	The process of breaking through to unprecedented levels of performance. Identify projects for improvement, organize support for the projects, diagnose causes, implement remedies, and provide control to maintain improvements.

U.S. had been using quality control techniques since the 1950s, Japan's overall quality levels grew faster than those of the U.S. because Japan's quality planning and improvement efforts were much greater.

Many characteristics, though, of the Deming, Crosby, and Juran philosophies are quite similar. All three focus on top management commitment, the need for continuous improvement efforts, training, and the use of statistical methods for quality control purposes.

The Malcolm Baldrige National Quality Award

The **U.S. Baldrige Quality Award** was signed into law on August 20, 1987, and is named in honor of then U.S. President Reagan's Secretary of Commerce, who helped draft an early version of the award, and who was tragically killed in a rodeo accident shortly before the award was enacted. The objectives of the award, which by the way is given only to U.S. firms, are to stimulate U.S. firms to improve quality and productivity, to recognize firms for their quality achievements, to establish criteria and guidelines so that organizations can independently evaluate their quality improvement efforts, and to provide examples and guidance to those companies wanting to learn how to manage and improve quality and productivity.

The Baldrige Award is managed by the Baldrige Performance Excellence Program, and administered by the National Institute of Standards and Technology (NIST). Up to eighteen awards are given annually and are presented by the President of the U.S. to organizations across six sectors: small businesses, service, manufacturing, education, healthcare, and nonprofit/government. The applicants are evaluated in seven areas: leadership; strategic planning; customer focus; measurement, analysis, and knowledge management; workforce focus; operations focus; and results.[51] Table 8.8 shows the ninety-nine Baldrige Award winners from 1988 through 2012.

All Malcolm Baldrige Award applications receive from 300 to 1000 hours of review by quality professional volunteers and are scored in the seven areas listed above. Finalists are visited wherein performance is reassessed and final scores tabulated, with the winners selected from this group. Over 1,500 organizations have applied for the Baldrige Award and six have won it twice. Companies may obtain a copy of the Baldrige Award criteria and perform self-assessments using the form and its point scoring guidelines. Completing a self-assessment using the Baldrige Award criteria identifies the firm's strengths and weaknesses and can aid in implementing various quality and productivity improvement initiatives. To date, thousands of firms have requested copies of the official application.

The ISO 9000 and 14000 Families of Management Standards

In 1946, delegates from twenty-five countries met in London and decided to create a new international organization, with the objective "to facilitate the international coordination and unification of industrial standards." The new organization, called the International Organization for Standardization or ISO, officially began operations on February 23, 1947. The ISO is the world's largest developer of voluntary international standards. Now located in Geneva, Switzerland, the ISO today has 163 member countries.[52]

ISO standards are voluntary, are developed in response to market demand, and are based on consensus among the member countries. This ensures widespread applicability

Table 8.8 Malcolm Baldrige National Quality Award Recipients (1988–2012)

YEAR	SMALL BUSINESS	MANUFACTURING	SERVICE	EDUCATION	HEALTH CARE	NONPROFIT/ GOV'T
1988	Globe Metallurgical	Motorola; Westinghouse Comm. Nuclear Fuel Div.				
1989		Xerox Bus. Products and Sys.; Milliken & Co.				
1990	Wallace Co.	Cadillac Motor Car Co.; IBM Rochester	FedEx Corp.			
1991	Marlow Industries	Solectron Corp.; Zytec Corp.				
1992	Granite Rock Co.	AT&T Network Sys. Group; Texas Instr. Def. Sys. & Electronics Grp.	AT&T Universal Card Svcs.; The Ritz-Carlton Hotel Co.			
1993	Ames Rubber Corp.	Eastman Chemical Co.				
1994	Wainwright Indus.		AT&T Consumer Comm Svcs.; GTE Directories			
1995		Armstrong World Ind. Bldg. Prod. Ops.; Corning Telecomm. Prod. Div.				
1996	Custom Research; Trident Precision Mfg.	ADAC Laboratories	Dana Comm. Credit			
1997		3M Dental Prod. Div.; Solectron	Merrill Lynch Credit; Xerox Business Svcs.			
1998	Texas Nameplate	Boeing Airlift and Tanker Programs; Solar Turbines				
1999	Sunny Fresh Foods	STMicroelectronics—Region Americas	BI; The Ritz-Carlton Hotel Co.			
2000	Los Alamos Nat'l. Bank	Dana Corp.—Spicer Drvshft Div.; KARLEE	Operations Mgt. Int'l.			
2001	Pal's Sudden Svc.	Clarke American Checks		Chugach Sch. Dist.; Pearl River Sch. Dist.; Univ. of Wisc.-Stout		
2002	Branch-Smith Printing Div.	Motorola Comm., Gov't., and Indus. Sol. Sector			SSM Health Care	
2003	Stoner	MEDRAD	Boeing Aerospace Support; Caterpillar Financial Svcs. Corp.	Community Consol. Sch. Dist. 15	Baptist Hosp.; St. Luke's Hosp. of Kan. City	
2004	Texas Nameplate	The Bama Companies		K. W. Monfort Coll. of Bus.	R. W. Johnson Univ. Hosp.	

Table 8.8 Malcolm Baldrige National Quality Award Recipients (1988–2012) (continued)

YEAR	SMALL BUSINESS	MANUFACTURING	SERVICE	EDUCATION	HEALTH CARE	NONPROFIT/ GOV'T
2005	Park Place Lexus	Sunny Fresh Foods	DynMcDermott Petroleum Opns.	Jenks Public Schools; Richland College	Bronson Meth. Hosp.	
2006	MESA Products		Premier		N. Mississippi Medical Center	
2007	PRO-TEC Coating				Mercy Health Sys.; Sharp HealthCare	City of Coral Springs; US Army ARDEC
2008		Cargill Corn Milling		Iredell-Statesville Schools	Poudre Valley Health System	
2009	MidwayUSA	Honeywell Federal Mfg. & Technologies			Heartland Health	VA Cooperative Studies Program
2010	Studer Grp.; Freese and Nichols; K&N Mgt.	MEDRAD; Nestle Purina PetCare		Montgomery Cty. Pub. Sch.	Advocate Good Sam. Hosp.	
2011					Henry Ford Health Sys.; Schneck Med. Ctr.; Southcentral Fndn.	Concordia Publishing House
2012	MESA	Lockheed Missiles and Fire Cont.			N. Miss. Health Svcs.	City of Irving, TX

of the standards. ISO considers evolving technology and member interests by requiring a review of its standards at least every five years to decide whether they should be maintained, updated, or withdrawn. In this way, ISO standards retain their position as state of the art.

ISO standards are technical agreements that provide the framework for compatible technology worldwide. Developing consensus on this international scale is a major operation. In all, there are some 3,000 ISO technical groups with approximately 50,000 experts participating annually to develop ISO standards. To date, ISO has published over 19,500 international standards. Examples include standards for agriculture and construction, mechanical engineering, medical devices, and information technology developments such as the digital coding of audio–visual signals for multimedia applications.

In 1987, ISO adopted the ISO 9000 family of international quality standards, and revises them every five years. ISO 9001:2008 sets out the criteria for a quality management system and is the only standard in the family with a certification for organizations. It can be used by any organization, large or small, regardless of its field of activity. It has been implemented by over 1 million organizations in over 170 countries. The standards have been adopted in the U.S. by the American National Standards Institute (ANSI) and the American Society for Quality (ASQ). In many cases worldwide, companies will not buy from suppliers who do not possess an ISO 9000 certification.

After the rapid acceptance of ISO 9000 and the increase of environmental standards around the world, ISO assessed the need for international environmental management standards. They formed an advisory group for the environment in 1991, which eventually led to the adoption of the ISO 14000 family of international environmental management standards in 1997. ISO 14001:2004 sets out the criteria for an environmental management system and offers organizations a certification. Some of the more recently adopted 14000 standards are the ISO 14006 standard for the management of ecodesign, ISO 14031, which provides guidance on the design and use of environmental performance evaluation, and the ISO 14064 standard for greenhouse gas accounting and verification.

Together, the ISO 9000 and 14000 families of certifications are the most widely used standards of ISO, with more than 1.2 million organizations in 175 countries holding one or both types of certifications. The standards that have earned the ISO 9000 and ISO 14000 families a worldwide reputation are known as "generic management system standards," meaning that the same standards can be applied to any type of organization.

The DMAIC Improvement Cycle

Figure 8.5 shows the five-step DMAIC improvement cycle, an important element of Six Sigma, listing the sequence of steps necessary to drive process improvement. The cycle can be applied to any process or project, both in services and manufacturing firms. The improvement cycle begins with customer requirements and then seeks to analyze and modify processes or projects so that they meet those requirements.

Each of the steps is described below:

1. *Define*: Identify customers and their service or product requirements critical to achieving customer satisfaction [also known as **critical-to-quality (CTQ) characteristics**]. Identify any gaps between the CTQ characteristics and process outputs. Where gaps exist, create Six Sigma projects to alleviate the gaps.
2. *Measure*: Prepare a data-collection plan to quantify process performance. Determine what to measure for each process gap and how to measure it. Use check sheets to organize measurements.

Figure 8.5 The DMAIC Improvement Cycle

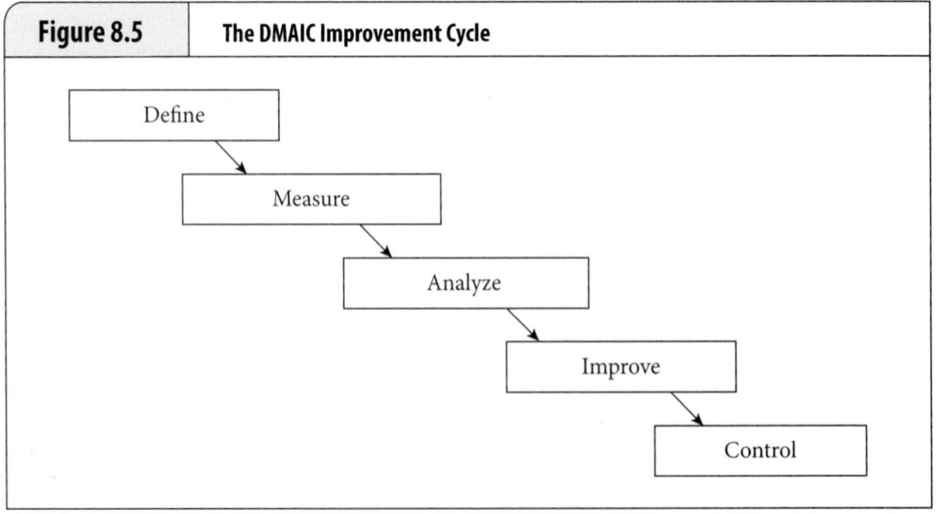

3. *Analyze*: Perform a process analysis using the performance data collected. Use Pareto charts and fishbone diagrams to identify the root causes of the process variations or defects.
4. *Improve*: Design an improvement plan and then remove the causes of process variation by implementing the improvement plan. This will require modifying, redesigning, or reengineering the process. Document the improvement and confirm that process gaps have been significantly reduced or eliminated.
5. *Control*: Monitor the process to assure that performance levels are maintained. Design and use statistical process control charts to continuously monitor and control the process. When performance gaps are once again identified, repeat Steps 1–5.

Using the DMAIC improvement cycle allows the firm to continuously monitor and improve processes that are keys to customer satisfaction. By concentrating on these key processes and the CTQ characteristics, firms can make large and radical improvements in processes, products, and customer satisfaction. Deaconess Health System, a six hospital system in Indiana, has used the DMAIC cycle since 2011 to improve contractual reimbursements from its managed care plans. After five months, its dollars collected per day had increased by over $3,800, and this had been sustained for seven months when the article was published. The simple DMAIC cycle allowed it to organize its efforts.[53]

Six Sigma Training Levels

In order to develop and successfully complete Six Sigma improvement projects, specific training in quality improvement methods is available. A number of organizations offer courses and certifications in Six Sigma methods, and the somewhat standardized training levels are summarized in Table 8.9. Global manufacturing giant GE began using Six Sigma in the 1980s, and, today, all GE employees are receiving training in the strategy, statistical

Table 8.9 The Six Sigma Training Levels[55]

TRAINING LEVELS	DESCRIPTION
Yellow Belt	Basic understanding of the Six Sigma Methodology and the tools within the DMAIC problem-solving process, including process mapping, cause-and-effect tools, simple data analysis, and process improvement and control methods. Role is to be an effective team member on process improvement project teams.
Green Belt	A specially trained team member allowed to work on small, carefully defined Six Sigma projects, requiring less than a Black Belt's full-time commitment. Has enhanced problem-solving skills, and can gather data and execute experiments in support of a Black Belt project. They spend approximately 25 percent of their time on Six Sigma projects of their own or in support of Black Belt projects.
Black Belt	Has a thorough knowledge of Six Sigma principles. Exhibits leadership, understands team dynamics, and assigns team members with roles and responsibilities. Has a complete understanding of the DMAIC model, a basic knowledge of lean concepts, and can quickly identify "nonvalue-added" activities. Coaches project teams and provide group assessments. Identifies projects, selects project team members, acts as an internal consultant, mentors Green Belts, and provides feedback to management.
Master Black Belt	A proven mastery of process variability reduction and waste reduction. Can effectively provide training at all levels. Challenges conventional wisdom through the demonstration of the application of Six Sigma principles and provides guidance and knowledge to lead and change organizations. Directs Black and Green Belts on the performance of their Six Sigma projects and also provides guidance and direction to management teams regarding the selection of projects and the overall health of a Six Sigma program.

tools, and techniques of Six Sigma. Eventually, all employees earn their Six Sigma Green Belt designations. Training courses are offered at various levels including basic Six Sigma awareness seminars, team training, Master Black Belt, Black Belt, and Green Belt training.[54] Several of the statistical tools of Six Sigma are discussed next.

THE STATISTICAL TOOLS OF SIX SIGMA

Flow Diagrams

Also called **process diagrams** or **process maps**, this tool is the necessary first step to evaluating any manufacturing or service process. **Flow diagrams** use annotated boxes representing process action elements and ovals representing wait periods, connected by arrows to show the flow of products or customers through the process. Once a process or series of processes is mapped out, potential problem areas can be identified and further evaluated for excess inventories, wait times, or capacity problems. A simple example of a customer flow diagram for a restaurant is shown in Figure 8.6. Using the diagram, restaurant managers could then observe each process activity and wait period element, looking for potential problems requiring further analysis.

Check Sheets

Check sheets allow users to determine the frequencies of specific problems. For the restaurant example shown in Figure 8.6, managers could make a list of potential problems based on experience and observation, and then direct employees to keep counts of each problem on check sheets for a given period of time (long enough to allow for true problem level determinations). At the end of the data-collection period, problem areas can be reviewed and compared. Figure 8.7 shows a typical check sheet that might be used in a restaurant.

Figure 8.6 Flow Diagram for a Restaurant

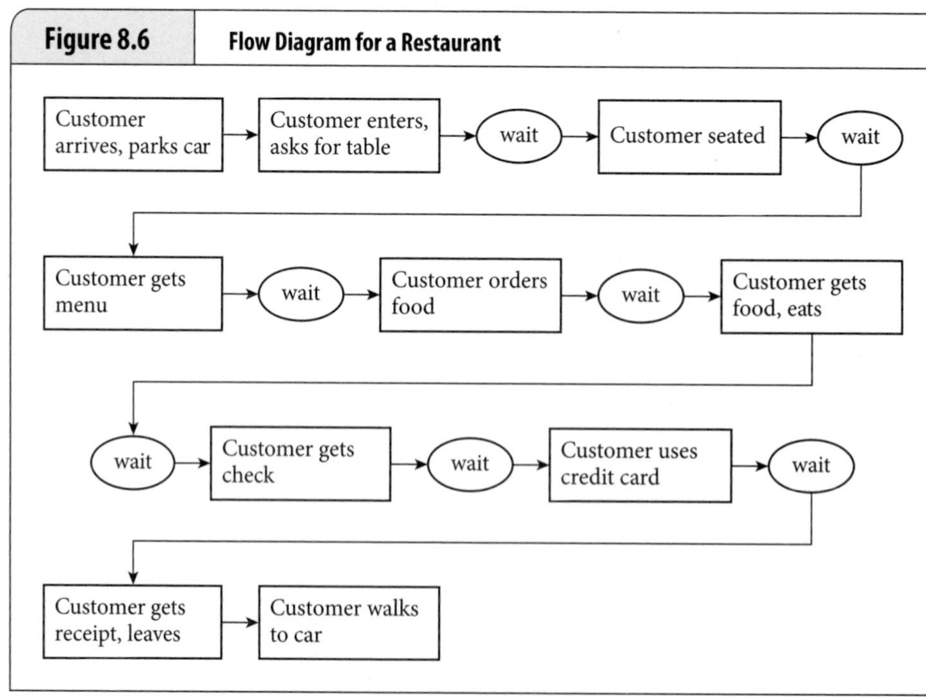

Figure 8.7 Check Sheet for Problems at a Restaurant

Problem	Mon.	Tues.	Wed.	Thurs.	Fri.	Sat.	Sun.	Totals	% of Total
long wait	//////	/////	////////	//////	/////////	//////////	////	48	26.5
cold food		//	/	/	///	//		9	5.0
bad food	//	/	///		/	////		11	6.1
wrong food	/////	//	/	//	/////	///	/	19	10.5
bad server	//////	///	/////	/	//////	//	/	24	13.3
bad table		/	//		/	///	/	8	4.4
room temp.			//	///	/////	/////		15	8.3
too expensive	/	//	/	/	///	///		11	6.1
no parking			//		/////	///////		14	7.7
wrong change	//////	/	////		////	///		18	9.9
other		/	//			/		4	2.2
Totals	26	18	31	14	42	43	7	181	100

Pareto Charts

Pareto charts, useful for many applications, are based at least initially, on the work of Vilfredo Pareto, a nineteenth-century Italian economist. In 1906, Pareto described the unequal distribution of wealth in his country, observing that 20 percent of the people owned about 80 percent of the wealth. Decades later, Joseph Juran described what he called the **Pareto Principle** referring to the observation that 20 percent of something is typically responsible for 80 percent of the results. Eventually this became widely known as the Pareto Principle or 80/20 Rule.[56] Applied to quality improvement, this refers to the common observation that a few of a firm's problems account for most of the problem occurrences. In other words, firms should fix the few big problems first.

The Pareto chart shown in Figure 8.8 is useful for presenting data in an organized fashion, indicating process problems from most to least severe. The top two restaurant problems in Figure 8.7 account for about 40 percent of the instances where problems were observed. Two Pareto charts are shown in Figure 8.7. Note that we could look at the total problem events either from a problem-type or day-of-the-week perspective and see that *long wait* and *bad server* are the two largest problems, while Saturdays and Fridays are the days when most of the problem events occur. Finding the causes and implementing solutions for these two problems would significantly decrease the number of problem events at the restaurant.

Cause-and-Effect Diagrams

Once a problem has been identified, **cause-and-effect diagrams** (also called **fishbone diagrams** or **Ishikawa diagrams**) can be used to aid in brainstorming and isolating the causes of a problem. Figure 8.9 illustrates a cause-and-effect diagram for the most troublesome *long wait* problem of Figure 8.8. The problem is shown at the front end of the diagram. Each of the four diagonals or fishbones of the diagram represents potential groups of causes. The four groups of causes shown, Material, Machine, Methods, and Manpower, commonly referred to as **the 4 Ms**, are the standard classifications of problem causes and

Figure 8.8 Pareto Charts for Problems in Figure 8.7

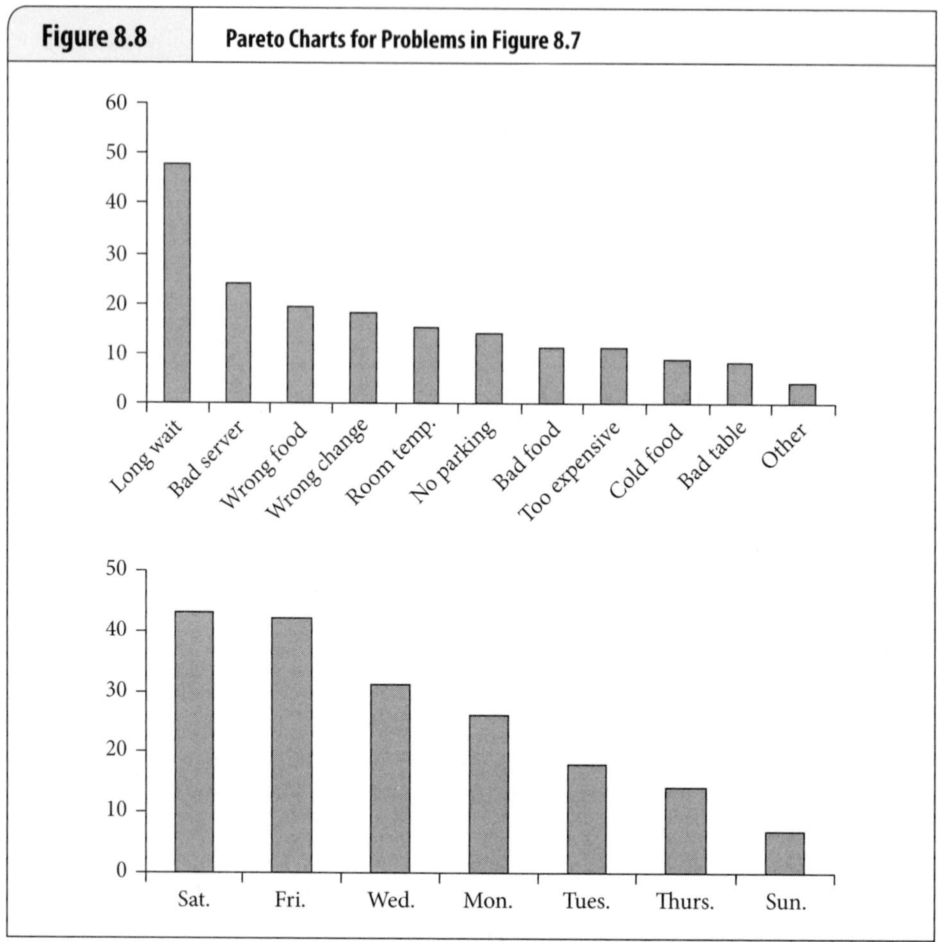

represent a very thorough list for problem–cause analyses. In almost all cases, problem causes will be in one or more of these four areas.

Typically, Six Sigma team members will gather and brainstorm the potential causes for a problem in these four areas. Each branch on the four diagonals represents one potential cause. Subcauses are also part of the brainstorming process and are shown as smaller branches attached to each of the primary causes. Breaking a problem down like this into its causes and subcauses allows workers to then go back to the process and determine the relative significance of each cause and subcause using more specific checklists and Pareto charts once again. Eventually, the firm begins working to eliminate the causes of the problem, starting with the most significant **root causes** and subcauses, until most of the problem's impact disappears.

A properly thought-out cause-and-effect diagram can be a very powerful tool for use in Six Sigma efforts. Without its use, workers and management risk trying to eliminate causes that have little to do with the problem at hand, or working on problems that are quite minor compared to other, more significant problems. Once most of a problem's causes are identified and eliminated, the associated process should be back under control and meeting customer requirements. At this point, firms can design and begin using statistical process control charts, discussed next.

Figure 8.10 $\bar{x}$ **and R charts for the Hayley Girl Soup Co.**

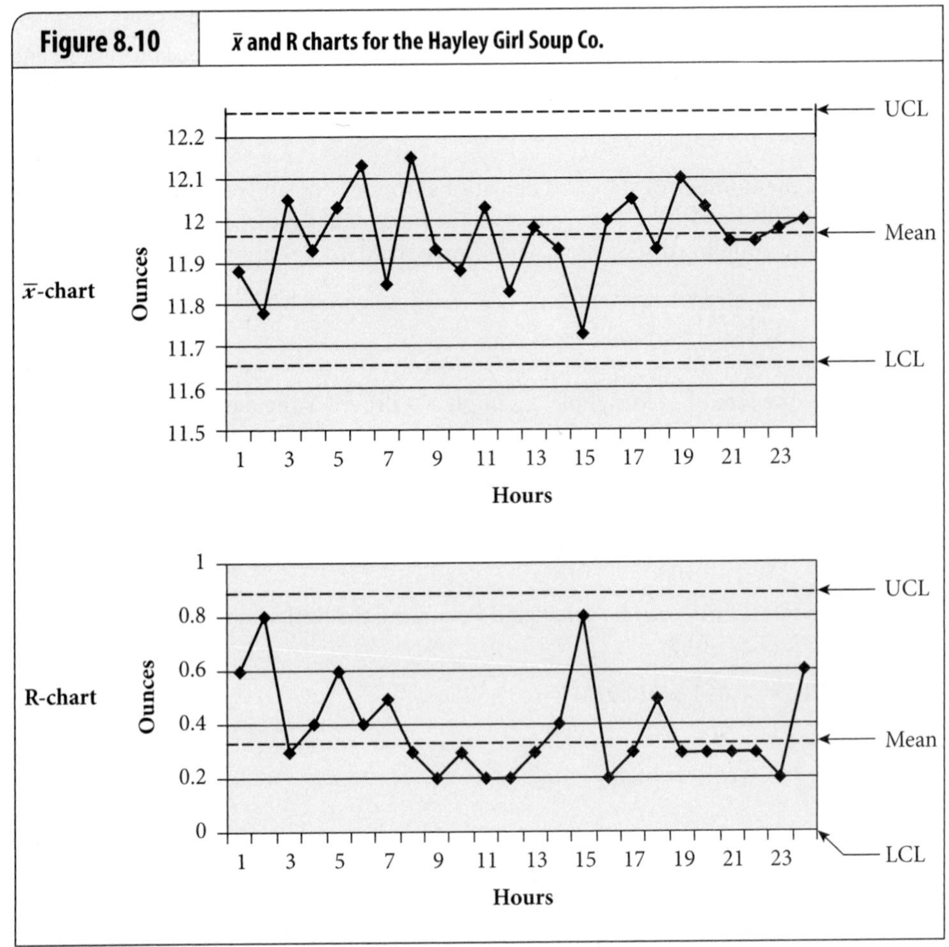

Attribute Data Control Charts

When collecting attribute data regarding whether or not a process is producing good or bad (nondefective or defective) output, use of $\bar{x}$ and R charts no longer applies. In these cases, either **P charts**, which monitor the *percent defective* in each sample, or **C charts**, which count the *number of defects* per unit of output, are used. Each of these is discussed next.

Using and Constructing P Charts

This is the most commonly used attribute control chart. If large sample sizes are used when collecting data, they are assumed to be normally distributed and the following formulas can be used to calculate the center line ($\bar{P}$) and the upper and lower control limits for the P chart:

$$\bar{P} = \frac{\sum_{i=1}^{k} P_i}{k},$$

where $\bar{P}$ is the mean fraction defective for all samples collected, k represents the number of samples, P is the fraction defective in one sample, and i represents the specific sample; and

$$UCL_P = \bar{P} + z\sigma_P$$
$$LCL_P = \bar{P} - z\sigma_P,$$

where z is the number of standard deviations from the mean (recall when $z = 3$, the control limits will contain 99.73 percent of all the sample data plots) and σ_P is the standard deviation of the sampling distribution. The sample standard deviation is calculated using

$$\sigma_P = \sqrt{\frac{(\bar{P})(1-\bar{P})}{n}},$$

where n is the size of each sample. Example 8.4 provides the data used to determine $\bar{P}$, σ_P, and the control limits for the P chart.

As shown in Example 8.4, $\bar{P} = 0.014$. Calculating σ_P:

$$\sigma_P = \sqrt{\frac{(0.014)(0.986)}{100}} = 0.012.$$

Now the control limits can be calculated (assuming the limits contain 99.73 percent of the data points, or $z = 3$):

$$UCL_P = 0.014 + 3(0.012) = 0.05,$$

and

$$LCL_P = 0.014 - 3(0.012) = 0.$$

Example 8.4 Attribute Data for the CeeJay Lightbulb Co.

The CeeJay Lightbulb Co. makes 40-watt light bulbs, and it has decided to begin monitoring its quality using a P chart. So, over the past thirty days, it has collected and tested 100 bulbs each day. The chart below shows the fraction defectives for each sample and the overall average fraction defective, or $\bar{P}$.

DAY	FRACTION DEFECTIVE	DAY	FRACTION DEFECTIVE
1	0.01	16	0.04
2	0.02	17	0
3	0	18	0
4	0.03	19	0.01
5	0	20	0.03
6	0.01	21	0.02
7	0.04	22	0
8	0	23	0.01
9	0	24	0.02
10	0.02	25	0.01
11	0.02	26	0.03
12	0.03	27	0
13	0	28	0.02
14	0.04	29	0.01
15	0.01	30	0
			$\bar{P} = \mathbf{0.014}$

Figure 8.11 P-Chart for the CeeJay Lightbulb Co.

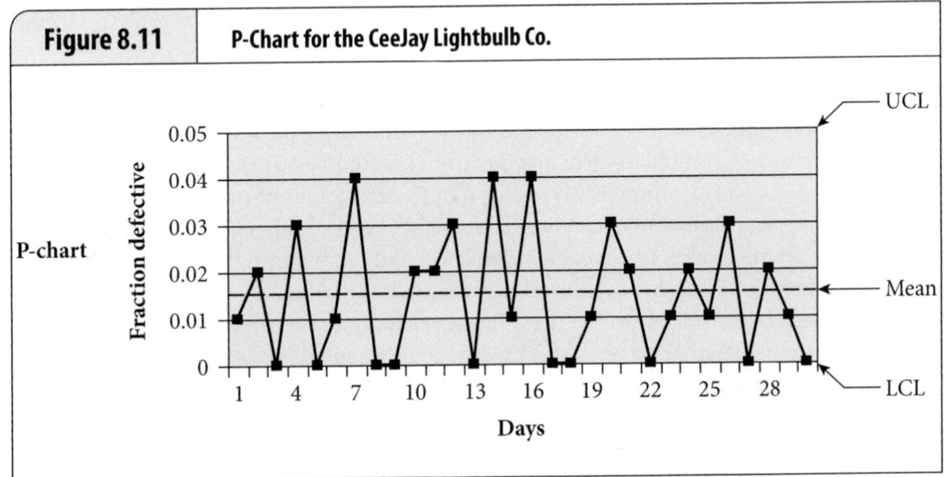

Note that the lower control limit is truncated at zero, as is the case in most P charts. Figure 8.11 shows the P chart for the CeeJay Lightbulb Co. with the fraction defectives from Example 8.4. Viewing the chart, the process appears to be in control, since the data points are randomly dispersed around the centerline and about half the data points are on each side of the centerline. Thus, the CeeJay Lightbulb Co. can begin using this control chart to monitor its lightbulb quality.

Using C Charts

When multiple errors can occur in a process resulting in a defective unit, then we can use C charts to control the *number* of defects per unit of output. C charts are useful when a number of mistakes or errors can occur per unit of output, but they occur infrequently. Examples can include a hotel stay, a printed textbook, or a construction project. The control limits for C charts are based on the assumption of a Poisson probability distribution of the item of interest (commonly used when defects are infrequent). In this case, the distribution variance is equal to its mean. For C charts then,

$\bar{c}$ = mean errors per unit of measure (and also the sample variance),

$\sqrt{c}$ = sample standard deviation, and

$\bar{c} \pm 3\sqrt{c}$ = control limits.

Example 8.5 can be used to illustrate the calculation of the C chart's control limits. In the example, the units of measure are days, thus the average daily defects are 29.1 (the centerline and also the variance). The upper and lower control limits are 45.3 and 12.9, respectively. The Casey Publishing Co. can now use the C chart centerline and control limits based on the 30-day error data to monitor its daily editorial error rate.

Example 8.5 Monitoring Editorial Defects at Casey Publishing, Inc.

Eight editorial assistants are monitored for defects in the firm's printed work on a monthly basis. Over the past thirty days, a total number of 872 editorial mistakes were found. Computing the centerline and control limits, we find:

$$\bar{c} = \frac{872}{30} = 29.1 \text{ mistakes per day, and the}$$

$$UCL_c = 29.1 + 3\sqrt{29.1} = 45.3 \text{ and } LCL_c = 29.1 - 3\sqrt{29.1} = 12.9.$$

Acceptance Sampling

When shipments of a product are received from suppliers, or before they are shipped to customers, samples can be taken from the shipment and measured against some quality acceptance standard. The quality of the sample is then assumed to represent the quality of the entire shipment (particularly when shipments contain many units of product, sampling is far less time consuming than testing every unit to determine the overall quality of an incoming or outgoing shipment). Ideally, if strategic alliance members within a supply chain are using Six Sigma quality improvement tools to build quality into the products they provide, acceptance sampling can be eliminated and used only when new or untested suppliers furnish products or materials to the firm. In these situations, **acceptance sampling** can be used to determine whether or not a shipment will be accepted, returned to the supplier, or used for billback purposes when defects are fixed or units are eliminated by the buyer.

One topic that arises is how big to make the test sample. One way to assure that the quality of the sample represents the quality of the entire shipment is to make the sample size equal to the size of the shipment (in other words, examine every unit). Since this is usually impractical, firms must assume the risk of incorrectly judging the quality of the shipment based on the size of the sample: the smaller the sample size, the greater the risk of incorrectly judging a shipment's quality.

There is a cost to both the supplier and buyer when incorrect quality assessments are made. When a buyer rejects a shipment of high-quality units because the sample quality level *did not* meet the acceptance standard, this is termed **producer's risk**. When this happens, it is called a **type-I error**. Conversely, when a buyer accepts a shipment of low-quality units because the sample *did* meet the acceptance standard, this is termed **consumer's risk** and is the result of a **type-II error**. Obviously, trading partners wish to avoid or minimize the occurrence of both of these types of outcomes. To minimize type-I and type-II errors, buyers and sellers must derive an acceptable sampling plan by agreeing on unacceptable defect levels and a sample size big enough to result in minimal numbers of type-I and type-II errors.

Statistical Process Control and Supply Chain Management

Ideally, long-standing strategic supply chain partners would not need to monitor their inbound and outbound product quality—quality would already be extremely high, and employees could spend their time in more productive pursuits. However, most processes and suppliers are not yet perfect, and the level of competition is so fierce in most industries that firms find they must continually be assessing and reassessing process and product quality levels. Managers should identify processes that are critical to achieving the firm's objectives, decide how to monitor process performance, gather data and create the appropriate control charts, and create policies for collecting process samples and monitoring process and product quality over time. Managers must also work to create a culture where quality improvements are encouraged and employees are empowered to make the changes that will result in improved product and service quality.

SUMMARY

Supply chain management, lean thinking, and Six Sigma quality make up a hierarchy for breakthrough competitive advantage. In order for supply chain management to reach its full potential and provide benefits to its members, trading partners must adopt a lean operating philosophy. Similarly, the primary ingredient in the success of a lean program is the use of Six Sigma quality improvement tools. There are a number of practices mentioned within each of these topics that overlap or are very similar such as top management support, workforce involvement, and continuous improvement. This is not surprising given the close ties between supply chain management, lean, and Six Sigma. Considerable time has been spent here, covering lean and Six Sigma because of their critical importance in achieving successful supply chain management and it is hoped that you have gained an appreciation for the topics presented here.

KEY TERMS

acceptance sampling, 286
assignable variations, 280
attribute data, 280
C charts, 283
cause-and-effect diagrams, 277
check sheets, 276
consumer's risk, 286
control charts, 279
critical-to-quality (CTQ) characteristics, 274
defects per million opportunities (DPMO), 264
efficient consumer response (ECR), 248
equipment setups, 258
fishbone diagrams, 277
Five-Ss, 254
flow diagrams, 276
Ishikawa diagrams, 277
just-in-time, 249
kaizen, 261
kaizen blitz, 262
kanban, 250
keiretsu relationships, 248
lean layouts, 256
lean manufacturing, 249
lean production, 249
lean Six, 266
lean Six Sigma, 266
lean supply chain relationships, 256
lean thinking, 249
manufacturing cells, 257
muda, 250
natural variations, 280
opportunities for a defect to occur (OFD), 265
P charts, 283
Pareto charts, 277
Pareto Principle, 277
part families, 257
poka-yoke, 251
process diagrams, 276
process maps, 276
producer's risk, 286
production kanban, 260
pull system, 260
quick response (QR), 248
R chart, 280
root causes, 278
seven wastes, 254
sigma drift, 264
Six Sigma, 249
statistical process control (SPC), 279
the 4 Ms, 277
total quality management (TQM), 264
Toyota Production System, 249
type-I error, 286
type-II error, 286
U.S. Baldrige Quality Award, 271
variable data, 280
waste reduction, 254
work cells, 257
$\bar{x}$ chart, 280
yokoten, 252

DISCUSSION QUESTIONS

1. Explain why lean thinking and Six Sigma are so important to successful supply chain management.
2. Briefly explain the primary concerns and objectives of lean production.

3. How is lean production associated with JIT?
4. What does the Toyota Production System have to do with JIT and lean production?
5. What person or people at Toyota is (are) most responsible for the development of the JIT concept?
6. Why was Toyota's first U.S. car such a failure? What did they learn from this experience?
7. Who was responsible for first using the term *lean* as it related to the auto industry?
8. How is lean thinking associated with supply chain management?
9. Use an example to show how you could use lean thinking with a supplier and a customer.
10. What is yokoten, and what does it have to do with lean thinking?
11. Which do you think is the most important element of lean thinking?
12. What are the seven wastes, and can you discuss these in terms of a business you are familiar with?
13. What are the five Ss? Apply these to improve how you could complete your daily homework or study assignments.
14. What are the advantages of close supplier and customer relationships, when practicing lean?
15. What are the advantages and disadvantages of making small, frequent purchases from just a few suppliers? How do we overcome the disadvantages?
16. Why should lean layouts be "visual"?
17. What are manufacturing cells, and why are they important in lean production?
18. Reducing lot sizes and increasing setups are common practices in most lean production settings. Why?
19. What is the origin of the term *kanbans*, and why are they used in lean systems?
20. Why are lean systems also known as pull systems?
21. What is kaizen, and why is it so important for successful lean production? What is a kaizen blitz?
22. Discuss the linkage between lean systems and environmental sustainability.
23. Describe Six Sigma's origins and the main parties involved. Why is the concept called "Six Sigma"?
24. How is Six Sigma different from TQM?
25. Describe the Lean Six Sigma approach.
26. Describe three ways by which your university could improve quality using elements of Six Sigma.
27. Describe Deming's Theory of Management, and how it can be used to improve quality.
28. Which of Deming's fourteen points might be the most important? Why?
29. Which do you like better—Deming's, Crosby's, or Juran's approach to quality?

30. Why do you think the Baldrige Award is available only to U.S. companies?

31. In viewing the Baldrige Award's seven performance categories, how would your firm stack up in these areas (use the university or your most recent employer if you are not currently employed).

32. What are the two most widely used ISO standards, and why are they so popular? If you are working, is your firm ISO certified? Is McDonald's?

33. What are critical-to-quality characteristics, and how are they used in Six Sigma?

34. What is the DMAIC improvement cycle, and how could you use it to improve your college study habits?

35. Construct a flow diagram of the ticket purchase/football game attendance process at your university. What areas would you investigate further, to identify problems?

36. Construct a cause-and-effect diagram for the following problem: The university course registration and payment process takes too long. Brainstorm some potential causes.

37. What are the two types of process variation, and which one does statistical process control seek to eliminate? What can be done with the other one?

38. Define "variable data," and explain why two control charts are needed to assure that these types of processes are under control.

39. Can a process exhibit sample measurements that are all inside the control limits and still be considered out of control? Explain.

40. What are some variable data and attribute data that could be collected to track the quality of education at your university?

41. How could P charts be used in a manufacturing facility?

42. Can a process be considered in control but *incapable* of meeting design requirements? Explain.

43. If one goal of a supplier partnership is to eliminate acceptance sampling, then when would it get done?

ESSAY/PROJECT QUESTIONS

1. Go to the Baldrige Award website (http://www.quality.nist.gov), and find out which organizations have won the award since this book was published. Report on any new developments with respect to the Baldrige Award and its recipients—have any declared bankruptcy, or are any in financial trouble?

2. Write a report on Toyota and its recent quality and recall problems since 2009.

3. Search the Internet and article databases at your university for the terms *sustainability* and *supply chain management* and write a report on the importance of sustainability in the practice of supply chain management, using company examples.

4. Discuss the implementation of lean and Six Sigma among Thai and Vietnamese companies.

5. Search the Internet and article databases at your university for the term *Lean Six* and write a report on the latest uses of this method using company examples.

PROBLEMS

1. Mejza Compressors uses a lean production assembly line to make its compressors. In one assembly area, the demand is 100 parts per eight-hour day. It uses a container that holds eight parts. It typically takes about six hours to round-trip a container from one work center to the next and back again. Mejza also desires to hold 15 percent safety stock of this part in the system. How many containers should Mejza Compressors be using?

2. Using the information from Problem 1, if Mejza desires to reduce its number of containers to eight, how does this impact the system? What has to be changed, if it is assumed that demand, container size, and safety stock percentage do not change, and what is that change?

3. Eakins Enterprises makes model boats, and it is switching to a lean manufacturing process. At one assembly area, Eakins is using one part container that holds 250 parts, and it wants the output to be approximately 100 finished parts per hour; they also desire a 10 percent safety stock for this part. How fast will the container have to make it through the system to accomplish this?

4. Jim Corner, owner of Corner Bike Rentals, wants to start analyzing his company's quality. For each bike rental, there are four types of customer complaints: (1) bike not working properly, (2) wrong bike size, (3) bike uncomfortable, and (4) bike broken during operation. During the past week, his company rented 280 bikes. He received a total of twenty-six complaints.

   a. What is his company's DPMO for the past week?
   b. What is its Six Sigma operating level?

5. Julie works at Gentry Flower Shoppe, which operates at the 4 sigma level, with about 6,000 DPMO, which was determined recently. At that time, Gentry was found to have 1,500 total defects. It wants to improve to the 5 sigma level, or about 500 DPMO. Assuming nothing else changes, what would its new total defect level have to be?

6. The following sample information was obtained by taking four doughnuts per hour for twelve hours from Fawcett Bakery's doughnut process and weighing them:

HOUR	WEIGHTS (GRAMS)	HOUR	WEIGHT (GRAMS)
1	110, 105, 98, 100	7	89, 102, 101, 99
2	79, 102, 100, 104	8	100, 101, 98, 96
3	100, 102, 100, 96	9	98, 95, 101, 100
4	94, 98, 99, 101	10	99, 100, 97, 102
5	98, 104, 97, 100	11	102, 97, 100, 101
6	104, 97, 99, 100	12	98, 100, 100, 97

   For the data shown above,

   a. Find the $\bar{x}$ and R for each sample.
   b. Find the $\bar{\bar{x}}$ and $\bar{R}$ for the twelve samples.
   c. Find the 3-sigma UCL and LCL for the mean and range charts.
   d. Does the process appear to be in statistical control. Why or why not?

7. Through process measuring a number of pizza delivery times, Mary Jane's Pizzeria finds the mean of all samples to be 27.4 minutes, with an average sample range of 5.2 minutes. It tracked four deliveries per hour for eighteen hours to obtain its samples.

a. Is this an example of variable or attribute sampling data?
b. Find the UCL and LCL for both the $\bar{x}$ and R charts.

8. A company produces 8-pound bags of rice. As shown below, it gathered five samples with six bags in each sample for quality control purposes. The weights of each of the bags are listed below.
Bags in each sample

SAMPLE	1	2	3	4	5	6
1	7.98	8.34	8.02	7.94	8.44	7.68
2	8.33	8.22	8.08	8.51	8.41	8.28
3	7.89	7.77	7.91	8.04	8	7.89
4	8.24	8.18	7.83	8.05	7.9	8.16
5	7.87	8.13	7.92	7.99	8.1	7.81

a. Find the $\bar{x}$ and R for each of the five samples.
b. Find the $\bar{\bar{x}}$ and $\bar{R}$.
c. Find the 3-sigma UCL and LCL for the mean and range charts.
d. Does the process appear to be in statistical control. Why or why not?

9. Ten customers per hour were asked by the cashier at Stanley's Deli if they liked their meal, and the fraction that said "no" are shown below, for a twelve-hour period.

HOUR	FRACTION DEFECTIVE	HOUR	FRACTION DEFECTIVE
1	0	7	0.1
2	0.2	8	0
3	0.4	9	0
4	0.1	10	0.2
5	0.1	11	0
6	0.2	12	0.1

For the data shown above, find
a. $\bar{P}$.
b. σ_P.
c. The 3-sigma UCL and LCL.
d. Does customer satisfaction at Stanley's appear to be in statistical control? How could we improve the analysis?

10. A company collects twenty samples with 100 eggs in each sample. It wants to construct a P chart to track the proportion of broken eggs in each sample. The table below shows the number of defective eggs per sample.

SAMPLE	EGGS	SAMPLE	EGGS	SAMPLE	EGGS
1	3	**8**	6	**15**	5
2	5	**9**	4	**16**	0
3	3	**10**	9	**17**	2
4	4	**11**	2	**18**	6
5	2	**12**	6	**19**	2
6	4	**13**	5	**20**	1
7	2	**14**	1	**TOTAL**	**72**

a. Determine $\bar{P}$.
b. Determine. σ_P.
c. Determine the 3-sigma UCL and LCL.
d. Does the egg process appear to be in statistical control?

11. Roberto's Steakhouse tracks customer complaints every day and then follows up with its customers to resolve problems. For the past thirty days, it received a total of twenty complaints from unhappy customers. Using this information, calculate
 a. $\bar{c}$.
 b. The 3-sigma control limits.

ADDITIONAL RESOURCES

Burt, D. N., D. W. Dobler, and S. L. Starling, *World Class Supply Management: The Key to Supply Chain Management*, 7th ed. New York: McGraw-Hill, 2003.

Crosby, P. B., *Quality Is Free*. New York: McGraw-Hill, 1979.

Crosby, P. B., *Quality Without Tears*. New York: McGraw-Hill, 1984.

Deming, W. E., *Out of the Crisis*. Cambridge, MA: MIT Center for Advanced Engineering Study, 1986.

Evans, J. R., and W. M. Lindsay, *The Management and Control of Quality*, 4th ed. Cincinnati, OH: South-Western, 1999.

Heizer, J., and B. Render, *Principles of Operations Management*, 4th ed. Upper Saddle River, NJ: Prentice Hall, 2000.

Jacobs, F., and R. Chase, *Operations and Supply Management: The Core*. New York: McGraw-Hill/ Irwin, 2008.

Juran, J., and A. Godfrey, *Juran´s Quality Handbook*. New York: McGraw-Hill, 2000.

Krajewski, L., L. Ritzman, and M. Malhotra, *Operations Management: Processes and Value Chains*, 8th ed. Upper Saddle River, NJ: Pearson/Prentice Hall, 2007.

Lucier, G., and S. Seshadri, "GE Takes Six Sigma Beyond the Bottom Line," *Strategic Finance* 82(11), 2001: 40–46.

Smith, G., *Statistical Process Control and Quality Improvement*. New York: Macmillan, 1991.

Vokurka, R. J., and R. R. Lummus, "The Role of Just-in-Time in Supply Chain Management," *International Journal of Logistics Management* 11(1), 2000: 89–98.

ENDNOTES

1. Selko, A., "Pharmaceutical's Lean Prescription," *Industry Week* 260(7), 2011: 1.
2. Anonymous, "Six Sigma Helps During Economic Downturn," *ASQ Six Sigma Forum Magazine* 10(4), 2011: 32.
3. Brandt, D., "Lean Six Sigma and the City," *Industrial Engineer* 43(7), 2011: 50–52.
4. Reed, J., and B. Simon, "Toyota's Long Climb Comes to an Abrupt Halt." *Financial Times*, February 6, 2010: 9.
5. For histories of lean and the Toyota Production System, see, for instance, Becker, R., "Learning to Think Lean: Lean Manufacturing and the Toyota Production System," *Automotive Manufacturing & Production* 113(6), 2001: 64–65; Dahlgaard, J., and S. Dahlgaard-Park, "Lean Production, Six Sigma Quality, TQM and Company Culture," *TQM Magazine* 18(3), 2006: 263–277.
6. Information on the Ford manufacturing system was found at www.lean.org
7. Arndorfer, J., C. Atkinson, J. Bloom, and M. Cardona, "The Biggest Moments in the Last 75 Years of Advertising History," *Advertising Age* 76(13), 2005: 12–15; and Reed and Simon, ref. 4.
8. Manivannan, S., "Error-Proofing Enhances Quality," *Manufacturing Engineering* 137(5), 2006: 99–105.

9. Nakamoto, M., and J. Reed, "Toyota Claims Global Top Spot from GM," *FT.com*, April 24, 2007: 1.

10. See http://oica.net/wp-content/uploads/ranking-without-china-30-nov-12.pdf

11. Womack, J., D. Jones, and D. Roos, *The Machine that Changed the World*. New York, NY: Maxwell MacMillan International, 1990.

12. Greathouse, D., "Managing a Lean Enterprise," *Material Handling Management* 65(7), 2010: 1–3.

13. Minter, S., "Measuring the Success of Lean," *Industry Week* 259(2), 2010: 32.

14. Gebhart, F., "Lean Management Generates Substantial Pharmacy Savings," *Drug Topics* 154(10), 2010: 43.

15. Anonymous, "A Small Company Makes Big Gains Implementing Lean." *Management Services* 50(3), 2006: 28–31.

16. Napolitano, M., "Still Doing More with Less," *Logistics Management* 50(11), 2011: 44–52.

17. Jargon, J., "Latest Starbucks Buzzword: 'Lean' Japanese Techniques." *Wall Street Journal*, August 4, 2009: A1.

18. Jusko, J., "Lean Confusion," *Industry Week* 259(9), 2010: 32.

19. Sedam, S., "Building Lean—Beyond Value Engineering," *Professional Builder*, September 2010: 1.

20. Carper, J., "Making Ice Cream the Safe Way," *Dairy Foods* 113(10), 2012: 52–61.

21. Anonymous, "Tool for Productivity, Quality, Throughput, Safety," *Management Services* 50(3), 2006: 16–18; Becker, J., "Implementing 5S: To Promote Safety & Housekeeping," *Professional Safety* 46(8), 2001: 29–31.

22. Beason, M., "Lean Machining—Integrating the Supply Chain," *Manufacturing Engineering* 151(2), 2013: 75–79.

23. Avery, S., "Suppliers are Continuing Source of Innovation for P&G," *Purchasing* 138(8), 2009: 14.

24. Katz, J., "Going Lean Revives Circuit Board Manufacturer," *Material Handling & Logistics*, January 17, 2012: 1.

25. Jovag, L., "Connect Process Flows to Become Lean," *Manufacturing Engineering*, May 2011: 97–106.

26. Anonymous, "Going Deep with a Four-Way Valve," *Manufacturing Engineering* 142(5), 2009: 39–42.

27. Harriman, F., "Origins of the Term 'KANBAN' from Conversations with Chihiro Nakao." Found at www.fredharriman.com/resources/OriginsofKanban (February 22, 2010).

28. Graban, M., K. Nexus, and J. Swartz, "Feel Human Again," *ASQ Six Sigma Forum Magazine* 12(1), 2012: 16–20.

29. English, P., "Jump Starting a Safety Program with Lean Manufacturing," *EHS Today*, January 5, 2012: 1.

30. Robinson, A., and D. Shroeder, "The Role of Front-Line Ideas in Lean Performance Improvement," *The Quality Management Journal* 16(4), 2009: 27–40.

31. King, A., and M. Lenox, "Lean and Green? An Empirical Examination of the Relationship Between Lean Production and Environmental Performance," *Production and Operations Management* 10(3), 2001: 244–256.

32. Pallavi, J., "Lean and Green Manufacturing," *Flexible Packaging* 14(9), 2012: 42–45; and Smith, L., "Making Lean Green," *ASQ Six Sigma Forum Magazine* 11(2), 2012: 25–26.

33. Phillips, E., "Six Sigma: The Breakthrough Management Strategy Revolutionizing the World's Top Corporations," *Consulting to Management* 13(4), 2002: 57–59. Also see the SSA & Co. website: www.ssaandco.com

34. Information about Six Sigma and sigma drift can be found at multiple locations, for example, www.isixsigma.com or www.wikipedia.org/Six_Sigma

35. Pulakanam, V., "Costs and Savings of Six Sigma Programs: An Empirical Study," *The Quality Management Journal* 19(4), 2012: 39–54.

36. Boulanger, M., "Six Sigma Standard: Panacea or Albatross?" *ASQ Six Sigma Forum Magazine* 12(1), 2012: 28–29.

37. Kelly, M., "Continuous Improvement Goes Global," *ASQ Six Sigma Forum Magazine* 9(4), 2010: 34–35.

38. Spindelndrier, D., F. Lesmeister, and R. Schmitt, "People Matter Most," *Industrial Management* 54(6), 2012: 12–17.

39. See, for example, *CRN* June 4, 2007: 12; Ante, S., "Motorola Is Split Into Two," *The Wall Street Journal*, January 5, 2011: 1; and *Google Official Blog: "We've acquired Motorola Mobility"* Google, (retrieved May 22, 2012).

40. "Business Brief—Primary PDC Inc.: Joint Bankruptcy Plan Filed to Dissolve Former Polaroid," *Wall Street Journal*, January 17, 2003: B-3.

41. Anonymous, "Lean is Crushing Six Sigma," *Manufacturing Engineering* 144(4), 2010: 19–20.

42. See, for example, Brodshy, R., "Deep-Sixing Waste," *Government Executive* 41(12), 2009: 19–20; Kucner, R., "Staying Seaworthy," *Six Sigma Forum Magazine* 8(2), 2009: 25–31; and Westervelt, R., "Clariant Rebuilds Momentum," *Chemical Week* 171(10), 2009: 41.

43. Anonymous, "Lean Six Sigma Saves Lives," *Management Services* 55(4), 2011: 37–39.

44. Gilbert, J., and J. Wisner, "Mattel, Lead Paint, and Magnets: Ethics and Supply Chain Management," *Ethics & Behavior* 20(1), 2010: 33–46.

45. Carbone, J., "Jabil Circuit Uses Six Sigma Quality Criteria to Rate Supplier Performance," *Purchasing* 139(1), 2010: 1.

46. Deming, W. E., *Out of the Crisis*. MIT Press, 1986.

47. See www.deming.org for more information.

48. *Quality is Free* is out of print; Crosby, P. B., *Quality Without Tears*. McGraw Hill, 1984.

49. Juran, J. M., and A. B., Godfrey, *Juran's Quality Handbook*. ASQ Press, 1999.

50. Butman, J., and J. Roessner, *An Immigrant's Gift: The Life of Quality Pioneer Joseph M. Juran*. PBS Documentary Video, produced by Howland Blackiston, copyright WoodsEnd, Inc.

51. Baldrige information was obtained from www.nist.gov/baldrige

52. ISO information was obtained from the organization's website, www.iso.org

53. Cash, B., "Getting It All," *ASQ Six Sigma Forum Magazine* 12(2), 2013: 9–14.

54. Information found at www.ge.com/sixsigma

55. Descriptions found at www.isixsigma.com, www.asq.org, and www.xlp.com

56. Found at http://management.about.com/cs/generalmanagement/a/Pareto081202

57. Adapted from Table 27 of the ASTM STP 15D ASTM *Manual on Presentation of Data and Control Chart Analysis*, © 1976 American Society for Testing and Materials, Philadelphia, PA.

PART 4

Distribution Issues in Supply Chain Management

Chapter 9

DOMESTIC U.S. AND GLOBAL LOGISTICS

I've always said the easiest way to become a millionaire is to start out as a billionaire and then go into the airline business.

— Sir Richard Branson, founder of Virgin Group[1]

Hopefully within 10 years' time, anyone placing an order online from anywhere in China will receive their goods within eight hours, allowing for the virtual urbanization of every village across China. In order to achieve this, we will need to establish a modern, 21st century logistics network.

— Jack Ma, chairman and CEO of Alibaba Group[2]

Learning Objectives

After completing this chapter, you should be able to

- Understand the strategic importance of the logistics elements and describe how they affect supply chain management.
- Compare and contrast the various modes of transportation and their impacts on costs.
- Understand how U.S. regulation and deregulation have impacted transportation.
- Discuss the global aspects of logistics.
- Examine and understand the interrelatedness of transportation, warehousing, and material handling.
- Identify a number of third-party logistics service providers.
- Describe the various reverse logistics activities.
- Discuss some of the e-commerce issues in logistics management.
- Explain how the various logistics software applications assist the firm in its supply chain management efforts.

Chapter Outline

SCM Profile — Biggest, Longest, Fastest

In transportation, bigger, longer, and faster usually means better. Since economies of scale in transportation can mean fewer trips, less fuel consumed, better equipment utilization, and lower labor costs, logistics providers have occasionally utilized enormous capacities to gain the benefits of transportation scale economies. And, with the continuing demand for greater shipping speed, some companies are designing ever-faster systems to satisfy demand. Several examples are provided here.

MOTOR CARRIERS

In Australia, large tractor units pull three, four, and even more trailers along long stretches of open road between cities in unpopulated areas with no rail service. These long tractor/trailer combinations are known as road trains. In Australia, road trains can legally be up to 180 feet in length, barreling along at speeds of up to 65 mph. In 2006, the record was set in Clifton, Queensland, Australia, for road train length when a Mack Titan tractor pulled 112 semi-trailers measuring 4,836 feet, weighing 2,900,000 pounds, for 328 feet.[3]

RAIL CARRIERS

If you want high-speed and on-time train service, the Japanese Shinkansen bullet train is the way to go. Started in 1964, the bullet train was an instant success, traveling 125 mph from Tokyo to Osaka and carrying 1 billion passengers by 1976. Shinkansen trains today reach speeds of 200 mph between a number of Japanese cities. Japan is now in the testing phase for its L-Zero magnetic levitation train, which has reached speeds of 310 mph. It is scheduled for completion in 2027, at a projected cost of $52 billion.[4]

AIR CARRIERS

The new Airbus A380 jetliner and the old Spruce Goose may be big, but they are nowhere near the biggest—that title belongs to the Antonov An-225 commercial jet freighter. It was built in 1988 for the Soviet space program to airlift rocket boosters and their space shuttle. When the Soviet Union collapsed in 1990, the aircraft was temporarily mothballed, and then eventually refurbished and put back into service in 2001 for Antonov Airlines. It has transported things once thought impossible by air, such as locomotives and 150-ton generators. It also has allowed vast quantities of relief supplies to be quickly transported to disaster areas, such as quake-stricken Haiti in February 2010. The An-225 can carry up to 550,000 pounds, cruise at 500 mph and travel up to 9,500 miles.[5]

WATER CARRIERS

The largest supertanker ever built was the *Seawise Giant*, built by Sumitomo Heavy Industries in 1979. The ship was 1,504 feet long with 340,000 square feet of deck, and was too big to pass through the English Channel, the Suez Canal, or the Panama Canal. Fully loaded, the ship weighed 646,000 tons and standing on end, it would be taller than the Empire State Building. The ship was by far the largest ship ever built and had a number of owners and names over the years, but was simply too big; it was scrapped in 2010. The largest containership ever built was the *Emma Maersk*, built in 2006 by the Moller-Maersk Group. It can carry up to 15,000 standard 20-foot containers, is 1,300 feet long, and can cruise at about 29 mph.[6]

PIPELINE CARRIERS

In the North Sea, the world's longest underwater pipeline, finished in 2007 by Norsk Hydro ASA, delivers natural gas from Norway's offshore gas fields to processing plants 746 miles away in the U.K. The sections of pipe were assembled and welded together using the world's largest pipeline-laying ships and then laid continuously on the seafloor, in depths up to 3,000 feet. The world's longest on-land pipeline was completed in December 2012, built by the China National Petroleum Corporation and stretching 5,400 miles from the central part of China to Shanghai in the east and Guangzhou and Hong Kong in the south. The pipeline cost $22.5 billion to build and will help bring power to 500 million people.[7]

INTRODUCTION

Logistics is necessary for moving purchased materials from suppliers to buyers, moving work-in-process materials within a firm, moving finished goods to customers, returning or recycling goods, and also storing these items along the way in supply chains. Effective logistics systems are needed for commerce to exist in any industrialized society. Products have little value to customers until they are moved to customers' usage areas at a point in time when they are needed. Logistics thus provides what are termed **time utility** and **place utility**. Time utility is created when customers get products delivered at precisely the right time, not earlier and not later. The logistics function creates time utility by determining how deliveries can be made in a timely manner and where items should be held prior to delivery. Place utility is created when customers get things delivered to their desired locations.

The official definition of **logistics** from the globally recognized Council of Supply Chain Management Professionals is:

> *The process of planning, implementing, and controlling procedures for the efficient and effective transportation and storage of goods including services, and related information from the point of origin to the point of consumption for the purpose of conforming to customer requirements.*[8]

So it can be seen that transportation, warehousing, information systems, and customer service play very significant roles in the logistics function. For supply chains in particular, logistics is what creates the flow of goods between supply chain partners, such that costs, service requirements, competitive advantage, and profits can be optimized.

When moving around within a city, between cities, or between countries, it is impossible to ignore the business of logistics, whether it be large trucks ambling along the roadways; trains pulling boxcars, cattle cars, and tankers next to highways; warehouses storing goods in cities' industrial sections; airplanes taking off at airports; container ships unloading cargo; or barges floating slowly down rivers. In the U.S. and other highly industrialized nations, the movement of goods is ever-pervasive. Without it, we as consumers would never have opportunities to find what we want, when we want it, at the many retail outlets we routinely visit each day.

Using the latest available statistics from the U.S. Department of Transportation, at the end of 2011 the total annual U.S. for-hire logistics services contribution to the U.S. gross

Table 9.1 Total U.S. For-Hire Logistics Services Contribution to GDP ($ billions)

	1980	1985	1990	1995	2000	2005	2007	2009	2011
Total U.S. GDP	2788	4218	5801	7415	9952	12623	14029	13974	15076
For-Hire Logistics Services GDP (% U.S. GDP)	102.6 (3.7)	137.1 (3.3)	172.8 (3.0)	231.7 (3.1)	301.4 (3.0)	369.5 (2.9)	404.9 (2.9)	396.6 (2.8)	447.9 (3.0)
Truck GDP (% For-Hire GDP)	28.4 (27.7)	39.4 (28.7)	49.7 (28.8)	69.3 (29.9)	97.0 (32.2)	119.6 (32.4)	127.2 (31.4)	114.8 (28.9)	126.0 (28.1)
Rail GDP (% For-Hire GDP)	20.2 (19.7)	21.0 (15.3)	18.6 (10.8)	21.1 (9.1)	22.8 (7.6)	27.0 (7.3)	31.7 (7.8)	31.0 (7.8)	36.7 (8.2)
Water GDP (% For-Hire GDP)	3.5 (3.5)	4.0 (2.9)	5.1 (3.0)	6.3 (2.7)	8.1 (2.7)	8.9 (2.4)	12.8 (3.2)	13.9 (3.5)	14.5 (3.2)
Air GDP (% For-Hire GDP)	13.1 (12.8)	19.3 (13.9)	31.3 (18.1)	46.2 (19.9)	53.1 (17.6)	55.7 (15.1)	60.2 (14.9)	59.4 (15.0)	69.6 (15.5)
Pipeline GDP (% For-Hire GDP)	5.1 (5.0)	7.3 (5.3)	6.0 (3.5)	6.7 (2.9)	9.1 (3.0)	10.4 (2.8)	12.5 (3.1)	13.2 (3.3)	21.1 (4.7)
Warehouse GDP (% For-Hire GDP)	6.4 (6.2)	9.5 (6.9)	13.0 (7.5)	18.8 (8.1)	25.8 (8.6)	34.8 (9.4)	39.6 (9.8)	42.8 (10.8)	45.6 (10.2)
Other Trans. GDP[a] (% For-Hire GDP)	26.0 (25.3)	36.6 (26.7)	48.9 (28.3)	63.4 (27.4)	85.3 (28.3)	113.2 (30.6)	120.9 (29.9)	121.6 (30.7)	134.5 (30.0)

Source: U.S. Dept. of Commerce, Bureau of Transp. Statistics, www.bts.gov/publications.
[a] Includes transit, ground passenger, and other transportation and support activities.

domestic product (GDP) was approximately 3.0 percent, or $448 billion. Table 9.1 shows the growth of for-hire logistics expenditures in the U.S., which has more than quadrupled in thirty-one years. Notice that logistics expenditures decreased during the recent recession but have recovered nicely in 2011. Also note that warehousing, pipeline, and water expenditures have been growing lately.

In this chapter, the many logistics activities are discussed, along with logistics nomenclature and related events affecting businesses each day. Included are discussions of the modes of transportation, transportation regulation and deregulation, warehousing and distribution, a number of logistics decisions firms must make, the impact of logistics on supply chain management, the global issues affecting logistics, the impact of e-commerce on logistics activities, and the management of product returns, also called reverse logistics. Some of the transportation basics are reviewed next.

TRANSPORTATION FUNDAMENTALS

This section reviews a number of important transportation elements within the logistics function, including the objective of transportation, legal forms of transportation, the modes of transportation, intermodal transportation, transportation pricing, transportation security, and transportation regulation and deregulation in the U.S. This provides a good foundation for discussing the remaining topics in the chapter, as well as an appreciation for the complex nature of transportation issues in logistics.

The Objective of Transportation

Although one might think the overriding objective of transportation is obvious—that is, moving people and things from one place to another—for-hire transportation services can go broke doing this inefficiently. For example, over the past twenty years, a number of U.S. passenger airlines have sought bankruptcy protection and asked for concessions from labor unions to keep operating. Some of these airlines include American, Ryan International, United, Continental, America West, US Airways, Delta, Northwest, Hawaiian, and Aloha. The steep economic downturn from 2008 to 2011, combined with steadily rising fuel prices, only made things more troublesome for transportation companies. As a matter of fact, by 2011, fuel costs accounted for 35 percent of U.S. airline operating costs (this was triple the percent of cost compared to 2000). During this same period, over 8,500 U.S. trucking companies went bankrupt, taking about 325,000 trucks off the road.[9]

Logistics managers seek to maximize value for their employers by correctly communicating the firm's service needs to transportation providers. Additionally, services and prices are negotiated such that the transportation provider's delivery costs are covered while allowing them an acceptable profit contribution. Finally, logistics managers must ensure the desired services are performed effectively. In the transportation industry, competitive prices may not be high enough to cover firms' fixed and variable costs, and this has created a tremendous problem for a number of airlines and trucking companies as mentioned above. In the most general terms, transportation objectives should then be to *satisfy customer requirements while minimizing costs and making a reasonable profit*. For logistics or perhaps supply chain managers, this also means deciding which forms of transportation, material handling, and storage, along with the most appropriate vehicle scheduling and routing, to use.

Legal Forms of Transportation

For-hire transportation service companies are classified legally as common, contract, exempt, or private carriers. The distinguishing characteristics of each of these classifications are discussed below.

Common Carriers

Common carriers offer transportation services to all shippers at published rates between designated locations. Common carriers *must offer* their transportation services to the general public without discrimination, meaning they must charge the same rates for the same service to all customers. In the U.S., a common carrier is legally bound to carry all passengers or freight as long as there is enough space, the fee is paid, and no reasonable grounds to refuse exist. Because common carriers serve the general public, they are the most heavily regulated of all carrier classifications. Some U.S. examples of common carriers are Southwest Air, Amtrak, Greyhound, and Carnival Cruise Lines.

Contract Carriers

Contract carriers might also be common carriers; however, as such, they are not bound to serve the general public. Instead, contract carriers serve specific customers under contractual agreements. Typical contracts are for movement of a specified cargo for a negotiated and agreed-upon price. Some contract carriers have specific capabilities that allow them to offer lower prices than common carriers might charge for the same service. For instance, Southwest Air might enter into a contractual agreement with the Dallas Cowboys football team to provide transportation for the team's out-of-town games. Shippers and carriers are free to negotiate contractual agreements for price, the commodity carried, liability, delivery timing, and types of service. Delta Airlines, for example, provides contract services to a number of professional sports teams as described in the nearby SCM Profile.

Contract Carriers for the Pros

One flight served grilled halibut with mashed potatoes and Dove ice cream bars. On another, passengers had large tables for card games and beds big enough to accommodate 7-footers. Forget first class and private jets—too cramped and understaffed. If you want the pinnacle of air travel today, fly with a professional sports team.

Airlines cater to teams with tricked-out jets, handpicked flight attendants, and meals from players' favorite restaurants. Many teams ban alcohol, have nutritionists select menus, and set up plane interiors so coaches can study game films and players can sleep. "They just want to get where they are going," said Denny Yaider, a charter coordinator for Delta. Among Mr. Yaider's duties: coordinating bus service and security screening, towing planes and refueling jets if regular workers don't show up, and hunting down and returning items left behind. These include everything from cellphones and cash-filled wallets to a tooth left behind by a hockey player.

Delta takes eight of its jets out of regular passenger service in October and installs special interiors for the NBA. Instead of 126 seats, there are only 54. The plane is split into three cabins—the front for players, with sixteen seats that fold out into beds for 7-footers, ten seats in the middle for coaches, and twenty-eight in the rear for team staff, security, and beat reporters.

In 2012, Delta flew twenty-one NBA teams, fifteen Major League Baseball teams, and fifteen NFL teams. The airline also carried two NHL teams, thirty-five college football teams, and forty college basketball teams. Domestic team flights typically cost $75,000 to $200,000 each way, Delta says. For teams, the convenience of postgame charters can ease the grind of frequent travel and keep players fresher for the next game. "Travel can be a big thing affecting the outcome of a game," said former MLB pitcher Rick Sutcliffe, now an analyst with ESPN. "If it helps you win one game, one game can be all the difference between making the playoffs or not."[10]

Exempt Carriers

Exempt carriers are also for-hire carriers, but they are exempt from regulation of services and rates. Carriers are classified as exempt if they transport certain exempt products such as produce, livestock, coal, garbage, or newspapers. School buses, taxis, and ambulances are also examples of exempt carriers. The exempt status was originally established to allow farmers to transport agricultural products on public roads, but today the status has been broadened to include a number of commodities. Rail carriers hauling coal between specific locations are exempt from economic regulation, for instance. All carriers can also act as exempt carriers for these specific commodities and routes.

Private Carrier

A **private carrier** is not subject to economic regulation and typically transports goods for the company owning the carrier. Firms transporting their own products typically own and operate fleets large enough to make the cost of transportation less than what it would be if the firm hired a transportation provider. Flexibility and control of product movements also play major roles in the ownership of a private carrier. Walmart, for instance, with its private fleet of trucks, was able to respond even quicker than U.S. government relief workers after Hurricane Katrina struck the Louisiana Gulf Coast in the summer of 2005. Immediately after the disaster, Walmart began hauling food, water, and other relief supplies with its private fleet of trucks to community members and other organizations in the affected areas. In three weeks, it hauled 2,500 truckloads of supplies to these areas; additionally, it was able to reopen its stores quickly in the hardest hit areas. Shortly after the hurricane, New Orleans Sheriff Harry Lee was quoted as saying, "If [the] American government would have responded like Walmart has responded, we wouldn't be in this crisis."[11]

The Modes of Transportation

There are five modes of transportation: motor (truck), rail, air, water, and pipeline carriers. These modes and the amount of freight they hauled each year between 1980 and 2011 in the U.S. are shown in Table 9.1. Each of these modes offers distinct advantages to customers, and their selection depends on a number of factors including the goods to be transported, how quickly the goods are needed, the price shippers are willing to pay, and the locations of shippers and customers. Discussion of each of the modes follows.

Motor Carriers

Motor carriers (or trucks) are the most flexible mode of transportation and, as shown in Table 9.1, account for about 28 percent of all U.S. for-hire transportation expenditures, which is by far the largest of the five modes. Motor carriers offer door-to-door service, local pickup and delivery, and small as well as large shipment hauling. It has very low fixed and variable costs, can compete favorably with rail and air carriers for short to medium hauls (distances shorter than 1,000 miles), and is still competitive with other forms of transportation for long cross-country shipments, particularly if there are multiple delivery locations. Motor carriers can also offer a variety of specialized services from refrigerated, to livestock, to automobile hauling.

The primary disadvantages for motor carriers are weather and traffic problems. The tragic collapse of the eight-lane Minneapolis, Minnesota, I-35 West bridge over the Mississippi River in August 2007 killed thirteen people and provided a painful reminder of the importance of a nation's transportation infrastructure. Per day, more than 140,000 vehicles, including approximately 5,700 commercial vehicles, used Minnesota's busiest bridge. (In 2005, the bridge was inspected and received a low rating, indicating that it should have been either repaired or replaced.[12] The replacement bridge opened to traffic on September 18, 2008.[13])

Motor carriers are most often classified as **less-than-truckload (LTL) carriers** or **truckload (TL) carriers**. LTL carriers move small packages or shipments that take up less than one truckload, and the shipping fees are higher per hundred weight (cwt) than TL fees, since the carrier must consolidate many small shipments into one truckload and then break the truckload back down into individual shipments at the destinations for individual deliveries. For many shippers, using LTL carriers is a much less expensive alternative than using a TL carrier. The LTL industry amounts to only about 5 percent of total trucking revenues and, in the U.S., is comprised of a few very large, national LTL carriers along with a sizeable number of small regional carriers. As of the end of 2012, the five largest LTL carriers in the U.S. in terms of revenue were FedEx Freight ($5 billion), Con-Way Freight ($3.3 billion), YRC Freight ($3.2 billion), UPS Freight ($2.4 billion), and Old Dominion Freight ($1.9 billion). Most of the regional carriers are small, privately owned companies that specialize in overnight and second-day deliveries. Since 2010, the LTL industry has been consolidating with capacities decreasing as carriers reduce expenditures on new trucks and equipment. Today, the top five carriers represent about 45 percent of the market.[14]

TL carriers, on the other hand, have trailers dedicated to a single shipper's cargo. A TL customer loads a trailer full, wherein the TL company transports the shipment to a final destination where it is received and unloaded. At the end of 2012, the top five TL carriers in terms of revenues were J.B. Hunt ($5.1 billion), Swift ($3.5 billion), Schneider ($3.3 billion), Landstar ($3.0 billion), and Werner ($2.0 billion). The industry is quite fragmented—about 70 percent of the companies operate fewer than five trucks. In contrast to the LTL market, the top five TL carriers represent only about 5 percent of the market.[15]

Motor carriers can also be classified based on the types of goods they haul. **General freight carriers** carry the majority of goods shipped in the U.S. and include common carriers, whereas **specialized carriers** transport liquid petroleum, household goods, agricultural commodities, building materials, and other specialized items. In Australia, extra-long truck and trailer combinations (referred to as **road trains**) transport goods between geographically dispersed communities not served by rail (see the chapter opening SCM Profile for discussions of this and other unique transportation services).

Rail Carriers

Rail carriers compete most favorably when the distance is long and the shipments are heavy or bulky. At one time in the U.S., rail carriers transported the majority of goods shipped; however, since World War II, their share of the transportation market has steadily fallen. Today, U.S. railroads account for only 8 percent of total annual for-hire transportation expenditures, as shown in Table 9.1.

Rail service is relatively slow and inflexible; however, rail carriers are less expensive than air and motor carriers and can compete fairly well on long hauls. To better compete, railroads have purchased trucking companies and can thus offer point-to-point pickup and delivery service using motor carrier trailers and rail flatcars that carry the trailers (known as **trailer-on-flatcar service** or TOFC service). Railroads are also at somewhat of a disadvantage compared with motor carriers with respect to shipment damages, equipment availability, and service frequency.

Because of their abundance, rail companies use each other's rail cars; however, keeping track of the rail cars and getting them where they are needed can be problematic. With advances in railroad routing and scheduling software and rail car identification systems, this has become less of a problem for rail carriers. **Real-time location systems (RTLSs)** on rail cars use active, Wi-Fi-enabled radio frequency identification (RFID) tags to allow tracking of rail cars (and their assets) in real time. The tag is programmed to broadcast a signal identifying its location at regular time intervals. Sensors can also be added to the RTLS tags to monitor the temperature inside refrigerated cars, for example, and transmit a signal if the temperature goes out of a preset range.[16]

In the U.S., railroad infrastructure and aging equipment have also been problems for the railroads; however, there has been a spending resurgence since the mid-1980s to replace worn track segments and rail cars, to upgrade terminals, and to consolidate through mergers and acquisitions. Unfortunately, train derailments have begun occurring more frequently, which is forcing the issue of replacing old rail track. In Bridgeport, Connecticut, an eastbound commuter train, for instance, derailed in March 2012, coming to rest in the path of a westbound train that sideswiped it, injuring 70 people and tearing up significant amounts of track. As a result, the Connecticut Department of Transportation is spending over $100 million to upgrade 56 miles of track along its New York commuter rail corridor.[17]

One of the trends in rail transportation is the use of **high-speed trains**. Today, they are operated in the U.S. by Amtrak along the northeast corridor (Boston–New

York–Washington D.C.). Bombardier Inc., a Montreal-based transportation and aerospace company, designed and manufactured Amtrak's Acela Express, an electric high-speed train. These trains can make the Washington D.C. to Boston trip in about 5.5 hours, averaging approximately 85 miles per hour, although top speeds can reach 120 miles per hour (other, slower trains and lack of straight-line track have tended to reduce the average speeds).[18] Eventually, with further improvements, speeds are expected to reach 160 mph.[19]

While the Acela Express is the only high-speed railroad operating in the U.S., other states such as California and Illinois are considering use of high-speed trains. In fact, the Obama administration unveiled a $53 billion plan in 2011 to give 80 percent of Americans access to high-speed rail within 25 years. China, new to the high-speed rail market, today operates the longest high-speed rail network (about 13,000 km) and is interested in helping the U.S. develop theirs. "This historic investment in America's high-speed rail network keeps us on track toward economic opportunity and competitiveness in the 21st century," said Ray LaHood, the U.S. Secretary of Transportation.[20]

Other countries such as France and Japan also have extensive high-speed rail lines operating. The inaugural high-speed French rail service between Paris and Lyon was in 1981 and has since expanded to connect cities across France and in neighboring countries. The Japanese Shinkansen high-speed rail began operations in 1964 between Tokyo and Osaka. A number of other European countries also use high-speed rail. China's massive $300 billion, 16,000 km high-speed rail network will connect many of China's largest cities and is expected to be complete by 2020. Malaysia and Singapore recently announced their plans to build a high-speed line connecting Kuala Lumpur and Singapore. It is due for completion in 2020. High-speed rail can provide an attractive alternative to air and other forms of ground transportation, depending on the cost and location of terminals.[21]

Air Carriers

Transporting goods by air is very expensive relative to other modes but also very fast, particularly for long distances. Looking again at Table 9.1, it can be seen that **air carriers** account for approximately 15 percent of the total annual U.S. for-hire transportation expenditures. The amount of freight hauled, however, is quite small, since airlines cannot carry extremely heavy or bulky cargo (an exception is the world's largest commercial cargo airliner, the Ukrainian-built Antonov An-225, described in the chapter-opening SCM Profile). For light, high-value goods that need to travel long distances quickly, air transportation is the best of the modal alternatives. For movements over water, the only other modal alternative is water carriage, where the transportation decision is based on timing, cost, and shipment weight. Though the incidence of shipment damage is quite low and schedule frequency is good, air transportation is limited in terms of geographic coverage. Most small cities in the U.S., for example, do not have airports or regularly scheduled air service; therefore, air transportation service must be combined with motor carrier service for these locations.

Today, about half of the goods transported by air are carried by freight-only airlines like FedEx, the world's largest air cargo airline. This represents a significant change since the late 1960s when most air cargo was hauled by passenger airlines. Today, most passenger air carriers are opting to use smaller, more fuel-efficient aircraft, which has reduced their ability to haul cargo. Economic growth in markets such as China has continued to fuel increases in international air cargo and air passenger demand, although other big markets such as India, Brazil, and the U.S. continue to shrink due to increasing fuel prices and the recent economic recession. U.S. carriers are trimming capacity while Air China is boosting capacity by 50 percent in 2013 compared to 2012, and China Southern is adding 73 percent more capacity.[22]

Water Carriers

Shipping goods by **water carrier** is very inexpensive but also very slow and inflexible. There are several types of water transportation including inland waterway, lake, coastal and intercoastal ocean, and global deep-sea carriers. Most of the inland waterway transportation is used to haul heavy, bulky, low-value materials such as coal, grain, and sand and competes primarily with rail and pipeline carriers. Inland water transport is obviously limited to areas accessible by water, and hence growth in this area of transportation is also limited. Based on information from Table 9.1, water transportation as a percent of total for-hire logistics services has remained fairly steady at about 3 percent for the past 30 years. Like rail and air transportation, water carriers are typically paired with motor carriers to enable door-to-door pick-up and delivery service.

In the U.K., efforts are underway to increase inland waterway carrier usage, as this has less environmental impact when compared to motor freight carriers. British Waterways, the organization responsible for managing U.K. waterways, is investing heavily to reduce highway congestion and pollution by increasing trade along its inland waterways. For example, a single river barge can carry the equivalent of 24 truckloads of freight. Freight on inland waterways also produces lower emissions, less noise, and is visually unobtrusive. The nearby SCM Profile describes water freight activities between Manchester and Liverpool in the U.K.

There have also been developments in **deep-sea transportation** that have made water transportation cheaper and more desirable, even with the slow transportation times. The development and use of supertankers and containerships has added a new dimension to water transportation. Many of today's oil supertankers are more than 1,200 feet long (that's four U.S. football fields) and carry over 2 million barrels of oil. The largest oil supertanker was the *Seawise Giant* (as described in the chapter opening SCM Profile). Oil-producing

SCM Profile | New Life for an Old Waterway

Barge travel is not a mode of transport generally associated with efficiency and modern logistics. But in northwest England, the Manchester Ship Canal is making a comeback 119 years after it was built. This one-time artery of imperial trade between Manchester and Liverpool is being promoted as a cheap and green alternative to clogged motorways.

Container traffic on the waterway has increased fivefold in the past three years. Kellogg returned to the waterway in 2011 and is planning to add still more tons of boxed cereals in 2013. This will cut 85 percent of road miles from its supply chain, saving 61 tons of carbon dioxide, the company says. Stephen Carr, head of business development at Peel Ports, which owns the canal, said: "It's back to the future. The canal was built when road transport was expensive and difficult. Everyone is telling us road transport is getting expensive and difficult again. [The canal] is a cost efficient, environmentally friendly alternative."

Peel Port's Atlantic Gateway development foresees £14 billion of investment in the area by 2030, creating 140,000 jobs. The group plans to invest almost £1billion directly into the ship canal. This includes a logistics system to bring goods in or out by barge via the expanded container terminal north of Liverpool and transfer them to road or rail at new or refurbished facilities at the ports at Salford, Warrington, and Ellesmere Port. Container traffic has risen from 3,000 containers in 2009 to 15,000 in 2012 and the company hopes to hit 100,000 within a decade.[23]

nations can now cheaply ship large quantities of oil anywhere around the globe where demand exists, and even small shippers can ship items overseas cheaply, because of the ability to consolidate small shipments in containers that are placed on board containerships.

Shipping containers allow almost any packaged product to be shipped overseas, and they add an element of protection to the cargo. Containerships carry the majority of the world's water-transported manufactured goods, and they can carry more than 10,000 standard 20-foot containers (these are normally 20 feet in length, 8.5 feet in height, and 8 feet wide but can vary), holding up to 52,000 pounds each, with a total containership value sometimes as high as $300 million. At any given time, there are approximately 5 to 6 million containers being shipped around the globe.[24]

Pipeline Carriers

Pipeline carriers are very specialized with respect to the products they can carry; however, once the initial investment of the pipeline is recovered, there is very little additional maintenance cost, so long-term pipeline transportation tends to be very inexpensive. Pipelines can haul materials that are only in a liquid or gaseous state and so the growth potential for pipelines is quite limited. One of the items pipelines haul is coal, and they do this by first pulverizing coal into small particles and then suspending it in water to form **coal slurry**. When the coal slurry reaches its destination, the coal and water are separated. Other items transported include water, oil, gasoline, and natural gas. The continuous nature of pipeline flow is what makes it unique. Once the product reaches its destination, it is continuously available. Pipelines are today being constructed to haul large quantities of natural gas and oil from desolate areas to existing processing facilities hundreds and even thousands of miles away (see the chapter-opening SCM Profile for more discussion of pipelines). So long as the world remains dependent on energy products such as coal, oil, and natural gas, there will be a need for pipeline transportation.

One of the more controversial pipelines is the proposed Keystone XL pipeline, which would transport 830,000 barrels per day of crude oil from the oil sands region of Alberta, Canada, to the U.S. gulf coast. Several state governments along with a number of U.S. government politicians are touting the benefits (lower gas prices and more jobs) as well as the costs to the environment (oil spills and native habitat destruction). To date, no decision has been reached on the project.[25]

Intermodal Transportation

Intermodal transportation, or the use of combinations of the various transportation modes, is a very popular transportation arrangement and can make the movement of goods cheaper, quicker, and more secure. Intermodal transportation dates at least to the early 1800s, when wooden containers were used to transport coal on the Bridgewater Canal in England. Horse-drawn vehicles were used to transfer the coal to and from the canal barges. During World War II, pallets were used to transfer U.S. military equipment quickly between warehouses, trucks, trains, ships, and airplanes. The reduced freight handling meant fewer personnel and faster shipping times. The use of standardized containers grew quickly in the U.S. when the Interstate Commerce Commission ruled in 1954 that railroads could carry truck trailers and containers on rail flatcars. In the 1970s, third-party shipper agents began moving shippers' goods in trailers and then using railroads for part of the transportation. The early success of these agents spawned hundreds of similar companies, driving the growth of intermodal traffic. Finally, deregulation of the transportation industry spurred intermodal growth to the levels of today.[26]

Most large intermodal transportation companies today such as U.S. companies J.B. Hunt, Hub Group, and RJW Transport offer one-stop, door-to-door shipping capabilities—they transport shippers' goods for a price and then determine the best intermodal transportation and warehousing arrangements to *meet customer requirements as cheaply as possible*. Here is a fictitious shipping example using a number of intermodal combinations:

> A manufacturing company packs a standard eight-foot container for shipment to an overseas customer. The container is sealed and connected to a motor carrier trailer for transport to a nearby rail terminal. The container is then loaded onto a flatcar and double-stacked with another container, where it is then transported to a seaport on the U.S. West Coast. Upon arrival, the container is placed aboard a container ship and transported to Japan. In Japan, the container is off-loaded and moves through customs, where it is then loaded onto another motor carrier trailer for transport to its final destination, where it finally is unsealed, inspected and unpacked. In this example, goods were packed, securely sealed, unsealed and unpacked one time. The container was used in three modes of transportation and was unsealed when customs authorities examined and accepted the goods.

The above example highlights a number of intermodal transportation combinations. The most common combinations are truck **trailer-on-flatcar (TOFC)** and **container-on-flatcar (COFC)**, also called **piggyback service**. The same containers can be placed on board containerships and freight airliners. These combinations attempt to combine the flexibility of motor carriers with the economy of rail and/or water carriers. The BNSF Railway, headquartered in Texas, operates one of the largest railroad networks in North America, with over 32,500 track miles covering twenty-eight states and two Canadian provinces. BNSF moves 10 percent of all the oil in the U.S. and moves about 4.7 million intermodal shipments per year. In 2013, BNSF had 41,000 employees, 6,900 locomotives, and more than 190,000 freight cars.[27]

Another example of intermodal transportation are **ROROs**, or roll-on-roll-off, vessels. These allow truck trailers, automobiles, heavy equipment, and specialty cargo to be directly driven on and off the ship, into secured below-deck garages without use of cranes. The New Jersey-based Atlantic Container Line operates the largest and most versatile combination RORO/containerships in the world, capable of carrying a wide variety of cargo. Their combination G-3 vessels are 1,000 feet long, and can carry 1,000 automobiles below deck, with 1,850 standard 20-foot containers above deck.[28]

Transportation Pricing

The two basic pricing strategies used by logistics service providers are **cost-of-service pricing** and **value-of-service pricing**. Further, when the shipments are large enough, carriers and shippers enter into **negotiated pricing**. Obviously, shippers want low prices and carriers want high profits, and these desires are often at odds with one another. Not too many years ago, logistics companies like UPS simply distributed their costs evenly and charged a uniform rate to all customers. As computer pricing models improved, companies were able to more closely identify their costs for various types of customers and differential pricing became more the norm, with small shippers and infrequent users seeing significant price increases. More recently, poor economic conditions caused excess capacity due to lower shipping demand, which allowed shippers to negotiate better terms.[29] These and other pricing topics are discussed below.

Cost-of-Service Pricing

Cost-of-service pricing is used when carriers establish prices based on their fixed and variable costs of transportation. To do this, carriers must be able to identify the relevant costs and then accurately allocate these to each shipment. Cost-of-service pricing varies based on volume and distance. As shipping volume increases, the portion of fixed costs that are allocated to each shipment goes down, allowing the carrier to reduce its prices. Large-volume shipments also allow carriers to charge carload or truckload rates instead of less-than-carload or less-than-truckload rates. Cost-of-service pricing represents the base, or lowest, shipping price for carriers, and in a highly competitive market, carriers will price just above these levels to maintain some minimal level of profitability. As occurred during the recent global recession, many carriers were unable to maintain prices at even these lowest levels, resulting in a number of bankruptcies as described earlier.

Value-of-Service Pricing

In this case, transportation providers price their services at the highest levels the market will bear. Prices are thus based on the level of competition and the current demand for each service. This is a profit-maximizing pricing approach. If a carrier has a service that is in high demand with little competition, prices will consequently be quite high. As other logistics companies notice the high profit potential of this service, competition will eventually increase, causing prices to fall. As the level of competition increases, carriers will seek ways to reduce their costs to maintain profitability.

In the highly competitive passenger airline industry, for example, Southwest Airlines has been able to keep its costs low by using only one type of airplane, flying relatively short distances between stops, concentrating on providing excellent customer service, keeping its planes in the air, and using fuel price hedging strategies, which have enabled it to remain profitable for forty consecutive years.[30] Online booking capabilities for airlines, combined with revenue management software to control prices as demand fluctuates, have allowed airlines to use value-of-service pricing to maximize revenues.

Negotiated Pricing

Since the deregulation of transportation in the U.S., negotiating transportation prices has become much more common among business shippers and logistics providers. In addition, shippers today are inclined to develop alliances with logistics companies because of the key role they play in allowing firms and their supply chains to be more responsive to changing demand. This has also tended to increase the use of negotiated prices. Shippers want carriers to use cost-of-service pricing, while carriers want to use value-of-service pricing. To maintain an equitable partnership, prices are negotiated such that they fall somewhere between these two levels, allowing carriers to cover their fixed and variable costs and make a reasonable profit, and allowing shippers to get the logistics services they want at reasonable prices.

Terms of Sale

In many cases, suppliers' terms of sale affect transportation costs. When products are purchased from a supplier, it may quote a price that includes transportation to the buyer's location. This is known as **FOB destination pricing**, or "free-on-board" to the shipment's destination. This also means that the supplier will be the legal owner of the product until it safely reaches its destination. For high-value shipments, small shipments, or when the buyer has little transportation expertise, FOB destination pricing is typically preferred.

Otherwise, the buyer may decide to purchase goods and supply its own transportation to the shipping destination; in this case, the supplier quotes the lower **FOB origin pricing.** The goods then become the legal responsibility of the buyer at the supplier's finished goods pickup location.

Rate Categories

Carrier prices or rates can be classified in a number of different ways. **Line haul rates** are the charges for moving goods to a nonlocal destination (e.g., between cities), and these can be further classified as *class rates, exception rates, commodity rates,* and *miscellaneous rates.* In the U.S., **class rates** are published annually by the National Motor Freight Traffic Association (NMFTA), a nonprofit group of motor carrier companies. The class rate standards, called the National Motor Freight Classification (NMFC), are based on an evaluation of four transportation characteristics: density, stowability, handling, and liability. Together, these characteristics establish a shipment's "transportability." There are eighteen classes numbered from 50 to 500—the higher the class rating, the higher the price.[31] **Exception rates** are rates that are lower than the NMFC class rates for specific origin-destination locations or volumes and generally are established on an account-by-account basis. **Commodity rates** apply to minimum quantities of products that are shipped between two specified locations. **Miscellaneous rates** apply to contract rates that are negotiated between two parties and to shipments containing a variety of products (in this case, the rate is based on the overall weight of the shipment). Today, many of the rates carriers charge are classified as miscellaneous, since negotiated rates tend to be used primarily for large shipments.

Transportation Security

Transportation security in the U.S., particularly **airline security**, has become a very important issue since September 11, 2001. Congress passed the Aviation and Transportation Security Act in November 2001, creating a large organization (the Transportation Security Administration, or TSA) to oversee transportation security. Today, the TSA's nearly 50,000 transportation security officers screen more than 1.8 million passengers every day at more than 450 airports nationwide and conduct all of the cargo screening on domestic and international-outbound passenger aircraft.[32] In addition to the TSA, Congress passed the Homeland Security Act in November 2002, creating the Department of Homeland Security (DHS) to further coordinate and unify national homeland security efforts. It includes the TSA along with twenty-one other federal departments and agencies and has 240,000 employees with an annual budget of about $60 billion to provide overall U.S. security leadership.[33]

A number of problems and actions have resulted from this heightened emphasis on transportation security in the U.S. The TSA has had numerous agency chiefs since 9/11 and has spent more than $12 billion to improve security on airplanes and in airports. One of the latest TSA initiatives began in 2010—the placement and use of advanced imaging technology (AIT) body scanning machines in hundreds of U.S. airports. Travelers are required to walk through these full-body scanners, which can identify any harmful devices hidden beneath clothing. The AITs use harmless millimeter wave technology to generate images reflected from the bodies being scanned. Currently, the TSA is spending additional millions to upgrade these AITs to eliminate passenger-specific images.[34] Air cargo transported on passenger aircraft is also subjected to high levels of security checks in the U.S. Today, 100 percent of air cargo must be prescreened, as mandated by the Improving America's Security Act of 2007.

With respect to the other modes of transportation, the TSA has been working with railroads to reduce the number of hours that toxic chemicals can spend in transit, resulting in a 54 percent reduction since 2006 in the overall risk of rail tanker explosions or spills. The TSA also has a Pipeline Security Division, which essentially mandates all pipeline operators to implement a pipeline security program. For many truckers and other transportation workers such as U.S. deepwater port workers, one of the latest transportation security initiatives is the use of the **Transportation Worker Identification Credential (TWIC)**, which was mandated by the Maritime Transportation Security Act of 2002 and the Safe Port Act of 2006. The TWIC became mandatory for all port workers in 2009.[35]

Another type of security initiative is the use of PrePass, offered by the nonprofit organization HELP, which allows prequalified U.S. motor carriers to bypass state inspection and weigh stations at highway speeds, using automated vehicle identification technology. Today, over 450,000 prequalified commercial vehicles can bypass more than 300 inspection facilities using PrePass, allowing inspection personnel to spend more of their time inspecting other vehicles. Additionally, PrePass saves drivers five to eight minutes and a half gallon of fuel per bypass.[36]

Transportation Regulation and Deregulation in the U.S.

The transportation industry in the U.S. has gone through periods of both government regulation and deregulation. On the one hand, **transportation regulation** is argued by many to be good in that it tends to ensure adequate transportation service throughout the country while protecting consumers in terms of monopoly pricing, safety, and liability. On the other hand, **transportation deregulation** is also argued to be good because it encourages competition and allows prices to adjust as supply, demand, and negotiations dictate. In addition, antitrust laws already in place tend to protect transportation consumers. This debate was the subject of a study in 1994 to determine the impact deregulation had on the U.S. motor carrier industry. The study concluded that transportation deregulation has resulted in greater use of cost-of-service pricing, rising freight rates for LTL shipments, and more safety problems, as operators tended to let fleets age and reduce maintenance levels.[37] Today, the U.S. transportation industry remains essentially deregulated; however, a number of regulations (primarily safety and security regulations) still exist and continue to be revised. Over the past few years, as financial losses mounted and consolidations occurred particularly in the airline industry, new calls for entire industry reregulation have also emerged. Some of the history of transportation regulation and deregulation in the U.S. is reviewed next.

Transportation Regulation

Table 9.2 summarizes the major transportation regulations in the U.S., starting with the Granger Laws of the 1870s, which led to the Interstate Commerce Act of 1887. Before this time, the railroads in the U.S. were charging high rates and discriminating against small shippers. So a number of Midwestern states passed laws to broadly regulate the railroads to establish maximum rates, prohibit local discrimination, forbid rail mergers (to encourage competition), and prohibit free passes to public officials. Though the U.S. Supreme Court later struck down these laws, the Granger movement made Congress realize the impacts of railroad monopolies. This led to the passage of the Interstate Commerce Act of 1887.

The 1887 act created the Interstate Commerce Commission (ICC), which required rail carriers to charge and publish reasonable rates, file them with the ICC, and make them available to the public and which prohibited discriminatory practices (charging some

Table 9.2 U.S. Transportation Regulation

DATE	REGULATION	SUMMARY
1870s	Granger Laws	Midwestern states passed laws to establish maximum rates, prohibit discrimination, and forbid mergers for railroads (RRs).
1887	Interstate Commerce Act	States cannot regulate transportation; established Interstate Commerce Commission (ICC); regulated and published rates, outlawed discriminatory pricing, prohibited pooling agreements.
1920	Transportation Act	Instructed the ICC to establish rates that allowed RRs to earn a fair return; established minimum rates; allowed ICC to set intrastate rates; allowed pooling agreements if they were in the public's best interest.
1935	Motor Carrier Act	Extended the ICA of 1887 to include motor carriers and brought them under ICC control; established five classes of operators: common, contract, private, exempt, and broker; mergers must be OK'd by ICC.
1938	Civil Aeronautics Act	Established the Civil Aeronautics Board (CAB) to regulate air carriers; new entrants had to get CAB approval; CAB controlled rates; Civil Aeronautics Administration controlled air safety.
1940	Transportation Act	Extended the ICA of 1887 to include ICC control over domestic water transportation; ICC controlled entry, rates, and services.
1942	Freight Forwarders Act	Extended the ICA of 1887 to include ICC control over freight forwarders; ICC controlled entry, rates, and services.
1948	Reed-Bulwinkle Act	Amendment to the ICA of 1887 legalizing rate bureaus or conferences.
1958	Transportation Act	Amended the rule of rate making by stating that rates couldn't be held up to protect the traffic of any other mode.
1958	Federal Aviation Act	Created the Federal Aviation Agency to assume the mission of the CAA; FAA empowered to manage and develop U.S. airspace and plan the U.S. airport system.
1966	Dept. of Transportation Act	Assumed mission of FAA and a number of other agencies for research, promotion, safety, and administration of transportation; organized into nine operating and six administrative divisions; also established the National Transportation Safety Board.
1970	Railway Passenger Service Act	Created the National Railroad Passenger Corp. to preserve and upgrade intercity rail passenger service; resulted in the creation of Amtrak.
1975	Hazardous Materials Transportation Act	Strengthened laws to fight illegal dumping. Created a cradle-to-grave responsibility for hazardous materials. Established minimum standards for transport by all modes. Regulated by DOT.

shippers less than others for the same service). The act also prohibited agreements between railroads to pool traffic or revenues. Between 1887 and 1910, a number of amendments made to the 1887 act increased the ICC's control and enforcement power. These amendments restricted railroads from providing rates and services that were not in the public's best interest, created penalties for failure to follow published rates or for offering and accepting rebates, set maximum rates, and prevented railroads from owning pipelines or water carriers, unless approved by the ICC.

By 1917, increased competition combined with the rate restrictions had created a rail system unable to offer the efficient service the U.S. government needed in its war efforts, and thus the federal government seized the railroads. Railroad companies were guaranteed a profit while the government poured large sums of money into upgrading the rail system. By the end of World War I, Congress had come to realize that all of the negative controls placed on railroads were unhealthy for the industry. They wanted to return the railroads to private ownership. This brought about the first of a number of regulations aimed at positive control, namely the **Transportation Act of 1920**.

The 1920 act instructed the ICC to ensure that rates were high enough to provide a fair return for the railroads each year (Congress initially set this at 6 percent return per year). When companies made more than the prescribed 6 percent, half of the excess was taken and used to fund low-interest loans to the weaker operators for updating their systems and increasing efficiency. The act also allowed the ICC to set minimum rates, allowed joint use of terminal facilities, allowed railroads to enter into pooling agreements, and allowed rail company acquisitions and consolidations. Finally, to keep the railroads from becoming overcapitalized, the act prohibited railroads from issuing securities without ICC approval. The rail system thus became a regulated monopoly.

From 1935 to 1942, regulations were passed that applied to other modes of transportation and these were similar in nature to the 1920 act. A great deal of money was spent during the 1920s and during the Depression building the U.S. highway system. The time became ripe, then, for the emergence of for-hire motor carriers. The number of small trucking companies grew tremendously during this period, creating competition for the railroads, as shippers opted to use the cheaper for-hire motor carriers. The **Motor Carrier Act of 1935** brought motor carriers under ICC control, thus controlling entry into the market, establishing motor carrier classes of operation, setting reasonable rates, mandating ICC approval for any mergers or acquisitions, and controlling the issuance of securities.

In 1938, the federal government enacted another extension of the Interstate Commerce Act by including regulation of air carriers in the **Civil Aeronautics Act of 1938**. This act promoted the development of the air transportation system and the air safety and airline efficiency by establishing the Civil Aeronautics Board to oversee market entry, establish routes with appropriate levels of competition, develop regional feeder airlines, and set reasonable rates. The Civil Aeronautics Administration was also established to regulate air safety.

The **Transportation Act of 1940** further extended the Interstate Commerce Act of 1887 by establishing ICC control over domestic water transportation. The provisions for domestic water carriers were similar to those imposed on rail and motor carriers. In 1942, the 1887 act was once again extended to cover freight forwarders, with the usual entry, rate, and service controls of the ICC. Freight forwarders were also prohibited from owning any carriers.

A number of other congressional enactments occurred up through 1970, further strengthening and refining the control of the transportation market. In 1948, the **Reed-Bulwinkle Act** gave groups of carriers the ability to form rate bureaus or conferences wherein they could propose rate changes to the ICC. The **Transportation Act of 1958** established temporary loan guarantees to railroads, liberalized control over intrastate rail rates, amended the rule of rate-making to ensure more intermodal competition, and clarified the differences between private and for-hire motor carriers. The **Federal Aviation Act of 1958** replaced the Civil Aeronautics Administration with the Federal Aviation Administration (FAA) and gave the FAA authority to prescribe air traffic rules, make safety regulations, and plan the national airport system. In 1966, the **Department of Transportation Act** created the Department of Transportation (DOT) to coordinate the executive functions of all government entities dealing with transportation-related matters. It was hoped that centralized coordination of all the transportation agencies would lead to more effective transportation promotion and planning. Finally, to preserve and improve the rail system's ability to service passengers, the **Railway Passenger Service Act** was passed in 1970, thus creating Amtrak.

As discussed earlier, there have been a number of transportation regulations dealing with safety and security, and only the 1975 Hazardous Materials Transportation Act is shown in Table 9.2. Prior to this time, many landfills began refusing to accept hazardous waste, which created a rash of midnight dumping activities along roadways and in vacant lots. Poor coordination and lack of personnel created poor enforcement of existing laws. This law established minimum standards of regulation for transportation of hazardous materials, administered by the DOT. All hazardous waste transporters were forced to register with the proper state and federal agencies, must track all pick-ups and deliveries, and must cleanup any spills during transport.

Transportation Deregulation

Commencing in 1976, Congress enacted a number of laws to reduce and eliminate many transportation regulations. These are summarized in Table 9.3. This began the movement toward less economic regulation by allowing market forces to determine prices, entry, and services. At this point in U.S. transportation history, consumers and politicians had the opinion that transportation economic regulations were administered more for the benefit of the carriers than the public. In addition, with the bankruptcy filings of a number of railroads in the mid-1970s combined with the Arab oil embargo of the same time period, regulation was receiving much of the blame for an inefficient transportation system.

The **Railroad Revitalization and Regulatory Reform Act**, commonly known as the 4-R Act, was passed in 1976 and made several regulatory changes to help the railroads. First, railroads were allowed to change rates without ICC approval, limited by *threshold costs* on one end and *market dominance* on the other. Threshold costs were defined as the firm's variable costs and the ICC determined whether the firm was in a market dominant position (absence of market competition). A number of ICC procedures were also sped up to aid transportation manager decision making. These same ideas appeared again in later deregulation efforts.

Air freight was deregulated in 1977. No longer were there any barriers to entry provided the firms were deemed fit by the Civil Aeronautics Board. Size restrictions were also lifted and carriers were free to charge any rate provided there was no discrimination. Finally, carriers did not have to file freight rates with the CAB. This was followed soon after by deregulation of air passenger service in 1978. The targeted beneficiary of passenger

Table 9.3 U.S. Transportation Deregulation

DATE	DEREGULATION	SUMMARY
1976	Railroad Revitalization and Regulatory Reform Act	The "4-R Act." Railroads were allowed to change rates without ICC approval, within limits; ICC procedures were sped up.
1977	Air Cargo Deregulation Act	Freed all air cargo carriers from CAB regulations.
1978	Air Passenger Deregulation Act	Airlines freed to expand routes, change fares within limits; small community routes were subsidized; CAB ceases to exist in 1985.
1980	Motor Carrier Act	Fewer restrictions on entry, routes, rates, and private carriers.
1980	Staggers Rail Act	Freed railroads to further establish rates within limits; legalized contract rates; shortened ICC procedure turnaround.
1982	Bus Regulatory Reform Act	Amended the 1980 MCA to include buses.
1984	Shipping Act	Partial deregulation of ocean transportation.
1994	Trucking Industry Regulatory Reform Act	Motor carriers freed from filing rates with the ICC.
1994	FAA Authorization Act	Freed intermodal air carriers from economic regulation by the states.
1995	ICC Termination Act	Eliminated the ICC and moved regulatory duties to Dept. of Transportation.
1998	Ocean Shipping Reform Act	Deregulated ocean liner shipping; allowed contract shipping; rate filing not required.

airline deregulation was the traveler. In introducing the bill to the Senate floor, Senator Ted Kennedy, one of the bill's principal sponsors, proclaimed, "This bill, while preserving the government's authority to regulate health and safety, frees airlines to do what business is supposed to do—serve consumers better for less." This was a phased-in approach, wherein carriers could slowly add routes to their systems while protecting other routes from competition. Fares could be adjusted within limits without CAB approval. To protect small communities from losing service, all cities with service in 1977 were guaranteed service for ten additional years. In 1981, all route restrictions were to be released, allowing any carrier to operate any route. Airline rates and mergers were to be released from regulation in 1983. Finally, the CAB was to shut down in 1985.

The impacts of deregulation on the U.S. airline industry were enormous—there were thirty-four air passenger carriers in 1977, and only five years later the number had increased to ninety. Some fares dropped substantially, while other fares went up, and routes to low-demand areas decreased substantially. By 1981, among the major U.S. airlines, only American, Delta, and TWA were making a profit. A number of notable airline failures also occurred in the years following deregulation. Braniff, for instance, after deregulation expanded rapidly in the U.S. and abroad, purchased a large number of planes, loaded up on debt, and then declared bankruptcy in 1982. They emerged from bankruptcy as a smaller airline; then seven years later declared bankruptcy again, after failing to obtain financing. A short time later, Braniff ceased operations completely. People Express, a new low-fare, no-frills airline that began right after deregulation, followed the Braniff large-expansion-high-debt model, and similarly had trouble operating by 1986, eventually selling out to rival Texas Air, which itself filed for bankruptcy in 1990. In all, some 150 airlines came and went during this period.[38]

Motor carriers were deregulated in 1980. The objectives of this act were to promote competitive as well as safe and efficient motor transportation. Entry regulations were relaxed to make it easier to enter the market—firms had only to show a "useful public purpose" would be served. Route restrictions were removed and restrictions deemed to be wasteful of fuel, inefficient, or contrary to public interest were also removed. And, as with air passenger deregulation, a large number of new motor carriers began service. By 1981, more than 2,400 new motor carrier companies had started up in the U.S. Unfortunately, by 1990, 11,490 of these companies had declared bankruptcy. This was more than the number of motor carrier bankruptcies in the forty-five years leading up to deregulation in 1980.[39]

Railroads were further deregulated with the **Staggers Rail Act of 1980**. The financial condition of railroads was worsening and this act was aimed at improving finances for the rail industry. With this act, rail carriers were free to change rates within a zone of rate freedom, but the ceiling or market dominance rate was established more definitively as 160 percent of variable costs and varied up to 180 percent depending on ICC cost formulas. After 1984, rate increases were to be tied to the rate of inflation. Contract rates were also allowed between railroads and shippers.

The **Shipping Act of 1984** marked the end of the initial push by Congress to deregulate the entire U.S. transportation industry. This act allowed ocean carriers to pool or share shipments, assign ports, publish rates, and enter into contracts with shippers. More recently, with the passage of the **ICC Termination Act of 1995** and the **Ocean Shipping Reform Act of 1998**, the Interstate Commerce Commission was eliminated and the requirement for ocean carriers to file rates with the Federal Maritime Commission also came to an end.

Thus, a number of changes in the U.S. transportation industry over the past century have occurred. Economic regulation of transportation occurred for several reasons. Initial transportation regulations were instituted to *establish the ground rules* as new forms of transportation developed and to *control prices, services, and routes* when monopoly power existed in the industry. Later, deregulation was used to *encourage competition* and *increase efficiency and safety*. Arguments remain as to the success and need for both transportation regulation and deregulation. In the future, as economic conditions change and as technology, political, and social changes occur, transportation regulations will also continue to change.

WAREHOUSING AND DISTRIBUTION

Warehouses provide very strategic supply chain services—they enable firms to store their purchases, work-in-progress, and finished goods, as well as perform breakbulk and assembly activities, while allowing faster and more frequent deliveries of finished products to customers, which in turn can result in better customer service. Today, companies view warehouses as a competitive resource. Amazon.com, for example, has dramatically expanded its warehouse network over the years to compete better and to offer same-day service in some areas. They have also entered into other logistics areas to enhance revenues as described in the nearby SCM Profile.

As disposable income increases, consumers buy more goods that must move through various distribution systems. In fast growing economies like India and China, this means the demand for warehouses is growing rapidly. In the U.S. as well, the number of warehouses

SCM Profile

Amazon: The New FedEx?

In the near future, Amazon.com's main competitors will likely be logistics companies like UPS and FedEx. Amazon garners billions a year in revenue from selling e-books and household items. Retailing, though, can be a difficult low-margin business.

As a result, Amazon has invested heavily in its back-end systems to cut operational costs. It even leverages these capabilities for revenue. It recently bought Kiva Systems, which makes robots for warehouses. Its cloud services emerged because it had excess capacity on its computer networks. Amazon also provides logistics services for third-party retailers that use its site as an electronic mall. But that is where a potential conflict comes in. Companies usually can adopt one of two strategies: sell products to consumers or sell products to other businesses and let them beat each other up trying to reach consumers.

Over the years, FedEx has lost a bit of its glow. Now, most people think of FedEx as simply the place they run to at 4:57 p.m. And Amazon has expertise in computing systems and artificial intelligence that exceeds what others in logistics likely cannot match. By positioning itself as the store behind a store, Amazon can function almost like a hyperspecialized IBM.

At first glance, Amazon competing with FedEx might seem like a stretch. Right now, FedEx is one of Amazon's primary delivery companies. One is a retailer with big warehouses, and the other is a big shipping company with similarly big warehouses. But if you think of both moving into logistics, the science of getting box A to destination B more efficiently, it makes more sense. Amazon has started to test market pick-up stations where customers can get packages delivered. FedEx, meanwhile, has inched steadily into higher-value delivery services like healthcare distribution and export consulting. It will be interesting to see how it all shakes out.[40]

is growing, and they are becoming larger too. Five years ago in the U.S., the average commercial warehouse size was approximately 250,000 square feet. Today, 400,000-square-foot warehouses are becoming more prevalent (that is almost five soccer fields).[41] Walmart is a good example—in 2013, Walmart operated over forty regional distribution centers in the U.S. with an average size exceeding 1 million square feet, with 35 feet of stacking height.[42]

In many cases today, warehouses are not used to store things, but rather to receive bulk shipments, break them down, repackage various items into outgoing orders, and then distribute these orders to a manufacturing location or retail center. These activities are collectively referred to as **crossdocking**. In this case, the warehouse is more accurately described as a **distribution center**. In other cases, firms are moving warehouses closer to suppliers, closer to customers, or to more centralized locations, depending on the storage objectives and customer service requirements. So, warehouses are still very much in use—some just to store things and others to provide efficient throughput of goods. This section discusses a number of warehousing issues including their importance and the types of warehouses, risk pooling and warehouse location, and lean warehousing.

The Importance and Types of Warehouses

Firms hold inventories for a number of reasons as explained in Chapter 6—warehouses are used to support purchasing, production, and distribution activities. Firms order raw materials, parts, and assemblies, which are typically shipped to a warehouse location close to or inside the buyer's location, and then eventually transferred to the buyer's various operations as needed. In a retail setting, a warehouse might be regionally located, with the retailer receiving bulk shipments at the warehouse from many suppliers, then breaking these down and reassembling outgoing orders for delivery to each retail location, while using a private fleet of trucks or for-hire transportation providers to move the orders to the retail locations. Similar distribution centers are used when manufacturers deliver bulk shipments to regional market areas and then break these down and ship LTL order quantities to customers.

Firms might operate **consolidation warehouses** to collect large numbers of LTL shipments from nearby regional sources of supply, and then consolidate and transport in TL or CL quantities to a manufacturing or user facility located at some distance from the consolidation warehouse. The use of consolidation warehouses and distribution centers allows firms to realize both purchase economies and transportation economies. Firms can buy goods in bulk at lower unit costs and then ship these goods at TL or CL rates either to a distribution center or directly to a manufacturing center. They can also purchase and move small quantity purchases at LTL rates to nearby consolidation warehouses.

Private Warehouses

Just as with the private forms of transportation, **private warehouses** refer to warehouses that are privately owned and used by an organization. For firms with large volumes of goods to store or transfer, private warehouses represent an opportunity to reduce the costs of warehousing as well as control the levels of service provided to customers. Currently, one of the largest e-commerce companies, the Alibaba Group, is building a network of private warehouses across China at a cost of $3 to $4.5 billion, to elevate its level of customer service and to meet rapidly growing demand.[43] Firms are free to decide what to store, what to process, what types of security to provide, and the types of equipment to use, among other operational aspects. Private warehousing can also enable the firm to better utilize its workforce and expertise in terms of transportation, warehousing, and distribution center activities. Also, as supply chains become more global to take advantage of cheaper sources of supply or labor, the use of private warehouses tends to increase. Finally, private warehouses can generate income and tax advantages through leasing of excess capacity and/or asset depreciation. For these reasons, private warehousing accounts for the vast majority of overall warehouse space in the U.S.[44]

Private warehouses can be truly massive. Several of the largest private warehouses include Target's import warehouse in Lacey, Washington. This gargantuan 2,000,000 square feet facility (about the size of forty U.S. football fields) was built to distribute imported products to regional Target warehouses. Constellation Europe, a liquor wholesaler, has a private warehouse in Bristol, England totaling just under 1,000,000 square feet. It can house up to 57 million bottles of wine at one time. Finally, the U.S. Army's Camp Carroll warehouse in South Korea is about 350,000 square feet and is used to store military vehicles and other defense equipment.[45]

Owning warehouses, though, can also represent a significant financial risk and loss of flexibility to the firm. The costs to build, equip, and then operate a warehouse can be very high and most small- to moderate-sized firms simply cannot afford private warehouses. Private warehouses also bind firms to locations that may not prove optimal as time passes. Warehouse size or capacity is also somewhat inflexible, at least in the short term. Another problem can be insurance. Insurance companies, in many cases, do not like insuring goods in private warehouses, simply because security levels can be meager or nonexistent, creating a significant concern regarding fires or thefts of goods. Storing fine art in private warehouses is one such example. "We have all this exposure at the private warehouses, where we might have half a billion or $800 million of art, but we know nothing about how they're operated and how they're secured," says Thomas Burns, vice president at fine art insurer Fortress Corp.[46]

Public Warehouses

As the name implies, **public warehouses** are for-profit organizations that contract or lease a wide range of light manufacturing, warehousing, and distribution services to other companies. Public warehouses provide a number of specialized services that firms can use to create customized services for various shipments and goods. These services include the following:

- *Breakbulk*—large-quantity shipments are broken down so that items can be combined into specific customer orders and then shipped out.
- *Repackaging*—after breakbulk, items are repackaged for specific customer orders. Warehouses can also do individual product packaging and labeling.
- *Assembly*—some public warehouses provide final assembly operations to satisfy customer requests and to create customized final products.
- *Quality inspections*—warehouse personnel can perform incoming and outgoing quality inspections.
- *Material handling, equipment maintenance, and documentation services.*
- *Short- and long-term storage.*

Besides the services shown here, public warehouses provide the short-term flexibility and investment cost savings that private warehouses cannot offer. If a firm's demand changes or its products change, the short-term commitments required at public warehouses allow the firm to quickly change warehouse locations. Public warehouses allow firms to test market areas and withdraw quickly if demand does not materialize as expected. The cost for firms to use a public warehouse can also be very small if their capacity requirements are minimal.

One of the latest demands for public warehousing involves the growing global market for pharmaceuticals. Pharmaceutical companies utilize so-called third-party **cold chains** to ensure their product reaches buyers in good shape. Cold chains refer to temperature-controlled transportation, transfers, and warehousing. The World Health Organization, for example, estimates that about half of all vaccines are wasted due to poor cold chain control. Currently, about half of the best selling drugs require cold chains.[47] BNSF is the only major railroad that is responding to the demand for temperature-controlled shipments. Since 2005, BNSF has experienced a double-digit growth rate in the demand for temperature-controlled intermodal shipping. BNSF boasts a door-to-door, on-time consistency of 97 percent, and delivery speeds that are 20 percent faster than the next leading intermodal provider, according to the Association of American Railroads.[48]

One of the main disadvantages associated with public warehouses is the lack of control provided to the goods owners. Other problems include lack of communication with warehouse personnel, lack of specialized services or capacity at the desired locations, and the lack of care and security that might be given to products.

Firms might find it advantageous to use public warehouses in some locations and private warehouses in others. For large, established markets and relatively mature products, large firms may decide that owning and operating a warehouse makes the most sense, whereas the same firm may lease space and pay for services at public warehouses in developing markets and low-demand areas.

Risk Pooling and Warehouse Location

One of the more important decisions regarding private warehouses is where to locate them. The location decision affects the number of warehouses needed, required capacities, system inventory levels, customer service levels, and warehousing system costs. For a given market area, as the number of warehouses used increases, the system becomes more *decentralized*. In a **decentralized warehousing system**, responsiveness and delivery service levels will increase since goods can be delivered more quickly to customers; however, warehousing system operating and inventory costs will also increase. Other costs that come into play here are outgoing transportation costs to customers and the transportation costs associated with the incoming deliveries of goods to each warehouse. Thus, the trade-off between costs and customer service must be carefully considered as the firm makes its warehouse location decisions. In a **centralized warehousing system**, fewer warehouses means that outbound transportation costs will be higher. This brings up the very important topic of **risk pooling**, which is discussed below.

Risk Pooling

Risk pooling describes the relationship between the number of warehouses, system inventories, and customer service, and it can be explained as follows:

> When market demand is random, it is very likely that higher-than-average demand from some customers will be offset by lower-than-average demand from other customers. As the number of customers served by a single warehouse increases, these demand variabilities will tend to offset each other more often, thus reducing overall demand variance and the likelihood of stockouts. Consequently, the amount of safety stock in a warehouse system required to guard against stockouts decreases. Thus, the more *centralized* a warehousing system is, the *lower the safety stock* required to achieve a given system-wide customer service level (recall that in inventory parlance the customer service level is inversely proportional to the number of stockouts per period).

As mentioned above, risk pooling assumes that demand at the markets served by a warehouse system is negatively correlated (higher-than-average demand in one market area tends to be offset by lower-than-average demand in another market area). In smaller market areas served by warehouses, this may not hold true, and warehouses would then require higher levels of safety stock. This is why a smaller number of centralized warehouses serving large market areas require lower overall system inventories, compared to a larger number of decentralized warehouses serving the same markets.

A good illustration of this principle occurred in Europe after the formation of the European Union in 1993. Prior to that time, European logistics systems were formed along national lines. In other words, each country's distribution systems operated independently of the others, with warehouses located in each country. With the arrival of a single European market in 1993, these distribution systems no longer made economic sense. For example, Becton Dickinson, an American manufacturer of diagnostics equipment, was burdened in Europe in the early 1990s with just this type of country-specific and costly distribution system. After the formation of the European Union, the company closed its distribution centers in Sweden, France, Germany, and Belgium and shifted all of its distribution operations to a single automated center in Belgium. In less than a year, average stock levels were down 45 percent, write-offs fell by 65 percent, and stockouts were reduced by 75 percent. Other companies in Europe had similar results.[49]

The effect of risk pooling can be estimated numerically by the **square root rule**, which suggests that the system average inventory (as impacted by changing the number of warehouses in the system) is equal to the original system inventory times the ratio of the square root of the new number of warehouses to the square root of the original number of warehouses.[50] A simple illustration of risk pooling is shown in Example 9.1. In the example, reducing the number of warehouses from two to one causes a reduction in average inventory of approximately 29 percent.

The differences between centralized and decentralized warehousing systems can be summarized as follows:

- *Safety stock and average system inventory*—as the firm moves toward fewer warehouses and a more centralized warehousing system, safety stocks and thus average inventory levels across the system are decreased. The magnitude of the reduction depends on the demand correlations in the various market areas.
- *Responsiveness*—as warehouse centralization increases, delivery lead times increase, increasing the risk of late deliveries to customers and reducing the ability of the organization to respond quickly to changes in demand. Customer service levels may thus be impacted because of issues such as traffic problems and weather delays.
- *Customer service to the warehouse*—as centralization increases, customer service levels provided by the warehouses' suppliers are likely to increase, reducing the likelihood of stockouts for a given level of average system warehouse inventory.
- *Transportation costs*—as centralization increases, outbound transportation costs increase, as LTL shipments must travel farther to reach customers. Inbound transportation costs decrease, since manufacturers and other suppliers are able to ship larger quantities at TL rates to fewer warehouse locations. The overall impact on transportation costs thus depends on the specific warehouse locations, the goods stored, the locations of suppliers, and the modes of transportation used.
- *Warehouse system capital and operating costs*—as centralization increases, warehouse capital and operating costs decrease because there are fewer warehouses, fewer employees, less equipment, and less maintenance costs.

Example 9.1 Risk Pooling at Perkins Boots

Perkins Western Boot Emporium currently owns two warehouses in Houston and Seattle to store its boots before shipping them out to various retail customers across the western U.S. Greg Perkins, the owner, is considering a change to one centralized warehouse in Denver to service all of their retail customers, and is curious to know the impact this will have on their system inventory requirements. Their current average inventory level is approximately 6,000 boots at each warehouse. He has found that this level of stock will result in warehouse stockouts approximately one percent of the time. Using the square root rule, he calculates the new average inventory level needed at the central Denver warehouse to maintain the same low level of stockouts:

$$S_2 = \frac{\sqrt{N_2}}{\sqrt{N_1}}(S_1) = \frac{1.0}{1.41}(12{,}000) = 8{,}511 \text{ boots},$$

where

S_1 = total system stock of boots for the N_1 warehouses;
S_2 = total system stock of boots for the N_2 warehouses;
N_1 = number of warehouses in the original system; and
N_2 = number of warehouses in the proposed system.

His total system inventory is thus reduced from 12,000 to 8,511, or by:

$$\% \text{ reduction} = \frac{(12{,}000 - 8{,}511)}{12{,}000} = 0.291 = 29.1\%$$

Warehouse Location

A number of location models and theories have been proposed over the years to optimally locate factories, services, and warehouses. In Chapter 11, a number of location analysis tools are discussed, and these can certainly be useful for locating warehouses. Early in the development of modern transportation and warehousing networks, several well-known economists posited theories regarding warehouse locations that are discussed in this section.

German economist Johann Heinrich von Thünen, who is often regarded as the "father of location theory," argued in the 1820s that transportation costs alone should be minimized when considering facility locations.[51] His model assumed that market prices and manufacturing costs would be identical regardless of the location of the warehouse, so the optimum location would be the one that resulted in the minimum transportation costs. Another German economist a century later, Alfred Weber, proposed an industrial location theory very similar to von Thünen's; he argued that the optimum location would be found when the sum of the inbound and outbound transportation costs was minimized.[52]

In the 1940s, Edgar Hoover recommended three types of location strategies: the market positioned, product positioned, and intermediately positioned strategies.[53] The **market positioned strategy** locates warehouses close to customers, to maximize customer service levels. This strategy is recommended when there are high levels of distribution flexibility and customer service. The **product positioned strategy** locates warehouses close to the sources of supply to enable the firm to collect various goods while minimizing inbound transportation costs. This strategy works well when there are large numbers of goods purchased from many sources of supply and assortments of goods ordered by customers. The **intermediately positioned strategy** places warehouses midway between the sources of supply and the customers. This strategy is recommended when distribution service requirements are relatively high and customers order product assortments purchased from many suppliers.

In the 1950s, Melvin Greenhut's location theory was based on profit instead of transportation costs.[54] He argued that the optimum location would be the one that maximized profits, which may not coincide with the minimum cost location, because demand and prices can potentially vary based on location.

Several location heuristics have been developed based on transportation costs, one of which is the center-of-gravity approach, discussed in Chapter 11. The weakness of this approach, as well as some of those discussed here, is that they fail to consider a number of other factors such as labor availability, labor rates, land cost, building codes, tax structure, construction costs, utility costs, and the local environment. Additionally, if a firm is using a public warehouse, the location selection criteria would need to include warehouse services, lease costs, communication capabilities, reporting frequency, and the operator's reputation. These factors may best be addressed using a weighted factor location analysis, also discussed in Chapter 11.

Lean Warehousing

As firms develop their supply chain management capabilities, items will be moving more quickly through inbound and outbound warehouses and distribution centers. These warehouses and distribution centers will thus have to develop leaner capabilities. Some examples of these capabilities include the following:

- *Greater emphasis on crossdocking*—warehouse employees must receive shipments and mix these quickly into outgoing shipments. Far fewer goods will be stored for any appreciable time and average warehouse inventory levels will decrease, while the number of stockkeeping units will increase.
- *Reduced lot sizes and shipping quantities*—inbound and/or outbound shipping quantities are likely to be smaller and more frequent, containing mixed quantities of goods and thus requiring more handling.
- *A commitment to customers and service quality*—warehouse employees must perform warehouse activities so as to meet the requirements of their inbound and outbound suppliers and customers.
- *Increased automation*—to improve handling speed and reliability, more warehouse activities will become automated, from scanner/barcode computer tracking systems, to warehouse management software applications, to automated storage and retrieval systems.
- *Increased assembly operations*—as more firms implement lean systems and mass customization, warehouses will be called upon to perform final assembly operations to meet specific customer requirements. This will change the skill requirements of warehouse employees, along with equipment requirements.
- *A tendency to be green*—since lean operations, by their nature, tend to produce less waste, a natural byproduct of lean warehousing is green warehousing.

Most distribution centers have adopted many **lean warehousing** concepts. Indiana-based Prime Distribution Services (PDS) offers distribution services to suppliers in club-store grocery supply chains. They offer warehousing, crossdocking, packaging, and freight consolidation to suppliers who are looking to increase speed and reduce costs as much as possible to compete in the extremely low-profit-margin grocery industry. Consequently, PDS distribution capabilities have had to evolve to survive. They combined several distribution centers into one 1.2 million square feet, heavily automated facility that provided greater control over inventory, more responsive order management, and easier building of mixed SKU pallets. They have a state-of-the-art warehouse management system to manage picking operations, and automated barcode scanning, sorting, and routing capabilities to divert orders to packing stations. "Our leadership and our organization are geared toward a lean warehousing operation," says Scott

Zurawski, director of PDS warehouse operations. "We're trying to build sustainability and quality into every process."[55] Pennsylvania-based manufacturer Crown Holdings changed its layout to eliminate the need to transport items between facilities, saving over 20,000 transportation miles, 27 tons of greenhouse gases, and many hours of labor time annually.[56]

THE IMPACTS OF LOGISTICS ON SUPPLY CHAIN MANAGEMENT

As mentioned in this chapter's introduction, logistics refers to the movement and storage of products from point of origin to point of consumption within the firm and throughout the supply chain and is thus responsible for creating time utility and place utility. In a managed supply chain setting, these logistics elements are extremely important in that products must be routinely delivered to each supply chain customer on time, to the correct location, at the desired level of quality, and at a reasonable cost. As mistakes occur in deliveries along the supply chain, more safety stocks must be held, impacting both customer service levels and costs. To make up for lost time, overnight deliveries might also have to be used, adding yet more costs to the transportation bill.

For global supply chains, the logistics function is even more critical. Providing adequate transportation and storage, getting items through customs, delivering to foreign locations in a timely fashion, and logistics pricing can all impact the ability of a supply chain to serve a foreign market competitively. In many cases, firms are forced to use outside agents or **third-party logistics services (3PLs)** to move items into foreign locations effectively.

Purchases from foreign suppliers are also similarly affected by logistics considerations. When firms begin evaluating and using foreign suppliers, logistics costs and timing become critical factors in the sourcing decision. For instance, Chinese suppliers delivering goods to buyers along the U.S. East Coast are in many cases favoring an all-water route through the Panama Canal, rather than dealing with port and traffic congestion on the U.S. West Coast, followed by trucking and rail transportation within the U.S. Buyers get cheaper freight rates and can plan on shipments arriving at a specific time when using an all-water route, whereas the chances of domestic U.S. shipments being held up because of port and traffic congestion and missed rail connections can be significant. All-water shipments have risen significantly since the early 1990s.[57] Containerized cargo numbers are up in every eastern U.S. port. Primarily, the growth has been the result of increased growth in global trade in general and an increase specifically in Asia–Pacific trade. The Port of Virginia, for example, has over fifty distribution centers and has seen its business increase as retailers have goods shipped to the port and then transported to East Coast distribution centers.[58]

Thus, the value created for supply chains by logistics can readily be seen. It is what effectively links each supply chain partner. Poor logistics management can literally bring a supply chain to its knees, regardless of the production cost or quality of the products. Alternatively, good logistics management can be one of the elements creating a competitive advantage for supply chains. A number of these topics are explored further in this section.

Third-Party Logistics (3PL) Services

Most logistics service companies offer both transportation and warehousing services, allowing firms to make better use of distribution alternatives such as transportation mode, storage location, and customs clearance. Some 3PLs provide complete end-to-end supply chain management services, including network optimization, light manufacturing, and other value-added services. In the U.S., two recent trends impacting 3PLs are the near-shoring of manufacturing and the development of oil and gas production in the North

Dakota Bakken Formation. Companies with the flexibility to offer logistics services in these areas are taking advantage of the increased service demand. Large 3PLs such as Con-way Multimodal and BNSF Logistics have developed significant Mexico–U.S. cross border capabilities in recent years to deal with the near-shoring trend and are working with producers in North Dakota to offer the logistics services needed there.[59]

For small firms with no internal logistics expertise and large firms with many sizeable and varied logistics needs, outsourcing logistics requirements to 3PLs can help firms get the services they require at reasonable prices. Many firms outsource some or all of their logistics needs to allow more attention to be placed on core competencies. In tough economic times, firms used 3PLs to help reduce costs while maintaining customer service levels. In 2009, 80 percent of U.S. companies used a 3PL for at least one area of their supply chains. In Europe, about 66 percent of every logistics euro spent was on outsourcing.[60] Today, use of 3PLs continues to grow, as companies respond to changing global markets, market uncertainties, and security issues. Logistics consulting firm Tompkins International projects 3PL growth in the U.S. to be three to four times the GDP growth.[61] Whatever the reason, demand for 3PL services is growing rapidly.

Studies performed by the Georgia Institute of Technology indicate a clear advantage gained by outsourcing logistics functions to 3PLs. One of their studies found that companies using 3PLs realized a 13 percent logistics cost savings. Supply chain management professor C. John Langley at the Georgia Institute of Technology argues that firms should increase the number of services outsourced to 3PLs. "Shippers want to outsource activities that are more routine and repetitive rather than customer-focused. As long as this continues, shippers are not exploiting the full range of services they can benefit from," he says.

Outsourcing End-to-End Supply Chain Management Activities

In some cases, firms may opt to partner with a 3PL for the provision of most or all supply chain management activities. For small firms, it may be a question of lack of expertise. The sheer scale of supply chain activities and cost may also attract very large firms that prefer to free up valuable resources for other activities. For example, global automaker General Motors formed a joint venture with CNF, Inc. (now renamed Con-way Inc. and based in California) to manage the automaker's entire supply chain, specifically all of GM's existing third-party logistics providers for both inbound and outbound movements over a three-year transition period. The joint venture company, Vector SCM, termed a **lead logistics provider** or **fourth-party logistics provider (4PL)**, managed all of GM's worldwide 3PL providers.[62] Vector also assumed responsibility for managing some 180 million pounds of materials from GM's 12,000 worldwide suppliers every day. (Later, as GM reorganized, it bought control of Vector from Con-way).[63]

3PL Supply Base Reduction

As discussed in Chapter 4 of this text, reducing the supply base can provide a number of advantages for the organization. With 3PL suppliers, the discussion is very similar—using fewer 3PLs enables the firm to select and use only the best-performing 3PLs as well as to give these 3PLs a bigger share of the firm's logistics needs. This, in turn, results in better levels of service and potentially cheaper prices. The larger share of business given to each 3PL can be used as leverage when negotiating prices, shipping schedules, and services. By the end of 2005, for instance, Hewlett-Packard had halved the number of 3PLs it was using and continued to reduce this number even further. Other companies are similarly seeking to achieve an "irreducible minimum" number of 3PL suppliers.[64] Thus, 3PL supply base reduction should become an integral part of an effective logistics management strategy particularly in markets characterized by numerous 3PL choices.

Mode and 3PL Selection

To minimize logistics costs while meeting customer service requirements, firms identify the most desirable transportation modes and 3PL services available for the various markets they serve as well as for their inbound purchased materials. Other costs will also be affected by this decision, including inventory-in-transit carrying costs, packaging costs, warehousing costs, and shipment damage costs. Part 2 of this text discussed the topic of evaluating and selecting suppliers, and again, the topic here is very similar. Firms use a mix of quantitative and qualitative factors to evaluate and select 3PLs, and there are a number of comparative methods available to aid in the decision process, the most common of which is the weighted factor analysis. In a number of surveys conducted, important selection factors were found to be transit-time reliability, transportation rates, total transit time, willingness to negotiate rates and services, damage-free delivery frequency, financial stability, use of electronic data interchange, and willingness to expedite deliveries.[65]

Creating Strategic Logistics Alliances

Building an effective supply chain very often includes the creation of strategic alliances with providers of logistics services. In fact, in several surveys of various businesses and industries, transportation and warehousing companies were included as supply chain partners in more than 50 percent of the survey respondents who were actively managing their supply chains.[66] In today's business climate, partnering with a 3PL makes even more sense. "Now, more and more companies are moving from their costly and older processes to outsource their logistics in favor of focusing on their core competencies," says Tony Zasimovich, vice president of logistics services at California-based APL Logistics.[67]

SCM Profile | C.H. Robinson Partners with United Solar

Solar panel manufacturer United Solar has facilities in Mexico, the U.S., and Canada. Its fast growth presented a number of daunting supply chain challenges back in 2008. Up until that time, United Solar used a manual process to ship its inbound freight through multiple transportation providers. Each of its plants independently managed all of its inbound vendor shipments. Orders were not always being routed via the most cost effective method. Missed optimization opportunities resulted in inefficiencies and lost savings. "Nearly every trade lane had its own carrier and mode of service," claims logistics manager Steve Britt. As a consequence, some destinations were underserved, and many physical movements of goods were uncoordinated. Additionally, limited visibility to freight in-transit made it difficult to answer shipper queries or assess carrier performance.

With United Solar's plants already running around the clock, demand for expedited services threw more complications into the mix. So, 3PL provider C.H. Robinson began collaborating with United Solar's managers and vendors, coordinating the inbound freight to each facility. United Solar now has a "gate keeper" who ensures suppliers are shipping appropriately. "There are no more shipments simply showing up at our doors," Britt says. With the current structure of checks and balances, however, this no longer happens.

When a specific project requires United Solar to arrange distribution for its customer, C.H. Robinson allows it to quickly quote and reliably move products. As with its inbound material flow, it now has greater visibility to the movements, and is able to provide customers with service options and competitive costs to meet the requirements of its projects.[68]

These partnerships underscore the importance and role played by logistics in supply chain management. A few examples are given here.

Automobile supply chains are getting longer and more complex as companies search for lower-cost and higher-quality suppliers. This has made collaborations with 3PLs even more important. Not too long ago, U.S. automakers focused on squeezing logistics suppliers for cost reductions. "They considered logistics a commodity," says Gregory Hines, president of National Logistics Management, a Michigan-based 3PL. "The right cost is not necessarily the lowest cost. One company can't do everything and partnership alliances are a key," he adds.[69] Partnerships between railroads and automakers in the U.S. mean that seven out of every ten vehicles produced are moved by rail to dealerships, along with a large percentage of the vehicle parts moving to assembly plants. Railroads have invested billions of dollars fabricating special boxcars designed to the automakers' specifications—autorack rail cars with premium cushioning, auto-carrier trucks, a network of vehicle distribution centers, and information systems that allow railroad companies to function as an integral part of automakers' organizations.[70]

Ohio-based bowling supplies distributor Ace Mitchell Bowlers Mart partnered with 3PL provider C.H. Robinson in 2007 to see if it could find improvements in its annual LTL transportation costs. "We thought we had a pretty good handle on things," says Todd Williams, Ace's vice president. In reality, C.H. Robinson found out that Ace's LTL carriers were shipping products on their own schedules with little coordination, creating many small load trips. Worst of all, they found that workers were stacking skids of bowling balls on top of each other and actually puncturing boxes, resulting in product being delivered in damaged condition. The Robinson team designed a coordinated delivery system to combine LTL shipments into the more efficient TL moves, and provide some direct-to-customer intermodal moves as well, resulting in a 20 percent reduction in annual transportation costs and much less product damage.[71] C.H. Robinson also partnered with a solar panel manufacturer to create a more effective logistics system, and this discussion appears in the nearby SCM Profile.

Other Transportation Intermediaries

In some cases, companies utilize **transportation intermediaries**, which may not own any significant logistics capital assets, to find the most appropriate transportation mode or 3PL service. For many small companies with limited logistics expertise, and in some cases for large companies, where the scale of logistics needs are great, use of these transportation services can make good economic sense. A few of these intermediaries are discussed next.

Freight Forwarders

Freight forwarders consolidate large numbers of small shipments to fill entire truck trailers or rail cars to achieve truckload or carload transportation rates. They can also provide air transportation consolidation services. These companies pass some of the savings on to the small shippers and then keep the rest as fees. Thus, freight forwarders provide valuable services to both the shipper (lower shipping costs) and the carrier (extra business and higher equipment utilization). Freight forwarders typically specialize in either domestic or global shipments, as well as air or ground shipments. These companies also provide documentation services, special freight handling, and customs clearance.

Lately, the freight forwarding business has been booming as shippers look for ways to further reduce costs. FedEx Trade Networks, the air freight forwarder subsidiary of FedEx, now has over 140 freight forwarding offices in twenty-seven countries around the world to take advantage of their growing demand for this service.[72] Use of web-based regulatory compliance software by freight forwarders shifted into high gear as the Importer Security Filing mandate of the U.S. Customs and Border Protection Program went into effect early in 2010. Importers and carriers must file twelve data elements before a U.S.-bound container can be loaded aboard a ship at a foreign port. This is the first all-electronic trade program of U.S. Customs and points the way toward their paperless future. Trade compliance has thus become the latest expertise area for freight forwarders.[73]

Logistics Brokers

Also referred to as **freight brokers** and **transportation brokers**, **logistics brokers** bring shippers and carriers together. The logistics broker is legally authorized to act on either the shipper's or carrier's behalf, and typically these companies are hired because of their knowledge of the many transportation alternatives available or the many shippers needing transportation. Besides helping goods move efficiently, brokers also handle cargo claims, obtain specialized equipment, use dependable carriers, and track deliveries in real time. Unfortunately, bad logistics brokers expose shippers and carriers to significant liability, risk the double payment of freight charges, reduce on-time delivery rates, and harm reputations. Accordingly, shippers and carriers must carefully screen and select their logistics brokers.

Typical arrangements might find small businesses using a broker to handle many of their shipping needs, or trucking companies using brokers to find a back-haul job after a delivery is completed. A number of logistics broker directories exist, enabling shippers and carriers to find one meeting their needs. FreightQuote.com and Direct Freight Services are just two examples. FreightQuote.com is the largest online U.S. freight shipping provider—it allows shippers to obtain and compare quotes from hundreds of logistics companies. It moves over 1 million shipments per year in North America. Direct Freight allows shippers to search for carriers and carriers to search for shippers for a monthly fee.[74]

Shippers' Associations

The American Institute for Shippers' Associations (AISA) defines **shippers' associations** as "non-profit membership cooperatives which make domestic or international arrangements for the movement of members' cargo." Thus, their job is to consolidate their members' shipments into full carloads, truckloads, or container loads to achieve volume discounts for the members, and to negotiate improved terms of service. These associations also benefit the carriers, in that they help to better utilize their equipment. Because shippers' associations do not identify themselves as 3PLs, brokers, or transportation providers, they are not required to publish or adhere to a number of U.S. transportation regulations and can keep service contracts confidential. Some of the disadvantages of membership include required minimum shipment volumes to receive the benefits of reduced rates. Additionally, some carriers refuse to do business with shippers' associations. A number of these cooperatives exist for different industries. For example, the Midwest Shippers' Association specializes in the shipping of specialty grains, and has members such as grain processors, traders, seed and equipment suppliers, and logistics providers. The International Shippers' Association is dedicated to international shippers and forwarders of commercial, military and government household goods, unaccompanied baggage, and general commodities.[75]

Intermodal Marketing Companies

Intermodal marketing companies (IMCs) are companies that act as intermediaries between intermodal railroad companies and shippers. They typically purchase large blocks of flatcars for piggyback service and then find shippers to fill containers, or motor carriers with truckloads, to load the flatcars. Essentially these are transportation brokers for the rail industry. They get volume discounts from the railroads and pass some of this on to the shippers. These companies facilitate intermodal shipping and have become an important service to railroads. Shifting 25 percent of truckload freight to the railways, for instance, would result in the savings of 16 billion gallons of fuel and 800,000 fewer tons of air pollution—1 ton of freight can move 830 miles on a *single* gallon of diesel fuel.[76] Many IMCs utilize Internet, cell phone, and satellite transmissions to allow real-time communications among themselves, the carriers, and the shippers. For example, Illinois-based Hub Group is the largest IMC in North America, and its automated online network allows electronic order entries and continuous shipment visibility.[77]

ENVIRONMENTAL SUSTAINABILITY IN LOGISTICS

Today, firms are facing growing pressure to improve environmental performance from customers as well as local, state, and federal governing bodies. Further, an enormous portion of the world's oil reserves is consumed to move goods around the globe (data analyst form Datamonitor estimates the total global cost of logistics to be $4 trillion for 2013).[78] Today, company managers understand the negative impacts of transportation on carbon footprints, total costs, and overall oil consumption, and are doing something about it. Shifting motor carrier freight to railroads, as described above, is one strategy that reduces carbon emissions. Governments are also taking note of voter sentiment and beginning to enact more stringent environmental protection laws regarding transportation. Some examples are provided here.

In logistics, one of the big energy wastes comes from trucks returning from their deliveries empty (referred to as **empty miles**). LeanLogistics, a Michigan-based transportation management systems provider, introduced GreenLanes in 2009, a freight optimization system designed to reduce empty miles for carriers. Shippers and carriers both use the software-as-a-service system, and GreenLanes matches empty carriers with shipper needs to optimize hauling across 24 million loads per year across 21,000 U.S. locations. "GreenLanes was developed as a sustainable business model that reduces wasted capacity and takes unneeded trucks off the road," says Chris Timmer, vice president of marketing at LeanLogistics.[79]

A number of nonprofit organizations have been formed to help logistics companies with their sustainability efforts. In the U.S., the Environmental Protection Agency (EPA) launched SmartWay in 2004, a certification program that reduces transportation emissions and improves supply chain efficiency. The SmartWay brand signifies a service that reduces transportation-related emissions. The SmartWay website allows users to locate alternative fuel station locations, identify greener vehicles to purchase, and select certified SmartWay transportation companies. The EPA also guides other countries seeking to develop freight sustainability programs.[80] The Coalition for Responsible Transportation (CRT), which began in 2007, includes importers, exporters, trucking companies, clean truck manufacturers, and ocean carriers. Through their Clean Truck Initiative, members of CRT work in partnership with U.S. ports to implement clean truck programs that are both environmentally and economically sustainable. CRT members invest millions of dollars in new clean equipment in partnership with federal and state governments, and local ports around the country. By partnering together, ports and their customers can improve the environmental quality of port communities.[81]

Europe's 3PLs and ports have been leading the way toward sustainability by introducing a number of green management initiatives. Damco, the logistics arm of Denmark's

AP Moller-Maersk Group, launched a carbon footprint tracker in 2009 called the Supply Chain Carbon Dashboard that allows users to track their supply chain carbon footprint. "It immediately allows you to identify carbon hotspots in your supply chain," says Erling Nielsen, head of Maersk's supply chain development team. Global freight management company Geodis Wilson of the Netherlands has a tool called GreenService that measures the environmental impact of its customers' logistics solutions. It might find, for example, that a shipment to the U.S. from Gothenburg, Sweden, could reduce carbon emissions by 16 percent compared to one originating in Rotterdam. German logistics company DB Schenker's EcoTransIT World Internet application allows customers to compare the energy consumption, CO_2 and pollutant emissions of all modes of transportation available, given the origination, destination, shipment volume, and freight being transported. Shippers can then select the best route and obtain all the emissions and energy data. Finally, EcoPorts, managed by the European Sea Ports Organization, is a nonprofit association with a current membership of sixty-eight European ports and acts as a network platform to create effective collaborations addressing sustainability issues in European ports and supply chains. The "EcoPort" status is obtained by any European port upon completion of a Self Diagnosis Method (SDM) checklist. Additional credit is provided to ports that are certified with PERS, the only port-sector specific environmental management standard, and ISO 14001.[82]

LOGISTICS MANAGEMENT SOFTWARE APPLICATIONS

As mentioned briefly in Chapter 6, logistics management software applications can be added to ERP software suites of applications, as the firm's needs and the users' level of experience dictates. Some of the more popular logistics management applications (aside from the more specific environmental applications discussed above) include **transportation management systems**, **warehouse management systems**, and **global trade management systems**. Companies typically find significant benefits with these logistics execution systems. Many shippers have been opting to use fee-based Internet logistics management portals instead of outright purchases of logistics software to further manage cost outlays. Still, the use of some form of logistics software remains significant. According to an industry survey conducted early in 2013, 34 percent of the respondents were currently using logistics management software (which is down from recent years due to the recession), and 21 percent indicated they planned to buy new logistics applications or upgrade during the year. For companies with ERP systems, about 79 percent said their systems included a warehouse management application, while 35 percent said their ERP systems included a transportation management application.[83] These systems are briefly discussed next.

Transportation Management Systems

Transportation costs are a significant portion of total logistics costs for many organizations. To help reduce these costs while optimizing service levels, transportation management system (TMS) applications allow firms to find carriers, select the best mix of transportation services and pricing to determine the best use of containers or truck trailers, better manage transportation contracts, rank transportation options, clear customs, track fuel usage and product movements, and track carrier performance. Additionally, regulatory bodies, shippers, and customers want to know the locations of goods in-transit; thus, real-time information about a shipment's location while it is being transported to a final destination is required. Consequently, information may need to be provided by the manufacturer, 3PLs, agents, freight forwarders, and others as products move through global supply chains. Technologies employed to provide this visibility include barcode scanners, RFID tags, the

Internet, and GPS devices. Assisting in the management of all this transportation-related information is the job of a TMS. Missouri-based manufacturer American Railcar Industries, for example, was having difficulty tracking its inbound shipments from suppliers. "We had visibility when the product was ready at suppliers, but then it went into a black hole once it left our vendors' docks until it arrived at our location," says American Railcar purchasing agent Brent Roever. In 2009, it incorporated a web-based TMS solution into its purchasing and logistics processes. Now, all of its purchase orders flow from its ERP system into the TMS, where a preselected list of suppliers can view the orders. Suppliers respond to the orders and indicate how and when the order will be shipped. The system then notifies the purchasing team at American Railcar when the shipment was picked up and when it is expected at the specified location based on established delivery times.[84]

The desire to secure national borders against unwanted shipments is causing a number of governments to more closely regulate the flow of goods across their countries' borders. This has potentially added transportation delay problems to shipments as companies deal with an added layer of bureaucracy and reporting at various border entry sites. To help mitigate delay problems, many TMS software applications now have capabilities for customs declaration; calculation and payment of tariffs, duties, and duty drawbacks; and advanced filing of shipment manifests.

Warehouse Management Systems

Many firms are purchasing ERP systems that include a TMS coupled with a warehouse management system (WMS) to further enhance their supply chain management effectiveness. For example, a company might use its TMS to forecast shipping volumes based on data provided by its WMS and then recommend the most efficient modes of shipping. The WMS could then pick and schedule warehouse usage based on TMS shipping information. Warehouse management systems track and control the flow of goods from the receiving dock of a warehouse or distribution center until the item is loaded for outbound shipment to the customer. RFID tags placed on products and pallets within the distribution center are used to control the flow of goods. The goals of a WMS include reducing distribution center labor costs, streamlining the flow of goods, reducing the time products spend in the distribution center, managing distribution center capacity, reducing paperwork, and managing the crossdocking process. A WMS can improve warehouse productivity by repositioning products to reduce the distance that products and pickers must travel. Reducing these travel times can improve warehouse productivity by 10 to 20 percent.

Nebraska-based retailer Cabela's recently incorporated a WMS for its three distribution centers, two return centers, and twenty retail stores. It uses the system to track inventories in its retail locations, replenishes stock as sales occur, and monitors receiving and returns. The system helps Cabela's handle 300,000 SKUs from 5,000 vendors at all of its facilities. It has realized improvements in operating costs, customer service, information visibility, and the ability to make configuration changes for its multichannel network. "In the past, configuration changes took days or weeks to complete," says Baloo Eledath, director of enterprise solutions at Cabela's. "We now handle them within an hour with our WMS."[85]

Use of TMSs and WMSs has increased the use of RFID tags and technologies. EastPack, for instance, New Zealand's largest Kiwi fruit pack house, must meet strict food traceability regulations. The company uses RFID tags on all pallets of food it ships, in order to track the locations of each pallet throughout its operations in real time. Pallet locations are reported to EastPack's WMS. Within two months of going live with the system, EastPack was able to move 30 percent more fruit trays per day with fewer lift trucks.[86]

Global Trade Management Systems

As the desire to better manage complex global supply chains becomes more common, the need to comply with foreign and domestic security regulations also increases. This, combined with the continued search for cheaper supplies and reduced logistics expenditures, has brought about the need for global trade management (GTM) systems. "The more borders you cross, the more documents you have to file," says William McNeill, research analyst with business research firm AMR Research. "No one wants to make mistakes because once you get caught up in customs you lose money while your competitors' products sail through the supply chain," he adds.

For many firms, the new U.S. Customs and Border Protection (CBP) security filing requirement (shippers and carriers must submit cargo information to the CBP 24 hours prior to ocean freight being loaded onto a vessel bound for the U.S.) has only added to the import documentation headaches. Illinois-based fastener importer, XL Screw Corp., with 100 to 300 import filings per month, decided it needed an in-house GTM system. The system proved to be a simple answer to CBP requirements. The biggest benefit for XL Screw is the ability to enter data for a specific shipment, store it in the system, and then use it to complete forms for other shipments.[87] Paper and plastic packaging supplier Bunzl Distribution USA adopted a GTM platform in 2009 to make its import supply chain more compliant and transparent. Used in over fifty branch offices in the U.S. and Canada, its GTM application improves visibility of its inbound shipments, monitors carrier and supplier performance, and automates customs entry, which improves customer service and reduces brokerage fees while improving compliance with international trade regulations.[88]

GLOBAL LOGISTICS

For global goods movements, logistics managers must be aware of a number of issues not impacting domestic movements such as regulatory requirements, import/export limitations, port and warehousing issues, and the modes of transportation available. In the U.S., freight movement to Europe or Asia involves either air or water transportation and then most likely motor and/or rail transportation to the final destination. Between most contiguous countries, rail and motor carrier shipments tend to be the most common modes of transportation. There are also many logistics problems and infrastructure differences found as goods are moved from one country to another. In Europe, rail transportation tends to be much more prevalent and reliable than rail transportation in the U.S., because European tracks, facilities, and equipment are newer and better maintained. This is partly because most transportation modes in Europe are government owned. Water carriers may be the dominant mode of transportation in countries with a great deal of coastline and developed inland waterways. In under- and undeveloped countries, ports may be very poorly maintained and equipped and the highway system may be almost nonexistent. A number of these and other global logistics topics are discussed next.

Global Freight Security

While a number of logistics security topics have already been discussed, one issue needing further discussion is motor freight security at U.S. border crossings. In the past few years, the trucking industry has worked with U.S. Customs to develop the **Customs-Trade Partnership Against Terrorism program (C-TPAT)** and its security program called the **Free and Secure Trade program (FAST)**. The overall goal is to ensure the security of global supply chains in general and international trucking in particular. To participate in

FAST, motor carriers must become C-TPAT certified, and their commercial drivers must complete an application and undergo a background check. FAST participants receive expedited cargo clearance provided their customers are also C-TPAT certified and they receive access to a dedicated FAST lane at border crossings. Today, over 10,000 companies have become C-TPAT certified, and other countries are adopting similar certifications.[89]

These and other customs clearance requirements are causing a high level of congestion at both U.S. borders (Canada and Mexico). "Free trade is being threatened by a thickening of the border," says Gerry Fedchun, president of the Canadian Automotive Parts Manufacturers' Association.[90] More than 80 percent of all Canadian export trade goes to the U.S. and 70 percent of what flows to the U.S. from Canada goes by way of trucks crossing the border. On many days, trucks are lined up for hours crossing into the U.S. from Canada. And, at the Mexican border, things have been much worse but are improving. Recently, the primary bridge allowing truck crossings into Laredo, Texas, has increased truck lanes from eight to fifteen, reducing crossing wait times from days to hours. Additionally, in 2011, Mexico and the U.S. reached an agreement to allow Mexican trucking companies to deliver goods anywhere in the U.S., reversing an imposed 20-mile commercial zone inside the U.S. that had been in effect since the start of NAFTA in 1994.[91]

Global Logistics Intermediaries

Global logistics intermediaries provide global shipping, consolidation, and import/export services for firms and offer expertise that can prove very useful for most organizations involved in global commerce. A number of these intermediaries that have not already been discussed are briefly discussed here.

Customs Brokers

Customs brokers move global shipments through customs for companies as well as handle the necessary documentation required to accompany the shipments. These specialists are often used by companies requiring expertise in exporting goods to foreign countries. Their knowledge of the many import requirements of various countries can significantly reduce the time required to move goods internationally and clear them through customs.

International or Foreign Freight Forwarders

These services move goods for companies from domestic production facilities to foreign destinations (or vice versa) using surface and air transportation and warehousing. They consolidate small shipments into larger TL or CL shipments, decide what transportation modes and methods to use, handle all of the documentation requirements, and then disperse the shipments at their destination. They also determine the best routing to use; oversee storage, breakbulk and repackaging requirements; and provide for any other logistics requirements of the seller. Use of **foreign freight forwarders** can reduce logistics costs, increase customer service, and allow shippers to focus resources on other activities. Many companies exporting or importing goods use the services of foreign freight forwarders because of their expertise and presence in foreign markets.

Until recently, many shippers were importing and shipping high-quality, low-cost goods from "far-shore" operations (e.g., U.S. buyers purchasing goods from Chinese manufacturers). Today, some buyers are utilizing a strategy called **right-shoring**. Right-shoring combines near-shore, far-shore, and domestic opportunities into a single, flexible, and cost-driven approach to purchasing and logistics. As crude oil prices fluctuate, for example, buyers find they must be much more flexible regarding where products are purchased. This has created an even greater need for globally connected freight forwarders.[92]

Trading Companies

Trading companies put buyers and sellers from different countries together and handle all of the export/import arrangements, documentation, and transportation for both goods and services. Most trading companies are involved in exporting and they usually take title to the goods until sold to foreign buyers. They enjoy economies of scale when exporting goods as they ship large quantities of consolidated shipments, using established transportation and warehousing services. In the U.S., the Export Trading Company Act was signed into law in 1982 to promote U.S. exports and to help U.S. exporters improve their competitiveness. Within the U.S. Department of Commerce, the Export Trading Company Affairs (ETCA) office helps promote the development of joint ventures between U.S. and foreign companies and the use of export trade intermediaries. The ETCA office was created by the Export Trading Company Act of 1982.[93]

Non-Vessel Operating Common Carriers

Also referred to as NVOCCs or simply NVOs, **non-vessel operating common carriers** operate very similarly to foreign freight forwarders but normally use only scheduled ocean liners. They consolidate small international shipments from a number of shippers into full container loads and then handle all of the documentation and transportation arrangements from the shippers' dock area. NVOCCs assume responsibility for cargo from point of origin to final destination; however, they do not own any vessels. They enter into contracts with ocean liners, which may then subcontract with rail or motor carriers for land travel.

Foreign-Trade Zones

Foreign-trade zones (FTZs) are secure sites within the U.S. under the supervision of the U.S. Customs Service. These sites are authorized by the Foreign-Trade Zones Board, chaired by the U.S. Secretary of Commerce, and are comparable to the so-called *free trade zones* that exist in many other countries today. FTZs are considered to be outside U.S. Customs territory, where foreign or domestic merchandise can enter without formal customs entry or payment of duties or excise taxes. Companies operating in FTZs bring goods and materials into the site and might use storage, assembly, testing, packaging, repairing, and export services. No retail activities are allowed, however. If the final product is exported out of the U.S., no domestic duties or excise taxes are levied. If the final product is imported into the U.S. from the FTZ, duties and taxes are paid at the time the goods leave the FTZ.

Congress established the Foreign-Trade Zones Board in 1934 to encourage U.S. firms to participate in global trade. As of 2013, there were over 250 active FTZs in the U.S. located in all fifty states, bringing in about 12 percent of all imported goods (75 percent of which was crude oil). The FTZs are used by about 3,200 companies and directly support over 320,000 U.S. workers with more than $300 billion in merchandise moving through these areas each year. In addition to petroleum, pharmaceutical, automotive, and electronics companies are the largest users of U.S. FTZs.[94]

The North American Free Trade Agreement

The **North American Free Trade Agreement (NAFTA)** was initially agreed upon in December 1992, with the U.S. Congress passing it in November 1993, and put into effect on January 1, 1994. By 2008, it had removed all duties and quantitative restrictions within the three countries. NAFTA forms the world's second-largest open market with a combined economy of more than $17 trillion and a population exceeding 450 million people (the European Union is a bit larger, with a population of over 500 million and an economy of $18 trillion). The objectives of NAFTA are to facilitate cross-border trade among the three countries, increase investment opportunities, and promote fair trade. Trade has soared between the three countries since NAFTA was implemented. Today, Canada and Mexico are the top two purchasers of U.S. exports, and these exports have grown 149 percent since 1994. Similarly, Canada and Mexico are the second and third largest suppliers of goods to the U.S. (China is number one), and imports from Canada and Mexico have grown 184 percent since 1994.

NAFTA has not been without its detractors. U.S. labor groups have argued that jobs are being lost as companies move to Mexico to take advantage of cheap foreign labor, undermining labor union negotiating power. U.S. environmental groups have been concerned that pollution and food safety laws have become more difficult to enforce. Others argue that because of subsidized agricultural exports to Mexico, the small Mexican farmer is being run out of business. Some in the U.S. saw NAFTA as a way to grow the Mexican economy and curb illegal immigration into the U.S. However, migration into the U.S., both legal and illegal, has increased since NAFTA began, mainly due to the Mexican peso crisis, enduring poverty in southern Mexico, and the most recent economic recession. In response to these and other concerns, supplementary agreements continue to be added to NAFTA.[95]

REVERSE LOGISTICS

Reverse logistics (sometimes also known as **returns management**) refers to the backward flow of goods *from* customers in the supply chain occurring when goods are returned, either by the end-product consumer or by a business customer within the supply chain. In other words, reverse logistics refers to the movement, storage, and processing of returned goods. Returns are increasing, in part, today because of the growth of online shopping, direct-to-store shipments, and direct-to-home shipments. Occasionally, the use of cheap and untested foreign suppliers causes a number of product recalls. On August 1, 2007, for example, California-based Mattel, the world's biggest toymaker, recalled almost 1 million Chinese-made toys because they were covered with paint containing high levels of lead. Mattel's primary Chinese supplier had subcontracted the work to a small Chinese toy manufacturer. The very next week, Mattel again was forced to announce a large recall for Chinese-manufactured toys containing small magnets that posed a choking hazard. In fact, eight of Mattel's nine toy recalls from 2004 to 2007 were for Chinese-made products.[96]

Traditional retail customer returns can account for 6 to 10 percent of sales, while returns to retail websites are 20 to 30 percent of sales. According to the Reverse Logistics Association, the sheer volume of returns in the U.S. alone is $150 to $200 billion per year *at cost*. Additionally, the logistical costs to process these returns can also be very high—now running approximately $100 billion each year in the U.S. for transportation, handling, refurbishment, repackaging, remarketing, disposal, and lost sales. Besides the significant impact on costs, returns also can have a direct negative impact on the environment, customer service, the firm's reputation, and profitability if not managed properly. "Reverse logistics is all about damage control and making the process as customer-friendly as possible," says Lou Cerny, vice president of Sedlak Management Consultants. "You've already disappointed the customer once, now you have to close the loop as soon as possible."[97]

Some companies view returns as *zombie inventory* (inventory that just won't die). It sits unsold in storerooms, takes up space on store shelves, or creates bottlenecks in distribution centers, as workers try to determine what should be recycled, repaired, or discarded. However, other companies take a hidden-profit view of returns. "Reverse logistics enables the extension of the life of a product, so that its return is not a 100 percent loss," says Jim Gerard, a segment manager at UPS. "It's a process of receiving goods back for the purpose of preparing them for resale or to recapture the valuable part of the unit for reuse or resale in an entirely different area of the after-market," he adds.[98]

Many firms hire a 3PL company specializing in reverse logistics to ensure these items are managed correctly. Texas-based computer maker Dell, Inc., contracted with Genco Supply Chain Solutions to manage its testing, repairing, and remanufacturing services. Texas-based InteliSol provides parts-harvesting and other recovery services for Dell within the same returns management facility. As a matter of fact, in its inaugural corporate sustainability index, New Hampshire-based Technology Business Research, Inc., announced that Dell received top honors for 2009 particularly for its recycling and renewable energy use.[99]

The Impact of Reverse Logistics on the Supply Chain

Returns can represent significant challenges to a supply chain. In many cases, reverse logistics is viewed as an unwanted activity of supply chain management. In these cases, reverse logistics is seen simply as a cost of doing business or a regulatory compliance issue. Problems include the inability of information systems to handle returns or monitor reverse product flow, lack of worker training in reverse logistics procedures, little or no identification on returned packages, the need for adequate inspection and testing of returns, and the placing of potentially damaged returned products into sales stocks. A poor reverse logistics system can affect the entire supply chain financially and can have a large impact on how a consumer views a product brand, potentially impacting future sales. A recent report by global business consulting company Accenture found that reverse logistics costs four to five times more than forward logistics and on average requires twelve times as many processing steps. Their findings, though, also suggest that reverse logistics represents a huge source of untapped value.[100]

From a marketing perspective, an effective returns process can create goodwill and enhance customers' perceptions of product quality and purchase risk. From a quality perspective, product failure and returns information can be used by quality personnel in root cause analyses and by design personnel to reduce future design errors (the number one reason for a product return is a defective or damaged item). From a logistics perspective, returned products can still create value as original products, refurbished products, or repair parts. This also tends to reduce disposal costs. Thus, while 46 percent of companies report losing money on product returns, about 8 percent actually report making money. Online shoe merchant Zappos has a very high return rate (about 35 percent) but views this as a competitive advantage—they provide free returns with no questions asked, but also boast very high repurchase rates.[101]

Reverse Logistics and the Environment

Reverse logistics can have a positive impact on the environment through activities such as recycling, reusing materials and products, or refurbishing used products. **Green reverse logistics programs** include reducing the environmental impact of certain modes of transportation used for returns, reducing the amount of disposed packaging and product materials by redesigning products and processes, and making use of reusable totes and pallets. "Sustainability is playing an important role in reverse logistics," says Paul Vassallo, marketing director for UPS. "More and more companies are looking to reduce their impact on the environment and search for carbon-neutral ways to dispose of product."[102]

Traditionally, organizations have used landfills for routine product and material disposal, but today, landfills have become much more expensive to use. Local, state, and federal governments are also imposing stricter rules and higher costs regarding the use of landfills. These changes have led to innovative ways of dealing with used products or product waste. The Campbell Soup Company now uses a system that tears soup cans into small strips and then washes and separates the metal. It also crushes and washes glass containers. The remaining vegetable matter is dried and sold as feed to local farmers.[103] Advanced Micro Devices, based in Texas, works with its suppliers to find ways to decrease packaging waste and handling activities. In one instance, the company had traditionally used 55-gallon drums to store some of its bulk chemicals but changed to 300-gallon totes and eventually to bulk tankers to reduce packaging waste that would eventually be delivered to a landfill.[104]

SUMMARY

This chapter has discussed the important role logistics plays in general and to supply chains in particular. Though this is a very broad topic, we have attempted to review the elements within U.S. domestic and global logistics to give the reader an adequate understanding of the entire field of logistics and its relationship to supply chain management. These elements include the basics of transportation, third-party transportation providers, warehousing, sustainability in logistics, global logistics, and reverse logistics. It is hoped that readers have gained an understanding of the many elements within the broad topic of logistics and why these are so important to the successful management of supply chains.

KEY TERMS

DISCUSSION QUESTIONS AND EXERCISES

1. What is logistics and how does it provide time and place utility?
2. Why are logistics issues important to business success?
3. What are the important activities or elements in logistics?
4. Why has it been so difficult for transportation companies to make profits lately?
5. List the legal forms and modes of transportation. Which mode is the least expensive? Which mode carries the most freight? Which mode is growing the fastest? Shrinking the fastest?
6. What are the modes of transportation? What are some intermodal transportation alternatives?
7. What does "piggyback service" refer to?
8. Why are LTL shipping fees higher per cwt than TL shipping fees?
9. Why is it that the fastest trains are found outside the U.S.? Is this a problem for the U.S.?
10. When would you want to use value-of-service pricing instead of cost-of-service pricing? When would you like to use negotiated pricing?
11. What is FOB destination pricing, and when would you want to use it?
12. What does transportation security refer to, and which mode of transportation is most affected by security concerns?
13. Is government regulation of transportation good or bad? Why?
14. Is transportation in the U.S. regulated today or deregulated? Why?
15. Describe three different types of warehouses and the advantages of each.
16. If storing goods in a warehouse is bad, since it increases inventory carrying costs, why are the number and size of warehouses increasing in the U.S.?
17. What is the difference between a distribution center and a warehouse?
18. What are cold chains and what type of warehouse is used for these?
19. Define risk pooling and the advantages and disadvantages of centralized warehousing. What assumption does risk pooling make?
20. For which situation does risk pooling result in less safety stock? Why?

21. *Chapter Problem:* For the following warehouse system information, determine the average inventory levels for three warehouses and then one warehouse, using the square root rule:

    Current warehouse system—six warehouses with 3,000 units at each warehouse.

22. What type of warehouse location strategy do you think Amazon uses? Why?
23. What is a lean warehouse? When are they used?
24. Why is logistics so important for successful supply chain management?
25. What are 3PLs and why are they used? What types of companies use them? Why is their use growing so rapidly? What are 4PLs and why are they used?
26. Can 3PLs be effective supply chain partners? Why?
27. Are transportation intermediaries also a form of 3PL? Explain.
28. Describe several kinds of transportation intermediary.
29. What are the impacts of logistics on environmental sustainability? How can these impacts be minimized?
30. What are empty miles and how can carriers reduce them?
31. What are the most common logistics management software applications and why are they beneficial to users?
32. Could you have a TMS without an ERP system? Or without a WMS?
33. Describe what C-TPAT and FAST are. Which transportation modes use these?
34. What do you think the most pressing global logistics problem is? Why?
35. Describe several global logistics intermediaries. Could they also be considered 3PLs?
36. What are foreign trade zones? How are they different from free trade zones? What benefits do they provide?
37. How has NAFTA affected trade among the U.S., Canada, and Mexico? Is NAFTA good for domestic U.S. and Mexican producers?
38. What is reverse logistics? How does it impact supply chain management?
39. How can reverse logistics have a positive impact on the environment? On profits? On customer service? On repeat purchases?

ESSAY/PROJECT QUESTIONS

1. Go to the BNSF website (www.bnsf.com) and describe the types of intermodal services offered.
2. Search on the term "green logistics" or "sustainable logistics" and write a report on logistics strategies used to reduce carbon emissions.
3. Write a report on Walmart's warehousing system around the globe.
4. Search on the term "port security software" and describe how these software applications help to assure port security and global cargo security.

ADDITIONAL READINGS

Bloomberg, D. J., S. LeMay, and J. B. Hanna, *Logistics*, Upper Saddle River, NJ: Prentice Hall, 2002.

Coyle, J. J., E. J. Bardi, and C. J. Langley, *The Management of Business Logistics*. St. Paul, MN: West Publishing, 1996.

Lambert, D. M., J. R. Stock, and L. M. Ellram, *Fundamentals of Logistics Management*. New York: McGraw-Hill, 1998.

Sampson, R. J., Farris, M. T., and Shrock, D. L., *Domestic Transportation: Practice, Theory, and Policy*. 5th ed. Boston: Houghton Mifflin, 1985.

Stock, J. R., and Lambert, D. M., *Strategic Logistics Management*. 4th ed. New York: McGraw-Hill, 2001.

ENDNOTES

1. McArthur, T., "How to Become a Millionaire," *Motley Fool* [blog], February 6, 2013. Found at http://www.fool.com.au/2013/02/06/how-to-become-a-millionaire-2/

2. Anonymous, "Alibaba to Spend Billions on Warehouse Network in China," *Material Handling & Logistics* online edition, January 20, 2011. Found at http://mhlnews.com/global-supply-chain/alibaba-spend-billions-warehouse-network-china

3. Material for road trains came from www.outback-australia-travel-secrets.com/australian-road-trains.html, www.truckersnews.com/riding-the-down-under-express and www.ourterritory.com/katherine_region/road_trains.htm.

4. Material for the Shinkansen train came from www.japaneselifestyle.com.au/travel/shinkansen_nozomi.htm, www.japan-guide.com/e/e2018.html and www.railway-technology.com/projects/shinkansen. Material for the L-Zero train came from http://www.ibtimes.com/worlds-fastest-train-reaches-310-mph-trials-japans-l-zero-maglev-train-open-2027-1403464.

5. Material for the Antonov An-225 came from Spaeth, A., "When Size Matters," *Air International*, December 2009: 29; www.theaviationzone.com/factsheets/an225.asp; www.airbususa380.tripod.com/id6.html; and www.antonov.com/products/air/transport.html.

6. Material for the largest water carriers came from www.globalsecurity.org/military/systems/ship/jahre-viking.html; www.blupulzz.com/?Id=2245; http://mentalfloss.com/article/27877/seawise-giant-you-cant-keep-good-ship-down, and www.emma-maersk.info.

7. Material for the largest pipelines came from Anonymous, "China Begins Using World's Longest Gas Pipeline," found at www.pennenergy.com/articles/pennenergy/2012/12/china-begins-using-worlds-longest-gas-pipeline.html; Wise, J., "World's Longest Underwater Pipeline Will Tap the Sea," *Popular Mechanics*, June 2007, found at www.popularmechanics.com/science/extreme_machines.

8. Council of Supply Chain Management Professionals, www.cscmp.org/aboutcscmp/definitions

9. "Number of Trucking Companies Declaring Bankruptcy Significantly Declines Last Quarter," found at http://www.roadscholar.com/blog/number-of-trucking-companies-declaring-bankruptcy-significantly-declines-last-quarter/; Hasbrouck, E., "FAQ About Airline Bankruptcies," *The Practical Nomad*, found at www.hasbrouck.org/articles/bankruptcy.html; Keeton, A., "Corporate News: Air Industry Faces Grim Year Ahead," *Wall Street Journal*, September 16, 2009: B3.

10. McCartney, S., "Teams Score Elite Service in the Sky," *The Wall Street Journal Online*, October 24, 2012; found at http://online.wsj.com/article/SB10001424052970203897404578076574126494236.html

11. Horowitz, S., "Wal-Mart to the Rescue: Private Enterprise's Response to Hurricane Katrina," *The Independent Review* 13(4), 2009: 511–528.

12. "Swift Currents, Debris Slow Recovery Effort," found at www.npr.org, August 13, 2007.

13. See http://www.dot.state.mn.us/i35wbridge/traffic_changes.html

14. Anonymous, "The 15 Biggest LTL Carriers," found at http://www.thelogisticsoflogistics.com/tag/top-25-ltl-carriers

15. Anonymous, "Top 50 Trucking Companies," found at http://www.joc.com/trucking-logistics/top-50-trucking-companies-2012. Also see http://www.thelogisticsoflogistics.com/2013/07/the-5-largest-truckload-carriers

16. Trebilcock, B., "RTLS: Find a Needle in a Haystack," *Modern Materials Handling* 61(7), 2006: 42.

17. Mann, T., "Rail Corridor Hit with Major Outage," *Wall Street Journal*, May 20, 2013: A3.

18. "Acela Express, USA," found at www.railway-technology.com/projects/amtrak/

19. Mitchell, J., "Amtrak Seeking Florida's Rail Funds," *Wall Street Journal*, April 28, 2011: A9.

20. Anonymous, "Chinese Train Makers Eye Part in US$53Bln U.S. Rail Plan," *Asia Pulse*, February 12, 2011: 1.

21. Macklem, K., "Is There a Fast Train Coming?" *MacLean's* 116(8), 2003: 24–25; Yong Chia, W., "KL-SG High-speed Rail Proposal—Drawing Closer for Mutual Benefit?" *Shares Investment: Facts & Figures*, September 21, 2013: 1; Spegele, B., and B. Davis, "High-speed Train Links Beijing, Shanghai—Cornerstone of China's Rail Expansion Illustrates Megaprojects' Speed Bumps," *Wall Street Journal*, June 29, 2011: A11.

22. Cameron, D., "Chia Spurs Rebound in Airline Traffic Growth," *Wall Street Journal*, April 3, 2013: 1.

23. Bounds, A., "Freight Travels Back to Future on Manchester Canal," *Financial Times*, April 23, 2013: 4.

24. Information found at en.wikipedia.org/wiki/Container_ship

25. Harper, D., and S. Nykolaishen, "A Canadian Perspective on the Keystone XL Pipeline," *Trends: ABA Section of Environment, Energy, and Resources Newsletter* 44(6), 2013: 2–5.

26. Martin, J., "Intermodal Transportation: Evolving Toward the 21st Century," *Transportation & Distribution* 37(2), 1996: 1–9.

27. BNSF website: www.bnsf.com

28. Atlantic Container Line website: www.aclcargo.com

29. Richardson, H., "Pricing/Costing Series Part III—Pricing: Carriers Calculate Their Risks," *Transportation & Distribution* 35(3), 1994: 29–31.

30. See www.southwest.com earnings reports.

31. See www.nmfta.org

32. See www.tsa.gov

33. See www.dhs.gov

34. Anonymous, "DHS Rolls Out Airport Body Scanners," *Informationweek—Online*, March 5, 2010. Found at http://www.informationweek.com/news/government/security/showArticle.jhtml?articleID=223101697&cid=RSSfeed_IWK_News; Anonymous, "North America Report," *Air Transport World* 48(10), 2011: 12.

35. See the following: Edmonson, R., "TWICs Technology Challenge," *Journal of Commerce*, February 22, 2010: 1; Staff, "Risk of Train Terror Attack Reduced: DHS IG," *Journal of Commerce*, March 2, 2009: 1.

36. Whistler, D., "More State Trucking Associations Endorse PrePass Service," *Fleet Owner*, July 2, 2013: 1.

37. Jerman, R., and R. Anderson, "Regulatory Issues: Shipper Versus Motor Carrier," *Transportation Journal* 33(3), 1994: 15–23.

38. See, for instance, Dempsey, P., "The Disaster of Airline Deregulation," *Wall Street Journal*, May 9, 1991: A15; Leonard, W., "Airline Deregulation: Grand Design or Gross Debacle?" *Journal of Economic Issues* 17(2), 1983: 453–465; O'Brian, B., and C. Solomon, "Braniff Files for Protection from Creditors," *Wall Street Journal*, September 29, 1989: 1; Staff, "Texas Air Provides $10 Million in Aid to People Express," *Wall Street Journal*, October 16, 1986: 1; and Staff, "Business Brief—Texas Air Corp," *Wall Street Journal*, June 7, 1990: A1.

39. Barlett, D., and J. Steele, "The High Cost of Deregulation: Joblessness, Bankruptcy, Debt," *The Inquirer*, October 24, 1991; found at www.philly.com/philly/news

40. Kanellos, M., "Will Amazon Become the Next FedEx?" *Forbes.com*, March 26, 2012; found at http://www.forbes.com/sites/michaelkanellos/2012/03/26/will-amazon-become-the-next-fedex/

41. Cassidy, W., "Bigger Faster," *Journal of Commerce*, June 23, 2008: 1.

42. Information found at www.mwpvl.com/html/walmart.html

43. Anonymous, "Alibaba to Spend Billions on Warehouse Network in China," *Material Handling & Logistics* online edition, January 20, 2011.

44. Feare, T., "Jazzing Up the Warehouse," *Modern Material Handling* 56(7), 2001: 71–72.

45. Found at www.universal-storage.co.za/largest-warehouses.asp

46. Gregor, A., "Precious Works Housed in Armour," *Financial Times*, November 4, 2008: 10.

47. Burnson, P., "Conquering the Cold Chain," *Logistics Management* 52(4), 2013: 36–38.

48. Dutton, G., "Intermodal is Viable—and Growing—for Cold Shipping," *World Trade* 26(1), 2013: 41–43.

49. Brown, M., "The Slow Boat to Europe," *Management Today*, June 1997: 83–86.

50. Maister, D. H., "Centralization of Inventories and the 'Square Root Law,' " *International Journal of Physical Distribution and Materials Management* 6(3), 1976: 124–134.

51. Warnenburg, C. M., trans., and P. Hall, ed., *Von Thunen's Isolated State*. Oxford, UK: Pergamon Press, 1966.

52. Friedrich, C. J., trans., *Alfred Weber's Theory of the Location of Industries.* Chicago: University of Chicago Press, 1929.

53. Hoover, E. M., *The Location of Economic Activity.* New York: McGraw-Hill, 1948.

54. Greenhut, M. L., *Plant Location in Theory and in Practice.* Chapel Hill: University of North Carolina Press, 1956.

55. Trebilcock, B., "Distribution Evolution at PDS," *Modern Materials Handling* 65(2), 2010: 14–15.

56. Trunick, P., "The 3 W's of Green Warehouses," *World Trade* 26(4), 2013: 40–43.

57. Fabey, M., "Changing Trade Winds," *Traffic World* 263(8), 2000: 41–42.

58. MacDonald, A., "What Business Leaders Need to Know About: Atlantic Maritime," *World Trade* 19(4), 2006: 42–48.

59. Burnson, P., "Top 50 3PLs: Seeing Into the Future," *Logistics Management* 52(6), 2013: 56S.

60. Blanchard, D., "When You'd Rather Not Do It Yourself," *Material Handling Management*, October 2009: 48.

61. Andel, T., "3PL Growth Outpacing GDP," *Material Handling & Logistics*, October 8, 2013: 1.

62. Hannon, D., "GM Hatches Plan to Cut 70 Days from Order Cycle Time," *Purchasing* 130(13), 2001: 61–62.

63. Schulz, J., "GM Buys Out Vector SCM, Brings Logistics Back In-House," *Logistics Management Online*, August 1, 2006; found at www.logisticsmgmt.com/index.asp?layout=articlePrint&articleID=CA6365036

64. Kerr, J., "What´s the Right Role for Global 3PLs?" *Logistics Management* 45(2), 2006: 51–54.

65. See, for example, Abshire, R., and S. Premeaux, "Motor Carrier Selection Criteria: Perceptual Differences Between Shippers and Carriers," *Transportation Journal* 31(1), 1991: 31–35; Bardi, E., P. Bagchi, and T. Raghunathan, "Motor Carrier Selection in a Deregulated Environment," *Transportation Journal* 29(1), 1989: 4–11; Foster, J., and S. Strasser, "Carrier/Modal Selection Factors: The Shipper/Carrier Paradox," *Transportation Research Forum* 31(1), 1990: 206–212; and Murphy, P., J. Daley, and P. Hall, "Carrier Selection: Do Shippers and Carriers Agree, or Not?" *Transportation Research* 33E(1), 1997: 67–72.

66. Mejza, M. C., and J. D. Wisner, "The Scope and Span of Supply Chain Management," *The International Journal of Logistics Management* 12(2), 2001: 37–56; Tan, K. C., and J. D. Wisner, "A Comparison of the Supply Chain Management Approaches of U.S. Regional and Global Businesses," *Supply Chain Forum* 2(2), 2001: 20–28.

67. Terreri, A., "Delivering Supply Chain Excellence," *World Trade* 23(3), 2010: 24–28.

68. Burnson, P., "United Solar's Enlightened Partnership," *Logistics Management* 50(3), 2012: 26–30.

69. Field, A., "Spirit of Cooperation," *Journal of Commerce*, October 2, 2006: 1.

70. Dutton, G., "Collaborative Transportation Management," *World Trade* 16(2), 2003: 40–43.

71. Schulz, J., "Cutting LTL Costs: Going to the Bench," *Logistics Management* 48(2), 2009: 35.

72. Found at www.ftn.fedex.com/news/NewsBulletinDisplay.jsp?url=101713&lang=en

73. Biederman, D., "Visibility into Compliance," *Journal of Commerce*, April 5, 2010: 1.

74. Obtained from the following sites: www.redbooktrucking.com, www.freightquote.com, and www.directfreight.com

75. Information obtained from www.midwestshippers.com and www.isaship.org

76. See www.trinitylogistics.com/freight-services/intermodal

77. Information obtained from www.hubgroup.com and Boyd, J., "Intermodal Takes Separate Tracks," *Journal of Commerce*, February 22, 2010: 1.

78. See www.mhlnews.com/global-supply-chain/global-logistics-market-hits-bottom-could-rise-4-trillion-2013

79. See www.leanlogistics.com/news/LeanLogistics-Receives-Going-Green-Award-by-Corp.html

80. See www.epa.gov/smartway

81. See www.responsibletrans.org

82. See www.godiswilson.com, www.dcvelocity.com, www.dbschenkerusa.com, and www.ecoports.com

83. McCrea, B., "11th Annual Software Users Survey: Caution Remains," *Logistics Management* 52(6), 2013: 36–40.

84. Hannon, D., "American Railcar Uses TMS to Shine Light on Inbound Supply Chain," *Purchasing* 139(3), 2010: 13.

85. McCrea, B., "WMS: Prompt Payback," *Logistics Management* 48(5), 2009: 40.

86. Andel, T. "No Failure to Communicate," *Modern Materials Handling* 64(10), 2009: 15.

87. McCrea, B., "GTM Has Arrived," *Logistics Management* 49(1), 2010: 34.

88. Anonymous, "Management Dynamics; Brunzl Distribution USA Implements Global Trade Management Platform," *Economics Week*, September 4, 2009: 13.

89. Russell, S., "'Robust' Security for Crossborder Trucking," *Traffic World*, July 2, 2007: 1; and Quinn, F., "Supply Chain Security in a High-Risk World," *Logistics Management* 50(1), 2011: 54–58.

90. Simon, B., "Border Snarls Put Brakes on Canada Trade," *Financial Times*, September 4, 2007: 24.

91. See, for instance, Cassidy, W., "House Members Rip Cross-Border Trucking," *Journal of Commerce*, April 14, 2010: 1; MacDonald, A., "NAFTA: A Delicate Balance," *World Trade* 22(10), 2009: 30–33; Moens, A., "The Peace Bridge Project and the Need to Harmonize Canada–US Border Security," *The Canadian Manager* 32(2), 2007: 20–22; and Krizner, K., "NAFTA Trade and Traffic on the Rise," *World Trade* 24(7), 2011: 50.

92. Anonymous, "Freight Forwarders Best Foreign Performance," *Logistics Management* 48(8), 2009: 44.

93. U.S. Dept. of Commerce website: www.ita.doc.gov/td/oetca/staff.html

94. See Anonymous, "National Association of Foreign-Trade Zones Promotes Benefits of FTZs," *Economics Week*, September 25, 2009: 29; the U.S. Dept. of Commerce Foreign-Trade Zones Board website: http://ia.ita.doc.gov/ftzpage/index; and Bolle, M., and B. Williams, "U.S. Foreign-Trade Zones: Background and Issues for Congress," September 5, 2012, found at http://www.fas.org/sgp/crs/misc/R42686.pdf

95. Bedell, D., "Can NAFTA Fill the Gap?" *Global Finance* 24(3), 2010: 30–32; Schot, J., "North American Free Trade Agreement (NAFTA)," *The Princeton Encyclopedia of the World Economy* 2, 2009: 851–855; www.ustr.gov/trade-agreements; and www.europa.eu

96. Lawrence, D., "China Issues Food, Toy Recall Rules to Tighten Safety," *Bloomberg.com News*, August 31, 2007, www.bloomberg.com/apps/news?pid=20601080&sid=asUaOAct_vrc&refer=asia

97. Rogers, L., "Going in Reverse to Move Forward," *Modern Materials Handling* 64(9), 2009: 28; Rogers, D., R. Lembke, and J. Benardino, "Reverse Logistics: A New Core Competency," *Supply Chain Management Review* 17(3), 2013: 40–47.

98. McCue, D., "Dealing with Zombie Inventory," *World Trade* 26(3), 2013: 39–42.

99. Gallagher, T., "GENCO Contracts for Dell Remanufacturing," *Journal of Commerce*, July 22, 2009: 1; and www.content.dell.com/us/en/corp/d/press-releases

100. Blanchard, D., "Moving Ahead by Mastering the Reverse Supply Chain," *Industry Week* 258(6), 2009: 58.

101. Martinez, R., "Best Practices in Returns Management," *Multichannel Merchant* 26(12), 2010: 29.

102. Rogers, L., "Going in Reverse to Move Forward."

103. More information on this case can be found at http://web.indstate.edu/recycle/9505.html

104. Trowbridge, P., "A Case Study of Green Supply-Chain Management," *Greener Management International*, Autumn 2001: 121–135.

Chapter 10

CUSTOMER RELATIONSHIP MANAGEMENT

The customer is more in charge today than they ever have been in the past. They want their information when and how they want it, and it's our job to figure out the best way to spread the information across the board.

— ***Ralph Bright, vice president–marketing, Interpower Corp.***[1]

For travel agencies, accurate and easily accessible customer information is critical to providing outstanding customer service, creating smart, efficient processes and fueling CRM systems.

— ***Chris Kroeger, senior vice president, Sabre Travel Network***[2]

Learning Objectives

After completing this chapter you should be able to:

- Discuss the strategic importance of CRM.
- Describe the components of a CRM initiative.
- Calculate customer lifetime value.
- Discuss the implementation procedures for CRM programs.
- Describe how information is used to create customer satisfaction and greater profits for the firm.
- Discuss the importance of data security in CRM.
- Describe how social media and cloud computing have impacted CRM.

Chapter Outline

SCM Profile Templeton & Company's Integrated CRM System

Over the last decade, "practice management" has become an industry unto itself, with a proliferation of task-specific software. As a result, accounting firms now find themselves operating with multiple systems and various applications that don't always work. Staff must be trained and retrained, and as new tools are added, firms must reinvest in IT expertise.

Even more frustrating, a cobbled network of practice management software does little to build a firm's business through client development and opportunity management. In today's business environment, client retention and cross-selling of services are paramount. The proven solution is customer relationship management (CRM). Yet, many firms in the accounting industry have been reluctant to invest in what they see as yet another costly layer of IT complexity. Florida-based accounting firm Templeton & Company's own study found less than 5 percent have given CRM systems a try.

But what if CRM included all the necessary tools of practice management? Why not a single solution? One completely integrated system that seamlessly combined everything needed in practice management with everything desired from CRM. Templeton asked that question and ultimately partnered with Microsoft to create a single comprehensive system for every aspect of practice management plus CRM.

First, it needed to be simple. A single log-in system that was intuitive, easy to learn, and operate on the same familiar Microsoft Outlook format. It had to be fully integrated to handle, for example, time and billing, accounting and reporting, tracking and project management, and personnel scheduling. Additionally, Templeton required built-in account management capabilities with a range of up-selling, cross-selling, and opportunity management CRM features. Most importantly, this integrated program had to be tailored to the nuanced needs of a busy accounting firm, such as Templeton.

Today, Templeton operates with a simple turnkey system that takes practice management not just to another level but to a new dimension. The program, named TC Practice Management, finally solves the old quandary of how to build a viable business development strategy within the often fragmented environment of an accounting practice that is structured on individual partnerships and "silos." This new system puts everyone on the same page and keeps them reading from the same book.

It did not take long for the new system to attract interest from frustrated executives, many of whom cope with two or three practice management software tools and no built-in CRM capability. What they immediately perceive are two things: the lower cost and convenience of one unified system, and the chance to create and sustain real "brand loyalty."

In the commercial marketplace, brand is king. And the linchpin is CRM technology to consistently "remember and reward" loyal customers, while cross-selling additional goods or services. Practice management software alone cannot address this dynamic customer relationship management role; and, until now, CRM could not do the essential work of a dedicated practice management system for accounting firms.[3]

INTRODUCTION

Customer relationship management becomes necessary as soon as a company finds a market and some customers for its products and services. To keep customers satisfied, coming back and telling others, firms must continually develop new products and services while discovering ways to add more value to existing products and services. This is particularly true in today's tough economic climate, which has made customers smarter and more willing to switch company allegiances. The often-told story that "finding a new customer costs five times as much as keeping an old customer" is one of the motivations behind customer relationship management. Over time, value continues to be demonstrated to customers through reliable on-time delivery, high-quality products and services, competitive pricing, innovative new products and services, attention to varying customer needs, and the flexibility to respond to those needs adequately. Managing and improving customer relationships start with building core competencies that focus on customer requirements, and then continuing with delivering products and services in a manner resulting in high levels of customer satisfaction.

Customer relationship management, or simply CRM, has come to be associated with automated transaction and communication applications—a suite of software modules or a portion of the larger enterprise resource planning system as described in Chapter 7. The global market for CRM applications is growing rapidly—it was approximately $18 billion in 2012 and growing at a 12.5 percent per year pace. Most large firms have made sizeable investments in CRM applications along with company websites that capture data in an effort to automate the customer relationship process, and in some respects these have provided significant benefits to the companies and their customers. Additionally, 40 percent of all CRM software sold in 2012 was software-as-a-service (SaaS) or cloud-based. These were from firms seeking easier-to-deploy systems or to replace their legacy or outdated CRM platforms.[4]

The growth of CRM is expected to continue. In a Gartner survey of European companies, 48 percent stated they planned to increase their CRM investments in 2013. "The upward trend we are witnessing confirms organizations' commitment to improving the management of their customer relationships, despite the volatile economic environment across Europe," says Jim Davies, research director at Gartner. For the third consecutive year, the number one objective for CRM investments was increasing customer satisfaction.[5]

Customers today like the convenience of communicating or transacting over the Internet; however, individualized contact between a company and its customers is also needed to ultimately keep customers satisfied and coming back. Two of the most recent trends in CRM are use of social networks and cloud computing, and both of these will be discussed in this chapter. Companies are using both as a means to build better customer relationships. Some applications allow a company, for instance, to extract information automatically about people from a social network like LinkedIn and load it directly into one of its CRM systems. Other applications include the use of a service provider's eMarketing cloud to send e-mail "blasts" to thousands of customers.

Businesses are rediscovering the need to provide personalized services to their customers. Today we see that a firm's Internet presence and software applications, though desirable for many types of information or product transactions, are not sufficient to satisfy most customers in a wide range of industries. Touching products and talking face-to-face with company representatives remain integral parts of the customer experience. Thus, CRM must still include talking to customers, understanding their behavior and their requirements, and then building a system to satisfy those requirements. CRM must be more than just software.

With the rapid pace of technological change comes many new and exciting ways to obtain and utilize customer information, and many of these will be highlighted throughout this chapter. While company–customer interactions are becoming more automated and as more e-services are created, organizations will still find they must continue to identify and develop new ways to add value to customer relationships in order to maintain a competitive advantage. Cultivating the human element in customer relationships will always remain a necessary factor in creating that value. Ultimately CRM, if used effectively, allows both sides to win—customers get what they want from businesses, while businesses continue to find new customers and satisfy old ones.

CUSTOMER RELATIONSHIP MANAGEMENT DEFINED

Simply put, customer relationship management refers to *building and maintaining profitable long-term customer relationships.* The elements comprising CRM vary based on the industry, the size of the company, and familiarity with CRM software applications. In the final analysis though, all forms of CRM seek to keep the firm's customers satisfied, which creates profits and other benefits for the firm. A few specific definitions of CRM are provided here:

- "The infrastructure that enables the delineation of, and increase in customer value, and the correct means by which to motivate valuable customers to remain loyal—indeed to buy again."[6]
- "... managing the relationships among people within an organization and between customers and the company's customer service representatives in order to improve the bottom line."[7]
- "... a core business strategy for managing and optimizing all customer interactions across an organization's traditional and electronic interfaces."[8]

Because of the intense competition in most markets today, CRM has become one of the leading business strategies—and potentially one of the most costly. Most executives, who haven't already implemented CRM applications, are planning on investing in them soon. And while investments in CRM are in the tens of billions of dollars each year as previously stated, it appears that some of this investment is not fundamentally improving customer relationships, making customers more loyal, or resulting in positive returns for the companies implementing CRM. In a recent U.S. survey of 800 marketers and salespeople, more than 80 percent thought CRM systems didn't always capture or provide the information needed to close the bigger and higher-margin deals. Additionally, while 87 percent of respondents said they were required to use their firms' CRM systems to track their sales activities, 79 percent agreed they simply "checked the boxes."[9] In another survey, while many CRM projects made money for the firms and met expectations, 70 percent of the projects either resulted in business losses or created no bottom line improvements.[10]

So why are many CRM programs failing? Several researchers who have studied this problem refer to the "seven deadly sins of CRM failure." These are viewing CRM primarily from a technology perspective, a lack of customer-centric vision, not understanding the concept of a customer's lifetime value, insufficient top management support, not reengineering business processes, underestimating the challenges in integrating various sources of data, and underestimating the challenge in effecting change.[11] Thus it is the people aspect of CRM that is often lacking. In one example, a researcher talked to hundreds of employees of a large global technology organization that had branded its CRM efforts a failure after three years and a $300 million investment. He found that only 24 percent of the employees had even heard of the program, and only 15 percent of those involved with the implementation had been asked to provide any input.[12] Given these findings, should the program's failure have been a surprise? Though corporations may collect customers' purchase, credit, and personal information, place it on a database, and use it to initiate some type of direct marketing activity, no substantive efforts are put forth to engender a customer's trust and loyalty—*to build customer relationships*. If building and maintaining relationships were truly what companies were seeking, they would, for instance, return phone messages, make it easy to return or service products, and make it easy for customers to get accurate information and contact the right people inside the organization. Consider this—how often, in your dealings with organizations, have you been made to feel valued?

Too often, companies today have delegated customer relationship management, certainly one of the most important activities of the firm, to third-party CRM services, software developers, and internal IT departments whose goal is to collect data, design databases, and use models to predict consumer buying patterns, for instance. Though it is a potentially valuable support element in CRM programs, data mining alone does not build the customer relationship. A number of years ago, Ms. Jessica Keyes, a well-known information system author and consultant, stated in an interview in the magazine *Infotrends*, "Technology does not beget a competitive advantage, any more than paint and canvas beget a Van Gogh."[13] These kinds of activities should be used in tandem with individual attention to build genuine long-term value for customers. Successful CRM programs require cultural change, effective CRM project management, and employee engagement, leading to strategies that cultivate long-term relationships with customers, aided by the information gathered from CRM applications.

SCM Profile | Amazon Provides CRM to its Merchant Customers

Under the guidance of CEO Jeff Bezos, Amazon has become the world's largest online retailer, with more than $61 billion in 2012 sales. Today, the company has more than 180 million active accounts and more than 2 million merchants selling on its website. Recently, the company launched Amazon Marketing Services, which includes several free services—Brand Pages, Brand Posts, Analytics, and eCommerce Ads—to help businesses sell more via their online portal.

Brand Pages is a service that lets companies create their own microsites within Amazon's website. Brand Posts lets companies engage audiences on Facebook and other social media sites and enhance their sites with social content. Analytics ties it all together, providing companies with insights into their pages and posts, including views, reach, purchase lift, and the online shopping behavior of customers. Finally, eCommerce Ads helps companies promote their products on Amazon.

Amazon also empowers its merchants with its Amazon Web Services (AWS) cloud platform. In 2012, Amazon supplemented its cloud platform with 159 new features and services, including AWS Trusted Advisor, which monitors merchant configurations, compares them to known best practices, and then notifies merchants where opportunities exist to improve performance, enhance security, or save money.

These offerings certainly bolster the Amazon cloud. Though Amazon doesn't list its AWS revenue separately, many analysts have estimated it at $2 billion a year, strongly positioning Amazon to take on the likes of IBM, Microsoft, HP, and Oracle. And that's just the way Jeff Bezos likes it.[14]

Simply put, companies need to *treat their customers right*. Not only does this mean providing the products and services they want at competitive prices, but it also means providing support services and other offerings that add value and create customer satisfaction. Because customers are not all the same, firms must identify and segment their customers and then provide different sets of desired products and services to each segment. As noted CRM consultant Barton Goldenberg has been telling clients for years—a successful CRM initiative is 50 percent people, 30 percent process, and 20 percent technology.[15]

Thus, a successful CRM program is both simple and complex—it is simple in that it involves training users and treating customers right, to make them feel valued. It is complex in that it also means finding affordable ways to identify (potentially millions of) customers and their needs, and then designing customer contact strategies geared toward creating customer satisfaction and loyalty. Doing these things right will produce bottom line results.

The services of online retailer Amazon.com are very simple for the consumer, for example, though actually some very complicated CRM tasks take place behind the scenes. "I think what ensured that Amazon was a dotcom winner was being dedicated to the initial principle of focusing on the customer," says Ms. Rakhi Parekh, group product manager at Amazon.co.uk. "We started off by passing-on the cost advantage of the model to consumers, with low prices, then extended that to clever use of their data so that we could work out what else they might enjoy."[16] Today, Amazon continues to search for better ways to serve not only its consumer-customers, but its merchant-customers as well. The nearby SCM Profile describes Amazon's current CRM efforts for merchants.

KEY TOOLS AND COMPONENTS OF CRM

A number of elements are required for the development of effective CRM initiatives, and these include segmenting customers, predicting customer behaviors, determining customer value, personalizing customer communications, automating the sales force, and managing customer service capabilities. Each of these elements is discussed in detail below.

Segmenting Customers

One of the most basic activities in CRM is to **segment customers**. Companies group customers in varieties of ways so that customized communications and marketing efforts can be directed to specific customer groups. Efforts to up-sell and cross-sell can be directed to some groups, while efforts to discourage further purchases might be made to others. The recent global recession may also have changed some customer preferences, which is in turn changing how firms are segmenting and marketing to these segments. Anything with the potential to change buying habits will eventually result in a different form of segmentation.

Customer segmentation can occur based on sales territory or region, preferred sales channel, profitability, products purchased, sales history, demographic information, desired product features, and service preferences, just to name a few. Analyzing customer information can tell companies something about customer preferences and the likelihood of their responding to various types of **target marketing** efforts. By targeting specific customer segments, firms can save money by avoiding marketing efforts aimed at the wrong customers. Additionally, firms can avoid becoming a nuisance to some customers, which may drive them to competitors. Global retailer Tesco sends out millions of mailers each month to its customers with promotional offers, using 150,000 variants of the mailer to appeal to the varied lifestyles of its many demographic segments.[17] The global insurance and financial services company Hartford Financial Services Group, for example, has provided auto and homeowner insurance to people above the age of sixty for more than twenty years. Their call center's automated voice answering system features a low-pitched male voice to allow words to be heard very clearly; speech recognition has been incorporated into its touch tone system; and the company has nine gerontologists on staff to advise the firm on everything from service to product design to marketing.[18]

Permission Marketing

An extension of target marketing is **relationship marketing** or **permission marketing**. The idea is to let customers select the type and time of communication with organizations. These days, consumers are bombarded with thousands of commercial messages each day in every form of communication imaginable. The general consensus is that there are simply far too many ads, consumers ignore most of them, and no one is really trying to do anything to reduce them. On the contrary, the advertising industry seems forever on the lookout for new ways to introduce commercial messages.

One example of new advertising is **mobile marketing**, or placing advertising messages on mobile phones. Users opt-in to get all of their services on cell phones, including advertising. "Mobile phones are the one thing that people carry with them all of the time and it's the most intimate of device because advertisers can target consumers individually and offer them coupons and come-ons to buy products or services literally when they're around the corner from a store," says Bill Jones, president of Air2Web, a mobile advertising firm.[19] The newest form of mobile marketing is the use of quick response codes, or **QR codes**. It involves using the camera function on a smartphone and installing a QR code reader on the phone. Suppose you're on your way to the airport and want an update on your flight. You could simply point your phone camera at a QR code on your boarding pass and instantly receive a flight update on your phone. Even better, you could take a photo of the flight's QR code on your computer screen and have the e-boarding pass sent directly to your phone.[20]

Thus in permission marketing, customers choose to be placed on (opt-in) and then taken off (opt-out) of e-mail or traditional mailing lists for information about goods and services. It is becoming possible on websites for consumers to specify exactly what they are interested in, when they want information, what type of information they want, and how they want it communicated. This kind of customer self-segmenting requires sophisticated software capabilities to track individual customers and their interaction preferences as well as the capability to update these preferences over time. With this capability, firms can better design multiple, parallel marketing campaigns around small, specific segments of their customer base, automate portions of the marketing process, and simultaneously free up time previously spent manually managing the marketing process.

Facebook, Web.com, and iPage, for example, allow users to create their own customized web pages that potential consumers choose to visit. Because visitors to these pages are self-selecting, this essentially amounts to permission marketing. This enables companies to identify interested consumers, engage them in dialogues, and market goods and services to them. As of 2013, the Toyota Prius Facebook site, for example, had more than 430,000 "likes."[21] One of the most popular websites of 2013 was www.outgrow.me, which featured products that were ready for orders from Kickstarter and Indiegogo. If they're shown on outgrow.me, then products have received enough funding and are available.

Cross-Selling

Cross-selling occurs when customers are sold additional products as the result of an initial purchase. The initial purchase allows the seller to segment the customer. E-mails to customers from Amazon.com describing other products purchased by people who purchased the same product a customer just bought, is an attempt at cross-selling. If the additional products or services purchased are even more profitable than the original purchase, this can provide significant add-on profits for the firm. In addition, if firms are successful at cross-selling the right products at the right time to the right customers, then customers perceive this as individualized attention, and it results in more satisfied and loyal customers.

When Bank of America acquired Merrill Lynch in 2009 for $50 billion, a number of cross-selling opportunities arose, since its wealth management employees could view each customer's savings and checking accounts along with their investment portfolios. One year later, these cross-selling opportunities were bearing fruit—global wealth management business had increased for Bank of America and profit margins were in excess of 20 percent—significantly higher than industry averages.[22] For banks, cross-selling to existing customers as a growth strategy makes sense. A 2009 survey by market research company Forrester found that 60 percent of consumers said they were unlikely to switch their banking provider, making new customer acquisitions expensive for banks. "It costs a lot less to mail to 10 percent of your best customers than it does to mail to 100,000 prospects," says Grover Pagano, vice president for Analytics at Texas-based Harland Clarke, a direct marketing service.[23]

Predicting Customer Behaviors

By understanding customers' current purchasing behaviors, future behaviors can be predicted. Using data mining software and customer behavior analytics allows firms to predict which products customers are likely to purchase next and how much they would be willing to pay. In this way, companies can revise pricing policies, offer discounts, and design promotions to specific customer segments. Sheldon Gilbert, the creator of Proclivity, a behavior predicting software used by New York-based Proclivity Systems, knows all about you—your favorite color, how many times you added that flat screen TV to your online shopping cart without buying it, and what you like to do in your spare time. Sheldon explains, "Every time you click a link, it's a request for information you're making to a server. We can then mine the data stored on the servers to create a profile of a person's likes and dislikes or proclivities." Using this information to advise which offers should be presented to which customers, Gilbert's company has increased online sales by as much as 30 percent for clients like upscale department store Barney's New York.[24] Along with determining what customers might purchase next, another desirable CRM attribute is **customer defection analysis**.

Customer Defection Analysis

Reducing customer defections (also referred to as **customer churn**) is another component of managing long-term customer relationships. And it can pay handsomely as well. According to Harvard Business School research, a 5 percent improvement in customer retention can result in a 75 percent increase in profits.[25] Today, competition in almost every product category is very high, and along with it, customer savvy. "The average consumer has more information at his fingertips with which to make informed decisions about a relationship with companies than he has had in the past," says Jonathan Trichel, principal of customer and market strategy at Deloitte Consulting.

Knowing which customers have quit purchasing and why can be very valuable information for organizations. Recent research has found that the top four reasons for customer defections are rude employees/poor attitudes, overall poor service, employees socializing and not paying attention to customers, and slow service.[26] Not only can these customers be approached to encourage additional purchases, but the knowledge gained can be used to reduce future defections. "If I've got an 80 percent satisfaction rate, the focus needs to be on the 20 percent of dissatisfied customers," says Bob Furniss, president of CRM consultancy Touchpoint Associates of Tennessee. "If I can understand what's occurring in the 20 percent, then my impact is much more profound than being satisfied with the satisfaction rate."[27]

Offers of money or free minutes from telephone service companies are examples of efforts to regain customers who have defected to another phone service. In some cases, though, organizations may actually want some customers (unprofitable ones) to defect. By determining the value or profitability of each of the defecting customers, firms can design appropriate policies for retaining or regaining some customers as well as policies to discourage additional purchases from other customers (also termed *firing customers*). In some department stores, for instance, customers who repeatedly return merchandise are at some point given only store credit instead of cash. By monitoring purchase histories, firms can see if this type of discouragement makes customers quit returning merchandise.

Customer Value Determination

Until recently, determining **customer value** or **customer profitability** was difficult for most CRM systems. Today, though, by integrating with ERP systems, capturing customer profitability information is possible. However, improper use of this information can cause poor decisions to be made. For instance, some customers who are unprofitable now, may become profitable later. A health club, for instance, may have some unmarried members who rarely make other purchases at the club but frequently visit and use the facility. While this type of member might be seen as unprofitable, it is likely that if these members are satisfied with the club, they will tell others, and at some point they may marry and upgrade to a family membership. Thus, it is necessary to determine **customer lifetime value (CLV)** such that appropriate benefits, communications, services, or policies can be directed toward (or withheld from) customers or customer segments.

Unless a firm has knowledge of customer profitability, they may be directing sizeable resources catering to customers who are actually unprofitable. For instance, in a study published by consultant and database marketing author Arthur Middleton Hughes, he described how Boston-based Fleet Bank's marketing staff was working hard trying to retain customers who were actually unprofitable. In fact, half of Fleet's customers were deemed unprofitable, with the bottom 28 percent gobbling up 22 percent of the bank's total annual profits.[28] Calculating CLV is based on a projection of a customer's lifetime purchases, the average profit margin on the items purchased, and the net present value of the customer's projected profits. Example 10.1 illustrates this calculation.

Estimating customers' total lifetime purchases can also help to focus resources on managing the right customers. Consider two business customers, for example, one with purchases of $2 million per year and the other with annual purchases of $1 million. At first glance, the first customer might seem more valuable; however, if that customer's total purchases from all suppliers for similar products is $3 million whereas the second firm's total purchases of similar products is $20 million, then the second firm suddenly has much more potential for additional sales and should be managed with that potential in mind.

Example 10.1 Calculating Customer Lifetime Value

The Kentucky Bluegrass Seed Company sells grass seed and other Kentucky-area plant seeds to area plant nurseries. They have decided to begin calculating the expected lifetime profitability of each of their nursery customers in order to design differential grass and plant seed promotions. Their top two customers have the following characteristics:

	AVG. ANNUAL SALES	AVG. PROFIT MARGIN	EXPECTED LIFETIME
Nursery A:	\$22,000	20%	5 years
Nursery B:	\$16,000	15%	15 years

Using a discount rate of 8 percent, and treating the average sales figures as annuities, the present value of the two nursery lifetime values is:

$$NPV_A = a\left[\frac{(1+i)^n - 1}{i(1+i)^n}\right] = \$22{,}000\,(.2)\left[\frac{(1+.08)^5 - 1}{.08(1+.08)^5}\right] = \$4{,}400\left[\frac{0.469}{0.118}\right] = \$17{,}488$$

$$NPV_B = a\left[\frac{(1+i)^n - 1}{i(1+i)^n}\right] = \$16{,}000\,(.15)\left[\frac{(1+.08)^{15} - 1}{.08(1+.08)^{15}}\right] = \$2{,}400\left[\frac{2.172}{0.254}\right] = \$20{,}522$$

where

a = average annual profit, or the (annual sales) × (profit margin)
i = annual discount rate
n = expected lifetime in years.

Based on these calculations, Nursery B is the more important customer because of the higher expected lifetime value.

Personalizing Customer Communications

Knowledge of customers, their behaviors, and their preferences allows firms to customize communications aimed at specific groups of customers. Referring to customers by their first name, or suggesting services used in the past, communicates value to the customer and is likely to result in greater levels of sales. The Ritz-Carlton Hotel, for instance, profiles its customers in order to provide the accommodations each person prefers on subsequent visits. The nearby SCM Profile describes these customer efforts in greater detail.

CRM software that can analyze customers' **clickstreams**, or how they navigate a website, can tailor a website's images, ads, or discounts based on past usage of the site. Website businesses may also send personalized e-mails, for instance, with incentives to lure customers back, if it has been a while since their last purchase. A quick-change oil and lube shop might send a postcard to a customer's address every ninety days, reminding them it's time for an oil change while offering a discount on the next visit. On the same card, it may also offer discounts on other services that the customer has used in the past, such as a radiator flush, a tune-up, or a tire rotation. With time, this customization capability improves, as the firm learns of additional services, products, and purchasing behaviors exhibited by various customers.

Event-Based Marketing

Another form of personalized communication comes with the ability to offer individual promotions tied to specific events. Banks, for example, may try to market automated mortgage payment services to all of their customers who have recently applied for and received a home mortgage loan. The same bank might offer home improvement loans to customers once their mortgages reach an age of five years. The idea with **event-based marketing** (also referred to as trigger-based or event-driven marketing) is to offer the right products and services to customers at just the right time. When entertainment venues or restaurants

Ritz-Carlton's Use of Customer Profiles

Homey coziness is not exactly the prevailing atmosphere outside the Ritz's door on Central Park South in New York. The hotel itself is neither particularly small nor time-worn. All rooms facing the park come equipped with telescopes and a field guide to birds of New York, for those craving a bit of treetop ornithology before rushing off to their breakfast meetings. In the corridors, the 1920s-style house telephones with porcelain handles and brass cradles evoke the Gatsby era. But it takes more than furnishings to maintain five-star ambience in the heart of Manhattan, says Scott Geraghty, general manager. "Satisfying the unexpressed wishes of our guests is our highest calling," he says.

To divine these whims, Ritz employees turn to the Internet, drawing up profiles of soon-to-be-arriving guests and coming up with extracurricular activities or amenities to enhance their stays. "We are Google masters," Geraghty boasts. Spotting that a retired military officer was arriving during New York's Fleet Week, Geraghty arranged a private tour of some of the visiting vessels. A guest with an equestrian passion got an unanticipated trot with New York Police Department mounted police. The Arab sheikhs who frequent the Royal Suite on the twenty-second floor find prayer rugs awaiting them, as well as room layouts that offer royal family members some privacy from their entourage of cooks, physicians, and body guards.

Newcomers stay at the Ritz to be part of the tradition, not to change it. At least that is Geraghty's doctrine. Revenue per room in U.S. luxury hotels crashed by 24 percent in 2009, and the Ritz-Carlton has had to make some layoffs; but three immaculately groomed concierges still stand on duty at the front desk, ready to cater to guests' every need.[29]

ask for the birth dates of their customers as they purchase tickets or meals, for instance, they can direct future discounts to occur on days they are likely to be celebrating. Or when bank customers call to determine the payout on an existing home mortgage, this indicates the customer is considering a different bank—an event-based tactic might be to transfer the caller to a special customer-save group at the call center. With large volumes of customers, event-based promotion strategies are impossible without computer automation, so event-based marketing capabilities tend to be popular among firms seeking to purchase CRM systems.

Automated Sales Force Tools

Sales force automation (SFA) products are used for documenting field activities, communicating with the home office, and retrieval of sales history and other company-specific documents in the field. Today, sales personnel need better ways to manage their accounts, their business opportunities, and their communications while away from the office. To supply these capabilities, firms have been using CRM tools since the early 1990s to help management and sales personnel keep up with the ever-more complicated layers of information that are required as customers and prospects increase. When field sales personnel have ready access to the latest forecasts, sales, inventory, marketing plans, and account information, it allows more accurate and timely decisions to be made in the field, ultimately increasing sales force productivity and improving customer service capabilities.

North Carolina bottling company Coca-Cola Bottling Co., for example, reorganized to improve the execution of its sales force. It split the team, with one part specializing in distribution while the other focused on improving sales. With this change, it had to address communication between the two groups as well as enable the sales group to handle more products, new product information, marketing materials, and in-store execution capabilities. To handle these needs, the company rolled out new mobile devices, featuring a custom-built sales force automation solution. Orders are taken on the new handheld devices, wirelessly transmitted to the company's network, and then prepared for delivery.[30] Some of the desired CRM capabilities in the area of sales force automation are discussed next.

Sales Activity Management

These tools are customized to each firm's sales policies and procedures and offer sales personnel a sequence of activities guiding them through their sales processes with customers. These standardized steps assure the proper sales activities are performed and also put forth a uniform sales process across the entire organization. The use of a **sales activity management system** reduces errors, improves sales force productivity, and boosts customer satisfaction. Along with the prescribed sales steps, field sales reps can be reminded of key customer activities as they are needed, generate mailings for inactive customers, be assigned tasks by management, and generate to-do lists. Pennsylvania pharmaceutical distributor AmerisourceBergen, for instance, needed an easy way to reach customers with a consistent message. With the help of a consultant and an automated message management software application, it created an interactive portal on its internal network for its sales reps. This allowed sales personnel to customize presentation slides, brochures, proposals, e-mail, follow-up letters, and other forms of client communication. "It's true situational selling," says Scan Markey, vice president of business operations at AmerisourceBergen. "And it's cool how it saves time, not having to mill through a myriad of collateral or making your own sales pieces."[31]

Sales Territory Management

Sales territory management systems allow sales managers to obtain current information and reporting capabilities regarding each sales person's activities on each customer's account, total sales in general for each sales rep, their sales territories, and any ongoing sales initiatives. Using these tools, sales managers can create sales teams specifically suited to a customer's needs, generate profiles of sales personnel, track performance, and keep up with new leads generated in the field. Poorly planned sales territories, for example, can reduce face time for sales personnel, resulting in lower sales.

Lead Management

Using a **lead management system** allows sales reps to follow prescribed sales tactics when dealing with sales prospects or opportunities, to aid in closing the deal. These applications can generate additional steps as needed to help refine the deal closing and negotiation process. During this process, sales personnel can generate product configurations and price quotes directly, using laptops or handheld devices remotely linked to the firm's server. In addition, leads can be assigned to field sales personnel as they are generated, based on the requirements of the prospect and the skill sets of the sales reps. Thus, lead management capabilities should result in higher deal closing success rates in less time. Another common characteristic allows managers to track the closing success of sales personnel and the future orders generated by each lead.

Another type of lead management system is for use with company websites. "Roughly three-out-of-four Internet leads fall through the cracks because businesses don't have a website that captures contacts nor simple tools for lead conversion," says ReachLocal chief product officer Kris Barton. The California-based ReachEdge system, for example, converts website visitors into leads through visitor engagement. The system sends automated staff reminders, including full lead details and call recordings, which helps ensure no leads go unseen or unaddressed. The system also automatically sends a series of customized marketing e-mails to prospects to keep the merchant top of mind until they are ready to buy.[32]

Knowledge Management

Sales personnel require access to a variety of information before, during, and after a sale, including information on contracts, client and competitor profiles, client sales histories, corporate policies, expense reimbursement forms, regulatory issues and laws, sales presentations, promotional materials, and previous client correspondence. Easy access to this information enables quick decision-making, better customer service, and a better-equipped and more productive sales staff. When sales and other skilled personnel leave an organization, years of accumulated knowledge walk out the door with them, unless a system is in place to capture this information for further use. A **knowledge management system** gives the organization this capability. Iowa-based Dupaco Community Credit Union installed several CRM tools including a knowledge management system. "We've seen a clear improvement in consistency of message and we understand situations better thanks to our CRM tools. Members don't have to repeat themselves when talking with different staff about service delivery or issue resolution because all employees have the notes from previous conversations at their fingertips," says Steve Ervolino, senior vice president of information services.[33]

Managing Customer Service Capabilities

A key objective for any CRM initiative is the ability to provide good customer service. In fact, with any process dealing with the customer, a primary objective is always to provide adequate levels of customer service. But what does customer service actually mean? In Chapter 7, customer service was discussed in terms of safety stock and managing inventory. In Chapter 9, customer service was tied to delivering goods on time. And as mentioned earlier in this chapter, customer service can also mean answering customers' questions and having disputes or product and service problems resolved appropriately and quickly. Thus, many definitions of customer service can be found. As a matter of fact, numerous customer service rankings exist and are published each year. Unfortunately, complaints about shoddy customer service abound in many organizations today, and this represents one area where organizations can create real competitive advantage, if customer service processes are designed and operated correctly. The next segment defines customer service and discusses several elements of customer service.

Customer Service Defined

One **customer service** definition covers most of the elements mentioned above, and that is the "**Seven Rs Rule.**"[34] The seven Rs stand for having the *right* product, in the *right* quantity, in the *right* condition, at the *right* place, at the *right* time, for the *right* customer, and at the *right* cost. In logistics parlance, for instance, a **perfect order** occurs when all seven Rs are satisfied. This customer service definition can be applied to any service provider or manufacturer, and for any customer. A misstep in any of the seven areas results in lower levels of customer service. Consequently, competitive advantage can be engendered by creating an organization that routinely satisfies the seven Rs.

Organizational performance measures are often designed around satisfying some of the seven Rs. For example, reducing stockouts to 1 percent means that customers get the product or service they want 99 percent of the time, and having an on-time delivery performance of 97 percent means that customers get their orders at the right time 97 percent of the time. Other customer service measures are typically designed to measure *flexibility* (responding to changes in customer orders), *response* (responding to requests for information), *recovery* (the ability to solve customer problems), and *post-sales support* (providing operating information, parts, equipment, and repairs). In the airline industry, customer service is measured using frequencies of lost or damaged baggage, bumped passengers, canceled flights, on-time flights, and customer complaints. In North America, Alaska Airlines, JetBlue, Southwest, and Delta were the top-rated air carriers in terms of customer service in 2012, while US Air and Frontier were rated the worst according to a 2012 survey by J.D. Power and Associates.[35] The nearby SCM Profile describes the award-winning service of Etihad Airways.

Providing award-winning services to customers keeps them returning; however, this also comes at a cost. Firms must consider the costs of providing good customer service (e.g., faster transport, greater safety stock levels, more service provider training, and better comforts as described in the SCM Profile) as well as the benefits (keeping customers' future profit streams). In organized supply chain relationships, firms often work together in determining (and paying for) adequate customer service, because the costs of poor customer service can be substantial.

Etihad Airways Knows Customer Service

Abu Dhabi–based Etihad Airways has emerged as the personification of what it means to put the customer first. Since its inception, the carrier has worked to embed a culture of excellence at the core of the business. Its benchmarks are not other airlines, but rather five-star hotels and restaurants.

As part of its Inspired Service initiative, Etihad introduced onboard food and beverage managers who are exclusively dedicated to serving the business class cabin; and onboard chefs for its first-class cabin. Etihad also installed luxurious individual suites in the first-class cabin. Accessed by a separate sliding door, the leather seat extends to a fully flat bed and includes a personal wardrobe and mini bar, as well as a 23-inch entertainment flat screen. Business class also features fully flat beds. Premium lounges offer any time, a la carte dining and buffet cuisine, business and relaxation areas, and a complimentary spa, champagne, and cigar bar.

Etihad also offers a range of novel services on the ground. At Abu Dhabi airport, for example, the airline has its own terminal with porter and concierge facilities. Remarkable passenger service throughout the travel and across all cabins, and an ability to blend global, contemporary service with genuine Arabian hospitality make Etihad a deserving winner of the Air Transport World Passenger Service Award.[36]

Customer service elements can be classified as **pretransaction**, **transaction**, and **posttransaction elements**. Each of these is briefly discussed next.

- *Pretransaction elements*: These customer service elements precede the actual product or service purchase; examples are customer service policies, the organization's service structure, and the service system's flexibility.
- *Transaction elements*: These elements occur during the sale of the product or service and include the order lead time, the order processing capabilities, and the distribution system accuracy.
- *Posttransaction elements*: These elements refer to the after-sale services and include warranty repair capabilities, complaint resolution, product returns, and operating information.

To provide high levels of service and value to customers, firms seek to continually satisfy the seven Rs while also developing adequate customer service capabilities before, during, and after the sale. Call centers have been used in many organizations to improve customer service and supply chain performance and this topic is discussed next.

Call Centers

Call centers or **customer contact centers** have existed for many years, and some organizations have used these effectively to satisfy and keep customers loyal, while others have seen them as a necessary cost of doing business and viewed them as a drain on profits. As call centers became automated, customer service representatives were able to quickly see how similar questions were answered in the past, and resolve problems more quickly, resulting in greater call center effectiveness. Call center systems can categorize calls, determine average resolution time, and forecast future call volumes. These automated systems can reduce call center labor costs and training times, and improve the overall productivity of the staff, while improving customer service levels.

Within the past ten years, call centers implemented virtual queuing systems, and most callers see this as a convenient call center characteristic. The virtual queue allows callers to request a callback from an agent without losing their place in the phone queue, which frees up callers' time, reduces caller frustration, and also reduces call center toll charges for keeping callers on hold. More recently, call centers have created interfaces with mobile applications to further enhance the customer experience. When a mobile customer can't complete his or her transaction, the application automatically forwards the entire history of the customer's mobile session to the contact center. The contact center then places the customer in a virtual queue and sends the customer a notice of when an agent will call. The customer has the option of taking the callback as scheduled or rescheduling it to a more convenient time. Either way, there are no wasted cell minutes. The agent also knows what steps the customer has already gone through and was attempting to do when the app issue popped up. When the call to the customer is made, the agent knows the entire transaction context, who the customer is, and his or her purchase history.[37]

Aside from solving customer problems, call centers today are also viewed increasingly as a source of revenue for the firm. In fact, a survey of managers at U.K. and U.S. in-house call centers revealed that 60 percent viewed their call centers as profit centers. Today, call center staff are expected to pursue cross-sell and up-sell opportunities. Additionally, 86 percent of the managers stated that reps needed a broader range of skills to deliver these revenues. "With more and more consumers opting out of direct marketing (telephone, mail, and e-mail), companies are realizing that they need to take advantage of every customer interaction; not only to serve the customers' needs, but to engage with them individually, build relationships and extend the customer lifetime value through effective up-sell and cross-sell," says Mark Smith, executive vice president at Portrait Software, a CRM software provider.[38]

While the practice of call center outsourcing has been around several decades, in the latter 1990s and the 2000s outsourcing call centers to offshore companies really exploded. The growth of the Internet, a boom in telecommunications capacity, cheap available labor, and education systems in areas like the Philippines, India, and Pakistan that encouraged the development of an English-speaking workforce all acted to create a perfect environment for the offshoring of call centers (along with other types of businesses). Today, though, as unemployment levels remain high and wage levels have come down in the U.S. relative to prerecession levels, and as labor costs have increased in popular offshore locations like India, this trend is reversing. Security issues are also hastening this trend. A report issued by the Communication Workers of America cites several examples of call center security breaches that were reported in the international media:

- Call center employees in India were caught stealing from Citibank customers by getting them to reveal their passwords;
- An undercover journalist bought the personal information, including passwords, of 1,000 British Bank customers from an Indian call center worker; and
- A Pakistani woman threatened to post patient records on the Internet unless she got a raise.

Finally, the use of an at-home workforce in the U.S. has helped to increase customer satisfaction with call centers. Cynthia Phillips, vice president of marketing for Colorado-based contact center provider Alpine Access, which uses home-based agents exclusively, says they can hire agents with more education and experience because they can recruit from a much broader base of applicants.[39]

Measuring Customer Satisfaction

Measuring customer satisfaction remains somewhat of a tricky proposition. Customers are frequently given opportunities to provide feedback about a product, service, or organization through customer feedback cards placed at cash registers or on tables. Customer surveys are also provided with purchased products or shown on firm websites. In most cases, though, the only time these forms are filled out is when customers are experiencing a problem. Given this, companies still can find valuable uses for the information. Responses can be analyzed and used to find solutions for the most commonly occurring problems. In CRM applications, customer satisfaction surveys can be personalized to fit specific customer segments, and responses can be matched to respondents' profiles to provide the company direction on improving its communication and service capabilities for various groups of customers.

The design of the surveys themselves can be a particular problem. In many cases, surveys don't ask the questions customers want to answer. On many website surveys, customers are more often asked about the design of the website instead of how the firm is performing or what the customer may be happy or unhappy about. In a study of both brick-and-mortar and Internet banks, for instance, less than half of all the banks studied even used customer comment cards or surveys, and only two banks in the study (both were Internet banks) offered service quality surveys.[40]

On the other hand, actually talking with and listening to customers and then taking action based on what customers are saying lets customers know the firm is completely engaged. Domino's Pizza, for example, completely redesigned its product after listening to unflattering customer comments. According to new product development expert and author Don Adams, many companies are designing a new product, testing it with some potential customers, and then measuring their success by watching sales. Instead, companies should initiate feedback from customers prior to designing products. "There's no substitute for respectful dialogue with customers," says Adams. "People inside companies tend to get defensive about their products and processes," he adds. "It's only human. But when you can cut through that defensiveness and show them 'Hey, this really isn't working for our customers,' well that's where true service and value finally begin."[41]

In this section of the chapter, the common elements necessary for successful CRM programs were reviewed. Many of these involve the use of technology and software. But having numerous software applications does not necessarily guarantee CRM success. A number of other factors come into play before, during, and after programs are implemented that must be adhered to, in order to give the firm and its CRM program a good chance of finding and keeping profitable customers. The next section will discuss this very important aspect of CRM.

DESIGNING AND IMPLEMENTING A SUCCESSFUL CRM PROGRAM

Designing and then implementing a CRM program can be a real challenge, because it requires an understanding of and commitment to the firm's customers, adherence to CRM goals, knowledge of the tools available to aid in CRM, support from the firm's top executives and the various departments that will be using the CRM tools, and a continuous awareness of customers' changing requirements. Poor planning is typically the cause for most unsuccessful CRM initiatives, because of the temptation to start working on a solution or to purchase several CRM applications before understanding the problem. The firm must first answer this question: *What are the problems a CRM program is going to solve?* This must involve employees from all functional groupings across the firm, as well as input from the firm's key customers. Putting together a sound CRM plan will force the organization to think about CRM needs, technology alternatives, and the providers that sell them. Selecting the right tools and providers is an important step but should not occur until a CRM plan is completed.

Aside from creating a CRM plan and getting the firm's employees to buy-in to the idea and uses of CRM tools, managers must also consider any existing CRM initiatives implemented in piecemeal fashion across the firm. Integrating new and existing applications into one enterprise-wide initiative should be one of the primary objectives of the CRM implementation process. Additionally, the firm must decide on specific performance outcomes and assessments for the program and provide adequate training to the CRM application users.

Creating the CRM Plan

Putting together a solid plan for a CRM project is crucial as an aid both to purchasing and implementing CRM applications and to obtaining executive management approval and funding for the project. The plan should include the objectives of the CRM program; its fit with corporate strategy; new applications to be purchased or used; the integration or replacement of existing methods or legacy CRM systems; the requirements for personnel, training, policies, upgrades, and maintenance; and the costs and time frame for implementation. Once this document is completed, the firm will have a roadmap for guiding the purchase and implementation process, as well as the organizational performance measures to be used once the program is in place.

New York–based Travel Dynamics International, for instance, a luxury small-ship charter cruise operator, had multiple software systems to handle customer-oriented processes, and it realized that some customers were not being served adequately. "Clients were slipping through the cracks. We were not efficient, and there were process gaps," says Nikos Papagapitos, manager of technology and special projects at Travel Dynamics. It ended up merging a Microsoft CRM application with its legacy application in December 2008. "It was a complete 180 from before, instead of looking in four or five places, we had one integrated database for everything. Now if a person calls in, we can see their history with us, and can record what made them choose us in the first place," Papagapitos explains.[42]

The objectives of any CRM initiative should be customer-focused. Examples might include increasing sales per customer, improving overall customer satisfaction, more closely integrating the firm's key customers with internal processes, or increasing supply chain responsiveness. These will vary somewhat based on the overall strategic focus of the firm. Once these objectives are in place, tactical goals and plans can be instituted at the functional level, consistent with the CRM objectives. Finally, tactical performance measures can be used to track the ongoing performance of the CRM program. This performance will serve to justify the initial and ongoing costs of the program.

Involving CRM Users from the Outset

In order to get acceptance of a new CRM initiative, employee involvement and support is required. This comes about by enlisting the help of everyone affected by the initiative from the very beginning. Employees need to understand how the CRM initiative will affect their jobs before they will buy-in to the program. Creating a project team with members from sales, customer service, marketing, finance, and production, for instance, will tremendously aid in the selection, training, use, and acceptance of the CRM program. The team can contact CRM application providers and collect information regarding capabilities and costs, and they can also collect baseline or current customer service, sales, complaint, and other meaningful performance information. The team should also be heavily involved in evaluating and selecting the CRM applications and then implementing and integrating the applications in each department. As the implementation process continues, closely monitoring system performance will keep users convinced of the value of the initiative and keep everyone committed to its success.

Quite a bit of research has been conducted to study CRM implementations, and most studies have found a direct relationship between program success and employee involvement. Several researchers in New Zealand, for instance, talked with managers at three banks that had implemented CRM programs several years earlier. Two of the banks had failed to focus on employee buy-in while the third bank introduced a new sales culture to complement its CRM project, to win employee support. Eventually, the third bank's CRM system proved to be much more successful. In another example, Beene Garter, a Michigan area accounting firm, designed an internal contest to "sell" CRM to its employees. "Teams were assigned 'homework' on client records and the software tracked who entered updates," says Den Ouden of Beene Garter. "The contest mirrored components of the Olympics and was called 'Go for the Gold' to tie into the software name, GoldMine," she adds. Their success was remarkable. Users' attitudes about the CRM project changed from anxiety associated with entering all the data to familiarity that created easy adoption and continuous use.[43]

Selecting the Right Application and Provider

Once the organization has completed its plan for CRM, it should have a fairly good idea of what it is going to do and which activities will require automation or technology. The job then becomes one of finding an appropriate application and deciding how much customization will be required to get the job done.

Finding the best application and supplier can be accomplished a number of ways including:

- visiting a CRM-oriented tradeshow
- using a CRM consulting firm
- searching CRM or business publications such as *Customer Magazine*, *Call Center Helper*, and *Inside Supply Management*
- using the knowledge of internal IT personnel, who already know the market, and
- searching the many CRM supplier directories and websites

Firms should seek help from a number of these alternatives, and internal IT personnel should be viewed as internal consultants in the application and supplier identification and selection process. Firms must analyze and compare the various products available. In her CRM handbook, Dychè recommends comparing the following software characteristics:[44]

- integration and connection requirements (the hardware, software, and networking capabilities)
- processing and performance requirements (the volume of data and number of users it can support)
- security requirements
- reporting requirements (preformatted and customized reporting capabilities)
- usability requirements (ability for users to customize the software, display graphics, and print information)
- function-enabling features (workflow management, e-mail response engine, predictive modeling capabilities), and
- performance capabilities (response times for various queries)

Comparing these CRM capabilities should narrow the list of qualified vendors substantially. When finally selecting a supplier for the application, one of the primary criteria for firms to consider is the support available from the application provider. Vendors offering implementation and after-sale user support that meets the needs of the firm should be valued more highly than other vendors. Suppliers offering free trial usage to verify their products' capabilities is another element that needs to be considered. Finally, cost and contract negotiations should be carefully considered. Pepperdine University recently purchased a CRM solution, and a discussion of this appears in the nearby SCM Profile.

Integrating Existing CRM Applications

In most firms, CRM systems are not one single product, but rather a suite of various applications that have been implemented over time. One of the biggest mistakes made is that departments across the firm implement various CRM applications without

SCM Profile — Pepperdine Uses a CRM System for Student Recruitment

Pepperdine University in California has a well-deserved reputation for personal attention to its students, leading to successful graduates and loyal alumni. As a result, it is always evaluating practices that personalize the student recruitment process. "We need to be responsive to the information our prospects provide to us and then have the ability to build relationships with those students based on targeted, personal communication," says Michael Truschke, Pepperdine dean of Admission and Enrollment Management.

Pepperdine's undergraduate enrollment office began searching for a CRM system, and it eventually chose Recruitment CRM from TargetX. TargetX's system helps colleges manage, integrate, and automate the process of student recruitment from the first point of contact through enrollment. Among its strengths is built-in electronic communication, including an e-mail broadcasting tool. It is also fully integrated with a powerful event manager and online application.

Pepperdine implemented TargetX's system to help its undergraduate school recruit traditional students. "TargetX will allow us to connect more effectively with prospective students and their families," says Truschke. One of Pepperdine's goals in selecting a CRM solution was the ability to track student contact more efficiently. "Currently that process is not as streamlined as we would like it to be," Truschke said. "With the TargetX CRM, we will be able to record, track and make informed data-driven decisions about the effectiveness of our recruitment activities."[45]

communicating these actions to other departments. Eventually, these systems will interfere with each other, as they communicate with the same customer, sending confusing and irritating signals that can chase customers away quickly.

Customer contact mechanisms need to be coordinated so that every CRM application user within the firm knows about all the contact activity for each customer. Today, this lack of integration is leading to real problems as call centers and sales offices seek to please and retain customers by adopting customer loyalty programs, customer tracking mechanisms, and various customer contact mechanisms like Twitter and Facebook, without making this information widely known and available within the firm. Additionally, multiple stand-alone CRM applications throughout the company result in duplication of effort, incompatible formats, wasted money, and disgruntled customers. Compatible CRM modules are needed that are linked to one centralized database or **data warehouse** containing all customer information. Thus, from one database, users in the organization can retrieve information on a customer's profile, purchase history, promotion responses, payment history, web visitations, merchandise returns, warranty repairs, and call center contacts.

By integrating CRM information obtained throughout the firm, managers can analyze the information and make much more customer-focused decisions. Using predictive models and statistical analyses, firms can identify customers most likely to purchase certain products, respond to a new promotion, or churn. As the number of customers grow, however, their transactions and the desire to analyze all of this information is referred to as **big data analytics**. In some companies, the volume of customer data is monumental—in four hours on "black Friday" 2012, Walmart handled 10 million cash register transactions, or 5,000 items per second; UPS receives over 39 million tracking requests per day from customers; and VISA processes more than 172 million card transactions each day.[46]

Some experts argue that trying to make sense of some big data like social media interactions can cause poor decision-making, as managers ignore the more routine "little" data, such as financial, customer, and product quality information. In 2012, for example, CEO Ron Johnson of retailer J.C. Penney drastically changed how it presented and priced merchandise, based on data showing that its customers didn't buy until items were marked down by 27 percent, and that customers didn't buy much of its private label. Within 18 months, Johnson was fired, primarily because Penney sales were down more than 25 percent. Johnson's replacement, Myron Ullman, looked at the same data and declared their private label merchandise to be their most profitable, so he is bringing their old clothing lines back and using Penney's old promotional tactics. Recent sales figures seemed to prove that Ullman's strategies were working.[47]

With interest income shrinking and loan demand weakening at banks, bankers today are rethinking how they can broaden customer relationships. According to Alabama-based consulting firm Bancography, a bank customer using one product will stay with that bank for about 18 months, but when adding two more products the expected customer lifetime jumps to about 6.8 years. MidSouth Bank in Louisiana recently converted to a new Oracle CRM system that gathers all customer information into a central database, allowing product innovations to be aligned with customer needs. "It's the 360-degree view of the customer you hear about," says the bank's marketing officer Alex Calicchia. "It's about giving the frontline in particular, the ability to look at a given moment, what's in the customer's wallet today and what's missing from that wallet."[48]

Establishing Performance Measures

Performance measures linked to CRM program objectives (and customers) allow managers to monitor the progression of the system in meeting its objectives. It also serves to keep everyone excited and informed about the benefits of a well-designed program and will identify any implementation or usage problems as they occur, allowing causes to be found and solutions to be implemented quickly.

At the organizational level, performance measures should concentrate on areas deemed strategically important, such as CRM program productivity, new customers added, or sales generated from the CRM program. Some examples of these measures are listed in Table 10.1. Note that the performance measures are spread between the customers, the CRM program itself, and the users. Additionally, all of the metrics should be transparent and easy to measure. At the user level, other more tactical performance measures should be developed and tracked, supporting the firm-wide strategic measures. Linking performance measures in this way will give the firm the best chance of a successful program implementation and continued management of the program into the future.

Training for CRM Users

Another important step in the implementation process is to provide and require training for all of the initial system users, and then provide ongoing training as applications are added or as other personnel begin to see the benefits of the CRM system. Training can also help convince key users such as sales, call center, and marketing personnel of the benefits and uses of CRM applications. Training is one area crucial to CRM program success. Unfortunately, in a recent survey conducted by *Customer Relationship Management* magazine, 43 percent of the respondents said their user training "needed improvement."[50] Unless the users are shown the personal gains they'll receive for taking time to learn the software and its capabilities, the CRM applications will most likely go unused or underused. Karen

Table 10.1 CRM Program Performance Measures[49]

PERFORMANCE MEASUREMENT TYPE	DEPARTMENT OR USER-LEVEL PERFORMANCE MEASURES		
	FIELD SALES	CALL CENTER	MARKETING
Customer Loyalty	1. % customer repurchases 2. avg. # repurchases 3. # customer referrals	1. # customer product information requests 2. # customer praises	1. % existing customers responding to promotions 2. # customer referrals
Customer Satisfaction	1. avg. # customer visits to resolve problem 2. # field service visits per customer	1. # complaints per customer 2. % first call resolution	1. % customers responding more than once to promotions 2. # customers engaged using social contacts
Average Sales Revenue per Customer	1. # sales quotas met 2. % repeat visits resulting in sales	1. sales per customer call 2. cross-sales and up-sales per customer call 3. % calls converted	1. # website/social visits per customer 2. website/social purchases per customer
CRM Productivity	1. % sales quotas met 2. # new leads generated 3. % new leads closed	1. avg. caller time 2. # complaints resolved 3. sales/call/hr. 4. transactions/agent/hr.	1. # segment catalogs produced 2. # promotional e-mails sent 3. # marketing campaigns 4. avg. campaign response rate
CRM User Satisfaction	1. sales rep. satisfaction score	1. call center agent satisfaction score	1. user satisfaction score
CRM User Training	1. hrs. training per year per rep. 2. # CRM applications trained per rep.	1. hrs. training per year per agent 2. # CRM applications trained per agent	1. hrs. training per year per user 2. # CRM applications trained per user

Ainley, product manager at U.K.-based CRM software developer Sage, emphasizes that shortcuts in training can ultimately prove costly. "The perception that CRM is so easy to use that you don't need training is a fallacy. By dismissing the need for training in the hope that users will simply 'learn on the job' and adapt their way of working, companies really are limiting the software's potential."[51]

Training managers and users in the key customer contact areas can also help the firm decide what customizations to the CRM applications are required, before the system is put into use. This is particularly important for larger firms where supply chains and the sales and marketing processes are complex. In many cases, CRM system implementation means that other systems already in place will be phased out or merged with the new system. Training can help personnel decide how best to phase out old systems and phase in the new ones. CRM consultant Barton Goldenberg suggests that firms should create a training profile for each of their CRM system users to provide training before, during, and after the implementation process in one or more of these areas: computer literacy training, business process training, CRM application training, remedial training, and new user training.[52]

RECENT TRENDS IN CRM

Customer Data Privacy

A number of trends are affecting the way CRM programs are designed today, and these trends will likely continue to influence CRM programs, application providers, the companies that use them, and finally the customers themselves. One of these is **data privacy**. As the use of the Internet grows, there is growing concern about customers' personal information becoming compromised or being shared with other companies in order to generate income. New privacy regulations are springing up as consumer protection groups continue to push for stronger Internet regulatory measures. As consumer fears mount, companies must take a proactive stand at reassuring their customers that their information will be protected, as well as convincing them to allow information to be used in the first place.

Unfortunately, customer data is sometimes compromised, and this news frequently hits the popular media outlets. For example, international banking company HSBC Holdings PLC announced that an employee stole 24,000 Swiss account records in 2007 and tried selling the information to foreign governments interested in finding tax dodgers. French authorities finally captured the culprit and retrieved the data in 2008 and returned it to HSBC. Later, the bank pledged to spend $100 million to upgrade security. Data breaches in the U.S. are a huge concern—according to the California-based consumer advocacy group Privacy Rights Clearinghouse, 2,500 breaches involving over 600 million records occurred from 2005 through 2010. Additionally, the Federal Trade Commission estimates that 9 million people have their identities stolen each year. And these breaches are expensive—the average cost to manage and repair a data breach is about $6.3 million.[53]

Safeguarding customer information is a legal and ethical responsibility for any company collecting, processing, and transmitting sensitive customer data. Data privacy laws such as the Data Protection Act in the U.K., The Internet Privacy Law in the E.U., and the U.S. Patriot Act, just to name a few, provide laws for protecting customer information and require compliance by all firms engaged in handling customer information. Unfortunately, it has been over ten years since the U.S. passed a cybersecurity law, although virtually every state has passed some form of one. Some of the independent measures firms can take to improve information security are to develop a privacy policy and post it on the company website as well as on other information-gathering forms; allow customers to opt-in and out of mailing lists and promotional campaigns; allow customers to access their accounts online so they can view the information collected about them; require customers to state their privacy preferences, build this into their profiles, and use these preferences when developing one-to-one promotions; make someone in the firm responsible for enforcing privacy policies and communicating these to employees and customers; and continuously monitor employee desktop applications, website activity, e-mails, instant messages, and phone calls.

Social CRM

Not too many years ago, employees were banned from visiting **social media** sites deemed unsuitable for conducting business, such as Facebook, Twitter, LinkedIn, and Pinterest. Today, companies are beginning to see potential value in these and other social media applications. Additionally, a 2012 survey found that 71 percent of 16–24 year olds and 65 percent of 25–34 year olds search for a solution online first, when they encounter a product problem. Another survey by New York–based customer polling agency Harris Interactive found that people are increasingly using social media sites to share good and bad business experiences. Finally, in a 2012 survey of contact center professionals, 42 percent were found to communicate with customers via social sites like Twitter and Facebook.

With this growth in use of the Internet and social media, CRM is evolving into **social CRM**. According to noted CRM author and customer strategy consultant Paul Greenberg, social CRM is "designed to engage the customer in a collaborative conversation in order to provide mutually beneficial value in a trusted and transparent business environment." This type of engagement leads to customer satisfaction and loyalty. Firms can use social media sites to create user forums where technical support and other customer questions are answered by other customers. In many cases, companies are finding this to be an improvement over answers given by the firms' own help desks. Companies like Intel and Linksys have found that the investment to create these social communities can be recouped in less than a year, given the zero labor cost of the social media sites.[54]

Business examples of social networking success and failure can easily be found. Copart, Inc., a Texas-based provider of online vehicle auction services, found success with social media when it tried a new strategy to reach new audiences. Copart teamed up with racing driver Carl Edwards for an online charity auction of his personal memorabilia. Participation in the auction came from all over the world as potential buyers joined in to place their bids. Copart used a new Facebook page, YouTube, and other online advertising sources, along with blogging to introduce fans to Copart.com. The social platforms drove people to become members for free and, if interested, participate in the charity auction. More than 50 percent of the buyers who bid on Edwards' memorabilia were new buyers acquired from the promotion. A mere three weeks after launching this strategy, Copart's Facebook fan base doubled in size. "As a technology-driven company, a strong social media presence is imminent to the future of our business," said Jay Adair, CEO, Copart, Inc. "We are eager and excited about what lies ahead , and where this new strategy will take Copart, as we continue to develop our presence on the social networking scene."[55]

In another example from March 2010, one of food product manufacturing giant Nestle's Facebook friends used a negatively modified Nestle logo as her Facebook photo, and others soon did likewise, as a way to criticize Nestle's use of palm oil in some of its products. Nestle's response was to delete these comments from its Facebook fan page while adding a warning to those who might be breaking trademark laws. Environmental activist group Greenpeace soon joined the Facebook discussion about Nestle's use of palm oil, along with many other activists, arguing that the company was contributing to the destruction of Indonesian rainforests when purchasing palm oil. The fan page quickly got out of control as large numbers of negative comments took over the site. Eventually, Nestle apologized and announced it had partnered with The Forest Trust to ensure that its palm oil products would be 100 percent sustainable by 2015. Since that time, Nestle's Facebook page has been much more fan-friendly.[56]

Really talking to, or engaging customers, is the value of social media. The concept of owning customers is fading as companies realize that customers' jobs, families, and friends are much more important than the brands they buy. Companies wanting to succeed with social media need to use it to listen to their customers. "Listening is the infrastructure that enables you to collect all this information and process it and analyze it," says Suresh Vittal, an analyst at Forrester Research.[57] General Motors, for instance, is talking and listening. After enduring a Chapter 11 bankruptcy, a government bailout, and several miserable sales years, GM began using Facebook and Twitter to raise brand awareness and rebuild some goodwill. "The way we look at it is, Twitter is almost the beginning of the conversation. It's a cocktail party. You walk in, and you're pretty much talking to anyone who's there. Facebook is the dinner party, where it's people you know a little bit, who have opted in to become part of your brand. Twitter conversations are a lot more open and a free-for-all, but there's value in both," says Chris Barger, director of global social media for GM.[58]

CRM Cloud Applications

Another current CRM trend is in the use of **on-demand** or **cloud computing**. Salesforce.com first introduced the concept of Internet-based, cloud computing back in 1999 in a San Francisco garage. To this company, "no software" was the motto. Within two years,

Salesforce.com had 3,500 customers, 53,000 subscribers, and was named the fastest growing online CRM company by Morgan Stanley. By the end of 2012, they had over 100,000 customers and 9,800 employees. In 2013, *Forbes* named Salesforce.com the most innovative company in the U.S. In a world dominated by expensive CRM software, high implementation costs, and with questionable success rates, Salesforce.com's model was simple—online basic CRM applications, low costs, quick implementation, and good results.[59]

Today, there are a large number of these **application service providers (ASPs)** providing cloud applications (not just for CRM), also referred to as the **software-as-a-service model**, or **SaaS model**. Worldwide, total cloud computing service revenues were $58.6 billion in 2009 and are expected to exceed $148 billion by 2014, so the potential market is huge for ASPs.[60] Perhaps as many as 50 percent of all CRM programs are now designed and maintained for clients by ASPs. In many cases, firms without the resources, time, knowledge, or infrastructure to buy and build an effective CRM system, use the cloud-based CRM services. For small companies with limited resources needing some basic CRM functions, the cloud applications have proved very useful. For larger companies with thousands of users seeking a wider range of functionality and customization, purchased CRM applications are still the desired platform and may prove less costly in the long run, since user subscription fees for cloud services are continuous and can become quite costly over time.

As more and more customers seek cloud computing applications, full-service business application providers like Cisco, SAP, IBM, Oracle, Microsoft, and Salesforce.com are scrambling to acquire and develop additional cloud computing products. These providers hope to be one-stop shops where customers can purchase software, hardware, and networking capabilities to build and manage dedicated, internal, or **private clouds** (where the data centers are owned by the corporate users and managed in-house, or a dedicated space is designed and provided by an ASP) or just subscribe to various public cloud applications as needed. "With a private cloud, I can control some of the aspects that bother me about a public cloud, such as security or the system going down," says Gary Matuszak, global chairman for KPMG's information, communications, and entertainment practices.[61]

Cosmetics maker Revlon, for example, was using twenty-one different ERP systems globally, according to its CIO David Giambruno. It is in the process of consolidating all its data and apps onto to a global, private cloud infrastructure. The project is following a massive infrastructure upgrade and master data management project. Revlon has already documented more than $70 million in annual cost avoidance and savings from the total project.[62]

SUMMARY

In this chapter, we introduced and discussed the elements of CRM, its place within the field of supply chain management, the requirements for successful CRM program implementation, and the current trends in CRM. As we learned in this chapter, customer relationship management is really all about listening to customers and treating them right. For as long as there have been businesses, some firms have been very successful at keeping customers satisfied and coming back, while others have not. For the past ten or fifteen years, though, both the level of competition in the market place as well as available computer technology and software capabilities have been increasing quite dramatically. Thus, we have seen a shift in CRM toward use of technology, software, and the Internet to better analyze, segment, and serve customers with the objective of maximizing long-term customer profitability.

Firms today are learning how to combine many channels of customer contact to better serve customers, resulting in better customer satisfaction and more sales. Though many traditional CRM applications are expensive, firms can use a structured approach to design an appropriate plan, and then analyze and select the right applications and vendors to implement a successful CRM program. Cloud-based CRM applications have also become a major consideration in the development of many firms' CRM efforts.

KEY TERMS

application service providers (ASPs), 373

big data analytics, 368

call centers, 363

clickstream, 358

cloud computing, 372

cross-selling, 356

customer churn, 356

customer contact centers, 363

customer defection analysis, 356

customer lifetime value (CLV), 357

customer profitability, 357

customer service, 361

customer value, 357

data privacy, 370

data warehouse, 368

event-based marketing, 358

knowledge management system, 361

lead management system, 360

mobile marketing, 355

on-demand computing, 372

perfect order, 361

permission marketing, 355

posttransaction elements, 363

pretransaction, 363

private clouds, 373

QR codes, 355

relationship marketing, 355

sales activity management system, 360

sales force automation, 359

sales territory management systems, 360

segment customers, 354

Seven Rs Rule, 361

social CRM, 371

social media, 371

software-as-a-service (SaaS) model, 373

target marketing, 354

transaction, 363

DISCUSSION QUESTIONS AND EXERCISES

1. Define the term *customer relationship management*, and what has impacted the way companies view CRM over the past fifteen or twenty years.

2. How does the actual practice of CRM differ from the use of CRM software?

3. Why have so many CRM efforts failed? Can you cite a personal example of a good or bad CRM effort?

4. Describe why CRM is so important in managing supply chains. What do firms with good CRM programs do? Can you cite an example aside from the ones mentioned in this chapter?

5. What is *segmenting customers*, and why is it perhaps the most important activity in CRM? What do firms typically do with the segments of customers?

6. Define these terms: permission marketing, cross-selling, and churn reduction.

7. How would an analysis of customer defections help the firm become more competitive?

8. Why is the determination of customer lifetime value important?

9. *Discussion Problem:* From the information given, rank the customers in terms of their lifetime value.

	AVG. ANNUAL SALES ($)	AVG. PROFIT MARGIN (%)	EXPECTED LIFETIME (YEARS)
Customer A:	2,500	17	8
Customer B:	4,000	12	6
Customer C:	1,200	30	12

Use a discount rate of 6 percent and treat the average annual sales figures as annuities. Should any of these customers be fired?

10. Pick a specific company near your residence and describe how it could personalize its communications with you, the customer.

11. Describe several ways that CRM applications can increase the effectiveness and productivity of a firm's sales force.

12. How does *your definition* of customer service compare to the *Seven Rs Rule*?

13. Describe some businesses in your area providing good customer service, and then list some providing poor customer service.

14. Describe the types of customer service that come before, during, and after the sale. Why are they important to CRM?

15. Are call centers good or bad for the firm? What has been your experience with call centers?

16. Do you think call center outsourcing negatively affects customer service? Explain.

17. Could self-service websites be used in place of call centers?

18. How should customer satisfaction be measured at a bank? A restaurant? A manufacturing firm? A retailer?

19. Do you think CRM applications unnecessarily invade customers' privacy? Explain.

20. Describe the steps necessary for designing and implementing a successful CRM program.

21. What is the most common mistake made, when designing and implementing a CRM program?

22. How do you think CRM performance should be measured? Suggest several performance measures for a specific company.

23. What sort of problems can occur with a firm's existing or legacy CRM applications?

24. What do *big data* and *big data analytics* refer to?
25. Why is CRM program user training so important?
26. How can firms help to ensure the privacy and security of their customers' information and data?
27. How do various social media impact an organization's CRM methods? Should firms use social media for attracting new customers?
28. What do you think the true value of social CRM is?
29. What is *cloud computing*, and what are its advantages for CRM?
30. What is the difference between on-demand computing, the software-as-a-service model, and cloud computing?

ESSAY AND PROJECT QUESTIONS

1. Go to the International Customer Management Institute's website, www.icmi.com, and look at several news stories. Describe a new development in call center usage or technology.
2. Identify an on-demand Internet CRM provider and see if you can determine what is "free" and what is not.
3. Search on the term "call center technology," and describe a few of the latest uses of technology in call centers.
4. What are some of the latest developments in Internet privacy laws?
5. Identify some of this year's best and worst customer service providers. Have you dealt with any of these companies?

ADDITIONAL RESOURCES

Barnes, J. G., *Secrets of Customer Relationship Management.* New York: McGraw-Hill, 2001.

Bergeron, B., *Essentials of CRM: A Guide to Customer Relationship Management.* New York: John Wiley & Sons, 2002.

Bloomberg, D. J., S. LeMay, and J. B. Hanna, *Logistics.* Upper Saddle River, NJ: Prentice Hall, 2002.

Dychè, J., *The CRM Handbook: A Business Guide to Customer Relationship Management.* Upper Saddle River, NJ: Addison-Wesley, 2002.

Fitzsimmons, J., and M. Fitzsimmons, *Service Management for Competitive Advantage.* New York: McGraw-Hill, 1994.

Lawrence, F. B., D. F. Jennings, and B. E. Reynolds, *EDistribution.* Mason, OH: South-Western, 2003.

Metters, R., K. King-Metters, and M. Pullman, *Successful Service Operations Management.* Mason, OH: South-Western.

ENDNOTES

1. Woolard, C., "How Interpower Builds Its Pipeline Through Virtual Events," *B to B* 98(5), 2013: 8.
2. Anonymous, "Sabre Travel Network Delivers Innovative New Customer Profile Management System," *Marketing Weekly News*, September 24, 2011: 825.

3. Gryskiewicz, C., "Practice Management with CRM: Can You Have It All?" *CPA Practice Management Forum* 7(6), 2011: 12–13.
4. Columbus, L., "2013 CRM Market Share Update," *Forbes.com*, April 26, 2013, found at www.forbes.com/sites/louiscolumbus/2013/04/26/2013-crm-market-share-update-40-of-crm-systems-sold-are-saas-based
5. van der Meulen, R., "Gartner Survey Shows European CRM Budgets Remain Strong in 2013," *Gartner Press Release*, February 28, 2013, found at www.gartner.com/newsroom/id/2352815
6. Dychè, J., *The CRM Handbook: A Business Guide to Customer Relationship Management*. Upper Saddle River, NJ: Addison-Wesley, 2002.
7. Bergeron, B., *Essentials of CRM: A Guide to Customer Relationship Management*. New York: John Wiley & Sons, 2002.
8. Ragins, E., and A. Greco, "Customer Relationship Management and e-Business: More than a Software Solution," *Review of Business* 24(1), 2003: 25–30.
9. Anonymous, "Corporate Visions, Inc.; Corporate Visions Survey," *Marketing Weekly News*, August 17, 2013: 104.
10. Foss, B., "What Makes for CRM System Success—Or Failure?" *Journal of Database Marketing & Customer Strategy Management* 15(2), 2008: 68–79.
11. Vella, J., and A. Caruana, "Encouraging CRM Systems Usage: A Study Among Bank Managers," *Management Systems Review* 35(2), 2012: 121–133.
12. Anonymous, "E-Business Disaster: Why an Ambitious and Expensive Project Failed," *Strategic Direction* 25(5), 2009: 21–22.
13. Dickie, J., "Fueling the CRM Engine," *Customer Relationship Management* 11(4), 2007: 10.
14. Anonymous, "The 2013 CRM Influential Leaders," *Customer Relationship Management* 17(8), 2013: 42–45.
15. Goldenberg, B., "Your People Are Half the Battle," *Customer Relationship Management* 14(4), 2010: 6.
16. Anonymous, "NMA @ 10: Secrets of Success," *New Media Age*, June 16, 2005: 18.
17. Mukerjee, K., and K. Singh, "CRM: A Strategic Approach," *IUP Journal of Management Research* 8(2), 2009: 65–82.
18. Bailor, C., "Elder Effect," *Customer Relationship Management* 10(11), 2006: 36–40.
19. Ostroff, J., "Internet Ad Trends Favor Consumers," *KiplingerForecasts.com*, May 9, 2008: 1.
20. Fernando, A., "Start Talking in Code!" *Communication World* 27(1), 2010: 8–9.
21. The Toyota Prius Facebook page is www.facebook.com/prius
22. Hintze, J., "A Wealth of Progress," *USBanker* 120(4), 2010: 32–33.
23. Anonymous, "Maximizing Growth and Retention with Cross-Selling," *Texas Banking* 98(11), 2009: 24.
24. Kanu, K., "Get In Or Get Left Behind," *Black Enterprise* 39(4), 2008: 76–80.

25. Nadeem, M., "How e-Business Leadership Results in Customer Satisfaction and Customer Lifetime Value," *The Business Review, Cambridge* 6(1), 2006: 218–224.

26. Helms, M., and D. Mayo, "Assessing Poor Quality Service: Perceptions of Customer Service Representatives," *Managing Service Quality* 18(6), 2008: 610–618.

27. Bailor, C., "Not Fade Away," *Customer Relationship Management* 11(2), 2007: 22–26.

28. Collieer, S., "Another Way to Look at 'Member Value,'" *Credit Union Magazine* 73(1), 2007: 9A.

29. Taub, S., "Ritz-Carlton, Central Park, New York," *Institutional Investor*, December 2010: 1.

30. Fuhrman, E., "Bottler of the Year: Coca-Cola Bottling Co. Consolidated," *Beverage Industry* 101(1), 2010: 30–35.

31. Hosford, C., "AmerisourceBergen Saves with Automated Sales Info," *B to B* 91(13), 2006: 18.

32. Anonymous, "ReachLocal Launches Small Business Marketing System to Attract, Capture and Convert More Customers," *Marketing Weekly News*, October 12, 2013: 68.

33. Dahl, J., "Save the Smarts," *Credit Union Magazine* 75(9), 2009: 68–69.

34. Shaprio, R. D., and J. L. Heskett, *Logistics Strategy: Cases and Concepts*. St. Paul, MN: West Publishing Co., 1985.

35. Go to www.jdpower.com/content/press-release/5sYQtpZ/2013-north-america-airline-satisfaction-study.html

36. Taub, S., "Ritz-Carlton, Central Park, New York," *Institutional Investor*, December 2010: 1.

37. Finneran, M., and B. Herrington, "Excelling at Mobile Customer Service," *Customer* 31(2), 2012: 42.

38. Terney, J., "Survey: Call Centers Now Profit Centers," *Multichannel Merchant*, December 21, 2010: 1.

39. Engebretson, J., "Outsourced Call Centers Pose Serious Security Threat," *Connected Planet*, December 19, 2011: 1; and Bernier, P., "In Retrospect: The History and Advancement of the Contact Center and the Customer Experience," *Customer Inter@ction Solutions* 30(13), 2012: 24–33.

40. Wisner, J. D., and W. J. Corney, "Comparing Practices for Capturing Bank Customer Feedback," *Benchmarking: An International Journal* 8(3), 2001: 240–250.

41. Anonymous, "Lessons from the Domino's Turnaround," *Restaurant Hospitality* 94(6), 2010: 30.

42. Lager, M., "Smooth Sailing," *Customer Relationship Management* 13(7), 2009: 45.

43. Shum, P., L. Bove, and S. Auh, "Employees' Affective Commitment to Change: The Key to Successful CRM Implementation," *European Journal of Marketing* 42(11/12), 2008: 1346–1371; Lassar, W., S. Lassar, and N. Rauseo, "Developing a CRM Strategy in Your Firm," *Journal of Accountancy* 206(2), (A2008): 68–73.

44. Dychè, J., *The CRM Handbook: A Business Guide to Customer Relationship Management*. Upper Saddle River, NJ: Addison-Wesley, 2002.

45. Anonymous, "Pepperdine University Selects Recruitment CRM from Higher Education Company TargetX," *Marketing Weekly News*, November 10, 2012: 187.

46. See www.news.walmart.com/news-archive/2012/11/23/walmart-us-reports-best-ever-black-friday-events; and www.sas.com/big-data

47. Healey, M., "Blinded By Big Data," *InformationWeek*, August 19, 2013: 6–12; and www.reuters.com/article/2013/11/20/jcpenney-results-idUSL2N0J50MX20131120

48. Keenan, C., "In Search of Wallet Share," *USBanker* 120(3), 2010: 20–25.

49. Stockford, P., and J. Staples, "Contact Center Metrics that Matter," *Customer* 31(11), 2013: 44–45; Hughes, A., "How to Measure CRM Success," found at www.dbmarketing.com/articles

50. Dickie, J., "Don't Confuse Implementation with Adoption," *Customer Relationship Management* 13(5), 2009: 10.

51. Davey, N., "CRM Training's Most Common Calamities," *MyCustomer.com* September 19, 2011: 1–10.

52. Goldenberg, B., "A CRM Initiative's Bermuda Triangle," *Customer Relationship Management* 11(5), 2007: 10.

53. Prosch, M., "Preventing Identity Theft Throughout the Data Life Cycle," *Journal of Accountancy* 207(1), 2009: 58–63; Ball, D. and D. Gauthier-Villars, "France Got Stolen HSBC Data," *The Wall Street Journal*, March 12, 2010: C1; Kirby, P., "Sony Breach Spurs Lawmakers to Eye Dada Security Legislation," *Cybersecurity Policy Report*, May 9, 2011: 1.

54. Kaser, D., "Plotting Social Media's Bottom Line," *Information Today* 26(9), 2009: 16; O'Brien, W., "Crowdsourcing for Customer Service," *Customer* 31(9), 2013: 32.

55. Anonymous, "Auto Dealership Companies; Online Vehicle Auction Company Copart," *Marketing Weekly News*, December 11, 2010: 569.

56. McCarthy, C., "After Facebook Backlash, Nestle Steps Up Sustainability," *The Social CNET News*, May 17, 2010: 1.

57. McKay, L., "Strategy and Social Media: Everything's Social (Now)," *Customer Relationship Management* 13(6), 2009: 24–28.

58. Wassermaan, T., "Why Micro-Blogging Is What's Good for General Motors," *Brandweek* 51(7), 2010: 29.

59. Company information from www.salesforce.com; see http://www.forbes.com/companies/salesforce/ for rankings; also see Pombriant, D., "The Man Who Moved a Paradigm," *Customer Relationship Management* 13(11), 2009: 6.

60. Hickey, A., Cloud Computing Services Market to Near $150 Billion in 2014," *CRN*, June 22, 2010: 1.

61. Veverka, M., "Sky's the Limit," *Barron's* 90(1), 2010: 19–21.

62. Henschen, D., "Microsoft Gains Enterprise Clout with ERP, CRM," *Information Week–Online*, March 21, 2013: 1.

Chapter 11
GLOBAL LOCATION DECISIONS

The global landscape for foreign direct investment is changing considerably as companies are adapting their global footprints to rapidly changing operating conditions and new opportunities around the world. As a result, we are witnessing a marked reconfiguration of where foreign direct investment is going. While the United States is seeing greater near-shoring, China is experiencing a transformation of its role in the global economy, and other emerging economies are positioning themselves as new key investment destinations. In this context, companies need to embrace strategic footprint planning and structure their global operations into agile and integrated enterprises that are able to adapt to changing conditions and opportunities across the world.

— *Jacob Dencik and Roel Spee, IBM Global Services*[1]

No two countries that both had McDonald's had fought a war against each other since each got its McDonald's.

— *Thomas Friedman, renowned columnist and author, in* The Lexus and the Olive Tree[2]

There is a whole shopping list of things that companies would typically look for when they try to plan a location: access to labor, access to capital, access to clients, well-placed and well-located real estate. Then, of course the cost of doing business in that market place.

— *Sheila Botting, partner and national leader, Deloitte LLP*[3]

Learning Objectives

After completing this chapter, you should be able to

- Explain the impact of global location decisions on a supply chain.
- Identify the factors influencing location decisions.
- Understand the impact of the regional trade agreements on location decisions.
- Use several location evaluation models.
- Understand the advantages of business clusters.
- Explain the impact of sustainable development on facility location.

Chapter Outline

SCM Profile An Optimal Location for Marriott's Shared Services Center[4]

Marriott wanted to consolidate the field operations of its accounting and other support positions at a centralized facility in the U.S. The following items were identified by Marriott as important locational factors:

- Availability of accountants, accounting clerks, and other entry-level clerical staff
- Local wages below the U.S. average
- Nonstop air service to Washington, DC
- Availability of a 50,000 square foot office building
- Access to a local university and two-year college with a good supply of accounting graduates
- Excellent telecommunications infrastructure
- Safe from natural disasters
- Favorable tax environment with no accounts receivable taxes
- Attractive quality of life
- Below-average cost of living

WDG Consulting, which was hired by Marriott, used a two-phase approach for the project. In Phase One, the goal was to develop a shortlist of three promising locations for further evaluation. WDG Consulting used its national database of U.S. metro areas and published data sources such as the U.S. Bureau of Labor Statistics, demographic vendors like Claritas, and specialized sources for disaster risk like ESRI to support its research. Based on WDG Consulting's factor weighting/area scoring model, three metro areas in Tennessee, Florida, and Kansas were identified for study in Phase Two. In Phase Two, the study was focused on the service center's most important operating requirements. The three metro areas were analyzed on short- and long-term attractiveness on the following criteria:

- Labor market: availability, quality, stability, salaries
- Business costs (multiyear): payroll, occupancy, taxes, travel, incentives
- Quality of life/transferee appeal: education/training, unionization, telecommunications, air services, taxation

The report of the three metro areas was presented to Marriott. After reviewing the report, Marriott decided to locate its shared services center in Knoxville, Tennessee. The following are indicators of the success of the location decision:

- Abundant access to skilled workers such as accountants and accounting clerks
- Low turnover of less than 20 percent
- Customized training programs conducted by the local community college
- Relatively short commutes to work for employees
- Wages approximately 15 percent below national average

INTRODUCTION

Locating a facility is an important decision affecting the efficiency and effectiveness of managing supply chains, the level of service provided to customers, and a firm's overall competitive advantage. A supply chain is a network of facilities, and the location of production facilities, offices, distribution centers, and retail sites determines the efficient flow of goods to and from these facilities. Once a decision on locating a facility is made, it is costly to move or shut down that facility. Thus, facility location has a long-term impact on the supply chain and must be an integral part of a firm's supply chain strategy. With increased globalization and investments in technology infrastructure, faster transportation, improved communications, and open markets, companies can locate anywhere in the world—previously thought to be impossible.

It would appear that easy access to global markets and corporate networks makes the role of location less important as a source of competitive advantage. However, successful business clusters in areas such as Silicon Valley, Wall Street, the California wine region, and the Italian leather fashion center show that location still matters. The existence of business clusters in many industries provides clear evidence that innovation and successful competition are concentrated geographically. Dr. Michael Porter suggests that the immediate business environment is just as important as the issues impacting companies internally, in affecting location decisions.[5] Business clusters are discussed in detail later in this chapter.

Global location decisions involve determining the location of the facility, defining its strategic role, and identifying markets to be served by the facility. For example, Honda's global location strategy of building cost-effective manufacturing facilities in areas that best meet the requirements of local customers has served the company well. Honda's "Small Born" manufacturing strategy is to start small and expand production as local demand increases. This approach allows the company to be efficient and profitable, even when production volumes are low. Honda's first auto plant in the U.S. was built in Marysville, Ohio. Then the company added a second factory in East Liberty, Ohio. As demand for Honda automobiles continued to increase, Honda opened a facility to assemble the Odyssey minivans in Alabama and an auto plant producing Civic GX Natural Gas Vehicles in Indiana. Honda's Ridgeline trucks, which were built previously in Canada, are today produced in the Alabama plant. Toyota, Nissan, Mercedes, BMW, Volkswagen, Kia Motors, and Hyundai have also built assembly plants in the U.S. to cater to the local automobile markets.[6]

GLOBAL LOCATION STRATEGIES

Global location decisions are made to optimize the performance of the supply chain and be consistent with the firm's competitive strategy. According to Frank Kern, Senior Vice President, IBM Global Business Services, "Corporations today are faced with unprecedented pressures to adapt and reinvent themselves to survive and prosper in a new economic environment. This comes with profound implications for how they approach their physical infrastructures and global operations. An emphasis on gaining access to new and growing markets is being replaced in their current location strategies by consolidation and cost reduction. In their search for lower costs, companies have reduced their overall level of investment, but have also widened the scope of their search to encompass new and more cost efficient locations. For example, some African countries have seen their share of global investment grow, as they are increasingly seen as locations that offer attractive operating environments and costs."[7] A firm competing on cost is more likely to select a location that provides a cost advantage. For instance, Amazon.com, as discussed in the nearby

SCM Profile: Amazon's Facility Network

Jeff Bezos founded Amazon.com in 1995. Amazon's corporate mission is "to be Earth's most customer-centric company for four primary customer sets: consumers, sellers, enterprises, and content creators."[8] The company's global operations are in Canada, China, France, Germany, Japan, and the U.K. In 2013, Amazon's total net sales amounted to $74.452 billion with about 40 percent coming from international sales.[9]

The early belief in electronic commerce was that millions of customers could be served without requiring the infrastructure of a Sears or Walmart. However, online retailers are finding that without their own warehouses and shipping capabilities, customer service could suffer. In the late 1990s, Amazon went on a warehouse-building spree, adding facilities in Nevada, Kentucky, and Kansas to its distribution system. The objective was to improve logistics and cut shipping times to customers. Amazon now offers "Guaranteed Accelerated Delivery" dates on selected items with one- or two-day express shipping. While recognizing that distribution systems will help companies manage their delivery processes better, there is still a need to turn a profit. With heavy investments in distribution centers (DCs) worldwide, companies are finding that the flow of goods through their distribution systems must be improved to reduce costs.

Amazon uses a network management software system to organize the movement of products through its global transportation network. The system determines which of Amazon's DCs to retain or expand and the quantity of each product to keep in stock. In addition, the software schedules deliveries, tracks shipments, computes the shipping cost for an item from the country of origin to the Amazon storage location, plans the shipping of products between a supplier and an Amazon facility, and decides which items can be delivered in the same container. The company currently has fulfillment centers in nine U.S. states. Fulfillment centers in Europe are located in France, Germany, Italy, Spain, and the U.K. In Asia, the fulfillment centers are found in China and Japan. By early 2014, Amazon had fifty-four fulfillment centers in North America exceeding 41.5 million square feet with fifty more centers outside of North America exceeding 28.6 million square feet of space.[10] By strategically locating its DCs and improving operations, Amazon is able to enhance its supply chain capabilities.

Today, Amazon is pushing the envelope with its next-day shipping at an attractive price. Ten percent of Amazon's customers are using this service, which is five times the industry average. Without a large number of fulfillment centers, next-day delivery would be prohibitively expensive. For example, a retailer with one DC offering next-day delivery might cost $27 per package; with ten DCs the cost could drop to $10, and with thirty-five DCs the cost could go down to below $5.[11]

SCM Profile, locates warehouses in areas that will minimize logistics and inventory costs. Many toy manufacturers have also moved their factories to Vietnam, Thailand, or China because of cost advantages provided by these countries.

A firm that competes on speed of delivery, such as the FedEx Corporation, uses the hub-and-spoke approach to location determination. FedEx's first and largest hub in the U.S. is in Memphis, Tennessee. This site has the capacity to sort 160,000 packages per hour and 265,000 documents per hour. It has 42 miles of conveyors, 108 gates for wide body planes, 44 gates for narrow body planes, and 44 gates for small "feeder" planes. Planes land at the rate of one every ninety seconds. In addition to the flagship hub in Memphis, FedEx has hubs in Indianapolis, Indiana; Newark, New Jersey; Oakland, California; Fort Worth,

Texas; Anchorage, Alaska; Miami, Florida; Toronto, Canada; Paris, France; Cologne, Germany; and Guangzhou, China.[12] Each of the hubs has been picked for its central location and easy access to customers.

To get the most out of foreign-based facilities, managers must treat these plants as a source of competitive advantage. These foreign facilities have a strategic role to perform. Professor Kasra Ferdows of Georgetown University suggests a framework consisting of six strategic roles depending on the strategic reason for the facility's location and the scope of its activities:[13]

- *Offshore factory*: An **offshore factory** manufactures products at low cost with minimum investment in technical and managerial resources. These products tend to be exported. An offshore factory imports or locally acquires parts and then exports all of the finished products. The primary objective is simply to take advantage of low labor costs. For example, in the early 1970s, Intel built a labor-intensive offshore factory to produce simple, low-cost components in Penang, Malaysia.
- *Source factory*: A **source factory** has a broader strategic role than an offshore factory with plant management heavily involved in supplier selection and production planning. The source factory's location is dictated by low production cost, fairly developed infrastructure, and availability of skilled workers. Hewlett-Packard's plant in Singapore started as an offshore plant in 1970 but with significant investments over a ten-year period was able to become a source factory for calculators and keyboards.[14]
- *Server factory*: A **server factory** is set up primarily to take advantage of government incentives, minimize exchange risk, avoid tariff barriers, and reduce taxes and logistics costs to supply the regional market where the factory is located. An example would be Coca-Cola's international bottling plants, each serving a small geographic region.
- *Contributor factory*: The **contributor factory** plays a greater strategic role than a server factory by getting involved in product development and engineering, production planning, making critical procurement decisions, and developing suppliers. In 1973, Sony built a new server factory in Bridgend, Wales. By 1988, the factory was involved in the design and development of many of the products it produced and now serves as a contributor factory in Sony's global manufacturing network.[15]
- *Outpost factory*: The **outpost factory** is set up in a location with an abundance of advanced suppliers, competitors, research facilities, and knowledge centers to get access to the most current information on materials, components, technologies, and products. Since the facility normally produces something, its secondary role can be that of a server or an offshore factory. For example, Lego still produces molds and toys in Denmark, Germany, Switzerland, and the U.S. in spite of the higher manufacturing cost.[16] Lego's factories serve as outpost facilities with access to research facilities, institutions of higher learning, and sophisticated suppliers of plastic materials.
- *Lead factory*: A **lead factory** is a source of product and process innovation and competitive advantage for the entire organization. It translates its knowledge of the market, competitors, and customers into new products. In the early 1970s, both Intel and Hewlett-Packard established offshore factories in Southeast Asia. Over time, the strategic roles of these factories were upgraded to that of lead factories.

CRITICAL LOCATION FACTORS

One of the most challenging tasks as a company grows, relocates, or starts up, is where to position assets strategically to create a long-term competitive advantage. Some of the questions and concerns that need to be addressed for each potential location follow:

- What will be the reaction of shareholders, customers, competitors, and employees?
- Will the location provide a sustainable competitive advantage?
- What will be the impact on product or service quality?
- Can the right people be hired?
- What will be the effect on the supply chain?
- What is the projected cost?
- What will be the impact on delivery performance?
- How will the market react?
- Is the transfer of people necessary, and, if so, are employees willing to move?

There are basically three levels of location decisions: the global market or country selection, the subregion or state selection, and the community and site selection. The process starts with an analysis of the market region of the world that bears a strategic interest to the organization, and, eventually, a country is targeted. Once the country is selected, the focus shifts to finding a subregion or state within the country that best meets the company's location requirements. Finally, the community and site for the facility are selected. The weighted-factor rating model, which is discussed later in this chapter, can be used to make a location decision at each of the levels we have mentioned. Table 11.1 lists a number of factors affecting each of the three levels of location decisions and a discussion of each of these factors follows.

Regional Trade Agreements and the World Trade Organization

An understanding of regional trade agreements and the **World Trade Organization** (WTO) is critical to the facility location decision process because of their impact on tariffs, costs, and the free flow of goods and services. The WTO is the successor to the General Agreement on Tariffs and Trade (GATT), which was responsible for setting up the multilateral trading system after World War II. Today, the WTO is the "only global international organization dealing with the rules of trade between nations"[17] and has 159 members. The goal of the WTO is to help producers of goods and services, exporters, and importers conduct their business. Its functions include administering the WTO agreements, providing a forum for trade negotiations, handling trade disputes, monitoring national trade policies, providing technical assistance and training programs for developing countries, and cooperating with other international organizations.

There are 377 regional trade agreements under the WTO in force today.[18] Examples of the better-known regional trade agreements are the **European Union (EU)**, the **North American Free Trade Agreement** (NAFTA), the **Southern Common Market (MERCOSUR)**, the **Association of Southeast Asian Nations (ASEAN)**, and the

Table 11.1 Important Factors in the Location Decision Process

LOCATION FACTOR	COUNTRY	REGION/STATE	COMMUNITY
Regional trade agreements—trade barriers, tariff, and import duties	X		
Competitiveness of nations—economic performance, government efficiency, business efficiency and infrastructure	X		
Government taxes and incentives	X		
Currency stability	X		
Environmental issues	X	X	X
Access and proximity to markets	X	X	X
Labor issues	X	X	X
Access to suppliers	X	X	X
Transportation issues	X	X	X
Utility availability and cost	X	X	X
Quality-of-life issues	X	X	X
State taxes and incentives		X	X
Right-to-work laws		X	X
Local taxes and incentives			X
Land availability and cost			X

Common Market for Eastern and Southern Africa (COMESA). Several of these are discussed here:

- *The European Union (EU):* Set up after World War II, the European Union was officially launched on May 9, 1950, with France's proposal to create a European federation consisting of six countries: Belgium, Germany, France, Italy, Luxembourg, and the Netherlands. A series of accessions in 1973 (Denmark, Ireland, and the U.K.), 1981 (Greece), 1986 (Spain and Portugal), 1995 (Austria, Finland, and Sweden), 2004 (Czech Republic, Estonia, Cyprus, Latvia, Lithuania, Hungary, Malta, Poland, Slovenia, and Slovakia), 2007 (Bulgaria and Romania), and 2013 (Croatia) has resulted in a total of twenty-eight member states. Currently, the EU has five candidate countries—Iceland, Montenegro, Serbia, Republic of Macedonia, and Turkey.[19] Two highlights of the EU are the establishment of the single market in 1993 and the introduction of the euro notes and coins on January 1, 2002. The EU has a population of more than half a billion people, third largest after China and India and with a GDP more than that of the U.S.
- *The North American Free Trade Agreement (NAFTA):* This trade agreement among the U.S., Canada, and Mexico was implemented on January 1, 1994. NAFTA created the world's largest free trade area, currently with over 440 million people and producing more than US$17 trillion of goods and services annually.[20] Many tariffs were eliminated with an immediate effect, while others were phased out over periods ranging from five to fifteen years. Twenty years after the agreement, Canada has expanded at the fastest average rate and Mexico has been the slowest.[21] While NAFTA has led to increased intraregional trade between Canada, Mexico, and the U.S., it has fallen short of creating jobs and the

regional economic integration its supporters promised decades ago. One benefit of NAFTA is that U.S. trade with Mexico and Canada exceeds that with Japan, South Korea, Brazil, Russia, India, and China combined.[22]

- *The Southern Common Market (MERCOSUR):* This economic and political agreement among Argentina, Brazil, Paraguay, and Uruguay was formed in March 1991 with the signing of the Treaty of Asuncion. The agreement was created with the goal of forming a common market/customs union between the participating countries and was based on economic cooperation between Argentina and Brazil that had been in place since 1986. After Paraguay was suspended in 2012 for violating the Democratic Clause of Mercosur, Venezuela was added as a full member. Associate members include Bolivia, Chile, Colombia, Ecuador, Guyana, Peru, and Suriname. The total population of the five member states is more than 275 million.[23]
- *The Association of Southeast Asian Nations (ASEAN):* This association was created in 1967 and is comprised of the ten countries in the Southeast Asian region: Brunei, Cambodia, Indonesia, Laos, Malaysia, Myanmar, Philippines, Singapore, Thailand, and Vietnam. The primary objective of ASEAN is "to accelerate the economic growth, social progress and cultural development in the region through joint endeavors in the spirit of equality and partnership in order to strengthen the foundation for a prosperous and peaceful community of Southeast Asian Nations.[24]
- *Common Market for Eastern and Southern Africa (COMESA):* COMESA was established in 1994 "as an organization of free independent sovereign states which have agreed to co-operate in developing their natural and human resources for the good of all their people."[25] COMESA has nineteen member states, population of over 389 million, and annual imports of around US$32 billion with exports of US$82 billion and forms a major market for both internal and external trading. The member countries are Burundi, Comoros, D.R. Congo, Djibouti, Egypt, Eritrea, Ethiopia, Kenya, Libya, Madagascar, Malawi, Mauritius, Rwanda, Seychelles, Sudan, Swaziland, Uganda, Zambia, and Zimbabwe.[26]

Competitiveness of Nations

A nation's competitiveness (in international trade) is defined by the Organization of Economic Cooperation and Development (OECD) as "a measure of a country's advantage or disadvantage in selling its products in international markets."[27] There are two competing sources for national competitiveness rankings. One is the *World Competitiveness Yearbook* published annually by the Swiss business school IMD, and the other is *The Global Competitiveness Report*, prepared by the World Economic Forum. Since the two organizations use different criteria for their rankings, the lists vary somewhat. The rankings from both publications are shown in Table 11.2.

IMD's World Competitiveness Yearbook features fifty-eight industrialized and emerging economies and provides businesses with the basic information on location decisions. There are 327 criteria, which are broadly grouped into four competitiveness factors:[28]

- *Economic Performance* (5 subfactors): "Macro-economic evaluation of the domestic economy: Domestic Economy, International Trade, International Investment, Employment, and Prices."
- *Government Efficiency* (5 subfactors): "Extent to which government policies are conducive to competitiveness: Public Finance, Fiscal Policy, Institutional Framework, Business Legislation and Societal Framework."

Table 11.2 International Competitiveness Ranking

RANKING	2013–14 GLOBAL COMPETITIVENESS REPORT	2013 WORLD COMPETITIVENESS YEARBOOK
1.	Switzerland	United States
2.	Singapore	Switzerland
3.	Finland	Hong Kong
4.	Germany	Sweden
5.	United States	Singapore
6.	Sweden	Norway
7.	Hong Kong SAR	Canada
8.	Netherlands	United Arab Emirates
9.	Japan	Germany
10.	United Kingdom	Qatar
11.	Norway	Taiwan
12.	Taiwan	Denmark
13.	Qatar	Luxembourg
14.	Canada	Netherlands Austria
15.	Denmark	Malaysia
16.	Austria	Australia
17.	Belgium	Ireland
18.	New Zealand	United Kingdom
19.	United Arab Emirates	Israel
20.	Saudi Arabia	Finland

Sources: http://www3.weforum.org/docs/GCR2013-14/GCR_Rankings_2013-14.pdf; and http://www.imd.org/uupload/IMD.WebSite/wcc/WCYResults/1/scoreboard.pdf

- *Business Efficiency* (5 subfactors): "Extent to which the national environment encourages enterprises to perform in an innovative, profitable, and responsible manner: Productivity and Efficiency, Labor Market, Finance, Management Practices, and Attitudes and Values."
- *Infrastructure* (5 subfactors): "Extent to which basic, technological, scientific, and human resources meet the needs of business: Basic Infrastructure, Technological Infrastructure, Scientific Infrastructure, Health, and Environment and Education."

The yearbook provides an analysis of the data collected and ranks nations according to their abilities to create and maintain an organization's competitiveness. Data from the report can be used to compare countries globally, to see five-year trends, to understand strengths and weaknesses, and to examine factors and subfactors. In addition, businesses can use the yearbook to determine investment plans and assess locations for new operations. The U.S. regained the top ranking in 2013, mostly due to an improving financial sector, a richness of technological innovation and successful companies.[29]

The World Economic Forum defines competitiveness as "the set of institutions, policies, and factors that determine the level of productivity of a country."[30] Their Global Competitiveness Report examines 148 economies in the 2013–2014 issue and uses what the Forum describes as their "12 Pillars of Competitiveness" to determine the rankings. These are briefly described below.

The World Economic Forum's 12 Pillars of Competitiveness

1. Institutions—the legal and administrative framework.
2. Infrastructure—the transportation, telecommunications, and power networks.
3. Macroeconomic environment—the stability of the macroeconomic environment is important for business and includes such issues as fiscal deficits, inflation rates, unemployment, and GDP growth rates.
4. Health and primary education—investment in health services and quantity and quality of basic education.
5. Higher education and training—amount of secondary, tertiary, vocational, and on-the-job training in the workforce.
6. Goods market efficiency—overall environment for exchange of goods.
7. Labor market efficiency—the environment for male and female workers.
8. Financial market development—how resources are channeled to businesses.
9. Technological readiness—how readily the economy adapts to new technologies.
10. Market size—the availability of domestic and international markets for firms.
11. Business sophistication—the quality of the overall business networks and quality of individual firms' operations and strategies.
12. Innovation—overall support for innovative activities.

The top five countries according to the Global Competitiveness Report for 2013–2014 are Switzerland, Singapore, Finland, Germany, and the U.S. The criteria covered in the World Competitiveness Report represent issues that organizations would like to know about before making a country location decision. All things equal, a country that has a higher competitiveness ranking would provide a better business climate for locating a facility than another country that is listed as less competitive.

In yet another competitiveness ranking, the global audit and tax service KPMG's *Competitive Alternatives* study examines business competitiveness in 112 major cities in ten countries: Australia, Canada, France, Germany, Italy, Japan, Mexico, the Netherlands, the U.K., and the U.S.[31] The study analyzes twenty-six major cost factors such as labor, taxes, real estate, and utilities over a ten-year planning horizon and presents an independent assessment of international business location costs. While the study is limited to ten countries, it nonetheless provides a useful guide for organizations considering locating in these countries. For 2014, the lowest-cost country ranking is as follows: (1) Mexico, (2) Canada, (3) Netherlands, (4) the U.K., (5) France, (6) Italy, (7) Japan, (8) Australia, (9) the U.S., and (10) Germany.

Government Taxes and Incentives

Government incentives, business attitude, economic stability, and taxes are important location factors. Several levels of government must be considered when evaluating potential locations. At the federal level, a *tariff* is a tax imposed by the government on imported goods to protect local industries, support the country's balance of payments, or raise revenue. Thus, countries with high tariffs discourage companies from importing goods into the country. At the same time, high tariffs encourage multinational corporations to set up factories to produce locally. However, membership in the WTO requires countries to open up their markets and to reduce the tariffs imposed on imported goods. Regional trade agreements such as NAFTA, MERCOSUR, and EU also serve to reduce tariffs among member nations to promote free movement of goods. Many countries have set up *foreign trade zones (FTZs)* where materials can be imported duty-free as long as the imports are used as inputs to production of goods that are eventually exported. If the goods are sold domestically, no duty is paid until they leave the free trade zones.

In the U.S., forty-one states have a broad-based personal income tax, and forty-six states have a corporate income tax. For example, Nevada is a business-friendly state that does not have a corporate income tax, state personal income tax, corporate franchise tax, or inventory tax. Companies such as Amazon.com have taken advantage of this by setting up warehouses in Nevada. The other states that do not have an individual income tax are Alaska, Florida, South Dakota, Texas, Washington, and Wyoming.[32] New Hampshire and Tennessee have a limited income tax on individuals. These two states tax dividends and interest. Location incentives at the state and local government levels are also important.

Currency Stability

One factor that impacts business costs and consequently location decisions is any instability in currency exchange rates. Any organization involved with international business will be subjected to the risk of currency fluctuation. For example, Amazon.com is exposed to foreign exchange rate fluctuations and risks associated with its international operations as reported in its annual report as shown here:[33]

> **Foreign Exchange Rate**
> During 2013, net sales from our International segment accounted for 40% of our consolidated revenues. Net sales and related expenses generated from our international websites, as well as those relating to www.amazon.ca (which is included in our North America segment), are denominated in the functional currencies of the corresponding websites and primarily include Euros, British Pounds, Japanese Yen, and Chinese Yuan. The functional currency of our subsidiaries that either operate or support these websites is the same as the corresponding local currency. The results of operations of, and certain of our intercompany balances associated with, our internationally-focused websites are exposed to foreign exchange rate fluctuations. Upon consolidation, as exchange rates vary, net sales and other operating results may differ materially from expectations, and we may record significant gains or losses on the remeasurement of intercompany balances. For example, as a result of fluctuations in foreign exchange rates during 2013, International segment revenues decreased $1.3 billion in comparison with the prior year.

Environmental Issues

How the environment is managed has a significant impact on human health. The inability to dispose of solid and hazardous waste, plus the presence of illegal waste, contributes to high incidences of diseases such as hepatitis A and amebiasis. Global warming, air pollution, and acid rain are issues that are increasingly being debated as the price to pay for industrialization. Millions of people live in cities with unsafe air and with asthma cases at an all-time high. In response to rising environmental concerns, the Clinton Administration negotiated the North American Agreement on Environmental Cooperation (NAAEC) as a supplementary environmental agreement to NAFTA. The key objectives of the agreement are to "foster the protection and improvement of the environment in the territories of the Parties for the well-being of present and future generations and promote sustainable development based on cooperation and mutually supportive environmental and economic policies."[34] The agreement provides a framework for the three NAFTA countries to conserve, protect, and enhance the North American environment and to effectively enforce the environmental laws.

With trade liberalization, there is a need for environmental cooperation. The WTO agreement makes direct reference to sustainable development and the desire to protect and preserve the environment. WTO members understand that "their relations in the field of trade and economic endeavor should be conducted with a view to raising standards of living, ensuring full employment and a large and steadily growing volume of real income and effective demand, and expanding the production of and trade in goods and services, while allowing for the optimal use of the world's resources in accordance with the objective of sustainable development, seeking both to protect and preserve the environment and to enhance the means for doing so in a manner consistent with their respective needs and concerns at different levels of economic development."[35]

Consumers and nongovernment agencies are now pressuring multinationals to be more environmentally conscious. Global organizations are assessing their total environmental footprints by focusing on carbon and life-cycle analysis. The life-cycle approach looks beyond just the carbon footprint since it focuses on a cradle-to-grave analysis of how products and services affect the environment. Walmart has a program to assist suppliers in managing their energy and materials usage and carbon emissions, and now companies such as Procter & Gamble, IBM, and Pacific Gas & Electric have adopted this approach.

Access and Proximity to Markets

Initially, many companies outsourced their manufacturing to China because of its cost competitiveness. However, as China's per capita income continues to rise, more and more companies are indicating that their main reason for being in China is to have access to the local markets rather than for export reasons. As such, many companies are now expanding into China not only to take advantage of the lower costs but also to access the local market. Likewise, Honda is a global company that aims to build plants in locations that best satisfy the needs of local customers. Honda has assembly plants in the U.S., Japan, Malaysia, China, and Indonesia, to name a few markets where Honda sells its vehicles.

In the service industry, proximity to customers is even more critical. Few customers will frequent a remotely located gas station or a supermarket if another more accessible alternative is available. Similarly, fast-food restaurants are well situated next to busy highway intersections to take advantage of heavy traffic areas. Walmart's early supercenters were located in predominantly rural markets to avoid direct competition with major discount stores in large metropolitan areas. Many regional chains, such as Jamesway, Bradlees, Caldor, Venture, and Hills went out of business because they were not competitive with larger and more efficient chains such as Walmart and Target. More recently, Walmart has changed its location strategy to include urban locations in the west and northeast regions of the U.S. In China, Walmart's location strategy has focused more on downtown areas, where most of the customers are located.

Ashley Furniture's decision to invest $80 million to build a new plant south of Winston-Salem, North Carolina, that will employ 500 people is an example of reshoring of a traditional industry that had lost jobs to China. Ashley recognizes that speed in meeting customer demands is becoming more critical. "Today the expectation is that you'd better be there in a week and it had better be perfect," Wanek, Ashley's CEO, says.[36] While the company still sources items such as glass and mirrors globally, larger and heavier components and upholstery are made in the U.S.

Labor Issues

Issues such as labor availability, productivity, and skill; unemployment and underemployment rates; wage rates; turnover rates; labor force competitors; and employment trends are key labor factors in making facility location decisions. Mexico has long competed on cheap labor but cannot continue to depend on this source of competitive advantage because of the emergence of lower labor cost countries like China. While China's labor cost is low compared to many countries, inflation and high economic growth has contributed to a sharp increase in wages there. Consequently, the apparel industry, which depends heavily on cheap labor, is beginning to see a shift in production from the "textile hub" in southern China to Vietnam because of the comparatively cheaper labor cost there.

Although it is true that low labor cost is an important factor in making location decisions, sustainable competitive advantage depends on productive use of inputs and continual product and process innovations. Singapore is an example of a country that first relied on cheap labor to attract foreign direct investments. Over time, Singaporeans were able to

International Business Location Costs[37]

Competitive Alternatives 2012 provides a comprehensive guide for comparing business costs in more than 110 cities in fourteen countries. The study also takes into account noncost factors such as labor availability and skills, economic conditions, innovation, infrastructure, regulatory environment, cost of living, and personal quality of life. The U.S. is used as the baseline for the study. The major cost categories are shown below:

- Labor is the single largest location-sensitive cost factor for all industries examined and is lowest in India, China, and Mexico.
- Facility cost is dependent on location and type of business. Industrial facility lease costs average 5 percent for manufacturing compared to 10 percent for service operations. Industrial leases are lowest in India, Canada, the U.S., and China. Office leases are lowest in India, the Netherlands, Mexico, and Germany.
- Transportation costs vary between 6 and 22 percent of location-sensitive costs. They are lowest in Asia (India, Japan, China) and Europe (France and the Netherlands).
- Utility cost (electricity and natural gas) is about 8 percent of total location-sensitive costs. The lowest utility cost is in Russia, followed by the U.S., Canada, and Mexico.

Overall, the U.K., the Netherlands, and Canada are the low-cost leaders for the mature markets with business costs that are about 5 percent lower than the U.S.. The reason is the drop in the euro and pound against the U.S. dollar.

For the first time, the study also looks at the business costs in the high-growth (BRIC) countries of Brazil, Russia, India, and China. The issues more related to high-growth markets include population/demographics, education/skilled labor, innovation, and infrastructure. China and India are the cost leaders among the high-growth countries, with overall business costs 25.8 and 25.3 percent, respectively, below the U.S. There is little difference in business costs between Mexico and Russia. Mexico is third among the countries, with business costs 21 percent below the U.S. Russia is ranked fourth with business costs at 19.7 percent below the U.S. baseline. Costs in Brazil approach the cost levels of the leading mature countries. Brazil's wage levels, including minimum wage standards, are the highest of the other four high-growth countries studied. Brazil also has high direct and indirect taxes that affect total cost performance.

increase the level of worker skills and develop human resource capabilities. The country moved from a producer of low-cost goods to one making high value-added products.

Access to Suppliers

Many firms prefer locations close to suppliers because of material availability and transportation cost reasons. The proximity of suppliers has an impact on the delivery of materials and, consequently, the effectiveness of the supply chain. Japanese electronics makers are finding that China is a better place to set up manufacturing facilities even though it means the cost to transport finished products to the U.S. market is higher. The reason is that a high proportion of components needed to make finished electronic products are made in China. Apple's iPhones, for example, are produced by Foxconn in China.

Utility Availability and Cost

The availability and cost of electricity, water, and gas are also important location considerations. In economically emerging countries, it is not unusual that the supply of electricity has not kept pace with the high speed of development, resulting in work stoppages due to electrical outages. Even developed countries, such as the U.S., are not immune to energy problems, although for different reasons. The largest blackout in U.S. history occurred in 2003, with more than 50 million people without power in the Northeast, Midwest, and parts of Canada. The primary cause of the blackout was a software problem in the control room of the FirstEnergy Corporation in Ohio. Energy experts are concerned with the weakness of the U.S. power grid and predict that the U.S. could be one big catastrophic event away from a total meltdown in the country.[38]

In heavy industries such as steel and aluminum mills, the availability and cost of energy are critical considerations. The concern for companies is to have the power available when needed, at an affordable price. Consequently, areas such as upstate New York, the Tennessee Valley, and parts of Canada, which provide low-cost power, are gaining in location popularity because of their plentiful energy supply. With the explosive growth in energy-intensive industries such as machinery, auto, and steel, demand for electricity has outpaced the generation capacity in China and the country has experienced power shortages in the past. However, the power generated by the completed Three Gorges Dam Project, the world's largest hydropower complex,[39] will help meet China's rapidly growing energy needs. With an increasing number of manufacturing facilities being added in China, the country must continue to invest in clean power-generating plants.

Quality-of-Life Issues

Quality of life can be defined as "general well-being of individuals and societies."[40] So what exactly are the issues affecting quality of life? While there is no definitive agreement on a set of **quality-of-life factors**, the Chamber of Commerce in Jacksonville, Florida, has annually prepared a report on the overall quality of life in the metropolitan area based on a comprehensive set of factors, which include the following:[41]

- *Achieving Educational Excellence:* Performance in terms of high-school graduation rates, college entrance test scores, teacher salaries, student–teacher ratios, and number of degrees awarded at universities and higher-education institutions provides an indicator of the quality of the education system.

- *Growing a Vibrant Economy:* Performance indicators such as net employment growth, new housing starts, and the unemployment rate show the economic health of the community. The economy must also be sufficiently diverse to allow for long-term careers for both spouses.
- *Preserving the Natural Environment:* Performance indicators include an air-quality index, average daily water use, and the amount of recycled waste diverted from landfills. A viable recycling program and clean air indicate a community's commitment to a green environment and the future health of the community.
- *Promoting Social Well-being and Harmony:* Performance indicators include whether racism is a problem, number of births to single mothers, volunteerism rate, and homeless survey count. A community where people and organizations contribute time and money to helping others in need shows a happy, affluent, and caring environment.
- *Enjoying Arts, Culture, and Recreation:* Performance measures include the public and private support for the arts, number of public performances and events, and library circulation. A community that offers choice in terms of cultural, entertainment, recreational, and sporting activities is a more attractive location than one that offers fewer of these options.
- *Sustaining a Healthy Community:* Performance indicators include the infant mortality rate, number of people without health insurance, cancer death rate, suicide rate, and new HIV cases. Recently, the U.S. medical profession has been facing a dramatic increase in malpractice insurance premiums in many states, with the result that many medical doctors are moving to areas with lower malpractice insurance costs. The ability to access good, affordable medical care provides residents with peace of mind and determines whether the community is a desirable place to live.
- *Maintaining Responsive Government:* Performance measures in this category include voter turnout, satisfaction rate with city services, number of neighborhood organizations, and a diverse and representative government. In the current economic situation, many state and local governments in the U.S. have been struggling to balance their budgets due to a slow growth economy and are considering cutting services and increasing taxes. This, in turn, will tend to negatively impact the quality of life.
- *Moving Around Efficiently and Safely:* This factor can be measured by indicators such as the average commute time to work, bus ridership, number of airport passengers, and the motor vehicle accident rate. If the roads are constantly jammed with traffic, this causes huge losses of productive time. In the warehousing and distribution industry, the quality of the highways, railways, waterways, and airways has a significant impact on the performance of the supply chain in such areas as transportation cost, speed of delivery, and customer satisfaction. The ability to travel easily within the area and to other locations affects the quality of life of the residents.
- *Keeping the Community Safe:* Performance indicators here include violent crime rate, percentage of people who feel safe in their neighborhood, people reporting being victims of crime, and the murder rate. In the U.S., there has been a trend toward suburban living because of the perception of safer neighborhoods and, therefore, a better place to live. In Mexico, especially in towns close to the U.S. border, many foreign businesses are concerned about the crime rate and the

safety of expatriates working in *maquiladora* industries. While there has been a decline in murders in Mexico's ongoing brutal drug war, the number of kidnappings is increasing and, as a result, vigilante militias taking justice into their own hands are on the rise.[42] Thus, the presence of crime could frighten off firms considering locating in Mexico.

Right-to-Work Laws

In the U.S. today, there are twenty-four states with **right-to-work laws**: Alabama, Arizona, Arkansas, Florida, Georgia, Idaho, Indiana, Iowa, Kansas, Louisiana, Mississippi, Nebraska, Nevada, North Carolina, Michigan, North Dakota, Oklahoma, South Carolina, South Dakota, Tennessee, Texas, Utah, Virginia, and Wyoming. A right-to-work law "secures the right of employees to decide for themselves whether or not to join or financially support a union."[43] In the last few decades, there has been a shift in the U.S. auto industry to the South, with assembly plants built in Tennessee, South Carolina, and Alabama, all of which are right-to-work states. Dubbed the *Southern Auto Corridor*, this cluster represents a new era in U.S. auto manufacturing. The trend to locate in the sunny, incentive-friendly, nonunionized South will most likely continue to grow.

Land Availability and Cost

As land and construction costs in most big cities continue to escalate, the trend is to locate in the suburbs and rural areas. Suburban locations can be attractive because of the cost and wide choice of land, available workforce, and developed transportation network. As mentioned earlier, when Honda first decided to set up a factory in the U.S., it located in Marysville, a small town about 40 miles from Columbus, Ohio. Affordable land near the highway was readily available, and Honda could draw its workforce from several communities around Marysville. Similarly, when Honda built its assembly plant in Alabama to meet the increased demand for its Odyssey minivans and sport utility vehicles, the site was located in Lincoln, 40 miles east of Birmingham. When Honeywell decided to move its manufacturing facility in Phoenix, Arizona, to China, the decision was to go to Suzhou, a city about 30 miles from Shanghai. Although the Pudong industrial zone in Shanghai was an attractive site, Suzhou had lower land and labor costs, which were deemed important decision factors.

FACILITY LOCATION TECHNIQUES

Two techniques that are commonly used by organizations to assist in making global location decisions are described here: the weighted-factor rating model and the break-even model. The two techniques are discussed below.

The Weighted-Factor Rating Model

The **weighted-factor rating model** is a method commonly used to compare the attractiveness of several locations along a number of quantitative and qualitative dimensions. Selecting a facility location using this approach involves the following steps:

1. Identify the factors that are considered important to the facility location decision.
2. Assign weights to each factor in terms of their relative importance. Typically, the weights sum to 1.

3. Determine a relative performance score for each factor considered. Typically, the scores vary from 1 to 100, although other scoring schemes can be used.
4. Multiply the factor score by the weight associated with each factor, and sum the weighted scores across all factors.
5. The location with the highest total weighted score is the recommended location.

Since the factors, the individual weights, and the scores are subject to interpretation and bias by the analyst, it is highly recommended that a team approach be used when performing this type of analysis. Ideally, the team should include representatives from marketing, purchasing, production, finance, and transportation, and possibly a key supplier and customer impacted by the location.

Determining the scores for each factor can include several intermediate steps. Comparing a labor cost score, for instance, might include determining an acceptable wage scale, along with insurance, taxes, and training costs and any other associated labor costs for each potential location. Then the total labor costs can be compared and translated into the final labor cost scores for each location by assigning the lowest-cost location the maximum score and then assigning the other locations a score based on their respective labor costs. Example 11.1 illustrates the use of the weighted-factor location model.

Example 11.1 Using the Weighted-Factor Location Model

The following factors have been identified as critical to making a location decision among three countries: China, Singapore, and Indonesia. A group of functional managers has determined the factors, weights, and scores to be used in the analysis.

IMPORTANT LOCATION FACTORS	FACTOR WEIGHTS (SUM TO 1)	CHINA SCORES (1–100)	SINGAPORE SCORES (1–100)	INDONESIA SCORES (1–100)
Labor cost	0.20	100	40	90
Proximity to market	0.15	100	60	80
Supply chain compatibility	0.25	80	80	60
Quality of life	0.30	70	90	60
Stability of government	0.10	80	100	50

To determine where the new facility should be located, the weighted scores for the three countries are calculated as follows:

China = 0.20(100) + 0.15(100) + 0.25(80) + 0.30(70) + 0.10(80) = 20 + 15 + 20 + 21 + 8 = 84.
Singapore = 0.20(40) + 0.15(60) + 0.25(80) + 0.30(90) + 0.10(100) = 8+ 9 + 20 + 27 + 10 = 74.
Indonesia = 0.20(90) + 0.15(80) + 0.25(60) + 0.30(60) + 0.10(50) = 18 + 12 + 15 + 18 + 5 = 68.

Based on the total weighted score, China would be the recommended country in which to locate the new facility.

The Break-Even Model

The **break-even model** is a useful location analysis technique when fixed and variable costs can be determined for each potential location. This method involves the following steps:

1. Identify the locations to be considered.
2. Determine the fixed cost for each facility. The components of fixed cost are the costs of land, property taxes, insurance, equipment, and buildings.
3. Determine the unit variable cost for each facility. The components of variable cost are the costs of labor, materials, utilities, and transportation.
4. Construct the total cost lines for each location on a graph.

Example 11.2 Using the Break-Even Model

Three locations have been identified as suitable candidates for building a new factory. The fixed and unit variable costs for each of three potential locations have been estimated and are shown in the following table.

LOCATION	ANNUAL FIXED COST ($)	UNIT VARIABLE COST ($)
A	500,000	300
B	750,000	200
C	900,000	100

Given a forecasted demand of 3,000 units per year, the best location can be found by first plotting the three total cost curves, represented by

$$TC_A = 500{,}000 + 300Q$$
$$TC_B = 750{,}000 + 200Q$$
$$TC_C = 900{,}000 + 100Q$$

The three curves are shown in Figure 11.1.

Next, the break-even point between Location A and Location B is determined:

$$TC_A = TC_B$$
$$500{,}000 + 300Q = 750{,}000 + 200Q$$
$$100Q = 250{,}000 \text{ and then } Q = 2{,}500 \text{ units.}$$

This indicates that producing less than 2,500 units per year would be cheaper at Location A (when the lower fixed cost predominates), while producing more than 2,500 units per year would be cheaper at Location B (when the lower variable cost predominates).

Next, the break-even point between Location B and Location C is determined:

$$TC_B = TC_C$$
$$750{,}000 + 200Q = 900{,}000 + 100Q$$
$$100Q = 150{,}000 \text{ and then } Q = 1{,}500 \text{ units.}$$

This indicates that producing less than 1,500 units per year would be cheaper at Location B, while producing more than 1,500 units per year would be cheaper at Location C.

Finally, the break-even point between Location A and Location C is determined:

$$TC_A = TC_C$$
$$500{,}000 + 300Q = 900{,}000 + 100Q$$
$$200Q = 400{,}000 \text{ and then } Q = 2{,}000 \text{ units.}$$

This indicates that producing less than 2,000 units per year would be cheaper at Location A, while producing more than 2,000 units per year would be cheaper at Location C.

Based on the cost curves shown in Figure 11.1, Location C has the lowest total cost when producing the forecasted quantity of 3,000 units per year. If, however, the annual demand forecast was 1,000 units, then Location A would be preferred. From Figure 11.1, it can be seen that Location B would never be the preferred location when comparing the costs of all three sites simultaneously.

5. Determine the break-even points on the graph. Alternatively, the break-even points can be solved algebraically.
6. Identify the range over which each location has the lowest cost.

Example 11.2 illustrates the use of the break-even model.

HELPFUL WEBSITE INFORMATION FOR LOCATION ANALYSIS

Two websites are available that provide useful information for location analysis:

1. *Development Alliance, The Site Selectors' Portal for Community Information*—found at www.developmentalliance.com: The Development Alliance website is developed by Conway Data, Inc., publishers of *Site Selection* magazine, which is the official publication of the Industrial Asset Management Council. The Development

Figure 11.1 Break-Even Graph

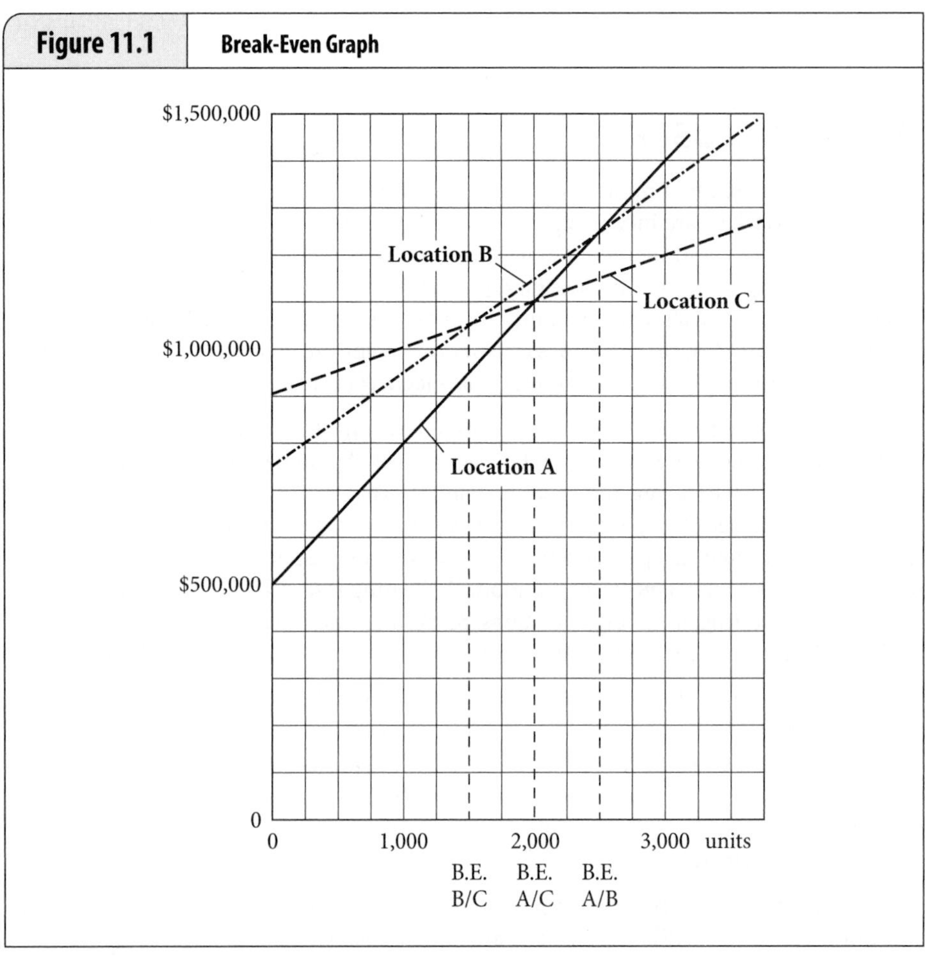

Alliance website is a portal for community information on finding the best global business location and includes the following:

- Metro and Micro Data—micropolitan and metropolitan statistical data for companies seeking new business locations.
- IEDN (Interactive Economic Development Network) Criteria-Based Search—use up to nineteen criteria to find and compare counties throughout the U.S.
- State of the States—from Alabama through Wyoming. Includes state contact information.
- Doing Business Database—World Bank's tool for evaluating the impacts on business and property rights protection of regulatory schemes in 175 countries.
- Property Marketplace—listings of properties for sale or lease in the U.S., Canada, and Mexico.

2. *Mapping Analytics*—found at www.mappinganalytics.com/site-selection/site-selection.html. The focus of Mapping Analytics is "business management, including sales, marketing, real estate, strategic planning, and GIS consulting."[44] Its clients are from a wide variety of businesses including manufacturing/distribution, banking/finance, retail, real estate, restaurants, marketing/media/advertising, insurance, and healthcare. The key site selection services provided by the company are customer profiling, mapping customer locations, competitive analysis, trade area development

and mapping, demographic, census and market data analysis, market potential analysis, and analysis of site impact on overall store network in the U.S.

BUSINESS CLUSTERS

Over the last decade, a number of trends have dramatically impacted the facility location process. Markets are increasingly globalized due to the liberalization of trade, technological advances, and increased demand from many regions of the world. Countries compete against one another for foreign direct investment. Having the necessary information to compare countries across a multitude of factors will help managers make better location decisions. Today, more **business clusters** are being created globally. Research parks and special economic/industrial zones serve as magnets for business clusters.

The concept of business clusters represents a new way of thinking about location decisions, challenges conventional logic on how companies should be configured, and provides a different approach to organizing a supply chain. So what exactly are these *business clusters?* According to Michael Porter, "clusters are geographic concentrations of interconnected companies and institutions in a particular field. Clusters encompass an array of linked industries and other entities important to competition."[45] Locating research and development, component manufacturing, assembly operations, marketing, and other associated businesses in one area can improve the supply chain, technology sharing, and information sharing.

Silicon Valley and Hollywood in California are probably the two most well-known and successful business clusters. Another high-tech cluster fashioned after Silicon Valley is Massachusetts' Route 128. A competitiveness study conducted by the U.K. government found that "business development is often strongest when firms cluster together, creating a critical mass of growth, collaboration, and competition and opportunities for investment and knowledge sharing."[46]

Governments today recognize the need to develop existing clusters of similar businesses into world-class units. Although clusters are more prevalent in advanced economies such as in the U.S. and Europe, countries such as Mexico, Singapore, India, and Taiwan have also created high-tech clusters with the participation of foreign companies. A discussion of each of these countries follows:

- *Mexico:* Mexico has long been a hotbed for electronic manufacturers, with many located in cities such as Tijuana, Mexicali, Tecate, Chihuahua, Saltillo, Reynosa, and Guadalajara. Examples of major global companies operating in Mexico are IBM, Motorola, Hewlett-Packard, Siemens, Ericsson, Samsung, LG Electronics, Sony, and Panasonic. With NAFTA, goods can be exported duty-free to North America, allowing Mexico to become an electronics manufacturing center for the Americas. Mexico, for example, produces nearly one-quarter of the world's television receivers.
- *Singapore:* Singapore has replaced Japan as the most attractive country for U.S. high-tech manufacturing investment in the Asia Pacific region. Singapore has the greatest technology penetration rates in Asia, the highest per capita GDP in Asia, and a highly skilled workforce. Approximately half of the world's computer disk drives are produced in Singapore.
- *Taiwan:* Taiwan, dubbed the "Silicon Island" by *Forbes*, is a leading manufacturer of computer hardware and has the largest global market share for motherboards, modems, and scanners. Intel and Compaq are two major investors in Taiwan, due partly to the large pool of engineers possessing technical degrees.
- *India:* India is a major player in the software industry and country of choice for customized software development. India has the world's third-largest pool of

scientific and technical personnel. India also provides a significant cost advantage due to its low labor cost. Companies such as IBM, Microsoft, Oracle, and Motorola have built facilities in India's silicon valleys: Bangalore, Hyderabad, and Mumbai.

There are many reasons why clusters are successful. One is the close cooperation, coordination, and trust among clustered companies in related industries. Another reason is the fierce competition for customers among rival companies located in the cluster. Companies are more productive in their operations because of access to the local supplier base, information, and technology. Companies are able to recruit from the local pool of skilled and experienced workers, thus reducing hiring costs. Professor Harald Bathelt (University of Toronto), who has studied industry clusters extensively, said, "The less that is known about another country, or another area they want to move into, the less uncertainty they will have if they move closer to a cluster."[47] Due to the intensity of competition within the business cluster, peer pressure, and constant comparison among rivals, companies tend to respond quicker to customer needs and trends. Clusters thus provide the competitive environment that promotes increasing innovation and profitability. In a study by Statistics Canada on clusters, the following findings were reported:[48]

- Not all manufacturing plants benefit from clustering—the phenomenon favors large firms.
- Startup and smaller firms in cluster areas do not make productivity gains.
- Startup and smaller firms could potentially benefit from knowledge transfers.

Not all clusters are successful. For example, Michigan suffered through plant closings and employee layoffs in the auto industry due to the industry's overreliance on gas-guzzling auto designs and the oil shock in the 1970s. The groupthink mentality among the cluster participants of General Motors, Ford, and Chrysler in Detroit made it more difficult for individual companies to try new ideas and see the need for radical innovation in fuel economy automobile designs.

SUSTAINABLE DEVELOPMENT AND FACILITY LOCATION

The World Commission on Environment and Development (the Brundtland Commission) defines **sustainable development** as "development that meets the needs of the present without compromising the ability of future generations to meet their own needs."[49] Sustainable development is important because what we do today will affect future generations. The critical issues in sustainable development are energy consumption/production, air pollution, and climate change. These issues are strongly related to one another and need to be considered in an integrated manner and linked to economic, social, and environmental policies. Luis Alberto Ferraté Felice, minister of the environment and natural resources of Guatemala, and the United Nations Commission on Sustainable Development Chair, said that "Sustainable development requires a transformation of values and principles that directly influence development strategies and lifestyles."[50] The increased global consumption of fossil fuels has increased global warming. In addition, prices of crude oil have continued to rise as demand has increased. More expensive oil translates to increased cost of production of goods and delivery of services. Ultimately this is affecting supply chain costs. This calls for the development of cleaner, more fuel-efficient and affordable energy technologies as well as renewable energy technologies.

It is clear that industrial development is the engine for economic growth and eradicating poverty in emerging countries. However, resource efficiency and technology innovation are opportunities for reducing cost and increasing competitiveness and employment, issues that are central to managing an effective supply chain. Air pollution has serious impacts on human health, environment, and the economy. A related issue is climate change and preserving the world's ecosystem. Due to the importance of climate change, most countries joined an international treaty, the United Nations Framework Convention on Climate Change (UNFCCC) "to begin to consider what can be done to reduce global warming and to cope with whatever temperature increases are inevitable."[51] Two groups of scientists reported that global warming caused by greenhouse gases has led to destabilization of the ice sheet in the West Antarctic glaciers. "This is really happening," Thomas P. Wagner, who runs NASA's programs on polar ice, said. "There's nothing to stop it now. But you are still limited by the physics of how fast the ice can flow."[52]

Another project with environmental implications is the Keystone XL pipeline, which is projected to move heavy oil sands oil from Alberta, Canada to the U.S. Gulf Coast. Environmentalists have been fighting to stop this controversial project because of the impact that processing this Canadian heavy oil might have on climate change and public health in the event of oil spills. Supporters of the project argue that jobs will be created and that the Alberta oil will be extracted and transported to markets whether the Keystone XL pipeline is built or not.[53] As of mid-2014, the U.S. government had not given the final go ahead with the project. Complicating the issue is the recent ruling by a judge in Nebraska blocking the pipeline's planned route through the state. Due to the uncertainty of the Keystone XL pipeline, a Canadian environmental and economic review panel approved plans for the alternative Enbridge Northern Gateway pipeline linking the oil sands to the Canadian west coast, which would cost $7.4 billion.[54] The panel concluded that Canadians would be better off with the Enbridge pipeline than without it. Currently, oil companies are processing this oil and moving it using trucks and trains, which are also argued to be creating high levels of greenhouse gases, along with oil spills.

A similar term, **green development**, has been used to describe environmentally friendly development. The difference between green development and sustainable development is that green development "prioritizes what its proponents consider to be environmental sustainability over economic and cultural considerations."[55] An example would be the installation of a state-of-the-art waste treatment plant with very high maintenance cost in a poor country. Due to the high maintenance cost, the ideal plant from an environmental standpoint may not be sustainable and likely will be shut down. From a sustainable development perspective, it would be acceptable to have a less effective environmental technology but one that can be maintained by the users of the equipment. When decision makers consider both economic and social issues in addition to environmental concerns, then sustainable development is more logical.

ADDITIVE MANUFACTURING AND ITS IMPACT ON FACILITY LOCATION

New technology developed recently may well change the landscape for manufacturing. **Additive manufacturing** or **3D printing** is a "process of making a three-dimensional solid object of virtually any shape from a digital model."[56] The technology was first developed by MIT, funded by grants from the Office of Naval Research and the National Science Foundation. Production using a 3D printer involves laying down a very thin layer of stainless steel or ceramic powder and using liquid binder to fuse the different layers to form the final product. The technology is applicable to wide range of industries such as defense, aerospace, automotive, medical, and metals manufacturing. Initially, 3D printing was used for rapid prototyping, but new developments make it possible for use in actual production. Benefits of additive manufacturing include shorter lead times, mass customization, reduced parts count, more complex shapes, parts on demand, efficient material use, and lower energy consumption. The National Additive Manufacturing Innovation Institute (NAMII) in Youngstown, Ohio, has been rebranded to America Makes, an organization that is focused on helping the U.S. enhance and grow in the area of 3D printing by facilitating collaboration among leaders from business, academia, nonprofit organizations, and government agencies. The goal of America Makes is to help the U.S. 3D printing industry become more globally competitive.[57]

Digital dentistry is one growth area for the technology where "dentists use 3D printers to produce models, dentures, braces, and implants, while foregoing the gooey pastes and gels that are traditionally used to make them."[58] In digital dentistry, there is no need to make physical impressions. Dentists can use intraoral scanners to provide a full view of the anatomy of the mouth, jaws, and teeth, and allow accurate models to be built by 3D printers that fit with high accuracy, minimum discomfort, and beautiful cosmetics. 3D printers enable on-site production at the dental clinics, which is faster, more economical, and predictable than ordering the implant from an outside vendor.

The affordability of 3D printers could keep businesses from going overseas for their manufacturing needs. A small business or an entrepreneur (such as a dentist) can now afford to have its own little factory. More companies are today experimenting with 3D printers, which will likely move the technology closer to the mainstream market and make the technology even more affordable. Shown below are several examples of companies using 3D printers to create new products, improve old ones, and improve their business processes:[59]

- **General Electric**
  General Electric has invested heavily in 3D printing to enable production of more than 85,000 fuel nozzles for its new Leap jet engines. The printers can make the nozzles in one metal piece that is stronger and lighter than the ones made in a traditional assembly plant.
- **Boeing**
  The airline company was an early adopter of 3D printing technology. For example, the 787 Dreamliner has thirty 3D printed parts, including air ducts and hinges, which is an industry record. Boeing has also printed an entire cabin using Stratasys 3D printers.
- **Ford**
  Ford, which has been using 3D printing technology since the 1980s, produced engine covers for the 2015 Ford Mustang with 3D printers. Ford estimates with 3D printing, it would take four days and cost $3,000 compared to four months and $500,000 using traditional methods to produce the engine cover for the new Ford Mustang.
- **Nike**
  The Nike Vapor Laser Talon, which are shoes designed for football players running the 40 yard dash on football turf, has a 3D printed plate and cleats made from selective laser sintering technology and weighing only 5.6 ounces.
- **MakieLab**
  Customers can design their unique Makie Doll selecting features such as face, eyes, jaw, smile, and hair. MakieLab then 3D prints the flexible fashion dolls from thermoplastics in its London headquarters and ships globally. The company promotes the dolls as environmentally friendly because custom printing produces less waste and the packaging is made from recyclable materials.

SUMMARY

Facility location decisions can provide organizations with a competitive advantage and, therefore, must be an integral part of their overall strategic plans. The effectiveness of a supply chain is influenced greatly by facility locations. Increased globalization and improved technologies have resulted in a variety of options for companies to locate their facilities. Today, companies must consider a number of factors when analyzing potential locations; several comparison methods are available when considering the country, region, and community for a facility location. Business clusters often provide for strong business development, collaboration, growth opportunities, and improved supply chain management. The existence of successful clusters suggests that innovation and competition are concentrated geographically. China today represents an attractive location for many of the world's top companies due to its inexpensive labor and huge market. There has been much discussion about sustainable development and the greening of the supply chain and its effect on global location decisions. Finally, emerging technologies such as 3D printing will have a major impact on how companies view manufacturing and where they locate production facilities.

KEY TERMS

3D printing , 402

additive manufacturing, 402

Association of Southeast Asian Nations (ASEAN), 386

break-even model, 397

business clusters, 400

Common Market for Eastern and Southern Africa (COMESA), 387

contributor factory, 385

European Union (EU), 386

green development, 402

lead factory, 385

North American Free Trade Agreement (NAFTA), 386

offshore factory, 385

outpost factory, 385

quality-of-life factors, 394

right-to-work laws, 396

server factory, 385

source factory, 385

Southern Common Market (MERCOSUR), 386

sustainable development, 401

weighted-factor rating model, 396

World Trade Organization (WTO), 386

DISCUSSION QUESTIONS

1. What is the impact of facility decisions on a supply chain?
2. Why is demand management important for effective supply chain management?
3. What are business clusters? Provide several examples of business clusters in a variety of countries. What are the advantages of clustering?
4. What are the factors influencing facility location?
5. Discuss the major regional trade agreements in Asia, Africa, Europe, Latin America, and North America.
6. What is the World Trade Organization, and what is its role in world trade?
7. What are the critical factors in making community and site decisions?
8. Discuss Walmart's location strategy.
9. Define *quality of life*. Why is quality of life an important factor in facility location? Is the set of quality-of-life factors used by the Chamber of Commerce in Jacksonville, Florida, a good one? Please explain.

10. What is a right-to-work state? What are the advantages or disadvantages of doing business in a right-to-work state?
11. Why is China an attractive location for many businesses?
12. What are the challenges of doing business in China?
13. Discuss the six strategic roles of a foreign facility.
14. What is sustainable development, and why is this policy important to a country and the world at large?
15. What is the difference between green development and sustainable development?
16. Explain why 3D printing may lead to a revival of manufacturing in the U.S.

ESSAY/PROJECT QUESTIONS

1. What are the key factors used in the World Competitiveness Ranking? Go to the website of IMD—World Competitiveness Yearbook at http://www.imd.org/wcc/wcy-world-competitiveness-yearbook/. Select any three countries in the Asia Pacific region. Prepare a report discussing the pros and cons for each of these countries to locate a business there.
2. What are the factors used in the Global Competitiveness Report? Go to the World Economic Forum website at http://www.weforum.org/issues/global-competitivenessGlobal%20Competitivenss%20Report/. Select any three countries in South America. Prepare a report discussing the pros and cons for each of these countries to locate a business there.
3. Go to the website of the World Trade Organization at www.wto.org. Outline the development that led to China's entry into the WTO. What is the impact of China's accession into WTO on U.S. companies?
4. Go to the website of the U.S. Commercial Service at http://export.gov/export/index.asp. First, select a country you wish to study. Next, retrieve the country commercial guide posted under the Doing Business in XXX menu option, where XXX is the country you selected. Then, based on the country commercial guide, prepare an assessment of the suitability of the country for doing business in the particular industry you picked earlier.
5. Go to the website http://www.reshorenow.org/, and prepare a report on why U.S. companies should move manufacturing back to the U.S.

PROBLEMS

1. The Soft Toys Company has collected information on fixed and variable costs for four potential plant locations.

LOCATION	ANNUAL FIXED COST ($)	UNIT VARIABLE COST ($)
A	200,000	50
B	300,000	45
C	400,000	25
D	600,000	20

   a. Plot the total cost curves for the four plant locations on a single graph.
   b. Find the break-even points and determine the range of demand for which each location has a cost advantage.
   c. Which plant location is best if demand is 30,000 units?

2. The Bruhaha Brewery is planning to expand internationally. The company has identified five critical location factors and their relative weights. The scores for each of the three potential sites are shown in the following table. Which site should be selected?

CRITICAL LOCATION FACTORS	FACTOR WEIGHT (SUM TO 1)	COLUMBUS SCORES (1–100)	LAS VEGAS SCORES (1–100)	SPOKANE SCORES (1–100)
Labor cost	0.15	70	90	50
Proximity to market	0.25	100	90	80
Supplier base	0.20	80	100	70
Quality of life	0.30	90	60	60
Taxes	0.10	60	80	90

ENDNOTES

1. Densik, J., and R. Spee, "Global Location Trends—2013 Annual Report," IBM Global Services; http://www-01.ibm.com/common/ssi/cgi-bin/ssialias?subtype=XB&infotype=PM&appname=GBSE_GB_TI_USEN&htmlfid=GBE03582USEN

2. See, for example, http://www.thomaslfriedman.com/bookshelf/the-lexus-and-the-olive-tree.

3. Senger, E., "The Pros and Cons of Business Clusters," HSBC Global Connections; https://globalconnections.hsbc.com/canada/en/articles/pros-and-cons-business-clusters

4. Project Case: Marriott, Wadley Donovan Gutshaw Consulting; http://www.wdgconsulting.com/WDGC_Project_case_studies_Marriot.htm

5. Porter, M., "Clusters and the New Economics of Competition," *Harvard Business Review*, November–December 1998.

6. "List of automotive assembly plants in the United States," Wikipedia; http://en.wikipedia.org/wiki/List_of_automotive_assembly_plants_in_the_United_States

7. Global Location Trend—Annual Report, IBM Global Business Service, October 2009.

8. Amazon Investor Relations; http://phx.corporate-ir.net/phoenix.zhtml?c=97664&p=irol-irhome

9. 2013 Amazon.com Annual Report; available from http://phx.corporate-ir.net/phoenix.zhtml?c=97664&p=irol-proxy

10. "Amazon Global Fulfillment Center Network," MWPVL international Supply Chain Experience; http://www.mwpvl.com/html/amazon_com.html

11. "Next-Day Shipping Wars: Can Etailers Compete with Amazon," *Forbes*, December 18, 2013; http://www.forbes.com/sites/mckinsey/2013/12/18/next-day-shipping-wars-can-etailers-compete-with-amazon/

12. "FedEx Facts," FedEx; http://about.van.fedex.com/fedex-facts

13. K. Ferdows, "Making the Most of Foreign Factories," *Harvard Business Review*, March–April 1997: 73–88.

14. Ibid.

15. Ibid.

16. Ibid.

17. "What Is the WTO?" available from http://www.wto.org/english/thewto_e/whatis_e/whatis_e.htm

18. Regional Trade Agreements; available from www.wto.org/english/tratop_e/region_e/region_e.htm

19. "The European Union at a Glance, Member States of the EU"; available from http://europa.eu/abc/european_countries/index_en.htm

20. "North American Free Trade Agreement (NAFTA)," Office of the United States Trade Representative; http://www.ustr.gov/trade-agreements/free-trade-agreements/north-american-free-trade-agreement-nafta

21. Sergie, M. A., "NAFTA's Economic Impact," Council of Foreign Relations; http://www.cfr.org/trade/naftas-economic-impact/p15790

22. Ibid.

23. MERCOSUR; available from http://en.wikipedia.org/wiki/Mercosur

24. Association of South East Asian Nations (ASEAN); available from http://www.aseansec.org/overview/

25. Common Market for Eastern and Southern Africa (COMESA); available from www.comesa.int/

26. Ibid.

27. "Glossary of Statistical Terms," OECED; http://stats.oecd.org/glossary/detail.asp?ID=399

28. World Competitiveness Report, Methodology and Principles of Analysis; available from www.imd.ch/research/publications/wcy/upload/methodology.pdf

29. "IMD Releases Its 25th Anniversary World Competitiveness Rankings," IMD; http://www.imd.org/news/World-Competitiveness-2013.cfm

30. Global Competitiveness Report 2009–2010, World Economic Forum; available from www.weforum.org/pdf/GCR09/GCR20092010fullreport.pdf

31. "Competitive Alternatives," KPMG; http://www.competitivealternatives.com/

32. Bell, K., "7 States That Don't Have a State Income Tax (And Two That Don't Tax Wage Income)," ABC News; http://abcnews.go.com/Business/states-income-tax-us/story?id=21490926#

33. 2013 Amazon.com Annual Report; http://phx.corporate-ir.net/phoenix.zhtml?c=97664&p=irol-reportsannual

34. Objectives—North American Agreement on Environmental Cooperation; available from www.cec.org/Page.asp?PageID=122&ContentID=2730&SiteNodeID=567&BL_ExpandID=

35. "Sustainable Development," WTO; http://www.wto.org/english/tratop_e/envir_e/sust_dev_e.htm

36. Foroohar, R., and B. Saporlto, "Made in the U.S.A.," *Time*, April 22, 2013; http://business.time.com/made-in-the-u-s-a/

37. "Competitive Alternatives," KPMG's Guide to International Business Location Costs,: 2012 Edition, KPNG; http://www.competitivealternatives.com/reports/2012_compalt_report_vol1_en.pdf

38. Pennington, T., "Are You Ready Series: Rolling Blackouts," Ready Nutrition; http://readynutrition.com/resources/are-you-ready-series-rolling-blackouts_12012014/

39. "List of Largest Hydroelectric Power Stations," Wikipedia; http://en.wikipedia.org/wiki/List_of_largest_hydroelectric_power_stations

40. "Quality of Life," Wikipedia; http://en.wikipedia.org/wiki/Quality_of_life

41. Indicators—Quality of Life Progress Report, Jacksonville Community Council Inc.; available from www.jcci.org/jcciwebsite/pages/indicators.html

42. "Mexico's Drug War Leads to Kidnappings, Vigilante Violence," *Time*; http://world.time.com/2014/01/17/mexico-drug-war-kidnapping/

43. "Right-to-Work States"; available from www.nrtw.org/rtws.htm

44. About Mapping Analytics; available from www.mappinganalytics.com/about/about.html

45. Porter, M., "Clusters and the New Economics of Competition."

46. "Business Clusters in the UK—A First Assessment"; available from www.dti.gov.uk/clusters/map/graphics/forintro.pdf

47. Senger, E., "The Pros and Cons of Business Clusters," HSBC Global Connections; https://globalconnections.hsbc.com/canada/en/articles/pros-and-cons-business-clusters

48. Ibid.

49. The World Commission on Environment and Development (the Brundtland Commission) Definition of Sustainable Development; available from www.unngosustainability.org/CSD_Definitions SD.htm

50. "Sustainable Development Discussions to Focus on Smart Use of Resources," Economic and Social Council of UN; available from www.un.org/News/Press/docs/2010/envdev1123.doc.htm

51. The United Nations Framework Convention on Climate Change; available from http://unfccc.int/2860.php

52. Gillis, J., and K. Chang,"Scientists Warn of Rising Oceans from Polar Melt," *New York Times*, May 12, 2014; http://www.nytimes.com/2014/05/13/science/earth/collapse-of-parts-of-west-antarctica-ice-sheet-has-begun-scientists-say.html?_r=0

53. Davenport, C., "No Conflict of Interest Found in Favorable Review of Keystone Pipeline," *The New York Times*, February 26, 2014; http://www.nytimes.com/2014/02/27/opinion/obamas-pipeline.html

54. Austin, J., "Canadian Review Panel Approves Plans for an Oil Pipeline," *The New York Times*, December 19, 2013; http://www.nytimes.com/2013/12/20/business/international/canadian-review-panel-approves-plans-for-an-oil-pipeline.html?_r=0

55. "Sustainable Development"; http://en.wikipedia.org/wiki/Sustainable_development

56. 3D Printing, Wikipedia; http://en.wikipedia.org/wiki/3D_printing

57. America Makes; http://americamakes.us/

58. Shamah, D., "New Niche for 3D Printers in Dentistry," *Start-Up Israel*, March 3, 2014; http://www.timesofisrael.com/new-niche-for-3d-printers-in-dentistry/

59. Gilpin, L., "3D printing: 10 companies Using It in Ground-Breaking Ways," March 26, 2014; http://www.techrepublic.com/article/3d-printing-10-companies-using-it-in-ground-breaking-ways/#

Chapter 12
SERVICE RESPONSE LOGISTICS

We know retailers want to reach their targets across every possible channel, and that means activating the best retail experience across a much wider path.

— ***Sharon Love, CEO at retail marketing agency, TPN.***[1]

By improving our social media analytics capabilities, we're engaging with our customers on a 1:1 basis, to address and anticipate their needs more cohesively.

— ***Eugene Liebenberg, head of Retail Business Intelligence, Nedbank.***[2]

Learning Objectives

After completing this chapter, you should be able to

- Understand how supply chain management in services differs from supply chain management in manufacturing.
- Define service response logistics and describe all of its elements.
- Understand the importance of service locations and layouts and perform a layout analysis using several techniques.
- Describe the strategies for managing capacity, wait times, distribution, and quality in services.
- Understand queuing system design issues, and calculate queue characteristics.
- Use various techniques for managing customers' perceived waiting times.
- Understand the different distribution channels available for services.
- Define service quality, and describe how to measure it and improve it.

Chapter Outline

SCM Profile Global Expansion of the INTA

Etienne Sanz de Acedo became the New York-based International Trademark Association's (INTA) new CEO in 2013. One of his first priorities, he stated, was to expand the organization's activities into developing markets. In an interview, Sanz de Acedo said his key priorities included ambitiously pursuing growth in Asia, Africa, Latin America, and the Middle East.

Spanish-born Sanz de Acedo is uniquely placed to lead this expansion. He speaks four languages, is the child of a French mother and a Spanish father, and grew up speaking both his parents' native tongues. He learned English at school and improved his proficiency during summer vacations to the U.K. He developed a passion for the Italian language and gained fluency over a span of five summers in Italy.

Sanz de Acedo was quick to acknowledge the challenges of his new role. Increasing trademark protection globally will not be helped by a sluggish recovery from the global economic crisis and ever-changing issues online. "When we go somewhere new, we need first to respect the culture of the country," he said. "Shaping the Association for the future means looking at the markets and the trends. The world is global, the economy is global. We are in an information-sharing era."

Sanz de Acedo also recognized the need to widen the scope of INTA's communication to the general public in response to recent Internet protests against intellectual property (IP), brand, and trademark legislation. "We tend to talk broadly within our IP community, and then we need to reach public opinion outside of that and explain how brands are important to investment and to growth," he said. "This will probably be by means of partnerships, by cooperating with associations that might not be IP-related." He also hopes to increase INTA's membership within the IP world, particularly among corporate counsel and lawyers who take a more informal approach to participating in the INTA's annual meetings. "I think that we need to find ways to help people understand that actually participating in the Annual Meeting is contributing to the efforts INTA is making on their behalf," he said. "It's a question of solidarity."[3]

INTRODUCTION

While most of the concepts of supply chain management discussed up to this point in the text can be applied to service organizations, this chapter introduces and discusses supply chain management concepts suited particularly to services and the service activities of manufacturers. Service firms differ from manufacturers in a number of ways including the tangibility of the end product, the involvement of the customer in the production process, the assessment of product quality, the labor content contained in the end products, and facility location considerations. Many services are considered **pure services**, offering few, if any, tangible products to customers. Examples are consultants, lawyers, entertainers, and stockbrokers. Other services may offer end products containing a tangible component such as restaurants, repair facilities, transportation providers, and public warehouses. Most manufacturers, on the other hand, have tangible products with a relatively small service component that might include maintenance, warranty repair, and delivery services, along with customer call centers.

In most services, customers are either directly or indirectly involved in the production of the service itself. In this sense, services are said to provide **state utility**, meaning that services do something to things that are owned by the customer (such as transport and store their supplies, repair their machines, cut their hair, and provide their healthcare). Managing the interactions between service firms and their customers while the service is being performed is the topic of this chapter and is of paramount importance to the ultimate success of service organizations.

To generate initial and repeat customer visits, service firms must be located near their customers, they must know what their customers want, and they must be able to satisfy these needs quickly and in a cost-effective manner. This requires service firms to adequately hire, train, and schedule service representatives; to acquire technologies and equipment to aid in the provision of services; and to provide the right facility, network, and procedures to continually satisfy customers. Problems or mistakes that occur during the delivery of services most likely mean an increase in service delivery time, a reduction in customer satisfaction, lower perceived service quality, and lost current and future sales.

The important role services play in the global economy is becoming more evident today as developed countries become increasingly service oriented and as the Internet creates global "e-preneurs" whose businesses exist solely on the Internet. Service jobs are replacing those in manufacturing as productivity gains in manufacturing mean fewer laborers are needed to make the same numbers of products. In the U.S., for instance, services accounted for about 79 percent of the nation's gross domestic product (GDP) in 2011, which is up from 77 percent in 2007. In the U.K., services provided about 78 percent of GDP; in France, 79 percent; and in Japan, 73 percent. As a contrast, in underdeveloped countries such as Afghanistan, Cambodia, Ethiopia, and Indonesia, services accounted for 52 percent, 40 percent, 43 percent, and 38 percent of GDP, respectively.[4]

Successful firms today are busy identifying and improving the customer-desired service elements in their product offerings, in order to provide better value through attention to these elements. These efforts are at the heart of service operations and the topic of service response logistics. Let's first review service operations in general and then move on to discuss service response logistics in particular.

AN OVERVIEW OF SERVICE OPERATIONS

Services include organizations such as retailers, wholesalers, transportation and storage companies, healthcare providers, financial institutions, schools, real estate companies, government agencies, hotels, and consulting companies. Since the 1950s, the ratio of services to manufacturing and agriculture in terms of its share of the U.S. workforce has been increasing quite dramatically, and it is extremely likely that current university graduates entering the job market will be employed in some service role. In the U.S. and other developed economies, as the population has generated more wealth, they have continued to demand more services. In 1960, for example, Americans were spending about 46 percent of their personal consumption income on services. Today, Americans spend more than 67 percent on services.[5]

On the other hand, India, the world's second largest emerging economy (after China), has experienced a continued growth of its service sector. Its economy has shifted away from an agrarian economy toward a more service-oriented economy, which has improved the standard of living in India and boosted domestic consumption. This has helped to bolster overall productivity and competitiveness of companies in India, creating higher-value jobs.

SCM Profile: MPS Limited Sees Rapid Revenue Increases in India

The only major publishing service listed on India's stock exchanges is MPS Limited. They saw a dramatic increase in market capitalization in 2012 due to a surge in revenue and profits. "We acquired a great company with a rich legacy from Macmillan and have successfully turned it around. We have also built a strong suite of products and services with organic growth well underway," says CEO Nishith Arora. MPS employs 2,600 people and has a large production footprint in Bangalore, Chennai, Gurgaon, Delhi, and Dehradun.

With more than forty-two years of presence in the industry, MPS has evolved to offer every stage in the author-to-reader publishing process. Platform solutions are Arora's current focus. MPS's DigiCore platform, in particular the online editing component DigiEdit, has undergone considerable upgrading. Another platform, MediaSuite, now supports HTML in addition to Flash and delivers a variety of mobile formats. Content can be developed on this platform and pivoted to classrooms and all types of whiteboards. "We are making rapid inroads into the higher education space with our integrated print and digital asset production model, leveraging our established relationships with publishers and our vast portfolio of book production services," says Arora, adding that the surge in content production resulting from open access has certainly benefited his company.[6]

Services now account for about 57 percent of India's GDP.[7] Multinational restaurant chains are moving into India rapidly. Yum! Brands Inc., owner of Taco Bell, KFC, and Pizza Hut, has plans to more than quadruple its locations in India, from 230 at the end of 2009 to 1,000 by 2015. Dominos Pizza already has over 300 stores in India and is planning more.[8] Among many other services, the publishing services industry is also doing well in India, as evidenced by the nearby SCM Profile of MPS Limited.

Some of the differences between goods and services are listed below:

- Services *cannot be inventoried.* Typically, services are produced and consumed simultaneously—once an airliner has landed, or surgical operations are performed, or legal advice is given, customers have "consumed" the service. For this reason, services often struggle to find ways to utilize their employees during low-demand periods and to serve customers effectively during busy periods.
- Services are often *unique.* High-quality service providers with well-trained and motivated employees have the capability of customizing services to satisfy each customer—insurance policies, legal services, and even fast-food services can be uniquely designed and then delivered to customers. Thus, hiring and training become important issues for satisfying individual customer needs.
- Services have *high customer–server interactions.* Services often require high levels of server attention, whether it means delivering purchased products to a specific location at the buyer's facility, analyzing data, answering customer questions, resolving complaints, or repairing machinery. Many services today are finding ways to automate or standardize services, or to utilize customers to provide some of the service, to reduce costs and improve productivity. For instance, the past few years have seen a rapid growth in automated, self-serve services such as purchasing books or performing banking chores online, and completing one's tax forms.

- Services are *decentralized.* Service facilities must be decentralized because of their inability to inventory their services. Therefore, finding good, high-traffic locations is extremely important (even Internet-based services must locate their advertisements where they will be easily seen by people using search engines).

Thus, services, whether they are stand-alone organizations or departments in goods-producing firms, must be managed in ways that will take into account these various service characteristics. A number of service elements are discussed next.

Service Productivity

The basic measure of productivity is shown by the following formula:

$$\text{Productivity} = \frac{\text{Outputs produced}}{\text{Inputs used}},$$

where service outputs produced might be customers served, the number of services performed, or simply sales dollars, and inputs might be shown as labor hours or labor dollars (for a **single-factor productivity** measure). Alternately, inputs can be shown as the sum of labor, material, energy, and capital costs (for a **multiple-factor productivity** measure). The productivity measures used in an organization might be based on manager preferences or industry standards. Further, firms measure productivity to gauge their successes in employee training, equipment or technology investments, and cost reduction efforts.

Productivity and its growth over time are commonly used indicators of a firm's (or a country's) economic success. For most services, automation can be a troublesome issue when calculating productivities, and the labor content per unit of output can be quite high relative to manufactured goods. These two things can lead to a declining productivity growth rate as a nation's economy becomes less manufacturing oriented and more service oriented (as discussed above in reference to the U.S. and other economies). This productivity growth problem has been termed **Baumol's disease**, named after noted U.S. economist William Baumol. In the 1960s, he and his colleague, William Bowen, argued that productivity growth tends to be low in service-oriented economies. And, in fact, this effect was realized in the U.S. from the mid-1970s through the mid-1990s as productivity growth averaged a relatively low 1.5 percent per year. Since the mid-1990s, however, productivity growth in the U.S. has been up and down, leading to other theories such as the **Walmart effect**, which postulates that the booming growth in information technology has allowed many big-box retailers such as Walmart to realize large productivity growth rates. Today, some economists are even saying that Baumol's disease has been cured.[9] A service productivity example appears in Example 12.1.

In services with high labor costs, there is often a desire to reduce labor costs to improve productivity (since labor cost is considered a productivity input). This can lead companies to relocate to lower labor cost areas, outsource jobs to other, lower cost service providers, or lay off workers. These can be risky strategies, since relocating can create added and unforeseen costs, outsourcing reduces managerial control, and reducing the workforce can adversely affect morale, service quality, and service availability.

Other strategies for increasing service productivity attack the numerator of the productivity equation. One example is the use of technology to increase outputs. Adam Fein, president of Pennsylvania-based Pembroke Consulting, states, "In the warehouse, the productivity improvements from wireless networks come from substituting technology for potentially error-prone human activities such as order processing, inventory control

Example 12.1 Productivity at the Ultra Ski Shop

The Ultra Ski Shop rents snow skis 15 weeks per year and employs five people. The owner wants to track productivity performance measures using the data shown below.

INPUTS AND OUTPUTS	2012
Skis rental revenue	\$66,000
Labor cost	\$10,800
Lease payments	\$24,000
INPUTS AND OUTPUTS	**2013**
Skis rental revenue	\$69,500
Labor cost	\$11,600
Lease payments	\$24,500

Single-factor productivities

2012: Labor productivity = \$66,000 sales/\$10,800 = 6.11 sales \$ per labor \$; lease productivity = \$66,000/\$24,000 = 2.75 sales \$ per lease \$.

2013: Labor productivity = \$69,500 sales/\$11,600 = 5.99 sales \$ per labor \$; lease productivity = \$69,500/\$24,500 = 2.84 sales \$ per lease \$.

Multiple-factor productivities

2012: \$66,000 sales/[\$10,800 + \$24,000] = 1.90 sales \$ per input \$.

2013 \$69,500 sales/[\$11,600 + \$24,500] = 1.93 sales \$ per input \$.

Labor productivity grew from 2012 to 2013 by (5.99 − 6.11)/6.11 = −0.02 or −2%. The lease productivity grew from 2012 to 2013 by (2.84 − 2.75)/2.75 = 0.033 or 3.3%. The multiple-factor productivity grew by (1.93 − 1.90)/1.90 = 0.016 or 1.6%. Ultra management should look into why labor cost grew faster than ski revenue from 2012 to 2013.

SCM Profile Improving Productivity in the Utility Industry

As utility linemen are tasked with upgrading a nation's aging infrastructure, they are demanding tools that will not only help them to get more work done in less time, but also improve ergonomics so they can work a longer career in the field with fewer injuries.

In the past, linemen had no other choice but to rely on manual tools that, over time, could inflict injuries to workers. Today, manufacturers have come out with tools that are lighter, faster, and easier to operate with less fatigue. For example, at North Carolina-based Duke Energy, a fifteen- to twenty-minute hole-drilling operation for a utility pole has now become a one-minute job with a battery-operated hammer drill. "Ergonomically speaking, the handheld tools were rough on the elbows and shoulders," says Keith Meza, a distribution line tech for Duke. "Our seasoned linemen aren't getting any younger, and these tools help to improve productivity. Our company has spared no expense in getting us what we need."

At the Kansas City Power & Light service center, linemen stock their bucket truck bins with ergonomic tools like shotgun sticks for working on energized lines and strap hoists to pull new wire to the proper tension following a storm. With the wire tension at more than 1,000 lb (454 kg), it would be impossible to perform this task by hand.[10]

or picking."[11] The nearby SCM Profile describes how the use of better tools is helping to improve the labor productivity of utility industry work crews.

Productivity improvements can also be realized through better education and training, which can ultimately impact both inputs and outputs in the productivity equation. Hallmark Consumer Services, a U.K. logistics company, purchased a warehouse management software application and then provided its warehouse employees with the necessary training to operate the system. "The training cost us £7,500 and the productivity gains alone were £7,000 our first year," says Chris Hall, managing director of Hallmark. "The WMS software was an investment of £20,000 and will have paid for itself in less than three years on labor savings alone."[12]

Improving service productivity can be quite challenging because of the desire in many cases for customized, labor-intensive services and because of the difficulty of assessing service quality (e.g., was the car fixed properly? Was the client properly defended? Was the hired comedian funny?). A complete discussion of service quality appears later in the chapter.

Global Service Issues

The growth and export of services are occurring everywhere as world economies improve and the demand for services increases. Even during the global recession a few years ago, a number of services were finding ways to stay competitive and expand. Just a few examples include—the expansion of Florida-based ZeroChaos, a workforce solutions provider, to the Nordic and European regions. "The Swedish market and the Nordic region remain attractive for expansion," says Harold Mills, CEO of ZeroChaos. "The exceptional market stability and nearly five percent GDP growth has provided numerous opportunities for our growth initiatives," he added. Small business funding specialist firm Bibby Financial Services of the U.K. expanded its presence in the Asia Pacific region by opening its first location in Singapore in 2012. It launched its Hong Kong and New Zealand operations in 2011. "Our overarching goal is to support the funding requirements of a greater number of small- and medium-sized businesses across the globe, and this latest venture will ensure we continue to develop our flexible trade finance packages," says global CEO Simon Featherstone. The U.K.-based deVere Group, a financial advisory service, started opening another 100 locations worldwide in 2011. "This is part of deVere's continued geographic expansion initiative to increase our presence in key growth markets and support our global growth strategy," says CEO Nigel Green.[13]

Successfully managing services as they expand into foreign markets involves a number of issues:

- *Labor, facilities, and infrastructure support.* Cultural differences, education, and expertise levels can prove to be problematic for firms unfamiliar with local human resources. Firms must also become adept at locating the most appropriate support facilities, suppliers, transportation providers, communication systems, and housing.
- *Legal and political issues.* Local laws may restrict foreign competitors, limit use of certain resources, attach tariffs to prices, or otherwise impose barriers to foreign services. Some countries require foreign companies to form joint ventures with domestic business partners.
- *Domestic competitors and the economic climate.* Company managers must be aware of their local competitors, the services they offer, their pricing structures, and the current state of the local economy. Firms can devise competitive

strategies by modifying their services to gain a local or regional competitive advantage.

- *Identifying global customers.* Perhaps most importantly, managers must find out where potential global customers are, through use of the Internet, foreign government agencies, trading partners, or foreign trade intermediaries. Once potential customers are identified, managers can begin modifying their service products to meet the needs of these customers.

More on global service expansion can be found later in the chapter.

Service Strategy Development

Manufacturing and service organizations use one or more of the three generic competitive strategies: cost leadership, differentiation, and focus.[14] Each of these is briefly discussed below in relation to services.

Cost Leadership Strategy

Using a **cost leadership strategy** often requires a large capital investment in automated production equipment and significant efforts in the areas of controlling and reducing costs, doing things right the first time, standardizing services, and aiming marketing efforts at cost-conscious consumers. Residential electricity provider Constellation Energy, headquartered in Maryland, used green energy to help it underbid Commonwealth Edison by 38 percent in 2012, to provide electricity to the city of Evanston, Illinois.[15]

Differentiation Strategy

Implementing a **differentiation strategy** is based on creating a service that is considered unique. The uniqueness can take many forms including customer service excellence (Ritz-Carlton hotels), brand image (the Google logo and its variations for holidays), variety (Best Buy's merchandise), and use of technology (Southwest Airlines' ticketing website and its "ding" notifications). Differentiation strategies are often created as the result of companies listening to their customers. Services are beginning to engage customers more effectively through various touch-points such as the phone, store locations, catalogs, social media, and online stores. New York–based Citigroup is well-known for its social media savvy. "Money is a highly sensitive topic," says Michelle Peluso, Citigroup's global consumer chief marketing and Internet officer. "One of the things social media allows us to do is to listen in to hear what people say about our brand, our competitors, our industry, products and services, and our people."[16] Differentiation does not necessarily mean higher costs; it merely refers to the ability of the service to offer unique elements in their services. In many cases, though, it may mean the customer is willing to pay more for the service. Advertisements, logos, awards, and company reputations all play a part in creating the perception of uniqueness among a service's potential customers.

Focus Strategy

A **focus strategy** refers to a service that can effectively serve a narrow target market or niche better than other firms trying to serve an entire market. Companies specializing in these market niches can provide customized services and expertise to suit the specific needs of these customers. For instance, a neighborhood hobby shop is more likely to serve the needs of hobby enthusiasts than a big-box retailer like Carrefour or Walmart, even though they might sell some of the same merchandise. Within each market niche, firms can then exhibit characteristics of differentiation or cost leadership. Florida-based French Fry Heaven, a gourmet french fry restaurant, started in 2011 and sells fifty types of French fries. They have found success serving this narrow fast-food niche. Their mission is: To serve the best fries on earth, be everywhere people are hungry, leave you with a smile on your face, and make a significant positive impact on the world![17]

The Service Delivery System

Customers actually purchase a bundle of attributes when purchasing services, including the *explicit service* itself (storage and use of your money at a bank), the *supporting facility* (the bank building, drive-up tellers, and website), *facilitating goods* (the deposit forms, monthly statements, and coffee in the lobby), and *implicit services* (the security provided, friendly atmosphere in the bank, privacy, and convenience). Successful services deliver this bundle of attributes in the most efficient way, while still satisfying customer requirements. Service managers define their **service bundles** and then design the most effective delivery system for each service bundle.

Service delivery systems fall along a continuum with mass-produced, low-customer-contact systems at one extreme (such as ATMs) and highly customized, high-customer contact systems at the other (such as an expensive beauty salon). Many delivery system designs seek to physically separate high-contact (front-of-the-house) operations from low-contact (back-of-the-house) operations to allow use of various management techniques to maximize performance of each area (such as in a restaurant). **Back-of-the-house operations** tend to be managed as manufacturing centers, where the emphasis is on maximizing quality outputs while achieving economies of scale. Technical people are hired for specific well-defined tasks, and technology is employed to increase productivity. On the other hand, **front-of-the-house operations** are characterized by hiring frontline service providers with good public relations skills, taking good care of customers, and giving employees the power and resources to solve customers' problems quickly and effectively.

Hospitals provide good examples of organizations characterized by a clear separation of high-contact and low-contact services. Administrative offices, labs, drug storage, laundry, and food preparation, for instance, are low-contact, back-of-the-house operations in a hospital. Managing these elements of the hospital service bundle can make a tremendous difference in profitability. No customer contact exists, so the emphasis is on materials management, space utilization, automation, and technical skills. However, patient care, prescription services, and emergency room and other high-contact services directly involve patients in the delivery of services. In these cases, customer–server interactions must be managed so that customers get what they need in an effective way.

Auditing the Service Delivery System

The service bundle delivery system should be audited periodically to assess the system's ability to meet customer expectations in a cost-effective way. Monitoring customer complaints, talking to and observing customers, and tracking customer feedback using customer comment cards and website comment forms (as well as looking at the bottom line) are ways to continually monitor the service delivery system. **Walk-through service audits** can be used to observe service system attributes from the time customers initially encounter the service until they leave. Several tools have been developed and used for this purpose, including service system surveys to be completed by managers, employees, and/or customers, and service process maps (as discussed in Chapter 8). The objective of the service audit is to identify service system problems or areas in need of improvement.

Service Location and Layout Strategies

Good locations provide barriers to entry and competitive positioning for services as well as generate high levels of demand. Once a location has been secured, firms can begin to consider layout strategies that help to maximize customer service, server productivity, and service efficiencies. Since location strategies and analysis models were discussed in Chapter 11, only a brief discussion of location considerations is included here, followed by the design of service layouts.

Location Strategies

Location decisions are extremely important for most services because they have a significant impact on customer visits and, consequently, the long-term profits of the company (how likely is it that customers would visit a clothing store, for instance, in an otherwise abandoned shopping center?). Location selection is viewed as a moderate- to long-term decision because of the typically high costs of construction, remodeling, and relocation. (Note: Here, it is assumed that service locations are permanent structures, although some services actually are not bound by this assumption, as with a small legal office renting space in an office building or a music teacher who visits customers.)

Global market opportunities, global competitors, and technological and demographic changes contribute to the importance of a good location. In all location evaluations, it is desirable to consider a number of relevant factors to reduce reliance on managerial intuition. Although intuition can certainly be a valuable location analysis tool, many disastrous location decisions have been made on the basis of intuition and not much more. For example, one-time Las Vegas gambler, entrepreneur, and self-proclaimed "Polish maverick" Bob Stupak built the 1,149-foot Stratosphere Hotel and Casino, which opened in a rundown neighborhood on the fringes of the famous Las Vegas Boulevard or "Strip" in 1996. Within just a few months, the hotel was in financial trouble, partly because of the lack of foot traffic in the area. Stupak defaulted on payments to the bondholders who had put up the construction funds, and corporate raider Carl Icahn subsequently bought the bonds for pennies on the dollar. He assumed control of the hotel in 1998. His company completed construction of the hotel and sold the property to Whitehall Street Real Estate Funds in 2008.[18]

A number of location analysis models can be used as aids in the location decision, and these include the weighted-factor location model, the location break-even model, and the center-of-gravity model (refer to Chapter 11 for use of these models).

Layout Strategies

Service layout strategies work in combination with location decisions to further support the overall business strategies of differentiation, low cost, or market focus. Office layouts tend to be departmentalized to allow specialists to share resources; many retailers such as U.K.-based Tesco PLC also tend to be departmentalized to assist customers in finding items to purchase, whereas others may have centers throughout the store to entice customers to try things out and buy on impulse; commercial airliner layouts segment customers, reduce the time to restock and service the galleys and lavatories, and allow for fast passenger boarding and exit (at least in theory!); casino layouts are designed to get customers in quickly and then keep them there by spacing out the attractions; and self-serve buffet restaurant layouts are designed to process customers quickly. These are just a few examples, and many service layouts use multiple layout strategies. As customer preferences, products, technologies, and service strategies change, layouts also tend to change. Several specific service layout design tools are illustrated below.

Departmental Layouts That Reduce Distances Traveled

Service layouts can be designed to reduce the travel times of customers or service workers when moving from one area to another. An example of a layout where this might be a primary consideration would be a health clinic. The waiting area is located in front where customers enter, and the examination rooms are located nearby. The doctors' offices might be centrally located, whereas the lab, storage, and x-ray rooms might be located farther to the back of the clinic away from most of the patients. A primary consideration is how far nurses, doctors, and patients have to walk to reach the various areas within the clinic. The objective would be to place high-traffic volume departments close to each other to minimize the total distances traveled per day. Example 12.2 illustrates a design tool for this type of layout.

Example 12.2 Layout of Bryson Health Clinic

The Bryson Health Clinic wants to see whether there is a better layout that will reduce the time doctors and nurses spend walking throughout the clinic. The existing layout is shown below, along with the number of trips and the distances between each department.

Existing Layout

Storage (F)	Doctor's offices (C)	Exam rooms (B)	Lobby & waiting area (A)
Nurses (E)	Lab & x-ray (D)		

Interdepartmental Doctors' and Nurses' Trips/Day

	B	C	D	E	F
A	55	0	0	50	0
B		40	15	40	0
C			15	60	10
D				30	0
E					18

Distances between Departments (meters)

	B	C	D	E	F
A	20	40	40	60	60
B		20	20	40	40
C			10	20	20
D				20	20
E					10

To analyze the existing layout, the total distance traveled per day is calculated as follows:

Total distance traveled $\sum_{i=1}^{n} \sum_{j=1}^{n} T_{ij} D_{ij}$

Where n = number of departments

i,j = individual departments

T_{ij} = number of trips between departments i and j

D_{ij} = distance from department i to department j

The objective is to find the layout resulting in the lowest total distance traveled per day. For the layout shown above, we find:

Total distance traveled per day = 55(20) + 50(60) + 40(20) + 15(20) + 40(40) + 15(10) + 60(20) + 10(20) + 30(20) + 18(10) = 9,130 meters

Example 12.2 Layout of Bryson Health Clinic (Continued)

From the layout and the trips and distances shown, it can be seen that the nursing station should be closer to the lobby and waiting area, closer to the exam rooms and closer to the doctors' offices. This can be accomplished by switching departments E and D (nurses and lab/x-ray). This also creates a trade-off, since now departments C, B, and A will all be farther from department D. To calculate the new total distance traveled per day, the distance table must be modified as shown below. The asterisks denote changes made to the table.

Distances between Departments

	B	C	D	E	F
A	20	40	60*	40*	60
B		20	40*	20*	40
C			20*	10*	20
D				20	10*
E					20*

The new total distance can then be calculated as follows:

Total distance traveled per day = 55(20) + 50(40) + 40(20) + 15(40) + 40(20) + 15(20) + 60(10) + 10(20) + 30(20) + 18(20) = 7,360 meters

This is a better layout (not necessarily the best) and only one of a large number of potential layouts. Typically a number of layouts are evaluated as shown here, until either the lowest-total-distance layout or some reasonable alternative lower-distance layout is found.

Departmental Layouts That Maximize Closeness Desirability

Designing service layouts to place certain desirable pairs of departments closer to one another is another useful type of layout analysis tool and is often used for retail or office layouts. Here, the importance is placed on the relationships between various departments. In a convenience store, for instance, it would be extremely important to have the cashier close to the entrance and the cold food items in the back, close to the cold storage areas and the rear loading doors of the store. In an office setting, it might be desirable to have the receptionist close to the office entrance and the file room, with the managers close to the conference room. For each department pair, a **closeness desirability rating** must be determined, with the objective being to design a layout that maximizes an overall desirability rating for the entire facility. Example 12.3 illustrates this concept. It should also be noted that it can be advantageous to use both of the analyses illustrated in Examples 12.2 and 12.3 for a given layout problem; in this way, the evaluation team could consider the best layout from both a distance traveled and closeness desirability perspective.

Example 12.3 Closeness Desirability Rating for an Office Layout

Existing Office Layout

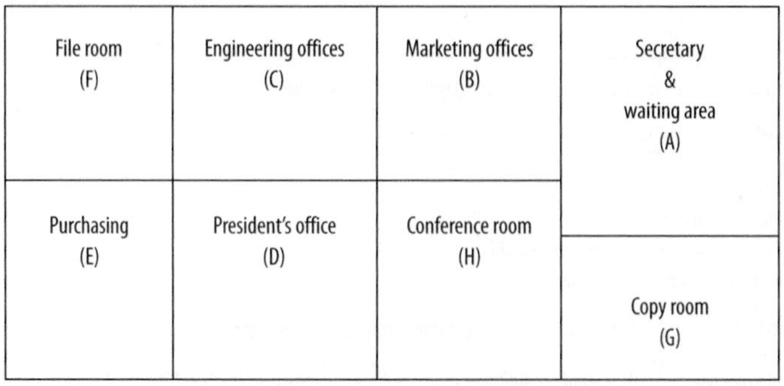

<table>
<tr><td>File room
(F)</td><td>Engineering offices
(C)</td><td>Marketing offices
(B)</td><td rowspan="2">Secretary
&
waiting area
(A)</td></tr>
<tr><td rowspan="2">Purchasing
(E)</td><td rowspan="2">President's office
(D)</td><td rowspan="2">Conference room
(H)</td></tr>
<tr><td>Copy room
(G)</td></tr>
</table>

Desirability Ratings

	B	C	D	E	F	G	H
A	2	0	−1	2	2	3	−1
B		0	2	1	1	0	3
C			2	2	0	0	1
D				1	−1	−1	3
E					3	1	2
F						3	1
G							0

The desirability ratings are based on a (−1 to 3) scale, where −1 = undesirable, 0 = unimportant, 1 = slightly important, 2 = moderately important, and 3 = very important. To calculate the score for the above layout, we count the closeness desirability score only when departments are adjacent to each other. For this layout:

Closeness desirability score = (A/B:2) + (A/H:−1) + (A/G:3) + (B/C:0) + (B/H:3) + (C/F:0) + (C/D:2) + (D/E:1) + (D/H:3) + (E/F:3) + (G/H:0)= 16 points

Note that department pairs are not counted twice and are also not counted if only the corners are touching. To find a better layout, we could place the department pairs with a rating of 3 adjacent to each other, and place adjacent pairs with a rating of −1 such that they are not adjacent. For instance, the file room (F) could be moved adjacent to the copy room (G), and the conference room (H) could be moved farther away from the secretary and waiting area (A).

The new layout might look like this:

New Office Layout

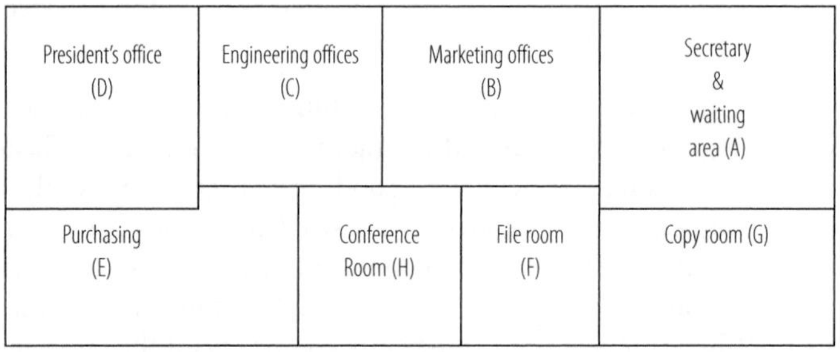

President's office (D)
Engineering offices (C)
Marketing offices (B)
Secretary & waiting area (A)
Purchasing (E)
Conference Room (H)
File room (F)
Copy room (G)

The closeness desirability score for the new layout shown above would then be:

Closeness desirability score = (A/B:2) + (A/F:2) + (A/G:3) + (B/C:0) + (B/H:3) + (B/F:1) + (C/D:2) + (C/E:2) + (C/H:1) + (D/E:1) + (E/H:2) + (H/F:1) + (F/G:3) = 23 points

On the basis of this analysis, it can be concluded that the second layout is better; like the previous example, though, there are many potential layouts, so a number of those should be evaluated prior to selecting the most appropriate one.

SUPPLY CHAIN MANAGEMENT IN SERVICES

In many respects, service-producing organizations are like goods-producing organizations: Both make purchases and therefore deal with suppliers; incur order costs and inventory carrying costs; and transport, count, store, and assess the quality of their purchased inventories. For some services, purchased items are part of the service provided and are extremely important sources of competitive advantage (as with a retailer or restaurant), whereas for others, this may be a less important concern (for example, law offices and barber shops). Service firms also purchase **facilitating products** such as computers, furniture, and office supplies that are not part of the services sold but rather consumed inside the firm,

Table 12.1 Transportation, Warehousing, and Inventory Considerations in Services

Services	Transportation	Warehousing and Inventory
Banks	• Movements of checks, coins/cash among branches and operations centers • Movement of checks to cities with Federal Reserve processing centers	• Office supplies and coins/cash • Furniture and computers • Files
Hospitals	• Movement of medical supplies to stockrooms • Transfers of patients • Movement of medical records, test results, and films among units	• Surgical/medical supplies • Pharmaceutical supplies • Office furniture • Medical equipment
Telephone Cos.	• Inbound transportation of switches, parts, and equipment to warehouses • Transportation of construction equipment and supplies to job sites • Routing of consumer products to retail outlets	• Parts, equipment, consumer products • Repair truck parts and equipment • Construction supplies

Adapted from Drazen, E. L., R. E. Moll, and M. F. Roetter. *Logistics in Service Industries*. Oak Brook, IL: Council of Logistics Management, 1991: 24–26.

and these materials must also be managed. Table 12.1 shows some typical transportation, warehousing, and inventory considerations at several different types of services.

In other respects, though, service firms are unlike goods-producing organizations, in that services typically deal with the end customers in their supply chains, whereas most goods-producing firms deal with wholesalers, distributors, other manufacturers, or retailers. In other words, service products are typically not passed on to customers further down a distribution channel. Thus, any goods that are delivered as part of the service are typically consumed or used by the immediate customers.

Service firms also interact closely with their customers, and the services performed in many cases contain higher labor content than manufactured products. Customers probably have no idea what resources or facilitating goods were used to deliver the services they purchase; rather, customers' primary concerns are with the service itself and the way it is delivered. For this reason, the distribution elements of interest to services revolve around customers and how they are being served. A good example of this can be found in the transportation industry. When shippers want things moved, they want the move performed at a specific time, delivered to a specific place, delivered on time, and performed as economically as possible. Most large transportation companies today have sophisticated information systems to allow customers to track deliveries as well as determine the best combination of warehousing, transportation method, port-of-entry, routing, pricing, and consolidation. FedEx's ground distribution hub in Hagerstown, Maryland, for example, speeds 7,500 packages per hour through an automated tracking process that involves two sorts and twelve scans before packages reach their destinations. "At the hub, after a package is unloaded from a trailer, the next time it is touched by human hands is at the loading dock," says Ken Spangler, CIO at FedEx Ground. "Everything in between is automated," he adds.[19]

Service Quality and Customers

The satisfaction or perceived level of quality a customer experiences with regard to the service is of paramount concern to most services. The concept of **service quality** includes many elements, and these can change over time—recently, for example, customers of many businesses include sustainability as an element in their definitions of service quality. "We are in a commodity world, and 'green' allows you to emerge from the pack," says Andrew Winston, author of *Green Recovery*. "It is a tie-breaker, and it can even be a deal-breaker,"

SCM Profile | **Green Is Soaring for Concessions**

Georgia-based Concessions International (CI) operates about forty different restaurant locations at seven U.S. airports. The company's portfolio includes Boar's Head Deli, Caribou Coffee, Nathan's Famous, New Belgium Hub Bar & Grill, and Panda Express. Many airports are requiring companies to be green if they want operating contracts. The Atlanta airport, for example, has mandated 100 percent compostable packaging for all of its concessions. Chicago's airport is also going green—it is banning Styrofoam and calling for recycling and composting.

These requirements impact CI in that it sets a high standard that has to be sustained. Anthony Joseph, president of Concessions International, is excited to see this trend accelerate. "I think it actually aids us, because if there are concepts out there that want to be part of our proposal, they have to offer [compostable packaging]. It has galvanized the industry [to become more green]. It comes from the airport, yes, but I think there's growing appreciation for going green in our customer base," says Joseph. Business travelers are among the best trendsetters because they experience different concepts from around the world. "That's the customer you want to satisfy. There's a higher expectation," adds Joseph.[20]

he adds.[21] The nearby SCM Profile describes the green trends at airports and the experiences of restaurant firm Concessions International.

Service quality assessments vary based on both the tangible and intangible elements of the services supplied and the satisfaction of the customers receiving the services. Call centers that fail to satisfy customers, for example, provide opportunities for improvement in service quality. With respect to call centers, the "gold standard" of service quality is their *first call resolution score* or the percent of callers whose problem is solved on their first call. Companies like Canada-based Service Quality Measurement Group survey call center customers and then identify what call centers with the highest first call resolution score are doing right. These best practices are then communicated to their call center clients.[22]

All the elements of supply chain management including supplier selection, transportation, warehousing, process management, quality assessment, distribution, and customer service hold strategic importance for the long-term success of service organizations. While the previous chapter sections above have discussed many of these elements, the remainder of this chapter is devoted to the portion of supply chain management of greatest concern to service organizations and the service arms of goods-producing companies—namely, the activities associated with the production and delivery of the actual service.

THE PRIMARY CONCERNS OF SERVICE RESPONSE LOGISTICS

Service response logistics is defined as the management and coordination of the organization's activities that occur while the service is being performed.[23] Managing these activities often means the difference between a successful service experience and a failure. The four primary activities of concern in service response logistics are the management of service capacity, waiting times, distribution channels, and service quality. Since a service cannot be inventoried, managing service capacity enables the firm to meet variable demand—perhaps the most important concern of all services. When demand variability cannot be adequately met, the firm must resort to managing queues or waiting times to keep customers satisfied. Demand management tactics also play a role in the service firm's ability to satisfy varying levels of demand. Customer waiting times are closely related to the customer's view of service quality and, ultimately, customer satisfaction. Since services usually must be decentralized to attract customers while providing adequate service delivery times, use of various distribution channels also becomes important to the delivery of service products. Each of these service elements is discussed in detail in the following sections.

Managing Service Capacity

Service capacity is most often defined as the number of customers per day the firm's service delivery systems *are designed to serve*, although it could also be some other period of time such as customers per hour or customers per shift. Capacity measures can be stated somewhat differently too, depending on the service industry standard—for instance, airline companies define capacity in terms of available seat miles per day. Most services desire to operate with some excess capacity to reduce the likelihood of having queues and long waiting times develop. For service employees dealing directly with customers, service capacity is largely dependent on the number of employees providing the services and the equipment they use in these activities.

Since service outputs can't be inventoried, firms are forced to either turn away customers when demand exceeds capacity, make them wait in line, or hire additional personnel. Since hiring, training, supervising, and equipping service personnel are quite costly (in many cases, 75 percent of total operating costs), the decision of how many service personnel to hire greatly affects costs, productivity, and ultimately sales and profits. Ideally, firms want enough service capacity (or service personnel) to satisfy variable demand, without having too much excess (and costly) capacity. This can be a tricky proposition if demand varies substantially throughout the day, week, or month, as is typical in a great many services. So an important part of a service manager's job is to forecast demand for various segments of time and customer service processes, and then provide enough capacity to meet the forecasted demand.

When things work out right, a service operates at an optimal **capacity utilization**. Capacity utilization is defined as:

$$\text{Capacity utilization} = \frac{\text{Actual customers served per period}}{\text{Capacity}}.$$

As utilization approaches (and sometimes even exceeds) 1.0, services become more congested, service times increase, wait times increase, and the perceived quality of service deteriorates. With utilization close to 1.0, even a slightly greater than average service time for several customers can cause queues to become very long (some readers may recall, for instance, waiting one or two hours beyond an appointment time to see a busy doctor). Thus, an optimal utilization would leave some level of capacity unutilized (perhaps 15 to 25 percent depending on the volatility of demand), so that variations in service times and customer demand won't severely affect customer wait times. In the trucking industry, the recent economic recession caused a dramatic decrease in trucking capacity, as some companies went out of business while others reduced drivers and equipment to reduce costs. Today, most trucking companies are reporting high utilizations with no capacity reserves; and new truck purchases have only covered replacement needs. There is also a shortage of about 30,000 drivers nationwide. The Cass Truckload Linehaul Index report projects that driver shortages could climb to as much as 100,000 as shipping demand increases, which will push up wages and benefits to attract and retain drivers.[24]

The two most basic strategies for managing capacity are to use a **level demand strategy** (when the firm utilizes a constant amount of capacity regardless of demand variations) or a **chase demand strategy** (when the amount of capacity varies with demand). When a level demand strategy is used, the firm is required to use **demand management** or **queue management** tactics to deal with excess customers. When a chase demand strategy is used, effective plans must be in place to utilize, transfer, or reduce service capacity when there is excess available and to develop or borrow capacity quickly when demand exceeds capacity. Capacity management techniques that are useful when demand exceeds available service capacity are discussed next, followed by a discussion of capacity management when service capacity exceeds demand.

Capacity Management When Demand Exceeds Capacity

An initial observation might be to simply let customers wait, or hire workers when demand exceeds existing capacity and then lay them off when capacity exceeds demand. Most likely, though, firms would like to avoid these options because of the expenses of finding, hiring, training, and supervising new workers; the loss of current and future business when people wait too long in queues; as well as the expense and damage to the firm's reputation when laying off workers. Instead, a number of other methods can be employed to minimize the costs of hiring and laying off workers, and the cost of letting customers wait in line. These methods include cross-training and sharing employees, using part-time employees, using customers, using technology, using employee scheduling strategies and, finally, using demand management techniques to smooth or shift demand. Each of these methods is discussed next.

Cross-Training and Sharing Employees

Have you ever been waiting in line to pay for items at a retail store and thought to yourself, "Why don't they use some of these other workers that are just standing around to ring up customers' purchases?" Many service firms, though, do make wide use of this employee-sharing strategy. Quite often in many service firms, some processes are temporarily overutilized while other processes remain under- or unutilized. Rather than hiring someone to add capacity to the overutilized processes, progressive firms have adequately hired and cross-trained workers to be proficient in a number of different process functions. Thus, when demand temporarily exceeds service capacity in one area, creating a customer queue, idle workers can quickly move to that process to help serve customers and reduce the time customers spend waiting in a queue.

By sharing employees among a number of processes, firms create the capability to quickly expand capacity as demand dictates while simultaneously minimizing the costs of having customers wait or hiring and laying off workers. This type of resource sharing arrangement can occur in almost any type of organization, from retailers to banks, hospitals, and universities.

Using Part-Time Employees

Use of part-time employees is also seen as a low-cost way to vary capacity. The hourly wages and costs of fringe benefits are typically lower than those of full-time employees. Firms use full-time employees to serve that stable portion of daily demand, while scheduling part-timers for those historically busy periods (such as lunch and dinner times, holidays, weekends, or busy seasons). Part-time employees can also be used to fill in during the vacation periods, off days, and sick days of full-time employees. Laying off part-time employees during slower periods is also viewed as more acceptable to the permanent full-time workforce and is somewhat expected by the part-time employees.

Using Customers

As the need to contain costs and improve productivity and competitiveness continues, firms are finding that customers themselves can be used to provide certain services, as long as it is seen by customers as value enhancing. The benefits of self-service include faster service, more customized service, and lower prices, since firms need fewer employees. The benefits for the companies include lower labor costs and additional service capacity. In this sense, customers are "hidden employees," allowing the firm to hire fewer workers and to vary capacity to some extent as needed. The trade-off for customers is that they expect to pay less for these services, since they are doing some of the work. This include services such as bagging groceries, filling soda cups, and filing taxes.

In other cases, though, customers might actually pay the same or more for the service as when using self-checkout at grocery stores or using 24-hour automated teller machines, if customers perceive the work they perform as saving time or providing some other benefit. Thus, if firms can identify service process jobs that customers can perform, if they can provide process directions that are easy to understand and learn, and if they can adequately satisfy customers who are being asked to perform the work, then using customers as service providers creates yet another method for managing capacity. U.K.-based Photo-Me International, which owns 25,000 self-service photo booths in a number of European countries, is expanding into self-service launderettes. It currently operates about 400 units but plans to have 2,000 in operation by 2015, in France and Belgium, to meet demand.[25]

Using Technology

Providing technological assistance in the form of computers, software applications, or other equipment to service company personnel can improve the ability of servers to process customers, resulting in more service capacity, faster service completion times, better service quality, and the need for fewer employees. Voice-activated telephone response systems; online banking, purchasing, selling, and comment systems; and field sales software applications are just a few examples of technology helping the provision of services. Some forms of technology may completely replace the need for sales or other types of customer service personnel as in the case of Amazon.com and other online retailers. Advances in software capabilities and cloud computing have also allowed services to share use of expensive software systems like reservation systems and property management systems, which greatly improve productivity while reducing labor and software development costs. Retailers are also increasingly using workforce management solutions to create a better customer experience while ensuring the right associates are available at the right place and the right time. Workforce management solutions align workforce schedules with demand forecasts and enterprise initiatives, such as promotions and markdowns.[26]

Technology can also enable service standardization—providing the service exactly the same way every time, as with automated teller machines or ticketing machines. In many cases, service standardization is viewed as a high-quality characteristic by customers seeking specific, periodic services. Standardization allows services to be accessed anywhere at any time, without the need for relearning the service process.

Using Employee Scheduling Policies

As mentioned briefly above, properly scheduling workers allows firms to adjust capacity to accommodate varying demand. Businesses forecast demand in short time increments during the day and then convert the demand to staffing requirements for each period, given the average service capabilities for workers. The problem of assigning workers to shifts is complicated by the number of hours each day and the number of days each week the business

Example 12.4 Workforce Scheduling at Nyoman's Plumbing Supply

The manager of Nyoman's Plumbing Supply has determined her workforce requirements as shown below for the five-day workweek. Given these requirements, she sees that she needs two full-time employees working all five days, resulting in the part-time requirements as shown (found by subtracting two from each workday requirement). To satisfy these requirements with the fewest number of part-time employees, she begins by assigning Part-timer No. 1 to the maximum number of workdays (Monday, Thursday, and Friday). Part-timer No. 2 is assigned to the maximum number of workdays remaining (Monday and Friday). Then Part-timers 3 and 4 are assigned to the remaining workday (Friday).

	MONDAY	TUESDAY	WEDNESDAY	THURSDAY	FRIDAY
Workers Required	4	2	2	3	6
Full-time Workers	2	2	2	2	2
Part-time Workers	2	0	0	1	4
Part-timer No. 1	1			1	1
Part-timer No. 2	1				1
Part-timer No. 3					1
Part-timer No. 4					1

is open, the timing of days off and consecutive days off, and employee shift preferences. The objective of worker scheduling is to adequately serve customers with the minimum number of employees while also assigning equitable work shifts to employees. Employee scheduling software is available to provide managers with multiple scheduling solutions to this problem.

Use of part-time workers, as stated earlier, makes scheduling easier and is illustrated in Example 12.4. In the example, the manager finds a need for two full-time workers and four part-time workers.

Using Demand Management Techniques

Even when accurate forecasting and good capacity management techniques are used, there are many occasions when demand exceeds available capacity. As stated earlier, forcing customers to wait in line for a long period of time may result in lost current and future business and damage to the firm's reputation. Organizations can try to reduce demand during busy periods using several short-term **demand management** techniques. These include raising prices during busy periods to reduce demand and shift it to less busy periods, taking reservations or appointments to schedule demand for less busy periods, discouraging undesirable demand through use of screening procedures and marketing ads, and segmenting demand to facilitate better service (examples include use of first-class and economy-class seating and use of express and regular checkout stations). These tactics are combined with the capacity management techniques discussed earlier to provide the firm with the ability to better serve customers. The next section describes capacity management techniques for periods when service capacity exceeds demand.

Capacity management when capacity exceeds demand

When capacity exceeds demand, the firm is faced with the problem of how to utilize excess capacity. Too much excess capacity means higher fixed costs, resulting in higher prices for the services provided, and may also affect customers' perceptions of quality (readers may recall their own quality perceptions when walking into a mostly deserted restaurant at peak dinner hours). Besides the obvious long-term solution of laying workers off and location size, firms may be able to find other uses for service capacity and use demand management techniques to stimulate demand.

Finding other uses for capacity

One way to utilize excess capacity is to develop additional service products. Periodic lack of demand might be particularly troublesome for services with seasonal demand such as hotels, airlines, and ski resorts. For these services, management may try to develop service products that the firm can provide during their characteristically slow periods. This might include airlines partnering with resorts to provide vacation packages during off-peak seasonal periods, hotels booking business conferences during slow periods, or ski resorts designing mountain bike trails or building cement luge runs for summer use. Firms can also make use of cross-training to shift or transfer employees to other areas temporarily needing more capacity. For instance, swimming pool builders might train and then use their construction workers to build pool enclosures during the winter months. In an interesting use of excess electricity capacity, Canada is gearing up for handling the electricity demand for electric cars, estimated to be 500,000 units by 2018. Currently, Canada's hydro, coal, natural gas, and nuclear power sources go largely unused during nighttime hours, and this power can't easily be turned off. It thus becomes wasted power. Consequently, Canada is developing smart electricity meters to charge users drastically cheaper rates for power usage during off-peak hours, which will allow electric cars to be cheaply recharged at night. "We have the resources and the electricity," says Al Cormier, executive director of the not-for-profit organization Electric Mobility Canada. "We should take advantage of this opportunity."[27]

Using demand management techniques

When capacity exceeds demand, demand management techniques can be used to stimulate demand. These include lowering prices during off-peak periods, as in early-bird dinner specials or mid-week hotel rates, as well as designing aggressive marketing campaigns for use during slow business periods. Gatwick airport in the U.K. eliminated its landing fees during the slow winter months to encourage more use of the airport during this period. This strategy increased passenger traffic by 3.3 percent in 2011, compared to the year earlier, when the policy was not in effect.[28]

Managing capacity in services thus involves techniques to adjust capacity and either stimulate or shift demand to match capacity to demand. When an oversupply or undersupply of capacity exists, service times, waiting times, cost, and service quality all suffer, all of which ultimately impact the competitiveness of the firm. The second concern in service response logistics is discussed next—managing queue times.

Managing Queue Times

Queue times are frequently encountered every day by consumers including waiting at checkout counters, waiting for a table at a restaurant, and waiting on hold on the telephone. Ideally, service managers would like to design **queuing systems** such that customers never have to wait in a queue; however, the cost of maintaining enough service capacity to handle peak demand and unexpectedly high levels of demand is simply too expensive. Thus, managers use information they have about their customers as well as their service employees to design adequate queuing systems and then couple this with management of customers' perceived waiting times to minimize the negative impact of waiting in line. Thus, good queue management consists of the management of *actual waiting time* and *perceived waiting time.* To accomplish this, managers must consider a number of issues:

- What is the average arrival rate of the customers?
- In what order will customers be serviced?
- What is the average service rate of the service providers?

- What is the average service time requirement of customers?
- How are customers' arrival and service times distributed?
- How long will customers actually wait in a queue before they either leave or lower their perceptions of service quality?
- How can customers be kept in line even longer without lowering their perceptions of service quality?

Answers to these questions will allow the firm to adequately design a queuing system that will provide acceptable service to most customers while minimizing the service system cost and the cost of lost and disgruntled customers. Properly thought-out and designed queuing systems decrease waiting times and subsequently the need for further managing waiting times; however, occasionally, waiting time management tactics must be utilized to decrease perceived waiting times. The design of queuing systems is discussed first, followed by a discussion of managing perceived waiting times.

Queuing System Design

The four types of queuing system configurations are shown in Figure 12.1. The most appropriate queuing system depends on the volume of customers to be served, the willingness of customers to wait in a queue, the physical constraints imposed by the service

Figure 12.1 **Queuing System Configurations**

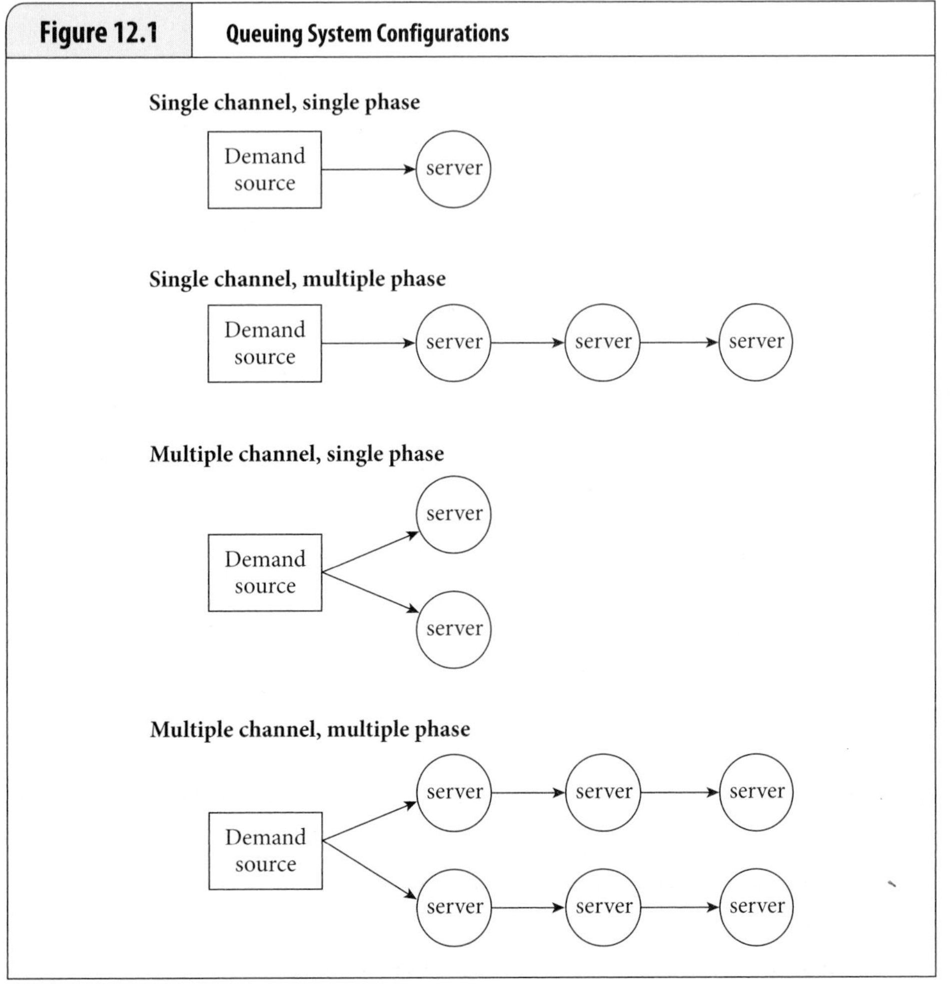

structure, and the number and sequence of services to be performed. The outputs from various queuing systems that managers need to compare are the average number of customers in line and in the system, the average waiting time in line and in the system, and the average server utilization. As alluded to earlier, the primary elements of all queuing systems are the *input process*, the *queue characteristics*, and the *service characteristics*. These elements are discussed next, along with several applications.

The Input Process

Customer arrivals are referred to here as the **demand source**. The size of the demand source can be considered either infinite or finite. Many situations (along with the examples covered later) assume an unlimited or infinite demand source such as customers arriving at a retail outlet, whereas other situations have a finite-sized demand source, such as ticketed customers showing up for a concert at an arena.

Customers also arrive at a service according to an **arrival pattern**. When students show up for a scheduled class, this is an example of a known or *deterministic interarrival time*. In many cases as in a retail establishment, customers show up in a random pattern, and the *Poisson distribution* (named after the 19th-century French mathematician Siméon Denis Poisson) is commonly used to describe these customer arrivals. Using the Poisson distribution, the probability of x customers arriving within some time period, T, is expressed as:

$$P_{x(T)} = \frac{e^{-\lambda T}(\lambda T)^x}{x!}$$

where λ = average customer arrivals in time period T
e = 2.71828 (natural log base), and
$x! = x$ factorial $= x(x-1)(x-2)\ldots(1)$.

Example 12.5 illustrates the use of this formula.

If we assume the number of arrivals per time period is Poisson distributed with a mean arrival rate of λ, then the interarrival time (time between arrivals) is described by the *negative exponential distribution*, with a mean interarrival time of $1/\lambda$ (so if the mean arrival rate is 10 per hour, then the mean interarrival time is 60 minutes/10 arrivals, or 6 minutes/arrival).

Example 12.5 Arrivals per Hour at Jay's Quick Lube Shop

Jay's Quick Lube Shop can service an average of four cars per hour with a partial crew of three employees, and the owner Jay is interested in calculating the probability they can handle all the customers on Saturdays with the partial crew, instead of his usual full crew of five. Given an average arrival rate of three customers per hour on Saturdays, he uses the Poisson distribution to calculate the probabilities of various customer arrivals per hour, shown below.

NUMBER OF ARRIVALS, X	$P_x(\text{for } T = 1 \text{ hour}) = \frac{e^{-3}3^x}{x!}$	CUMULATIVE PROBABILITY
0	0.0498	0.0498
1	0.1494	0.1992
2	0.2240	0.4232
3	0.2240	0.6472
4	0.1680	0.8152

By summing the probabilities for each of the arrival levels, Jay figures that he can handle the demand per hour approximately 82 percent of the time. Conversely, he figures that approximately 18 percent of the time, demand per hour will be greater than four customers, causing queues to develop.

Most queuing models assume that customers stay in the queue once they join it. In other words, customers do not exhibit **balking** (refusing to join the queue once they see how long it is) or **reneging** (leaving the queue before completing the service). Though most people have done this at one time or another, queuing analysis becomes much more complex when these arrival characteristics are allowed.

The Queue Characteristics

Queuing models generally assume the length of a queue can grow to an infinite length, although for some situations this is not appropriate (e.g., people with tickets waiting to enter a concert). Queuing configurations can contain single or multiple queues (e.g., the single winding queue at Wendy's versus the multiple queues at most McDonald's). Another queue characteristic is the **queue discipline**. The discipline describes the order in which customers are served. The most common queue discipline is first-come-first-served, although other examples include most-needy-first-served (in emergency rooms) and most-important-first-served (a VIP queue at a nightclub).

Virtual Queues

Technology is impacting queuing systems such that **virtual queues** are becoming more commonplace. Customers' places in the queue are tracked by a computerized system that allows them to roam the premises until their handheld monitor lights up. This reduces balking and reneging while allowing customers to make better use of their time. For instance, the Lavi Industries' Qtrac system registers customers via a touch-screen kiosk (in shopping malls), which prints a ticket that includes expected waiting time. Customers are then free to shop until their name appears on an LCD monitor. In hospitals in Shanghai, waiting patients can input their cell phone numbers into a computer system that sends them a text message when they become fifth in line, allowing them to leave without fear that they will miss an appointment.[29]

Increasingly, companies are allowing queue-jumping, which can happen invisibly in virtual queues. Call centers, for example, can prioritize callers in a telephone queue once they have been identified. Customers willing to pay extra can, in many cases, jump queues. Banks, airlines, and credit card companies have elite call centers, and some doctors give patients priority if they pay extra. U.K.-based Lo-Q operates handheld devices (called Q-bots) that allow theme park visitors in twenty theme parks worldwide to reserve a spot in line. A premium option allows visitors to jump the queues.[30]

The Service Characteristics

Services can be provided either by a single server or by multiple servers that act in series or in parallel. Multiple servers acting in parallel is referred to as a **multiple-channel queuing system**. Multiple servers acting in series is referred to as a **multiple-phase queuing system**. Figure 12.1, above, shows these queuing configurations.

The *single-channel, single-phase* configuration is the most basic. For standard distribution patterns of customer arrival and service times, the formulas to evaluate this type of system are very straightforward. An example is the one-person retail shop (such as a comic book shop or gift shop). The *single-channel, multiple-phase* queuing system is the next configuration shown. For this system, customers all contact the same servers, but receive more than one service and encounter a queue at each service. An example of this type of service is a dentist's office where customers are checked-in by a receptionist, get their teeth cleaned by a dental hygienist, get their teeth x-rayed by a dental assistant, and then get a dental exam

Example 12.6 Service Times at Jay's Quick Lube Shop

Jay's Quick Lube Shop can service an average of four customers per hour, or one customer every fifteen minutes, with a crew of three service personnel. The average customer arrival rate on Saturdays is three customers per hour, or one customer every twenty minutes. Jay is interested in calculating the probability that actual service time, *t*, will be within a specific time period, *T*, and he develops a chart showing these probabilities below, using the negative exponential distribution.

SPECIFIC TIME PERIOD	$P(t \leq T\ hrs.) = 1 - e^{-4T}$
15 min. (.25 hrs.)	$1 - e^{-4(.25)} = 0.6321$
20 min. (.33 hrs.)	$1 - e^{-4(.33)} = 0.7329$
30 min. (.5 hrs.)	$1 - e^{-4(.5)} = 0.8647$
40 min. (.67 hrs.)	$1 - e^{-4(.67)} = 0.9314$
45 min. (.75 hrs.)	$1 - e^{-4(.75)} = 0.9502$

Thus, Jay thinks that almost 75 percent of the time, they will be able to service a customer in less than or equal to twenty minutes.

by a dentist. For each service, longer-than-average service times by the preceding customer or during one phase of the service can mean waiting line buildups within the entire system. The third configuration shown is the *multiple-channel, single-phase* system. Customers enter the system, receive one service from any one of a number of servers, and then exit. Examples of this are retailers' checkout stands or banks' teller windows. These systems can have queues at each channel or one winding queue where all channels receive customers from one line. The final configuration shown is the *multiple-channel, multiple-phase* queuing system. In this example, customers all receive more than one service in sequence from more than one set or channel of servers. An example here might be a large medical clinic where patients are checked in by one of several assistants, have their vital signs recorded by one of several nurses, and receive a medical consultation and service by one of several doctors.

Another characteristic of a service are the times required to complete each of the services provided. For each phase in the system, service times are described by a mean time and a probability distribution. Frequently, the negative exponential distribution is used to describe the randomness of service time distributions. To determine the probability that the service time, *t*, will be less than or equal to some specified time, *T*, the following formula can be used:

$$P(t \leq T) = 1 - e^{-\mu T}$$

where $e = 2.71828$ (natural log base), and
μ = the average service rate.

Example 12.6 illustrates the use of this formula for calculating the probability of completing service within a specified time period.

For single-channel systems, the average arrival and service rates can be used to calculate average capacity utilization, by dividing the customer arrival rate by the customer service rate. For example, if the arrival rate is three per hour and the service rate is four per hour, then the average capacity utilization is 75 percent. Although, as can be seen in Example 12.4, there will likely be times when utilization for periods during the day approaches or exceeds 100 percent. Now that all of the important elements of queuing systems have been reviewed, various applications of the models can be discussed and these are presented next.

Queuing System Applications

When using queuing models, managers collect arrival rate and service rate data by observing over time how many customers actually arrive for service and how many customers are actually served. Depending on the service, it may take a number of days or weeks to compile meaningful information. Presented below are applications of the single-channel, single-phase queuing model and the multiple-channel, single-phase queuing model. These are meant only to be introductory applications. Examples for the other queuing systems and applications can be quite complicated and are beyond the scope of this text. Interested readers are encouraged to examine management science or operations research texts for more advanced treatments of this topic. Several references are provided at the end of this chapter for this purpose.

A Single-Channel, Single-Phase Queuing System Application

This is the most widely used and simplest of all queuing systems. The assumptions for the system are:

- Customers come from an infinite population and are Poisson distributed over time.
- Customers are served in first-come-first-served sequence.
- No balking or reneging occurs.
- Service times are distributed according to the negative exponential distribution.
- The average service rate is greater than the average arrival rate.

The symbols and equations used to determine the operating characteristics for the single-channel, single-phase queuing model are:

λ = average arrival rate
μ = average service rate
ρ = average server utilization = λ/μ
L_s = expected number of customers in the system = $\lambda/(\mu-\lambda)$
L_q = expected number of customers in the queue = $\lambda^2/[\mu(\mu-\lambda)] = L_s - \lambda/\mu$
W_s = expected waiting time in the system = $1/(\mu-\lambda) = L_s/\lambda$
W_q = expected waiting time in the queue = $\lambda/[\mu(\mu-\lambda)] = L_q/\lambda$
P_n = probability that there are n units in the queuing system = $(\lambda/\mu)^n(1-\lambda/\mu)$

Example 12.7 illustrates the calculations of operating characteristics for a single-channel, single-phase service.

A Multiple-Channel, Single-Phase Queuing System Application

All of the assumptions shown above still apply for the multiple-channel, single-phase system, except that the number of servers is now greater than one, and the queuing system consists of multiple servers serving customers from multiple queues. The operating characteristics of this queuing system are as follows:

λ = average arrival rate
$s\mu$ = average service rate, where s = number of service channels

ρ = average server utilization = $\lambda/s\mu$
P_0 = probability of zero customers in the system

$$= \frac{1}{\sum_{n=0}^{s=1} \frac{(\lambda/\mu)^n}{n!} + \frac{(\lambda/\mu)^s}{s!}\left[\frac{1}{1-(\lambda/s\mu)}\right]}, \text{ for } s\mu > \lambda$$

Example 12.7 Operating Characteristics for Kathy's Sewing Shop

Kathy's Sewing Shop can serve about five customers per hour. For the past two weeks Kathy has kept track of the customer arrival rate, and the average has been four customers per hour. Kathy is interested in calculating the operating characteristics for her store. So she asks one of her customers, a business student at the local university, to help her. The student provides the following information:

$\lambda = 4$ customers per hour
$\mu = 5$ customers per hour
$\rho = 4/5 = 0.8$ or 80% utilization
$L_s = \lambda/(\mu-\lambda) = 4/(5-4) = 4$ customers
$L_q = L_s - \lambda/\mu = 4 - 4/5 = 3.2$ customers
$W_s = L_s/\lambda = 4/4 = 1$ hour $= 60$ minutes
$W_q = L_q/\lambda = 3.2/4 = 0.8$ hours $= 48$ minutes

Kathy also wants to know how likely it will be that more than four customers will be in her shop at one time. So the student thinks about this and decides to determine the probabilities of zero, one, two, three, and four customers in the shop, and then subtract their sum from 1. So, she provides the following information:

For $n = 0$ $P_0 = (4/5)^0(1-4/5) = 0.200$
$n = 1$ $P_1 = (4/5)^1(1-4/5) = 0.160$
$n = 2$ $P_2 = (4/5)^2(1-4/5) = 0.128$
$n = 3$ $P_3 = (4/5)^3(1-4/5) = 0.102$
$n = 4$ $P_4 = (4/5)^4(1-4/5) = 0.082$
For $n > 4$ $P_{n>4} = 1-(P_0+P_1+P_2+P_3+P_4) = 1-(.2+.16+.128+.102+.082) = 1-.672 = 0.328$

So Kathy can expect that there will be more than four people in her shop about 33 percent of the time.
Kathy can also purchase a barcode scanner with an automated cash register that will increase her service rate to ten customers per hour. She wants to know how this will change the average wait time in the queue and in the system. The student then shows her the very significant change this will make:

$L_s = \lambda/(\mu-\lambda) = 4/(10-4) = 0.67$ customers
$W_q = \lambda/[\mu(\mu-\lambda)] = 4/[10(6)] = 0.067$ hours $= 4$ minutes
$W_s = 1/(\mu-\lambda) = 1/6$ hour $= 10$ minutes

$$P_n = \text{probability of } n \text{ customers in the system}$$
$$= P_0\frac{(\lambda/\mu)^n}{n!}, \text{ for } n \le s$$
$$= P_0\frac{(\lambda/\mu)^n}{s!\,s^{n-s}}, \text{ for } n > s$$
$$L_q = \text{expected number of customers in the queue}$$
$$= P_0\frac{(\lambda/\mu)^s(\lambda/s\mu)}{s!\,(1-\lambda/s\mu)^2}$$
$$L_s = \text{expected number of customers in the system}$$
$$= L_q + \lambda/\mu$$
$$W_q = \text{expected waiting time in the queue}$$
$$= L_q/\lambda$$
$$W_s = \text{expected waiting time in the system}$$
$$= W_q + 1/\mu$$

Example 12.8, below, extends the single-channel, single-phase shop, to the two-channel, single-phase shop, for comparison purposes.

Managing Perceived Waiting Times

The final topic of discussion in managing queue times management of **perceived waiting times** (sometimes, customers perceive the wait time to be much longer or shorter

Example 12.8 Operating Characteristics for Kathy's Expanded Sewing Shop

Kathy's Sewing Shop has decided to hire a second worker and buy a second checkout stand with cash register for the shop. Both Kathy and the second worker can serve five customers per hour and the average arrival rate is four customers per hour. Kathy again wants to know all of the operating characteristics of the new configuration. Once again, her student-customer helps her out:

$\rho = 4/10 = 0.4$, or 40 percent utilization

$$P_0 = \frac{1}{\frac{(4/5)^0}{0!} + \frac{(4/5)^1}{1!} + \frac{(4/5)^2}{2!}\left(\frac{1}{1\,(4/10)}\right)} = \frac{1}{1 + 0.8 + 0.32(1.67)} = \frac{1}{2.33} = 0.428$$

$$L_q = \frac{(4/5)^2(4/10)}{2(1-4/10)^2}(0.428) = 0.152 \text{ customers}$$

$L_s = 0.152 + 4/5 = 0.952$ customers
$W_q = 0.152/4 = 0.038$ hours, or 2.28 minutes
$W_s = 0.038 + 0.2 = 0.238$ hours, or 14.28 minutes

Note that because of the mean service time and distribution differences, having a two-channel, two-queue system serving customers with an average service rate of five customers per hour per channel is not the same as having a one-channel, one-queue system that serves at a rate of ten customers per hour.

than it really is). Even though an admirable job may be done designing a queuing system, there are still likely to be times when demand exceeds the queuing system's capacity (recall the mention earlier of the two-hour wait in a doctor's office). For these time periods, service firms must have other tools at their disposal to influence customers' perceptions of the waiting times. In a well-known paper written on the topic of waiting time, noted professor and author Dr. David Maister presented some very interesting observations starting with his **First and Second Laws of Service**:[31]

> *Law #1: Satisfaction = perception – expectation*
>
> When customers expect a certain level of service and then perceive the service they actually received to be higher, they will be satisfied. Conversely, when customers' service expectations are higher than their perceptions once the service has been completed, they are unsatisfied.
>
> *Law #2: It is hard to play catch-up ball*
>
> If customers start out happy when the service is first encountered, it is easy to keep them happy. If they start out disgruntled or become that way during the service, it is almost impossible to turn things around.

Service Law #1 is interesting in that expectations and perceptions are not necessarily based on reality. For example, customer expectations are formed based on previous experiences, marketing campaigns, signs, information from other people, and the location, while customer perceptions can be affected during the service encounter by a friendly server, mood music, visually pleasant surroundings, and a host of other things. A common practice coming out of Law #1 is to "under-promise and over-deliver." Service Law #2 is good for firms to remember when they are trying to improve service. Investments in service improvements might best be placed at the initial contact or early stages of the service to make sure the service encounter gets off to a good start.

Firms can manage both customer expectations and perceptions by observing and understanding how they are affected when customers wait for service. Waiting time management techniques resulting from this understanding include keeping customers occupied, starting the service quickly, relieving customer anxiety, keeping customers informed, grouping customers together, and designing a fair waiting system.[32] Each of these is briefly discussed next.

SCM Profile: Occupying Customers at Pizza Hut

Pizza Hut is introducing Hut TV, a video network that is being introduced in many of its restaurant locations. Pizza Hut is looking to offset stagnant same-store sales by positioning itself as a solution for home meals with new menu items, and enhancing the in-store experience for the customer. "We're in the middle of the transformation of the Pizza Hut brand, both in terms of how our store looks and creating a different consumer experience we're calling The Hut," said Bob Kraut, vice president of marketing for Pizza Hut. "Hut TV is a way to engage and entertain customers and make those who own our stores feel better about Pizza Hut."

Hut TV's video content is designed to enhance the in-store experience by entertaining customers, decreasing perceived wait time, increasing frequency of visits and promoting specials. The largest of the screen's three sections features entertainment (trivia or games) or short customized segments from CBS-produced programs such as Wheel of Fortune or Entertainment Tonight. CBS also provides a news ticker at the bottom of the screen.[33]

Keeping Customers Occupied

Firms can benefit by keeping customers occupied while waiting in line. This is why magazines, televisions, and toys for children to play with, are often seen in office waiting areas. Other attention-keepers such as music, windows, mirrors, or menus to look at keep customers' minds off the passage of time. In amusement parks such as Disneyland where long lines can be a big problem, customers waiting in line might get entertained by Mickey Mouse, a mime, or a juggler, for instance. The nearby SCM Profile describes Pizza Hut's HutTV to keep customers engaged and occupied. All these techniques try to lessen the perceived passage of time and influence customer satisfaction with the waiting experience. At the largest pediatric healthcare office in the U.S., Houston's Texas Children's Pediatric Associates serves 250,000 patients with about 160 doctors making queue times a big concern. Internet connectivity allows parents to work while they wait; activity centers and an interactive video wall keep children occupied; and moving from an outer waiting area to an inner one keeps families moving. "Perception is reality," says Kay Tittle, group president.[34]

Starting the Service Quickly

Giving waiting customers menus, forms to complete, drinks from the bar, or programs to read all act to give customers the impression the service has started. When firms acknowledge receipt of an order via telephone, mail, or e-mail, this is another example of beginning the service. If organizations can design preprocess activities that begin quickly once a customer encounters a queue, this will act to keep customers occupied and make long waits seem much shorter. The London-based Carphone Warehouse (CPW), a mobile phone retailer, has turned to Facebook and Twitter to engage customers quickly and keep them satisfied. They have found that it allows them to address complaints more quickly, offer quick feedback on problems, and to positively impact customer satisfaction. If a customer wants to know whether a certain city has a retail location, CPW can tweet a link to the store; if a customer wants to know how to remove a SIM card, CPW can tweet the solution.[35]

Relieving Customer Anxiety

Customer anxiety is created in many waiting situations; for example, when customers are afraid they've been forgotten, when they don't know how long their wait is going to be, when they don't know what to do, or when they fear they've entered the wrong line. Managers need to observe customers, learn what is likely causing anxiety, then develop plans for relieving their concerns. These plans might include simply having employees reassure customers, announcing how much longer a caller on hold is likely to wait, announcing the lateness of a plane yet to arrive, or using signs to direct customers to the correct line.

Keeping Customers Informed

Managers can derail customer anxieties before they even begin by giving customers information as their preprocess and in-process waits progress. When receptionists tell patients that their doctor was called to an emergency, when pilots tell passengers that the plane is waiting to be cleared for gate departure, when work crews place a flashing sign on the road warning drivers to expect delays during a certain period of time, and when amusement parks place signs in the queue telling customers the waiting time from that point forward, this information makes waiting customers much more patient because they know that a delay will occur and the reasons for the delay. Consequently, they are much more willing to stay in line, remain satisfied, and complete the service.

Grouping Customers

Customers generally prefer waiting together in queues, rather than waiting alone. Customers act to alleviate their own and others' anxieties, fears, and problems while waiting in line by talking to each other, sharing concerns, and helping out if possible. This sense of togetherness reduces perceived waiting times and may even add enjoyment to the waiting experience. Managers should think of ways to create or encourage group waiting instead of solo waiting such as closer seating, single queues instead of multiple queues, and use of numbered tickets or virtual queues so that people don't have to physically stand in the queue.

Designing a Fair Waiting System

"Taking cuts" or queue-jumping is something that can cause significant irritation to others already waiting, particularly if it is seen as unfair. In an emergency room, most people waiting will likely accept that others coming into the queue later might be taken care of first (the queue discipline is most-critical-first-served). Alternately, taking cuts in a long queue at a retail store or amusement park could result in grumbling and shouting from those already waiting (recall our earlier discussion about virtual queues removing some of these problems). Whenever the queue discipline is something other than first-come-first-served, managers need to be aware of the potential problems this causes and take steps to reduce the feeling of unfairness or segment customers such that the queue discipline is not obvious. Examples include physically separating customers such as in first-class versus economy-class seating on airplanes, taking names and group sizes at a restaurant while concealing the list, and putting up signs like "six items or less" at retail checkout stands. In many cases, customers will understand and accept the reasons for using a particular queue discipline if they are informed of it. The next concern of service response logistics is the management of distribution channels.

Managing Distribution Channels

This next topic within service response logistics describes several distribution channels and strategies a service can use to deliver its services and products to customers. Table 12.2

Table 12.2 Service Distribution Channels

Service	Distribution Channel
Retailer	• Freestanding • Mall • Internet • Mail order
Bank	• Main office/headquarters • Freestanding branches • Sites in malls • Sites in retail locations • ATMs • Internet • Telephone
Auto Repair Business	• Freestanding • Attached to a large retailer • Franchised outlets • Mobile repair van
University/College	• Public • Private • Specialized/general • Traditional/adult education • Main campus • Branches • Internet • Day/Evening • Television

lists a number of distribution alternatives for a retailer, a bank, an auto repair facility, and a university. Many of these distribution alternatives are the traditional ones everyone is used to seeing; however, services today are experimenting with other, nontraditional distribution channels as customer preferences and habits, demographics, technology and competition change.

Some distribution channels have revolutionized the way services do business. For instance, ATMs, debit cards, and the Internet have completely changed the financial services industry; many customers almost never set foot inside a bank or stockbroker's office. Today, many people have come to expect these things, and many services have responded.

Other distribution strategies have arisen because new technologies made them possible, and because customers were asking for them. In the grocery industry, Amazon.com's grocery delivery service AmazonFresh has been operating since 2007 and promises same-day and next-day delivery of groceries (depending on when the order is placed) to customers in Seattle, Washington, and Los Angeles and San Francisco, California. Even though grocery home delivery businesses have failed in the past, materials handling technologies such as robotics and refrigerated totes, Amazon's mobile app, and the deep pockets of Amazon.com give it a good chance of succeeding this time around.[36] Several of the distribution channel alternatives and issues facing services today are discussed next.

Eatertainment, Entertailing, and Edutainment

As service distribution concepts change, new words have been coined to describe these concepts. **Eatertainment** is the combination of restaurant and entertainment elements.

Many of these services incorporate elements of local culture or history into their design themes and offer the capabilities of eating, drinking, entertainment, and shopping all in one venue. For over thirty years, fast food restaurants like McDonalds and Burger King have incorporated children play areas in their restaurants; Chuck E. Cheese restaurants are another example of the eatertainment concept. In Fairmont, New York, the Golf Play Café offers personal caddies that take food and beverage orders and assist customers at one of the 50-plus golf course simulators available. The simulators deliver a realistic interactive golf experience by rendering all the courses in 3D based on terrain, reference data, and calibrated satellite photos. The simulators can also measure the spin and axis of the golf ball and accurately detect a slice, hook, cut, or fade.[37]

Entertailing refers to retail locations with entertainment elements. Many shopping malls are designed today to offer entertainment such as ice skating, rock climbing, and amusement park rides. Since opening in 1992, Bloomington, Minnesota's Mall of America boasts 4.2 million square feet of enclosed area, a theme park, an aquarium, a Lego play area, a mini-golf park, a flight simulator center, 500+ retailers, over 400 events per year, and 11,000 employees. The Body Shop in London is a prototype for a new "experience-based" store. The retailer, with 2,600 locations in more than sixty countries, is testing the new entertailing model that includes information and conversation areas designed to encourage customers to linger as they flow through the store. Shoppers can receive hand massages while listening to stories at the "story table" and test a variety of products for sale, including ointments, lotions, and makeup. "We found that the average amount of time a consumer spends in our prototype stores has doubled, from an average of five minutes to more than 10. This shows a depth of interaction and communication we have witnessed," says Sophie Gasperment, CEO of Body Shop International.[38]

Museums, parks, radio shows, movies, and a host of service providers are also getting into the act with **edutainment** or **infotainment** to attract more customers, create a learning experience, and increase revenues. Edutainment combines learning with entertainment to appeal to customers looking for education along with play. In the U.S., state and national park employees entertain and inform tourists with indigenous animal lectures and shows or campfire stories in the evenings. For many years, documentary movies have been shown to educate and entertain, and radio shows like the U.K. radio soap opera *The Archers* have been educating its audience (in this case, on agricultural matters). Theme parks, such as Legoland in San Diego, offer attractions that combine fun and education aimed at the two- to twelve-year-old audience. Finally, television shows such as *The Electric Company* and software aimed at teaching math and foreign languages in an engaging way also fall into this category.[39]

Franchising

Franchising allows services to expand quickly into dispersed geographic markets, protect existing markets, and build market share. When the owners have limited financial resources, franchising is a good strategy for expansion. Franchisees are required to invest some of their own capital, while paying a small percentage of sales to the franchisor in return for the brand name, start-up help, advertising, training, and assistance in meeting specific operating standards. Many services such as fast food restaurants, accounting and tax businesses, auto rental agencies, beauty salons, clothing stores, ice cream shops, motels, and other small service businesses use franchising as a strategy for growing and competing.

Control problems are one of the biggest issues in franchising. Franchisors periodically perform financial and quality audits on the franchisees along with making frequent visits to facilities to assure that franchisees are continuing to comply with operating standards of the company. The idea of control, however, is something that some new franchisors are experimenting with. The Massachusetts-based Wings Over franchise chain, for instance, lets franchisees make changes to their stores in order to lend an element of uniqueness to each restaurant. The franchise in Boston is called Wings Over Boston and has a citrus chipotle sauce among others; several in North Carolina offer dry rub sauces; and in college towns, many Wings Over restaurants don't open until 4:00 p.m., and they close at 3:00 or 4:00 a.m. This gives franchisees the flexibility to compete with local businesses.[40]

RUMA Invests in Microfranchises in Indonesia

Microfranchising is an effective tool for helping low-income people in developing countries gain hope, skills, and money. RUMA, an Indonesian enterprise is doing just that. RUMA, which stands for Rekan Usaha Mikro Anda, or "Your Micro Business Partner," provides its franchisees a turn-key, prepackaged mobile phone service.

In the past decade cell phone use in Indonesia has skyrocketed, even for poor villagers. The problem these users run into, however, is paying for their minutes. That's where RUMA comes in. RUMA gives franchisees a mobile phone, marketing materials, training on business operations, working capital loans, and mentoring services. It provides the franchisees with everything necessary to help them be successful. The franchisees can then start selling airtime to members of their community. The most innovative characteristic of RUMA's model is its ability to use the mobile phones as the transaction mechanism.

By the end of April 2011, RUMA had a network of over 7,200 village phone operators serving 680,000 customers, with customer growth at 6 percent per month. RUMA has proven to be profitable and sustainable as it continues to grow, create jobs, and reach new markets. RUMA is showing the business community that investing in building up the poor can be profitable for everyone.[41]

The **microfranchise** is another type of franchising concept and is seen as a good way for economically disadvantaged people to make a living. It offers readymade, low-risk starter jobs for people with little or no education and little available capital, while giving established companies additional distribution avenues. Drishtee, for example, is an India-based microfranchise. Its small kiosks can be seen in thousands of rural Indian villages selling basic healthcare, financial, educational, and retail products and services. Drishtee brings financiers and franchisees together for small start-up loans, and the kiosks can earn the franchisees about $30 per month in profits.[42] In the nearby SCM Profile, the Indonesian microfranchisor RUMA is discussed.

International Expansion

The search for larger and additional markets has driven services to expand globally. Since the world today has become essentially borderless because of the Internet and other communication mediums, more freedom of movement, greater use of common currencies, and the expansion that has already taken place, services today compete in a global economy.

Global service expansion most likely means operating with partners who are familiar with the region's culture, markets, suppliers, competitors, infrastructure, and government regulations. For instance, when McDonald's opened its first restaurant in Moscow, an entire food supply chain had to be designed and implemented. McDonald's had to train farmers to produce the type and quality of crops needed to supply the business and then find buyers for the excess food the farmers produced (e.g., Moscow hotels and embassies).[43]

China's service sector is emerging as a key driver of the Chinese economy—the service sector has now surpassed agriculture in terms of contribution to annual GDP, and is growing annually by about 13 percent. Consequently, many foreign services are looking to become involved in Chinese markets. For instance, Chinaco Healthcare, the very successful Tennessee-based hospital chain, has recently opened its first hospital in the Chinese city of Cixi. It is operating the CHC International Hospital in a joint venture with the municipal government of Cixi. Chinaco has three other Chinese hospitals in its pipeline. "Until 2009, the hospital industry was a nonchanging industry," says Sheldon Dorenforest, founder of Dorenforest China Healthcare Group. Today though, "the growth is unlimited. The opportunity is so great, investors are saying, now is the time," he adds.[44]

Exposure to foreign currency exchange rate fluctuations can also pose a problem for expanding service firms, requiring them to use financial hedging strategies to reduce exchange rate risk. Firms can operate in several different countries to offset currency problems, since economic downturns in one country can often be offset by positive economic conditions in other countries.

Language barriers, cultural problems, and the varying needs of different regional cultures also must be addressed when expanding. Local management must be allowed to vary services, signage, and accompanying products to suit local tastes. Restaurants, for instance, typically add local favorites to menus to increase acceptability. Companies must become familiar with language translations in order to properly change the wording on signs and advertisements to increase readability and understanding. The Coca-Cola name in China, for example, was initially rendered as "ke-kou-ke-la" on thousands of signs before it was found that the meaning of the phrase was either "bite the wax tadpole" or "female horse stuffed with wax" depending on the regional dialect. Coke personnel eventually studied 40,000 characters to find the phonetic equivalent "ko-kou-ko-le," which translates into "happiness in the mouth." Similarly, Japan's second-largest tourist agency, Kinki Nippon Tourist Co. felt compelled to change its U.S. name after it began getting requests from American customers for unusual sex-oriented trips.[45]

Internet Distribution Strategies

Internet-based "dot com" companies exploded on the scene during the latter part of the 1990s, pushing the NASDAQ to historic highs and promising to enrich anyone with an idea, good or bad, for a website that could generate revenues on the Internet. E-commerce was touted as the coming trillion dollar revolution in retailing. But as it turned out, most of the dot-com companies of that era are gone today. Still, Internet retailing is growing faster than traditional retailing. In the third quarter of 2013, e-commerce accounted for $67 billion in U.S. retail sales, or approximately 6 percent of total U.S. retail sales for the quarter. This reflects an increase of 17 percent from 2012 third quarter. By 2017, it is projected that about 10 percent of all retail sales will be online purchases. Commercial listings on eBay, for instance, have surged so rapidly that its website briefly crashed on November 21, 2009.[46]

One of the primary advantages of the Internet is its ability to offer convenient sources of real-time information, integration, feedback, and comparison shopping. Individual consumers use Internet search engines to look for jobs, find and communicate with businesses, find the nearest movie theater, find products, sell things, and barter goods. And they can do all this in the privacy of their homes. Globally, approximately 2.17 trillion online Google searches occurred in 2013, for example.[47] Businesses, too, use the Internet to communicate, find and then purchase items from suppliers, and sell or provide goods and services to individual consumers and other businesses. Today, most businesses either have a website or are thinking about building one. Many individuals also have their own websites, since domain names can be purchased for as little as $10 per year. Many retailers today sell products exclusively over the Internet (a *pure strategy*), while others use it as a supplemental distribution channel (a *mixed strategy*).

The **pure Internet distribution strategy** can have several distinct advantages over traditional brick-and-mortar services. Internet companies can become more centralized, reducing labor, capital, and inventory costs while using the Internet to decentralize their marketing efforts to reach a vastly distributed audience of business or individual consumers. Amazon.com falls into this category. Today, though, the **mixed Internet distribution strategy** of combining traditional retailing with Internet retailing seems to be emerging as the stronger business model. Firms such as JCPenney sell items in retail outlets and also from Internet and store catalogs. Customers can either pick up their purchases at the store or have them delivered. Southwest Airlines was the first airline to establish a home page on the Internet, and by the end of 2013, approximately 80 percent of its passenger revenue was generated by online bookings via its industry leading website, www.southwest.com.[48]

Developing good customer service capabilities can be challenging, however. JCPenney representatives, for instance, must be able to perform customer service functions over the Internet, in-person, and via mail and telephone. Companies are addressing this problem by developing sophisticated **customer contact centers**. These centers integrate their websites and traditional call centers to offer 24/7 support where customers and potential customers can contact the firm and each other using telephone, e-mail, chat rooms, and e-bulletin boards. These contact centers allow firms to serve a large number of geographically dispersed customers with a relatively small number of customer service agents.

Just as services have to be concerned with managing service capacity and queues, firms must also invest in designing the necessary distribution channels to compete in today's marketplaces. The final element of the service response logistics discussion affects all elements of the service itself and the way it is distributed, and that is the management of service quality. Although this topic was initially addressed in Chapter 8, the quality management topics geared strictly toward services need further discussion, and this topic is presented below.

Managing Service Quality

The fourth and final topic area in service response logistics is the management of service quality. For services, quality occurs during the service delivery process and typically involves interactions between a customer and service company personnel. In other words, service quality is closely tied to customer satisfaction. Customer satisfaction with the service depends not only on the ability of the firm to deliver what customers want, but on the customers' perceptions of the quality of service received. When customer expectations are met or exceeded, the service is deemed to possess high quality; and when expectations are not met, the perception of quality is poor (recall Maister's First Law of Service). Thus, service quality is highly dependent upon the ability of the firm's employees and service systems to meet or exceed customers' varying expectations. Because of the variable nature of customer expectations, perceptions, and happiness, services must continually be monitoring their service delivery systems using the tools described in Chapter 8 while concurrently observing, communicating with, and surveying customers to adequately assess and improve quality.

The Five Dimensions of Service Quality

Some of the most highly quoted studies of service quality are those done by Drs. Parasuraman, Zeithaml, and Berry.[49] Surveying customers of a number of different services and situations, they identified **five dimensions of service quality** generally used by customers to rate service quality—reliability, responsiveness, assurance, empathy, and tangibles. Reliability was consistently reported in their study as the most important quality dimension.

- *Reliability*: consistently performing the service correctly and dependably.
- *Responsiveness*: providing the service promptly or in a timely manner.
- *Assurance*: using knowledgeable, competent, and courteous employees who convey trust and confidence to customers.
- *Empathy*: providing caring and individual attention to customers.
- *Tangibles*: the physical characteristics of the service including the facilities, servers, equipment, associated goods, and other customers.

Using their survey, the three researchers were able to identify any differences occurring between customer expectations in the five dimensions listed above and customer perceptions of what was actually received during the service encounter. These differences were referred to as service quality "gaps," and can thus be used in actual situations to highlight areas in need of service improvement.

What this research shows is that organizations should develop specific, measurable criteria relating to the five service quality dimensions and then collect data using customer comment cards and mailed or e-mailed surveys of customer satisfaction regarding each of the quality dimensions. This will allow managers to measure overall service quality performance. Table 12.3 presents criteria that might be used in each of the five quality dimensions. Obviously, these would vary by industry, products, and company. When weaknesses or gaps are encountered in any of the performance criteria, managers can institute improvements in the areas indicated.

World-class service companies realize they must get to know their customers, and they invest considerable time and efforts gathering information about customer expectations and perceptions. This information is used to design services and delivery systems that satisfy customers, capture market share, and create profits for the firm. These organizations understand that one of the most important elements affecting long-term competitiveness and profits is the quality of their goods and services relative to their competitors. Nebraska-based Union Pacific Railroad is a good example of a world-class service provider. They recently received Eastman Chemical Company's Supplier Excellence Award for overall company performance, the highest level of all awards presented in the Eastman Supplier Excellence Program. Union Pacific earned this award for the second consecutive year and remains the only railroad to be so honored. The award recognizes consistent performance in providing Eastman with high-quality services and for working on Eastman's behalf to improve its efficiency and competitiveness in the changing market. "We are extremely

Table 12.3 Examples of Service Quality Criteria

Service Quality Dimensions	Criteria
Reliability	• billing accuracy • order accuracy • on-time completion • promises kept
Responsiveness	• on-time appointment • timely callback • timely confirmation of order
Assurance	• skills of employees • training provided to employees • honesty of employees • reputation of firm
Empathy	• customized service capabilities • customer recognition • degree of server–customer contact • knowledge of the customer
Tangibles	• appearance of the employees • appearance of the facility • appearance of customers • quality of equipment and other goods used

proud to receive Eastman's Supplier Excellence Award again this year," said Diane Duren, Union Pacific vice president and general manager. "We are committed to providing great service and earning this recognition from one of our customers is a real compliment to our entire support team in operations and dispatching, as well as marketing and sales."[50]

Recovering from Poor Service Quality

There will undoubtedly, from time to time, be occasions when an organization's products and services do not meet a customer's expectations. In most cases, quick recovery from these service failures can keep customers loyal and coming back, and may even serve as good word-of-mouth advertising for the firm, as customers pass on their stories of good service recoveries. Most importantly, when service failures do occur, firms must be able to recover quickly and forcefully to satisfy customers. This involves empowering frontline service personnel to identify problems and then provide solutions quickly and in an empathetic way.

Good services offer guarantees to their customers and empower employees to provide quick and meaningful solutions when customers invoke the guarantee. In the U.S., the great majority of retailers offer money-back guarantees if customers are not satisfied, and about half offer low-price guarantees where customers are refunded the price difference for a period of time after purchase.[51] In many cases, quick solutions to service problems are designed into service processes and become part of a service firm's marketing efforts. Firms that anticipate where service failures can occur, develop recovery procedures, train employees in these procedures, and then empower employees to remedy customer problems can assure they have the best service recovery system possible.

Florida-based resort management company Kelco Management incorporates service failure response into its training regimen. "Guests who share their concerns with us provide us with an opportunity to respond to and resolve situations. When we do this right, we can retain our guest loyalty. When we do this wrong, our guests will take their business to our competitors. And, worse yet, disgruntled guests will air their negative impressions in one of the online review sites," says Ray Hobbs, vice president of operations. When Kelco executives realized their goal of outstanding service quality was not being achieved, they found the disconnect to be linked to their associates. Kelco has now changed its training programs to provide each associate a service recovery guideline at the very beginning of training. This training instills confidence and empowers them to respond properly, quickly resolve or offer solutions to guest issues, and follow through to initiate actions needed from others.[52]

SUMMARY

Services constitute a large and growing segment of the global economy. Managing the supply chains of services is thus an important part of an overall competitive strategy for services. Since service customers are most often the final consumers of the services provided, successfully managing service encounters involves managing productive capacity, managing queues, managing distribution channels, and managing service quality. These four concerns are the foundations of service response logistics and were the primary focus of this chapter.

Service companies must accurately forecast demand, design capacity to adequately meet demand, employ queuing systems to serve customers as quickly and effectively as possible, utilize distribution systems to best serve the firm's customers, and then take steps to assure service quality and customer satisfaction throughout the service process. Provided that managers have selected a good location, designed an effective layout, hired, trained, and properly scheduled service personnel, and then employed effective service response logistics strategies, firms and their supply chains should be able to maintain competitiveness, market share, and profitability.

KEY TERMS

arrival pattern, 432
back-of-the-house operations, 419
balking, 433
Baumol's disease, 415
capacity utilization, 426
chase demand strategy, 427
closeness desirability rating, 422
cost leadership strategy, 418
customer contact centers, 444
demand management, 427
demand source, 432
differentiation strategy, 418
eatertainment, 440
edutainment, 441
entertailing, 441
facilitating products, 423
First and Second Laws of Service, 437
five dimensions of service quality, 445
focus strategy, 418
franchising, 441
front-of-the-house operations, 419
infotainment, 441
level demand strategy, 427
microfranchise, 442
mixed Internet distribution strategy, 444
multiple-channel queuing system, 433
multiple-factor productivity, 415
multiple-phase queuing system, 433
perceived waiting times, 436
pure Internet distribution strategy, 444
pure services, 412
queue discipline, 433
queue management, 427
queue times, 430
queuing systems, 430
reneging, 433
service bundles, 419
service capacity, 426
service delivery systems, 419
service layout strategies, 420
service quality, 424
service response logistics, 425
single-factor productivity, 415
state utility, 412
virtual queues, 433
walk-through service audits, 419
Walmart effect, 415

DISCUSSION QUESTIONS

1. Is your university a pure service? Explain.
2. Why is the service sector in the U.S. and other highly developed economies growing more rapidly than the manufacturing sector?
3. Describe the primary differences between goods and service firms.

4. Using the formula for productivity, describe all the ways that firms can increase productivity. Which of these ways might be considered risky?
5. Describe several single- and multiple-factor productivity measures that could be used at your university.
6. Define Baumol's disease and the Walmart effect, and how they affect service-oriented economies like the U.S.
7. Discuss the primary issues in the management of global services.
8. What sorts of problems must services overcome as they expand into foreign markets?
9. What are the three generic strategies that services use to compete? Give examples.
10. When a service competes using a cost leadership strategy, does this mean the service is low quality? Explain.
11. When customers purchase a service, they are actually getting a bundle of service attributes. List and describe these attributes using a car rental agency, a convenience store, and a radio station.
12. How would you characterize your university's service delivery system?
13. Provide some examples of front-of-the-house and back-of-the-house service operations.
14. What are some things service firms can do to monitor customer satisfaction?
15. Why are service locations so important?
16. What strategy do you think was used in selecting the location of your university? Could there be a better location?
17. Discuss the principal design objectives for service layouts.
18. How do supply chain management activities differ between services and manufacturing companies? In what ways are these activities alike?
19. What are the four concerns of service response logistics?
20. Define service capacity, and provide three examples of it that were not listed in the text.
21. What is the capacity of your class's classroom?
22. Define capacity utilization. What is an ideal utilization? Can utilization ever be greater than 100 percent? Explain.
23. Describe how you would use a level and a chase demand capacity utilization strategy. Which one does your university use?
24. What are some alternatives to hiring and laying off workers to vary service capacity as demand varies?
25. Can customers be used to provide extra service capacity? Explain.
26. Describe some demand management techniques that are used when demand exceeds capacity and when capacity exceeds demand. Your university has periods of time when both of these situations exist. What do they do?
27. How can firms make use of excess capacity?
28. What are the two elements managers must pay attention to when managing queues so as to maximize customer satisfaction?

29. What are the primary elements to consider when designing any queuing system?

30. What type of queuing system configuration is used at a restaurant? A car dealer? At Zappos?

31. Define the terms "balking" and "reneging." How could a firm minimize them?

32. What is a virtual queue? When might one be used?

33. What type of queuing system does a three-channel, four-phase system refer to?

34. What are the advantages and disadvantages of increasing the number of channels?

35. What queue discipline is used to register students at your university? What about seating patrons at a fancy nightclub?

36. Explain and give examples of Maister's First and Second Laws of Service. Use your personal experiences.

37. If your firm has designed an effective queuing system, why is it still necessary to practice waiting time management on some occasions?

38. What are the distribution channel alternatives for a weather service? A souvenir shop? A marriage counselor? How about your university?

39. What is a microfranchise? Would these be good for a developing country? For the U.S.?

40. What is edutainment? Does your university use it? How?

41. Describe the important issues in the international expansion of services.

42. Describe and give examples of a pure Internet distribution strategy and a mixed Internet distribution strategy. Find your examples on the Internet.

43. How is service quality related to customer service and satisfaction?

44. Describe the five dimensions of service quality for a dentist's office, how performance in these dimensions might be measured, and how recoveries might be handled for failures in each of the service quality dimensions.

45. Can recovery from a poor service quality incident be a good thing? Explain.

ESSAY/PROJECT QUESTIONS

1. Search the Internet for additional examples of eatertainment, entertailing, and edutainment, and describe them in a report.

2. Search the Internet for examples of microfranchising and report on several of these.

3. Search the Internet for the terms "McDonald's carbon footprint" or "McDonald's green initiatives," and write a report on this firm's efforts.

4. Write a paper on Walmart's location and layout strategies in the U.S. and other countries.

5. Search for examples of virtual queuing systems and report on several of these, explaining how they work.

PROBLEMS

1. For the previous month, the Bichsel Lounge served 1,500 customers with very few complaints. Its labor cost was $3,000, material cost was $800, energy cost was $200, and the building's lease cost was $1,500. It was open twenty-six days during the month, and the lounge has twenty seats. They are open six hours per day, and the average customer stay is one hour.
   a. Calculate the single-factor productivities and the overall multiple-factor productivity. How could it improve the productivity?
   b. Calculate the monthly capacity and the capacity utilization.
2. The Iarussi Legal Aide office assisted 126 people in June 2013, with a staff labor cost of $3,240. In June 2014, the office provided assistance to 145 people with a labor cost of $3,960. What was its productivity growth over this one-year period?
3. For the office layout shown below and the accompanying trip and distance matrices, determine the total distance traveled per day. Find another layout that results in a lower total distance traveled per day.

Management (1)	Production (2)	Engineering (3)	Reception (4)
Files (5)	Accounting (6)	Purchasing (7)	Sales (8)

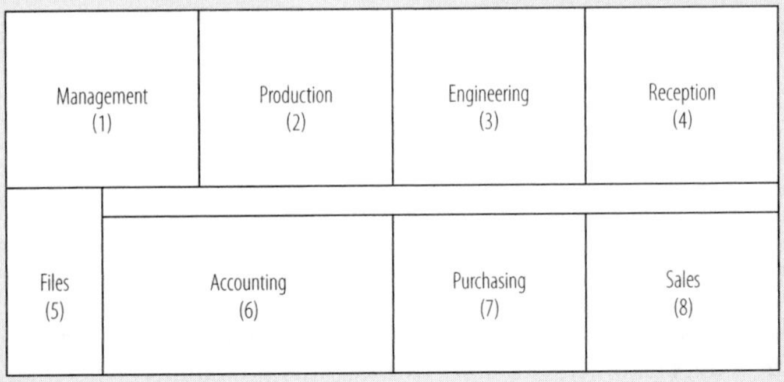

Interdepartmental Trips per Day

	(2)	(3)	(4)	(5)	(6)	(7)	(8)
(1)	6	5	2	1	7	6	15
(2)		12	4	5	2	10	5
(3)			2	9	2	10	8
(4)				18	12	4	2
(5)					0	0	0
(6)						6	14
(7)							6

Distances Between Departments (Meters)

	(2)	(3)	(4)	(5)	(6)	(7)	(8)
(1)	15	30	45	10	20	35	50
(2)		15	30	20	10	20	35
(3)			15	40	20	10	20
(4)				60	50	30	10
(5)					10	30	50
(6)						20	40
(7)							20

4. For the office layout shown in question 3, determine the closeness desirability rating using the rating table below. Treat the hallway as if it doesn't exist (i.e., the Production and Accounting Departments touch each other). Can you find a more desirable layout? How could you use both the total distance traveled and the closeness desirability in assessing the layout alternatives? Can you find a layout resulting in relatively good scores using both types of criteria?

Closeness Desirabilities Between Departments

	(2)	(3)	(4)	(5)	(6)	(7)	(8)
(1)	2	2	−1	0	1	3	3
(2)		3	0	0	0	3	1
(3)			0	2	0	2	3
(4)				3	1	2	2
(5)					2	2	1
(6)						0	2
(7)							1

5. Corner's Cat Care needs help in its grooming business as shown below for the five-day workweek. Determine a full- and part-time work schedule for the business using the fewest number of workers.

	MONDAY	TUESDAY	WEDNESDAY	THURSDAY	FRIDAY
Workers Required	2	3	3	4	5

6. Given an average service rate of twelve customers per hour, what is the probability the business can handle all the customers when the average arrival rate is ten customers per hour? Use the Poisson distribution to calculate the probabilities for various customer arrivals.

7. With an average service rate of twelve customers per hour and an average customer arrival rate of ten customers per hour, calculate the probability that actual service time will be less than or equal to six minutes.

8. Theresa can handle about ten customers per hour at her one-person comic book store. The customer arrival rate averages about six customers per hour. Theresa is interested in knowing the operating characteristics of her single-channel, single-phase queuing system.

9. How would Theresa's queuing system operating characteristics change for the problem above if she added another cashier and increased her service rate to twenty customers per hour?

ADDITIONAL RESOURCES

Anderson, D., D. Sweeney and T. Williams. *An Introduction to Management Science*. Mason, OH: South-Western, 2003.

Davis, M., N. Aquilano and R. Chase. *Fundamentals of Operations Management*. New York: McGraw-Hill, 1999.

Drazen, E., R. Moll and M. Roetter. *Logistics in Service Industries*. Oak Brook, IL: Council of Logistics Management, 1991.

Fitzsimmons, J. and M. Fitzsimmons. *Service Management for Competitive Advantage*. New York: McGraw-Hill, 1994.

Heizer, B. and B. Render. *Principles of Operations Management*. Upper Saddle River, NJ: Prentice Hall, 2001.

Markland, R., S. Vickery and R. Davis. *Operations Management*. Mason, OH: South-Western, 1998.

Metters, R., K. King-Metters and M. Pullman. *Successful Service Operations Management*. Mason, OH: South-Western, 2003.

Rodriguez, C. *International Management: A Cultural Approach*. Mason, OH: South-Western, 2001.

Taha, H. A. *Operations Research: An Introduction*. Upper Saddle River, NJ: Prentice Hall, 2003.

Taylor, B. *Introduction to Management Science*. Upper Saddle River, NJ: Prentice Hall, 2002.

ENDNOTES

1. Anonymous, "TPN to Enhance Service Offering," *Marketing Weekly News*, February 9, 2013: 224.
2. Anonymous, "Nedbank Taps into IBM Analytics," *Marketing Weekly News*, January 25, 2014: 150.
3. Pyrah, A., "New INTA CEO to Push Global Expansion of the INTA," *Managing Intellectual Property*, May 2013: 1.
4. World Bank information found at: http://data.worldbank.org/indicator/NV.SRV.TETC.ZS
5. McCully, C., "Trends in Consumer Spending and Personal Saving, 1959–2009," *Survey of Current Business* 91(6), 2011: 14–23.
6. Tan, T., "We've Got the Transformation Power: Digital Solutions in India 2013," *Publishers Weekly* 260(15), 2013: 1.
7. World Bank information found at: http://data.worldbank.org/indicator/NV.SRV.TETC.ZS
8. Liddle, A., "India Beckons US Brands," *Nation's Restaurant News* 44(8), 2010: 10.
9. Blackstone, B., "Is Productivity Growth Back in Grips of Baumol's Disease?" *Wall Street Journal*, August 13, 2007: A2.
10. Fishbach, A., "Labor-Saving Tools Fuel Productivity," *Transmission & Distribution World*, September 2013: 8.
11. Cain, R., "Finding the Right Fit," *Journal of Commerce*, May 10, 2010: 1.
12. Pollitt, D., "Warehouse Team Develops IT Skills One Stage at a Time," *Training & Management Development Methods* 23(3), 2009: 525–530.
13. Anonymous, "ZeroChaos Continues Growth and Expansion," *Economics & Business Week*, August 13, 2011: 1366; Zafar, A., "deVere Unveils Global Expansion Plan," *Financial Advisor*, November 12, 2011: 1; Anonymous, "Bibby Financial Services Continues Global Expansion," *The Secured Lender* 68(10), 2012: 14–15.
14. Porter, M., *Competitive Strategy: Techniques for Analyzing Industries and Competitors*. New York: The Free Press, 1980.
15. Anonymous, "Constellation Energy Chosen by Evanston, Illinois," *Marketing Weekly News*, May 29, 2012: 471.
16. Melone, L., "Tiptoeing into Social Media," *Computerworld* 47(2), 2013: 26–28.
17. See frenchfryheaven.com for information.

18. Ainlay, T., and J. Gabaldon, *Las Vegas: The Fabulous First Century*. Mt. Pleasant, SC: Arcadia Publishing, 2003; Land, B., and M. Land, *A Short History of Las Vegas*. Reno: University of Nevada Press, 2004; http://www.golflink.com/about_4669_history-stratosphere-hotel-las-vegas.html

19. King, J., "Extreme Automation," *Computerworld* 45(11), 2011: 16–23.

20. Dostal, E., "Going Local, Green Takes Off for Concessions International," *Nation's Restaurant News* July 17, 2013: 1.

21. Levin, A., "Green Gets Going," *Foodservice Equipment & Supplies* 62(3), 2010: 18.

22. Warren, M., "Simply Irresistible," *Profit* 29(3), 2010: 68–69.

23. Drazen, E. L., R. E. Moll, and M. F. Roetter, *Logistics in Service Industries*. Oak Brooks, IL: Council of Logistics Management, 1991: 34.

24. Whisler, D., "Truckload Costs Up While Capacity Remains Tight," *Fleet Owner*, July 16, 2013: 1.

25. Green, K., "Photo-Me Washes Up Nicely," *Investors Chronicle*, December 11, 2013: 1.

26. Anonymous, "Labor Management: Automated Solutions Take Center Stage," *Chain Store Age* 89(3), 2013: 25.

27. Li, H., "Charging Cars for Pennies," *Canadian Business* 82(19), 2009: 24.

28. Jacobs, R., "Gatwick Beats Rival in Battle for Passengers," *FT.com*, November 29, 2011: 1.

29. Anonymous, "Lavi Industries Inc.," *Marketing Weekly News*, March 27, 2010: 200; Anonymous, "North Asia Office Carat China, Shanghai," *Media*, December 17, 2009: 36.

30. Morris, J., "The Waiting Game," *Management Today*, January 2013: 44–47.

31. Maister, D., "The Psychology of Waiting Lines," In J. A. Czepiel, M. R. Solomon, and C. F. Surprenant, *The Service Encounter*. Lexington, MA: Lexington Books, D.C. Heath & Co., 1985.

32. Ibid.

33. Bachman, K., "TV with Your Pie?" *Mediaweek* 19(23), 2009: 10.

34. Okie, S., "Form Follows Function: A Redesigned Pediatric Office," *Health Affairs* 29(5), 2010: 979–981.

35. Petouhoff, N., "The Social Customer Economy," *Customer Relationship Management* 14(3), 2010: 14. Also see www.carphonewarehouse.com.

36. Andel, T., "Can Amazon Succeed at Grocery Delivery?" *Modern Materials Handling* 62(9), 2007: 15. Also see their website: http://fresh.amazon.com

37. See http://rochester.golflocal.com/what-is-eatertainment/

38. Anonymous, "The Body Shop Tests 'Entertailing' in Britain," www.retailcustomerexperience.com, May 2012; www.mallofamerica.com/about

39. See http://www.bbc.co.uk/programmes/b006qpgr/features/about for more on The Archers; see http://kidstvmovies.about.com/od/theelectriccompany/fr/ElectricCor.htm for more on The Electric Company

40. See www.wingsover.com

41. Farnsworth, T., "Microfanchising: An Example through RUMA," *The Microfranchise Blog*, July 12, 2012, found at http://themicrofranchisingblog.wordpress .com/2012/07/12/microfranchising-an-example-through-ruma

42. See www.drishtee.org

43. Byrne, H., "Welcome to McWorld," *Barron's* 74(35), 1994: 25–28.

44. Kutscher, B., "Eastern Opportunities: HCA Founders Look to Nascent Chinese Market," *Modern Healthcare* 43(5), 2013: 20–21.

45. Hoffman, G., "On Foreign Expansion," *Progressive Grocer* 75(9), 1996: 156.

46. Enright, A., "E-Retail on a Roll: Online Retail Sales Jumped 17.5% in Q3," *Internet Retailer*, November 22, 2013: 1; Dusto, A., "60% of U.S. Retail Sales Will Involve the Web by 2017," *Internet Retailer*, October 30, 2013: 1; Anonymous, "Business: Bleak Friday; Retail v E-tail in America," *The Economist* 393(8659), 2009: 69.

47. Anonymous, "Google Annual Search Statistics," January 1, 2014, found at http://www .statisticbrain.com/google-searches/

48. Rooney, K., "Consumer-Driven Healthcare Marketing: Using the Web to Get Up Close and Personal," *Journal of Healthcare Management* 54(4), 2009: 241–251; also see www .swamedia.com/channels/Corporate-Fact-Sheet/pages/corporate-fact-sheet

49. See, for instance, Parasuraman, A., V. A. Zeithaml, and L. L. Berry, "SERVQUAL: A Multiple-Item Scale for Measuring Consumer Perceptions of Service Quality," *Journal of Retailing* 64(1), 1988: 12–40; Parasuraman, A., V. A. Zeithaml, and L. L. Berry, "Conceptual Model of Service Quality and Its Implications for Future Research," *Journal of Marketing* 49, Fall 1985: 41–50.

50. Anonymous, "Union Pacific Railroad Earns Eastman Chemical's Highest Level Supplier Excellence Award for Second Consecutive Year," *Marketing Weekly News*, May 21, 2011: 1640.

51. McWilliams, B., and E. Gerstner, "Offering Low Price Guarantees to Improve Customer Retention," *Journal of Retailing* 82(2), 2006: 105.

52. Feiertag, H., "Successful Service Recovery Is Key to Customer Retention," *Hotel Management* 228(10), 2013: 14.

Integration Issues in Supply Chain Management

Chapter 13
SUPPLY CHAIN PROCESS INTEGRATION

We've reached critical mass. Companies integrate today because they must react faster to remain competitive. Integration gives them the capacity to bring functions together from multiple applications in real-time data for better decision making.

— Sloan Zupan, senior product manager, Mitsubishi Electric[1]

In my former company, which was in the consumer electronics industry, we had eight or nine different systems that we used in the supply chain. As someone personally involved with this, I felt the pain. To get around this, companies find shortcuts and workarounds. Inevitably, this causes mistakes.

— James Vinson, CEO of VChain Solutions[2]

Learning Objectives

After completing this chapter, you should be able to

- Discuss the overall importance of process integration in supply chain management.
- Describe the advantages of, and obstacles to, process integration.
- Understand the important issues of internal and external process integration.
- Understand the role played by information systems in creating information visibility along the supply chain.
- Describe the various processes requiring integration along the supply chain.
- Understand the various causes of the bullwhip effect and how they impact process integration.
- Discuss the various issues associated with supply chain risk and security.

Chapter Outline

SCM Profile | IBM Uses Business Analytics to Integrate its Supply Chains

IBM's global supply chain encompasses thousands of suppliers and every product and service offering the company produces, from mainframe computers, servers, and other hardware to software, services, and spare parts. Orchestrating many supply chains while achieving integration is no small task.

There was a point in time when IBM let every business unit within the company run itself. Its supply chains were characterized by widely distributed infrastructures and procurement practices. Later, as IBM became a globally integrated enterprise, its supply chains changed as well. Today, all of IBM's global supply chain processes are fully integrated.

IBM's supply chains must be capable of handling their vast array of products. They must be capable of processing an order for a new mainframe computer, software orders, service orders, and orders for spare parts using the same worldwide systems. Additionally, there is the need to know, end to end, how its supply chains are performing and where the problem areas are. IBM recognizes that part of a supply chain's ability to perform depends on how much information the suppliers have at their fingertips so they can contribute to the success of the supply chains. "Collaboration with our suppliers and business partners is very important to us today," says Mike Ray, vice president of business integration for IBM. "In the old days, relationships with suppliers were almost adversarial at times. The buyer never gave much information to the supplier and the supplier wouldn't communicate much, either. What we learned is that everyone engaged in the supply chain, whether it is the buyer or the supplier or the logistics provider, needs visibility and information."

The rapidly changing dynamics of the supply chain and the global marketplace also demand a new generation of reporting, powered by business analytics. Business analytics for the supply chain, if properly designed and implemented, provides visibility into emerging supply chain issues before they become problems. When business analytics accomplishes this, it preempts supply chain interruptions from occurring. "These new analytics tools can create better supply chain visibility for everyone," says Ray. "This is why in some cases, we have implemented business analytics and have then provided these analytics tools to our suppliers to give them better supply chain visibility."

Like most global enterprises, IBM has gone through years of both evolution and transformation in its business and supply chain. Today's challenges require the company to be competitive and responsive in an ever-changing global marketplace. This focus demands a set of sound supply chain practices that will enable the company to reach its goals.[3]

INTRODUCTION

The ultimate goal in supply chain management is to create value for the services and products provided to end customers, which, in turn, provides benefits to the firms in the supply chain network. To accomplish this, firms in the supply chain must integrate their process activities internally and then with their trading partners. Throughout this textbook, the integration of key business processes along the supply chain has been a recurring theme. The term **process integration** (also sometimes called process collaboration) means sharing information and coordinating resources to jointly manage a process or processes. We have been introducing and discussing the various processes and issues concerning this time-consuming and somewhat daunting task throughout the text and have been alluding to the idea that key processes must somehow be coordinated, shared, or integrated among the supply chain members. In this chapter, some of these issues will be revisited and refined.

Additionally, the advantages, challenges, methods, and tools used to achieve process integration both within organizations and among their trading partners will be discussed. Today, process integration remains a significant problem for many organizations. In a 2011 survey of 190 executives representing a wide variety of global companies, only 6 percent of the executives said their firms' processes were "extremely integrated" and 25 percent said they were "not at all integrated." Additionally, about 72 percent of the small company (revenues less than $100 million per year) executives said their firms' supply chain integration levels were only slight or nonexistent.[4] Generally speaking, since process integration between departments is considered to be the necessary foundation for successful external integration between trading partners, it can then be understood that problems with internal integration have made external integration even more difficult to achieve.

Specifically, this chapter discusses the key business processes requiring integration, the impact of integration on the bullwhip effect, the importance of internal and external process integration in supply chain management, issues of supply chain risk and security that come about as information is shared and products are moved significant distances, and the important role played by information technology (IT) when integrating processes.

External process integration can be an extremely difficult task because it requires proper training and preparedness, willing and competent trading partners, trust, compatible information systems, potentially a change in one or more organizational cultures, and, as mentioned above, successful internal process integration. The benefits of collaboration and information sharing between trading partners can be significant: reduced supply chain costs, greater flexibility to respond to market changes, and fewer process problems, which means less supply chain safety stock, higher quality levels, reduced time to market, and better utilization of resources. It is hoped that this chapter will allow readers to recall and consider all of the previous chapters' topics, their contributions to successful supply chain management, and the means by which information sharing and process integration must occur to make supply chain management a success.

THE SUPPLY CHAIN MANAGEMENT INTEGRATION MODEL

Figure 13.1 presents a supply chain integration model, starting with the identification of key trading partners, the development of supply chain strategies, aligning the strategies with key process objectives, developing internal process performance measures, internally integrating these key processes, developing external supply chain performance measures for each process, externally integrating key processes with supply chain partners, extending process integration to second-tier supply chain participants, and then, finally, reevaluating the integration model periodically. Each of the elements in the model is discussed next.

Identify Critical Supply Chain Trading Partners

For each of the focal firm's products and services, it is important to identify the critical or **key trading partners** that will eventually enable the successful sale and delivery of end products to the final customers. Over time, companies identify these trading partners

Figure 13.1 **The Supply Chain Integration Model**

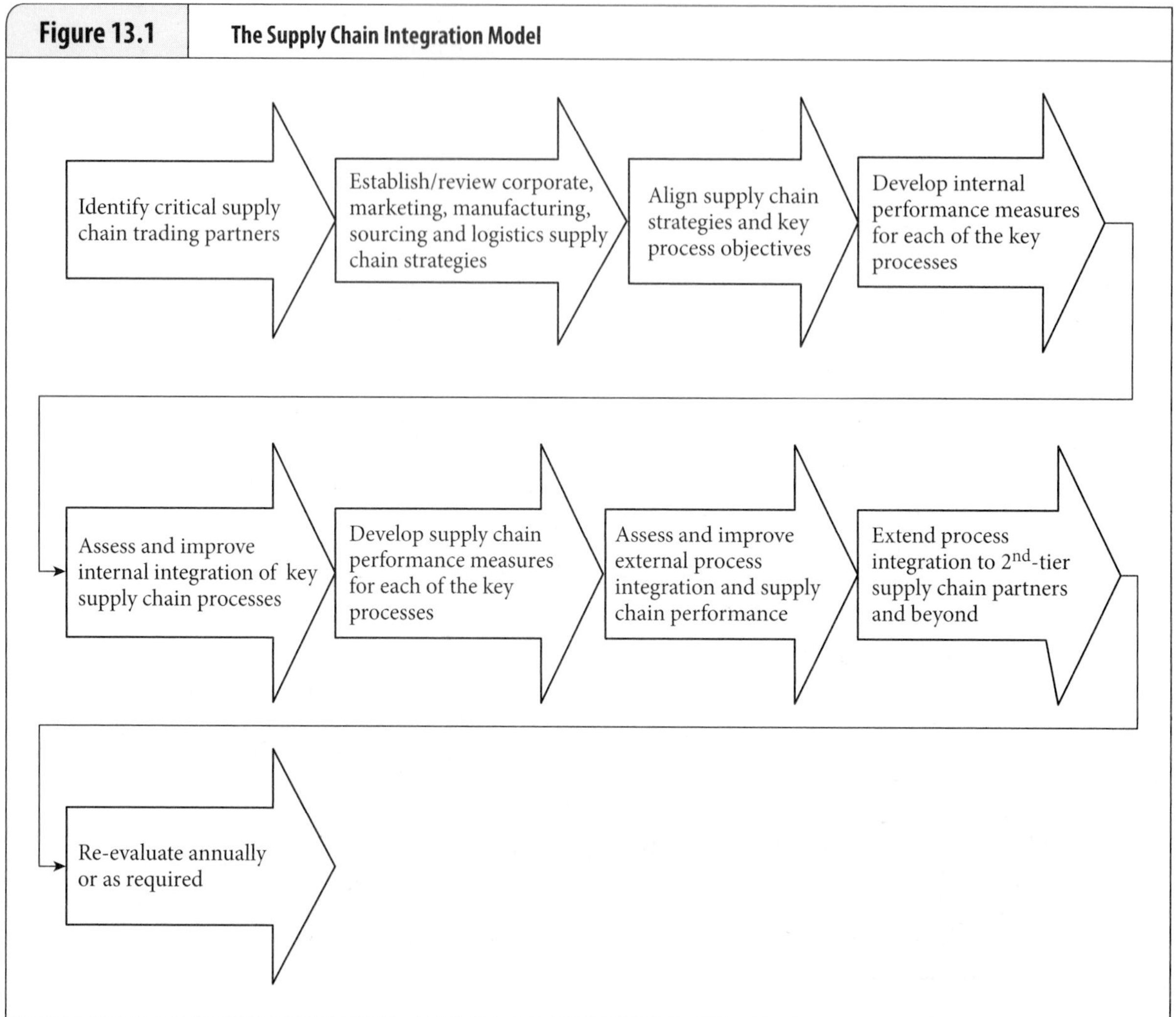

through successful business dealings—suppliers that have come to be trusted and that provide a large share of the firm's critical products and services; and repeat, satisfied customers that buy a significant portion of the firm's products. As the focal firm moves out to second- and third-tier suppliers and customers, trading partner numbers increase quite dramatically, which can greatly complicate integration efforts. Identifying only the first-tier primary trading partners allows the firm to concentrate its time and resources on managing important process links with these companies, enabling the larger supply chain to perform better. Including nonessential and minor supporting businesses will most likely prove counterproductive in terms of successful supply chain management. In a landmark supply chain article by Drs. Lambert, Cooper, and Pagh, they define primary or key trading partners as "all those autonomous companies or strategic business units who actually perform operational and/or managerial activities in the business processes designed to produce a specific output for a particular customer or market."[5]

Depending on where within a supply chain the focal firm is physically located (close to its key suppliers, close to end-product customers, or somewhere in between), the structure of the network of primary trading partners will vary. Mapping the network of primary trading partners is something that should be done to help the firm decide which businesses to include in its supply chain management efforts. For instance, a firm with a large number of key suppliers and customers might limit the number of integrative processes, leading to fewer second-tier relationships as well. Coordinating processes with its key suppliers was seen as so important to IBM, for example, that in 2006 it moved its global procurement headquarters to Shenzhen, China, from the U.S.[6]

Review and Establish Supply Chain Strategies

On an annual basis, management should identify the basic supply chain strategies associated with each of its trading partner's goods and services. If an end product is competing based on quality, then supply chain members should also be using strategies consistent with delivering high-quality products at competitive price and service levels. Product strategies should then translate into internal functional policies regarding the types of parts purchased and suppliers used, the manufacturing processes employed, the designs of goods and services, the warranty and return policies offered, and potentially the amount of outsourcing employed. In each of these areas, policies should be geared toward supporting the overall strategy of the supply chain.

Similarly, if end products are competing based on sustainability, then strategies and functional policies among each of the supply chain participants must be consistently aimed at achieving favorable environmental impacts or carbon footprints as intermediate goods and services are purchased, produced, and moved along the supply chain. Supply chain sustainability has become an important issue today as organizations seek better ways to compete. In 2012, for example, global food maker General Mills commissioned a study of its environmental dependence on natural resources across its supply chains and found that nearly two-thirds of greenhouse gas emissions and 99 percent of water use occurred outside its own operations—in the growth of raw materials and preparation of ingredients that General Mills uses to produce its products. Consequently, General Mills designed a sourcing plan to improve the sustainability of raw materials it uses and to manage the impact of water usage across its supply chains.[7]

Align Supply Chain Strategies with Key Supply Chain Process Objectives

Once the primary strategy has been identified for a supply chain end product, managers need to identify the important processes linking each of the supply chain trading partners and establish process objectives to assure that resources and efforts are effectively deployed within each firm to support the end-product strategy. The key processes and the methods used to integrate and manage process links among supply chain partners will vary based on the internal structure of each firm, the prevailing economic conditions in the marketplace, the degree to which **functional silos** exist in any of the trading partners, and the nature of existing relationships within the supply chain. In some cases, it may be best to integrate only one key process with one trading partner, while with other partners more processes would be integrated.

Based on the research of Lambert, Cooper, and Pagh, eight processes have been identified as important supply chain business processes. These **key supply chain processes** are shown in Table 13.1. A *process* can be defined as a set of activities designed to produce

Table 13.1 The Eight Key Supply Chain Business Processes[9]

Customer Relationship Management	Identifying key customer segments, tailoring product and service agreements to meet their needs, measuring customer profitability and firm's impact on customers.
Customer Service Management	Providing information to customers such as product availability, shipping dates, and order status; administering product and service agreements.
Demand Management	Balancing customer demand with the firm's output capacity; forecasting demand and coordinating with production, purchasing, and distribution.
Order Fulfillment	Meeting customer requirements by synchronizing the firm's marketing, production, and distribution plans.
Manufacturing Flow Management	Determining manufacturing process requirements to enable the right mix of flexibility and velocity to satisfy demand.
Supplier Relationship Management	Managing product and service agreements with suppliers; developing close working relationships with key suppliers.
Product Development and Commercialization	Developing new products frequently and getting them to market effectively; integrating suppliers and customers into the process to reduce time to market.
Returns Management	Managing used product disposition, product recalls, packaging requirements; and minimizing future returns.

a product or service for an internal or external customer. A discussion of each of these processes follows.

Customer Relationship Management

The **customer relationship management process** provides the firm with the structure for developing and managing customer relationships. As discussed in Chapter 10, key customers are identified, their needs are determined, and then products and services are developed to meet their needs. Over time, relationships with these key customers are solidified through the sharing of information; the formation of cross-company teams to improve product design, delivery, quality, and cost; the development of shared goals; and, finally, improved performance and profitability for the trading partners along with agreements on how to share these benefits. The firm should monitor the impact of customer relationship management (CRM) efforts in terms of both the financial impact of these efforts and customer satisfaction. Over time, CRM has come to be associated with software applications to aid the CRM process. In fact, in 2013, Microsoft was granted a patent for extending a "CRM eventing framework" to a cloud computing environment.[8]

Customer Service Management

The **customer service management process** is what imparts information to customers while also providing ongoing management of any product and service agreements between the firm and its customers. Information can be offered through a number of communication channels including websites, personal interactions, information system linkages, and printed media. Objectives and policies are developed to assure proper distribution of products and services to customers, to adequately respond to product and delivery failures and complaints, and to utilize the most effective means of communication to coordinate successful product, service, and information deliveries. The process also includes methods for monitoring and reporting customer service performance, allowing firms to understand the extent that their management efforts are achieving the process objectives. In Auburn University's 2009 State of the Retail Supply Chain study, executives from over forty retailers

SCM Profile — EasyJet Makes It Look Easy

London-based commercial airline EasyJet is using customer service as a weapon against rivals in the highly competitive airline market. Under CEO Carolyn McCall, raising the customer satisfaction bar has been placed at the heart of what EasyJet does, in its goal of becoming Europe's preferred short-haul airline.

The airline is pushing ahead with a program to transform company culture and the results have been evident: Its full year pretax profit increased 51 percent from 2012 to 2013. "As a low-cost airline it's where we can differentiate ourselves," says Angie Mullen, EasyJet's standards manager.

Ms. McCall has underscored the difference between it and the "stuffy" and more formal competition. "If you go on our planes, our crew will have a laugh with you," she says. "If it's appropriate, they'll have a joke—they're very easy."

Meanwhile, the list of initiatives to raise standards and burnish the "orange spirit" is lengthy and growing. Out has gone the old uniform with the garish orange men's shirt, in instead are touches of orange and a "fun" striped tie. There is a customer charter and scores of "customer champions." There is a pledge day, numerous internal awards, and a Spirit Awards Portal, where staff can commend colleagues. There are feel-good videos and behavior pins to be won by crew, for displaying certain behaviors toward passengers. Customer satisfaction is up, and the test now will be keeping the momentum going to stay ahead.[10]

thought the primary challenges today for retail supply chains were decreasing costs while improving customer service. To accomplish this, most of the retailers were trying to take innovative approaches to managing their supply chains—they were trying to improve workforce quality, break down internal and external silos, create more flexible capacities, and strengthen their distribution networks.[11] The nearby SCM Profile describes EasyJet's customer service efforts.

Demand Management

The **demand management process** is what balances customer demand and the firm's output capabilities. The specific demand management activities include forecasting demand and then utilizing techniques to vary capacity and demand within the purchasing, production, and distribution functions. Various forecasts can be used, based on the time frame, the knowledge of the forecaster, the ability to obtain point-of-sale information from customers, and the use of forecasting models contained in many ERP systems. The next step is to determine how to synchronize demand and productive capacity. As discussed in Chapters 5, 6, and 12, a number of effective techniques exist to smooth demand variabilities and increase or decrease capacity when disparities exist between demand and supply. Contingency plans must also be ready for use when demand management techniques fail or when forecasts are inaccurate. Performance measurement systems can prove quite useful here to increase the accuracy of forecasts and to track the success of various demand management activity implementations. After a terrible explosion at a Georgia-based Imperial Sugar refinery destroyed 60 percent of the plant's capacity in 2008, Imperial Sugar was able to rely on its demand management software to show everyone from production to sales, in real time, what could be delivered to which customers using available inventories. "It was our saving grace," said CIO George Muller.[12]

Order Fulfillment

The **order fulfillment process** is the set of activities that allows the firm to fill customer orders while providing the required levels of customer service at the lowest possible delivered cost. Thus, the order fulfillment process must integrate the firm's marketing, production, and distribution plans to be effective. More specifically, the firm's distribution system must be designed to provide adequate customer service levels, and their production system must be designed to produce at the required output levels, while marketing plans and promotions must consider the firm's output and distribution capabilities. Related order fulfillment issues are the location of suppliers, the modes of inbound and outbound transportation used, the location of production facilities and distribution centers, and the system used for entering, processing, communicating, picking, delivering, and documenting customer orders.

The order fulfillment process must integrate closely with customer relationship management, customer service management, supplier relationship management, and returns management to assure that customer requirements are being met, customer service levels are being maintained, suppliers are helping to minimize order lead times, and customers are getting undamaged, high-quality products. A 2013 survey of U.S. consumers and supply chain managers highlighted the importance of effective order fulfillment—89 percent of the consumer group said they would likely shop at a different retailer if an order was delivered late, and 54 percent of the supply chain mangers said that fulfillment issues have had a negative impact on their firms' revenues and profitability over the past few years.[13]

Manufacturing Flow Management

The **manufacturing flow management process** is the set of activities responsible for making the actual product, establishing the manufacturing flexibility required to adequately serve the markets, and designing the production system to meet cycle-time requirements. To be effective, manufacturing flow management activities must be interfaced with the demand management and customer relationship management processes, using customer requirements as inputs to the process. As customers and their requirements change, so too must the supply chain and the manufacturing flow processes change to maintain the firm's competitiveness. As was shown in Chapter 8, the flexibility and rapid response requirements in many supply chains result in the firm's use of lean systems in order to continue to meet customer requirements.

Manufacturing flow characteristics also impact supplier requirements. For instance, as manufacturing batch sizes and lead time requirements are reduced, supplier deliveries must become smaller and more frequent, causing supplier interactions and supplier relationships to potentially change. The importance of an adequate material requirements planning system should become evident here, as customer requirements must be translated into production capabilities and supplier requirements. As with other processes, a good set of performance metrics should also be utilized to track the capability of the manufacturing flow process to satisfy demand.

Supplier Relationship Management

The **supplier relationship management process** defines how the firm manages its relationships with suppliers. As was discussed in Chapters 2, 3, and 4, firms in actively managed supply chains seek out small numbers of the best-performing suppliers and establish ongoing, mutually beneficial, close relationships with these suppliers in order to meet cost, quality, and/or customer service objectives for key materials, products, and services. For nonessential items, firms may use reverse auctions, bid arrangements, or catalogues to select suppliers. Activities in this process include screening and selecting suppliers, negotiating product and service agreements, managing suppliers, and then monitoring supplier performance and improvement. Some companies may have a cross-functional team to manage suppliers' progress toward meeting the firm's current and long-term requirements and establishing records of performance improvement over time, while other suppliers may be managed little or not at all, depending on supply chain, company, or product requirements. Supplier relationship management personnel routinely communicate with production personnel to obtain feedback on supplier and purchased item performance, and with marketing personnel for customer feedback. Additionally, suppliers are frequently contacted for new product development and performance feedback purposes.

Product Development and Commercialization

The **product development and commercialization process** is responsible for developing new goods and services to meet changing customer requirements and then getting these products to market quickly and efficiently. In actively managed supply chains, customers and suppliers are involved in the new product development process to assure that products conform to customers' needs and purchased items meet manufacturing requirements. Activities in the product development and commercialization process include methods and incentives for generating new product ideas; the development of customer feedback mechanisms; the formation of new product development teams; assessing and selecting new product ideas based on financial impact, resource requirements, and fit with existing manufacturing and logistics infrastructure; designing and testing new product prototypes; determining marketing channels and rolling out the products; and, finally, assessing the success of each new product. Successful new product development requires inputs from external customers and suppliers, and from internal manufacturing, marketing, and finance personnel. In the U.S. beverage industry, 64 percent of the respondents to a 2012 beverage industry survey planned to increase their new product launches in 2013 in response to consumer demand, company growth, and trend developments. Additionally, 42 percent expected their research and development budgets to increase in 2013 due to the new products.[14]

Returns Management

The **returns management process**, discussed in Chapter 9, can be extremely beneficial for supply chain management in terms of maintaining acceptable levels of customer service and identifying product improvement opportunities. Returns management activities include environmental compliance with substance disposal and recycling, writing operating and repair instructions, troubleshooting and warranty repairs, developing disposition guidelines, designing an effective reverse logistics process, and collecting returns data. Returns management personnel frequently communicate with customers and personnel from customer relationship management, product development and commercialization, and supplier relationship management during the returns process.

One of the goals of returns management is to reduce returns. This is accomplished by communicating return and repair information to product development personnel, suppliers, and other potential contributors to any returns problems to guide the improvement of future product and purchased item designs. Logistics services may also be included in the returns feedback communication loop. In a recent reverse logistics survey by the Massachusetts-based business consultants Aberdeen Group, the companies best at reverse logistics were found to have a few things in common, including a standardized returns and repair process, the ability to recover costs from suppliers, real-time information reporting, and multichannel visibility.[15]

For each of the eight processes identified above, objectives or goals must be developed to help guide the firm toward its supply chain strategy. Additionally, consistent objectives within each functional area of the firm, for each process, help to integrate the processes internally, as well as focus efforts and firm resources on the supply chain strategy. For instance, if the supply chain strategy is to compete using low pricing, marketing objectives for the customer relationship management process might be to find cheaper delivery alternatives, develop vendor managed inventory (VMI) accounts, and automate the customer order process. Production objectives might be to develop bulk packaging solutions consistent with the modes of transportation and distribution systems used, to increase mass production capabilities, and to identify the lowest total cost manufacturing sites for specific products, while purchasing objectives might be to identify the cheapest materials and components that meet specifications and to utilize reverse auctions whenever possible. Firms should similarly progress through each of the key processes using teams of employees, suppliers, and customers to help develop process objectives.

Develop Internal Performance Measures for Key Process Effectiveness

As alluded to in each of the key processes above (and to be discussed at greater length in Chapter 14), procedures and metrics must be in place to collect and report internal performance data for the eight key processes. Thus, prior to measuring and comparing performance with their supply chain partners, firms must first build good internal performance measurement capabilities across functions. This can prove troublesome given that in recent surveys of Canadian manufacturing firms and e-businesses, only about half were found to have reasonably well-developed performance measurement systems.[16] Performance measures need to create a consistent emphasis on the overall supply chain strategy and corresponding process objectives. In order to ensure that processes are supporting the overall supply chain strategy, performance should be continuously monitored using a set of metrics designed for each process.

Continuing the discussion from the previous section where competing based on low pricing was the supply chain strategy, performance measures for the customer relationship management process would need to be designed for each of the firm's functional areas. The responsibility for designing these measures can also be assigned to the teams developing objectives for each of the functional areas. Since the objectives in this case are cost driven, the performance measures should reflect this as well. For the customer relationship management process, performance measures in marketing might be the average delivery cost, the number of new VMI accounts, the average cost of ordering and carrying inventories for the new VMI accounts, and the number of new automated order systems over the period of time studied. For production, performance measures might be the average packaging cost per order, the average daily output capability for each product, and the average unit cost per order. For purchasing, the performance measures for the customer relationship management objectives might be the average purchasing cost for each of the items purchased and the percentage of time that reverse auctions were used over the period of time studied. Performance measures would similarly be designed for each of the key processes and their corresponding functional objectives. In this way, firms have the capability to track the progress toward meeting each of the objectives for the key processes.

Assess and Improve Internal Integration of Key Supply Chain Processes

Successful supply chain management requires process coordination and collaboration internally between the firm's functional areas as well as externally between the firm and its trading partners. Achieving process integration within the firm requires a transition from the typical functional silos to one of teamwork and cooperation across business functions. Internal integration has been shown to provide significant benefits for the firm. In a survey of 500 U.S. organizations, for instance, good interdepartmental relationships were found to result in reduced cycle times and fewer stockouts.[17] To achieve internal integration, personnel must have management support, resources, and empowerment to make meaningful organizational changes to foster the type of cooperation necessary to support the overall supply chain strategy. The formation of cross-functional teams to develop the key process objectives and accompanying performance measures is a good starting point in achieving internal process integration.

The primary enabler of integration, though, is the firm's ERP system. In Chapter 6, the importance and capabilities of ERP systems were described, along with some of the various software applications or modules that are used today. ERP systems provide a view of the entire organization, enabling decision makers within each function to have information regarding customer orders, production plans, work-in-process and finished goods inventory levels, outbound goods in-transit, purchase orders, inbound goods in-transit, purchased item inventories, and financial and accounting information. ERP systems thus link business processes and facilitate communication and information sharing between the firm's departments. Since the key business processes overlay each of the functional areas, the firm eventually becomes process oriented rather than functionally oriented as ERP systems are deployed. It is this visibility of information across the organization that allows processes to become integrated within the firm.

To assess the current state of internal integration, firms should first develop an understanding of their **internal supply chains**. Internal supply chains can be complex, particularly if firms have multiple divisions and global organizational structures. Thus, firms should assess the makeup of the teams used in setting process objectives and performance measures—do they include representatives from each of the organization's divisions or business units? These cross-functional teams should adequately represent the firm's internal supply chain. During the recent economic downturn, internal integration was impacted as companies trimmed staff. As a result, managers have turned to team-based games to get departments working together again. "Many employees have been shifted into new job roles because of layoffs, and employers are using team-based business games to train workers in their new responsibilities and to increase their retention of new knowledge," says Elizabeth Treher, CEO of Minnesota-based The Learning Key. "Team-based business games result in better knowledge retention, provide focused, memorable learning and a more enjoyable learning atmosphere than traditional methods," Treher adds.[18]

Once the firm has an understanding of its internal supply chain, it can begin to assess the level of information access across functional boundaries. Does the firm have a single company-wide ERP system linking the functional areas? Are all of the firm's **legacy systems** linked to its ERP system? How easy is it to extract the information needed to make effective decisions? Are centralized **data warehouses** being used to collect data from the various divisions of the firm? Firms that are successfully integrating key business processes are using global ERP systems and data warehouses to make better, informed decisions. Data warehouses store information collected from ERP and legacy systems in one location, such that users can extract information as needed, analyze it, and use it to make decisions.

A globally linked ERP system allows the firm to use a common database from which to make product, customer, and supplier decisions. Information is captured once, reducing data input errors; information is available in real time, eliminating delays throughout the organization as information is shared; and, finally, information is visible throughout the organization—all transactions taking place can be seen and accessed by everyone on the system. As the firm moves away from legacy systems and toward a fully integrated ERP system, as organization-wide cross-functional teams are created to link key processes to the supply chain strategy, and as process performance is monitored and improved, the firm will become more focused on managing the key supply chain processes in an integrated fashion.

Develop Supply Chain Performance Measures for the Key Processes

As described earlier for internal performance measures, the firm should also develop external performance measures to monitor the links with trading partners regarding the key supply chain processes. And, as with the creation of internal performance measures, teams composed of members from primary trading partners should be created to design these measures to be consistent with overall supply chain strategies.

Continuing with the low-cost supply chain strategy example, trading partners should monitor a number of cost-oriented measures that are averaged across the member firms for each of the key supply chain processes. For the customer relationship management process, examples might include the average delivery cost, rush order cost, VMI carrying cost, finished-goods safety stock costs, returned order costs, and spoilage costs. Inbound and outbound logistics costs, in particular, have come under much greater scrutiny over the past few years, due to the rising cost of fuel. From 2005 to 2010, for example, gasoline prices increased by more than 50 percent in the U.S.[19] Fuel prices have thus placed increased pressure on trading partners to find cheaper ways to transport goods in a timely fashion, and this can be particularly problematic for supply chains following a low-cost strategy. External performance measures should align with internal performance measures, but may vary based on purchasing, production, distribution, customer service, and other variations across the participating firms. The topic of external performance measures is discussed further in Chapter 14.

Assess and Improve External Process Integration and Supply Chain Performance

Over time, firms eliminate poor-performing suppliers as well as unprofitable customers while concentrating efforts on developing beneficial relationships and strategic alliances with their remaining suppliers and customers. Building, maintaining, and strengthening these relationships is accomplished through use of external process integration. As process integration improves among supply chain partners, so too does supply chain performance. When firms have achieved a reasonably good measure of internal process integration, they are ready to move on to externally integrating key supply chain processes with trading partners.

Trading partners must be willing to share sales and forecast information, along with information on new products, expansion plans, new processes, and new marketing campaigns in order to ultimately satisfy end customers and maximize profits for all supply chain members. As with internal process integration, the teams formed to design and organize process performance measures should be viewed as a key resource for external process integration. These teams can set and revise supply chain process objectives, and the type of information that must be shared to achieve the objectives. Once the performance metrics are designed for each of the processes, they can be monitored to identify lack of process integration and supply chain competitive weaknesses. Firms should thus periodically communicate their levels of process performance and integration and collaborate on methods to improve both.

Once again, the way information is communicated plays an extremely important role in external process integration. Today, connecting buyers and suppliers via the Internet is the way supply chains are becoming integrated. More generally termed **knowledge management solutions**, Internet applications tied to desktop applications enable real-time collaboration and flow of information between supply chain partners, the ability to "see" into suppliers' and customers' operations, faster decision making, and the collection of supply chain performance metrics. The nearby SCM Profile describes GE's knowledge management initiative.

Supply chain communication and technologies must deal with handling the flows of goods and information between companies, negotiating and executing contracts, managing supply and demand problems, making and executing orders, and handling financial settlements, all with a high level of security. California-based home textile retailer Anna's Linens uses an Internet portal solution to communicate with over 100 of its key vendors and distributors. The system has enabled Anna's to make opportunistic purchases from other retail closures and immediately interpret global trends using real-time visibility within its supply chain.[21]

SCM Profile

GE's Knowledge Management Initiative

General Electric's knowledge management initiative, Access GE, encompasses all the "know how" that resides across its seven industrial segments. GE content includes perspectives, best practices, and papers from top industry partners.

Access GE began as a pilot in 2012 and grew to encompass the entire global GE network. Extending access to this network beyond employees, to all current customers, has increased the engagement of GE staff with customers around topics of interest to the customer. Think of it as a private social network designed to help customers face today's business challenges. There is even a mobile Access GE app so that users are never without access to video interviews, e-learning modules, economic analyses, or expert guidance.

Access GE uses a sponsor to validate categories of expertise, then identifies and connects additional experts to develop the content, and institutionalize the initiative. One or two champions are designated for each subdomain. Experts deliver their expertise through engagements or events. Initially, there may be only two to three experts per category, but the number can grow, depending upon customer demand.

The Access GE search functionalities present big picture concepts into which the user can drill down to find precisely the concept and document, person, or discussion that will answer the question at hand. The categories target almost every business issue to be encountered by any industry or size of organization. Connecting with colleagues to exchange ideas and insights is one of the reasons employees and customers turn to Access GE, selecting cohorts and communities based on an industry, an area of interest, or a particular business issue.[20]

Extend Process Integration to Second-Tier Supply Chain Partners

As supply chain relationships become more trusting and mature, and as the supply chain software used to link supply chain partners' information systems evolves and becomes more widely used and relied upon, the tendency will be to integrate processes to second-tier partners and beyond. Today, supply chain software suppliers are developing systems that integrate more easily with other applications, allowing trading partners to exchange ever more complex or detailed information on contracts, product designs, forecasts, sales, purchases, and inventories. Using these linkages, companies can, in real time, work with suppliers and customers to compare design ideas, forecasts, and order commitments; determine supply/demand mismatches; and analyze supplier performance.

Every major software developer today is trying to make its supply chain applications easier to integrate with existing systems and gather data anywhere along a firm's supply chain. One development is the **radio-frequency identification tag (RFID)**, discussed in Chapters 7 and 9. These microchip devices can be attached to pallets or cases to relay information on the products' whereabouts as they move through the supply chain. Thus, a firm's supply chain system can access real-time inventory information and instigate a replenishment order as inventories are drawn down.

The prices of RFID tags vary greatly depending on whether they are *active* or *passive*. **Passive RFID tags** don't contain a power source, require power from a tag reader, and cost from \$0.05 to \$1.00 each, depending on purchase volume, packaging, and how the tag is made. **Active RFID tags** draw power from an internal battery and are priced in the \$20 to \$70 range depending on the volume required and battery type. Both are finding applications. The passive variety are placed on pallets, cases, and even units of product and are used in many retail and warehousing environments. In fact, a 2011 study of fifty-eight suppliers and fifty-six retailers across North America, conducted by Accenture, reports that RFID technology is at a "tipping point" with more than 50 percent of the companies piloting or implementing item-level RFID within their organizations.[22]

The much more costly active tags are being used, for example, to track the whereabouts of expensive equipment in a hospital or for identification of fleet vehicles and shipping containers in and out of a facility. The U.S. Marines also use active tags to track container loads on international shipments. The Marines' vision is to have tags talk directly to logistics databases via network access points that will then communicate information to other locations via satellite.[23]

Prior to the development of these supply chain applications, integrating processes beyond first-tier suppliers and customers was somewhat more difficult and time-consuming. As discussed in Chapter 4, firms can develop relationships with their second-tier suppliers and then insist that their direct suppliers use these suppliers. They can also work closely with their key direct suppliers to solve second-tier supplier problems and help them, in turn, to better manage *their* direct suppliers. To stay on the competitive edge, firms today must use a combination of information system linkages and old-fashioned customer and supplier teamwork to identify and manage second-tier relationships along the supply chain.

Reevaluate the Integration Model Annually

In light of the dramatic and fast-paced changes occurring with the development of supply chain communication technologies and the frequent changes occurring with new products, new suppliers, and new markets, trading partners should revisit their integration model annually to identify changes within their supply chains and to assess the impact these changes are having on integration efforts. New suppliers may have entered the scene with better capabilities, more distribution choices, and better resources. Or perhaps the firm may be redesigning an older product, requiring different purchased components or supplier capabilities. Alternatively, the firm may be moving into a new foreign market, potentially requiring entirely different supply chains. These examples are common and should cause firms to reevaluate their supply chain strategies, objectives, processes, performance measures, and integration levels. Computer maker Dell, for example, is switching to use of additional ocean shipping in its supply chains to reduce logistics costs. Currently, Dell's highly regarded supply chain strategy has been to use costly air shipments to enable deliveries of customized computers within days of customer orders. It is shifting now to greater use of retail distribution, requiring more of a forecasting and make-to-stock supply chain, which ultimately will dramatically change its supply chain network and logistics partners. "We will limit the number of configuration choices where appropriate and move more of our products to a low-touch, fixed-configuration [ocean] ship model," explains Dell CFO Brian Gladden.[24]

OBSTACLES TO PROCESS INTEGRATION ALONG THE SUPPLY CHAIN

A number of factors can impede external process integration along the supply chain, causing loss of visibility, information distortion, longer cycle times, stockouts, and the bullwhip effect, resulting in higher overall costs and reduced customer service capabilities. Managers must try to identify these obstacles and take steps to eliminate them to improve profitability and competitiveness for a supply chain's members. Table 13.2 summarizes these obstacles. Each of these is discussed next.

The Silo Mentality

Too often, firms do not consider the impact of their actions on their supply chains and long-term competitiveness and profitability. An "I win, you lose" **silo mentality** can be evidenced when using the cheapest (or hungriest) suppliers, paying little attention to the needs of customers, and assigning few resources to new goods and services designs. Particularly with firms involved in global supply chains, silo mentalities can crop up as a result of cultural differences. The U.K. auto firm Rover is a case in point. In the 1980s, Rover formed a partnership with Japan-based Honda to provide products for its new model program. The arrogance of Rover managers and a lack of a learning culture at Rover prevented it from realizing any benefits from the partnership. Later, when the German firm BMW bought Rover, communications with German managers and political infighting was even worse. The managerial problems that surfaced when Chrysler and Daimler-Benz got together, leading to dissolution of that partnership, were similar.[25]

Eventually, lack of internal or external collaboration will create quality, cost, delivery timing, and other customer service problems that are detrimental to supply chains. In fact, Mr. Wayne Bourne, vice president of logistics and transportation at electronics retailer Best Buy, noted in an interview that the most significant obstacle to overcome in supply chain management was the silo mentality that exists in companies.[26]

Internally, the silo effect might be found between personnel of different departments. The transportation manager, for instance, may be trying to minimize total annual

Table 13.2 Obstacles to Supply Chain Integration

Silo mentality	Failing to see the big picture, and acting only in regard to a single department within a firm or a single firm within a supply chain.
Lack of supply chain visibility	The inability to easily share or retrieve trading partner information in real time, as desired by supply chain participants.
Lack of trust	Unwillingness to work together or share information because of the fear that the other party will take advantage of them or use the information unethically.
Lack of knowledge	Lack of process and information system skills and lack of knowledge regarding the benefits of SCM among management and other employees, within the firm and among partners.
Activities causing the bullwhip effect:	
Demand forecast updating	Using varying customer orders to create and update forecasts, production schedules, and purchase requirements.
Order batching	Making large orders for goods from suppliers on an infrequent basis to reduce order and transportation costs.
Price fluctuations	Offering price discounts to customers, causing erratic buying patterns.
Rationing and shortage gaming	Allocating short product supplies to customers, causing them to increase future orders beyond what they really need.

transportation costs against the wishes of the firm's sales manager. Delivery inconsistencies caused by use of the cheapest transportation providers might be deteriorating customer satisfaction and leading to a loss of customers.

To overcome these and other silo mentalities, firms must strive to align supply chain goals and their own goals and incentives. Functional decisions must be made while considering the impact on the firm's overall profits and those of the supply chain members. Performance reviews of managers should include the ability of their department to integrate processes internally and externally and meet overall supply chain goals. Outside the firm, managers must work to educate suppliers and customers regarding the overall impact of their actions on their supply chains and the end customers. This should be an important part of the supply chain partnership creation and management process. Additionally, suppliers should be annually evaluated and potentially replaced if their performance vis-à-vis supply chain objectives does not improve. California-based Sutter Health, a network of physicians, hospitals, and other healthcare providers, has long believed integration among all departments is the best and most efficient way to deliver care to patients. In fact, in a study by Dartmouth Medical School's Center for the Evaluative Clinical Sciences, Sutter's hospitals, physicians, home care, and hospice services were found to represent a national benchmark.[27]

Lack of Supply Chain Visibility

Lack of **information visibility** along a supply chain is also cited as a common process integration problem. In global supply chains, information visibility is particularly important. Product safety standards, trade agreements, and security requirements are changing almost daily, making information visibility critical for importers, shippers, and logistics providers. If trading partners have to carve out data from their information systems and then send it to one another where it then has to be uploaded to other systems prior to the data being shared and evaluated, the extra time can mean higher inventories, higher costs, longer response times, and lost customers. "Visibility is not just about watching stuff happen," says Melissa Irmen, vice president of products and strategy for North Carolina–based Integration Point, a provider of global trade solutions. "Things are changing so fast, and to have connectivity to all partners is just critical."[28]

Today, connectivity and visibility are becoming much easier with the use of **cloud-based communication platforms**. Cloud systems provide greater visibility, ensure faster time to market, and offer faster response to changing market dynamics and demands. Another key benefit to use of cloud-based communications is speed. Customers and suppliers can be up and running in minutes to days, not months to years. Del Monte Foods, one of the largest producers, distributors, and marketers of branded food and pet products for the U.S. retail market, has enhanced its global supply chain operating platform by using a cloud-based service. Del Monte has automated its inventory and document management processes with its international suppliers using a cloud-based system hosted by GT Nexus.[29]

As businesses expand their supply chains to accommodate foreign suppliers and markets, and as outsourcing of manufacturing and logistics services continues, the need to use systems that provide real-time information to trading partners increases. "It's not good enough to just take the order," says Beth Enslow of Massachusetts-based research company Aberdeen Group. "Now you have to provide a continuous stream of information about its status, feasibility, and total cost to customers and partners throughout the world. You don't want customers receiving unexpected transportation expenses or delays in shipments—or worse, receiving them without you knowing about it."[30]

RFID tags, as mentioned earlier, can be used to improve information visibility in supply chains. With the right equipment, users can determine the exact location of any product, anywhere in a supply chain, at any time. An RFID tag attached to an automobile seat or engine, for example, can be used to gather and exchange work-in-process data. Or, when a shipment of flowers drops below a safe temperature, an RFID system can alert packers to pull those cartons and send them to a closer destination. When a thief tries to break into a shipping container, an RFID-controlled monitor can send an alert to company representatives. These are all applications of RFID technology. "When you have bad data, you make bad decisions," says Kaushal Vyas, director of product development at Georgia-based Infor, a business software provider. "You must be able to source and mine data from all the different places in real time, so you can focus on the exceptions that you need to manage in order to boost your performance."[31]

Lack of Trust

Successful process integration between trading partners requires trust, and as with the silo mentality and lack of information visibility, the lack of trust is seen as a major stumbling block to process integration in supply chains. Trust develops over time between trading partners, as each organization follows through on promises made to the other firms. Even though this sounds cliché, relationships employing trust result in a win-win or win-win-win situation for the participants.

Unfortunately, old-fashioned company practices and purchasing habits don't change overnight. Until managers understand that it is in their firms' best interests to trust each other and collaborate, supply chain management will be an uphill battle. Organizations such as the medical treatment innovator Mayo Clinic build a collaborative culture by hiring professionals with collaborative attitudes and a common set of deeply held values regarding care for patients. At computing giant IBM, CEO Sam Palmisano transformed an extremely hierarchical culture based on individualism to one of collaboration by organizing online, town hall-type meetings involving tens of thousands of IBM employees and dozens of trading partners. Collaborative projects resulted from these meetings. IBM reinforced collaboration with "thanks awards," which are T-shirts, backpacks, and other similar gear emblazoned with the IBM logo and given by IBM employees.[32]

While reciprocal sharing of information among supply chain partners is growing in acceptance, many companies still have a long way to go. "We are early in the cycle, maybe in the second inning," says David Smith, head of human performance practice at Accenture, a global technology services consulting firm. "Companies are beginning to attack it. Very few are getting it right."[33]

Some useful advice for creating collaboration and trust is summed up nicely in an article appearing in *CIO* magazine, a business journal for IT and other business executives. They recommended six ways of "getting to yes:"[34]

1. *Start small*—Begin by collaborating on a small scale. Pick a project that is likely to provide a quick return on investment for both sides. Once you can show the benefits of trust and collaboration, then move to larger projects.
2. *Look inward*—The necessary precondition for establishing trust with outside partners is establishing trust with internal constituents. Break down the barriers to internal communication and integration.
3. *Gather 'round*—The best way to build trust is to meet face-to-face, around a table. Listen to objections, find out the agendas, and spring for lunch. Then do it all over again as people leave and as management changes.
4. *Go for the win-win*—Collaboration is a new way of doing business where the biggest companies don't bully their partners, but instead help create an environment that optimizes business for all supply chain members.
5. *Don't give away the store*—No one has to share all of their information. Some information should remain proprietary. The simple exchange of demand, purchase, and forecast information goes a long way.
6. *Just do it*—One of the best ways to build trust is to simply start sharing information. If all goes well, success breeds trust, allowing partners to progress to bigger things.

Lack of Knowledge

Companies have been slowly moving toward collaboration and process integration for years, and it is just within the past few years that technology has caught up with this vision, enabling process integration across extended supply chains. Getting a network of firms and their employees to work together successfully, though, requires managers to use subtle persuasion and education to get their own firms and their trading partners to do the right things. The cultural, trust, and process knowledge differences in firms are such that firms successfully managing their supply chains must spend significant time influencing and increasing the capabilities of their own employees as well as those of their trading partners.

Training of supply chain partner employees is also known as **collaborative education** and can result in more successful supply chains and higher partner returns. As technologies change, as outsourcing increases, and as supply chains are expanded to foreign sources and markets, the pressure to extend software and management training to trading partners increases. As Rick Behrens, senior manager of supplier development at Boeing Company's Integrated Defense Systems unit, explains, "We look at our suppliers as an extension of Boeing. So since we invest heavily in training and education of our employees, why wouldn't we invest in education and development for our suppliers?" Farm and construction equipment manufacturer John Deere, for example, has established a global learning and development center specifically for training its key suppliers.[35]

Change and information sharing can be threatening to people; they may fear losing control or losing their job, particularly if outsourcing accompanies process integration. Additionally, as firms construct their supply chain information infrastructure, they may find themselves with multiple ERP systems with various software applications that all need to be integrated both internally and externally. Thus, firms must realize that people using the systems should be involved early on in terms of the purchase decision, the implementation process, and training.

For all organizations, successful supply chain management requires a regimen of ongoing training. When education and training are curtailed, innovation cannot occur, and innovation fuels supply chain competitiveness. Poor decision making and other human errors can have a rippling effect in supply chains, causing loss of confidence and trust, and a magnification of the error and correction cost as it moves through the supply chain. Industry trade shows, conferences, and expos such as the Sensors Expo and Conference, the Annual Institute for Supply Management Conference, or the GSI Connect Conference can also be valuable sources of learning, exchanging ideas, and gathering new information about supply chain management.[36]

Activities Causing the Bullwhip Effect

As discussed in Chapter 1 of this textbook, the **bullwhip effect** can be a pervasive and expensive problem along supply chains and is caused by a number of factors that supply chain members can control. Recall that even though end item demand may be relatively constant, forecasts of trading partner demand, additions of safety stock, and the corresponding orders to suppliers as they are traced back up the supply chain can become amplified, causing what is termed the bullwhip effect. These amplified demand levels cause problems with capacity planning, inventory control, and workforce and production scheduling, and ultimately result in lower levels of customer service, greater overall levels of safety stock, and higher total supply chain costs. In an early publication on the bullwhip effect, Dr. Hau Lee and his associates identified four major causes of the bullwhip effect. More recently, Dr. Lee commented that the economic downturn a few years ago caused a number of bullwhips to again emerge, but that firms could still "tame the bullwhip" with hard work, understanding the causes of demand, gaining visibility, and investing in collaboration with partners.[37] The causes of the bullwhip effect and the methods used to counteract it are discussed below.

Demand Forecast Updating

Whenever a buying firm places a purchase order, its supplier uses that information as a predictor of future demand. Based on this information, suppliers update their demand forecasts, which then impact orders placed with their own suppliers. If lead times grow between orders placed and deliveries, then safety stocks also grow and impact purchase orders as well, which adds to the bullwhip effect. Thus, fluctuations are magnified as orders vary from period to period, and as the review periods change, causing frequent **demand forecast updating**. These are major contributors to the bullwhip effect.

One solution to this problem is for the buyer to make its actual demand data available to its suppliers. (Recall from Chapter 5 that this activity is part of collaborative planning, forecasting, and replenishment.) Better yet, if all point-of-sale data is made available to

SCM Profile — When Walmart Began Sharing Data with Suppliers

In the late 1980s, Mike Graen of Procter & Gamble moved to Arkansas to work on P&G's Walmart team. At that time, Walmart was P&G's fifth largest customer, and data sharing and collaboration between suppliers and retailers was in its infancy. Graen was charged with improving the economics between the two companies using information technology. According to Graen, "Within the first eight months, we made a $50 million swing in profitability."

Before this change, the only thing that P&G knew about Walmart's demand was that another order for a truckload of stuff had arrived. This new level of data sharing and collaboration allowed Graen to see, for the first time, inventory levels, store-level sales data, and everything from when P&G shipped an item to Walmart to when it was sold at their registers.

The legendary story of how Walmart profited from data sharing and how it improved the bullwhip effect through better forecasting and inventory management is well understood; however, it has not been replicated to the same level by other retailers to date. The information sharing had a network effect, as Walmart expanded its data sharing from P&G to every supplier that also wanted in.

The benefits of sharing information were improved forecasting and a reduced bullwhip effect, creating more efficient supply chain networks, and improved merchandizing. Sharing data also made Walmart the place where suppliers competed to innovate. Other retailers are just now beginning to share information and this is the future of success in retail—innovation and collaboration, not one-sided negotiations. Any retailer can hire great negotiators, but creating a culture of innovation and collaboration requires strategic thinking and analytical capabilities.[38]

the upstream tiers of suppliers, all supply chain members can then update their demand forecasts less frequently, using actual demand data. This real demand information also tends to reduce safety stocks among supply chain members, generating even less variability in supply chain orders. Thus, the importance of supply chain information visibility can again be seen.

Using the same forecasting techniques and buying practices also tends to smooth demand variabilities among supply chain members. In many cases, buyers allow some of their suppliers to observe actual demand, create a forecast, and determine their resupply schedules—a practice known as **vendor managed inventory** (discussed in Chapters 3 and 4). This practice can generally reduce inventories substantially.

Reducing the length of the supply chain can also lessen the bullwhip effect by reducing the number of occasions where forecasts are calculated and safety stocks are added. Examples of this are Drugstore.com, Amazon.com, and other firms that bypass distributors and resellers and sell directly to consumers. Firms can thus see actual end-customer demand, resulting in much more stable and accurate forecasts.

Finally, reducing the lead times from order to delivery will lessen the bullwhip effect. For example, developing just-in-time ordering and delivery capabilities results in smaller, more frequent orders being placed and delivered, which more closely matches supply to demand patterns, thus decreasing the need for safety stocks. The nearby SCM Profile describes Walmart's first use of data sharing with suppliers to reduce the bullwhip effect.

Order Batching

In a typical buyer–supplier scenario, demand draws down existing inventories until a reorder point is reached wherein the buyer places an order with the supplier. Inventory levels, prior delivery performance, and the desire to order full truckloads or container loads of materials may cause orders to be placed at varying time intervals. Thus, the supplier receives an order of some magnitude; then at some indeterminate future time period, another order is received from the buyer, for some quantity potentially much different in size from the prior order. This causes the supplier to hold extra safety stock. Thus, **order batching** tends to amplify demand variability, which creates greater use of safety stock, causing the bullwhip effect.

Another type of order batching can occur when salespeople need to fill end-of-quarter or end-of-year sales quotas, or when buyers desire to fully spend budget allocations at the end of their fiscal year. Generate production orders to meet sales quotas and making excess purchases to spend budget money causes erratic surges in consumption and production, again creating the bullwhip effect. If the timing of these surges is the same for many of the firm's customers, the resulting bullwhip effect can be severe.

As with forecast updating, more information visibility and frequent and smaller order sizes will reduce the order batching problem. When suppliers know that large orders are occurring because of the need to spend budgeted monies, for instance, they will not revise forecasts based on this information. Further, when using automated or computer-assisted order systems, order costs are reduced, allowing firms to order more frequently. To counteract the need to order full truckloads or container loads of an item, firms can order smaller quantities of a variety of items from a supplier, or use a freight forwarder to consolidate small shipments, to avoid the high unit cost of transporting at less-than-truckload or less-than-container load quantities.

Price Fluctuations

When suppliers offer special promotions, quantity discounts or other special discounts, these pricing fluctuations result in significant **forward buying** activities on the part of buyers, who "stock up" to take advantage of the low price offers. Forward buying can occur between retailers and consumers, between distributors and retailers, and between manufacturers and distributors due to pricing promotions at each stage in a supply chain, all contributing to erratic buying patterns, lower forecast accuracies, and consequently the bullwhip effect. If these pricing promotions become commonplace, customers will stop buying when prices are undiscounted and buy only when the discount prices are offered, even further contributing to the bullwhip effect. To deal with these surges in demand, manufacturers may have to vary capacity by scheduling overtime and undertime for employees, finding places to store stockpiles of inventory, paying more for transportation, and dealing with higher levels of inventory shrinkage as inventories are held for longer periods.

The obvious way to reduce the problems caused by fluctuating prices is to eliminate price discounting among a supply chain's members. Manufacturers can reduce forward buying by offering uniform wholesale prices to their customers. Many retailers have adopted this notion, termed **everyday low pricing** (EDLP), while eliminating promotions that cause forward buying. Similarly, buyers can negotiate with their own suppliers to offer EDLP. ASDA, a fast-growing grocery retailer in the U.K., for example, used an EDLP strategy to overtake competitor Sainsbury a few years ago, then went back to using promotions in an effort to further beef up its sales. That strategy failed and sent ASDA's sales into a slide. Its new CEO, Andy Clarke, said ASDA's loss of focus on EDLP was to blame and promised a return to that strategy.[39]

Rationing and Shortage Gaming

Rationing can occur when demand exceeds a supplier's finished goods available—in other words, the supplier might allocate units of product in proportion to what buyers ordered. Thus, if the supply on-hand is 75 percent of total demand, buyers would be allocated 75 percent of what they ordered. When buyers figure out the relationship between their orders and what is supplied, they inflate their orders to satisfy their real needs. This strategy is known as **shortage gaming**. Of course, this further exacerbates the supply problem, as the supplier and, in turn, its suppliers, struggle to keep up with these higher demand levels. When, on the other hand, production capacity eventually equals demand and orders are filled completely, orders suddenly drop to less than normal levels as the buying firms try to unload their excess inventories. This has occurred occasionally in the U.S. and elsewhere around the world—for instance, with gasoline supply shortages, and in 2012 with Hostess Twinkies. As soon as consumers think a gasoline shortage is looming, demand suddenly increases as people top off their tanks and otherwise try to stockpile gasoline, which itself creates a deeper shortage. In December 2012, when Hostess Brands entered Chapter 7 liquidation, it set off a period of mass panic as fans of Twinkies, Ding Dongs, and other Hostess baked goods flew off shelves.[40] When these types of shortages occur due to shortage gaming, suppliers can no longer discern their customers' true demand, and this can result in unnecessary additions to production capacity, warehouse space, and transportation costs.

One way to eliminate shortage gaming is for sellers to allocate short supplies based on the demand histories of their customers. In that way, customers are essentially not allowed to exaggerate orders. And once again, the sharing of capacity and inventory information between a manufacturer and its customers can also help to eliminate customers' fears regarding shortages and eliminate gaming. Also, sharing future order plans with suppliers allows suppliers to increase capacity if needed, thus avoiding a rationing situation.

Thus, it is seen that a number of decisions on the part of buyers and suppliers can cause the bullwhip effect in supply chains. When trading partners use the strategies discussed above to reduce the bullwhip effect, the growth of information sharing, collaboration, and process integration occurs along supply chains. Firms that strive to share data, forecasts, plans, and other information can significantly reduce the bullwhip effect.

MANAGING SUPPLY CHAIN RISK AND SECURITY

As supply chains grow to include more foreign suppliers and customers, there is a corresponding growth in supply chain disruptions caused by weather and traffic delays, infrastructural problems, political problems, and fears of, or actual, unlawful or terrorist-related activities. For example, in just the last few years there have been political upheavals and riots in Thailand and the Ukraine, terrorist concerns at the Sochi Winter Olympics, the cyber attack on the nonprofit Spamhaus, typhoon Haiyan in the Philippines, floods in India, the Sichuan earthquake in China, and numerous commercial airline crashes and suicide bombings. Besides the obvious impact on life and limb, these events add elements of financial, reputation, and customer service risk to global supply chains and the need for enhanced planning, change management, and security to mitigate that risk.

So, while lengthening supply chains may have resulted in cheaper labor and material costs, better product quality, and greater market coverage, it has also resulted in higher security costs and greater levels of risk, potentially leading to deteriorating profits and customer service levels. Managing risk and security along the supply chain is discussed in detail below.

Managing Supply Chain Risk

In a study commissioned by Rhode Island–based commercial insurer Factory Mutual Insurance Co., the three biggest threats facing companies, according to 500 North American and European company executives, were competition, supply chain disruptions, and property-related risks.[41] In another study by global management consulting company Accenture, 73 percent of the responding companies had experienced supply chain disruptions within the past five years, and over half had said the impact on customers was moderate to significant. These and other studies point to the fact that as more and more firms penetrate new and emerging markets, supply chain risk is increasing.

As the global economy continues to emerge from the 2008 recession, risk management appears to be an even greater concern than ever before. Information technology advances, for example, have made cyber attacks more and more common. "Obviously hackers and intruders can also affect the availability of a system, and that can come from any angle," says Thomas Srail, senior vice president at FINEX North America, a risk advisement service. Linda Conrad, director of strategic business risk for Zurich Global Corporate, says the effect from attackers getting access to companies' data along their supply chains can take the form of the loss of the data itself, reputation damage, regulatory issues, and fines. Zurich's disruption database shows that 52 percent of supply chain disruptions in the past year resulted from information technology or communications outages between buyer and supplier.[42]

Tom Ridge, the former governor of Pennsylvania, former secretary of Homeland Security in the U.S. and now CEO of risk management consulting firm Ridge Global, says that supply chains need to be vetted down to the second, third, and fourth tiers. No multinational firm "can afford to let anybody in the supply chain, no matter how far removed, view risk less seriously than it does," he says. The 2010 BP oil disaster in the Gulf of Mexico is a good example. Transocean was the oil rig operator, a supplier for BP in this case. Based on the finger-pointing in this disaster, Transocean was at least partially responsible for the explosion, rig destruction, worker deaths, and oil well blowout. If communication and due diligence can break down as badly as it did between BP and one of its primary direct suppliers, consider the potential financial, reputation, and customer service risks posed by the many second- and third-tier suppliers.[43]

A number of steps have been suggested for managing supply chain risk, and several good examples exist that highlight successful supply chain risk management. Table 13.3 describes these risk management activities, and they are discussed next.

Increase Safety Stocks and Forward Buying

If the firm fears a supply disruption, it may choose to carry some level of safety stock to provide the desired product until a suitable substitute supply source can be found. If the purchased item is readily available from other sources, the desired level of safety stock may be relatively small. On the other hand, if the item is scarce, if the supply disruption is likely to be lengthy, or if the firm fears a continued and lengthy price increase, it may decide to

Table 13.3 Activities Used to Manage Supply Chain Risk[44]

RISK MANAGEMENT ACTIVITY	DESCRIPTION
Increase safety stocks and forward buying	Can be costly. A stopgap alternative.
Identify backup suppliers and logistics services	Can create ill will with current partners; requires additional time and relationship building.
Diversify the supply base	Use of suppliers from geographically dispersed markets to minimize the impacts of disruptions.
Utilize a supply chain IT system	Collection and sharing of appropriate information with supply chain partners.
Develop a formal risk management program	Identifies potential disruptions and the appropriate response.

purchase large quantities of product, also known as **stockpiling** or **forward buying**. Safety stocks and forward buying should only be viewed as temporary solutions since they can dramatically increase inventory carrying costs, particularly for firms with large numbers of purchased items.

In some cases, though, stockpiling may be viewed as the only short-term solution for managing risk. In 2006, many organizations opted to stockpile the influenza drug Tamiflu to prepare for a potential avian influenza pandemic, since shortages of the drug worldwide had already been experienced. In the U.S., for example, 300 firms along with the government itself had already been engaged in significant stockpiling by the summer of 2006. Since then, supplies of antiviral drugs have increased, and the practice of stockpiling has decreased.[45]

Identify Backup Suppliers and Logistics Services

Another very simple strategy for guaranteeing a continuous supply of purchased items and logistics services is to identify suppliers, transportation and warehousing services, and other third-party services to use in case the preferred supplier or service becomes unavailable. This topic was discussed in relation to the use of sole or single sources in Chapter 2. The disadvantage of this strategy is that it requires additional time to find and qualify sources and to build trusting relationships. Additionally, this strategy may tend to damage existing supplier or logistics provider relationships. The backup source may see limited value in the relationship if they are providing only a small percentage of total demand; their price for the goods or services will likely be higher, and the existing firm may view the use of backup companies as a signal that their "piece of the pie" will continue to shrink. Additionally, use of multiple sources may allow proprietary designs or technologies to be copied, creating further risk.

Backup or **emergency sourcing** and multiple sourcing, though, may be a sound strategy in specific cases. During the 2002 U.S. West Coast dockworker strikes, airfreight capacity quickly ran out, causing freight rates to skyrocket and firms to be unable to quickly move freight. Companies that had already entered into contracts for emergency airfreight service, though, were able to maintain operations during the port disruptions.[46] Sainsbury's, a U.K. supermarket chain, uses multiple suppliers for the many products it buys as part of its business continuity plan, established in response to events such as the Irish Republican Army's bombing campaigns in the 1990s, the Y2K computer bug, the 2001 fuel shortage, and the foot-and-mouth cattle disease outbreaks in the U.K. Additionally, Sainsbury's works closely with key suppliers to ensure that they, too, have business continuity plans.[47]

Diversify the Supply Base

Madagascar, one-time provider of half of the world's vanilla supply, saw Cyclone Hudah destroy 30 percent of its vanilla bean vines in 2000. Additionally, a political problem in Madagascar caused its primary port to be closed for many weeks in 2002. These two events caused vanilla prices to skyrocket for an extended period of time until growers in Madagascar and other countries could increase their production. Buyers with vanilla supply contracts in multiple countries were able to avoid some of this pricing problem. Eventually, the market for vanilla became more diversified, creating a situation whereby vanilla buyers today have vanilla sources outside of Madagascar.[48] The supply of liquid natural gas, LNG, is at risk, since much of the supply of LNG comes from production plants in Arabian Gulf countries and Russia. LNG consumers are thus busy trying to diversify their purchases of LNG from other countries such as Norway, Algeria, and Libya. Further, new plans for construction of LNG shipping and receiving facilities, additional LNG vessels, and LNG regasification facilities will eventually allow for diversification of LNG supply and transportation services.[49] An earthquake and tsunami in Japan in 2011 halted automobile and parts production at a number of the country's manufacturing plants. In India, for example, Suzuki and Honda production and retail facilities had to cease operations for a time, since their parent companies and parts suppliers sustained damage from the tsunami.[50]

In all of the examples above, concentrating purchases with one supplier was seen as increasing supply risk, while purchasing the same or similar products from geographically dispersed suppliers could have the effect of spreading and hence reducing the risk of supply disruptions from political upheavals, weather-related disasters, and other widespread supply problems. Buyers, though, must also consider the impact of a geographically dispersed supply base on other supply chain risks. While potentially reducing the risk associated with geographic supply disruptions, the use of suppliers in multiple countries exposes buyers to additional political, customs clearance, exchange rate, and security risks.

Utilize a Supply Chain IT System

Chapter 6 discussed the importance of supply chain communication and information systems. As firms geographically expand their supply chains, they find customs clearance requirements and paperwork becoming increasingly complicated. Complying with these regulations requires information and data visibility among supply chain participants and involvement by all key supply chain partners. Accurate data transmissions, as discussed in Chapter 6, can also aid in the reduction of stockouts and the bullwhip effect caused by forecasting and order inaccuracies and late deliveries, which also pose significant risk and cost to supply chains.

Information systems should be designed to help mitigate supply chain risk. As stated by Julian Thomas, head of the supply chain advisory department at global auditing and advisory firm KPMG, "Risk should be on the agenda and as you build your systems, you need to put in place systems to monitor and evaluate risk continuously."[51] Farm and ranch equipment retailer Tractor Supply, headquartered in Tennessee, is a good example of a firm making use of information technologies to support flexible and quick decision making to reduce risk. For example, they use an on-demand transportation management system (TMS), an ERP system, and a voice-picking solution for their distribution centers. "In 2005, transportation capacity was really tight after Hurricane Katrina hit, but the way our TMS is configured we have the ability to escalate carrier service from low-cost to high-cost providers and sometimes when all the carriers in a market were taken, we had to take carriers in from another market," says Mike Graham, vice president of logistics at Tractor Supply. "We also have the flexibility within our DC network to react quickly if there is an event and move stores from one DC to another."[52]

Develop a Formal Risk Management Program

By far the most proactive risk management activity is to create a formal risk management plan encompassing the firm and its supply chain participants. Risk management should become an executive-level priority. Potential risks should be identified and prioritized, and appropriate responses should be designed that will minimize disruptions to supply chains. Additionally, mechanisms should be developed to recover quickly, efficiently, and with minimal damage to the firm's reputation and customer relationships. Finally, performance measures need to be developed to monitor the firm's ongoing risk management capabilities. "Risk happens," says Dr. Kate Vitasek, supply chain faculty member at the University of Tennessee. "Plan for it. Collaborate with your partners in the supply chain to mitigate and eliminate it, and don't bury your head in the sand."[53]

A supply chain risk management office should be created to oversee and coordinate the firm's risk management efforts. The risk manager provides guidance and support to department managers, is the interface between the firm and its trading partner risk managers, and possesses the knowledge to adequately identify, prioritize, and provide a plan to reduce risks. In 2005, Tractor Supply, for example, developed a disaster recovery plan as part of its overall risk management strategy. One year later, its Waco, Texas, distribution center was struck by a tornado in the evening, leaving 2 to 3 inches of water standing in the facility and product scattered across the landscape for miles. By the time logistics VP Mike Graham made it to his office the next day, plans were already in place to repair the damage, and within several hours all of the customers served by the Waco distribution center were linked to other facilities. "We did not miss a delivery the following week and May is actually a peak season for us," said Mr. Graham.[54]

Richard Sharman, a partner in KPMG's risk advisory services group, offers his advice for developing risk management plans—"Companies almost need to ask themselves the stupid questions to think about the full spectrum of business risks, and how they would manage them," he says. Another consideration is to know who the firm is doing business with, to assure they are using an appropriate labor force, complying with product safety guidelines, and generally using practices that fit with the firm's reputation. "Know your partner. There is no substitute for that," says Brian Joseph, partner at global business consultant PricewaterhouseCoopers.[55] When outsourcing to firms in foreign locales, it is also necessary to have adequate quality controls in place, and require suppliers to report periodically to the firm to ensure their products meet design requirements.

Managing Supply Chain Security

As supply chains become more global and technologically complex, so does the need to secure them. **Supply chain security management** is concerned with reducing the risk and impacts of intentionally created disruptions in supply chain operations including product and information theft and activities seeking to endanger personnel or sabotage supply chain infrastructure. The crash of Pan Am Flight 103 in Lockerbie, Scotland, in 1988 not only tragically illustrated the weaknesses of airline security systems at the time, but it also exposed the dependency of entire supply chains on each member's security capabilities. Pan Am's security processes did not fail in permitting a bomb onto Flight 103—it

Table 13.4 Supply Chain Security System Response[58]	
LEVEL OF SECURITY SYSTEM RESPONSE	DESCRIPTION
Basic initiatives	Physical security measures; personnel security; standard risk assessment; basic computing security; continuity plan; freight protection.
Reactive initiatives	Larger security organization; C-TPAT compliance; supply base analysis; supply continuity plan; limited training.
Proactive initiatives	Director of security; personnel with military or gov't. experience; formal security risk assessment; advanced computing security; participation in security groups.
Advanced initiatives	Customer/supplier collaboration; learning from the past; formal security strategy; supply chain drills, simulations, exercises; emergency control center.

was actually Malta's Luqa Airport's security system that allowed the luggage carrying the bomb into the baggage handling system that eventually led to the luggage being flown on an aircraft to London where it was placed aboard Flight 103.[56] In the U.S., the attacks of September 11, 2001, were a wakeup call to many businesses to begin assessing their needs for supply chain security systems. Prior to that time, most executives were aware that their operations might be vulnerable to security problems; however, most firms (as well as governments) chose to put off improving security practices.

The notion that a supply chain is only as secure as its weakest link is illustrated in the Pan Am example above. It is therefore necessary today for firms to manage not only their own security but the security practices of their supply chain partners as well. Supply chain security, though, is an extremely complex problem—security activities begin at the factory where goods are packaged and loaded, and then include the logistics companies transporting goods to ports, the port terminals and customs workers, the ocean carriers, the destination ports and customs workers, additional transportation companies, distribution centers and workers, and the final delivery companies. And integrating all of these participants are various information systems that also need to be protected.

Security management collaboration should include, for example, contractual requirements for secure systems, "standards of care" for movement and storage of products as they move along the supply chain, and the use of law enforcement officials or consultants in security planning, training, and incident investigation. James G. Liddy, internationally recognized expert on security, CEO of Virginia-based security firm Liddy International and son of famous Watergate burglar and talk-show host G. Gordon Liddy, says, "Focus on what your real vulnerabilities are and have in place a safety-and-preparedness plan for all hazards. When you enhance your safety procedures and integrate them into your security you create efficiencies."[57] Table 13.4 describes four increasing levels of supply chain security system preparedness, and these are discussed below.

Basic Initiatives

At the most basic level, security systems should include procedures and policies for securing offices, manufacturing plants, warehouses, and other physical facilities and additionally should provide security for personnel, computing systems, and freight shipments. Managers should consider use of security badges and guards, conducting background checks on applicants, using antivirus software and passwords, and using shipment tracking technologies.

Today, cargo theft is one of the biggest problems facing global supply chains, and some of the basic security approaches can be used to reduce this threat. Global loss estimates are tagged at $10 billion to $30 billion per year. And technology and lack of downside risk have enabled thieves to be more sophisticated and daring than ever before. Stolen goods can be moved to a warehouse, off-loaded, repackaged, remanifested, and placed on another vehicle before the theft is even discovered and reported. The existence of online marketers and auction sites even further facilitates the movement and sale of stolen merchandise.[59] Food items are frequently being targeted by cargo thieves, according to U.S. cargo consulting firm FreightWatch. In terms of the most stolen types of products, food and beverages topped the list in 2013, with the electronics industry running a close second. One reason foodstuffs are being stolen more frequently is that they are easy to resell, especially in the case of brand-name products, and their resale value is very high, around 70 cents on the dollar.[60]

Corruption is another potential problem organizations must begin to manage. Transparency International, a global group leading the fight against corruption, annually publishes its Corruption Perceptions Index to publicize the degree of corruption existing in a number of countries. The scale ranges from 0 (highly corrupt) to 100 (no corruption). The index combines multiple surveys of public sector employees' perceptions of the level of corruption. In the 2013 ranking, the U.K., Japan, and the U.S. ranked fourteenth, eighteenth, and nineteenth, respectively. Denmark, New Zealand, and Finland were the top-rated countries, while Afghanistan, North Korea, and Somalia were at the bottom of the 177-country list.[61]

Reactive Initiatives

Reactive security initiatives represent a somewhat deeper commitment to the idea of security management compared to basic initiatives, but still lack any significant efforts to organize a cohesive and firm-wide plan for security management. Many firms in this category, for example, implemented security systems in response to the terrorist attacks of September 11, 2001. These initiatives include becoming Customs-Trade Partnership Against Terrorism (C-TPAT) compliant, assessing suppliers' security practices, developing continuity plans for various events, and implementing specific training and education programs.

C-TPAT refers to a partnership among U.S. Customs, the International Cargo Security Council (a U.S. nonprofit association of companies and individuals involved in transportation), and Pinkerton (a global security advising company, headquartered in New Jersey), whereby companies agree to improve security in their supply chain in return for "fast lane" border crossings at both the Canadian and Mexican borders. This includes conducting self-assessments of the firm's and its partner facilities and updating security policies to meet C-TPAT security requirements, and then completing a C-TPAT application. As of the end of 2013, there were about 11,000 C-TPAT-certified companies. U.S. Customs and Border Protection states that nonparticipants are about six times more likely to receive a security-related container inspection at U.S. border crossings.[62] The U.S. government is currently working with other countries to implement similar programs. A number of other government initiatives also fall into the reactive category, such as the "10+2" or Importer Security Filing rule that requires a 48-hour notice for all ocean shipping containers coming into the U.S. and the Certified Cargo Screening Program (CCSP) regarding all air cargo loaded onto planes in the U.S.—as of 2010, all air cargo originating in the U.S. must be screened the same way as passenger luggage.[63]

Proactive Initiatives

Proactive security management initiatives venture outside the firm to include suppliers and customers, and also include a more formalized approach to security management within the firm. Security activities occurring among firms in this category include the creation of an executive-level position such as director of corporate security; the hiring of former military, intelligence, or law enforcement personnel with security management experience; a formal and comprehensive approach for assessing the firm's exposure to security risks; the use of cyber-intrusion detection systems and other advanced information security practices; the development of freight security plans in collaboration with 3PLs; and the active participation of employees in industry security associations and conferences. Home Depot, for example, uses a computer risk modeling approach to assess its supply chains' vulnerabilities and design appropriate security measures. "We look at 35 global risk elements and one of those is threat of terrorism," explains Benjamin Cook, senior manager for global trade service for Home Depot. "We use that technique to help us roll out a strategy that is most appropriate to the country we are sourcing from."[64]

Massachusetts-based life insurance company MassMutual wanted to ensure the security of its IT system, spread across a dozen applications, including its website as well as the 12 million business and individual customer accounts it managed. It named a vice president of information security to direct its information security efforts, and it put in place a fifty-person security group that included an internal consulting team with specific security item experts, an engineering team that supported firewalls, a security assurance team that analyzed security monitoring devices, and a team responsible for identity management. Finally, it purchased a security management software application to help its security team quickly assess and prioritize risks. It creates an aggregate risk score for each application and system it uses to determine which risks need to be addressed first.[65]

Advanced Initiatives

Firms with advanced security management systems are recognized as industry leaders with respect to their security initiatives. Activities within this category include full collaboration with key suppliers and customers in developing quick recovery and continuity plans for supply chain disruptions, consideration of past security failures of other firms in developing a more comprehensive and effective security system, the design of a complete supply chain security management plan that is implemented by all key trading partners, the undertaking of exercises designed to train participants and test the resilience of the supply chain to security disruptions, and the use of an emergency control center to manage responses to unexpected supply chain disruptions.

Industry security leaders, such as Michigan-based Dow Chemical, see supply chain security as simply good business. As Henry Ward, director of transportation security and safety at Dow, offers, "We view security as one of the steps we take to make sure we remain a reliable supplier of goods to the marketplace." Dow's efforts to improve supply chain visibility and security led to a 50 percent improvement in the time it takes to identify and resolve trade transit problems, and a 20 percent inventory reduction at receiving terminals. Dow uses RFID and a global positioning system (GPS) to track large intermodal containers as they move from North America to Asia. Dow also sees collaboration with governments and its supply chain partners as crucial to its success. "We take an integrated approach to supply chain security, which means we look at it holistically," says Ward.[66]

As described in this final section, supply chain participants are pulled by opposing objectives—one is to reduce supply chain costs and improve freight handling speed to improve competitiveness and profits; the other is to manage the risk and cost of security breaches. Unfortunately, as supply chains venture into countries in search of cheaper suppliers and implement practices to reduce transit times, the security risks grow. Tim Manahan, a vice president at supply management software provider Procuri, admits, "Very few companies have effective supply chain security systems in place, either for monitoring security issues, or for reacting to problems." Managers and government representatives understand the problem much better, though, today than ten years ago, and hopefully, this is beginning to lead to better management of risk and security.

SUMMARY

In this chapter, the topic of integrating processes within the firm and among supply chain partners was discussed, including the steps required to achieve internal and external process integration, the advantages of doing this, and the obstacles to overcome. Process integration should be considered the primary means to achieving successful supply chain management, but it is the one thing firms struggle with most when setting out to manage their supply chains. For without the proper support, training, tools, trust, and preparedness, process integration most likely will be impossible to ever fully achieve.

The supply chain integration model provides the framework for integrating processes first within the firm and then among trading partners, and this model served as the foundation of the chapter. The role played by performance measures in assessing and improving integration was also discussed. Finally, a discussion of supply chain risk and security management outlined the need for firms and their trading partners to collaborate in developing effective strategies for assessing the risk of supply chain disruptions and implementing solutions.

KEY TERMS

active RFID tags, 472
bullwhip effect, 477
cloud-based communication platforms, 475
collaborative education, 476
customer relationship management process, 464
customer service management process, 464
data warehouses, 469
demand forecast updating, 477
demand management process, 465
emergency sourcing, 482
everyday low pricing (EDLP), 479
forward buying, 479
functional silos, 463
information visibility, 474
internal supply chains, 469
key supply chain processes, 463
key trading partners, 461
knowledge management solutions, 471
legacy systems, 469
manufacturing flow management process, 466
order batching, 479
order fulfillment process, 466
passive RFID tags, 472
process integration, 460
product development and commercialization process, 467
radio-frequency identification tag (RFID), 472
rationing, 480
returns management process, 467
shortage gaming, 480
silo mentality, 473
stockpiling, 482
supplier relationship management process, 466
supply chain security management, 484
vendor managed inventory, 478

DISCUSSION QUESTIONS

1. What does process integration mean, and why is it difficult to achieve?
2. What makes a supplier or customer a key or primary trading partner? Describe why it is important to begin supply chain management efforts with only these key companies.
3. Describe the linkage between supply chain strategies and internal functional strategies and policies.
4. How do functional silos prevent process integration?

5. What are the eight key supply chain business processes, and why are they important when managing supply chains?
6. What is the difference between the customer service management process and the customer relationship management process?
7. Do you think customer service has improved over the years for retailers? Cite some examples.
8. What sort of demand management techniques would an exclusive restaurant use when demand exceeds its capacity? What about McDonald's?
9. Is it necessary to have internal performance measures for each of the supply chain business processes? Why or why not?
10. Which should come first—internal process integration or external process integration? Why?
11. Explain the differences between process integration, coordination, and collaboration.
12. Why is an ERP system important for both internal and external process integration? What other IT considerations are there?
13. Think of some supply chain (external) performance measures for several of the eight key supply chain business processes, assuming the overall strategy is superior customer service. What if the overall strategy is sustainability?
14. What is an internal supply chain? Do some firms not have any?
15. What are knowledge management solutions, and how can they support a firm's supply chain integration efforts? Give some examples.
16. How do organizations extend process integration to second-tier suppliers and customers?
17. How can RFID tags help to enable external process integration?
18. What is the difference between active and passive RFID tags?
19. Why is lack of trust an obstacle to supply chain management? How can we overcome this obstacle?
20. Why is visibility so important when integrating processes?
21. Define the bullwhip effect and describe how it impacts supply chain integration, or how integration impacts the bullwhip effect.
22. What is cloud-based supply chain management and how might it impact process integration?
23. What is the difference between supply chain management and supply chain process integration?
24. Define the term "collaborative education" and explain what this has to do with supply chain management.
25. Describe an incidence either personally or at work where you have been involved in shortage gaming.
26. What is order batching, and is this something that will reduce the bullwhip effect? Why or why not?

27. Why should reducing the length of the supply chain also reduce the bullwhip effect?
28. What is everyday low pricing, and how does it impact the bullwhip effect?
29. Have you ever experienced rationing and/or shortage gaming? Please describe an instance.
30. What is the difference between supply chain risk management and supply chain security management? Which do you think is most important?
31. What do most small businesses do to reduce supply chain risk? Could they do something more effective?
32. In Chapters 3 and 4, it was explained how some firms were successfully single- or sole-sourcing. Doesn't this increase supply chain risk?
33. What types of supply chains are most likely to be impacted by risk and security problems? Why?
34. Which is more important—risk management or security management?
35. List some steps firms can take to reduce supply chain risk and increase security.
36. What is C-TPAT, and which companies would benefit most from using it?

ESSAY/PROJECT QUESTIONS

1. Go to the Institute for Supply Management website, www.ism.ws, and find the listing for the latest ISM Annual International Supply Management Conference. Then find the Conference Proceedings, and report on a paper that was presented regarding a topic covered in this chapter.
2. Find a company online that is successfully using external process integration and report on its experiences.
3. Find the websites of several supply chain security and risk assessment firms, and report on their specialties and management experience.
4. Search on the term "Customs-Trade Partnership Against Terrorism" or "C-TPAT," and write a paper on the history of C-TPAT and how it is being used today.
5. Search on the term "supply chain security problems," and write a report on several current problems and how they are being addressed.

ADDITIONAL RESOURCES

Chopra, S., and P. Meindl. *Supply Chain Management: Strategy, Planning, and Operation*. Upper Saddle River, NJ: Prentice Hall, 2001.

Croxton, K. L., S. J. Garcia-Dastugue, D. M. Lambert, and D. S. Rogers. "The Supply Chain Management Processes," *International Journal of Logistics Management* 12(2), 2001: 13–36.

Handfield, R. B., and E. L. Nichols. *Supply Chain Redesign: Transforming Supply Chains into Integrated Value Systems*. Upper Saddle River, NJ: Financial Times Prentice Hall, 2002.

Lambert, D. M., M. C. Cooper, and J. D. Pagh, "Supply Chain Management: Implementation Issues and Research Opportunities," *International Journal of Logistics Management* 9(2), 1998: 1–19.

Simchi-Levi, D., P. Kaminsky, and E. Simchi-Levi. *Designing and Managing the Supply Chain*. New York: McGraw-Hill/Irwin, 2003.

ENDNOTES

1. Katzel, J., "Building an Integration Strategy," *Control Engineering*, December, 2013: 1.
2. Shacklett, M., "The Intelligent Supply Chain," *World Trade* 25(10), 2012: 20–24.
3. Shacklett, M., "IBM Evolves a Globally Integrated Supply Chain," *World Trade* 25(5), 2012: 32–35.
4. Shea, M. and B. Gilleon, "The Powerful Potential of Demand Management," *Supply Chain Management Review* 15(3), 2011: 18–27.
5. Lambert, D., M. Cooper, and J. Pagh, "Supply Chain Management: Implementation Issues and Research Opportunities," *International Journal of Logistics Management* 9(2), 1998: 1–19.
6. Siu, S., "CargoSmart Ltd," *Journal of Commerce*, January 8, 2007: 1.
7. Andel, T., "General Mills Releases Its Sustainable Supply Chain Strategy," *Material Handling & Logistics* April 30, 2013: 1.
8. Anonymous, "Microsoft Corporation—Patent Issued," *Marketing Weekly News*, October 12, 2013: 465.
9. These processes are discussed in detail in Lambert, D. M., M. C. Cooper, and J. D. Pagh, "Supply Chain Management: Implementation Issues and Research Opportunities," *International Journal of Logistics Management* 9(2), 1998: 1–19; and in Croxton, K. L., S. J. Garcia-Dastugue, and D. M. Lambert, "The Supply Chain Management Processes," *International Journal of Logistics Management* 12(2), 2001: 13–36.
10. Wild, J., "EasyJet Blazes Trail on Customer Service," *FT.com*, December 23, 2013: 1.
11. Anonymous, "Report: Retailers Turning to SCM," *Modern Materials Handling* 65(1), 2010: 9.
12. Overby, S., "Managing Demand After Disaster Strikes," *CIO* 23(9), 2010: 1.
13. Andel, T., "Many Retailers Not Ready for Holiday Order Fulfillment," *Material Handling & Logistics*, November 21, 2013: 1.
14. Cernivec, S., "2102 New Product Development Survey," *Beverage Industry* 104(1), 2013: 52–60.
15. Dutton, G., "Reverse Logistics: Money Tree or Money Pit?" *World Trade* 23(7), 20109: 28–32.
16. Henri, J., "Are Your Performance Measurement Systems Truly Performing?" *CMA Management* 80(7), 2006: 31–35; Hinton, M., and D. Barnes, "Discovering Effective Performance Measurement for e-Business," *International Journal of Productivity and Performance* 58(4), 2009: 329–340.
17. Wilding, R., "Playing the Tune of Shared Success," *Financial Times,* November 10, 2006: 2.
18. Anonymous, "Companies are Using Team-Based Business Games to Increase Productivity," *CPA Practice Management Forum* 6(5), 2010: 22.
19. www.eia.doe.gov/oil_gas/petroleum/data_publications
20. Keiser, B., "Knowledge Management at GE and CCH," *Online Searcher* 37(4), 2013: 20–22.
21. Wilson, M., "A Blanket Solution," *Chain Store Age* 86(1), 2010: 39.

22. Napolitano, M., "RFID Surges Ahead," *Logistics Management* 51(4), 2012: 47–49.

23. See, for instance, www.rfidinc.com, www.rfidjournal.com; Andel, T., "RFID: The Only Thing Passive About the Marines," *Modern Materials Handling* 62(8), 2007: 61; Fink, R., J. Gillett, and G. Grzeskiewicz, "Will RFID Change Inventory Assumptions?" *Strategic Finance* 89(4), 2007: 34–39; and *Joch, A.*, " 'Active' Assistance," *Hospitals & Health Networks* 6(3), 2007: 36–37.

24. Armbruster, W., "Dell Looks to the Ocean," *Journal of Commerce*, April 26, 2010: 1.

25. Lester, T., "Masters of Collaboration—How Well Do U.K. Businesses Work Together," *Financial Times,* June 29, 2007: 8.

26. Trunick, P., "It's Crunch Time," *Transportation & Distribution* 43(1), 2002: 5–6.

27. Anonymous, "Robert Reed on Hospital-Physician Integration," *Healthcare Financial Management* 64(6), 2010: 30.

28. Biederman, D., "Visibility into Compliance," *Journal of Commerce*, April 5, 2010: 1.

29. Anonymous, "Del Monte Looks to the Cloud for Inventory Visibility," *Material Handling & Logistics*, May 4, 2011: 1.

30. Beasty, C., "The Chain Gang," *Customer Relationship Management* 11(10), 2007: 32–36.

31. Field, A., "Sound the Alarm," *Journal of Commerce,* May 7, 2007: 1.

32. Maccoby, M., "Creating Collaboration," *Research Technology Management* 49(6), 2006: 60–62.

33. Roberts, B., "Counting on Collaboration," *HR Magazine* 52(10), 2007: 47–51.

34. Paul, L., "Suspicious Minds: Collaboration Among Trading Partners Can Unlock Great Value," *CIO* 16(7), 2003: 74–82.

35. Maylett, T., and K. Vitasek, "For Closer Collaboration, Try Education," *Supply Chain Management Review* 11(1), 2007: 58.

36. Information about these annual conferences can be found at www.sensorsexpo.com, www.ism.ws, and www.gs1us.org

37. Lee, H., V. Padmanabhan, and S. Whang, "The Bullwhip Effect in Supply Chains," *Sloan Management Review* 38(3), 1997: 93–102; Lee, H., "Taming the Bullwhip," *Journal of Supply Chain Management* 46(1), 2010: 7.

38. Waller, M., "How Sharing Data Drives Supply Chain Innovation," *Industry Week*, August 12, 2013: 1.

39. Rigby, E., "Netto Seen as Significant 'Step-Change' for ASDA," *Financial Times*, May 28, 2010: 20; Baker, R., "ASDA: Cheap Brings No Cheer for ASDA in the Post-Recession," *Marketing Week*, August 26, 2010: 10.

40. Hines, A., "Twinkie Shortage Shows Hostess Fans Went a Little Crazy Over Bankruptcy," *Huffington Post Business*, November 16, 2012, found at: http://www.huffingtonpost.com/tag/twinkies-shortage

41. Hofmann, M., "Financial Executives Rate Top Challenges Through 2009," *Business Insurance* 41(21), 2007: 4–5.

42. Zolkos, R., "Cyber Exposures Threaten Supply Chain Risk Management," *Business Insurance* 47(26), 2013: 4–29.

43. Anonymous, "A BP Lesson: Supply-Chain Risk," *Institutional Investor*, June 2010: 1.

44. Field, A., "How 'Free' Is Free Trade?" *Journal of Commerce*, December 18, 2006: 1–3; *Kline, J.*, "Managing Emerging Market Risk," *Logistics Management* 46(5), 2007: 41–44; Swaminathan, J., and B. Tomlin, "How to Avoid the Risk Management Pitfalls," *Supply Chain Management Review* 11(5), 2007: 34–43.

45. Esola, L., "Employers Questioned on Pandemic Drug Plan," *Business Insurance* 40(49), 2006: 4–5.

46. Swaminathan, J., and B. Tomlin, "How to Avoid the Risk Management Pitfalls," *Supply Chain Management Review* 11(5), 2007: 34–43.

47. Anonymous, "Supply Disruption Discussed," *Business Insurance* 37(22), 2003: 17.

48. Swaminathan, J., and B. Tomlin, "How to Avoid the Risk Management Pitfalls," *Supply Chain Management Review* 11(5), 2007: 34–43.

49. Anonymous, "Supply Diversity Cuts Risk Exposure," *Oil & Gas Journal* 105(17), 2007: 65–68.

50. Tieman, R., "It's About Common Sense," *Financial Times*, September 10, 2007: 5; Chauhan, C., "Importer of Japanese Automobiles, Spare Parts to Stop," *The Economic Times Online*, March 13, 2011: 1.

51. Tieman, R. (See note 50.)

52. Anonymous, "Flexing Supply Chain Muscle," *Chain Store Age* 83(9), 2007: 10A.

53. Shacklett, M., "What to Do About Risk," *World Trade* 26(10), 2013: 22–27.

54. See note 52.

55. Felsted, A., "Lessons from Barbie World," *Financial Times*, September 10, 2007: 1.

56. Rice, J., "Rethinking Security," *Logistics Management* 46(5), 2007: 28; Knowles, J., "The Lockerbie Judgments: A Short Analysis," *Case Western Reserve Journal of International Law* 36(2/3), 2004: 473–485.

57. Terreri, A., "How Do You Balance Shipment Speed with a Secure Supply Chain?" *World Trade* 19(11), 2006: 18–22.

58. Rice, J., "Rethinking Supply Chain Security," *Logistics Management*, May 1, 2007.

59. Anderson, B., "Prevent Cargo Theft," *Logistics Today* 48(5), 2007: 37–38.

60. Kilcarr, S., "Brand 'Damage' a Side Effect of Cargo Theft Issue, Expert Says," *Fleet Owner*, October 29, 2013: 1.

61. Information found at www.transparency.org

62. See, for example, the website www.cargosecurity.com/ncsc/education-CTPAT.asp

63. See https://www.securecargo.org/content/what-certified-cargo-screening-program-ccsp-0

64. Terreri, A., "How Do You Balance Shipment Speed with a Secure Supply Chain?"

65. Greenemeier, L., "MassMutual Gets Control of Its Security Data," *InformationWeek*, September 17, 2007: 108–109.

66. Michel, R., "Profit from Secure Supply Chains," *Manufacturing Business Technology* 24(11), 2006: 1.

Chapter 14

PERFORMANCE MEASUREMENT ALONG SUPPLY CHAINS

When high-performance analytics can solve the world's toughest business problems thousands of times faster, there's no limit to what organizations can achieve.

— Jim Goodnight, CEO, SAS Institute, Inc.[1]

Operational resilience will come to the forefront and underpin manufacturers' supply chain strategy moving forward. It will no longer be enough to be fast in terms of supply chain response; they will need to be accurately fast. That is clearly dependent upon being demand aware and data driven, but it is also about digital execution—leveraging data to broaden and extend supply chain intelligence.

— Simon Ellis, director for global supply chain strategies, IDC Manufacturing Insights[2]

Learning Objectives

After completing this chapter, you should be able to

- Discuss why managers need to assess the performance of their firms as well as their supply chains.
- Discuss the merits of financial and nonfinancial performance measures.
- List and describe a number of traditional and world-class performance measures.
- Describe how the Balanced Scorecard and the SCOR models work.
- Describe how to design a supply chain performance measurement system.

Chapter Outline

SCM Profile | The U.S. Sustainable Supply Chain Community of Practice

On October 5, 2009, President Obama signed an executive order entitled "Federal Leadership in Environmental, Energy, and Economic Performance." The order made greenhouse gas (GHG) emission reductions a priority for the government and tasked the General Services Administration (GSA) to reduce the GHGs from the federal supply chain. The result has been that businesses have found a strong economic case for sustainability. Increasingly, emphases on sustainable supply chains are seen as a competitive necessity. It is this awareness that is driving leading businesses to employ sustainable supply chain practices. Accordingly, the GSA announced in March 2012 the launch of a Sustainable Supply Chain Community of Practice. The goal of the initiative is to provide federal agencies and their small business suppliers an avenue to learn from companies that have some of the most advanced supply chains in the world.

In November 2010, the Council on Environmental Quality and GSA jointly launched the Green. Gov Supply Chain Partnership Program as an incentive for federal suppliers to complete GHG emissions inventories. As part of the program activities, the GSA held listening sessions around the country and the feedback was surprising. Many of the largest suppliers were not just tracking and publicly reporting GHG emissions as part of corporate social responsibility efforts, they were also starting to engage their suppliers. Along with GHGs, these same "top 100" suppliers were actively identifying and addressing additional environmental impacts within their supply chains.

The U.S. government spends approximately $535 billion each year on contracts for products and services. Increasing the federal supply chain's sustainability offers huge value to the taxpayer. Moving forward, the data.gov website will play an increasingly central role for the Sustainable Supply Chain Community of Practice. Established by the government to provide data sets for use by any person who registers to gain access to the site, data.gov already serves as the home to a number of other communities. The Sustainable Supply Chain Community of Practice seeks to share best practices from all who are active in supply chain sustainability. Examples of relevant practices include supplier codes of conducts, checklists, tutorials, and other supplier engagement tools. The Sustainable Supply Chain Community of Practice seeks to serve as an "Über community" for sustainable supply chain practices. Thanks to the backing of the federal government and its $535 billion in annual contract spending, the Sustainable Supply Chain Community of Practice has the scale and reach beyond any community of practice currently in existence.[3]

INTRODUCTION

This chapter discusses the role and importance of performance measurements for both the firm and its supply chains. The old adage "you can't improve what you aren't measuring" is certainly true for firms as well as their supply chains. In fact, for a number of years, the global business research firm Gartner has published a ranking of the world's most successful supply chains and has consistently found that firms with the best supply chains create hierarchies of precise performance measures at the execution level combined with distillation of meaning at the strategic level. These organizations realize that strategic goals at the top will only succeed if there is a clear path to performance measures at the transaction level to identify execution problems.[4] While several types of performance measures have been discussed or suggested in earlier chapters of this textbook, firms need to develop an entire system of meaningful performance measures to become and then remain competitive, particularly when managing supply chains is one of the imperatives.

Performance measurement systems vary substantially from company to company. For example, many firms' performance measures concentrate solely on the firm's costs and profits. While these measures are certainly important, managers must realize that making decisions while relying on financial performance alone gives no indication of the underlying causes of financial performance. Designing standards and then monitoring the many activities or processes indirectly or directly impacting financial performance can provide much better information for decision-making purposes.

Indeed, during the recent recession as global demand for goods and services languished, personnel relied on their supply chain management skills to drive costs out of their supply chains to improve profitability. According to a survey of global business managers, three of the activities receiving the most attention during this period were purchasing, logistics, and performance measurement.[5] Always the supply chain innovator, Walmart, for instance, decided to purchase up to 80 percent of its private label merchandise directly from manufacturers, saving billions of dollars.[6] Supply chain leaders are working closely with their trading partners to seek out and eliminate non-value-creating activities while identifying new customer requirements and turning these into product and service attributes. And, supporting and guiding these activities are good performance measurement systems.

Even for companies like Walmart (which by the way is a long-time member of the annual Top 25 Supply Chains published by Gartner) that rely on low prices to attract customers, cost performance alone is not enough to guarantee success without assuring that products are also available when needed and at acceptable levels of quality. Attaining world-class competitive status requires managers to realize that making process decisions to create or purchase products and services customers want, and then to distribute them in ways that will satisfy customers, requires careful monitoring of cost, quality, and customer service performance among all key supply chain trading partners. Achieving adequate performance and then continually improving on those measures are what firms aim toward. Using an adequate system of performance measures allows managers to pursue that vision.

Unfortunately, many firms and their supply chains today are not adequately measuring process performance. According to a survey of Canadian manufacturing firms performed in 2006, for instance, only about 50 percent of the firms had even moderately well-developed performance measurement systems. And in a more recent survey of business technologists, about 75 percent said their firms mainly relied on their suppliers to furnish them with inbound performance information.[7] In other cases, organizations are busy measuring everything in sight, and in so doing, they make poor measurements, measure the wrong things, and measure things that only make the firm look good—actions that can sometimes lead to misstatements and restatements, loss of confidence, and even prove dangerous (Enron and Worldcom might come to mind here). Managers need to realize the importance of creating a good, true set of performance measures, and this is the objective of this chapter.

When managing supply chains, assessing the performance of several tiers of suppliers and customers further complicates an already formidable performance measurement problem. With supply chains, performance measurement systems become much larger and are complicated by varied relationships, trust, and interactions. Performance at the end-customer level depends on the collective performance among the primary trading companies along the supply chain. Thus, performance measures must be visible and communicated to all participating members of the supply chain while managers collaborate to achieve results that allow firms to plan ahead, create value, and realize benefits. Indeed, it is likely that some member costs will be higher than otherwise would be the case to permit supply chains to offer what end customers want. It is only through cooperation and shared planning and benefits that an effective supply chain-wide performance measurement system can be designed and implemented.

This chapter will discuss the basics of performance measurement including cost-based and other traditional measurements, and then move on to discuss the more effective measurement systems typical of world-class organizations. From there, the discussion will move into measuring the performance of supply chains. Finally, the Balanced Scorecard and the SCOR model methods of performance measurement, which are being utilized effectively in supply chain settings, will be presented and discussed.

VIEWING SUPPLY CHAINS AS A COMPETITIVE FORCE

The eventual and ultimate goal of supply chains is to successfully deliver products and services to end customers. Traditionally, to meet customer service requirements, trading partners might simply load their retail shelves, warehouses, and factories with finished goods. Today, though, this strategy would ultimately lead to inventory carrying costs and product prices so high that the firms would no longer be competitive. For companies to be successful, supply chain customers and end-product users must be satisfied. Thus, firms must invest time and effort understanding supply chain partner and end-customer requirements and then adjust or acquire supply chain competencies to satisfy the needs of these customers. To obtain the resources to accomplish these tasks, top managers must become involved and support the firm's improvement efforts. Ultimately, well-designed performance measurement systems integrated among key trading partners must be implemented to control and enhance the capabilities of these firms and thus the supply chain.

Understanding End Customers

As discussed in Chapter 10, companies segment customers based on their service needs and then design production and distribution capabilities to meet segment needs. In other words, instead of taking a one-size-fits-all approach to product design and delivery, firms and their supply chains need to look at each segment of the markets they serve and determine the needs of those customers. Companies consider customer segment needs such as:

- The variety of products required
- The quantity and delivery frequency needed
- The product quality desired
- The level of sustainability sought, and
- The pricing of products.

Obviously, depending on the range of customers the company and its supply chains serve, there will be multiple customer segments and requirements. Computer maker Dell, for example, a leader in social marketing and support, integrates Twitter data to allow brand managers and support teams to actively track what's being said in tweets. The data can be codified to show microsegments of customers who are, for example, frequent visitors to coffee shops during their work day, commute ninety minutes or more, fly internationally during the week, stay in business hotels, are passionate about football, are eco-savvy, and watch a lot of TV.[8]

Understanding Supply Chain Partner Requirements

Once firms understand end customers' needs, the next step is determining how their supply chains can best satisfy those needs. Supply chain strategies must consider the potential trade-offs existing among the cost, quality, sustainability, and service requirements mentioned above. For instance, supply chain responsiveness (meeting due date, lead-time, and quantity requirements and providing high levels of customer service) can come at a cost. To achieve the desired level of responsiveness, companies along the supply chain may also have to become more responsive, potentially requiring investments in additional capacity and faster transportation. Likewise, supply chain quality or reliability may require investments in newer equipment, better technology, and higher-quality materials and components among participants in supply chains.

Conversely, increasing supply chain efficiency (enabling lower prices for goods) creates the need among supply chain partners to make adjustments in their purchasing, production, and delivery capabilities that will lower costs. This may include using slower transportation modes, buying and delivering in larger quantities, and reducing the quality of the parts and supplies purchased. Ultimately, firms within supply chains must collaborate and decide what combination of customer needs their supply chains can and should provide, both today and in the long term. Furniture retailer IKEA, for example, tries to use environmentally and socially responsible suppliers to better satisfy its retail customers. It has developed a code of conduct using life-cycle thinking for its many suppliers that includes resource use, sustainable forestry practices, and proper employee training.[9]

Adjusting Supply Chain Member Capabilities

Supply chain members can audit their capabilities and those of their trading partners to determine if what they do particularly well is consistent with the needs of the end customers and other supply chain members. Some companies may be well positioned to supply the desired levels of cost, quality, and customer service performance, while others may not be as well positioned. Matching or adjusting supply chain member capabilities with end customer requirements can be a very difficult task, particularly if the communication and cooperation levels among companies are not excellent, or if companies are serving multiple supply chains and customer segments requiring different sets of capabilities.

In many cases, a dominant company within the supply chain (e.g., Walmart) can use its buying power to leverage demands for suppliers to conform to its supply chain requirements. As customer tastes and competition change over time, supply chain members can reassess and redesign their strategies for meeting end-customer requirements and remaining competitive. Use of the Internet as a marketplace, for instance, has become a significant part of many firms' competitive strategies, allowing them to offer much greater product variety and convenience than ever before.

Matching supply chain capabilities to end-customer requirements means that firms and their supply chain partners must be continually reassessing their performance with respect to these changing end-customer requirements. This brings us back to the importance of performance measures and their ability to relay information regarding the performance of each member within the supply chain, along with the performance of the supply chain vis-à-vis the end customers. Now, more than ever before, successful supply chains are those that can continue to deliver the right combinations of cost, quality, sustainability, and customer service, as customer needs change. Weaknesses in any of these areas can mean loss of competitiveness and profits for all supply chain members. Today, the best supply chain performers are more responsive to customer needs, quicker to anticipate changes in the markets, and much better at controlling costs, resulting in greater supply chain profits. The next section discusses traditional performance measures.

TRADITIONAL PERFORMANCE MEASURES

Most performance measures used by firms today continue to be the traditional cost-based and financial statistics reported to shareholders in the form of annual report, balance sheet, and income statement data. This information is relied upon by potential investors and shareholders to make stock transaction decisions and forms the basis for many managers' performance bonuses. Unfortunately, financial statements and other cost-based information don't necessarily reflect the underlying performance of the productive systems of an

SCM Profile | Bernard Madoff's $50 Billion Fraud

Mr. Bernard Madoff, arrested in 2008, is today serving a 150-year prison sentence for fraudulently bilking clients out of more than $50 billion over several decades. Fifteen others have been criminally charged in the case, and nine have pleaded guilty.

Madoff's firm actually performed real stock trades in its so-called "House 5." Its fake trades occurred in a separate computer, known as "House 17," which processed information on securities allegedly bought for clients. The end results were phony trade confirmations on official-looking statements for 4,900 clients. According to the faked statements, these accounts typically yielded 11 to 17 percent returns annually.

Court-appointed trustee Irving Picard, charged with liquidating Madoff's assets, focused on House 17, where the Ponzi scheme was managed. Picard hired Joseph Looby, an accounting forensics expert, to determine how Madoff stole client funds.

House 5 supported Madoff's market-making operation and was networked to third parties outside the firm that supported a trading operation. "[House 5] was an [IBM] AS/400, consistent with a legitimate securities trading business," Looby wrote. House 17, though, was managed by Madoff's right-hand man Frank DiPascali Jr. Its sole purpose was to maintain phony records and crank out phony IRS 1099s and customer statements.

Here's how the fraud worked: Madoff employees fed House 17 with stock data, enough to support trades that would satisfy the expectations promised to clients. To support the fantasy returns, so-called baskets of stocks would be bought and sold on behalf of clients. The proceeds from the purported sales existed only on House 17 and on the statements it printed, which showed the funds were put into U.S. Treasury bonds. Meanwhile, actual investor funds were being diverted to a JPMorgan Chase bank account.

Looby verified that trades between 2002 and 2008 were fake by cross-checking with various clearing houses. He also compared the cleared trades on House 5, and "99.9 percent" of the fake trades on House 17 did not match.

In court, DiPascali confessed, "I helped Bernie Madoff and other people, carry out the fraud that hurt thousands of people." At the end of his confession and just prior to pleading to be released on bail, he said: "I hope my help will bring some small measure of comfort to those who have been harmed. I apologize for this catastrophe."[10]

organization. As readers might recall with the fraudulent practices at firms like Texas-based energy company Enron, Mississippi-based long-distance phone company WorldCom, and New York-based Bernard Madoff Investment Securities, cost and profit information can be hidden or manipulated to make performance seem far better than it really is.

Enron claimed revenues of $111 billion in 2000. That year, *Fortune* magazine named Enron "America's Most Innovative Company." The very next year, high-profile managers left the company, Enron declared bankruptcy, and its fraudulent corporate and accounting practices became public, and by 2004 it had become one of the costliest bankruptcy cases in U.S. history. Thousands of employees lost everything, executives ended up in jail, and the Arthur Andersen accounting company, associated with Enron during this period, was dissolved.[11] The nearby SCM Profile describes how Bernard Madoff used fraudulent reporting to hide its Ponzi scheme from investors for years.

As illustrated above, decisions that are made solely to make the firm look good don't necessarily mean the firm is performing well or will continue to perform well in the future. Business success depends on a firm's ability to turn internal competencies into products and services that customers want, while providing desired environmental, quality, and customer service levels at a reasonable price. Financial performance measures, while important, cannot adequately capture a firm's ability to excel in various process areas.

Use of Organization Costs, Revenue, and Profitability Measures

These might at first glance seem to be useful types of performance measures, but several problems are associated with using costs, revenues, and profits to gauge a firm's performance. Windfall profits that occur when prices rise due to sudden demand increases or supply interruptions, as has been the case at different times in the oil industry, are one example. When this happens, airlines and other transportation companies suddenly experience much higher costs and reductions in profits, while oil companies see suddenly rising profits. In 2012, for example, Exxon Mobil reported the highest profits in the world—$44.9 billion, while Royal Dutch Shell posted the highest sales—$481.7 billion. Exxon Mobil was also number one in profits in 2009 and 2011, while slipping to number two in 2010 and 2013. Several other oil companies also frequently make the top ten.[12] Similarly, many tourist destinations such as Las Vegas saw dramatic declines in visitor volumes during the 2008 to 2010 economic recession, causing hotels and theme parks to report much lower occupancies and profits during this period. Beginning in 2008, for instance, Las Vegas saw plunges in visitor volume, gaming revenues, occupancies, and average daily room rates for the first time since the Las Vegas Convention and Visitors Authority began tracking the numbers in 1970. Hotels laid off over 25,000 workers while several resorts filed for bankruptcy.[13] Thus, profits, as described here, were not necessarily the result of something the firms did or did not do particularly well; they were caused for the most part by uncontrollable environmental conditions. Changes in cost and profit statistics, in many cases, may not accurately reflect the true capabilities of the firm.

Another problem with the use of costs, revenues, or profits as performance measures is the difficulty in attributing cost, revenue, or profit contributions to the various functional units or underlying processes of the organization. Many departments and units are interdependent and share costs, equipment, labor, and revenues, making it extremely difficult to split out costs and revenues equitably. Additionally, using costs alone as a departmental or business unit performance measure can result in actions that actually hurt the organization. For example, rewarding the purchasing department for minimizing its purchasing costs might cause increased product return rates and warranty repair costs due to low-cost but poor-quality part purchases. Minimizing transportation costs might also look great on financial reports but may result in late deliveries and lower customer service levels, causing a loss of customers. Finally, the practice of allocating overhead costs based on a department's percentage of direct labor hours causes managers to waste time trying to reduce direct labor hours to lower overhead cost allocations when, today, direct labor accounts for only a small fraction of total manufacturing costs. In essence, these overhead costs merely get transferred somewhere else in the firm, leaving the organization no better off and perhaps in worse shape due to the loss of valuable labor resources.

Use of Performance Standards and Variances

Establishing standards for performance comparison purposes can be troublesome and particularly when the standards are unrealistic, damaging to an organization. Establishing output standards like 1,000 units/day or productivity standards like 10 units/labor hour establishes an ultimate goal that can drive employees and managers to do whatever it takes to reach their goals, even if it means producing shoddy work or "cooking the books." When performance expectations are not met, perfectly good products, employees, or departments can be branded as losers. Additionally, once goals are actually reached, there is no further incentive to keep improving.

When standards are not reached, a **performance variance** is created, which is the difference between the standard and actual performance. When organizations hold managers up to performance standards that then create performance variances, managers can be pressured to find ways to make up these variances, resulting in decisions that may not be in the long-term best interests of the firm. Decisions like producing to make an output quota regardless of current finished goods inventory levels, or purchasing unneeded supplies just to use up department budgets, are examples of things that can happen when performance standards are applied without considering the true benefits to the organization. When applied at the functional level, standards can reinforce the idea of **functional silos**. Departments are then assessed on meeting their performance standards instead of optimizing firm or supply chain performance.

Productivity and Utilization Measures

Overall **total productivity measures** such as $\frac{\text{output}}{\text{costs of (labor + capital + energy + material)}}$ and **single-factor productivity measures** such as $\frac{\text{output}}{\text{cost of labor}}$, while potentially useful, have the same problems as the use of costs and profits for performance measures. These measures, while allowing firms to view the impact of one or any number of the firm's inputs (e.g., the cost of labor) on the firm's outputs (e.g., units produced), do not allow the firm to determine the actual performance of any of the resources behind these elements. Decisions made to increase productivity may prove to actually increase a firm's costs and reduce quality or output in the long term, ultimately reducing productivity. For example, a business unit might be tempted to produce at output levels greater than demand to increase productivity, which also increases inventories and inventory carrying costs. Or managers might be inclined to lay off workers and buy the cheapest materials to decrease input costs and thus maximize their productivity without considering the impact on the firm's quality, customer service, and employee morale. In these ways, productivity measures can prove to be damaging. Example 14.1 provides a look at calculating productivity and the problems that can arise when making decisions based solely on productivity.

Example 14.1 Productivity Measures at Ultra Ski Manufacturing

The Ultra Ski company makes top-of-the-line custom snow skis for high-end ski shops as well as its own small retail shop and employs fifteen people. The owner has been adamant about finding a way to increase productivity because her sales have been flat for the past two seasons. Given the information shown below, she has calculated the annual single-factor and total productivity values as:

Labor productivity = 1,000 skis/10,800 hours = 0.093 skis per labor hour

Material productivity = 1,000 skis/$18,000 = 0.056 skis per dollar of materials

Lease productivity = 1,000 skis/$24,000 = 0.042 skis per lease dollar

INPUTS AND OUTPUTS	LAST YEAR
Skis produced	1,000
Labor hours	10,800
Materials purchased	$18,000
Lease payments	$24,000

She calculates the company's total productivity by multiplying the labor hours by its average wage of $17 per hour and finds:

Total productivity = 1,000 skis/[10,800($17) + $18,000 + $24,000]
= 0.0044 skis per dollar.

So the owner figures that she can get some great improvements in productivity by finding a low-cost supplier, moving to a cheaper location, and laying off six workers (reducing her workforce by 40 percent), making the new single-factor productivities:

Labor productivity = 1,000 skis/10,800(.6) hours = 0.154 (a 66 percent increase)
Material productivity = 1,000 skis/$12,000 = 0.083 (a 48 percent increase)
Lease productivity = 1,000/$18,000 = 0.056 (a 33 percent increase)

and the new total productivity:

Total productivity = 1,000 skis/[10,800($17)(.6) + $12,000 + $18,000]
= 0.0071 skis per dollar (a whopping 61 percent increase!)

Consequently, the owner decided to make the changes for the coming year. Unfortunately, they went out of business in six months due to poor-quality materials, a bad location, and overworked, low-morale employees.

Labor and machine utilization can be shown as $\frac{\text{actual units produced}}{\text{standard output level}}$ or $\frac{\text{actual hours utilized}}{\text{total hours available}}$. These performance measures, when used as performance goals, can encourage the firm, for instance, to reduce labor levels until everyone is overworked, causing queues of work or customers to develop, morale to suffer, and quality and customer service levels to erode. Additionally, when using the measures discussed above, there is a tendency to continue producing and adding to inventory just to keep machines and people busy. Less time is spent doing preventive maintenance, training, and projects that can lead to greater performance and profits in the future. While it is obviously beneficial to meet demand and keep labor costs at optimal levels, maximizing utilization can prove to be expensive for firms.

Thus, the emphasis on overall performance in terms of generalized criteria such as the firm's financial, productivity, or utilization characteristics does not tell the entire story. While it certainly is important for firms to possess financial strength and high levels of productivity and factory utilization, these measures do not reveal in detail the firm's underlying process performance. Using general and internally focused measures like these does not give many clues as to specific problems that may exist or how to go about solving those problems. Managers are left to guess at what types of actions are needed and have no way of knowing if any corrections made actually had the intended effect. What is needed is a set of detailed performance measures throughout the organization and extending to supply chain partners that are consistent with firm and supply chain strategies, allow managers to find root causes of performance failures, and, finally, lead managers to reasonable problem solutions.

Traditional performance measures also tend to be short-term oriented. To maximize profits in the upcoming quarter, for instance, firms may focus considerable efforts on delaying capital investments, selling assets, denying new project proposals, outsourcing work, and leasing instead of purchasing equipment. These actions, while reducing short-term costs, can also significantly reduce a firm's ability to develop new products and maintain competitiveness. New product research, new technology purchases, new facilities, and newly trained people all enhance the capabilities of the firm and position it to keep up with ever-changing customer requirements, but these things all initially worsen the performance measures discussed above. Without this infusion of ideas and capital expenditures, though, firms will ultimately perform poorly.

On the other hand, world-class organizations realize that long-term competitive advantage is created when strategies are geared toward continually meeting and exceeding customer expectations of product and service cost, quality, deliverability, flexibility, and sustainability—in other words, the creation of value. These firms realize that investments to improve capabilities in these areas will eventually bear fruit and position them to be successful in the long term. Effective performance measurement systems link current operating characteristics to these long-term strategies and objectives. Peoria, Arizona, for example, a city of 150,000 sitting just northwest of Phoenix, has been using performance measures for years and has won numerous awards for its efforts. Their most effective programs have used performance measures along with program descriptions and goals to tell a story. Many of the programs also incorporate satisfaction surveys to measure the extent to which outcomes are valued by customers. They also benchmark performance with some 150 other cities across the U.S. (Read more about Peoria in the SCM Profile later in this chapter.)[14]

WORLD-CLASS PERFORMANCE MEASUREMENT SYSTEMS

Businesses respond to increased competitive and marketplace pressures by developing and maintaining a distinctive competitive advantage, which creates the need to develop effective performance measurement systems linking firm strategies and operating decisions to customer requirements. Performance criteria that guide a firm's decision making to achieve strategic objectives must be easy to implement, understand, and measure; they must be flexible and consistent with the firm's objectives; and they must be implemented in areas that are viewed as critical to the creation of value for customers. Tennessee-based Mountain States Health Alliance operates thirteen hospitals in twenty-nine counties. As such, it considers corporate and individual hospital performance. Tamera Fields, vice president of quality, is creating a support structure that will place a director of quality and patient safety at the regional level for its hospitals. These directors review and discuss the factors that contribute to poorer-than-expected performance and share practices for helping to improve performance. "Each facility will be able to take away something they have learned from another facility. They will take back to their own facility actions, plans and practices that have worked in other hospitals and that can help get their performance scores up," explains Fields.[15]

An effective performance measurement system should consist of the traditional financial information for external reporting purposes along with tactical-level performance criteria used to assess the firm's competitive capabilities while directing its efforts to attain other desired capabilities. In short, good performance helps firms attain their goals. "Bottom line, without comparative data, we would have no way of learning how to get from point A to point B," says Mountain States Health Alliance CFO Martin Eichorn. Finally, a good performance measurement system should include measures that *assess what is important to customers.* In a recent survey of manufacturing and service company executives, researchers found that in firms with successful lean and Six Sigma programs, there was use of a wider variety of both financial and nonfinancial performance measures.[16]

Developing World-Class Performance Measures

Creating an effective performance measurement system involves the following steps:[17]

- Identify the firm's strategic objectives.
- Develop an understanding of each functional area's set of requirements for achieving the strategic objectives.

SCM Profile **Peoria is Becoming a Data-Driven City**

For a number of years now, the city of Peoria, Arizona, has been refining its performance measurement system to become a tool for budget decisions and promoting accountability throughout its organization. The city has received a number of awards for its efforts but still has a ways to go to become truly data-driven.

Peoria has a population of more than 150,000, a budget of more than $150 million, with more than 1,100 employees in fourteen departments. Peoria has been one of the fastest growing cities in the U.S., but its growth halted in 2008, along with growth-related revenues. The city's new reality required creative thinking and innovative tools.

Peoria's leadership embraced performance management as an important tool for managing programs and services and for allocating city resources. Performance measures are organized by program area, are based on service goals and objectives, and measure outcomes as well as efficiency.

The most effective programs use performance measures to tell a story. For these programs, an outsider would be able to pick up a performance report and quickly understand their purpose and key functions, and form opinions about whether they are achieving desired outcomes. Many of the city's successful programs have incorporated surveys to measure the extent that outcomes are satisfying customers.

The collection and reporting of good performance data is the foundation of a useful performance management program. However, unless this information is used to make decisions about resource allocation and service delivery, it is really little more than window dressing. Faced with a substantial budget deficit and the need to adapt to a new slow-growth revenue environment, Peoria's leadership has emphasized a reliance on performance management concepts. The focus of this effort has been to deliver core city services as efficiently and effectively as possible.[18]

- Design and document performance measures for each functional area that adequately track each required capability.
- Assure the compatibility and strategic focus of the performance measures to be used.
- Implement the new performance monitoring system.
- Identify internal and external trends likely to affect firm and functional area performance over time.
- Periodically reevaluate the firm's performance measurement system as these trends and other environmental changes occur.

In this way, world-class firms establish strategically oriented performance criteria among each of their functional areas, using the categories of quality, cost, and customer service, and then revisit these measures as problems are solved, competition and customer requirements change, and as supply chain and firm strategies change.

For instance, the San Diego Zoo in California, a world-class leader in conservation, audits among other things, its own waste recycling performance. The zoo initially became interested in waste recycling and other conservation efforts in response to customer and employee suggestions. In 2013, it recovered over 80 percent of all waste generated within the facility. Additionally, it found that most of the unrecycled waste was compostable. As a result, new programs including the zoo's sister location, Safari Park, have been developed that include composting to further improve its waste recovery performance.[19] The nearby SCM Profile describes the award-winning performance measurement practices of the city of Peoria, Arizona.

Table 14.1 lists a number of world-class performance measures that might be used in different functional areas of the firm to satisfy strategic objectives, enhance the value of the firm's products and services, and increase customer satisfaction. As firms become more proactive in managing their supply chains, performance measures must be incorporated into this effort. The next section discusses performance measurement in a supply chain setting.

SUPPLY CHAIN PERFORMANCE MEASUREMENT SYSTEMS

Performance measurement systems for supply chains must effectively link supply chain trading partners to achieve breakthrough performance in satisfying end users. At the local or interfirm level, performance measures similar to the ones presented in Table 14.1 are required for high-level performance. In a collaborative supply chain setting, these measures must overlay the entire supply chain to ensure that firms are all contributing to the supply chain strategy and the satisfaction of end customers. In successful supply chains, members jointly agree on appropriate supply chain performance measures. The focus of the system should be on value creation for end customers, since customer satisfaction drives sales for all of the supply chain's members.

While challenging to implement, the best managed supply chains are indeed pulling it off. In a major study by the Massachusetts-based Performance Measurement Group that looked at firms and their supply chains from 1995 to 2000, the top supply chain performers were found to be leading the way in terms of responsiveness and reliability performance, and total supply chain costs. In a 2008 survey of 287 companies and their supply chains conducted by Connecticut-based AMR Research, the most successful supply chains were

Table 14.1 World-Class Performance Measures

CAPABILITY AREAS	PERFORMANCE MEASURES
Quality	1. Number of defects per unit produced and per unit purchased 2. Number of product returns per units sold 3. Number of warranty claims per units sold 4. Number of suppliers used 5. Lead time from defect detection to correction 6. Number of workcenters using statistical process control 7. Number of suppliers that are quality certified 8. Number of quality awards applied for; number of awards won
Cost	1. Scrap or spoilage losses per workcenter 2. Average inventory turnover 3. Average setup time 4. Employee turnover 5. Average safety stock levels 6. Number of rush orders required for meeting delivery dates 7. Downtime due to machine breakdowns
Customer Service	*Flexibility* 1. Average number of labor skills 2. Average production lot size 3. Number of customized services available 4. Number of days to process special or rush orders *Dependability* 1. Average service response time or product lead time 2. Percentage of delivery promises kept 3. Average number of days late per shipment 4. Number of stockouts per product 5. Number of days to process a warranty claim 6. Average number of hours spent with customers by engineers *Innovation* 1. Annual investment in R&D 2. Percentage of automated processes 3. Number of new product or service introductions 4. Number of process steps required per product

found to be more centralized, integrated, global, and focused on measuring performance. And finally, in a ranking of the "Top 25" supply chains compiled each year since 2004 by business research firm Gartner, one of the common characteristics is a focus on measurements that matter; measures that will improve operational results.[20]

Supply Chain Environmental Performance

Environmental sustainability has been a recurring theme throughout this textbook, and as consumers, governments, and business leaders begin to address the need for protecting the environment and reducing greenhouse gas emissions, the demand for products and services will change, along with regulations impacting how supply chains operate. As a result, supply chain performance must begin to include assessments of environmental performance, as seen in the chapter opening profile.

Green supply chain management (GSCM) is the objective of an effective supply chain environmental performance system. The reach of GSCM extends across the organization and its trading partners, and includes the processes involved in purchasing, manufacturing and materials management, distribution, and reverse logistics. GSCM promotes the sharing of environmental responsibility along the supply chain in each of these areas such that environmentally sound practices predominate, and adverse impacts to global environments are minimized.[21] Perhaps the world's largest GSCM initiative is being implemented by Walmart—its goals are to be supplied 100 percent by renewable energy, to produce zero waste, and to sell products that sustain health and the environment. In 2011, 80.9 percent of its physical waste in the U.S. was recycled, and that this was worth some $231 million to its bottom line, due to recycling revenues and other cost avoidance. Also, in 2011, Walmart began to integrate a supplier Sustainability Index into its business by scoring vendor product offerings. It has developed scorecards to help its purchasing agents evaluate products and was expecting to develop scorecards for up to 100 major categories by the end of 2012.[22]

The design of an effective green supply chain performance system should be discussed by all key supply chain members and be compatible with existing performance monitoring systems. As discussed in earlier chapters, the ISO 14000 environmental management standards, typically associated with one organization's environmental compliance, can be a good starting point for building a green supply chain strategy among supply chain partners. Today, trading partners all realize that green supply chains are not only becoming a requirement but are also providing cost savings, additional profits, and cheaper prices to supply chain members and end-product customers. For these reasons, use of environmental sustainability assessments is a common practice.

Today, software is available that enables companies to analyze the **carbon footprints** of their supply chains and then evaluate design configurations and various options for reducing total carbon emissions. In many cases, this will also mean lower costs. A number of software suppliers are extending their existing software applications to measure and optimize areas such as transportation and inventory management, with explicit considerations for greening the supply chain.

French company EcoVadis, for example, has developed a sophisticated, easy-to-use rating platform for sustainable supply chain management. Pierre Francois Thaler, managing director of EcoVadis, has helped scores of multinational corporations assess the performance of their supply chains in terms of overall sustainability. "There's a bit of a difference between the U.S. use of the term 'sustainability' and the European definition, which takes in other aspects," Thaler says. "When you talk about sustainability of the supply chain in the U.S., what you're most often talking about is 'green procurement,' " he goes on to explain. "In Europe, although global companies like Johnson & Johnson and Coca-Cola talk about sustainability of their supply chains, what they are talking about clearly include other things—these companies understand sustainability encompasses a much broader agenda. Having said that, I think the biggest challenge companies, large and small, face when it comes to sustainability is having what efforts they are making cascade down to the lowest tiers of their supply chain," he says. "I think it's safe to say that most companies have good visibility when it comes to the activities of their tier-one suppliers. However, it's a far different story when you start talking about the suppliers or suppliers of suppliers. That's where the problems lay. That's the area where there's a clear challenge to be dealt with."[23]

To achieve the type of performance alluded to in this chapter, specific measures must be adopted by supply chain trading partners such that performance can be further aligned with supply chain objectives. A number of these are listed below.[24]

1. *Total Supply Chain Management Costs*: the costs to process orders, purchase materials, purchase energy, comply with environmental regulations, manage inventories and returns, and manage supply chain finance, planning, and information systems. Leading supply companies are spending from 4 to 5 percent of sales on supply chain management costs, while the average company spends about 5 to 6 percent.
2. *Supply Chain Cash-to-Cash Cycle Time*: the average number of days between paying for raw materials and getting paid for product, for the supply chain trading partners (calculated by inventory days of supply plus days of sales outstanding minus average payment period for material). This measure shows the impact of lower inventories on the speed of cash moving through firms and the supply chain. Top supply chain companies have a cash-to-cash cycle time of about thirty days, which is far less than the average company. These trading partners no longer view "slow paying" as a viable strategy.
3. *Supply Chain Production Flexibility*: the average time required for supply chain members to provide an unplanned, sustainable 20 percent increase in production. The ability for the supply chain to quickly react to unexpected demand spikes while still operating within financial targets provides tremendous competitive advantage. One common supply chain practice is to maintain stocks of component parts locally for supply chain customers to quickly respond to unexpected demand increases. Average production flexibility for best-in-class supply chains is from one to two weeks.
4. *Supply Chain Delivery Performance*: the average percentage of orders for the supply chain members that are filled on or before the requested delivery date. In the top-performing supply chains, delivery dates are being met from 94 to 100 percent of the time. For average firms, delivery performance is approximately 70 to 80 percent. Updating customers on the expected delivery dates of orders is becoming a common e-service for many supply chains.
5. *Supply Chain Perfect Order Fulfillment Performance*: the average percentage of orders among supply chain members that arrive on time, complete and damage-free. This is quickly becoming the standard for delivery performance and represents a significant source of competitive advantage for top-performing supply chains and their member companies.
6. *Supply Chain e-Business Performance*: the average percentage of electronic orders received for all supply chain members. In 1998, only about 2 percent of all firms' purchase orders were made over the Internet. By 2007, for example, office supply retailer Staples said that 90 percent of its orders came in electronically. Additionally, use of e-procurement can save up to 90 percent of the administrative costs of ordering.[25] Today, supply chain companies are investing heavily in e-based order-receipt systems, marketing strategies, and other forms of communication and research using the Internet.
7. *Supply Chain Environmental Performance*: the percentage of supply chain trading partners that have become ISO 14000 certified; the percentage of supply chain trading partners that have created a director of environmental sustainability; the average percentage of environmental goals met; the average number of policies adopted to reduce greenhouse gas emissions; and the average percentage of carbon footprints that have been offset by sound environmental practices. While these performance indicators may certainly vary by supply chain and industry, the measures here will provide a good starting point for collaboration on supply chain environmental performance.

When combined with the world-class performance measures of Table 14.1, the measures shown above can help global trading partners align themselves with supply chain strategies, creating competencies that lead to dominant positions in their markets. In fact, according to a financial analysis of the leading supply chain management companies and their closest competitors for the period 2004–2007, the analysis conclusively shows that the leading supply chain companies do, in fact, outperform their peers in most financial measures—even when accounting for other factors such as size and financial leverage. The leading supply chain companies also showed greater stock returns and economic value added, over the 2004–2007 timeframe.[26]

THE BALANCED SCORECARD

The **balanced scorecard** (BSC) approach to performance measurement was developed in 1992 by Drs. Robert Kaplan and David Norton and representatives from a number of companies as a way to align an organization's performance measures with its strategic plans and goals. The BSC thus allowed a firm to move away from reliance on merely financial measures, which effectively improved managerial decision making.[27]

Also referred to as simply **scorecarding**, BSC has become a widely used model with some 80 percent of large U.S. businesses either using it or having previously used it and a smaller but growing percentage of European businesses using it. Many companies have reported notable successes with the use of the BSC including Mobil Oil, Tenneco, Brown & Root, AT&T, Intel, Allstate, Ernst & Young, and KPMG Peat Marwick.[28] According to Shell Canada's human resource director John Hofmeister, "It gives us better and better alignment (between all operating units) and focuses attention on what's important and on results. In addition, the group's reward structure is linked directly to the scorecard."[29] Sir Terry Leahy, CEO of British retailer Tesco from 1997 to 2011, pioneered use of the BSC in his quest to drive profitability. "What made it so effective was the ability to link these concepts all the way down to individual stores," says Bernard Marr, chief executive of the Advanced Performance Institute, who worked with Sir Terry in developing the BSC across Tesco. "The success of Tesco has been down to Terry Leahy's ability to set corporate strategy through the Balanced Scorecard," he adds. Incidentally, during that time, Leahy took Tesco from the third largest retailer in Britain to the third largest in the world.[30]

There are some indications, though, that BSC use can be problematic, expensive, and even unsuccessful. Research from the U.S.-based benchmarking company Hackett Group indicated that while 82 percent of its company database reportedly used scorecards, only 27 percent of the systems were considered "mature." They concluded that most companies were having difficulty taking BSC from concept to reality. John McMahan, senior advisor at Hackett Group, said, "Most companies get very little out of scorecards because they haven't followed the basic rules that make them effective." For example, in the U.S., the average number of measures used is a very high and often confusing 132, while Kaplan and Norton suggest use of 20 to 30 measures.[31] Additionally, consultants are used in many cases to help map the organization's strategy and its effect on performance, and to assist in selecting performance measures. Further, information systems may have to be modified, sometimes at great expense, to supply the information necessary for the scorecards. Other weaknesses in the BSC include its inability to show what one's competitors are doing; exclusion of employee, supplier, and alliance partner contributions; and its reliance on top-down measures.[32]

Nevertheless, the BSC is widely used in helping organizations track performance and identify areas of weakness. Scorecarding is designed to provide managers with a formal

Figure 14.1 The Balanced Scorecard Framework

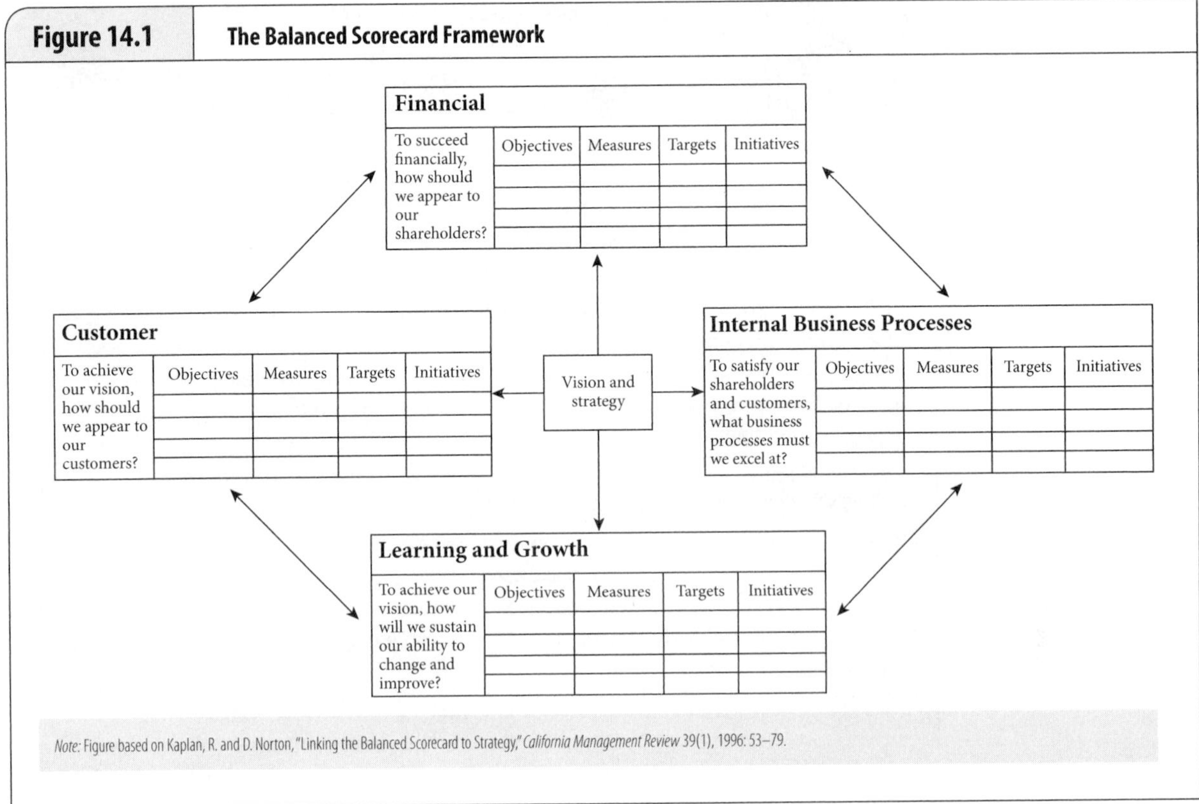

Note: Figure based on Kaplan, R. and D. Norton, "Linking the Balanced Scorecard to Strategy," *California Management Review* 39(1), 1996: 53–79.

framework for achieving a balance between nonfinancial and financial results across both short-term and long-term planning horizons. The BSC framework consists of four perspectives as shown in Figure 14.1:

- *Financial Perspective*—measures that address revenue and profitability growth, product mix, cost reduction, productivity, asset utilization, and investment strategies. Traditional financial measures are typically used.
- *Internal Business Process Perspective*—focuses on performance of the most critical internal business processes of the organization including quality, new product development, flexibility, innovative elements of processes, and time-based measures.
- *Customer Perspective*—measures that focus on customer requirements and satisfaction including customer satisfaction ratings, reliability and responsiveness, customer retention, new customer acquisition, customer-valued attributes, and customer profitability.
- *Learning and Growth Perspective*—measures concentrating on the organization's people, systems, and external environment and including retaining and training employees, enhancing information technology and systems, employee safety, and health and environmental sustainability issues.

These perspectives are all linked together using performance measures within each of the four areas. Measurements are developed for each goal in the organization's strategic plan and include both outcome measures and the performance drivers of those outcomes. In doing this, senior managers can channel the specific set of capabilities within the

SCM Profile | Balanced Scorecarding at CHP

"My history in health care told me that we had superb financial information, but not superb information on quality or community benefit, so that started our organization on a journey to collect that data," says Michael Connelly, CEO of Catholic Health Partners (CHP) in Cincinnati, Ohio. "It was fundamental to creating a scorecard that would give us a well-rounded picture of our ongoing progress toward achieving our mission and strategic priorities."

CHP began gathering internal performance information thirteen years ago, with a goal of achieving top performance. "From the beginning, we aimed to select a balanced set [of objectives]—quality, mission, human resources, physician partnerships or growth, and finance," says Jane Crowley, executive vice president of clinical integration. "For each measure, we established five levels of achievement—poor to excellent—specifically defined to help us understand performance expectations at each step along the way, so we would know ahead of time what excellent looked like," she added.

It decided on fifteen to eighteen system-wide measures to give it an overall view of performance. Measures are changed annually, based on progress toward achieving CHP's strategic plan. Over the years, it has added more quality measures and reduced the number of financial metrics. Over time, CHP has made its scorecard more complex and diverse in measuring achievements.

For instance, CHP in 2010 added a diversity measure to determine its retention rate for minority employees. By tracking why ethnically diverse employees were leaving CHP, managers were able to make changes that virtually eliminated the higher turnover rates for racially diverse employees. Improved outcomes and organizational alignment over the past thirteen years are the direct results from using a balanced scorecard.[33]

organization toward achieving the firm's goals. A properly constructed scorecard should support the firm's strategy and consists of a linked series of measures that are consistent and reinforcing. By developing suitable performance measures in each of the perspectives, firms can detect problem areas before they become significant, trace the problem to its root causes, and make improvements to alleviate the problem.

The process of developing a BSC begins with defining the firm's strategy. Once that strategy is understood and agreed upon by senior managers, the next step is to translate the strategy's goals into a system of relevant performance measures. Each of the four perspectives in the BSC require four to seven performance measures, resulting in a scorecard with about two dozen measures relating to one single strategy. As alluded to above, the potential for failure does exist if firms are not clear about what they are hoping to achieve and are not focused on ensuring that the best scorecards with the right performance measures linked to firm strategies are used.

The BSC can be also be utilized by firms in a collaborative supply chain setting by expanding the internal perspective of the scorecard to include interfunctional and partnership perspectives that characterize the supply chain. In this way, for instance, the firm's employees are motivated to view their firm's performance vis-à-vis the success of the entire supply chain. Supply chain–oriented performance measures, such as the ones described earlier, can thus be added to the more internally focused measures traditionally used in a balanced scorecard to help the firm as well as its supply chains meet their objectives.

Balanced scorecards are being used in the government and healthcare sectors, too, with many positive outcomes. One example is the U.S. Economic Development administration (EDA). The EDA has used the BSC to help develop its world-class performance measurement system. After adoption of the BSC approach, it aligned the organization around a common set of goals, improved the quality of its investments, enhanced efficiencies, and created higher-quality jobs. In 2004, it exceeded its target for new investment partners and improved its private sector investment leverage ratio by 500 percent.[34] Finally, the nearby SCM Profile describes the use of balanced scorecards at Catholic Health Partners of Ohio to achieve its strategic priorities.

Web-Based Scorecards

Today, a number of software applications are available to help design scorecards, which link via the web to a firm's enterprise software system. Web-based balanced scorecard applications are also sometimes referred to as **performance dashboards**. They enable users to retrieve data easily from ERP databases and also enable wide access by users at many locations, while providing desired security features. Performance dashboards are being used to track "big picture" corporate objectives as well as core process performance and more tactical, detailed data. Use of these web-based dashboards allows managers to see real-time progress toward organizational milestones and helps to ensure that decisions remain in sync with the firm's overall strategies.

Virtually all accounting applications, for example, provide BSC capabilities, including applications offered by Microsoft, SAP, IBM, and Oracle. Performance dashboard applications are becoming commonplace these days. For example, the U.S. Department of Veterans Affairs uses performance dashboards to give its IT employees a visual representation of its effectiveness in solving problems for customers. Some of the top supply chain companies use dashboards to compare team performances and find that this motivates teams to perform better. American energy company ConocoPhillips uses performance dashboards at a number of its oil and gas wells to let well operators know when plunger-lift operating cycles must be adjusted to eliminate fluid buildups that restrict the flow of gas. Using these dashboards has allowed production to increase by about 30 percent. The U.S. Environmental Protection Agency (EPA) uses state dashboards and comparative maps that provide the public with information about the performance of state and EPA enforcement and compliance programs across the country. "Transparency and access to information at all levels helps to drive improvements in environmental performance," says Cynthia Giles, assistant administrator for the EPA's Office of Enforcement and Compliance Assurance.[35]

THE SCOR MODEL

One of the more recognized methods for integrating supply chains and measuring performance is use of the Supply Chain Operations Reference (SCOR) model developed in 1996 by supply chain consulting firms Pittiglio, Rabin, Todd & McGrath and AMR Research. These firms also founded the Texas-based Supply Chain Council, a nonprofit global organization with a current membership of over 1,000 profit and nonprofit organizations on six continents. The purpose of the Supply Chain Council is to manage the SCOR model, while providing education opportunities for its members.[36]

The SCOR model helps to integrate the operations of supply chain members by linking the delivery operations of the seller to the sourcing operations of the buyer. Starting

Figure 14.2 The SCOR Model Processes and Linkages

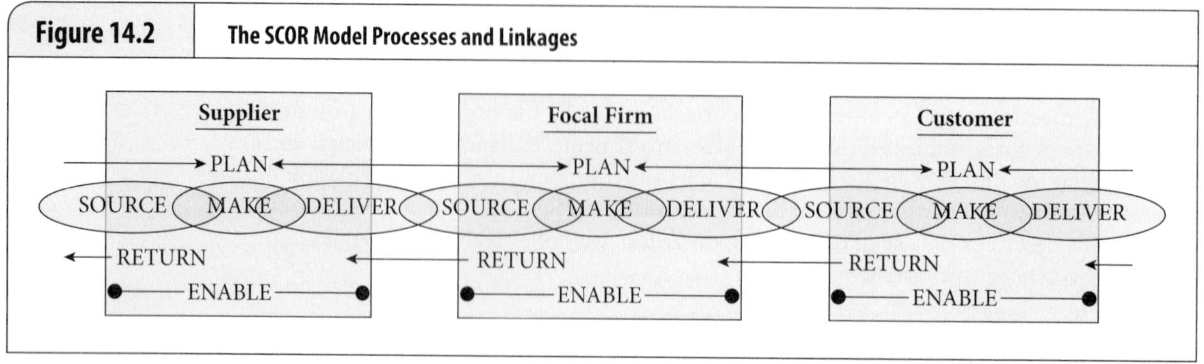

in 2013, members can obtain a professional certification in knowledge and methods of the SCOR model, termed a SCOR-P certification. Also new for 2013, the SCOR model's eleventh revision has added a new process category, ENABLE, as shown in the model in Figure 14.2.[37]

The SCOR model is used as a supply chain management diagnostic, benchmarking, and process improvement tool by manufacturing and service firms in a variety of industries around the globe. Some of the notable firms to have success using the SCOR model include Intel, IBM, 3M, Cisco, Siemens, and Bayer. Striving for the best telecommunications supply chain, Alcatel (now Alcatel-Lucent), for example, used SCOR metrics following the economic downturn of 2001 to measure and benchmark its performance. Major improvements were realized in delivery performance, sourcing cycle time, supply chain management cost, and inventory days of supply.[38] Cisco set out to revamp its supply chain in 2005 using the SCOR model as a way to monitor its growing global footprint. It eventually appointed a vice president responsible for the SCOR model's functions.[39] In 2010, German semiconductor manufacturer Infineon used the SCOR model to build an agile and adaptable supply chain. Hundreds of employees, customers, suppliers, and production partners were involved in the eighteen-month project. Results included improved flexibility and reduction of total finished goods inventory levels, leading to improved shareholder confidence and stock price.[40]

The SCOR model separates supply chain operations into six process categories: plan, source, make, deliver, return, and enable, as described below:[41]

- *PLAN*—Demand and supply planning including balancing resources with requirements; establishing/communicating plans for the supply chain; management of business rules, supply chain performance, data collection, inventory, capital assets, transportation, and regulatory requirements.
- *SOURCE*—Sourcing stocked, make-to-order, and engineer-to-order products including scheduling deliveries, receiving, verifying, and transferring product, authorizing supplier payments, identifying and selecting suppliers, assessing supplier performance, managing incoming inventory and supplier agreements.
- *MAKE*—Make-to-stock, make-to-order, and engineer-to-order production execution including scheduling production activities, producing, testing, packaging, staging, and releasing product for delivery, finalizing engineering for engineer-to-order products, managing work-in-process, equipment, facilities, and the production network.

- *DELIVER*—Order, warehouse, transportation, and installation management for stocked, make-to-order, and engineer-to-order product including all order management steps from order inquiries and quotes to routing shipments and selecting carriers, warehouse management from receiving and picking to loading and shipping product, invoicing customer, managing finished product inventories, and import/export requirements.
- *RETURN*—Returns of purchased materials to suppliers and receipt of finished goods returns from customers including authorizing and scheduling returns, receiving, verifying, and disposition of defective or excess products, return replacement or credit, and managing return inventories.
- *ENABLE*—The processes associated with establishing, maintaining, and monitoring information, relationships, resources, assets, business rules, compliance, and contracts required to operate supply chains. Enable processes support the design and management of the planning and execution processes of supply chains.

The SCOR model also uses five categories of performance attributes as shown in Table 14.2.[42] Implementing the SCOR model is no simple task. It requires a significant investment of time and open communications within the firm and among supply chain partners. However, the firms that use the model find it very beneficial. For instance, Joe Williams, director of global productivity at Mead Johnson Nutritionals, a division of Bristol-Myers Squibb, says the SCOR model is playing a big role in helping their unit measure its supply chain performance against other companies. But getting those measurements "is a big job," he says. "SCOR is definitive in some respects and open to interpretation in others."[43]

The SCOR model is designed to enable effective communication, performance measurement, and integration of processes between supply chain members. A standardized reference model helps management focus on management issues, serving internal and external customers, and instigating improvements along the supply chain. Using the SCOR software, virtually any supply chain can be configured, evaluated, and benchmarked against best practices, leading to continuous improvements and sustainable competitive advantage for the supply chain's participating members.

Table 14.2 SCOR Performance Categories and Attributes

PERFORMANCE CATEGORY	PERFORMANCE ATTRIBUTE
Reliability	1. On-time delivery performance 2. Order fill rates 3. Order accuracy rates
Responsiveness	1. Order lead times or speed
Agility	1. Response times for unforeseen events 2. Production flexibility
Cost	1. Supply chain management and logistics costs 2. Cost of goods sold 3. Warranty and returns processing costs
Asset Management	1. Cash-to-cash cycle time 2. Inventory days of supply 3. Asset turns

SCORmark is one of the newest tools of the Supply Chain Council, which allows member firms to benchmark performance against peer companies using a benchmarking portal at the Supply Chain Council's website. Benchmark data is supplied through an alliance with Performance Measurement Group, a wholly owned subsidiary of PricewaterhouseCoopers. Supply Chain Council members have access to confidential benchmarking based on the SCOR model metrics. Companies generally use SCOR-based benchmarking to:

- set reasonable performance goals based on the SCOR model
- calculate performance gaps against a global database
- develop company-specific roadmaps for supply chain competitive success

This has greatly reduced the time normally taken by firms to perform a benchmarking study—from months to weeks and, in some cases, days. The SCORmark portal removes cost barriers for members to obtain accurate and timely benchmark reports.

SUMMARY

Measuring the performance of companies and their supply chains is critical for identifying underlying problems and keeping end customers satisfied in today's highly competitive, rapidly changing marketplaces. Unfortunately, many firms have adopted performance measurement systems that measure the wrong things and are thus finding it difficult to achieve strategic goals and align their goals with those of the other supply chain members and the supply chain as a whole. Good performance measures allow firms to improve their processes, making their supply chains better as well.

Financial performance, while important to the firm and its shareholders, is argued to provide too little information regarding the firm's underlying ability to provide products and services that satisfy customers. Thus, measures that say something about the firm's quality, productivity, flexibility, and customer service capabilities have begun to be used successfully in many organizations. World-class organizations realize how important it is to align strategies with the performance of their people and processes, and performance measurement systems give these firms a means for directing efforts and firm capabilities toward what the firm is trying to do over the long haul—meet strategic objectives and satisfy customers.

As was discussed throughout the chapter, performance measurement systems should be a mix of financial, nonfinancial, quantitative, qualitative, process-oriented, environmentally oriented, and customer-oriented measures that effectively link the actions of the firm to the strategies defined by its executive managers. Firms actively managing their supply chains have an added layer of performance measurement requirements—measures must be added that link the operations of member firms as well as linking the actions of the firms to the competitive strategies of the supply chain. Several performance measurement models were presented and discussed in the chapter that have been successfully used in supply chains to monitor and link supply chain members' performance—namely the Balanced Scorecard and the Supply Chain Operations Reference models.

KEY TERMS

balanced scorecard, 510

carbon footprints, 508

environmental sustainability, 507

functional silos, 502

green supply chain management, 508

performance dashboards, 513

performance variance, 502

scorecarding, 510

single-factor productivity measures, 502

total productivity measures, 502

DISCUSSION QUESTIONS

1. Walmart's success is due to its low prices. Why would they need to monitor anything except price performance?
2. Do you think there is a relationship between performance measurement and a firm's competitiveness and profitability? Explain.
3. Why would IKEA be interested in sustainability performance measures?
4. What do customers have to do with good performance measures?
5. How should performance measures be viewed from a supply chain perspective?

6. In building supply chain competencies, what are the trade-offs that must be considered?
7. What risk do managers take when they view their firm's performance solely in financial terms?
8. List some of the traditional performance measures, and describe their value in today's competitive climate.
9. Discuss the use of performance standards and performance variances. Do schools and universities use them? How can they be damaging to the organization?
10. How can performance standards create functional silos?
11. What is the difference between a total productivity measure and a single-factor productivity measure? Provide an example.
12. List some single-factor and multiple-factor productivity measures for a restaurant, a quick-change oil garage, and an overnight delivery service.
13. Using the basic formula for productivity, (outputs)/(inputs), what are all the ways that productivity can be increased?
14. *Problem:* Cindy Jo's Hair Salon is concerned about its rising costs of supplies, energy, and labor, so it is considering investing in better equipment, which hopefully will reduce the time required to perform most hairstyles as well as result in better perceived quality by its customers. It predicts that the added investment will increase output levels as well as reduce energy costs, since some of the new equipment (hair dryers) use less electricity. Using the following information, determine the current and expected single-factor and total productivity measures. What is the percentage change in total productivity? What other items should be considered before making this capital investment? Do you think the increase in output will overcome the capital costs?

INPUTS AND OUTPUTS	CURRENT (THIS YEAR)	EXPECTED (NEXT YEAR)
Hairstyles per week	250	300
Labor costs per week	$960	$1,010
Energy costs per week	$400	$350
Material costs per week	$300	$325
Capital investment	$0	$12,000

15. What are the advantages and disadvantages of using labor utilization as a performance measure? Do these same arguments apply to machine utilization?
16. How could you increase labor productivity without increasing labor utilization?
17. Using the formulas provided for utilization, calculate the utilization of your classroom.
18. What do you think a good labor utilization would be for a factory? A restaurant? Why?
19. How do world-class performance measures differ from, say, financial performance measures?
20. Using the steps suggested for developing performance measures, create several world-class performance measures for a hotel's front-desk area, maintenance department, and room service personnel.

21. How should a firm extend its performance measures to include other supply chain members?

22. How could a company go about developing a sustainability performance measure?

23. How can you create performance measures for an entire supply chain?

24. Why should supply chains begin using green performance measures? Provide some examples of green supply chain performance measures. How would these differ from green performance measures for one firm?

25. What is a carbon footprint, and how can firms reduce theirs? How could you measure the carbon footprint for a supply chain?

26. What is perfect order fulfillment? Cash-to-cash cycle time?

27. Describe the four perspectives of the Balanced Scorecard. How is this model different from a set of world-class performance measures?

28. What are the steps in developing a balanced scorecard?

29. What are some weaknesses of the BSC?

30. How is a scorecard different from a dashboard?

31. What are the six process categories of the SCOR model, and which one do you think is the most important?

32. In what ways is the BSC similar to the SCOR model? Different from the SCOR model?

33. Which model do you think is best suited to measure supply chain performance—the BSC or the SCOR? Why?

34. How is SCORmark beneficial for member organizations?

ESSAY/PROJECT QUESTIONS

1. Using data obtained from the U.S. Bureau of Labor Statistics website (www.bls.gov), write a report on labor productivity in the U.S. compared to several other countries listed.

2. Find a company using sustainability performance measures to assess its own company as well as their suppliers, and write an essay on this company and their performance measures.

3. Pick a company from Gartner's annual listing of the Top 25 Supply Chains (see their listing at http://www.gartner.com/technology/supply-chain/top25.jsp), and discuss the performance measures it uses.

4. Find current examples of firms that are using Balanced Scorecards and the SCOR model, and report on their success.

ADDITIONAL RESOURCES

Kaplan, R. S., and D. P. Norton. "Linking the Balanced Scorecard to Strategy," *California Management Review* 39(1), 1996: 53–79.

Evans, J. R., and W. M. Lindsay. *The Management and Control of Quality*. Mason, OH: South-Western, 2002.

Metters, R., K. King-Metters, and M. Pullman. *Successful Service Operations Management*. Mason, OH: South-Western, 2003.

Nicholas, J. M. *Competitive Manufacturing Management*. New York: McGraw-Hill, 1998.

Wisner, J. D., and S. E. Fawcett. "Linking Firm Strategy to Operating Decisions Through Performance Measurement," *Production and Inventory Management Journal* 32(3), 1991: 5–11.

ENDNOTES

1. Anonymous, "SAS Achieves Record Revenue of $2.87 Billion in 2012," *Marketing Weekly News*, February 9, 2013: 202.
2. Kilcarr, S., "Resiliency and Reliability to be Main Supply Chain Focus in 2014," *Fleet Owner*, January 9, 2014: 1.
3. Laseter, T. and N. Gillis, "Collaborating for a More Sustainable Supply Chain," *Supply Chain Management Review* 16(5), 2012: 43–49.
4. Hofman,D., S. Aronow, and K. Nilles, "The 2013 Supply Chain Top 25: Learning from Leaders," *Supply Chain Management Review* 17(5), 2013: 12–21.
5. Poirier, C., M. Swink, and F. Quinn, "Progress Despite the Downturn," *Supply Chain Management Review* 13(7), 2009: 26.
6. Biederman, D., "The Customer Is King, Again," *Journal of Commerce,* May 10, 2010: 1.
7. Henri, J., "Are Your Performance Measurement Systems Truly Performing?" *CMA Management,* 80(7), 2006: 31–35; Biddick, M., "Time for a SaaS Strategy," *InformationWeek,* January 18, 2010: 27–30.
8. Woodcock, N., N. Broomfield, G. Downer, M. Starkey, "The Evolving Data Architecture of Social Customer Relationship Management," *Journal of Direct, Data and Digital Marketing Practice* 12(3), 2011: 249–266.
9. Balkau, F., and G. Sonnemann, "Managing Sustainability Performance Through the Value-Chain," *Corporate Governance* 10(1), 2010: 46–56.
10. Dodge, J., "The Technology Behind the Scam: Madoff Prosecutors Want to Find Out What Really Happened in 'House 17'," *The Investment Dealers' Digest* 75(42), 2009: 1; and Lattman, P., "Accountant Who Worked with Madoff for Years Is Indicted in Fraud," *New York Times,* September 27, 2013: B3.
11. Fusaro, P., and R. Miller, *What Went Wrong at Enron: Everyone's Guide to the Largest Bankruptcy in U.S. History.* Hoboken, NJ: Wiley, 2002.
12. Found at *CNN Money:* http://money.cnn.com/magazines/fortune/fortune500/2010/index.html
13. Stoessel, E., "Reaching New Heights," *Lodging Hospitality* 67(4), 2011: 1.
14. Christensen, P., and K. Gregory, "Becoming a Data-Driven Organization: City of Peoria, Arizona," *Government Finance Review* 26(2), 2010: 57–59.
15. Anonymous, "Hospital Strategies for Effective Performance Management," *Healthcare Financial Management* 65(1), 2011: H1–H6.

16. Debusk, G., and C. Debusk, "Characteristics of Successful Lean Six Sigma Organizations," *Cost Management* 24(1), 2010: 5–10.

17. Adapted from Nicholas, J. M. *Competitive Manufacturing Management.* New York: McGraw-Hill, 1998; and Wisner, J., and S. Fawcett, "Linking Firm Strategy to Operating Decisions Through Performance Measurement," *Production and Inventory Management Journal* 32(3), 1991: 5–11.

18. Christensen, P., and K. Gregory, "Becoming a Data-Driven Organization: City of Peoria, Arizona," *Government Finance Review* 26(2), 2010: 57–59.

19. Hae, E., and D. Ballou, "Raising the Recycling Rate at World-Class Zoo," *BioCycle* 50(10), 2009: 31–33. Also see p. 4 in http://www.sandiego.gov/environmental-services/pdf/geninfo/news/2013RecyclingAwardFS.pdf

20. Geary, S., and J. Zonnenburg, "What It Means to Be Best in Class," *Supply Chain Management Review,* July 2000: 42–50; Aquino, D., and K. O'Marah, "What Makes a Modern Supply Chain Professional?" *Supply Chain Management Review,* May 2009: 12–13; Hofman, D. and S. Aronow, "The Supply Chain Top 25 Raising the Bar," *Logistics Management* 51(9), 2012: 54–64.

21. Hervani, A., M. Helms, and J. Sarkis, "Performance Measurement for Green Supply Chain Management," *Benchmarking* 12(4), 2005: 330–354.

22. Editorial staff, "Green Supply Chain News: Walmart's Vast Efforts and Progress in Sustainability," found at http://www.thegreensupplychain.com/news/12-04-18-1.php, April 18, 2012.

23. McCue, D., "From Green to Black Ink," *World Trade* 26(5), 2013: 20–25.

24. Adapted from Geary, S., and J. P. Zonnenburg, "What It Means to Be Best in Class," *Supply Chain Management Review,* July 2000: 42–50.

25. Varmazis, M., "What to Look for in Online Office Supply Catalogs," *Purchasing* 136(11), 2007: 33.

26. Swink, M., R. Golecha, and T. Richardson, "Does Supply Chain Excellence Really Pay Off?" *Supply Chain Management Review* 14(2), 2010: 14.

27. See, for example, DeBusk, G., and A. Crabtree, "Does the Balanced Scorecard Improve Performance?" *Management Accounting Quarterly* 8(1), 2006: 44–48; Kaplan, R. S., and D. P. Norton, "The Balanced Scorecard—Measures That Drive Performance," 70(1), 1992: 71–79; Lester, T., "Measure for Measure, the Balanced Scorecard Remains a Widely Used Management Tool," *Financial Times,* October 6, 2004: 6; and Lawson, R., W. Stratton, and T. Hatch, "Scorecarding in the Public Sector: Fad or Tool of Choice?" *Government Finance Review* 23(3), 2007: 48–52.

28. Chow, C. W., D. Ganulin, K. Haddad, and J. Williamson, "The Balanced Scorecard: A Potent Tool for Energizing and Focusing Healthcare Organization Management," *Journal of Healthcare Management* 43(3), 1998: 263–280.

29. Lester, T., "Measure for Measure, the Balanced Scorecard Remains a Widely Used Management Tool."

30. Holmes, L., "Sir Terry Leahy," *Financial Management,* April 2013: 20–24.

31. Lester, T., "Measure for Measure, the Balanced Scorecard Remains a Widely Used Management Tool."

32. Alsyouf, I., "Measuring Maintenance Performance Using a Balanced Scorecard Approach," *Journal of Quality in Maintenance Engineering* 12(2), 2006: 133–143.

33. Totten, M., "Using Scorecard for Strategic Results," *Trustee* 66(10), 2013: 15–18.

34. Bush, P., "Strategic Performance Management in Government: Using the Balanced Scorecard," *Cost Management* 19(3), 2005: 24–31.

35. Anonymous, "New Look at State Enforcement of Regs," *Pollution Engineering* 45(3), 2013: 14–15; Blanco, E., "Seeing Is Believing: Harnessing the Power of Visualization," *Supply Chain Management Review* 17(5), 2013: 10–11; Henschen, D., "Drilling Down into Big Data," *InformationWeek,* September 9, 2013: 15–17; Mayor, T., "IT Takes on Bureaucracy," *Computerworld* 47(10), 2013: 24–26.

36. Interested readers can visit www.supply-chain.org for more information about the Supply Chain Council.

37. McCrea, B., "Certification: The Career Enhancer," *Supply Chain Management Review* 16(4), 2012: S3–S11; Anonymous, "SCOR Model Enhances How Supply Chains Are Enabled," *Material Handling & Logistics,* December 4, 2012: 1.

38. Taken from the online proceedings of the Supply-Chain World—Latin America 2002 conference, Mexico City, Mexico (www.supplychainworld.org/la2002/program.html).

39. Harbert, T., "Why the Leaders Love Value Chain Management," *Supply Chain Management Review* 13(8), 2009: 12–16.

40. Anonymous, "SCC Names Supply Chain Excellence Winners," *Material Handling & Logistics,* November 1, 2010: 1.

41. For more information, see www.supply-chain.org

42. For more information, see www.supply-chain.org. Also see, Myerson, P., "How Do You Know If Your Supply Chain Is Lean Enough?" *Material Handling & Logistics,* July 9, 2012: 1; Georgise, F., K. Thoben, and M. Siefert, "Adapting the SCOR Model to Suit the Different Scenarios: A Literature Review & Research Agenda," *International Journal of Business and Management* 7(6), 2012: 2–17.

43. Stedman, C., "Users Eye Standard for Supply Chain," *Computerworld News,* June 1, 1998 issue. Web page: www.computerworld.com/news/1998

Appendix 1

Areas Under the Normal Curve

This table gives the area under the curve to the left of x for various Z scores, or the number of standard deviations from the mean. For example, in the figure, if $Z = 1.96$, the value .97500 found in the body of the table is the total shaded area to the left of x.

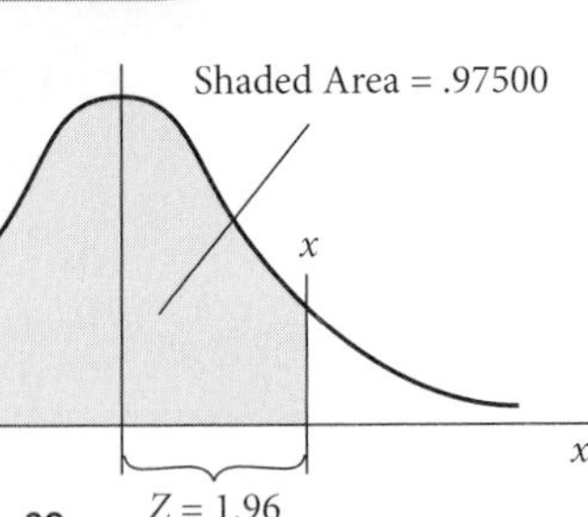

Z	.00	.01	.02	.03	.04	.05	.06	.07	.08	.09
.0	.50000	.50399	.50798	.51197	.51595	.51994	.52392	.52790	.53188	.53586
.1	.53983	.54380	.54776	.55172	.55567	.55962	.56356	.56749	.57142	.57535
.2	.57926	.58317	.58706	.59095	.59483	.59871	.60257	.60642	.61026	.61409
.3	.61791	.62172	.62552	.62930	.63307	.63683	.64058	.64431	.64803	.65173
.4	.65542	.65910	.66276	.66640	.67003	.67364	.67724	.68082	.68439	.68793
.5	.69146	.69497	.69847	.70194	.70540	.70884	.71226	.71566	.71904	.72240
.6	.72575	.72907	.73237	.73536	.73891	.74215	.74537	.74857	.75175	.75490
.7	.75804	.76115	.76424	.76730	.77035	.77337	.77637	.77935	.78230	.78524
.8	.78814	.79103	.79389	.79673	.79955	.80234	.80511	.80785	.81057	.81327
.9	.81594	.81859	.82121	.82381	.82639	.82894	.83147	.83398	.83646	.83891
1.0	.84134	.84375	.84614	.84849	.85083	.85314	.85543	.85769	.85993	.86241
1.1	.86433	.86650	.86864	.87076	.87286	.87493	.87698	.87900	.88100	.88298
1.2	.88493	.88686	.88877	.89065	.89251	.89435	.89617	.89796	.89973	.90147
1.3	.90320	.90490	.90658	.90824	.90988	.91149	.91309	.91466	.91621	.91774
1.4	.91924	.92073	.92220	.92364	.92507	.92647	.92785	.92922	.93056	.93189
1.5	.93319	.93448	.93574	.93699	.93822	.93943	.94062	.94179	.94295	.94408
1.6	.94520	.94630	.94738	.94845	.94950	.95053	.95154	.95254	.95352	.95449
1.7	.95543	.95637	.95728	.95818	.95907	.95994	.96080	.96164	.96246	.96327
1.8	.96407	.96485	.96562	.96638	.96712	.96784	.96856	.96926	.96995	.97062
1.9	.97128	.97193	.97257	.97320	.97381	.97441	.97500	.97558	.97615	.97670
2.0	.97725	.97784	.97831	.97882	.97932	.97982	.98030	.98077	.98124	.98169
2.1	.98214	.98257	.98300	.98341	.98382	.98422	.98461	.98500	.98537	.98574
2.2	.98610	.98645	.98679	.98713	.98745	.98778	.98809	.98840	.98870	.98899
2.3	.98928	.98956	.98983	.99010	.99036	.99061	.99086	.99111	.99134	.99158
2.4	.99180	.99202	.99224	.99245	.99266	.99286	.99305	.99324	.99343	.99361
2.5	.99379	.99396	.99413	.99430	.99446	.99461	.99477	.99492	.99506	.99520
2.6	.99534	.99547	.99560	.99573	.99585	.99598	.99606	.99621	.99632	.99643
2.7	.99653	.99664	.99674	.99683	.99693	.99702	.99711	.99720	.99728	.99736
2.8	.99744	.99752	.99760	.99767	.99774	.99781	.99788	.99795	.99801	.99807
2.9	.99813	.99819	.99825	.99831	.99836	.99841	.99846	.99851	.99856	.99861
3.0	.99865	.99869	.99874	.99878	.99882	.99886	.99889	.99893	.99896	.99900
3.1	.99903	.99906	.99910	.99913	.99916	.99918	.99921	.99924	.99926	.99929
3.2	.99931	.99934	.99936	.99938	.99940	.99942	.99944	.99946	.99948	.99950
3.3	.99952	.99953	.99955	.99957	.99958	.99960	.99961	.99962	.99964	.99965
3.4	.99966	.99968	.99969	.99970	.99971	.99972	.99973	.99974	.99975	.99976
3.5	.99977	.99978	.99978	.99979	.99980	.99981	.99981	.99982	.99983	.99983
3.6	.99984	.99985	.99985	.99986	.99986	.99987	.99987	.99988	.99988	.99989
3.7	.99989	.99990	.99990	.99990	.99991	.99991	.99992	.99992	.99992	.99992
3.8	.99993	.99993	.99993	.99994	.99994	.99994	.99994	.99995	.99995	.99995
3.9	.99995	.99995	.99996	.99996	.99996	.99996	.99996	.99996	.99997	.99997

Appendix 2

Answers to Selected End-of-Chapter Problems

CHAPTER 2

1. 8%
4. 5 times
10. a. 5,500 units, $69,000
    b. buy, $4,000
    c. make, $2,000

CHAPTER 3

19. The weighted score is 89. Supplier is classified as a Certified Vendor.

CHAPTER 4

27. 50,000 second-tier suppliers, then reduced to 2,000 second-tier suppliers.

CHAPTER 5

2. (1) 72,567, (2) 71,980, (3) 71,058

CHAPTER 6

1a. Chase production strategy

MONTH	JAN	FEB	MAR	APR	MAY	JUN
Demand	2000	3000	5000	6000	6000	2000
Production	2000	3000	5000	6000	6000	2000
Ending inventory	0	0	0	0	0	0
Workforce	20	30	50	60	60	20

1b. Level production strategy

MONTH	JAN	FEB	MAR	APR	MAY	JUN
Demand	2000	3000	5000	6000	6000	2000
Production	4000	4000	4000	4000	4000	4000
Ending inventory	2000	3000	2000	0	−2000	0
Workforce	40	40	40	40	40	40

−2000 indicates backlog of 2000 in May

4. ATP: D

WEEK		1	2	3	4	5	6	7	8
MODEL B									
MPS	BI = 20	20	0	20	20	0	20	20	20
Committed customer orders		10	10	10	10	10	0	0	10
ATP: D		20	0	10	0	0	20	20	10

7. Planned order releases and projected on-hand balances for component part Y.

PART Y		WEEK 1	WEEK 2	WEEK 3	WEEK 4	WEEK 5
Gross Requirements		80	50	90	0	80
Scheduled Receipts		160				
Projected Balance	120	200	150	60	60	20
Planned Order Releases				40*		

Q = 20, LT = 2 weeks, Safety Stock = 10
(*need to release an order of 40 units (2 × 20) in week 3 so that the projected balance on week 5 does not fall below the required safety stock of 10 units)

CHAPTER 7

1. 13.7 times
3. EOQ = 1,000
   Annual holding cost = annual order cost = $7,500
   Total annual inventory cost = $15,000 (not including $5,000,000 annual purchase cost)

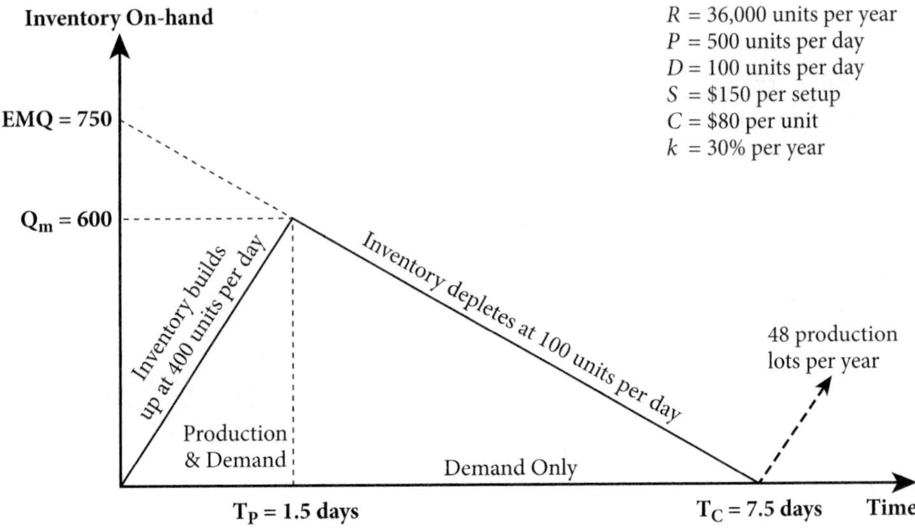

12. Safety stock = 117.6 units, Statistical reorder point = 767.6 units
14. Safety stock = 1,470 units, Statistical reorder point = 4,470 units

CHAPTER 8

2. The container round-trip time would have to be about 4.45 hours.
4. a. DPMO = 23,214 defects per million rentals.
   b. slightly less than 3.5

6. b. $\bar{\bar{x}} = 99.2$ and $\bar{R} = 8.4$
   c. $UCL_x = 105.3$, $LCL_x = 93.1$, $UCL_R = 19.2$, $LCL_R = 0$
9. a. $\bar{P} = .1167$
   b. $\sigma_p = .1015$
   c. UCL = 0.42; LCL = 0
11. a. $\bar{c} = 0.73$
   b. UCL = 3.30; LCL = 0

CHAPTER 9

21. The starting system with six warehouses has 18,000 total units; $S_2 = 12{,}728$ units total with three warehouses; and $S_3 = 7{,}348$ units total with one warehouse.

CHAPTER 10

9. $NPV_A = \$2{,}639$; $NPV_B = \$2{,}362$; $NPV_C = \$3{,}018$

CHAPTER 11

2. Columbus has the highest total weighted score of 84.5 and is the selected site.

CHAPTER 12

1. a. labor prod. = 0.5 cust. per labor \$; material prod. = 1.88 cust. per mat'l. \$; energy prod. = 7.5 cust. per energy \$; mult. fact. prod. = 0.38 cust. per \$.
   b. monthly capacity = 3,120 customers; capacity utilization = 48.1%
3. distance traveled = 5,545 m/day; you could put Depts. 4 and 5 closer together (switch 5 and 8), so the new distance = 3,805 m/day.
4. 19 points; try switching Depts. 5 and 8.
5. 2 full-time and 3 part-time workers would fill the requirements.
6. Probability = 0.7915
8. $L_s = 1.5$ customers; $L_q = 0.9$ customers
9. $P_0 = 1/(1 + .6 + .18(1.43)) = 0.538$; $L_q = .538((.36(.3) / (2(.7^2)) = .059$ customers

CHAPTER 14

14. Current total productivity = 250/\$1,660 = 0.151 haircuts/dollar
    Expected total productivity = 300/\$1,685 = 0.178 haircuts/dollar (an 18% productivity increase).

Glossary

A

ABC inventory control system A useful technique for determining which inventories should be managed more closely and which others should not (A-items are the most important).

ABC inventory matrix A diagram that illustrates whether a firm's physical inventory matches its inventory usage. It is derived by plotting an ABC analysis based on inventory usage classification on the vertical axis and an ABC analysis based on physical inventory classification on the horizontal axis.

acceptance sampling In purchasing, it is a statistical screening technique that can be used to determine whether or not a shipment will be accepted, returned to the supplier or used for billback purposes when defects are fixed or units are eliminated by the buyer.

active RFID tags An RFID tag that is equipped with an onboard power supply to power the integrated circuits and broadcast its signal to the tag reader.

additive manufacturing or 3D printing A process of making a three-dimensional solid object of virtually any shape from a digital model.

aggregate production plan (APP) A long-range production plan; it sets the aggregate output rate, workforce size, utilization, inventory and backlog levels for a plant.

air carriers For-hire airlines.

airline security Protection that is provided for airlines against terrorist attacks and other illegal activities.

analytic SRM A method that allows the company to analyze the complete supplier base.

application service providers (ASPs) A company that offers website services for a fee, such as self-serve reverse auction websites.

arrival pattern The frequency with which customers arrive at a business.

assignable variations Process variations that can be traced to a specific cause. Assignable variations are created by causes that can be identified and eliminated and thus become the objective of statistical process control efforts.

Association of Southeast Asian Nations (ASEAN) An economic and geopolitical organization created in 1967 that today comprises the following countries in the Southeast Asian region: Brunei, Cambodia, Indonesia, Laos, Malaysia, Myanmar, the Philippines, Singapore, Thailand and Vietnam. The primary objective of ASEAN is to promote economic, social and cultural development of the region through cooperative programs.

attribute data Yes/no kinds of data. These indicate the presence of some attribute such as color, satisfaction, workability or beauty (for instance, determining whether or not a car was painted the right color, if a customer liked the meal, if the lightbulb worked or if the dress was pretty).

available-to-promise (ATP) quantity The uncommitted portion of a firm's planned production. It is used to promise new customer orders.

B

back-of-the-house operations Those services that do not require customer contact.

back-shoring/near-shoring/right-shoring Moving their foreign production back home or close to home.

backward vertical integration Acquiring upstream suppliers.

balanced scorecard (BSC) A management system developed in the early 1990s by Robert Kaplan and David Norton that helps companies to continually refine their vision and strategy. The balanced scorecard uses a set of measures to provide feedback on internal business performance in order to continually improve strategic performance. Also referred to as scorecarding.

balking Refusing to join a queue once it is seen how long it is.

barter The complete exchange of goods and/or services of equal value without the exchange of currency. The seller can either consume the goods and/or services or resell the items.

Baumol's disease A productivity growth problem named after noted U.S. economist William Baumol in the 1960s. For most services, automation can be a troublesome issue, and the labor content per unit of output can be quite high relative to manufactured goods. These two things can lead to a declining productivity growth rate as a nation's economy becomes less manufacturing oriented and more service oriented.

benchmarking The practice of copying what other businesses do best; studying how things are done well in other firms to potentially make use of the same methods.

best-of-breed solution An ERP system that picks the best application or module for each individual function.

big data Collections of data sets that are too large and complex to be processed by traditional database management tools or data processing software applications.

big data analytics As the number of customers grows for large businesses, their transactions and the desire to analyze all of this information also grows, which requires big data analytics.

bill of materials (BOM) An engineering document that shows an inclusive listing of all component parts and assemblies making up the final product.

billback penalty A fee charged back to the supplier for services or products not received by the customer.

blank check purchase order A small value purchase order with a signed blank check attached, usually at the bottom of the purchase order.

blanket order release A form used to release a specific quantity against a prenegotiated blanket purchase order.

blanket purchase order A purchase order that covers a variety of items and is negotiated for repeated supply over a fixed time period, such as quarterly or yearly.

breakbulk When large-quantity shipments are broken down in a distribution center so that items can be combined into specific customer orders and then shipped out.

bullwhip effect A term referring to ineffective communication between buyers and suppliers and infrequent delivery of materials, combined with production based on poor forecasts along a supply chain that results in either too little or too much inventory at various points of storage and consumption. Simply, it causes an amplification of the variation in the demand pattern along the supply chain.

business clusters According to Dr. Michael Porter, "clusters are geographic concentrations of interconnected companies and institutions in a particular field. Clusters encompass an array of linked industries and other entities important to competition."

business cycle Alternating periods of expansion and contraction in economic activity.

business ethics The application of ethical principles to business situations.

business process reengineering (BPR) The radical rethinking and redesigning of business processes to reduce waste and increase performance.

Buy American Act Legislation mandating that U.S. government purchases and third-party purchases that utilize federal funds must buy domestically produced goods, if the price differential between the domestic product and an identical foreign-sourced product does not exceed a certain percentage amount.

C

C charts Counts the number of defects per unit of output.

call centers or customer contact centers Customer service departments that integrate all of themethods customers can use to contact a business, including telephone, mail, comment cards, email, and website messages and chat rooms.

capacity The output capabilities of a firm's labor and machine resources.

capacity requirements planning (CRP) A shortrange capacity planning technique that is used to check the feasibility of the material requirements plan.

carbon footprints A firm's or supply chain's total carbon emissions.

cause-and-effect diagrams Also called fishbone diagram or Ishikawa diagram. A method that is used to aid in brainstorming and isolating the causes of a problem. Typically there are four causes of problems (the 4-Ms).

cause-and-effect forecasting A forecasting method that uses one or more factors (independent variables) that are related to demand to predict future demand.

centralized purchasing A single purchasing department, usually located at the firm's corporate office, makes all the purchasing decisions, including order quantity, pricing policy, contracting, negotiations, and supplier selection and evaluation.

centralized warehousing system Fewer warehouses means that outbound transportation costs will be higher.

centralized–decentralized purchasing structure A hybrid purchasing structure that is centralized at the corporate level but decentralized at the individual business unit level.

chase demand strategy A strategy that is used when the amount of capacity varies with demand. See also chase production strategy.

chase production strategy A production strategy that adjusts output to match the demand pattern during each production period.

check sheets A tool that allows users to determine the frequencies of specific problems.

Civil Aeronautics Act of 1938 Legislation that promoted the development of the air transportation system, air safety, and airline efficiency by establishing the Civil Aeronautics Board to oversee market entry, establish routes with appropriate levels of competition, develop regional feeder airlines and establish reasonable rates. The Civil Aeronautics Administration was also established to regulate air safety.

class rates The transportation rates based on the particular class of the product transported; some products have higher published class rates than others. Rates are based on an evaluation of four transportation characteristics: density, stowability, handling and liability.

clickstreams A record of the items that a specific customer clicks on when visiting a website.

closed-loop MRP An MRP-based manufacturing planning and control system that incorporates aggregate production planning, master production scheduling, material requirements planning and capacity requirements planning.

closeness desirability rating A scale used to rate how desirable it is to have two departments close together. The objective is to design a layout that maximizes the desirability rating for the entire facility.

cloud-based communication platforms An internet-based platform that provides greater visibility, ensures faster time to market, and offers faster response to changing market dynamics and demands.

cloud computing/on-demand computing When shared resources and other information are made available to users over the Internet, usually for a subscription fee. It allows small businesses, for example, to make use of sophisticated software without actually making the purchase; also termed on-demand computing.

cloud-based forecasting Using supplier-hosted or software-as-a-service (SaaS) advanced forecasting applications that are provided to companies on a subscription basis.

coal slurry Pulverized coal that is suspended in water.

cold chains Refer to temperature controlled transportation, transfers, and warehousing.

collaboration Working together through information sharing with suppliers and customers on various activities.

collaborative education Providing training for supply chain partner employees.

collaborative negotiations/integrative or win–win negotiations The process that occurs when both sides work together to maximize the joint outcome, or to create a win-win result; also referred to as integrative negotiations.

collaborative planning, forecasting, and replenishment (CPFR) According to the Council of Supply Chain Professionals, "CPFR seeks cooperative management of inventory through joint visibility and replenishment of products throughout the supply chain. Information shared between suppliers and retailers aids in planning and satisfying customer demands through a supportive system of shared information. This allows for continuous updating of inventory and upcoming requirements, essentially making the end-to-end supply chain process more efficient. Efficiency is also created through the decrease expenditures for merchandising, inventory, logistics, and transportation across all trading partners."

co-managed inventories A somewhat more collaborative form of VMI; can also refer to JIT II buyer and supplier reach an agreement regarding how information is shared, order quantities, when an order is generated, and the delivery timing and location.

commodity rates Rates that apply to minimum quantities of specified products that are shipped between two specified locations.

common carriers Transportation providers that offer services to all shippers at published rates between designated locations.

Common Market for Eastern and Southern Africa (COMESA) A customs union established to foster economic growth among the member countries of Burundi, Comoros, D. R. Congo, Djibouti, Egypt, Eritrea, Ethiopia, Kenya, Libya, Madagascar, Malawi, Mauritius, Rwanda, Seychelles, Sudan, Swaziland, Uganda, Zambia, and Zimbabwe.

consolidation warehouses Warehouses that collect large numbers of LTL shipments from nearby regional sources of supply, then deliver in TL or CL quantities to a manufacturer.

consumer's risk The risk assumed when a buyer accepts a shipment of poor-quality units because the sample did meet the acceptance standard; this results in a type-II error.

container-on-flatcar (COFC) A form of intermodal transportation; standardized shipping containers are transported via rail flatcar, and they can also be placed on a truck chassis or on an ocean-going container ship.

continuous review system An inventory management system where the physical inventory levels are counted on a continuous or daily basis.

contract carriers For-hire carriers that are like common carriers but are not bound to serve the general public. They serve specific customers under contractual agreements.

Contracts for the International Sale of Goods (CISG) A set of rules established by the United Nations to govern the international transactions in goods.

contributor factory A manufacturing facility that plays a greater strategic role than a server factory by getting involved in product development and engineering, production planning, making critical procurement decisions and developing suppliers.

control charts A method that monitors process variabilities and then collects and plots sample measurements of the process over time. The means of these sample measures are plotted on the control charts.

corporate social responsibility (CSR) The practice of business ethics.

cost-of-service pricing A pricing strategy used when carriers desire to establish prices that vary based on their fixed and variable costs.

counterpurchase A trade arrangement whereby the original exporter either buys or finds a buyer to purchase a specified quantity of unrelated goods and/or services from the original importer.

countertrade A global sourcing process in which goods and/or services of domestic firms are exchanged for goods and/or services of equal value or in combination with currency from foreign firms. This type of arrangement is sometimes used by countries where there is a shortage of hard currency or as a means to acquire technologies.

critical-to-quality (CTQ) characteristics Those characteristics related to customers and their service or product requirements that are critical to achieving customer satisfaction.

crossdocking A continuous replenishment logistics process at a distribution center, where incoming goods are sorted and/or consolidated, and then shipped out to their final destinations, without the need to store the goods. Cross-docking generally takes place within 24 hours, sometimes less than an hour, after shipment arrivals and is used to replenish high demand inventories.

cross-selling Purchasing that occurs when customers are sold additional products as the result of an initial purchase.

customer churn The rate at which customers leave or stop using a firm.

customer defection analysis Information that analyzes why customers stop using a particular business.

customer lifetime value (CLV)/customer value or customer profitability Assigning a profit figure to each customer by summing the margins of all the products and services purchased over time, less the cost of marketing to and maintaining that customer, such as the costs of direct mail and sales calls and the service costs for each customer. Additionally, the firm forecasts future purchased quantities, profit margins, and marketing costs for each customer, discounts these back to the current date and then adds this projected profit quantity to the current profit amount. Also known as customer value or customer profitability.

customer relationship management Managing a firm's customer base such that customers remain satisfied and continue to purchase goods and services. Sometimes it also refers to CRM software applications.

customer relationship management process Provides the firm with the structure for developing and managing customer relationships.

customer service The provision of information, help, and/or technical support to customers in a way that meets or exceeds customer expectations.

customer service management process A process that provides information to customers while also providing ongoing management of any product and service agreements between the firm and its customers.

customs brokers Global logistics intermediaries that move international shipments through customs for companies as well as handle the necessary documentation required to accompany the shipments.

Customs-Trade Partnership Against Terrorism program (C TPAT) A partnership between U.S. Customs, the International Cargo Security Council (a U.S. nonprofit association of companies and individuals involved in transportation) and Pinkerton (a global security advising company, headquartered in New Jersey), whereby companies agree to improve security in their supply chain in return for "fast lane" border crossings.

cycle counting A commonly used technique in which physical inventory is counted on a periodic basis to ensure that physical inventory matches current inventory records.

D

data privacy The desire of customers to keep personal information from becoming compromised or being shared with other companies to generate income.

data warehouse Information system structures used to store data that was collected from the various divisions of the firm.

deep-sea transportation Ocean-going water carriers. The development and use of supertankers and containerships are examples.

decentralized purchasing Individual, local purchasing departments, such as at the plant level, make their own purchasing decisions.

decentralized warehousing system Used when faster delivery service is required. As the number of warehouses used increases, the system becomes more decentralized.

decentralized–centralized purchasing structure A hybrid purchasing structure that is decentralized at the corporate level but centralized at the individual business unit level.

deep-sea transportation Ocean-going shipping vessels, primarily carrying containers.

defects per million opportunities (DPMO) A Six Sigma quality metric.

demand forecast updating When buyers place purchase orders, suppliers use this information to revise their demand forecasts.

demand management A set of activities that range from determining or estimating the demand from customers through converting specific customer orders into promised delivery dates to help balance demand with supply.

demand management process The steps used for balancing customer demand and the firm's output capabilities.

demand source That part of the input process that deals with customer arrivals.

demand time fence A firmed planning segment that is used with the MRP application; it usually stretches from the current period to a period several weeks into the future.

Department of Defense (DOD) A major public buyer within the United States government.

Department of Transportation Act Legislation that created the Department of Transportation (DOT) in 1966 to coordinate the executive functions of all government entities dealing with transportation related matters.

dependent demand The internal demand for parts based on the demand of the final product in which the parts are used.

differentiation strategy A business approach that is based on creating a product or service that is considered unique. Usually associated with high quality.

direct costs Costs that are directly traceable to the unit produced, such as the amount of materials and labor used to produce a unit of the finished good.

direct offset A form of countertrade that usually involves coproduction, or a joint venture, and exchange of related goods and/or services.

distribution center A warehouse that performs break-bulk activities and then forms outbound specific product assortments that are then shipped to the customer.

distribution network The organization of a distribution system that ensures successful product delivery.

distribution requirements plan (DRP) A time-phased finished goods inventory replenishment plan in a distribution network.

distributive negotiations A negotiating objective that seeks an outcome that primarily favors the interests of one side.

E

early supplier involvement (ESI) Involving key suppliers during the product design and development stage to take advantage of their knowledge and technologies.

eatertainment The combining of restaurant and entertainment elements.

economic manufacturing quantity (EMQ) or production order quantity (POQ) model A variation of the classic EOQ model, used to determine the most economical number of units to produce.

economic order quantity (EOQ) model The classic independent demand inventory system that computes the optimal order quantity to minimize total inventory costs.

economies of scale A theory stating that the cost per unit decreases as the number of units purchased, produced or transported increases.

edutainment or infotainment The combining of learning with entertainment to appeal to customers looking for substance along with play.

efficient consumer response (ECR) developed by a U.S. grocery industry task force charged with making grocery supply chains more competitive. Point-of-purchase transactions at grocery stores were forwarded via computer to distributors and manufacturers, allowing the stores to keep stocks replenished while minimizing the need for safety stock inventories.

80/20 rule A theory originating from Pareto analysis, which suggests that most of a firm's problem "events" (80 percent) are accounted for by just a few (20 percent) of the problems; can also be applied to other areas, such as ABC inventory control, which says that 80 percent of the inventory dollars come from 20 percent of the inventory items.

electronic data interchange (EDI) A computer-to-computer exchange of business documents such as purchase orders, order status inquiries and reports, promotion announcements and shipping and billing notices.

electronic product code (EPC) A widely used RFID standard managed by EPC global, Inc.

emergency sourcing The act of maintaining a backup source of supply available to provide purchased items when the primary source has temporarily become unavailable.

empty miles The trucks that return empty after their delivery; these return journeys cause big energy wastes.

enterprise resource planning (ERP) A packaged business software system that lets a company automate and integrate the majority of its business processes, share common data and practices across the enterprise and produce and access information in a real-time environment.

entertailing The combining of retail locations with entertainment elements—such as offering ice skating, rock climbing and amusement park rides at a shopping mall.

environmental management system (EMS) The practices put in place by a firm to try to reduce environmental waste and improve environmental performance.

environmental sustainability The need to continually protect the environment and reduce greenhouse gas emissions.

equipment setups The steps required to prepare production equipment for the next product to be produced.

ethical and environmental certifications certifying companies according to ethical and environmental requirements. A number of certifying agencies can be used, such as the New York-based Rainforest Alliance and Trans-Fair USA.

ethical and sustainable sourcing Purchasing from suppliers that are governed by environmental sustainability and social and ethical practices.

ethical sourcing The practice of purchasing from suppliers that are governed by social and ethical practices.

Ethical Trading Initiative (ETI) An alliance of organizations seeking to take responsibility for improving working conditions and agreeing to implement the ETI Base Code, a standard for ethical practices for the firms and its suppliers.

European Union (EU) A European international trade organization designed to reduce tariff and nontariff barriers among member countries. Set up after the Second World War, the EU was officially launched on May 9, 1950, with France's proposal to create a European federation consisting of six countries: Belgium, Germany, France, Italy, Luxembourg, and the Netherlands. A series of accessions resulted in a total of 28 member states in 2013. Most recently, the EU has added Iceland, Montenegro, Serbia, Republic of Macedonia and Turkey.

event-based marketing A marketing strategy that offers the right products and services to customers at the right time.

everyday low pricing (EDLP) The elimination of price discounting and offering wholesale prices to customers. Helps reduce the bullwhip effect.

exception rates Published rates that are lower than class rates for specific origin-destination locations or volumes.

exempt carriers For-hire carriers that are exempt from the regulations of services and rates. They transport certain exempt products such as produce, livestock, coal, garbage, or newspapers.

expediting The act of contacting the supplier to speed up an overdue shipment.

F

facilitating products Products such as computers, furniture, and office supplies that are not part of the services sold but rather are consumed inside the firm and must also be managed.

fair trade products A product manufactured or grown by a disadvantaged producer in a developing country that receives a fair price for its goods.

Federal Acquisition Regulation (FAR) The primary set of rules issued by the U.S. government to govern the process through which the government purchases goods and services.

Federal Acquisition Streamlining Act (FASA) A federal act signed by President Clinton in October 1994 to remove many restrictions on government purchases that do not exceed $100,000.

Federal Aviation Act of 1958 Legislation that replaced the Civil Aeronautics Administration with the Federal Aviation Administration (FAA) and gave the FAA authority to prescribe air traffic rules, make safety regulations and plan the national airport system.

First and Second Laws of Service Two laws proposed by David Maister in a well-known paper written on the topic of waiting time: (1) Satisfaction=perceptions – expectations, and (2) It is hard to play catch-up ball.

five dimensions of service quality Five categories used by customers to rate service quality: reliability, responsiveness, assurance, empathy, and tangibles.

five-Ss Five Japanese words, coming originally from Toyota, that relate to industrial housekeeping. The idea is that by implementing the five-Ss, the workplace will be cleaner, more organized and safer, thereby reducing processing waste and improving productivity.

fixed costs Costs that are independent of the output quantity.

fixed order quantity models Independent demand inventory models that use fixed parameters to determine the optimal order quantity to minimize total inventory costs.

flow diagrams/process diagrams/process maps Tools that use annotated boxes representing process action elements and ovals representing wait periods, connected by arrows to show the flow of products or customers through the process. This tool is the necessary first step to evaluating any manufacturing or service process.

FOB destination pricing A price quotation that includes transportation to the buyer's location when products are purchased from a supplier.

FOB origin pricing A price quotation in which the buyer may decide to purchase goods and provide the transportation to the shipping destination; in this case, the supplier quotes are lower.

focus strategy A business approach incorporating the idea that a firm can serve a narrow target market or niche better than other firms that are trying to serve a broad market.

follow-up A proactive act to contact the supplier to ensure on-time delivery of the goods ordered.

forecast bias A measure of the tendency of a forecast to be consistently higher (negative bias) or lower (positive bias) than the actual demand.

forecast error The difference between actual demand and the forecast.

foreign freight forwarders Service providers that move goods for companies from domestic production facilities to foreign customer destinations, using surface and air transportation and warehouses. They consolidate small shipments into larger TL, CL or container shipments, decide what transportation modes and methods to use, handle all of the documentation requirements and then disperse the shipments at their destination.

foreign-trade zones (FTZs) Secure sites within the U.S. under the supervision of the U.S. Customs Service. These are where materials can be imported duty-free as long as the imports are used as inputs to production of goods that are eventually exported.

forward buying When buyers stock up to take advantage of low price offers.

forward vertical integration Acquiring downstream customers.

four Ms The standard classifications of problem causes and represent a very thorough list for problem–cause analyses. In almost all cases, problem causes will be in one or more of these four areas: Material, Machine, Methods, and Manpower.

franchising A business practice that allows services to expand quickly in dispersed geographic markets, protect existing markets and build market share. Franchisees are required to invest some of their own capital, while paying a small percentage of sales to the franchiser in return for the brand name, start-up help, advertising, training and assistance in meeting specific operating standards.

Free and Secure Trade program (FAST) A U.S. Customs' security program; the overall goal is to ensure the security of international supply chains and international trucking in particular. To participate in FAST, motor carriers must become C-TPAT certified and their commercial drivers must complete an application and undergo a background check.

freight brokers Legally authorized intermediaries that bring shippers and transportation companies (mainly truckers) together.

front-of-the-house operations Operations that are involved with interactions with customers, such as front desk operations.

functional products MRO items and other commonly purchased items and supplies. These items are characterized by low profit margins, relatively stable demands and high levels of competition.

functional silos Departments in a firm that are only concerned with what is going on in their department and not what is in the best interests of the firm.

G

general freight carriers The carriers transporting the majority of goods shipped in the U.S.; includes common carriers.

General Services Administration (GSA) A U.S. federal agency that is responsible for most federal purchases. It is based in Washington, D.C., and has 11 regional offices throughout the U.S.

global sourcing Purchasing from non-domestic suppliers.

global supply chains Supply chains with foreign trading partners.

global trade management systems Software that enables shippers and carriers to submit the correct import/export documents as goods are moved between countries.

green development The implementation of environmentally friendly development.

green power Electricity products that include large proportions of electricity generated from renewable and environmentally preferable energy sources such as wind and solar energy.

green purchasing A practice aimed at ensuring that purchasing personnel include environmental considerations and human health issues when making purchasing decisions; also termed green sourcing and sustainable procurement.

green purchasing/green sourcing/sustainable procurement/sustainable sourcing A practice aimed at ensuring that purchasing personnel include environmental considerations and human health issues when making purchasing decisions.

green reverse logistics programs Systems that focus on reducing the environmental impact of certain modes of transportation used for returns, reducing the amount of disposed packaging and product materials by redesigning products and processes, and making use of reusable totes and pallets.

green supply chain management (GSCM) An organizational approach that extends the concept of green logistics to include activities related to environmentally responsible product design, acquisition, production, distribution, use, reuse and disposal by partners within the supply chain.

H

high-speed trains Passenger trains that typically average 70 miles per hour or greater.

holding or carrying costs The costs incurred for holding inventory in storage.

hybrid purchasing organization A firm that uses either a centralized–decentralized or decentralized–centralized purchasing structure.

I

ICC Termination Act of 1995 Legislation that eliminated the Interstate Commerce Commission.

import broker or sales agent A firm that is set up to import goods for customers for a fee. An import broker does not take title to the goods.

import merchant A firm that imports and takes title to the good, and then resells them to a buyer.

incoterms (International Commercial Terms) A uniform set of rules created by the International Chamber of Commerce to simplify international transactions of goods with respect to shipping costs, risks and responsibilities of the buyer, seller and shipper.

indented bill of materials Indentations are used to present the level number within the bill of materials; also known as the multilevel bill of materials.

independent demand The demand for final products and service parts. It has a demand pattern that is affected by trends, seasonal patterns and general market conditions.

indirect costs Those costs that cannot be traced directly to the unit produced and are synonymous with manufacturing overhead.

indirect offset A form of countertrade that involves an exchange of goods and/or services unrelated to the initial purchase.

industrial buyers Buyers with a primary responsibility of purchasing raw materials for conversion purposes.

information visibility The degree that information is communicated and made available to various constituents, typically on the Internet.

innovative products Newly developed products characterized by short product life cycles, volatile demand, high profit margins and relatively less competition.

integration A shared-process view of the supply chain that spans multiple departments, processes and software applications for internal users and external partners.

intermediate or medium-range planning horizon A planning horizon that covers six to eighteen months.

intermediately positioned strategy A location strategy that places warehouses midway between the sources of supply and the customers.

intermodal marketing companies (IMCs) Companies that act as intermediaries between intermodal railroad companies and shippers.

intermodal transportation Two or more modes of transportation that combine to deliver a shipment of goods.

internal control An internal operational system that prevents, for example, abuse of purchasing funds.

internal supply chains An organization's network of internal suppliers and internal customers. Internal supply chains can be complex, particularly if the firm has multiple divisions and organizational structures around the globe.

inventory turnover The number of times a firm's inventory is utilized and replaced over an accounting period, such as a year.

inventory turnover ratio or inventory turnovers A widely used measure to analyze how efficiently a firm uses its inventory to generate revenue.

inventory visibility The ability of supply chain companies to see inventory quantities of the various members, typically using the Internet.

invitation for bid (IFB) A request for qualified suppliers to submit bids for a contract. Suppliers are asked to bid, given certain opening and closing dates of the bid. The basis for awarding a contract is preset and binding.

ISO 14000 A family of international standards for environmental management developed by the International Organization for Standardization (ISO).

ISO 9000 A series of management and quality assurance standards in design, development, production, installation and service developed by the International Organization for Standardization (ISO).

J

JIT warehousing/lean warehousing The process of moving inventory more quickly through inbound and outbound warehouses and distribution centers. As firms develop their supply chain management capabilities, warehouses and distribution centers will develop more JIT capabilities, like crossdocking; also termed lean warehousing.

just-in-time (JIT)/lean thinking Originally associated with Toyota managers like TaiichiOhno and his kanban system, JIT encompasses continuous problem solving to eliminate waste. Today it is also referred to as lean or lean thinking.

K

kaizen ways to reduce supplier delivery and quality problems, solve movement problems, visibility problems, machine breakdown problems, machine setup problems, and internal quality problems.

kaizen blitz A rapid improvement event or workshop, aimed at finding big improvements.

kanban A Japanese word for "card"; it is a visual tool used in lean production.

key supply chain processes The eight processes that are most important to integrate in the supply chain.

key trading partners Suppliers that have come to be trusted and that provide a large share of the firm's critical products and services; and repeat, satisfied customers that buy a significant portion of the firm's products.

keiretsu relationships partnership arrangements between Japanese manufacturers and suppliers.

knowledge management solutions A system that uses Internet applications tied to desktop applications that enable real-time collaboration and flow of information between supply chain partners.

knowledge management system A system that is able to capture the accumulated knowledge of experienced sales staff and other skilled personnel if they leave an organization.

L

lag capacity strategy A reactive approach that adjusts capacity in response to demand.

lead capacity strategy A proactive approach that adds or subtracts capacity in anticipation of future market condition and demand.

lead factory A source of product and process innovation and competitive advantage for the entire organization.

lead logistics provider Outside agents that manage all of a firm's 3PLs; also termed a 4PL.

lead management system A tool that allows sales reps to follow prescribed sales tactics when dealing with sales prospects or opportunities, to aid in closing the deal with a client.

lean layouts Arrangements that reduce wasted movements of workers, customers and/or workin-process (WIP), and achieve smooth product flow through the facility.

lean production/lean manufacturing/lean thinking Organizing work and analyzing the level of waste existing in operating machinery, warehouses and systems to fit a lean process flow. The goals are to reduce production throughput times and inventory levels, cut order lead times, increase quality and improve customer responsiveness with fewer people and other assets.

Lean Six Sigma/Lean Six A new term used to describe the melding of lean production and Six Sigma quality practices.

lean supply chain relationships The relationships that occur when the focal firm, its suppliers and its customers begin to work together to identify customer requirements, remove waste, reduce cost and improve quality and customer service.

lean warehousing When warehousing, crossdocking, packaging and freight consolidation is offered to companies who are looking to increase speed and reduce costs as much as possible to compete.

legacy MRP system A broad label used to describe an older information system that usually works at an operational level to schedule production within a single facility.

legacy systems A firm's existing software applications.

less-than-truckload (LTL) carriers Carriers that move small packages or shipments taking up less than one truckload; the shipping fees are higher per hundred weight (cwt) than TL fees, since the carrier must consolidate many small shipments into one truckload, then break the truckload back down into individual shipments at the destination for individual deliveries.

level demand strategy A theory for managing capacity that occurs when a firm utilizes a constant amount of capacity regardless of demand variations.

leveraging purchase volume The concentration of purchase volume to create quantity discounts, less-costly volume shipments and other more favorable purchase terms.

line haul rates The charges for moving goods to a nonlocal destination; these can be further classified as class rates, exception rates, commodity rates and miscellaneous rates.

linear trend forecast A forecasting method in which the trend can be estimated using simple linear regression to fit a line to a time series of historical data.

logistics The practice of moving and storing goods to meet customer requirements for the minimum cost.

logistics brokers Legally authorized intermediaries that bring shippers and transportation companies (mainly truckers) together.

long-range planning horizon A planning horizon that covers a year or more.

M

make or buy decision A strategic one that can impact an organization's competitive position. It is obvious that most organizations buy their MRO and office supplies rather than make the items themselves.

make-to-order manufacturing firms Firms that make custom products based on orders from customers, resulting in long lead times and higher unit costs.

make-to-stock Firms that typically emphasize immediate delivery of off-the-shelf, standard goods at relatively low prices compared to the chase strategy.

manufacturing cells or work cells Cells that are designed to process similar parts or components, saving duplication of equipment and labor as well as centralizing the area where units of the same purchased part are delivered.

manufacturing flow management process The set of activities responsible for making the actual product, establishing the manufacturing flexibility required to adequately serve the markets, and designing the production system to meet cycle time requirements.

manufacturing resource planning (MRP-II) An outgrowth and extension of the original closed loop MRP system.

market positioned strategy A location strategy that places warehouses close to customers, to maximize customer service and to allow the firm to generate transportation economies by using inbound TL and CL deliveries to each warehouse location.

master production schedule (MPS) A medium range production plan that is more detailed than the aggregate production plan.

match or tracking capacity strategy A moderate strategy that adjusts capacity in small amounts in response to demand and changing market conditions.

material requirements plan (MRP) A software application that has been available since the 1970s; it performs an analysis of the firm's existing internal conditions and reports back what the production and purchase requirements are for a given finished product manufacturing schedule.

material requisition (MR) An internal document initiated by the material user to request materials from the warehouse or purchasing department.

maximize competition The competition that is designed for ensuring the purchases of goods and services that are in strict compliance with statutes and policies, public procurement procedures.

mean absolute deviation (MAD) An indicator of forecast accuracy based on an average of the absolute value of the forecast errors over a given period of time. The measure indicates, on average, how many units the forecast is off from the actual data.

mean absolute percentage error (MAPE) An indicator of forecast accuracy based on the true magnitude of the forecast error. The monthly absolute forecast error divided by actual demand is summed, then divided by the number of months used in the forecast to derive an average, and lastly multiplied by 100. The measure indicates, on average, what percent the forecast is off from the actual data.

mean square error (MSE) An indicator of forecast accuracy. The forecast errors are squared and then summed and divided by the number of periods to determine the mean square error. The measure penalizes large errors more than small errors.

merchants Firms that buy goods in large quantities for resale purposes. Wholesalers and retailers are examples of merchants.

microfranchise A type of franchising concept that offers ready-made, low-risk starter jobs to people with no education and little available capital while giving established companies additional distribution avenues.

micro-purchases Government purchases of less than $2,500.

miscellaneous rates Contract rates that are negotiated between two parties involving shipments containing a variety of products (in the typical case, the rate is based on the overall weight of the shipment).

mixed Internet distribution strategy The combining of traditional retailing with Internet retailing.

mobile marketing An advertising technique that places advertising messages on mobile phones.

Motor Carrier Act of 1935 Legislation that brought motor carriers under ICC control, thus controlling entry into the market, establishing motor carrier classes of operation, setting reasonable rates, requiring ICC approval for any mergers or acquisitions, and controlling the issuance of securities.

motor carriers Trucks; the most flexible mode of transportation, accounting for almost one third of all U.S. for-hire transportation.

muda A Japanese word meaning waste or anything that does not add value.

multiple regression forecast A forecast technique using multiple regression.

multiple-channel queuing system A system in which multiple servers act in parallel.

multiple-factor productivity Inputs that can be represented by the sum of labor, material, energy and capital costs.

multiple-phase queuing system A system in which multiple servers act in series.

N

naïve forecast A forecasting approach where the actual demand for the immediate past period is used as a forecast for next period's demand.

natural variations Variations that are random and uncontrollable with no specific cause; also termed environmental noise or white noise.

near-shoring Moving foreign production to on-shore or nearby foreign locations.

negotiated pricing Transportation pricing that is agreed upon by both parties.

nontariff barriers Import quotas, licensing agreements, embargoes, laws, and other regulations imposed on imports and exports.

non-vessel operating common carriers (NVOCC) Carriers that operate very similarly to international freight forwarders but normally use scheduled ocean liners.

North American Free Trade Agreement (NAFTA) Legislation that began on January 1, 1994, and will eventually remove most barriers to trade and investment among the U.S., Canada and Mexico.

O

Ocean Shipping Reform Act of 1998 Legislation that eliminated the requirement for ocean carriers to file rates with the Federal Maritime Commission.

offset An exchange agreement for industrial goods and/or services as a condition of military- related export. It is also commonly used in the aerospace and defense sectors.

offshore factory A firm that manufactures products at low cost with minimum investment in technical and managerial resources in low labor cost countries, then exports all of its finished goods.

open-end purchase order A purchase order that covers a variety of items and is negotiated for repeated supply over a fixed time period, such as quarterly or yearly. Additional items and expiration dates can be renegotiated in an open-end purchase order.

opportunities for a defect to occur (OFD) The number of activities or steps in a product wherein a defect could occur. Used in the DPMO calculation.

optimization The highest level of processes and decision-making that occurs through enhanced analytical tools such as On-Line Analytical Processing (OLAP) tools. The method determines the best number of units to produce, store or purchase, among other things, given cost and service considerations.

option overplanning Raising the final requirements of component parts beyond 100 percent in a super bill of materials to cover uncertainty.

order batching A type of inventory control that occurs when small orders are combined into one large order. This amplifies demand variability and adds to the use of safety stock, creating the bullwhip effect.

order costs Direct variable costs associated with placing an order with a supplier.

order fulfillment process The set of activities that allows a firm to fill customer orders while providing the required levels of customer service at the lowest possible delivered cost.

outpost factory A manufacturing facility that is set up in a location with an abundance of advanced suppliers, competitors, research facilities and knowledge centers to get access to the latest information on materials, components, technologies and products.

outsource The process that occurs when a firm purchases materials or products instead of producing them in-house.

P

P charts Monitors the percent defective in each sample.

Pareto analysis A graphic technique that prioritizes the most frequently occurring problems or issues. The analysis recommends that problems falling into the most frequently occurring category be assigned the highest priority and managed closely.

Pareto charts A useful method for organizing applications of data in many formats; based on the work of Vilfredo Pareto, a nineteenth-century economist.

Pareto principle Refers to the observation that 20 percent of something is typically responsible for 80 percent of the results.

part families similarly processed parts in a manufacturing cell.

passive RFID tags RFID tags that are without an internal power source and require power from a tag reader.

payment bonds Bonds posted by the bidders to protect the buyer against any third-party liens not fulfilled by the successful bidder.

perceived waiting times An aspect of queue management that occurs when customers think the wait time is much longer or shorter than it really is.

perfect order An order that did arrive on time, complete and damage free.

performance bonds Bonds posted by the bidders to guarantee that the work done by the successful bidder meets specifications and is completed in the time specified.

performance dashboards Web-based balanced scorecard applications.

performance variance The difference between the standard and actual performance.

periodic review system A review of physical inventory at specific points in time.

petty cash A small cash reserve maintained by a midlevel manager or clerk.

piggyback service A type of intermodal transportation involving the loading of shipping containers or truck trailers on a rail flatbed car; also known as container-on-flat-car (COFC) and trailer-on-flat-car (TOFC).

pipeline carriers One of the five modes of transportation; carries oil, natural gas, coal slurry and other liquids/gases.

place utility A situation that is created when customers get things delivered to the desired location.

planned order releases The bottom line of an MRP part record. It designates when the specific quantity is to be ordered from the supplier or to begin being processed. These quantities also determine the gross requirements of the dependent or "children" parts going into this higher level part or product.

planning factor A calculation showing the number of units of a specific component required to make one unit of a higher-level part.

planning time fence A period typically stretching from the end of the firmed segment to several weeks farther into the future; also known as the tentative segment.

poka-yoke Error- or mistake-proofing.

posttransaction costs Costs are incurred after the goods are in the possession of the company, agents, or customers.

posttransaction elements Customer service activities that occur after a sale.

pretransaction costs Costs that are incurred prior to order and receipt of the purchased goods.

pretransaction elements Customer service activities that occur before a sale.

price break point The minimum quantity required to receive a quantity discount.

private carrier A form of transportation owned by a company, such as a fleet of trucks, which is used to ship that company's goods only.

private clouds A data center that is owned by the firm and managed in-house.

private warehouses Warehouses that are owned by the firm storing the goods.

process diagrams or process maps A tool that is the necessary first step to evaluating any manufacturing or service process; a drawing showing how products or people flow through a process; Also called a flow diagram.

process integration The sharing of information and coordinating resources to jointly manage a process.

procurement credit cards or corporate purchasing cards (P-cards) Credit cards with a predetermined credit limit, usually not more than $5,000 depending on the organization, issued to authorized personnel of the buying organization to make low-dollar purchases.

producer's risk The risk that occurs when a buyer rejects a shipment of good-quality units because the sample quality level did not meet the acceptance standard.

product development and commercialization process The development of new products to meet changing customer requirements and then getting these products to market quickly and efficiently.

product family A group consisting of different products that share similar characteristics, components or manufacturing processes.

product positioned strategy A location strategy that places warehouses close to the sources of supply, to enable the firm to collect various goods and then consolidate these into TL or CL quantities for shipment to customers.

production kanban A visual signal such as a light, flag or sign that is used to trigger production of certain components.

profit-leverage effect A purchasing performance measure that calculates the impact of a change in purchase spend on a firm's profit before taxes, assuming gross sales and other expenses remain unchanged.

public procurement or public purchasing The management of the purchasing and supply management function of the government and nonprofit sector, such as educational institutions, charitable organizations and the federal, state and local governments.

public warehouses An independent warehouse that is operated as a for-profit business.

pull system An operating system where synchronized work takes place only upon authorization from another downstream user in the system rather than strictly to a forecast. JIT systems or lean systems are typically referred to as pull systems.

purchase order (PO) A contractual commercial document issued by the buying firm to a supplier, indicating the type, quantities and agreed prices for products or services that the supplier will provide to the buying firm.

purchase requisition An internal document initiated by the material user to request the purchasing department to buy specific goods or services.

purchase spend The money a firm spends on goods and services.

pure Internet distribution strategy Selling goods or services strictly over the Internet.

pure services Services that offer few, if any, tangible products to customers.

Q

QR codes A form of mobile marketing that involves the use of the camera function on a smart phone and installing a QR (quick response) code reader on the phone.

qualitative forecasting methods Forecasts based on opinions and intuition.

quality-of-life factors Those issues that contribute to "a feeling of well-being, fulfillment or satisfaction resulting from factors in the external environments."

quantitative forecasting methods Forecasts based on mathematical models and relevant historical data.

quantity discount model or price-break model A variation of the classic EOQ model, wherein purchase price is allowed to vary with the quantity purchased.

queue discipline The order in which customers are served.

queue management A demand management strategy that is used to deal with excess customers.

queuing systems The processes used to align, prioritize and serve customers.

quick response (QR) "Developed by the U.S. textile industry in the mid-1980s as an offshoot of JIT and was based on merchandisers and suppliers working together to respond more quickly to consumer needs by sharing information, resulting in better customer service and less inventory and waste."

R

R chart Used to track sample ranges, or the variation of the measurements within each sample.

radio frequency identification (RFID) A technology that enables huge amounts of information to be stored on chips (called tags) and read at a distance by readers, without requiring line-ofsight scanning.

radio-frequency identification tag (RFID) The chips used to store information about a specific product or carton using RFID.

rail carriers Trains or railroads.

Railroad Revitalization and Regulatory Reform Act Commonly known as the 4-R Act; this legislation was passed in 1976 and made several regulatory changes to help the railroads.

Railway Passenger Service Act Legislation passed in 1970 that created Amtrak.

rationing A strategy that can occur when demand exceeds a supplier's finished goods available. In such cases, the supplier may allocate product in proportion to what buyers ordered.

real-time location systems (RTLSs) WiFi-enabled radio frequency identification (RFID) tags used on rail cars to allow tracking of rail cars (and their assets) in real-time.

Reed-Bulwinkle Act Legislation passed in 1948 that gave groups of carriers the ability to form rate bureaus or conferences wherein they could propose rate changes to the ICC.

relationship marketing or permission marketing An extension of target marketing; letting customers select the type and time of communication with organizations.

reneging Leaving a queue before receiving the service

reorder point (ROP) The lowest inventory level at which a new order must be placed to avoid a stockout during the order cycle time period.

request for proposal (RFP) A formal request for a project or product proposal issued by the buyer to qualified suppliers. The use of RFPs allows the supplier to develop part specifications based on their own knowledge of the materials and technology needed.

request for quotation (RFQ) A formal request for pricing from a supplier; commonly used when the purchasing requirements are clear.

resource requirements planning (RRP) A long range capacity planning module that is used to check whether aggregate resources are capable of satisfying the aggregate production plan.

return on assets (ROA)/return on investment (ROI) A financial ratio of a firm's net income in relation to its total assets.

returns management process A process that manages product returns. This can be extremely beneficial for supply chain management in terms of maintaining acceptable levels of customer service and identifying product improvement opportunities.

reverse logistics Returning products, warranty repairs, and recycling or disposing items. Also referred to as returns management.

rewarding suppliers Giving suppliers more business when their performance is deemed to be excellent.

rights and duties A theory stating that some actions are right in themselves without regard for the consequences.

right-shoring The combining of on-shore, near-shore and far-shore operations into a single, flexible, low-cost approach to supply chain management.

right-to-work laws State legislation that provides employees with the right to decide whether to join or support a union financially.

risk pooling The relationship between the number of warehouses, inventory and customer service; it can be explained intuitively as follows: when market demand is random, it is very likely that higher-than-average demand from some customers will be offset by lower-than-average demand from other customers. As the number of customers served by a single warehouse increases, these demand variabilities will tend to offset each other more often, thus reducing overall demand variance and the likelihood of stockouts.

road trains Trucks pulling more than two trailers; these are commonly seen in Australia where trucks are used instead of railroads in low population areas.

root causes The most significant/potential cause of a problem that impacts the process.

ROROs Roll-on-roll-off containerships that allow truck trailers and containers to be directly driven on and off the ship, without use of cranes.

rough-cut capacity plan (RCCP) A plan that is used to check the feasibility of the master production schedule.

running sum of forecast errors A measure of forecast bias—that is, whether the forecast tends to be consistently higher or lower than actual demand.

S

sales activity management system Software tools that give sales personnel a sequence of activities guiding them through their sales processes with customers. These standardized steps assure the proper sales activities are performed and also put forth a uniform sales process across the entire organization.

sales force automation (SFA) Software products used for documenting field activities, communicating with the home office, and retrieval of sales history and other company-specific documents in the field.

sales order A supplier's offer to sell goods and services at the supplier's terms and conditions. The sales order becomes a legally binding contract when accepted by the buyer.

sales territory management systems Software applications that allow sales managers to obtain current information and reporting capabilities regarding each salesperson's activities on each customer's account, total sales in general for each sales rep, their sales territories and any ongoing sales initiatives.

scorecarding A performance measure design technique such as the Balanced Scorecard that uses the scorecard model.

sealed bids A bid for business by a supplier in response to an invitation for bid sent by a buyer. The bid is kept sealed until all bids are received, whereupon they are opened and the low bidder is typically awarded the purchase contract.

second-tier customers A customer's customers.

second-tier suppliers A supplier's suppliers.

segment customers Placing customers in a behavioral class, such as males/females, age brackets and profitability, so as to better design marketing campaigns for each segment.

server factory A manufacturing facility that is set up primarily to take advantage of government incentives, minimize exchange risk, avoid tariff barriers and reduce taxes and logistics costs to supply the regional market where the factory is located.

service bundles A group of attributes that are offered to customers when purchasing services, including the explicit service itself, the supporting facility, facilitating goods and implicit services. Successful services are designed to deliver this bundle of attributes in the most efficient way, while still satisfying customer requirements.

service capacity The number of customers per day that a firm's service delivery systems are designed to serve, although it could also be some other period of time such as customers per hour or customers per shift.

service delivery systems A continuum of services that may range from mass-produced, low-customer-contact systems at one extreme (such as ATMs) to highly customized, high customer- contact systems at the other (such as expensive beauty salons).

service layout strategies A method that works in combination with location decisions to further support the overall business strategies of differentiation, low cost or market focus. Office layouts tend to be departmentalized; commercial airliner layouts segment customers; casino layouts are designed to get customers in quickly and then keep them there by spacing out the attractions; and self-serve restaurant buffet layouts are designed to process customers quickly.

service level The in-stock probability.

service quality The satisfaction or perceived level of quality a customer experiences with regard to a service. It includes many elements—for example, because of health and safety concerns, pharmacies are under intense pressure to provide high quality services to customers.

service response logistics The management and coordination of an organization's activities that occur while the service is being performed.

setup costs The costs associated with setting up machines and equipment to produce a batch of product; the term is often used in place of order costs.

Seven Rs Rule Having the right product, in the right quantity, in the right condition, at the right place, at the right time, for the right customer, at the right cost.

seven wastes A concept that encompasses things such as excess wait times, inventories, material and people movements, processing steps, variabilities and any other non-value-adding activity.

shippers' associations Nonprofit membership cooperatives that make domestic or international arrangements for the movement of members' cargo.

Shipping Act of 1984 Legislation that allowed ocean carriers to pool or share shipments, assign ports, publish rates and enter into contracts with shippers.

shortage gaming A strategy that occurs when buyers figure out the relationship between their orders and what is supplied, and they then tend to inflate their orders to satisfy their real needs.

short-range planning horizon A planning horizon that covers a weekly, daily, or hourly basis.

sigma drift A theory that assumes process variations will grow over time, as process measurements drift off target.

silo effect/silo mentality An I-win-you-lose organizational issue that causes a firm to be reactive and short-term-goal oriented. At this stage, no internal functional integration is occurring.

simple moving average forecast A method that uses historical data to generate a forecast; it works well when the demand is fairly stable over time.

simplification A reduction of the number of components, supplies, or standard materials used in a product or process.

single integrator solution An ERP system that uses all the desired applications from the same vendor.

single sourcing "Refers to the deliberate practice of concentrating purchases of an item with one source from a pool of viable suppliers."

single-factor productivity measures The output measure divided by a single input measure, such as labor cost.

Six Sigma A system that stresses a commitment by top management to enable a firm to identify customer expectations and excel in meeting and exceeding those expectations. A type of TQM method devised by Motorola.

social CRM Evolution of CRM in use of the Internet and social media.

social media Online social services such as LinkedIn, Twitter and Facebook.

software-as-a-service model (SaaS model) Also referred to as an application service provider (ASP) and cloud computing provider. Perhaps as many as 50 percent of all CRM programs are now designed and maintained for clients by ASPs. In many cases, firms do not have the time, knowledge or infrastructure to buy and build an effective CRM program, so they use Internet on-demand CRM services provided by an ASP. These providers also offer high levels of data security, which many firms find very attractive.

sole sourcing Refers to the situation when the supplier is the only available source.

source factory A manufacturing facility that has a broader strategic role than an offshore factory, with plant management heavily involved in supplier selection and production planning.

Southern Common Market (MERCOSUR) A regional trade agreement among Argentina, Brazil, Paraguay and Uruguay, formed in March 1991.

specialized carriers Carriers that transport liquid petroleum, household goods, agricultural commodities, building materials and other specialized items.

square root rule A rule suggesting that the system average inventory (impacted by adding or deleting warehouses) is equal to the old system inventory times the ratio of the square root of the new number of warehouses to the square root of the old number of warehouses.

Staggers Rail Act of 1980 Legislation aimed at improving finances for the rail industry.

state utility A situation that occurs when services do something to things that are owned by the customer, such as transport and store their supplies, repair their machines, cut their hair or provide their healthcare.

statistical process control (SPC) A method that allows firms to visually monitor process performance, compare the performance to desired levels or standards and take corrective steps quickly before process variabilities get out of control and damage products, services and customer relationships.

stockless buying or system contracting An extension of the blanket purchase order.

stockpiling To set aside or hoard purchased items, if it is thought that prices will soon increase. Also known as forward buying.

strategic alliance development Improving the capabilities of key trading partners.

strategic partnerships A close working relationship that develops among trading partner relationships.

strategic sourcing Strategically managing a firm's external resources and services to improve cost, quality, delivery, performance and competitive advantage.

strategic supplier alliances The creation of partnerships with key suppliers.

subcontracting The process of entering into a contractual agreement with a supplier to produce goods and/or services according to a specific set of terms and conditions.

super bill of materials Another type of bill of materials that is useful for planning purposes.

supplier certification Defined by the Institute of Supply Management as "an organization's process for evaluating the quality systems of key suppliers in an effort to eliminate incoming inspections."

supplier co-location Placing a supplier's employee within a buyer's firm, to perform purchasing activities. A type of VMI; also referred to as JIT II.

supplier development The efforts of a buying firm to improve the capabilities and performance of specific suppliers to better meet its needs.

supplier evaluation Determining the current capabilities of suppliers.

supplier management One of the most crucial issues within the topic of supply management— getting suppliers to do what the buyer's firm wants them to do.

supplier relationship management (SRM) Accenture defines SRM as "the systematic management of supplier relationships to optimize the value delivered through the relationship over their life cycle."

supplier relationship management process A process by which the firm manages its relationships with suppliers.

supply base or supplier base Refers to the list of suppliers that a firm uses to acquire its materials, services, supplies, and equipment.

supply base rationalization, supply base optimization, or supply base reduction Getting rid of poorly performing suppliers.

supply chain A network of trading partners that make products and services available to consumers, including all of the functions enabling the production, delivery and recycling of materials, components, end products and services

supply chain management (SCM) The integration of key business processes regarding the flow of materials from raw material suppliers to the final customer.

supply chain performance measurement Determining the performance of an entire supply chain.

supply chain security management A method that is concerned with reducing the risk of intentionally created disruptions in supply chain operations including product and information theft and activities seeking to endanger personnel or sabotage supply chain infrastructure.

supply management The identification, acquisition, access, positioning and management of resources the organization needs or potentially needs in the attainment of its strategic objectives.

surety bonds Bonds posted by bidders to ensure that the successful bidder will accept the contract.

sustainability A commitment to environmental responsibility.

sustainable development A development that meets the needs of the present without compromising the ability of future generations to meet their own needs.

sustainable sourcing A process of purchasing goods and services that takes into account the long-term impact on people, profits, and the planet.

system nervousness A situation where a small change in the upper- level production plan causes a major change in the lower-level production plan.

T

target marketing Targeting specific customer segments, with respect to promotional efforts.

tariff An official list or schedule showing the duties, taxes or customs imposed by a host country on imports or exports.

the 4 Ms Material, Machine, Methods, and Manpower

third-party logistics providers (3PLs) For-hire outside agents that provide transportation and other services including warehousing, document preparation, customs clearance, packaging, labeling and freight bill auditing.

fourth-party logistics services (4PLs) Outside agents that manage all of a firm's worldwide 3PL providers; also termed a lead logistics provider.

three P's Refers to people, planet, and profit.

time fence system Separates the planning horizon into two segments: a firmed and a tentative segment.

time series forecasting A prediction technique based on the assumption that the future is an extension of the past and that historical data can thus be used to forecast future demand.

time utility A state of well-being that is created when customers get products delivered at precisely the right time, not earlier and not later.

total cost of ownership (TCO) or total cost of acquisition Considers the unit price of the material, payment terms, cash discount, ordering cost, carrying cost, logistical costs, maintenance costs and other more qualitative costs that may not be easy to assess.

total productivity measures A measure of total outputs divided by total inputs.

total quality management (TQM) A focus on the customer, performance measurement, and formal training in quality control methods. Six Sigma embodies an organizational culture wherein everyone from CEO, to production worker, to frontline service employee is involved in quality assessment and improvement.

Toyota Production System A methodology created by Toyota Motor Company in the 1950s. The idea is to make the best use of an organization's time, assets and people in all processes in order to optimize productivity. Also known as JIT and lean production.

tracking signal A tool used to check the forecast bias.

trading companies A firm that puts buyers and sellers from different countries together and handles all of the export/import arrangements, documentation and transportation for both goods and services.

trailer-on-flatcar service or TOFC service Railroads that offer flatcars used to carry truck trailers.

transaction costs Costs include the cost of the goods/services and cost associated with placing and receiving the order.

transaction elements Activities that occur during the sale of a product or service.

transactional SRM A system that enables an organization to track supplier interactions such as order planning, order payment and returns. The volume of transactions involved may result in independent systems maintained by geographic region or business lines. Transactional SRM tends to focus on short-term reporting.

Transportation Act of 1920 Legislation that instructed the ICC to ensure that rates were high enough to provide a fair return for the railroads each year.

Transportation Act of 1940 Legislation that further extended the Interstate Commerce Act of 1887, establishing ICC control over domestic water transportation.

Transportation Act of 1958 Legislation that established temporary loan guarantees to railroads, liberalized control over intrastate rail rates, amended the rule of rate making to ensure more intermodal competition and clarified the differences between private and for hire motor carriers.

transportation brokers Legally authorized intermediaries that bring shippers and transportation companies (mainly truckers) together.

transportation deregulation The laws that seek to reduce government regulation in the transportation industry, allowing market forces to dictate services offered.

transportation intermediaries For-hire agencies that bring shippers and transportation providers together.

transportation management systems Software applications that allow firms to select the best mix of transportation services and pricing to determine the best use of containers or truck trailers, to better manage transportation contracts, to rank transportation options, to clear customs and to track fuel usage, product movements and carrier performance.

transportation regulation The laws that protect consumers in areas of transportation monopoly pricing, safety and liability.

transportation security Protection that is provided to transportation companies against unlawful activities such as terrorism.

Transportation Worker Identification Credential (TWIC) A transportation security initiative for transportation workers mandated by the Maritime Transportation Security Act of 2002 and the Safe Port Act of 2006.

traveling requisition A material requisition that is used for materials and standard parts that are requested on a recurring basis.

truckload (TL) carriers For-hire trucks that move shipments that take up one full truckload.

Type-I error When a process is mistakenly thought to be out of control and an improvement initiative is undertaken unnecessarily.

Type-II error When a process is thought to be exhibiting only natural variations and no improvement is undertaken, even though the process is actually out of control.

U

U.S. Baldrige Quality Award Legislation enacted in 1987, named in honor of Malcolm Baldrige, President Ronald Reagan's Secretary of Commerce, that seeks to recognize U.S. companies for service or product quality.

Uniform Commercial Code (UCC) Legislation that governs the purchase and sale of goods.

utilitarianism A theory that maintains an ethical act creates the greatest good for the greatest number of people.

V

value engineering Designing better quality and cost savings into the products originally.

value-of-service pricing A strategy that allows carriers to price their services at competitive levels the market will bear.

variable costs Expenses that vary as a function of the output level.

variable data Measurable data, such as weight, time and length (as in the weight of a box of cereal, the time to serve a customer or the length of a steel girder).

vendor managed inventory (VMI) A progressive partner-based approach to controlling inventory and reducing supply chain costs. Customers provide information to the key supplier, including historical usage, current inventory levels, minimum and maximum stock levels, sales forecasts and upcoming promotions, who then takes on the responsibility and risk for planning, managing and monitoring the replenishment of inventory. The supplier may even own the inventory until the product is sold.

virtual queues A queuing system in which customers' places in the queue are tracked by a computerized system that allows customers to roam the premises until their names are called.

visibility Information and process flows in and between organizations. Views are customized by role and aggregated via a single portal.

W

walk-through service audits A method of monitoring a service system that is performed by management and covers service system attributes from the time customers initially encounter the service until they leave.

Walmart effect A theory postulating that the booming growth in information technology has allowed many big-box retailers such as Wal-Mart to realize large productivity growth rates.

warehouse management systems Software applications facilitating the proper storage and movement of inventory and minor manufacturing such as assembly or labeling activities within the warehouse, and movement of shipments onto the transportation carrier.

waste reduction The process of reducing the waste from the productive systems to enhance value of the products.

water carrier A carrier using ships for transportation.

weighted-factor rating model A method commonly used to compare the attractiveness of several locations along a number of quantitative and qualitative dimensions.

World Trade Organization (WTO) The only international organization dealing with the rules of trade between nations. Its functions include administering the WTO agreements, providing a forum for trade negotiations, handling trade disputes, monitoring national trade policies, providing technical assistance and training programs for developing countries and cooperating with other international organizations.

X

$\bar{x}$ chart Used to track the central tendency of the sample means.

Y

yokoten A Japanese term meaning "across everywhere." In lean terminology, it is used to mean the sharing of best practices.

Author Index

Subject Index

Note: Figures, tables, and examples are indicated by page numbers including f, t, and e.

Q

T

U